The United States Government Manual 2017

For Reference

Not to be taken from this room

Bernan Press

Lanham • Boulder • New York • London

Bernan Press does not claim copyright in U.S. government information.

Published in the United States of America
by Bernan Press, a wholly owned subsidiary of
The Rowman & Littlefield Publishing Group, Inc.
4501 Forbes Boulevard, Suite 200
Lanham, Maryland 20706
http://www.rowman.com/bernanpress
1-800-462-6420
customercare@bernan.com

ISBN: 978-1-59888-977-2

♾™ The paper used in this publication meets the minimum requirements of American
National Standard for Information Sciences—Permanence of Paper for Printed Library
Materials, ANSI/NISO Z39.48-1992.

Manufactured in the United States of America.

Preface

As the official handbook of the Federal Government, *The United States Government Manual* provides comprehensive information on the agencies of the legislative, judicial, and executive branches. The Manual also includes information on quasiofficial agencies; international organizations in which the United States participates; and boards, commissions, and committees.

A typical agency description includes a list of principal officials, a summary statement of the agency's purpose and role in the Federal Government, a brief history of the agency, including its legislative or executive authority, a description of its programs and activities, and a "Sources of Information" section. This last section provides information on consumer activities, contracts and grants, employment, publications, and many other areas of public interest.

The Manual is also available and periodically updated on its own website. The U.S. Government Manual website (usgovernmentmanual.gov) is jointly administered by the Office of the Federal Register (OFR)/Government Printing Office (GPO) partnership. The website offers three ways to and information about Government agencies and organizations by entering a term in the keyword search box, browsing categories, or using "The Government of the United States" site map for an overview of the Government. For more information and to view The Manual online, go to www.usgovernmentmanual.gov.

Contents

EXECUTIVE BRANCH: DEPARTMENTS

EXECUTIVE BRANCH: INDEPENDENT AGENCIES AND GOVERNMENT CORPORATIONS

Declaration of Independence

Action of Second Continental Congress, July 4, 1776

IN CONGRESS, JULY 4, 1776.

THE UNANIMOUS DECLARATION of the thirteen united STATES OF AMERICA,

WHEN in the Course of human events, it becomes necessary for one people to dissolve the political bands which have connected them with another, and to assume among the powers of the earth, the separate and equal station to which the Laws of Nature and of Nature's God entitle them, a decent respect to the opinions of mankind requires that they should declare the causes which impel them to the separation.

We hold these truths to be self-evident, that all men are created equal, that they are endowed by their Creator with certain unalienable Rights, that among these are Life, Liberty and the pursuit of Happiness.—That to secure these rights, Governments are instituted among Men, deriving their just powers from the consent of the governed,— That whenever any Form of Government becomes destructive of these ends, it is the Right of the People to alter or to abolish it, and to institute new Government, laying its foundation on such principles and organizing its powers in such form, as to them shall seem most likely to effect their Safety and Happiness. Prudence, indeed, will dictate that Governments long established should not be changed for light and transient causes; and accordingly all experience hath shewn, that mankind are more disposed to suffer, while evils are sufferable, than to right themselves by abolishing the forms to which they are accustomed. But when a long train of abuses and usurpations, pursuing invariably the same Object evinces a design to reduce them under absolute Despotism, it is their right, it is their duty, to throw off such Government, and to provide new Guards for their future security.—Such has been the patient sufferance of these Colonies; and such is now the necessity which constrains them to alter their former Systems of Government. The history of the present King of Great Britain is a history of repeated injuries and usurpations, all having in direct object the establishment of an absolute Tyranny over these States. To prove this, let Facts be submitted to a candid world.—He has refused his Assent to Laws, the most wholesome and necessary for the public good.—He has forbidden his Governors to pass Laws of immediate and pressing importance, unless suspended in their operation till his Assent should be obtained; and when so suspended, he has utterly neglected to attend to them.—He has refused to pass other Laws for the accommodation of large districts of people, unless those people would relinquish the right of Representation in the Legislature, a right inestimable to them and formidable to tyrants only.—He has called together legislative bodies at places unusual, uncomfortable, and distant from the depository of their public Records, for the sole purpose of fatiguing them into compliance with his measures.—He has dissolved Representative Houses repeatedly, for opposing with manly firmness his invasions on the rights of the people.—He has refused for a long time, after such dissolutions, to cause others to be elected; whereby the Legislative powers, incapable of Annihilation, have returned to the People at large for their exercise; the State remaining in the mean time exposed to all the dangers of invasion from without, and convulsions within.—He has endeavoured to prevent the population of these States;

1

for that purpose obstructing the Laws for Naturalization of Foreigners; refusing to pass others to encourage their migrations hither, and raising the conditions of new Appropriations of Lands.—He has obstructed the Administration of Justice, by refusing his Assent to Laws for establishing Judiciary powers.—He has made Judges dependent on his Will alone, for the tenure of their offices, and the amount and payment of their salaries.—He has erected a multitude of New Offices, and sent hither swarms of Officers to harrass our people, and eat out their substance.—He has kept among us, in times of peace, Standing Armies without the Consent of our legislatures.—He has affected to render the Military independent of and superior to the Civil power.—He has combined with others to subject us to a jurisdiction foreign to our constitution, and unacknowledged by our laws; giving his Assent to their Acts of pretended Legislation:—For Quartering large bodies of armed troops among us:—For protecting them, by a mock Trial, from punishment for any Murders which they should commit on the Inhabitants of these States:—For cutting off our Trade with all parts of the world:—For imposing Taxes on us without our Consent:—For depriving us in many cases, of the benefits of Trial by Jury:—For transporting us beyond Seas to be tried for pretended offences—For abolishing the free System of English Laws in a neighbouring Province, establishing therein an Arbitrary government, and enlarging its Boundaries so as to render it at once an example and fit instrument for introducing the same absolute rule into these Colonies:—For taking away our Charters, abolishing our most valuable Laws, and altering fundamentally the Forms of our Governments:—For suspending our own Legislatures, and declaring themselves invested with power to legislate for us in all cases whatsoever.—He has abdicated Government here, by declaring us out of his Protection and waging War against us.—He has plundered our seas, ravaged our Coasts, burnt our towns, and destroyed the lives of our people.—He is at this time transporting large Armies of foreign Mercenaries to compleat the works of death, desolation and tyranny, already begun with circumstances of Cruelty & perfidy scarcely paralleled in the most barbarous ages, and totally unworthy the Head of a civilized nation.—He has constrained our fellow Citizens taken Captive on the high Seas to bear Arms against their Country, to become the executioners of their friends and Brethren, or to fall themselves by their Hands.—He has excited domestic insurrections amongst us, and has endeavoured to bring on the inhabitants of our frontiers, the merciless Indian Savages, whose known rule of warfare, is an undistinguished destruction of all ages, sexes and conditions.—In every stage of these Oppressions We have Petitioned for Redress in the most humble terms: Our repeated Petitions have been answered only by repeated injury. A Prince whose character is thus marked by every act which may define a Tyrant, is unfit to be the ruler of a free people.—Nor have We been wanting in attentions to our Brittish brethren. We have warned them from time to time of attempts by their legislature to extend an unwarrantable jurisdiction over us. We have reminded them of the circumstances of our emigration and settlement here. We have appealed to their native justice and magnanimity, and we have conjured them by the ties of our common kindred to disavow these usurpations, which, would inevitably interrupt our connections and correspondence. They too have been deaf to the voice of justice and of consanguinity. We must, therefore, acquiesce in the necessity, which denounces our Separation, and hold them, as we hold the rest of mankind, Enemies in War, in Peace Friends.

    WE, THEREFORE, THE REPRESENTATIVES OF THE UNITED STATES OF AMERICA, in General Congress, Assembled, appealing to the Supreme Judge of the world for the rectitude of our intentions, do, in the Name, and by Authority of the good People of these Colonies, solemnly publish and declare, That these United Colonies are, and of Right ought to be FREE AND INDEPENDENT STATES; that they are Absolved from all Allegiance to the British Crown, and that all political connection between them and the State of Great Britain, is and ought to be totally dissolved; and that as Free and Independent States, they have full Power to levy War, conclude Peace, contract Alliances, establish Commerce, and to do all other Acts and Things which Independent States may of right do. And for the support of this Declaration, with a firm reliance on the protection of divine Providence, we mutually pledge to each other our Lives, our Fortunes and our sacred Honor.

The 56 signatures on the Declaration appear in the positions indicated:

Column 1

Georgia:
  Button Gwinnett
  Lyman Hall
  George Walton

Column 2

North Carolina:
  William Hooper
  Joseph Hewes
  John Penn

South Carolina:
  Edward Rutledge
  Thomas Heyward, Jr.
  Thomas Lynch, Jr.
  Arthur Middleton

Column 3

Massachusetts:
  John Hancock

Maryland:
  Samuel Chase
  William Paca
  Thomas Stone
  Charles Carroll of
  Carrollton

Virginia:
  George Wythe
  Richard Henry Lee
  Thomas Jefferson
  Benjamin Harrison
  Thomas Nelson, Jr.
  Francis Lightfoot Lee
  Carter Braxton

Column 4

Pennsylvania:
  Robert Morris
  Benjamin Rush
  Benjamin Franklin
  John Morton
  George Clymer
  James Smith
  George Taylor
  James Wilson
  George Ross

Delaware:
  Caesar Rodney
  George Read
  Thomas McKean

Column 5

New York:
  William Floyd
  Philip Livingston
  Francis Lewis
  Lewis Morris

New Jersey:
  Richard Stockton
  John Witherspoon
  Francis Hopkinson
  John Hart
  Abraham Clark

Column 6

New Hampshire:
  Josiah Bartlett
  William Whipple

Massachusetts:
  Samuel Adams
  John Adams
  Robert Treat Paine
  Elbridge Gerry

Rhode Island:
  Stephen Hopkins
  William Ellery

Connecticut:
  Roger Sherman
  Samuel Huntington
  William Williams
  Oliver Wolcott

New Hampshire:
  Matthew Thornton

For more information on the Declaration of Independence and the Charters of Freedom, see http://archives.gov/exhibits/charters/declaration.html.

Constitution of the United States

Note: The following text is a transcription of the Constitution in its original form. Items that are underlined have since been amended or superseded.

Preamble

WE THE PEOPLE of the United States, in order to form a more perfect union, establish justice, insure domestic tranquility, provide for the common defense, promote the general welfare, and secure the blessings of liberty to ourselves and our posterity, do ordain and establish this Constitution for the United States of America.

Article I

Section 1. All legislative powers herein granted shall be vested in a Congress of the United States, which shall consist of a Senate and House of Representatives.

Section 2. The House of Representatives shall be composed of members chosen every second year by the people of the several states, and the electors in each state shall have the qualifications requisite for electors of the most numerous branch of the state legislature.

No person shall be a Representative who shall not have attained to the age of twenty five years, and been seven years a citizen of the United States, and who shall not, when elected, be an inhabitant of that state in which he shall be chosen.

Representatives and direct taxes shall be apportioned among the several states which may be included within this union, according to their respective numbers, which shall be determined by adding to the whole number of free persons, including those bound to service for a term of years, and excluding Indians not taxed, three fifths of all other Persons. The actual Enumeration shall be made within three years after the first meeting of the Congress of the United States, and within every subsequent term of ten years, in such manner as they shall by law direct. The number of Representatives shall not exceed one for every thirty thousand, but each state shall have at least one Representative; and until such enumeration shall be made, the state of New Hampshire shall be entitled to chuse three, Massachusetts eight, Rhode Island and Providence Plantations one, Connecticut five, New York six, New Jersey four, Pennsylvania eight, Delaware one, Maryland six, Virginia ten, North Carolina five, South Carolina five, and Georgia three.

When vacancies happen in the Representation from any state, the executive authority thereof shall issue writs of election to fill such vacancies.

The House of Representatives shall choose their speaker and other officers; and shall have the sole power of impeachment.

Section 3. The Senate of the United States shall be composed of two Senators from each state, chosen by the legislature thereof, for six years; and each Senator shall have one vote.

Immediately after they shall be assembled in consequence of the first election, they shall be divided as equally as may be into three classes. The seats of the Senators of the first class shall be vacated at the expiration of the second year, of the second class at the expiration of the fourth year, and the third class at the expiration of the sixth year, so that one third may be chosen every second year; and if vacancies happen by resignation, or otherwise, during the recess of the legislature of any state, the executive thereof may make temporary appointments until the next meeting of the legislature, which shall then fill such vacancies.

No person shall be a Senator who shall not have attained to the age of thirty years, and been nine years a citizen of the United States and who shall not, when elected, be an inhabitant of that state for which he shall be chosen.

The Vice President of the United States shall be President of the Senate, but shall have no vote, unless they be equally divided.

The Senate shall choose their other officers, and also a President pro tempore, in the absence of the Vice President, or when he shall exercise the office of President of the United States.

The Senate shall have the sole power to try all impeachments. When sitting for that purpose, they shall be on oath or affirmation. When the President of the United States is tried, the Chief Justice shall preside: And no person shall be convicted without the concurrence of two thirds of the members present.

Judgment in cases of impeachment shall not extend further than to removal from office, and disqualification to hold and enjoy any office of honor, trust or profit under the United States: but the party convicted shall nevertheless be liable and subject to indictment, trial, judgment and punishment, according to law.

Section 4. The times, places and manner of holding elections for Senators and Representatives, shall be prescribed in each state by the legislature thereof; but the Congress may at any time by law make or alter such regulations, except as to the places of choosing Senators.

The Congress shall assemble at least once in every year, and such meeting shall be on the first Monday in December, unless they shall by law appoint a different day.

Section 5. Each House shall be the judge of the elections, returns and qualifications of its own members, and a majority of each shall constitute a quorum to do business; but a smaller number may adjourn from day to day, and may be authorized to compel the attendance of absent members, in such manner, and under such penalties as each House may provide.

Each House may determine the rules of its proceedings, punish its members for disorderly behavior, and, with the concurrence of two thirds, expel a member.

Each House shall keep a journal of its proceedings, and from time to time publish the same, excepting such parts as may in their judgment require secrecy; and the yeas and nays of the members of either House on any question shall, at the desire of one fifth of those present, be entered on the journal.

Neither House, during the session of Congress, shall, without the consent of the other, adjourn for more than three days, nor to any other place than that in which the two Houses shall be sitting.

Section 6. The Senators and Representatives shall receive a compensation for their services, to be ascertained by law, and paid out of the treasury of the United States. They shall in all cases, except treason, felony and breach of the peace, be privileged from arrest during their attendance at the session of their respective Houses, and in going to and returning from the same; and for any speech or debate in either House, they shall not be questioned in any other place.

No Senator or Representative shall, during the time for which he was elected, be appointed to any civil office under the authority of the United States, which shall have been created, or the emoluments whereof shall have been increased during such time: and no person holding any office under the United States, shall be a member of either House during his continuance in office.

Section 7. All bills for raising revenue shall originate in the House of Representatives; but the Senate may propose or concur with amendments as on other Bills.

Every bill which shall have passed the House of Representatives and the Senate, shall, before it become a law, be presented to the President of the United States; if he approve he shall sign it, but if not he shall return it, with his objections to that House in which it shall have originated, who shall enter the objections at large on their journal, and proceed to reconsider it. If after such reconsideration two thirds of that House shall agree to pass the bill, it shall be sent, together with the objections, to the other House, by which it shall likewise be reconsidered, and if approved by two thirds of that House, it shall become a law. But in all such cases the votes of both Houses shall be determined by yeas and nays, and the names of the persons voting for and against the bill shall be entered on the journal of each House respectively. If any bill shall not be returned by the President within ten days (Sundays excepted) after it shall have been presented to him, the same shall be a law, in like manner as if he had signed it, unless the Congress by their adjournment prevent its return, in which case it shall not be a law.

Every order, resolution, or vote to which the concurrence of the Senate and House of Representatives may be necessary (except on a question of adjournment) shall be presented to the President of the United States; and before the same shall take effect, shall be approved by him, or being disapproved by him, shall be repassed by two thirds of the Senate and House of Representatives, according to the rules and limitations prescribed in the case of a bill.

Section 8. The Congress shall have power to lay and collect taxes, duties, imposts and excises, to pay the debts and provide for the common defense and general welfare of the United States; but all duties, imposts and excises shall be uniform throughout the United States;

To borrow money on the credit of the United States;

To regulate commerce with foreign nations, and among the several states, and with the Indian tribes;

To establish a uniform rule of naturalization, and uniform laws on the subject of bankruptcies throughout the United States;

To coin money, regulate the value thereof, and of foreign coin, and fix the standard of weights and measures;

To provide for the punishment of counterfeiting the securities and current coin of the United States;

To establish post offices and post roads;

To promote the progress of science and useful arts, by securing for limited times to authors and inventors the exclusive right to their respective writings and discoveries;

To constitute tribunals inferior to the Supreme Court;

To define and punish piracies and felonies committed on the high seas, and offenses against the law of nations;

To declare war, grant letters of marque and reprisal, and make rules concerning captures on land and water;

To raise and support armies, but no appropriation of money to that use shall be for a longer term than two years;

To provide and maintain a navy;

To make rules for the government and regulation of the land and naval forces;

To provide for calling forth the militia to execute the laws of the union, suppress insurrections and repel invasions;

To provide for organizing, arming, and disciplining, the militia, and for governing such part of them as may be employed in the service of the United States, reserving to the states respectively, the appointment of the officers, and the authority of training the militia according to the discipline prescribed by Congress;

To exercise exclusive legislation in all cases whatsoever, over such District (not exceeding ten miles square) as may, by cession of particular states, and the acceptance of Congress, become the seat of the government of the United States, and to exercise like authority over all places purchased by the consent of the legislature of the state in which the same shall be, for the erection of forts, magazines, arsenals, dockyards, and other needful buildings;—And

To make all laws which shall be necessary and proper for carrying into execution the foregoing powers, and all other powers vested by this Constitution in the government of the United States, or in any department or officer thereof.

Section 9. The migration or importation of such persons as any of the states now existing shall think proper to admit, shall not be prohibited by the Congress prior to the year one thousand eight hundred and eight, but a tax or duty may be imposed on such importation, not exceeding ten dollars for each person.

The privilege of the writ of habeas corpus shall not be suspended, unless when in cases of rebellion or invasion the public safety may require it.

No bill of attainder or ex post facto Law shall be passed.

No capitation, or other direct, tax shall be laid, unless in proportion to the census or enumeration herein before directed to be taken.

No tax or duty shall be laid on articles exported from any state.

No preference shall be given by any regulation of commerce or revenue to the ports of one state over those of another: nor shall vessels bound to, or from, one state, be obliged to enter, clear or pay duties in another.

No money shall be drawn from the treasury, but in consequence of appropriations made by law; and a regular statement and account of receipts and expenditures of all public money shall be published from time to time.

No title of nobility shall be granted by the United States: and no person holding any office of profit or trust under them, shall, without the consent of the Congress, accept of any present, emolument, office, or title, of any kind whatever, from any king, prince, or foreign state.

Section 10. No state shall enter into any treaty, alliance, or confederation; grant letters of marque and reprisal; coin money; emit bills of credit; make anything but gold and silver coin a tender in payment of debts; pass any bill of attainder, ex post facto law, or law impairing the obligation of contracts, or grant any title of nobility.

No state shall, without the consent of the Congress, lay any imposts or duties on imports or exports, except what may be absolutely necessary for executing it's inspection laws: and the net produce of all duties and imposts, laid by any state on imports or exports, shall be for the use of the treasury of the United States; and all such laws shall be subject to the revision and control of the Congress.

No state shall, without the consent of Congress, lay any duty of tonnage, keep troops, or ships of war in time of peace, enter into any agreement or compact with another state, or with a foreign power, or engage in war, unless actually invaded, or in such imminent danger as will not admit of delay.

Article II

Section 1. The executive power shall be vested in a President of the United States of America. He shall hold his office during the term of four years, and, together with the Vice President, chosen for the same term, be elected, as follows:

Each state shall appoint, in such manner as the Legislature thereof may direct, a number of electors, equal to the whole number of Senators and Representatives to which the State may be entitled in the Congress: but no Senator or Representative, or person holding an office of trust or profit under the United States, shall be appointed an elector.

The electors shall meet in their respective states, and vote by ballot for two persons, of whom one at least shall not be an inhabitant of the same state with themselves. And they shall make a list of all the persons voted for, and of the number of votes for each; which list they shall sign and certify, and transmit sealed to the seat of the government of the United States, directed to the President of the Senate. The President of the Senate shall, in the presence of the Senate and House of Representatives, open all the certificates, and the votes shall then be counted. The person having the greatest number of votes shall be the President, if such number be a majority of the whole number of electors appointed; and if there be more than one who have such majority, and have an equal number of votes, then the House of Representatives shall immediately choose by ballot one of them for President; and if no person have a majority, then from the five highest on the list the said House shall in like manner choose the President. But in choosing the President, the votes shall be taken by States, the representation from each state having one vote; A quorum for this purpose shall consist of a member or members from two thirds of the states, and a majority of all the states shall be necessary to a choice. In every case, after the choice of the President, the person having the greatest number of votes of the electors shall be the Vice President. But if there should remain two or more who have equal votes, the Senate shall choose from them by ballot the Vice President.

The Congress may determine the time of choosing the electors, and the day on which they shall give their votes; which day shall be the same throughout the United States.

No person except a natural born citizen, or a citizen of the United States, at the time of the adoption of this Constitution, shall be eligible to the office of President; neither shall any person be eligible to that office who shall not have attained to the age of thirty five years, and been fourteen Years a resident within the United States.

In case of the removal of the President from office, or of his death, resignation, or inability to discharge the powers and duties of the said office, the same shall devolve on the Vice President, and the Congress may by law provide for the case of removal, death, resignation or inability, both of the President and Vice President, declaring what officer shall then act as President, and such officer shall act accordingly, until the disability be removed, or a President shall be elected.

The President shall, at stated times, receive for his services, a compensation, which shall neither be increased nor diminished during the period for which he shall have been elected, and he shall not receive within that period any other emolument from the United States, or any of them.

Before he enter on the execution of his office, he shall take the following oath or affirmation:—"I do solemnly swear (or affirm) that I will faithfully execute the office of President of the United States, and will to the best of my ability, preserve, protect and defend the Constitution of the United States."

Section 2. The President shall be commander in chief of the Army and Navy of the United States, and of the militia of the several states, when called into the actual service of the United States; he may require the opinion, in writing, of the principal officer in each of the executive departments, upon any subject relating to the duties of their respective offices, and he shall have power to grant reprieves and pardons for offenses against the United States, except in cases of impeachment.

He shall have power, by and with the advice and consent of the Senate, to make treaties, provided two thirds of the Senators present concur; and he shall nominate, and by and with the advice and consent of the Senate, shall appoint ambassadors, other public ministers and consuls, judges of the Supreme Court, and all other officers of the United States, whose appointments are not herein otherwise provided for, and which shall be established by law: but the Congress may by law vest the appointment of such inferior officers, as they think proper, in the President alone, in the courts of law, or in the heads of departments.

The President shall have power to fill up all vacancies that may happen during the recess of the Senate, by granting commissions which shall expire at the end of their next session.

Section 3. He shall from time to time give to the Congress information of the state of the union, and recommend to their consideration such measures as he shall judge necessary and expedient; he may, on extraordinary occasions, convene both Houses, or either of them, and in case of disagreement between them, with respect to the time of adjournment, he may adjourn them to such time as he shall think proper; he shall receive ambassadors and other public ministers; he shall take care that the laws be faithfully executed, and shall commission all the officers of the United States.

Section 4. The President, Vice President and all civil officers of the United States, shall be removed from office on impeachment for, and conviction of, treason, bribery, or other high crimes and misdemeanors.

Article III

Section 1. The judicial power of the United States, shall be vested in one Supreme Court, and in such inferior courts as the Congress may from time to time ordain and establish. The judges, both of the supreme and inferior courts, shall hold their offices during good behaviour, and shall, at stated times, receive for their services, a compensation, which shall not be diminished during their continuance in office.

Section 2. The judicial power shall extend to all cases, in law and equity, arising under this Constitution, the laws of the United States, and treaties made, or which shall be made, under their authority;—to all cases affecting ambassadors, other public ministers and consuls;— to all cases of admiralty and maritime jurisdiction;—to controversies to which the United States shall be a party;—to controversies between two or more states;—<u>between a state and citizens of another state;</u>—between citizens of different states;—between citizens of the same state claiming lands under grants of different states, and between a state, or the citizens thereof, and foreign states, citizens or subjects.
   In all cases affecting ambassadors, other public ministers and consuls, and those in which a state shall be party, the Supreme Court shall have original jurisdiction. In all the other cases before mentioned, the Supreme Court shall have appellate jurisdiction, both as to law and fact, with such exceptions, and under such regulations as the Congress shall make.
   The trial of all crimes, except in cases of impeachment, shall be by jury; and such trial shall be held in the state where the said crimes shall have been committed; but when not committed within any state, the trial shall be at such place or places as the Congress may by law have directed.

Section 3. Treason against the United States, shall consist only in levying war against them, or in adhering to their enemies, giving them aid and comfort. No person shall be convicted of treason unless on the testimony of two witnesses to the same overt act, or on confession in open court.
   The Congress shall have power to declare the punishment of treason, but no attainder of treason shall work corruption of blood, or forfeiture except during the life of the person attainted.

Article IV

Section 1. Full faith and credit shall be given in each state to the public acts, records, and judicial proceedings of every other state. And the Congress may by general laws prescribe the manner in which such acts, records, and proceedings shall be proved, and the effect thereof.

Section 2. The citizens of each state shall be entitled to all privileges and immunities of citizens in the several states.

A person charged in any state with treason, felony, or other crime, who shall flee from justice, and be found in another state, shall on demand of the executive authority of the state from which he fled, be delivered up, to be removed to the state having jurisdiction of the crime.

No person held to service or labor in one state, under the laws thereof, escaping into another, shall, in consequence of any law or regulation therein, be discharged from such service or labor, but shall be delivered up on claim of the party to whom such service or labor may be due.

Section 3. New states may be admitted by the Congress into this union; but no new states shall be formed or erected within the jurisdiction of any other state; nor any state be formed by the junction of two or more states, or parts of states, without the consent of the legislatures of the states concerned as well as of the Congress.

The Congress shall have power to dispose of and make all needful rules and regulations respecting the territory or other property belonging to the United States; and nothing in this Constitution shall be so construed as to prejudice any claims of the United States, or of any particular state.

Section 4. The United States shall guarantee to every state in this union a republican form of government, and shall protect each of them against invasion; and on application of the legislature, or of the executive (when the legislature cannot be convened) against domestic violence.

Article V

The Congress, whenever two thirds of both houses shall deem it necessary, shall propose amendments to this Constitution, or, on the application of the legislatures of two thirds of the several states, shall call a convention for proposing amendments, which, in either case, shall be valid to all intents and purposes, as part of this Constitution, when ratified by the legislatures of three fourths of the several states, or by conventions in three fourths thereof, as the one or the other mode of ratification may be proposed by the Congress; provided that no amendment which may be made prior to the year one thousand eight hundred and eight shall in any manner affect the first and fourth clauses in the ninth section of the first article; and that no state, without its consent, shall be deprived of its equal suffrage in the Senate.

Article VI

All debts contracted and engagements entered into, before the adoption of this Constitution, shall be as valid against the United States under this Constitution, as under the Confederation.

This Constitution, and the laws of the United States which shall be made in pursuance thereof; and all treaties made, or which shall be made, under the authority of the United States, shall be the supreme law of the land; and the judges in every state shall be bound thereby, anything in the Constitution or laws of any State to the contrary notwithstanding.

The Senators and Representatives before mentioned, and the members of the several state legislatures, and all executive and judicial officers, both of the United States and of the several states, shall be bound by oath or affirmation, to support this Constitution; but no religious test shall ever be required as a qualification to any office or public trust under the United States.

Article VII

The ratification of the conventions of nine states, shall be sufficient for the establishment of this Constitution between the states so ratifying the same.

Signers

Done in convention by the unanimous consent of the states present the seventeenth day of September in the year of our Lord one thousand seven hundred and eighty seven and of the independence of the United States of America the twelfth. *In witness whereof We have hereunto subscribed our Names,*

G° Washington—Presid^t
and deputy from Virginia

New Hampshire	John Langdon Nicholas Gilman
Massachusetts	Nathaniel Gorham Rufus King
Connecticut	W^m: Saml Johnson Roger Sherman
New York	Alexander Hamilton
New Jersey	Wil: Livingston David Brearly Wm Paterson Jona: Dayton
Pennsylvania	B. Franklin Thomas Mifflin Robt Morris Geo. Clymer Thos FitzSimons Jared Ingersoll James Wilson Gouv Morris
Delaware	Geo: Read Gunning Bedford jun John Dickinson Richard Bassett Jaco: Broom
Maryland	James McHenry Dan of St Thos Jenifer Danl Carroll
Virginia	John Blair— James Madison Jr.

North Carolina	Wm Blount
	Richd Dobbs Spaight
	Hu Williamson
South Carolina	J. Rutledge
	Charles Cotesworth Pinckney
	Charles Pinckney
	Pierce Butler
Georgia	William Few
	Abr Baldwin

Amendments

Note: The first ten Amendments were ratified December 15, 1791, and form what is known as the Bill of Rights.

Amendment 1

Congress shall make no law respecting an establishment of religion, or prohibiting the free exercise thereof; or abridging the freedom of speech, or of the press; or the right of the people peaceably to assemble, and to petition the government for a redress of grievances.

Amendment 2

A well regulated militia, being necessary to the security of a free state, the right of the people to keep and bear arms, shall not be infringed.

Amendment 3

No soldier shall, in time of peace be quartered in any house, without the consent of the owner, nor in time of war, but in a manner to be prescribed by law.

Amendment 4

The right of the people to be secure in their persons, houses, papers, and effects, against unreasonable searches and seizures, shall not be violated, and no warrants shall issue, but upon probable cause, supported by oath or affirmation, and particularly describing the place to be searched, and the persons or things to be seized.

Amendment 5

No person shall be held to answer for a capital, or otherwise infamous crime, unless on a presentment or indictment of a grand jury, except in cases arising in the land or naval forces, or in the militia, when in actual service in time of war or public danger; nor shall any person be subject for the same offense to be twice put in jeopardy of life or limb; nor shall be compelled in any criminal case to be a witness against himself, nor be deprived of life, liberty, or property, without due process of law; nor shall private property be taken for public use, without just compensation.

Amendment 6

In all criminal prosecutions, the accused shall enjoy the right to a speedy and public trial, by an impartial jury of the state and district wherein the crime shall have been committed, which district shall have been previously ascertained by law, and to be informed of the nature and cause of the accusation; to be confronted with the witnesses against him; to have compulsory process for obtaining witnesses in his favor, and to have the assistance of counsel for his defense.

Amendment 7

In suits at common law, where the value in controversy shall exceed twenty dollars, the right of trial by jury shall be preserved, and no fact tried by a jury, shall be otherwise reexamined in any court of the United States, than according to the rules of the common law.

Amendment 8

Excessive bail shall not be required, nor excessive fines imposed, nor cruel and unusual punishments inflicted.

Amendment 9

The enumeration in the Constitution, of certain rights, shall not be construed to deny or disparage others retained by the people.

Amendment 10

The powers not delegated to the United States by the Constitution, nor prohibited by it to the states, are reserved to the states respectively, or to the people.

Amendment 11

(Ratified February 7, 1795)

The judicial power of the United States shall not be construed to extend to any suit in law or equity, commenced or prosecuted against one of the United States by citizens of another state, or by citizens or subjects of any foreign state.

Amendment 12

(Ratified July 27, 1804)

The electors shall meet in their respective states and vote by ballot for President and Vice-President, one of whom, at least, shall not be an inhabitant of the same state with themselves; they shall name in their ballots the person voted for as President, and in distinct ballots the person voted for as Vice-President, and they shall make distinct lists of all persons voted for as President, and of all persons voted for as Vice-President, and of the number of votes for each, which lists they shall sign and certify, and transmit sealed to the seat of the government of the United States, directed to the President of the Senate;—The President of the Senate shall, in the presence of the Senate and House of Representatives, open all the certificates and the votes shall then be counted;—the person having the greatest number of votes for President, shall be the President, if such number be a majority of the whole number of electors appointed; and if no person have such majority, then from the persons having the highest numbers not exceeding three on the list of those voted for as President, the House of Representatives shall choose immediately, by ballot, the President. But in choosing the President, the votes shall be taken by states, the representation from each state having one vote; a quorum for this purpose shall consist of a member or members from two-thirds of the states, and a majority of all the states shall be necessary to a choice. And if the House of Representatives shall not choose a President whenever the right of choice shall devolve upon them, before the fourth day of March next following, then the Vice-President shall act as President, as in the case of the death or other constitutional disability of the President. The person having the greatest number of votes as Vice-President, shall be the Vice-President, if such number be a majority of the whole number of electors appointed, and if no person have a majority, then from the two highest numbers on the list, the Senate shall choose the Vice-President; a quorum for the purpose shall consist of two-thirds of the whole number of Senators, and a majority of the whole number shall be necessary to a choice. But no person constitutionally ineligible to the office of President shall be eligible to that of VicePresident of the United States.

Amendment 13

(Ratified December 6, 1865)

Section 1. Neither slavery nor involuntary servitude, except as a punishment for crime whereof the party shall have been duly convicted, shall exist within the United States, or any place subject to their jurisdiction.

Section 2. Congress shall have power to enforce this article by appropriate legislation.

Amendment 14

(Ratified July 9, 1868)

Section 1. All persons born or naturalized in the United States, and subject to the jurisdiction thereof, are citizens of the United States and of the state wherein they reside. No state shall make or enforce any law which shall abridge the privileges or immunities of citizens of the United States; nor shall any state deprive any person of life, liberty, or property, without due process of law; nor deny to any person within its jurisdiction the equal protection of the laws.

Section 2. Representatives shall be apportioned among the several states according to their respective numbers, counting the whole number of persons in each state, excluding Indians not taxed. But when the right to vote at any election for the choice of electors for President and Vice President of the United States, Representatives in Congress, the executive and judicial officers of a state, or the members of the legislature thereof, is denied to any of the male inhabitants of such state, being twenty-one years of age, and citizens of the United States, or in any way abridged, except for participation in rebellion, or other crime, the basis of representation therein shall be reduced in the proportion which the number of such male citizens shall bear to the whole number of male citizens twenty-one years of age in such state.

Section 3. No person shall be a Senator or Representative in Congress, or elector of President and Vice President, or hold any office, civil or military, under the United States, or under any state, who, having previously taken an oath, as a member of Congress, or as an officer of the United States, or as a member of any state legislature, or as an executive or judicial officer of any state, to support the Constitution of the United States, shall have engaged in insurrection or rebellion against the same, or given aid or comfort to the enemies thereof. But Congress may by a vote of two-thirds of each House, remove such disability.

Section 4. The validity of the public debt of the United States, authorized by law, including debts incurred for payment of pensions and bounties for services in suppressing insurrection or rebellion, shall not be questioned. But neither the United States nor any state shall assume or pay any debt or obligation incurred in aid of insurrection or rebellion against the United States, or any claim for the loss or emancipation of any slave; but all such debts, obligations and claims shall be held illegal and void.

Section 5. The Congress shall have power to enforce, by appropriate legislation, the provisions of this article.

Amendment 15

(Ratified February 3, 1870)

Section 1. The right of citizens of the United States to vote shall not be denied or abridged by the United States or by any state on account of race, color, or previous condition of servitude.

Section 2. The Congress shall have power to enforce this article by appropriate legislation.

Amendment 16

(Ratified February 3, 1913)

The Congress shall have power to lay and collect taxes on incomes, from whatever source derived, without apportionment among the several states, and without regard to any census or enumeration.

Amendment 17

(Ratified April 8, 1913)

The Senate of the United States shall be composed of two Senators from each state, elected by the people thereof, for six years; and each Senator shall have one vote. The electors in each state shall have the qualifications requisite for electors of the most numerous branch of the state legislatures.

When vacancies happen in the representation of any state in the Senate, the executive authority of such state shall issue writs of election to fill such vacancies: Provided, that the legislature of any state may empower the executive thereof to make temporary appointments until the people fill the vacancies by election as the legislature may direct.

This amendment shall not be so construed as to affect the election or term of any Senator chosen before it becomes valid as part of the Constitution.

Amendment 18

(Ratified January 16, 1919. Repealed December 5, 1933 by Amendment 21)

Section 1. After one year from the ratification of this article the manufacture, sale, or transportation of intoxicating liquors within, the importation thereof into, or the exportation thereof from the United States and all territory subject to the jurisdiction thereof for beverage purposes is hereby prohibited.

Section 2. The Congress and the several states shall have concurrent power to enforce this article by appropriate legislation.

Section 3. This article shall be inoperative unless it shall have been ratified as an amendment to the Constitution by the legislatures of the several states, as provided in the Constitution, within seven years from the date of the submission hereof to the states by the Congress.

Amendment 19

(Ratified August 18, 1920)

The right of citizens of the United States to vote shall not be denied or abridged by the United States or by any state on account of sex.

Congress shall have power to enforce this article by appropriate legislation.

Amendment 20

(Ratified January 23, 1933)

Section 1. The terms of the President and Vice President shall end at noon on the 20th day of January, and the terms of Senators and Representatives at noon on the 3d day of January, of the years in which such terms would have ended if this article had not been ratified; and the terms of their successors shall then begin.

Section 2. The Congress shall assemble at least once in every year, and such meeting shall begin at noon on the 3d day of January, unless they shall by law appoint a different day.

Section 3. If, at the time fixed for the beginning of the term of the President, the President elect shall have died, the Vice President elect shall become President. If a President shall not have been chosen before the time fixed for the beginning of his term, or if the President elect shall have failed to qualify, then the Vice President elect shall act as President until a President shall have qualified; and the Congress may by law provide for the case wherein neither a President elect nor a Vice President elect shall have qualified, declaring who shall then act as President, or the manner in which one who is to act shall be selected, and such person shall act accordingly until a President or Vice President shall have qualified.

Section 4. The Congress may by law provide for the case of the death of any of the persons from whom the House of Representatives may choose a President whenever the right of choice shall have devolved upon them, and for the case of the death of any of the persons from whom the Senate may choose a Vice President whenever the right of choice shall have devolved upon them.

Section 5. Sections 1 and 2 shall take effect on the 15th day of October following the ratification of this article.

Section 6. This article shall be inoperative unless it shall have been ratified as an amendment to the Constitution by the legislatures of three-fourths of the several states within seven years from the date of its submission.

Amendment 21

(Ratified December 5, 1933)

Section 1. The eighteenth article of amendment to the Constitution of the United States is hereby repealed.

Section 2. The transportation or importation into any state, territory, or possession of the United States for delivery or use therein of intoxicating liquors, in violation of the laws thereof, is hereby prohibited.

Section 3. This article shall be inoperative unless it shall have been ratified as an amendment to the Constitution by conventions in the several states, as provided in the Constitution, within seven years from the date of the submission hereof to the states by the Congress.

Amendment 22

(Ratified February 27, 1951)

Section 1. No person shall be elected to the office of the President more than twice, and no person who has held the office of President, or acted as President, for more than two years of a term to which some other person was elected President shall be elected to the office of the President more than once. But this article shall not apply to any person holding the office of President when this article was proposed by the Congress, and shall not prevent any person who may be holding the office of President, or acting as President, during the term within which this article becomes operative from holding the office of President or acting as President during the remainder of such term.

Section 2. This article shall be inoperative unless it shall have been ratified as an amendment to the Constitution by the legislatures of three-fourths of the several states within seven years from the date of its submission to the states by the Congress.

Amendment 23

(Ratified March 29, 1961)

Section 1. The District constituting the seat of government of the United States shall appoint in such manner as the Congress may direct:
   A number of electors of President and Vice President equal to the whole number of Senators and Representatives in Congress to which the District would be entitled if it were a state, but in no event more than the least populous state; they shall be in addition to those

appointed by the states, but they shall be considered, for the purposes of the election of President and Vice President, to be electors appointed by a state; and they shall meet in the District and perform such duties as provided by the twelfth article of amendment.

Section 2. The Congress shall have power to enforce this article by appropriate legislation.

Amendment 24

(Ratified January 23, 1964)

Section 1. The right of citizens of the United States to vote in any primary or other election for President or Vice President, for electors for President or Vice President, or for Senator or Representative in Congress, shall not be denied or abridged by the United States or any state by reason of failure to pay any poll tax or other tax.

Section 2. The Congress shall have power to enforce this article by appropriate legislation.

Amendment 25

(Ratified February 10, 1967)

Section 1. In case of the removal of the President from office or of his death or resignation, the Vice President shall become President.

Section 2. Whenever there is a vacancy in the office of the Vice President, the President shall nominate a Vice President who shall take office upon confirmation by a majority vote of both Houses of Congress.

Section 3. Whenever the President transmits to the President pro tempore of the Senate and the Speaker of the House of Representatives his written declaration that he is unable to discharge the powers and duties of his office, and until he transmits to them a written declaration to the contrary, such powers and duties shall be discharged by the Vice President as Acting President.

Section 4. Whenever the Vice President and a majority of either the principal officers of the executive departments or of such other body as Congress may by law provide, transmit to the President pro tempore of the Senate and the Speaker of the House of Representatives their written declaration that the President is unable to discharge the powers and duties of his office, the Vice President shall immediately assume the powers and duties of the office as Acting President.

Thereafter, when the President transmits to the President pro tempore of the Senate and the Speaker of the House of Representatives his written declaration that no inability exists, he shall resume the powers and duties of his office unless the Vice President and a majority of either the principal officers of the executive department or of such other body as Congress may by law provide, transmit within four days to the President pro tempore of the Senate and the Speaker of the House of Representatives their written declaration that the President is unable to discharge the powers and duties of his office. Thereupon Congress shall decide the issue, assembling within forty-eight hours for that purpose if not in session. If the Congress, within twenty-one days after receipt of the latter written declaration, or, if Congress is not in session, within twenty-one days after Congress is required to assemble, determines by two-thirds vote of both Houses that the President is unable to discharge the powers and duties of his office, the Vice President shall continue to discharge the same as Acting President; otherwise, the President shall resume the powers and duties of his office.

Amendment 26

(Ratified July 1, 1971)

Section 1. The right of citizens of the United States, who are 18 years of age or older, to vote, shall not be denied or abridged by the United States or any state on account of age.

Section 2. The Congress shall have the power to enforce this article by appropriate legislation.

Amendment 27

(Ratified May 7, 1992)

No law, varying the compensation for the services of the Senators and Representatives, shall take effect, until an election of Representatives shall have intervened.

For more information on the Constitution of the United States and the Charters of Freedom, see http://archives.gov/ exhibits/charters/constitution.html.

THE GOVERNMENT OF THE UNITED STATES

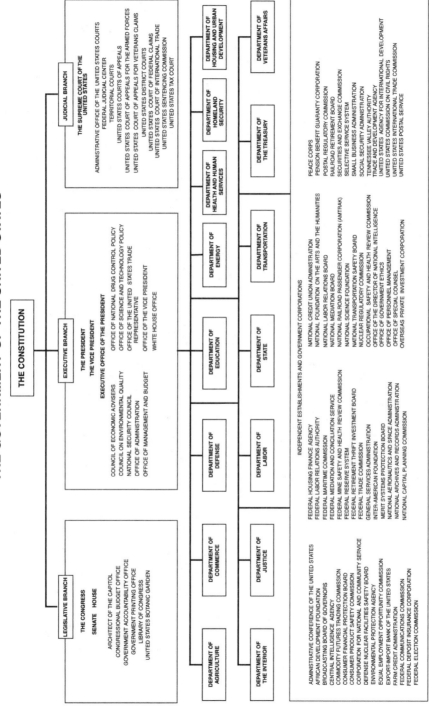

THE CONSTITUTION

LEGISLATIVE BRANCH

THE CONGRESS

SENATE   HOUSE

ARCHITECT OF THE CAPITOL
CONGRESSIONAL BUDGET OFFICE
GOVERNMENT ACCOUNTABILITY OFFICE
GOVERNMENT PRINTING OFFICE
LIBRARY OF CONGRESS
UNITED STATES BOTANIC GARDEN

EXECUTIVE BRANCH

THE PRESIDENT

THE VICE PRESIDENT

EXECUTIVE OFFICE OF THE PRESIDENT

COUNCIL OF ECONOMIC ADVISERS
COUNCIL ON ENVIRONMENTAL QUALITY
NATIONAL SECURITY COUNCIL
OFFICE OF ADMINISTRATION
OFFICE OF MANAGEMENT AND BUDGET

OFFICE OF NATIONAL DRUG CONTROL POLICY
OFFICE OF SCIENCE AND TECHNOLOGY POLICY
OFFICE OF THE UNITED STATES TRADE
REPRESENTATIVE
OFFICE OF THE VICE PRESIDENT
WHITE HOUSE OFFICE

JUDICIAL BRANCH

THE SUPREME COURT OF THE
UNITED STATES

ADMINISTRATIVE OFFICE OF THE UNITED STATES COURTS
FEDERAL JUDICIAL CENTER
TERRITORIAL COURTS
UNITED STATES COURTS OF APPEALS
UNITED STATES COURT OF APPEALS FOR THE ARMED FORCES
UNITED STATES COURT OF APPEALS FOR VETERANS CLAIMS
UNITED STATES DISTRICT COURTS
UNITED STATES COURT OF FEDERAL CLAIMS
UNITED STATES COURT OF INTERNATIONAL TRADE
UNITED STATES SENTENCING COMMISSION
UNITED STATES TAX COURT

DEPARTMENT OF AGRICULTURE

DEPARTMENT OF COMMERCE

DEPARTMENT OF DEFENSE

DEPARTMENT OF EDUCATION

DEPARTMENT OF ENERGY

DEPARTMENT OF HEALTH AND HUMAN SERVICES

DEPARTMENT OF HOMELAND SECURITY

DEPARTMENT OF HOUSING AND URBAN DEVELOPMENT

DEPARTMENT OF THE INTERIOR

DEPARTMENT OF JUSTICE

DEPARTMENT OF LABOR

DEPARTMENT OF STATE

DEPARTMENT OF TRANSPORTATION

DEPARTMENT OF THE TREASURY

DEPARTMENT OF VETERANS AFFAIRS

INDEPENDENT ESTABLISHMENTS AND GOVERNMENT CORPORATIONS

ADMINISTRATIVE CONFERENCE OF THE UNITED STATES
AFRICAN DEVELOPMENT FOUNDATION
BROADCASTING BOARD OF GOVERNORS
CENTRAL INTELLIGENCE AGENCY
COMMODITY FUTURES TRADING COMMISSION
CONSUMER FINANCIAL PROTECTION BOARD
CONSUMER PRODUCT SAFETY COMMISSION
CORPORATION FOR NATIONAL AND COMMUNITY SERVICE
DEFENSE NUCLEAR FACILITIES SAFETY BOARD
ENVIRONMENTAL PROTECTION AGENCY
EQUAL EMPLOYMENT OPPORTUNITY COMMISSION
EXPORT-IMPORT BANK OF THE UNITED STATES
FARM CREDIT ADMINISTRATION
FEDERAL COMMUNICATIONS COMMISSION
FEDERAL DEPOSIT INSURANCE CORPORATION
FEDERAL ELECTION COMMISSION

FEDERAL HOUSING FINANCE AGENCY
FEDERAL LABOR RELATIONS AUTHORITY
FEDERAL MARITIME COMMISSION
FEDERAL MEDIATION AND CONCILIATION SERVICE
FEDERAL MINE SAFETY AND HEALTH REVIEW COMMISSION
FEDERAL RESERVE SYSTEM
FEDERAL RETIREMENT THRIFT INVESTMENT BOARD
FEDERAL TRADE COMMISSION
GENERAL SERVICES ADMINISTRATION
INTER-AMERICAN FOUNDATION
MERIT SYSTEMS PROTECTION BOARD
NATIONAL AERONAUTICS AND SPACE ADMINISTRATION
NATIONAL ARCHIVES AND RECORDS ADMINISTRATION
NATIONAL CAPITAL PLANNING COMMISSION

NATIONAL CREDIT UNION ADMINISTRATION
NATIONAL FOUNDATION ON THE ARTS AND THE HUMANITIES
NATIONAL LABOR RELATIONS BOARD
NATIONAL MEDIATION BOARD
NATIONAL RAILROAD PASSENGER CORPORATION (AMTRAK)
NATIONAL SCIENCE FOUNDATION
NATIONAL TRANSPORTATION SAFETY BOARD
NUCLEAR REGULATORY COMMISSION
OCCUPATIONAL SAFETY AND HEALTH REVIEW COMMISSION
OFFICE OF THE DIRECTOR OF NATIONAL INTELLIGENCE
OFFICE OF GOVERNMENT ETHICS
OFFICE OF PERSONNEL MANAGEMENT
OFFICE OF SPECIAL COUNSEL
OVERSEAS PRIVATE INVESTMENT CORPORATION

PEACE CORPS
PENSION BENEFIT GUARANTY CORPORATION
POSTAL REGULATORY COMMISSION
RAILROAD RETIREMENT BOARD
SECURITIES AND EXCHANGE COMMISSION
SELECTIVE SERVICE SYSTEM
SMALL BUSINESS ADMINISTRATION
SOCIAL SECURITY ADMINISTRATION
TENNESSEE VALLEY AUTHORITY
TRADE AND DEVELOPMENT AGENCY
UNITED STATES AGENCY FOR INTERNATIONAL DEVELOPMENT
UNITED STATES COMMISSION ON CIVIL RIGHTS
UNITED STATES INTERNATIONAL TRADE COMMISSION
UNITED STATES POSTAL SERVICE

Legislative Branch

LEGISLATIVE BRANCH

CONGRESS

One Hundred and Fifteenth Congress, First Session, http://www.congress.gov

The Congress of the United States was created by Article I, section 1, of the Constitution, adopted by the Constitutional Convention on September 17, 1787, providing that "All legislative Powers herein granted shall be vested in a Congress of the United States, which shall consist of a Senate and House of Representatives."

The first Congress under the Constitution met on March 4, 1789, in the Federal Hall in New York City. The membership then consisted of 20 Senators and 59 Representatives.*

Congressional Record Proceedings of Congress are published in the Congressional Record, which is issued each day when Congress is in session. Publication of the Record began March 4, 1873. It was the first record of debate officially reported, printed, and published directly by the Federal Government. The Daily Digest of the Congressional Record, printed in the back of each issue of the Record, summarizes the proceedings of that day in each House and each of their committees and subcommittees, respectively. The Digest also presents the legislative program for each day and, at the end of the week, gives the program for the following week. Its publication was begun March 17, 1947.

Sessions Section 4 of Article I of the Constitution makes it mandatory that "The Congress shall assemble at least once in every Year. . . ." Under this provision, also, the date for convening Congress was designated originally as the first Monday in December, "unless they shall by Law appoint a different Day." Eighteen acts were passed, up to 1820, providing for the meeting of Congress on

other days of the year. From 1820 to 1934, however, Congress met regularly on the first Monday in December. In 1934 the 20th amendment changed the convening of Congress to January 3, unless Congress "shall by law appoint a different day." In addition, the President, according to Article II, section 3, of the Constitution "may, on extraordinary Occasions, convene both Houses, or either of them, and in Case of Disagreement between them, with Respect to the Time of Adjournment, he may adjourn them to such Time as he shall think proper. . . ."

Powers of Congress Article I, section 8, of the Constitution defines the powers of Congress. Included are the powers to assess and collect taxes—called the chief power; to regulate commerce, both interstate and foreign; to coin money; to establish post offices and post roads; to establish courts inferior to the Supreme Court; to declare war; and to raise and maintain an army and navy. Congress is further empowered "To provide for calling forth the Militia to execute the Laws of the Union, suppress Insurrections and repel Invasions;" and "To make all Laws which shall be necessary and proper for carrying into Execution the foregoing Powers, and all other Powers vested by this Constitution in the Government of the United States, or in any Department or Officer thereof."

---

*New York ratified the Constitution on July 26, 1788, but did not elect its Senators until July 15 and 16, 1789. North Carolina did not ratify the Constitution until November 21, 1789; Rhode Island ratified it on May 29, 1790.

25

Amendments to the Constitution   Another power vested in the Congress is the right to propose amendments to the Constitution, whenever two-thirds of both Houses shall deem it necessary. Should two-thirds of the State legislatures demand changes in the Constitution, it is the duty of Congress to call a constitutional convention. Proposed amendments shall be valid as part of the Constitution when ratified by the legislatures or by conventions of three-fourths of the States, as one or the other mode of ratification may be proposed by Congress.

Prohibitions Upon Congress   Section 9 of Article I of the Constitution also imposes prohibitions upon Congress. "The Privilege of the Writ of Habeas Corpus shall not be suspended, unless when in Cases of Rebellion or Invasion the public Safety may require it." A bill of attainder or an ex post facto law cannot be passed. No export duty can be imposed. Ports of one State cannot be given preference over those of another State. "No money shall be drawn from the Treasury, but in Consequence of Appropriations made by Law. . . ." No title of nobility may be granted.

Rights of Members   According to section 6 of Article I, Members of Congress are granted certain privileges. In no case, except in treason, felony, and breach of the peace, can Members be arrested while attending sessions of Congress "and in going to and returning from the same. . . ." Furthermore, the Members cannot be questioned in any other place for remarks made in Congress. Each House may expel a Member of its body by a two-thirds vote.

Enactment of Laws   In order to become law, all bills and joint resolutions, except those proposing a constitutional amendment, must pass both the House of Representatives and the Senate and either be signed by the President or be passed over the President's veto by a two-thirds vote of both Houses of Congress. Section 7 of Article I states: "If any Bill shall not be returned by the President within ten Days (Sundays excepted) after it shall have been presented to him, the Same shall be a Law, in like Manner as if he had signed it, unless the Congress by their Adjournment prevent its Return, in which Case it shall not be a Law." When a bill or joint resolution is introduced in the House, the usual procedure for its enactment into law is as follows: assignment to House committee having jurisdiction; if favorably considered, it is reported to the House either in its original form or with recommended amendments; if the bill or resolution is passed by the House, it is messaged to the Senate and referred to the committee having jurisdiction; in the Senate committee the bill, if favorably considered, may be reported in the form as received from the House, or with recommended amendments; the approved bill or resolution is reported to the Senate, and if passed by that body, is returned to the House; if one body does not accept the amendments to a bill by the other body, a conference committee comprised of Members of both bodies is usually appointed to effect a compromise; when the bill or joint resolution is finally approved by both Houses, it is signed by the Speaker (or Speaker pro tempore) and the Vice President (or President pro tempore or acting President pro tempore) and is presented to the President; and once the President's signature is affixed, the measure becomes a law. If the President vetoes the bill, it cannot become a law unless it is re-passed by a two-thirds vote of both Houses.

The Senate

The Capitol, Washington, DC 20510
Phone, 202-224-3121. Internet, http://www.senate.gov

Constitutionally Mandated Officers	
President of the Senate / Vice President of the United States	MICHAEL R. PENCE
President pro tempore	ORRIN G. HATCH
Political Party Leaders	
Majority Leader	A. MITCHELL McCONNELL
Minority Leader	CHARLES E. SCHUMER
Officers / Officials	
Chaplain	BARRY C. BLACK
Parliamentarian	ELIZABETH C. MacDONOUGH
Secretary for the Majority	LAURA C. DOVE
Secretary for the Minority	GARY B. MYRICK
Secretary of the Senate	JULIE E. ADAMS
Sergeant at Arms	FRANK J. LARKIN

Overview   The Senate comprises 100 Members, 2 from each State. Senators are elected to serve for a term of 6 years. There are three classes of Senators, and a new class is elected every 2 years. Senators were originally chosen by the State legislatures. The 17th amendment, which became part of the Constitution in 1913, made their election a function of the people.

A Senator must be a resident of the State that he or she represents. A Senator also must be at least 30 years of age and have been a U.S. citizen for at least 9 years.

Officers   The Vice President of the United States is the Presiding Officer of the Senate. In the Vice President's absence, the duties are taken over by a President pro tempore, elected by that body, or someone designated by the President pro tempore.

The positions of Senate Majority and Minority Leader have been in existence only since the early years of the 20th century. Leaders are elected at the beginning of each new Congress by a majority vote of the Senators in their political party. In cooperation with their party organizations, Leaders are responsible for the design and achievement of a legislative program. This involves managing the flow of legislation, expediting noncontroversial measures, and keeping Members informed regarding proposed action on pending business. Each Leader serves as an ex officio member of his party's policymaking and organizational bodies and is aided by an assistant floor leader (whip) and a party secretary.

The Secretary of the Senate, elected by vote of the Senate, performs the duties of the Presiding Officer of the Senate in the absence of the Vice President and pending the election of a President pro tempore. The Secretary is the custodian of the seal of the Senate, draws requisitions on the Secretary of the Treasury for moneys appropriated for the compensation of Senators, officers, and employees, and for the contingent expenses of the Senate, and is empowered to administer oaths to any officer of the Senate and to any witness produced before it. The Secretary's executive duties include certification of extracts from the Journal of the Senate; the attestation of bills and joint, concurrent, and Senate resolutions; in impeachment trials, issuance, under the authority of the Presiding Officer, of all orders, mandates, writs, and precepts authorized by the Senate; and certification to the President of the United States of the advice and consent of the Senate to ratification of treaties and the names of persons confirmed or rejected upon the nomination of the President.

The Sergeant at Arms, elected by vote of the Senate, serves as the executive, chief law enforcement, and protocol officer and is the principal administrative manager for most support services in the Senate. As executive officer, the Sergeant at Arms has custody of the Senate gavel; enforces Senate rules and regulations as they pertain to the Senate Chamber, the Senate wing of the Capitol, and the Senate office buildings; and

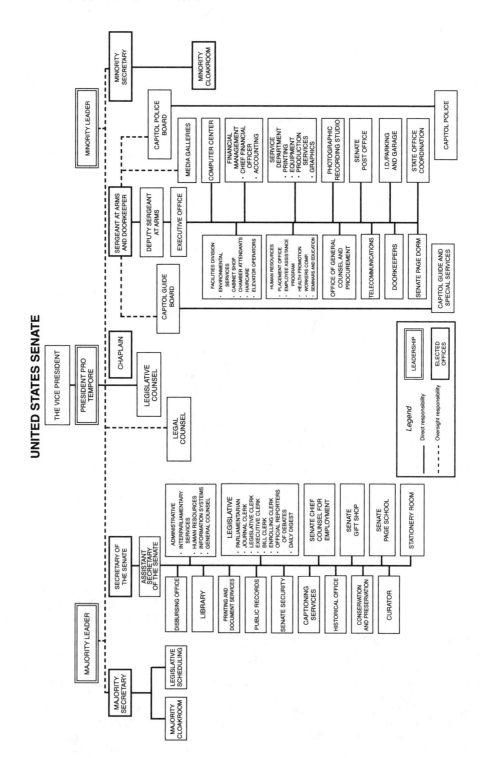

UNITED STATES SENATE

subject to the Presiding Officer, maintains order on the Senate floor, Chamber, and galleries. As chief law enforcement officer of the Senate, the Sergeant at Arms is authorized to maintain security in the Capitol and all Senate buildings, as well as to protect Senators; to arrest and detain any person violating Senate rules; and to locate absentee Senators for a quorum. The Sergeant at Arms serves as a member of the Capitol Police Board and as its chairman each odd year. As protocol officer, the Sergeant at Arms escorts the President and other heads of state or official guests of the Senate who are attending official functions in the Capitol; makes arrangements for funerals of Senators who die in office; and assists in planning the inauguration of the President and organizing the swearing-in and orientation programs for newly elected Senators.

Committees   The work of preparing and considering legislation is done largely by committees of both Houses of Congress. There are 16 standing committees in the Senate. The standing committees of the Senate are shown in the list below. In addition, there are two select committees in each House and various congressional commissions and joint committees composed of Members of both Houses. Each House may also appoint special investigating committees. The membership of the standing committees of each House is chosen by a vote of the entire body; members of other committees are appointed under the provisions of the measure establishing them.

Each bill and resolution is usually referred to the appropriate committee, which may report a bill out in its original form, favorably or unfavorably, recommend amendments, report original measures, or allow the proposed legislation to die in committee without action. http://www.senate.gov/general/common/generic/about_committees.htm

Standing Committees of the Senate

Committee	Chair	Web Site
Agriculture, Nutrition, and Forestry	C. Patrick Roberts	http://www.agriculture.senate.gov
Appropriations	W. Thad Cochran	http://www.appropriations.senate.gov
Armed Services	John S. McCain	http://www.armed-services.senate.gov
Banking, Housing, and Urban Affairs	Michael D. Crapo	http://www.banking.senate.gov
Budget	Michael B. Enzi	http://www.budget.senate.gov
Commerce, Science, and Transportation	John R. Thune	http://www.commerce.senate.gov
Energy and Natural Resources	Lisa A. Murkowski	https://www.energy.senate.gov
Environment and Public Works	John A. Barrasso	https://www.epw.senate.gov
Finance	Orrin G. Hatch	https://www.finance.senate.gov
Foreign Relations	Robert P. Corker, Jr.	http://www.foreign.senate.gov
Health, Education, Labor, and Pensions	A. Lamar Alexander, Jr.	http://www.help.senate.gov
Homeland Security and Governmental Affairs	Ronald H. Johnson	https://www.hsgac.senate.gov
Judiciary	Charles E. Grassley	https://www.judiciary.senate.gov
Rules and Administration	Richard C. Shelby	http://www.rules.senate.gov/public
Small Business and Entrepreneurship	James E. Risch	http://www.sbc.senate.gov
Veterans' Affairs	John H. Isakson	https://www.veterans.senate.gov

Special Powers   Under the Constitution, the Senate is granted certain powers not accorded to the House of Representatives. The Senate approves or disapproves certain Presidential appointments by majority vote, and treaties must be concurred in by a two-thirds vote.

List of U.S. Senators

State	Expiration Of Term—Party Affiliation	Contact Information
Alabama		
Richard C. Shelby	2023—Republican	http://www.shelby.senate.gov
Luther J. Strange III	2021—Republican	http://www.strange.senate.gov
Alaska		
Lisa A. Murkowski	2023—Republican	https://www.murkowski.senate.gov
Daniel S. Sullivan	2021—Republican	http://www.sullivan.senate.gov
Arizona		
Jeffry L. Flake	2019—Republican	http://www.flake.senate.gov
John S. McCain	2023—Republican	http://www.mccain.senate.gov
Arkansas		
John N. Boozman	2023—Republican	https://www.boozman.senate.gov
Thomas B. Cotton	2021—Republican	https://www.cotton.senate.gov
California		
Dianne Feinstein	2019—Democrat	http://www.feinstein.senate.gov
Kamala D. Harris	2023—Democrat	https://www.harris.senate.gov
Colorado		
Michael F. Bennet	2023—Democrat	https://www.bennet.senate.gov
Cory S. Gardner	2021—Republican	https://www.gardner.senate.gov
Connecticut		
Richard Blumenthal	2023—Democrat	https://www.blumenthal.senate.gov
Christopher S. Murphy	2019—Democrat	https://www.murphy.senate.gov
Delaware		
Thomas R. Carper	2019—Democrat	https://www.carper.senate.gov
Christopher A. Coons	2021—Democrat	https://www.coons.senate.gov
Florida		
C. William Nelson	2019—Democrat	https://www.billnelson.senate.gov
Marco A. Rubio	2023—Republican	http://www.rubio.senate.gov
Georgia		
John H. Isakson	2023—Republican	https://www.isakson.senate.gov
David A. Perdue, Jr.	2021—Republican	http://www.perdue.senate.gov
Hawaii		
Mazie K. Hirono	2019—Democrat	https://www.hirono.senate.gov
Brian E. Schatz	2023—Democrat	http://www.schatz.senate.gov
Idaho		
Michael D. Crapo	2023—Republican	http://www.crapo.senate.gov
James E. Risch	2021—Republican	http://www.risch.senate.gov
Illinois		
L. Tammy Duckworth	2023—Democrat	https://www.duckworth.senate.gov
Richard J. Durbin	2021—Democrat	http://www.durbin.senate.gov
Indiana		
Joseph S. Donnelly	2019—Democrat	http://www.donnelly.senate.gov
Todd C. Young	2023—Republican	https://www.young.senate.gov
Iowa		
Joni K. Ernst	2021—Republican	http://www.ernst.senate.gov
Charles E. Grassley	2023—Republican	http://www.grassley.senate.gov

List of U.S. Senators (*Continued*)

State	Expiration Of Term—Party Affiliation	Contact Information
Kansas		
Gerald W. Moran	2023—Republican	http://www.moran.senate.gov
C. Patrick Roberts	2021—Republican	http://www.roberts.senate.gov
Kentucky		
A. Mitchell McConnell	2021—Republican	http://www.mcconnell.senate.gov
Randal H. Paul	2023—Republican	https://www.paul.senate.gov
Louisiana		
William Cassidy	2021—Republican	http://www.cassidy.senate.gov
John N. Kennedy	2023—Republican	https://www.kennedy.senate.gov
Maine		
Susan M. Collins	2021—Republican	https://www.collins.senate.gov
Angus S. King, Jr.	2019—Independent	http://www.king.senate.gov
Maryland		
Benjamin L. Cardin	2019—Democrat	https://www.cardin.senate.gov
Christopher Van Hollen, Jr.	2023—Democrat	https://www.vanhollen.senate.gov
Massachusetts		
Edward J. Markey	2021—Democrat	http://www.markey.senate.gov
Elizabeth H. Warren	2019—Democrat	https://www.warren.senate.gov
Michigan		
Gary C. Peters	2021—Democrat	https://www.peters.senate.gov
Deborah A. Stabenow	2019—Democrat	http://www.stabenow.senate.gov
Minnesota		
Alan S. Franken	2021—Democrat	https://www.franken.senate.gov
Amy J. Klobuchar	2019—Democrat	https://www.klobuchar.senate.gov
Mississippi		
W. Thad Cochran	2021—Republican	http://www.cochran.senate.gov
Roger F. Wicker	2019—Republican	https://www.wicker.senate.gov
Missouri		
Roy D. Blunt	2023—Republican	http://www.blunt.senate.gov
Claire McCaskill	2019—Democrat	https://www.mccaskill.senate.gov
Montana		
Steven D. Daines	2021—Republican	https://www.daines.senate.gov
Jonathan Tester	2019—Democrat	http://www.tester.senate.gov
Nebraska		
Debra S. Fischer	2019—Republican	http://www.fischer.senate.gov
Benjamin E. Sasse	2021—Republican	http://www.sasse.senate.gov
Nevada		
Catherine Cortez Masto	2023—Democrat	https://www.cortezmasto.senate.gov
Dean A. Heller	2019—Republican	http://www.heller.senate.gov
New Hampshire		
Margaret Wood Hassan	2023—Democrat	https://www.hassan.senate.gov
Jeanne Shaheen	2021—Democrat	https://www.shaheen.senate.gov
New Jersey		
Cory A. Booker	2021—Democrat	http://www.booker.senate.gov
Robert Menendez	2019—Democrat	https://www.menendez.senate.gov

List of U.S. Senators (*Continued*)

State	Expiration Of Term—Party Affiliation	Contact Information
New Mexico		
Martin Heinrich	2019—Democrat	http://www.heinrich.senate.gov
Thomas S. Udall	2021—Democrat	http://www.tomudall.senate.gov
New York		
Kirsten E. Gillibrand	2019—Democrat	https://www.gillibrand.senate.gov
Charles E. Schumer	2023—Democrat	https://www.schumer.senate.gov
North Carolina		
Richard Burr	2023—Republican	http://www.burr.senate.gov
Thomas R. Tillis	2021—Republican	https://www.tillis.senate.gov
North Dakota		
Heidi Heitkamp	2019—Democrat	http://www.heitkamp.senate.gov
John H. Hoeven III	2023—Republican	https://www.hoeven.senate.gov
Ohio		
Sherrod C. Brown	2019—Democrat	https://www.brown.senate.gov
Robert J. Portman	2023—Republican	http://www.portman.senate.gov
Oklahoma		
James M. Inhofe	2021—Republican	http://www.inhofe.senate.gov
James Lankford	2023—Republican	https://www.lankford.senate.gov
Oregon		
Jeffrey A. Merkley	2021—Democrat	https://www.merkley.senate.gov
Ronald L. Wyden	2023—Democrat	https://www.wyden.senate.gov
Pennsylvania		
Robert P. Casey, Jr.	2019—Democrat	https://www.casey.senate.gov
Patrick J. Toomey	2023—Republican	http://www.toomey.senate.gov
Rhode Island		
John F. Reed	2021—Democrat	https://www.reed.senate.gov
Sheldon Whitehouse	2019—Democrat	https://www.whitehouse.senate.gov
South Carolina		
Lindsey O. Graham	2021—Republican	https://www.lgraham.senate.gov
Timothy E. Scott	2023—Republican	https://www.scott.senate.gov
South Dakota		
M. Michael Rounds	2021—Republican	https://www.rounds.senate.gov
John R. Thune	2023—Republican	https://www.thune.senate.gov
Tennessee		
A. Lamar Alexander, Jr.	2021—Republican	https://www.alexander.senate.gov
Robert P. Corker, Jr.	2019—Republican	https://www.corker.senate.gov
Texas		
John Cornyn III	2021—Republican	https://www.cornyn.senate.gov
R. Edward Cruz	2019—Republican	https://www.cruz.senate.gov
Utah		
Orrin G. Hatch	2019—Republican	http://www.hatch.senate.gov
Michael S. Lee	2023—Republican	https://www.lee.senate.gov
Vermont		
Patrick J. Leahy	2023—Democrat	https://www.leahy.senate.gov
Bernard Sanders	2019—Independent	https://www.sanders.senate.gov

List of U.S. Senators (*Continued*)

State	Expiration Of Term—Party Affiliation	Contact Information
Virginia		
Timothy M. Kaine	2019—Democrat	http://www.kaine.senate.gov
Mark R. Warner	2021—Democrat	http://www.warner.senate.gov
Washington		
Maria Cantwell	2019—Democrat	https://www.cantwell.senate.gov
Patricia L. Murray	2023—Democrat	http://www.murray.senate.gov
West Virginia		
Shelley Moore Capito	2021—Republican	https://www.capito.senate.gov
Joseph Manchin III	2019—Democrat	http://www.manchin.senate.gov
Wisconsin		
Tammy S. Baldwin	2019—Democrat	https://www.baldwin.senate.gov
Ronald H. Johnson	2023—Republican	https://www.ronjohnson.senate.gov
Wyoming		
John A. Barrasso	2019—Republican	https://www.barrasso.senate.gov
Michael B. Enzi	2021—Republican	http://www.enzi.senate.gov

The Above List Of 100 Senators Was Updated 09–2017. Republicans are 52; Democrats are 46; Independents are 2; and there are no vacancies. Information on Senate.gov may be more accurate and current. https://www.senate.gov

Sources of Information

Art   The Senate's collections of ephemera, decorative art, graphic art, paintings, and sculpture can be viewed online. http://www.senate.gov/pagelayout/art/one_item_and_teasers/Explore_Senate_Art.htm

Campaign Finance   The Federal Election Commission maintains a campaign finance database that contains information on candidates, including senatorial candidates, who file reports with the Commission. Users of the online "Candidate and Committee Viewer" can sort data and download them. The data presentations consist of biennial summaries, report summaries, and report images and downloads. http://www.fec.gov/finance/disclosure/candcmte_info.shtml?tabIndex=1

Campaign Web Sites   The Library of Congress maintains a database of "Archived Web Sites" that includes thousands of official campaign Web sites. Former senatorial candidates' Web sites are part of this collection. https://www.loc.gov/websites

Career Opportunities   Information on fellowships, internships, and job openings is available online. http://www.senate.gov/visiting/employment.htm

Committees   Information on Senate committees is available online. http://www.senate.gov/committees/committees_home.htm

Congressional Record   Starting with the year 1995, the official record of the proceedings and debates of the U.S. Congress is available on Congress.gov. https://www.congress.gov/congressional-record

Starting with the year 1994, the official record of the proceedings and debates of the U.S. Congress is available on the Government Publishing Office's Federal Digital System (FDsys) Web site. https://www.gpo.gov/fdsys/browse/collection.action?collectionCode=CREC

Contact a Senator   Phone numbers, postal addresses, and online forms are available for contacting a Senator. http://www.senate.gov/senators/contact

An online list of States also provides web forms for contacting a Senator via email. http://www.senate.gov/senators/states.htm

Directory   The online "Biographical Directory of the United States Congress, 1774–Present," allows visitors to search for Members of Congress—past and present—by first or last name, political affiliation, position, State, or year or Congress. http://bioguide.congress.gov/biosearch/biosearch.asp

Glossary   A Senate glossary is available online. http://www.senate.gov/reference/glossary.htm

History   The Senate Historical Office has told the history of the Senate, from the First Federal Congress of 1789 through the early 21st century; explained its traditions; described the individuals who served in its Chamber, and examined the major issues that confronted these national leaders. http://www.senate.gov/pagelayout/history/a_three_section_with_teasers/Explore_Senate_History.htm

Legislation / Records   Research guides and resources are available online. http://www.senate.gov/legislative/legislative_home.htm

Member Profiles   The "Members of the U.S. Congress" database contains profiles for Senators who have held office since 1973 or were still serving in the 93d Congress. Users of the database can filter profiles by chamber, Congress, political affiliation, and State or U.S. Territory. A Member profile includes the following: dates of service, State represented, party affiliation, and a picture when available, as well as a link to the Member's entry in the "Biographical Directory of the United States Congress, 1774–Present" and a link to remarks made in the "Congressional Record." A profile also includes the list of legislation that the Member sponsored and cosponsored. https://www.congress.gov/members

Membership / Party Divisions   The Office of the Clerk's "Congressional Profile" Web page keeps a tally of the number of Democrats, Independents, Republicans, and vacant seats in both the Senate and the House of Representatives. http://clerk.house.gov/member_info/cong.aspx

Publications   The Congressional Directory, the Senate Manual, and telephone directory for the U.S. Senate are available from the Government Publishing Office's bookstore. Phone, 202-512-0132. https://www.gpo.gov/about/bookstore.htm | Email: mainbks@gpo.gov

Web Sites   More information on legislation and the U.S. Senate is available on Congress.gov. https://www.congress.gov

More information also is available on the Government Publishing Office's Federal Digital System (FDsys) Web site. https://www.gpo.gov/fdsys/browse/collectiontab.action. http://www.senate.gov/general/contacting.htm.

For further information, contact the Secretary of the Senate, The Capitol, Washington, DC 20510. Phone, 202-224-2115.

The House of Representatives

The Capitol, Washington, DC 20515
Phone, 202-225-3121. Internet, http://www.house.gov

Constitutionally Mandated Officer	
Speaker of the House	PAUL D. RYAN
Political Party Leaders	
Majority Leader	KEVIN O. MCCARTHY
Minority Leader	NANCY P. PELOSI
Officers / Officials	
Chaplain	PATRICK J. CONROY
Chief Administrative Officer	Philip G. Kiko
Clerk	KAREN L. HAAS
Parliamentarian	THOMAS J. WICKHAM, JR.
Sergeant at Arms	PAUL D. IRVING

Overview   The House of Representatives comprises 435 Representatives. The number representing each State is determined by population, but every State is entitled to at least one Representative. Members are elected by the people for 2-year terms, all terms running for the same period. Representatives must be residents of the State from which they are chosen. In addition, a Representative must be at least 25 years of age and must have been a citizen for at least 7 years.

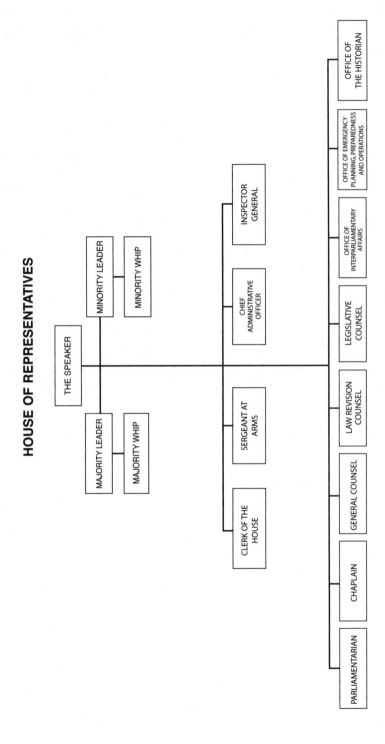

HOUSE OF REPRESENTATIVES

A Resident Commissioner from Puerto Rico (elected for a 4-year term) and Delegates from American Samoa, the District of Columbia, Guam, the Northern Mariana Islands, and the Virgin Islands complete the composition of the Congress of the United States. Delegates are elected for a term of 2 years. The Resident Commissioner and Delegates may take part in the floor discussions, but have no vote in the full House. They do, however, vote in the committees to which they are assigned.

Officers   The Presiding Officer of the House of Representatives, the Speaker, is elected by the House. The Speaker may designate any Member of the House to act in the Speaker's absence.

The House leadership is structured essentially the same as the Senate, with the Members in the political parties responsible for the election of their respective leader and whips.

The elected officers of the House of Representatives include the Clerk, the Sergeant at Arms, the Chief Administrative Officer, and the Chaplain.

The Clerk is custodian of the seal of the House and administers the primary legislative activities of the House. These duties include accepting the credentials of the Members-elect and calling the Members to order at the commencement of the first session of each Congress; keeping the Journal; taking all votes and certifying the passage of bills; and processing all legislation. Through various departments, the Clerk is also responsible for floor and committee reporting services; legislative information and reference services; the administration of House reports pursuant to House rules and certain legislation including the Ethics in Government Act and the Lobbying Disclosure Act of 1995; and the distribution of House documents. The Clerk is also charged with supervision of the offices vacated by Members due to death, resignation, or expulsion.

The Sergeant at Arms maintains the order of the House under the direction of the Speaker and is the keeper of the Mace. As a member of the U.S. Capitol Police Board, the Sergeant at Arms is the chief law enforcement officer for the House and serves as Board Chairman each even year. The ceremonial and protocol duties parallel those of the Senate Sergeant at Arms and include arranging the inauguration of the President of the United States, Joint Sessions of Congress, visits to the House of heads of state, and funerals of Members of Congress. The Sergeant at Arms enforces the rules relating to the privileges of the Hall of the House, including admission to the galleries, oversees garage and parking security of the House, and distributes all House staff identification cards.

Committees   The work of preparing and considering legislation is done largely by committees of both Houses of Congress. There are 19 standing committees in the House of Representatives. The standing committees of the House of Representatives are shown in the list below. In addition, there are two select committees in the House and various congressional commissions and joint committees composed of Members of both Houses. Each House may also appoint special investigating committees. The membership of the standing committees of each House is chosen by a vote of the entire body; members of other committees are appointed under the provisions of the measure establishing them.

Each bill and resolution is usually referred to the appropriate committee, which may report a bill out in its original form, favorably or unfavorably, recommend amendments, report original measures, or allow the proposed legislation to die in committee without action.

Standing Committees of The House of Representatives

Committee	Chair	Web Site
Agriculture	K. Michael Conaway	http://agriculture.house.gov
Appropriations	Rodney P. Frelinghuysen	http://appropriations.house.gov
Armed Services	W. McClellan Thornberry	https://armedservices.house.gov
Budget	Diane L. Black	http://budget.house.gov
Education and the Workforce	Virginia A. Foxx	http://edworkforce.house.gov

Standing Committees of The House of Representatives (*Continued*)

Energy and Commerce	Gregory P. Walden	https://energycommerce.house.gov
Ethics	Susan W. Brooks	http://ethics.house.gov
Financial Services	T. Jeb Hensarling	http://financialservices.house.gov
Foreign Affairs	Edward R. Royce	https://foreignaffairs.house.gov
Homeland Security	Michael T. McCaul	https://homeland.house.gov
House Administration	Gregory L. Harper	https://cha.house.gov
House Administration (Franking Office)	Rodney L. Davis	https://cha.house.gov/franking-commission
Judiciary	Robert W. Goodlatte	https://judiciary.house.gov
Natural Resources	Robert W. Bishop	http://naturalresources.house.gov
Oversight and Government Reform	Jason E. Chaffetz	https://oversight.house.gov
Rules	Peter A. Sessions	https://rules.house.gov
Rules (Minority)	Louise M. Slaughter (Ranking Member)	http://democrats.rules.house.gov
Science, Space, and Technology	Lamar S. Smith	https://science.house.gov
Small Business	Steven J. Chabot	http://smallbusiness.house.gov
Transportation and Infrastructure	William F. Shuster	http://transportation.house.gov
Veterans' Affairs	D. Phillip Roe	https://veterans.house.gov
Ways and Means	Kevin P. Brady	https://waysandmeans.house.gov

Special Powers The House of Representatives is granted the power of originating all bills for the raising of revenue. Both Houses of Congress act in impeachment proceedings, which, according to the Constitution, may be instituted against the President, Vice President, and all civil officers of the United States. The House of Representatives has the sole power of impeachment, and the Senate has the sole power to try impeachments.

List of U.S. Representatives

State / District	District—Party Affiliation	Contact Information
Alabama		
Bradley R. Byrne	01—Republican	https://byrne.house.gov
Martha Roby	02—Republican	http://roby.house.gov
Michael D. Rogers	03—Republican	https://mikerogers.house.gov
Robert B. Aderholt	04—Republican	https://aderholt.house.gov
Morris J. Brooks, Jr.	05—Republican	https://brooks.house.gov
Gary J. Palmer	06—Republican	https://palmer.house.gov
Terrycina A. Sewell	07—Democrat	https://sewell.house.gov
Alaska		
Donald E. Young	At Large—Republican	http://donyoung.house.gov
American Samoa		
Amata Coleman Radewagen—Delegate	At Large—Republican	https://radewagen.house.gov
Arizona		
Thomas C. O'Halleran	01—Democrat	https://ohalleran.house.gov
Martha McSally	02—Republican	https://mcsally.house.gov
Raúl M. Grijalva	03—Democrat	https://grijalva.house.gov
Paul A. Gosar	04—Republican	http://gosar.house.gov
Andrew S. Biggs	05—Republican	https://biggs.house.gov
David Schweikert	06—Republican	https://schweikert.house.gov
Ruben M. Gallego	07—Democrat	https://rubengallego.house.gov
H. Trent Franks	08—Republican	https://franks.house.gov
Kyrsten Sinema	09—Democrat	https://sinema.house.gov

List of U.S. Representatives (*Continued*)

State / District	District—Party Affiliation	Contact Information
Arkansas		
Eric A. Crawford	01—Republican	https://crawford.house.gov
J. French Hill	02—Republican	https://hill.house.gov
Stephen A. Womack	03—Republican	https://womack.house.gov
Bruce E. Westerman	04—Republican	https://westerman.house.gov
California		
Douglas L. LaMalfa	01—Republican	http://lamalfa.house.gov
Jared W. Huffman	02—Democrat	https://huffman.house.gov
John R. Garamendi	03—Democrat	https://garamendi.house.gov
Thomas M. McClintock	04—Republican	https://mcclintock.house.gov
Michael C. Thompson	05—Democrat	https://mikethompson.house.gov
Doris O. Matsui	06—Democrat	https://matsui.house.gov
Amerish B. Bera	07—Democrat	https://bera.house.gov
Paul J. Cook	08—Republican	https://cook.house.gov
Gerald M. McNerney	09—Democrat	https://mcnerney.house.gov
Jeffrey J. Denham	10—Republican	https://denham.house.gov
Mark J. DeSaulnier	11—Democrat	https://desaulnier.house.gov
Nancy P. Pelosi	12—Democrat	https://pelosi.house.gov
Barbara J. Lee	13—Democrat	https://lee.house.gov
K. Jacqueline Speier	14—Democrat	https://speier.house.gov
Eric M. Swalwell	15—Democrat	https://swalwell.house.gov
James M. Costa	16—Democrat	https://costa.house.gov
Ro Khanna	17—Democrat	https://khanna.house.gov
Anna G. Eshoo	18—Democrat	https://eshoo.house.gov
Zoe Lofgren	19—Democrat	https://lofgren.house.gov
James V. Panetta	20—Democrat	https://panetta.house.gov
David G. Valadao	21—Republican	https://valadao.house.gov
Devin G. Nunes	22—Republican	https://nunes.house.gov
Kevin O. McCarthy	23—Republican	https://kevinmccarthy.house.gov
Salud O. Carbajal	24—Democrat	https://carbajal.house.gov
Stephen T. Knight	25—Republican	https://knight.house.gov
Julia A. Brownley	26—Democrat	https://juliabrownley.house.gov
Judy M. Chu	27—Democrat	https://chu.house.gov
Adam B. Schiff	28—Democrat	https://schiff.house.gov
Antonio Cárdenas	29—Democrat	https://cardenas.house.gov
Bradley J. Sherman	30—Democrat	https://sherman.house.gov
Peter R. Aguilar	31—Democrat	https://aguilar.house.gov
Grace F. Napolitano	32—Democrat	https://napolitano.house.gov
Ted W. Lieu	33—Democrat	https://lieu.house.gov
Jimmy Gomez	34—Democrat	https://gomez.house.gov
Norma J. Torres	35—Democrat	https://torres.house.gov
Raul Ruiz	36—Democrat	https://ruiz.house.gov
Karen R. Bass	37—Democrat	https://bass.house.gov
Linda T. Sánchez	38—Democrat	https://lindasanchez.house.gov
Edward R. Royce	39—Republican	http://royce.house.gov
Lucille Roybal-Allard	40—Democrat	https://roybal-allard.house.gov
Mark A. Takano	41—Democrat	https://takano.house.gov
Kenneth S. Calvert	42—Republican	http://calvert.house.gov
Maxine M. Waters	43—Democrat	https://waters.house.gov
Nanette Diaz Barragán	44—Democrat	https://barragan.house.gov
Marian K. Walters	45—Republican	https://walters.house.gov

List of U.S. Representatives (*Continued*)

State / District	District—Party Affiliation	Contact Information
J. Luis Correa	46—Democrat	https://correa.house.gov
Alan S. Lowenthal	47—Democrat	http://lowenthal.house.gov
Dana T. Rohrabacher	48—Republican	https://rohrabacher.house.gov
Darrell E. Issa	49—Republican	https://issa.house.gov
Duncan D. Hunter	50—Republican	https://hunter.house.gov
Juan C. Vargas	51—Democrat	http://vargas.house.gov
Scott H. Peters	52—Democrat	http://scottpeters.house.gov
Susan A. Davis	53—Democrat	https://susandavis.house.gov
Colorado		
Diana L. DeGette	01—Democrat	http://degette.house.gov
Jared S. Polis	02—Democrat	http://polis.house.gov
Scott R. Tipton	03—Republican	http://tipton.house.gov
Kenneth R. Buck	04—Republican	https://buck.house.gov
Douglas L. Lamborn	05—Republican	http://lamborn.house.gov
Michael H. Coffman	06—Republican	http://coffman.house.gov
Edwin G. Perlmutter	07—Democrat	https://perlmutter.house.gov
Connecticut		
John B. Larson	01—Democrat	https://larson.house.gov
Joseph Courtney	02—Democrat	https://courtney.house.gov
Rosa L. DeLauro	03—Democrat	https://delauro.house.gov
James A. Himes	04—Democrat	https://himes.house.gov
Elizabeth H. Esty	05—Democrat	https://esty.house.gov
Delaware		
Lisa Blunt Rochester	At Large—Democrat	https://bluntrochester.house.gov
District of Columbia		
Eleanor Holmes Norton— Delegate	At Large—Democrat	https://norton.house.gov
Florida		
Matthew L. Gaetz II	01—Republican	https://gaetz.house.gov
Neal P. Dunn	02—Republican	https://dunn.house.gov
Theodore S. Yoho	03—Republican	http://yoho.house.gov
John H. Rutherford	04—Republican	https://rutherford.house.gov
Alfred J. Lawson, Jr.	05—Democrat	https://lawson.house.gov
Ronald D. DeSantis	06—Republican	https://desantis.house.gov
Stephanie N. Murphy	07—Democrat	https://stephaniemurphy.house.gov
William J. Posey	08—Republican	http://posey.house.gov
Darren M. Soto	09—Democrat	https://soto.house.gov
Valdez Butler Demings	10—Democrat	https://demings.house.gov
Daniel A. Webster	11—Republican	http://webster.house.gov
Gus M. Bilirakis	12—Republican	https://bilirakis.house.gov
Charlie J. Crist, Jr.	13—Democrat	https://crist.house.gov
Katherine A. Castor	14—Democrat	http://castor.house.gov
Dennis A. Ross	15—Republican	http://dennisross.house.gov
Vernon G. Buchanan	16—Republican	https://buchanan.house.gov
Thomas J. Rooney	17—Republican	https://rooney.house.gov
Brian J. Mast	18—Republican	https://mast.house.gov
L. Francis Rooney III	19—Republican	https://francisrooney.house.gov
Alcee L. Hastings	20—Democrat	http://alceehastings.house.gov
Lois J. Frankel	21—Democrat	http://frankel.house.gov

List of U.S. Representatives (*Continued*)

State / District	District—Party Affiliation	Contact Information
Theodore E. Deutch	22—Democrat	http://teddeutch.house.gov
Deborah Wasserman Schultz	23—Democrat	https://wassermanschultz.house.gov
Frederica S. Wilson	24—Democrat	https://wilson.house.gov
Mario R. Díaz-Balart	25—Republican	http://mariodiazbalart.house.gov
Carlos L. Curbelo	26—Republican	http://curbelo.house.gov
Ileana Ros-Lehtinen	27—Republican	http://ros-lehtinen.house.gov
Georgia		
Earl L. Carter	01—Republican	http://buddycarter.house.gov
Sanford D. Bishop, Jr.	02—Democrat	http://bishop.house.gov
A. Drew Ferguson IV	03—Republican	https://ferguson.house.gov
Henry C. Johnson, Jr.	04—Democrat	https://hankjohnson.house.gov
John R. Lewis	05—Democrat	https://johnlewis.house.gov
Karen C. Handel	06—Republican	https://handel.house.gov
W. Robert Woodall	07—Republican	https://woodall.house.gov
J. Austin Scott	08—Republican	https://austinscott.house.gov
Douglas A. Collins	09—Republican	https://dougcollins.house.gov
Jody B. Hice	10—Republican	https://hice.house.gov
Barry D. Loudermilk	11—Republican	http://loudermilk.house.gov
Richard W. Allen	12—Republican	http://allen.house.gov
David A. Scott	13—Democrat	http://davidscott.house.gov
J. Thomas Graves, Jr.	14—Republican	http://tomgraves.house.gov
Guam		
Madeleine Z. Bordallo— Delegate	At Large—Democrat	https://bordallo.house.gov
Hawaii		
Colleen W. Hanabusa	01—Democrat	https://hanabusa.house.gov
Tulsi Gabbard	02—Democrat	https://gabbard.house.gov
Idaho		
Raúl R. Labrador	01—Republican	https://labrador.house.gov
Michael K. Simpson	02—Republican	http://simpson.house.gov
Illinois		
Bobby L. Rush	01—Democrat	http://rush.house.gov
Robin L. Kelly	02—Democrat	https://robinkelly.house.gov
Daniel W. Lipinski	03—Democrat	https://lipinski.house.gov
Luis V. Gutiérrez	04—Democrat	https://gutierrez.house.gov
Michael B. Quigley	05—Democrat	https://quigley.house.gov
Peter J. Roskam	06—Republican	https://roskam.house.gov
Danny K. Davis	07—Democrat	https://davis.house.gov
S. Raja Krishnamoorthi	08—Democrat	https://krishnamoorthi.house.gov
Janice D. Schakowsky	09—Democrat	https://schakowsky.house.gov
Bradley S. Schneider	10—Democrat	https://schneider.house.gov
William G. Foster	11—Democrat	http://foster.house.gov
Michael J. Bost	12—Republican	https://bost.house.gov
Rodney L. Davis	13—Republican	http://rodneydavis.house.gov
Randall M. Hultgren	14—Republican	http://hultgren.house.gov
John M. Shimkus	15—Republican	https://shimkus.house.gov
Adam D. Kinzinger	16—Republican	http://kinzinger.house.gov
Cheryl C. Bustos	17—Democrat	https://bustos.house.gov
Darin M. LaHood	18—Republican	https://lahood.house.gov

List of U.S. Representatives (*Continued*)

State / District	District—Party Affiliation	Contact Information
Indiana		
Peter J. Visclosky	01—Democrat	https://visclosky.house.gov
Jacqueline S. Walorski	02—Republican	http://walorski.house.gov
James E. Banks	03—Republican	https://banks.house.gov
Theodore E. Rokita	04—Republican	http://rokita.house.gov
Susan W. Brooks	05—Republican	http://susanwbrooks.house.gov
A. Lucas Messer	06—Republican	https://messer.house.gov
André D. Carson	07—Democrat	http://carson.house.gov
Larry D. Bucshon	08—Republican	https://bucshon.house.gov
Joseph A. Hollingsworth III	09—Republican	https://hollingsworth.house.gov
Iowa		
Rodney L. Blum	01—Republican	https://blum.house.gov
David W. Loebsack	02—Democrat	http://loebsack.house.gov
David E. Young	03—Republican	https://davidyoung.house.gov
Steven A. King	04—Republican	https://steveking.house.gov
Kansas		
Roger W. Marshall	01—Republican	https://marshall.house.gov
Lynn M. Jenkins	02—Republican	https://lynnjenkins.house.gov
Kevin W. Yoder	03—Republican	http://yoder.house.gov
Ronald G. Estes	04—Republican	https://estes.house.gov
Kentucky		
James R. Comer	01—Republican	https://comer.house.gov
S. Brett Guthrie	02—Republican	https://guthrie.house.gov
John A. Yarmuth	03—Democrat	https://yarmuth.house.gov
Thomas H. Massie	04—Republican	https://massie.house.gov
Harold D. Rogers	05—Republican	https://halrogers.house.gov
Garland H. Barr IV	06—Republican	https://barr.house.gov
Louisiana		
Stephen J. Scalise	01—Republican	http://scalise.house.gov
Cedric L. Richmond	02—Democrat	https://richmond.house.gov
G. Clay Higgins	03—Republican	https://clayhiggins.house.gov
J. Michael Johnson	04—Republican	https://mikejohnson.house.gov
Ralph L. Abraham	05—Republican	https://abraham.house.gov
Garret N. Graves	06—Republican	https://garretgraves.house.gov
Maine		
Chellie M. Pingree	01—Democrat	https://pingree.house.gov
Bruce L. Poliquin	02—Republican	https://poliquin.house.gov
Maryland		
Andrew P. Harris	01—Republican	http://harris.house.gov
C.A. Dutch Ruppersberger	02—Democrat	http://ruppersberger.house.gov
John P. Sarbanes	03—Democrat	https://sarbanes.house.gov
Anthony G. Brown	04—Democrat	https://anthonybrown.house.gov
Steny H. Hoyer	05—Democrat	https://hoyer.house.gov
John K. Delaney	06—Democrat	http://delaney.house.gov
Elijah E. Cummings	07—Democrat	https://cummings.house.gov
Jamin B. Raskin	08—Democrat	https://raskin.house.gov
Massachusetts		
Richard E. Neal	01—Democrat	https://neal.house.gov
James P. McGovern	02—Democrat	http://mcgovern.house.gov

List of U.S. Representatives (*Continued*)

State / District	District—Party Affiliation	Contact Information
Nicola S. Tsongas	03—Democrat	https://tsongas.house.gov
Joseph P. Kennedy III	04—Democrat	https://kennedy.house.gov
Katherine M. Clark	05—Democrat	https://katherineclark.house.gov
Seth W. Moulton	06—Democrat	http://moulton.house.gov
Michael E. Capuano	07—Democrat	http://capuano.house.gov
Stephen F. Lynch	08—Democrat	http://lynch.house.gov
William R. Keating	09—Democrat	https://keating.house.gov
Michigan		
John W. Bergman	01—Republican	https://bergman.house.gov
William P. Huizenga	02—Republican	http://huizenga.house.gov
Justin A. Amash	03—Republican	http://amash.house.gov
John R. Moolenaar	04—Republican	https://moolenaar.house.gov
Daniel T. Kildee	05—Democrat	http://dankildee.house.gov
Frederick S. Upton	06—Republican	http://upton.house.gov
Timothy L. Walberg	07—Republican	http://walberg.house.gov
Michael D. Bishop	08—Republican	https://mikebishop.house.gov
Sander M. Levin	09—Democrat	http://levin.house.gov
Paul Mitchell III	10—Republican	https://mitchell.house.gov
David A. Trott	11—Republican	https://trott.house.gov
Deborah A. Dingell	12—Democrat	https://debbiedingell.house.gov
John J. Conyers, Jr.	13—Democrat	https://conyers.house.gov
Brenda L. Lawrence	14—Democrat	https://lawrence.house.gov
Minnesota		
Timothy J. Walz	01—Democrat	https://walz.house.gov
Jason M. Lewis	02—Republican	https://jasonlewis.house.gov
Erik P. Paulsen	03—Republican	https://paulsen.house.gov
Betty L. McCollum	04—Democrat	http://mccollum.house.gov
Keith M. Ellison	05—Democrat	https://ellison.house.gov
Thomas E. Emmer, Jr.	06—Republican	https://emmer.house.gov
Collin C. Peterson	07—Democrat	http://collinpeterson.house.gov
Richard M. Nolan	08—Democrat	http://nolan.house.gov
Mississippi		
J. Trent Kelly	01—Republican	https://trentkelly.house.gov
Bennie G. Thompson	02—Democrat	https://benniethompson.house.gov
Gregory L. Harper	03—Republican	http://harper.house.gov
Steven M. Palazzo	04—Republican	http://palazzo.house.gov
Missouri		
W. Lacy Clay, Jr.	01—Democrat	https://lacyclay.house.gov
Ann L. Wagner	02—Republican	http://wagner.house.gov
W. Blaine Luetkemeyer	03—Republican	http://luetkemeyer.house.gov
Vicky J. Hartzler	04—Republican	https://hartzler.house.gov
Emanuel Cleaver II	05—Democrat	http://cleaver.house.gov
Samuel B. Graves, Jr.	06—Republican	https://graves.house.gov
William H. Long	07—Republican	https://long.house.gov
Jason T. Smith	08—Republican	https://jasonsmith.house.gov
Montana		
Gregory R. Gianforte	At Large—Republican	https://gianforte.house.gov

List of U.S. Representatives (*Continued*)

State / District	District—Party Affiliation	Contact Information
Nebraska		
Jeffrey L. Fortenberry	01—Republican	https://fortenberry.house.gov
Donald J. Bacon	02—Republican	https://bacon.house.gov
Adrian M. Smith	03—Republican	http://adriansmith.house.gov
Nevada		
A. Costandina Titus	01—Democrat	https://titus.house.gov
Mark E. Amodei	02—Republican	https://amodei.house.gov
Jacklyn S. Rosen	03—Democrat	https://rosen.house.gov
Ruben J. Kihuen	04—Democrat	https://kihuen.house.gov
New Hampshire		
Carol Shea-Porter	01—Democrat	https://shea-porter.house.gov
Ann McLane Kuster	02—Democrat	http://kuster.house.gov
New Jersey		
Donald W. Norcross	01—Democrat	https://norcross.house.gov
Frank A. LoBiondo	02—Republican	http://lobiondo.house.gov
Thomas C. MacArthur	03—Republican	https://macarthur.house.gov
Christopher H. Smith	04—Republican	http://chrissmith.house.gov
Joshua S. Gottheimer	05—Democrat	https://gottheimer.house.gov
Frank J. Pallone, Jr.	06—Democrat	https://pallone.house.gov
Leonard J. Lance	07—Republican	http://lance.house.gov
Albio B. Sires	08—Democrat	https://sires.house.gov
William J. Pascrell, Jr.	09—Democrat	http://pascrell.house.gov
Donald M. Payne, Jr.	10—Democrat	http://payne.house.gov
Rodney P. Frelinghuysen	11—Republican	https://frelinghuysen.house.gov
Bonnie Watson Coleman	12—Democrat	https://watsoncoleman.house.gov
New Mexico		
Michelle Lujan Grisham	01—Democrat	https://lujangrisham.house.gov
Stevan E. Pearce	02—Republican	http://pearce.house.gov
Ben R. Luján	03—Democrat	https://lujan.house.gov
New York		
Lee M. Zeldin	01—Republican	https://zeldin.house.gov
Peter T. King	02—Republican	http://peteking.house.gov
Thomas R. Suozzi	03—Democrat	https://suozzi.house.gov
Kathleen M. Rice	04—Democrat	http://kathleenrice.house.gov
Gregory W. Meeks	05—Democrat	http://meeks.house.gov
Grace Meng	06—Democrat	http://meng.house.gov
Nydia M. Velázquez	07—Democrat	https://velazquez.house.gov
Hakeem S. Jeffries	08—Democrat	http://jeffries.house.gov
Yvette D. Clarke	09—Democrat	https://clarke.house.gov
Jerrold L. Nadler	10—Democrat	http://nadler.house.gov
Daniel M. Donovan, Jr.	11—Republican	https://donovan.house.gov
Carolyn B. Maloney	12—Democrat	http://maloney.house.gov
Adriano D. Espaillat	13—Democrat	https://espaillat.house.gov
Joseph Crowley	14—Democrat	http://crowley.house.gov
José E. Serrano	15—Democrat	https://serrano.house.gov
Eliot L. Engel	16—Democrat	https://engel.house.gov
Nita M. Lowey	17—Democrat	https://lowey.house.gov
Sean P. Maloney	18—Democrat	http://seanmaloney.house.gov
John J. Faso	19—Republican	https://faso.house.gov

List of U.S. Representatives *(Continued)*

State / District	District—Party Affiliation	Contact Information
Paul D. Tonko	20—Democrat	https://tonko.house.gov
Elise M. Stefanik	21—Republican	https://stefanik.house.gov
Claudia Tenney	22—Republican	https://tenney.house.gov
Thomas W. Reed II	23—Republican	https://reed.house.gov
John M. Katko	24—Republican	https://katko.house.gov
Louise McIntosh Slaughter	25—Democrat	https://louise.house.gov
Brian M. Higgins	26—Democrat	http://higgins.house.gov
Christopher C. Collins	27—Republican	https://chriscollins.house.gov
North Carolina		
George K. Butterfield	01—Democrat	http://butterfield.house.gov
George E.B. Holding	02—Republican	http://holding.house.gov
Walter B. Jones, Jr.	03—Republican	http://jones.house.gov
David E. Price	04—Democrat	https://price.house.gov
Virginia A. Foxx	05—Republican	http://foxx.house.gov
B. Mark Walker	06—Republican	https://walker.house.gov
David C. Rouzer	07—Republican	https://rouzer.house.gov
Richard L. Hudson, Jr.	08—Republican	https://hudson.house.gov
Robert M. Pittenger	09—Republican	https://pittenger.house.gov
Patrick T. McHenry	10—Republican	http://mchenry.house.gov
Mark R. Meadows	11—Republican	https://meadows.house.gov
Alma S. Adams	12—Democrat	http://adams.house.gov
Theodore P. Budd	13—Republican	https://budd.house.gov
North Dakota		
Kevin J. Cramer	At Large—Republican	http://cramer.house.gov
Northern Mariana Islands		
Gregorio Kilili Camacho Sablan—Delegate	At Large—Independent	http://sablan.house.gov
Ohio		
Steven J. Chabot	01—Republican	http://chabot.house.gov
Brad R. Wenstrup	02—Republican	http://wenstrup.house.gov
Joyce B. Beatty	03—Democrat	http://beatty.house.gov
James D. Jordan	04—Republican	http://jordan.house.gov
Robert E. Latta	05—Republican	http://latta.house.gov
William L. Johnson	06—Republican	http://billjohnson.house.gov
Robert B. Gibbs	07—Republican	https://gibbs.house.gov
Warren E. Davidson	08—Republican	https://davidson.house.gov
Marcia C. Kaptur	09—Democrat	https://kaptur.house.gov
Michael R. Turner	10—Republican	https://turner.house.gov
Marcia L. Fudge	11—Democrat	https://fudge.house.gov
Patrick J. Tiberi	12—Republican	http://tiberi.house.gov
Timothy J. Ryan	13—Democrat	http://timryan.house.gov
David P. Joyce	14—Republican	https://joyce.house.gov
Steven E. Stivers	15—Republican	http://stivers.house.gov
James B. Renacci	16—Republican	https://renacci.house.gov
Oklahoma		
James F. Bridenstine	01—Republican	http://bridenstine.house.gov
Markwayne Mullin	02—Republican	http://mullin.house.gov
Frank D. Lucas	03—Republican	http://lucas.house.gov
Thomas J. Cole	04—Republican	https://cole.house.gov
Steven D. Russell	05—Republican	https://russell.house.gov

List of U.S. Representatives (*Continued*)

State / District	District—Party Affiliation	Contact Information
Oregon		
Suzanne M. Bonamici	01—Democrat	http://bonamici.house.gov
Gregory P. Walden	02—Republican	https://walden.house.gov
Earl Blumenauer	03—Democrat	https://blumenauer.house.gov
Peter A. DeFazio	04—Democrat	http://defazio.house.gov
W. Kurt Schrader	05—Democrat	http://schrader.house.gov
Pennsylvania		
Robert A. Brady	01—Democrat	http://brady.house.gov
Dwight Evans	02—Democrat	https://evans.house.gov
George J. Kelly, Jr.	03—Republican	http://kelly.house.gov
Scott G. Perry	04—Republican	http://perry.house.gov
Glenn W. Thompson	05—Republican	http://thompson.house.gov
Ryan A. Costello	06—Republican	https://costello.house.gov
Patrick L. Meehan	07—Republican	https://meehan.house.gov
Brian K. Fitzpatrick	08—Republican	https://fitzpatrick.house.gov
William F. Shuster	09—Republican	https://shuster.house.gov
Thomas A. Marino	10—Republican	https://marino.house.gov
Louis J. Barletta	11—Republican	http://barletta.house.gov
Keith J. Rothfus	12—Republican	https://rothfus.house.gov
Brendan F. Boyle	13—Democrat	https://boyle.house.gov
Michael F. Doyle	14—Democrat	http://doyle.house.gov
Charles W. Dent	15—Republican	https://dent.house.gov
Lloyd K. Smucker	16—Republican	https://smucker.house.gov
Matthew A. Cartwright	17—Democrat	http://cartwright.house.gov
Timothy F. Murphy	18—Republican	https://murphy.house.gov
Puerto Rico		
Jenniffer A. González-Colón—Resident Commissioner	At Large—Republican	https://gonzalez-colon.house.gov
Rhode Island		
David N. Cicilline	01—Democrat	http://cicilline.house.gov
James R. Langevin	02—Democrat	http://langevin.house.gov
South Carolina		
Marshall C. Sanford, Jr.	01—Republican	https://sanford.house.gov
Addison G. Wilson	02—Republican	http://joewilson.house.gov
Jeffrey D. Duncan	03—Republican	http://jeffduncan.house.gov
Harold W. Gowdy III	04—Republican	https://gowdy.house.gov
Ralph W. Norman, Jr.	05—Republican	https://norman.house.gov
James E. Clyburn	06—Democrat	http://clyburn.house.gov
H. Thompson Rice, Jr.	07—Republican	http://rice.house.gov
South Dakota		
Kristi L. Noem	At Large—Republican	https://noem.house.gov
Tennessee		
D. Phillip Roe	01—Republican	http://roe.house.gov
John J. Duncan, Jr.	02—Republican	http://duncan.house.gov
Charles J. Fleischmann	03—Republican	http://fleischmann.house.gov
Scott E. DesJarlais	04—Republican	https://desjarlais.house.gov
James H.S. Cooper	05—Democrat	http://cooper.house.gov
Diane L. Black	06—Republican	http://black.house.gov
Marsha W. Blackburn	07—Republican	http://blackburn.house.gov

List of U.S. Representatives (*Continued*)

State / District	District—Party Affiliation	Contact Information
David F. Kustoff	08—Republican	https://kustoff.house.gov
Stephen I. Cohen	09—Democrat	https://cohen.house.gov
Texas		
Louis B. Gohmert, Jr.	01—Republican	https://gohmert.house.gov
L. Theodore Poe	02—Republican	https://poe.house.gov
Samuel R. Johnson	03—Republican	http://samjohnson.house.gov
John L. Ratcliffe	04—Republican	https://ratcliffe.house.gov
T. Jeb Hensarling	05—Republican	http://hensarling.house.gov
Joseph L. Barton	06—Republican	https://joebarton.house.gov
John A. Culberson	07—Republican	http://culberson.house.gov
Kevin P. Brady	08—Republican	http://kevinbrady.house.gov
Alexander N. Green	09—Democrat	http://algreen.house.gov
Michael T. McCaul	10—Republican	http://mccaul.house.gov
K. Michael Conaway	11—Republican	http://conaway.house.gov
Kay M. Granger	12—Republican	http://kaygranger.house.gov
W. McClellan Thornberry	13—Republican	http://thornberry.house.gov
Randy K. Weber, Sr.	14—Republican	http://weber.house.gov
Vicente Gonzalez	15—Democrat	https://gonzalez.house.gov
Robert F. O'Rourke	16—Democrat	http://orourke.house.gov
William H. Flores	17—Republican	http://flores.house.gov
Sheila Jackson Lee	18—Democrat	http://jacksonlee.house.gov
Jodey Cook Arrington	19—Republican	https://arrington.house.gov
Joaquin Castro	20—Democrat	https://castro.house.gov
Lamar S. Smith	21—Republican	http://lamarsmith.house.gov
Peter G. Olson	22—Republican	https://olson.house.gov
William B. Hurd	23—Republican	https://hurd.house.gov
Kenny E. Marchant	24—Republican	https://marchant.house.gov
J. Roger Williams	25—Republican	http://williams.house.gov
Michael C. Burgess	26—Republican	http://burgess.house.gov
R. Blake Farenthold	27—Republican	http://farenthold.house.gov
Enrique R. Cuellar	28—Democrat	http://cuellar.house.gov
R. Eugene Green	29—Democrat	https://green.house.gov
Eddie Bernice Johnson	30—Democrat	http://ebjohnson.house.gov
John R. Carter	31—Republican	https://carter.house.gov
Peter A. Sessions	32—Republican	https://sessions.house.gov
Marc A. Veasey	33—Democrat	http://veasey.house.gov
Filemón B. Vela, Jr.	34—Democrat	https://vela.house.gov
Lloyd A. Doggett II	35—Democrat	https://doggett.house.gov
Brian Babin	36—Republican	http://babin.house.gov
Utah		
Robert W. Bishop	01—Republican	http://robbishop.house.gov
Christopher D. Stewart	02—Republican	http://stewart.house.gov
Jason E. Chaffetz	03—Republican	https://chaffetz.house.gov
Ludmya B. Love	04—Republican	https://love.house.gov
Vermont		
Peter F. Welch	At Large—Democrat	https://welch.house.gov
Virgin Islands		
Stacey E. Plaskett—Delegate	At Large—Democrat	https://plaskett.house.gov

List of U.S. Representatives (*Continued*)

State / District	District—Party Affiliation	Contact Information
Virginia		
Robert J. Wittman	01—Republican	http://wittman.house.gov
Scott W. Taylor	02—Republican	https://taylor.house.gov
Robert C. Scott	03—Democrat	http://bobbyscott.house.gov
A. Donald McEachin	04—Democrat	https://mceachin.house.gov
Thomas A. Garrett, Jr.	05—Republican	https://tomgarrett.house.gov
Robert W. Goodlatte	06—Republican	https://goodlatte.house.gov
David A. Brat	07—Republican	http://brat.house.gov
Donald S. Beyer, Jr.	08—Democrat	http://beyer.house.gov
H. Morgan Griffith	09—Republican	http://morangriffith.house.gov
Barbara J. Comstock	10—Republican	https://comstock.house.gov
Gerald E. Connolly	11—Democrat	https://connolly.house.gov
Washington		
Suzan K. DelBene	01—Democrat	https://delbene.house.gov
Richard R. Larsen	02—Democrat	http://larsen.house.gov
Jaime L. Herrera Beutler	03—Republican	http://herrerabeutler.house.gov
Daniel M. Newhouse	04—Republican	https://newhouse.house.gov
Cathy A. McMorris Rodgers	05—Republican	http://mcmorris.house.gov
Derek C. Kilmer	06—Democrat	https://kilmer.house.gov
Pramila Jayapal	07—Democrat	https://jayapal.house.gov
David G. Reichert	08—Republican	http://reichert.house.gov
D. Adam Smith	09—Democrat	https://adamsmith.house.gov
Dennis L. Heck	10—Democrat	http://dennyheck.house.gov
West Virginia		
David B. McKinley	01—Republican	https://mckinley.house.gov
Alexander X. Mooney	02—Republican	https://mooney.house.gov
Evan H. Jenkins	03—Republican	https://evanjenkins.house.gov
Wisconsin		
Paul D. Ryan	01—Republican	http://paulryan.house.gov
Mark Pocan	02—Democrat	http://pocan.house.gov
Ronald J. Kind	03—Democrat	https://kind.house.gov
Gwendolynne S. Moore	04—Democrat	https://gwenmoore.house.gov
F. James Sensenbrenner, Jr.	05—Republican	http://sensenbrenner.house.gov
Glenn S. Grothman	06—Republican	http://grothman.house.gov
Sean P. Duffy	07—Republican	https://duffy.house.gov
Michael J. Gallagher	08—Republican	https://gallagher.house.gov
Wyoming		
Elizabeth L. Cheney	At Large—Republican	https://cheney.house.gov

The Above List of 435 Representatives was updated 07–2017. The Resident Commissioner and Delegates are not counted as Members. Republicans are 241; Democrats are 194; and there are 0 vacancies. Information on House. gov may be more accurate and current. https://www.house.gov

Sources of Information

Art Competition Each spring, the Congressional Institute sponsors a nationwide high school visual art competition to recognize and encourage artistic talent. Students submit their entries to their Representative's office, and panels of district artists select the winning artwork, which is displayed at the U.S. Capitol for 1 year. http://www.house.gov/content/educate/art_competition

Campaign Finance The Federal Election Commission maintains a campaign finance database that contains information on candidates, including congressional candidates, who file reports with the Commission. Users of the online "Candidate and Committee Viewer" can sort data and download them. The data presentations consist of biennial summaries, report summaries, and report images and downloads. http://www.fec.gov/finance/disclosure/candcmte_info.shtml?tabIndex=1

Campaign Web Sites   The Library of Congress maintains a database of "Archived Web Sites" that includes thousands of official campaign Web sites. Former congressional candidates' Web sites are part of this collection. https://www.loc.gov/websites

Career Opportunities   The House Vacancy Announcement and Placement Service assists House Members, committees, and leadership by posting job vacancies and maintaining a resume bank. The Service provides confidential referral of resumes when House offices request them. Information on submitting a resume is available online. http://www.house.gov/content/jobs/members_and_committees.php

To apply for positions with House organizations, read the individual vacancy announcements and follow the instructions. http://www.house.gov/content/jobs/vacancies.php

Committees   Information on House committees is available on House.gov. http://www.house.gov/committees

Additional information is available on the Office of the Clerk's Web site. http://clerk.house.gov/committee_info/index.aspx

Congressional Record   Starting with the year 1995, the official record of the proceedings and debates of the U.S. Congress is available on Congress.gov. https://www.congress.gov/congressional-record

Starting with the year 1994, the official record of the proceedings and debates of the U.S. Congress is available on the Government Publishing Office's Federal Digital System (FDsys) Web site. https://www.gpo.gov/fdsys/browse/collection.action?collectionCode=CREC

Directories   The Web site House.gov has a directory that contains the committee assignment, congressional district, name,

phone number, political affiliation, and room number of each Member of the U.S. House of Representatives, as well as the Uniform Resources Locator (URL) the leads to his or her Web site. http://www.house.gov/representatives

The online "Biographical Directory of the United States Congress, 1774–Present," allows visitors to search for Members of Congress—past and present—by first or last name, political affiliation, position, State, or year or Congress. http://bioguide.congress.gov/biosearch/biosearch.asp

Present and former Members of Congress have control numbers associated with their records in the "Biographical Directory of the United States Congress." Member IDs or "BioGuide IDs" serve as metadata within Congress.gov and legislative documents that the Government Publishing Office publishes. https://www.congress.gov/help/field-values/member-bioguide-ids

Find a Representative   A Zip code-based search tool is available on House.gov for locating a representative. http://www.house.gov/representatives/find

Educational Resources   The Office of the Clerk's Web site features educational and entertaining information on the legislative branch of the Government for students of all ages. Its Kids in the House Web site explains the role of the House of Representatives, describes the legislative process, and covers House history. http://kids.clerk.house.gov

Adults seeking to learn about commissions, committees, House history, House leadership, Representatives, rules, or a Representative's schedule may benefit from "The House Explained" section on House.gov. http://www.house.gov/content/learn

Glossary   The Office of the Clerk's Web site features a short glossary for children. http://kids.clerk.house.gov/young-learners/glossary.html

House.gov features a glossary of terms related to congressional records. http://history.house.gov/Records-and-Research/FAQs/Congressional-Glossary/

House.gov features a glossary of records management terms. http://history.house.gov/Records-and-Research/FAQs/Records-Glossary/

The "Statement of Disbursements" is a quarterly public report of all receipts and expenditures for U.S. House of Representatives committees, leadership, Members, and officers and offices. To help the general public read this report, House. gov maintains an online glossary. http:// disbursements.house.gov/glossary.shtml

History   The House of Representative's "History, Art and Archives" Web site features resources and a trove of information, including online collections, exhibitions, publications, and records. http://history.house.gov

Member Profiles   The "Members of the U.S. Congress" database contains profiles for Representatives who have held office since 1973 or were still serving in the 93d Congress. Users of the database can filter profiles by chamber, Congress, political affiliation, and State or U.S. Territory. A Member profile includes the following: dates of service, district number and State, party affiliation, and a picture when available, as well as a link to the Member's entry in the "Biographical Directory of the United States Congress, 1774–Present" and a link to remarks made in the "Congressional Record." A profile also includes the list of legislation that the Member sponsored and cosponsored. https://www.congress.gov/members

Membership / Party Divisions   The Office of the Clerk's "Congressional Profile" Web page keeps a tally of the number of Democrats, Independents, Republicans, and vacant seats in both the House of Representatives and the Senate. http://clerk. house.gov/member_info/cong.aspx

Publications   The Congressional Directory, Rules and Manual of the House of Representatives, and telephone directory for the House of Representatives are available from the Government Publishing Office's bookstore. Phone, 202-512-0132. https:// www.gpo.gov/about/bookstore.htm | Email: mainbks@gpo.gov

Schedule   The House's schedule and related resources are available in the "Legislative Activity" section on House.gov. http://www. house.gov/legislative

Site Map   House.gov features a site map that allows visitors to look for a specific topic or to browse content that aligns with their interests. http://www.house.gov/ content/site_tools/sitemap.php

Web Sites   More information on legislation and the U.S. House of Representatives is available on Congress.gov. https://www. congress.gov

More information also is available on House.gov. http://www.house.gov

More information also is available on the Government Publishing Office's Federal Digital System (FDsys) Web site. https:// www.gpo.gov/fdsys/search/home.action. http://clerk.house.gov

For further information, contact the Clerk, The Capitol, Washington, DC 20515. Phone, 202-225-7000.

Architect of the Capitol

U.S. Capitol Building, Washington, DC 20515
Phone, 202-228-1793. Internet, http://www.aoc.gov

Architect of the Capitol	STEPHEN T. AYERS
Deputy Architect of the Capitol / Chief Operating Officer	CHRISTINE A. MERDON
Assistant Architect of the Capitol	MICHAEL G. TURNBULL
Chief Administrative Officer	AMY JOHNSON
Chief Financial Officer	THOMAS CARROLL
General Counsel	JASON BALTIMORE
Inspector General	CHRISTOPHER FAILLA
Chief Executive Officer for Visitor Services, U.S. Capitol Visitor Center	BETH PLEMMONS
Director, Communications and Congressional Relations	MARY ANNE BITTNER
Director, Planning and Project Management	PETER W. MUELLER
Director, Safety, Fire and Environmental Programs	PATRICIA WILLIAMS
Director, Security Programs	KENNETH A. EADS
Director, Utilities and Power Plant Operations	CHRISTOPHER POTTER

Executive Director, U.S. Botanic Garden   Susan K. Pell, Acting
Facility Manager, Supreme Court Building and Grounds   Joseph A. Campbell
Superintendent, Capitol Building   Mark Reed
Superintendent, Capitol Grounds   Theodore R. Bechtol, Jr.
Superintendent, House Office Buildings   William M. Weidemeyer
Superintendent, Library Buildings and Grounds   Larry D. Brown
Superintendent, Senate Office Buildings   Takis Tzamaras

The above list of key personnel was updated 09–2017.

The Architect of the Capitol maintains the U.S. Capitol and the buildings and grounds of the Capitol campus.

Permanent authority for the care and maintenance of the U.S. Capitol was established by the act of August 15, 1876 (40 U.S.C. 162, 163). The title Architect of the Capitol (AOC) is the official title of both the agency and the person.

Historically, the President appointed the Architect of the Capitol for an indefinite term. Legislation enacted in 1989, however, provides that the President, with the advice and consent of the Senate, appoints the Architect for a 10-year term from a list of three candidates whom a congressional commission recommends. Upon confirmation by the Senate, the Architect becomes an official of the legislative branch as an officer of Congress. The Architect is eligible for reappointment at the end of his or her 10-year term. While overseeing the agency, the Architect also serves as the Acting Director of the U.S. Botanic Garden. https://www.aoc.gov/governance

The Architect of the Capitol serves the Congress and Supreme Court in its capacity as the builder and steward of the landmark buildings and grounds of Capitol Hill. AOC staff preserves and maintains the art, historic buildings, monuments, and inspirational gardens on the Capitol campus. The AOC team, comprising more than 2,000 employees and providing around-the-clock service, creates a safe environment and inspiring experiences for those who visit and work on Capitol Hill.

The AOC traces its beginnings to the laying of the Capitol cornerstone in 1793. The agency oversees the operations and care of more than 17.4 million square feet of facilities, 580 acres of grounds, and thousands of works of art. The Capitol campus accommodates 30,000 daily occupants and hosts more than 3 million visitors annually. https://www.aoc.gov/who-we-are

Sources of Information

Architecture   A trove of information on columns, materials, styles, and more is available on the AOC website. https://www.aoc.gov/architecture

Art   The AOC website includes pages on AOC art stories, artists, art by State, decorative arts, paintings and murals, and sculptures, as well as on African Americans, Native Americans, and women in art. https://www.aoc.gov/art

Blog   AOC experts write on the architecture, art, and work on the Capitol Hill. http://www.aoc.gov/blog

Business Opportunities   Information for contractors and small businesses—delivery instructions, procedures, procurement opportunities, and programs—is accessible online. https://www.aoc.gov/procurement

Career Opportunities   The AOC relies heavily on architects, carpenters, electricians, engineers, gardeners, masons, mechanics, painters and plasterers, plumbers, and sheet metal workers to maintain the U.S. Capitol and the buildings and grounds of the surrounding campus. https://www.aoc.gov/careers

In 2016, The AOC ranked 11th among 27 midsize Government agencies in the Best Places To Work Agency Rankings. http://bestplacestowork.org/BPTW/rankings/detail/AC00

Events   The AOC website contains pages of events associated with the U.S. Capitol and

Botanic Garden. Events include Christmas tree displays, concerts, lying in state, Presidential Inaugurations, and State of the Union addresses. https://www.aoc.gov/capitol-campus-events

Facts Capitol Hill facts are posted on the AOC website. https://www.aoc.gov/facts/capitol-hill

Gallery A multimedia gallery is available online. https://www.aoc.gov/multimedia-gallery

Grounds Frederick L. Olmsted planned the late 19th-century expansion and landscaping of the Capitol Grounds. Olmsted, who also designed Central Park in New York City, was regarded as the most talented American landscape architect of his day. The "About the Grounds" web page features an informative 4-minute video on his plan for the U.S. Capitol. https://www.aoc.gov/capitol-grounds/about-grounds

History President George Washington appointed commissioners to provide buildings and accommodations for Congress. The commissioners hired the French artist and engineer Major Pierre Charles L'Enfant, a Revolutionary War veteran, to lay out the new city. They also staged a competition for the design of the Capitol. Dr. William Thornton's entry won the competition. To learn more about the first "architect of the capitol" and the Architects that followed, visit the AOC's history web pages. https://www.aoc.gov/about-aoc/history-architect

Map A map of Capitol Hill is available online. https://www.aoc.gov/us-capitol-map

News The AOC posts news and notices on its website. https://www.aoc.gov/news

Organizational Directory An organizational directory is available online. https://www.aoc.gov/organizational-directory

Oversight The Office of the Inspector General from the AOC posts reports and data on Oversight.gov, a text-searchable repository of reports that Federal Inspectors General publish. The Council of the Inspectors General on Integrity and Efficiency operates and maintains the website to increase public access to independent and authoritative information on the Federal Government. https://oversight.gov

Planning a Visit Information on accessibility services, activities, tours, visiting hours, and where to shop and eat is available online. http://www.aoc.gov/plan-your-visit

Projects The AOC never lacks things to preserve or restore. Visit the "Projects" web page to learn about ongoing work. https://www.aoc.gov/projects

Publications The AOC publishes a variety of publications that are accessible online. https://www.aoc.gov/publications

Site Map The website map allows visitors to look for specific topics or to browse content that aligns with their interests. https://www.aoc.gov/sitemap

Social Media The AOC tweets announcements and other newsworthy items on Twitter. https://twitter.com/uscapitol

The AOC has a Facebook account. https://www.facebook.com/ArchitectoftheCapitol

The AOC posts videos on its YouTube channel. https://www.youtube.com/user/AOCgov

Trees Approximately 890 trees surround the Capitol Building on Capitol Square, and more than 4,300 trees grow throughout the 274-acre Capitol Grounds. A tree map is available on the "Trees on Capitol Grounds" web page. https://www.aoc.gov/trees. http://www.aoc.gov/contact-form

For further information, contact the Office of the Architect of the Capitol, U.S. Capitol Building, Washington, DC 20515. Phone, 202-228-1793.

Congressional Budget Office

Second and D Streets SW., Washington, DC 20515
Phone, 202-226-2600. Internet, http://www.cbo.gov

Director	KEITH HALL
Deputy Director	MARK P. HADLEY
Office of the Director	
Associate Director, Communications	DEBORAH KILROE
Associate Director, Economic Analysis	WENDY EDELBERG
Associate Director, Economic Analysis	JEFFREY KLING
Associate Director, Legislative Affairs	LEIGH ANGRES
General Counsel	T.J. MCGRATH
Senior Advisor	ROBERT A. SUNSHINE
Other Divisions	
Assistant Director, Budget Analysis	THERESA A. GULLO
Assistant Director, Financial Analysis	SEBASTIEN GAY
Assistant Director, Health, Retirement, and Long-Term Analysis	DAVID WEAVER
Assistant Director, Macroeconomic Analysis	JEFFREY F. WERLING
Assistant Director, Microeconomic Studies	JOSEPH KILE
Assistant Director, National Security	DAVID E. MOSHER
Assistant Director, Tax Analysis	JOHN MCCLELLAND
Chief Administrative Officer, Management, Business, and Information Services	JOSEPH E. EVANS, JR.

The Congressional Budget Office produces independent analyses of budgetary and economic issues to support the congressional budget process.

The Congressional Budget Office (CBO) was established by the Congressional Budget Act of 1974 (2 U.S.C. 601), which also created a procedure by which the Congress considers and acts on the annual Federal budget. This process enables the Congress to have an overview of the Federal budget and to make overall decisions on spending and taxation levels and on the deficit or surplus these levels generate. https://www.cbo.gov/about/founding

Activities

The CBO assists the congressional budget committees with drafting and enforcing the annual budget resolution, which serves as a blueprint for total levels of Government spending and revenues in a fiscal year. Once completed, the budget resolution guides the action of other congressional committees in drafting subsequent spending and revenue legislation within their jurisdiction.

To support this process, the CBO makes budgetary and economic projections, analyzes the proposals set forth in the President's budget request, and details

alternative spending and revenue options for lawmakers to consider. The CBO also provides cost estimates of bills approved by congressional committees and tracks the progress of spending and revenue legislation in a scorekeeping system. CBO cost estimates and scorekeeping help the budget committees determine whether the budgetary effects of individual proposals are consistent with the most recent spending and revenue targets.

Upon congressional request, the CBO also produces reports analyzing specific policy and program issues that are significant for the budget. In keeping with the Office's nonpartisan role, its analyses do not include policy recommendations, and they routinely disclose their underlying assumptions and methods. This open and nonpartisan stance has been instrumental in preserving the credibility of the Office's analyses. https://www.cbo.gov/about/products/RecurringReports

Analysis of the President's Budget   The CBO estimates the budgetary impact of the proposals in the President's budget using its own economic forecast and assumptions. The CBO's independent reestimate allows Congress to compare the administration's spending and revenue proposals with the CBO's baseline projections and other proposals using a consistent set of economic and technical assumptions. https://www.cbo.gov/about/products#2

Baseline Budget Projections and Economic Forecasts   Each year, the CBO issues reports on the budget and economic outlook that cover the 10-year period used in the congressional budget process. Those reports present and explain the CBO's baseline budget projections and economic forecast, which are generally based on current law regarding Federal spending and revenues. The reports also describe the differences between the current projections and previous ones, compare the CBO's economic forecast with those of other forecasters, and show the budgetary impact of some alternative policy assumptions. https://www.cbo.gov/about/products#1

Budgetary and Economic Policy Issues   The CBO also analyzes specific program and policy issues that affect the Federal budget and the economy. Generally, requests for these analyses come from the chair or ranking minority member of a committee or subcommittee or from the leadership of either party in the House or Senate. https://www.cbo.gov/topics/reports-policy-options

Cost Estimates for Bills   The CBO provides cost estimates of every bill to show how it would affect spending or revenues over the next 5 or 10 years, depending on the type of spending involved. The CBO also provides informal estimates at the committee level and other stages in the legislative process. https://www.cbo.gov/cost-estimates

Federal Mandates   As required by the Unfunded Mandates Reform Act of 1995, the CBO analyzes the costs that proposed legislation would impose on State, local, and tribal governments and on the private sector. The CBO produces mandate statements with its cost estimates for each committee-approved bill. https://www.cbo.gov/about/products#7

Scorekeeping   The CBO provides the budget and appropriations committees with frequent tabulations of congressional action affecting spending and revenues. Those scorekeeping reports provide information on whether legislative actions are consistent with the spending and revenue levels set by the budget resolution. https://www.cbo.gov/about/products#9

Sources of Information

Blog   The CBO Web site features a blog. https://www.cbo.gov/blog

Business Opportunities   Information to help vendors is available online. https://www.cbo.gov/about/business-opportunities | Email: acquisitions@cbo.gov

Cost Estimates   The CBO Web site features an online tool for searching cost estimates. https://www.cbo.gov/cost-estimates

Career Opportunities   A career at the CBO offers opportunities to analyze public policies and their budgetary and economic effects, to work with policy analysis experts, to support the Congress, and to provide nonpartisan and objective analysis. https://www.cbo.gov/about/careers | Email: careers@cbo.gov

Frequently Asked Questions (FAQs)   The CBO posts answers to the most common questions that people ask. https://www.cbo.gov/faqs

Glossary   The glossary is available online in Portable Document Format (PDF). It defines terms that are commonly used in CBO reports. Many of the entries conform to those published in "A Glossary of Terms Used in the Federal Budget Process" (Government Accountability Office, 2005). https://www.cbo.gov/publication/42904

Information Products   CBO informational, nonpartisan products include baseline projections for selected programs, budget and economic data, and major recurring reports. https://www.cbo.gov/about/products

Internships   Interns attend seminars, participate in an educational program, and contribute to the agency's output of analysis. https://www.cbo.gov/about/careers/internships | Email: careers@cbo.gov

Press Center   The CBO posts news and upcoming events online, as well as SlideShare presentations and YouTube videos. It also disseminates information via an RSS feed and by tweeting on Twitter. https://www.cbo.gov/about/press-center

Site Map   The CBO site map allows Internet visitors to look for keywords or to browse content that aligns with their interests. https://www.cbo.gov/sitemap

Topics   The CBO Web sites allows visitors to browse topics of analysis or to search for them with an online search tool. Topic categories include agriculture, budget, climate and environment, economy, education, energy and natural resources, health care, housing, immigration, income distribution, poverty and income security, social security, taxes, and more. https://www.cbo.gov/topics

Visiting Scholars   The CBO welcomes applications from analysts and scholars in all fields; however, it has a special interest in collaborating with experts in macroeconomics and financial, health, and public economics. https://www.cbo.gov/about/careers/visitingscholars | Email: careers@cbo.gov. https://www.cbo.gov/about/contact

For further information, contact the Management, Business, and Information Services Division, Congressional Budget Office, Second and D Streets SW., Washington, DC 20515. Phone, 202-226-2600. Fax, 202-226-2714.

Government Accountability Office

441 G Street NW., Washington, DC 20548
Phone, 202-512-3000. Internet, http://www.gao.gov

Comptroller General Of The United States	GENE L. DODARO
Chief Operating Officer	PATRICIA A. DALTON
Chief Quality Officer	TIMOTHY P. BOWLING
Managing Director, Continuous Process Improvement	THOMAS WILLIAMS
Managing Directors—Mission Teams	
Acquisition and Sourcing Management	MICHELE MACKIN
Applied Research and Methods	NANCY KINGSBURY
Defense Capabilities and Management	CATHLEEN A. BERRICK
Education, Workforce, and Income Security	BARBARA D. BOVBJERG
Financial Management and Assurance	GARY T. ENGEL
Financial Markets and Community Investment	ORICE WILLIAMS BROWN
Forensic Audits and Investigative Service	JOHANA R. AYERS
Health Care	NIKKI CLOWERS
Homeland Security and Justice	GEORGE A. SCOTT
Information Technology	VALERIE MELVIN
International Affairs and Trade	CHARLES M. JOHNSON, JR.
Natural Resources and Environment	MARK E. GAFFIGAN
Physical Infrastructure	DANIEL BERTONI
Strategic Issues	J. CHRISTOPHER MIHM
Chief Administrative Officer / Chief Financial Officer	KARL J. MASCHINO
Deputy Chief Administrative Officer	PAUL R. JOHNSON
Chief Human Capital Officer	WILLIAM WHITE
Chief Information Officer	HOWARD WILLIAMS, JR.
Deputy Chief Financial Officer / Controller	WILLIAM L. ANDERSON
Managing Directors	
Field Operations	LINDA M. CALBOM
Infrastructure Operations	TERRELL G. DORN
Professional Development Program	TERESA RIVERA RUSSELL
Managing Directors—Staff Offices	
Congressional Relations	KATHERINE A. SIGGERUD
Opportunity and Inclusiveness	REGINALD E. JONES
Public Affairs	CHARLES YOUNG
Strategic Planning and External Liaison	JAMES-CHRISTIAN BLOCKWOOD

General Counsel	SUSAN A. POLING
Deputy General Counsel / Ethics Counselor	THOMAS H. ARMSTRONG
Inspector General	ADAM TRZECIAK

The key personnel tables above were updated 10–2017.

The Government Accountability Office helps the Congress fulfill its constitutional responsibilities and heightens the Federal Government's accountability and performance.

The Government Accountability Office (GAO) is an independent, nonpartisan agency that works for the Congress. The GAO is often called the "congressional watchdog" because it investigates how the Federal Government spends taxpayer dollars. The GAO was established as the General Accounting Office by the Budget and Accounting Act of 1921 (31 U.S.C. 702). It was renamed the Government Accountability Office pursuant to the GAO Capital Reform Act of 2004 (31 U.S.C. 702 note).

Activities

The GAO gathers information that the Congress uses to determine how effective executive branch agencies are at carrying out their missions. Its efforts routinely center on answering basic questions: Are Government programs meeting their objectives? Are they providing services of value to the public? Ultimately, the GAO ensures that the Government is accountable to the American people.

To help Senators and Representatives make informed policy decisions, the GAO provides them with accurate, balanced, and timely information. The Office supports congressional oversight by evaluating Government policies and programs; auditing agency operations to ensure effective, efficient, and appropriate spending of Federal funds; investigating allegations of illegal and improper activities; and issuing legal decisions and opinions.

With virtually the entire Federal Government subject to its review, the GAO issues a steady stream of products, including hundreds of reports and testimonies by GAO officials each year. Its reports or "blue books" meet short-term, immediate needs for information on a wide range of Government operations. These reports help Members of Congress understand emerging, long-term issues with far-reaching effects. The GAO's work supports a wide variety of improvements in Government operations and legislative actions that save the American people billions of dollars. http://www.gao.gov/about

Sources of Information

At a Glance   The "GAO at a Glance" Web page offers a profile of the agency, including information on the scope and nature of its activities. http://www.gao.gov/about/gglance.html

Bid Protests   Bidders or other interested parties may protest Federal Government procurement contracts. The GAO provides an inexpensive and expeditious forum for the resolution of these protests. Two search tools are available on the "Bid Protests" Web page. One allows users to search and access all published bid protest decisions; the other allows users to search the bid protest docket to find status information on cases filed within the past 12 months. http://www.gao.gov/legal/bid-protests/search | Email: ProtestFinder@gao.gov

Blog   The GAO's Web site features "WatchBlog: Following the Federal Dollar." To receive electronic notifications of new posts, sign up by entering an email address in the appropriate text box on the "WatchBlog" Web page. https://blog.gao.gov

Career Opportunities   The GAO relies on attorneys, communications analysts, criminal investigators, economists, financial auditors, information technology analysts, and other professionals to carry out its mission. http://www.gao.gov/careers/index.html

The GAO offers an intern program for students. Appointments for intern positions are 10–16 weeks in length and normally held during summer months. A student must be enrolled on at least a half-time basis, as determined by his or her college or university. A GAO student intern receives an appointment on a nonpermanent basis; however, after completing 400 hours of service and meeting degree requirements, he or she may be eligible for a permanent position. Internships are open to undergraduate and graduate students. http://www.gao.gov/careers/student.html

The GAO was named again as an outstanding place to work in the Federal Government. Among midsize agencies, it shared the second highest ranking with the Peace Corps in the Partnership for Public Service's 2016 list of the Best Places To Work. http://bestplacestowork.org/BPTW/rankings/detail/GA00

FraudNet FraudNet helps people report suspicion of abuse, fraud, waste, or mismanagement of Federal funds to the appropriate authorities. It refers allegations to Federal, State, and local law enforcement, and to Offices of Inspector General, when appropriate; it supports congressional investigation and audit requests; it provides audit and investigative leads to GAO staff; and it offers support to government at all levels for establishing and operating hotlines. Phone, 800-424-5454. Fax, 202-512-3086. http://www.gao.gov/fraudnet | Email: fraudnet@gao.gov

Freedom of Information Act (FOIA) The GAO is not subject to the FOIA; however, its disclosure policy adheres to the spirit of the act while remaining consistent with its duties and functions as an agency whose primary responsibility is to the Congress. Fax, 202-512-5806. http://www.gao.gov/about/freedom_of_information_act | Email: RecordsRequest@gao.gov

Frequently Asked Questions (FAQs) The GAO posts answers to general questions about its legal decisions. http://www.gao.gov/legal/more/about

Good Governance The Center for Audit Excellence promotes good governance and builds the capacity of domestic and international accountability organizations. It provides high-quality training, technical assistance, and related products and services. http://www.gao.gov/resources/centerforauditexcellence/overview

History When World War I came to a close, the Federal Government's financial affairs lacked proper management. Wartime spending had inflated the national debt, and Congress needed reliable information and enhanced expenditure control. Its solution for the problem came in 1921 with passage of the Budget and Accounting Act. To learn more about how that piece of legislation helped Congress manage the Nation's fiscal affairs and the role that a new agency played—and would continue to play—in Federal financial management, visit the "The History of GAO" Web pages. http://www.gao.gov/about/history

Key Issues The "Key Issues" Web pages contain information on GAO's work on a range of national issues, and they highlight the agency's most relevant reports. http://www.gao.gov/key_issues/overview#t=0

Organizational Chart The GAO's organizational chart is available on its Web site. http://www.gao.gov/about/workforce/orgchart.html

Podcast Gallery Recorded, hosted, and produced by GAO staff, the "Watchdog Report" features interviews with agency officials on significant issues and new reports. http://www.gao.gov/multimedia/podcast

Products The best known GAO products—correspondence, legal decisions and opinions, reports, and testimonies—are available to the press and the public. http://www.gao.gov/about/products

Publications Most GAO products and publications are available online, free of charge. Charges for printed copies cover the printing, shipping, and handling costs. Phone, 202-512-6000 or 866-801-7077. TDD, 202-512-2537. http://www.gao.gov/ordering.htm

The GAO's Web site allows visitors to browse reports and testimonies by date and topic and by agency alphabetically or hierarchically. http://www.gao.gov/browse/date/week

The "Principles of Federal Appropriations Law," also known as the "Red Book," is a multivolume treatise on Federal fiscal law. It provides text discussions with references to specific legal authorities to illustrate legal principles, their applications, and exceptions. These references include GAO decisions and judicial decisions, opinions, statutory provisions, and other relevant sources. http://www.gao.gov/legal/red-book/overview

Recommendations Database The recommendations database contains report recommendations that still need to be addressed. GAO's recommendations help congressional and agency leaders prepare for appropriations and oversight activities, as well as improve Government operations. Recommendations remain open until designated as "closed-implemented" or "closed-not implemented." The public can explore open recommendations online by browsing or searching. http://www.gao.gov/recommendations

Resources The GAO Web site features resources that auditors and others promoting accountability may find useful. http://www.gao.gov/resources/auditors/overview

The GAO Web site features resources that Members of Congress and and their staff may find useful. http://www.gao.gov/resources/congress/overview

The GAO Web site features resources that Federal agency managers may find useful. http://www.gao.gov/resources/federal_managers/overview

The GAO Web site features resources that journalists may find useful. http://www.gao.gov/resources/journalists/overview

The GAO Web site features resources—search tips for locating GAO products on its website, information on using the data and images contained in them, suggestions for additional informational sources—that researchers may find useful. http://www.gao.gov/resources/researchers/overview

Social Media The GAO has a Facebook account. https://www.facebook.com/usgao

The GAO tweets announcements, news, and other noteworthy items on Twitter. https://twitter.com/usgao

The GAO posts videos on its YouTube channel. https://www.youtube.com/user/usgao

The GAO posts informational graphics and photographs on Flickr. https://www.flickr.com/photos/usgao

Site Map The Web site map allows visitors to look for specific topics or to browse content that aligns with their interests. http://www.gao.gov/sitemap.html

Telephone Directory The "Organizational Telephone Directory" (April 2017), a document that is updated often, contains contact information for agency personnel and is available online in Portable Document Format (PDF). http://www.gao.gov/about.gao/phonebook/orgphonebook.pdf

Updates A subscription form is available on the GAO's Web site to sign up for email updates on the latest reports. Daily or monthly electronic updates are options, too, as well as notifications about correspondence, reports, and testimony that fall within a specific topic area. http://www.gao.gov/subscribe/index.php

Video Gallery The GAO Web site features a video collection that is diverse and extensive, educational and informative. http://www.gao.gov/multimedia/video/#video_id=679942

Widgets Snippets of HTML code for embedding small news widgets that refresh automatically are available on the GAO Web site. Pasting the code into the desired location on a Web site makes the most recent reports and testimonies and legal decisions from GAO locally accessible. http://www.gao.gov/widgets_reports_and_legal.html. http://www.gao.gov/about/contact.html | Email: contact@gao.gov

For further information, contact the Office of Public Affairs, Government Accountability Office, 441 G Street NW., Washington, DC 20548. Phone, 202-512-4800.

Government Publishing Office

732 North Capitol Street NW., Washington, DC 20401
Phone, 202-512-1800. Internet, http://www.gpo.gov

Director	JAMES C. BRADLEY, ACTING
Deputy Director	JAMES C. BRADLEY
Equal Employment Opportunity Managing Director	JUANITA M. FLORES
Chief Administrative Officer	HERBERT H. JACKSON, JR.
Chief Financial Officer	STEVEN T. SHEDD
Chief of Staff	ANDREW M. SHERMAN
General Counsel	KERRY L. MILLER, ACTING
Superintendent of Documents	LAURIE HALL
Chief Officers	
Acquisition Services	LORNA BAPTISTE-JONES
Human Capital	(VACANCY)
Information	TRACEE BOXLEY
Public Relations	GARY SOMERSET
Technology	RICHARD G. DAVIS
Managing Directors	
Customer Services	SANDRA MACAFEE
Labor Relations	MELISSA HATFIELD
Library Services and Content Management	LAURIE HALL
Official Journals of Government	LYLE GREEN
Plant Operations	JOHN CRAWFORD
Security and Intelligent Documents	STEPHEN G. LEBLANC
Security Services	LAMONT VERNON

The above list of key personnel was updated 11–2017.

The Government Publishing Office produces, procures, and disseminates printed and electronic publications of the Congress, executive departments, and Federal agencies and establishments.

The Government Publishing Office (GPO) was created on June 23, 1860, by Congressional Joint Resolution 25. The Office opened for business on March 4, 1861. Its duties are defined in title 44 of the U.S. Code. The President appoints the Director, who is then confirmed by the Senate. https://www.gpo.gov/about/gpohistory

Activities

Headquartered in Washington, DC, with a total employment of approximately 1,700, the Office is responsible for the production and distribution of information products and services for the three branches of the Federal Government. It is the Federal Government's primary centralized resource for producing, procuring, cataloging, indexing, authenticating, disseminating, and

preserving the official information products of the U.S. Government in digital and tangible forms. https://www.gpo.gov/about

While many of the informational products, such as the "Congressional Record" and "Federal Register," are produced at the main GPO plant, most of the Government's printing is done in partnership with America's printing industry. The Office procures 75 percent of all printing orders through private sector vendors across the country, competitively buying products and services from thousands of businesses in all 50 States. The contracts cover the entire spectrum of printing and publishing services and are suitable for companies of all sizes.

The Office disseminates Federal information products through a sales program, distribution network of more than

1,200 Federal libraries nationwide, and the Federal Digital System (FDsys). The public can access more than 800,000 Federal Government document titles online by using the FDsys website. http://www.gpo.gov/fdsys/search/home.action

Sources of Information

Ben's Guide An educational website for children and young adults, Ben's Guide has learning adventures for the apprentice level (ages 4–8), journeyperson level (ages 9–13), and master level (ages 14 and older). https://bensguide.gpo.gov

Bookstore Printed copies of many documents, ranging from Supreme Court opinions to reports from the Bureau of Labor Statistics, may be purchased. To order in person, visit the GPO Main Bookstore at 710 North Capitol Street NW., Washington, DC (corner of North Capitol Street NW. and G Street), 8 a.m.–4 p.m. To order online, use the link below. To order by phone or inquire about an order, call 866-512-1800 or 202-512-1800 (Washington, DC–metropolitan area), 8 a.m.–5:30 p.m., eastern standard time. All orders require prepayment by an American Express, Discover/NOVUS, MasterCard, or VISA credit card; check or money order; or Superintendent of Documents (SOD) deposit account, which customers who purchase Government products on a recurring basis can open with the GPO. Fax, 202-512-2104. https://bookstore.gpo.gov | Email: contactcenter@gpo.gov

Business Opportunities Acquisition Services obtains the equipment, services, and supplies that GPO needs from external sources to accomplish its mission. Phone, 202-512-0937. https://www.gpo.gov/vendors/as.htm

Commercial printers seeking contract opportunities should contact Customer Services, Government Publishing Office, Washington, DC 20401. Phone, 202-512-0526. https://www.gpo.gov/vendors/index.htm | Email: ppdsmla@gpo.gov

Career Opportunities GPO vacancy announcements and information on benefits, career paths, and the application process are accessible online. https://www.gpo.gov/careers

In 2016, the GPO was ranked number 13 among midsize Government agencies in the Best Places To Work Agency Rankings. http://bestplacestowork.org/BPTW/rankings/detail/LP00

Catalog of U.S. Government Publications (CGP) The CGP is a searchable Federal publications catalog that contains descriptive information on recent and historical publications, as well as links to some complete documents. Users can search the catalog by agency, keywords, subject, and title. https://catalog.gpo.gov/F?RN=785806650

Congressional Relations The Office of Congressional Relations responds to congressional inquiries and requests. Phone, 202-512-1991. Fax, 202-512-1293. http://www.gpo.gov/congressional

Federal Digital System (FDsys) / Govinfo The FDsys website makes official publications from the executive, judicial, and legislative branches of Government accessible. The GPO provides user support for the System. Phone, 866-512-1800 or 202-512-1800 (Washington, DC–metropolitan area). http://www.gpo.gov/fdsysinfo/aboutfdsys.htm

In 2018, the GPO plans to replace the FDsys website with govinfo. Both websites are available online; however, the FDsys site will be retired from public service at some point. Like FDsys, govinfo provides free and public access to official publications from the executive, judicial, and legislative branches of Government. https://www.govinfo.gov

Frequently Asked Questions (FAQs) Answers to FAQs are available online. https://www.gpo.gov/about/faq.htm

History The GPO has collections of historic photographs on its website. These collections contain images of the building and former Public Printers, as well as GPO employees and officials, presses and equipment, and products. https://www.gpo.gov/about/gpohistory/historic_photo_gallery.htm

Newsroom The newsroom features high resolution images for downloading, news reports, press releases, and a video chronicling GPO from its beginnings to the digital future. Phone, 202-512-1957. Fax, 202-512-1998. http://www.gpo.gov/newsroom-media

Organizational Chart The GPO posts its organizational chart in Portable Document Format (PDF) for viewing and downloading. https://www.gpo.gov/pdfs/about/GPO_organization_1.17.pdf

Oversight   The Office of the Inspector General from the GPO posts reports and data on Oversight.gov, a text-searchable repository of reports that Federal Inspectors General publish. The Council of the Inspectors General on Integrity and Efficiency operates and maintains the website to increase public access to independent and authoritative information on the Federal Government. https://oversight.gov

Regional Offices   A list of regional offices, with contact information, is available on the GPO website. http://www.gpo.gov/customers/offices.htm

Site Map   The website map allows visitors to look for specific topics or to browse content that aligns with their interests. https://www.gpo.gov/etc/sitemap.htm

Social Media   The GPO maintains a Facebook account. https://www.facebook.com/USGPO

The GPO tweets announcements and other newsworthy items on Twitter. https://twitter.com/usgpo

The GPO posts videos on its YouTube channel. https://www.youtube.com/user/gpoprinter. https://www.gpo.gov/contact.htm | Email: ContactCenter@gpo.gov

For further information, contact Public Relations, Government Publishing Office, 732 North Capitol Street NW., Washington, DC 20401. Phone, 202-512-1957. Fax, 202-512-1998.

Library of Congress

101 Independence Avenue SE., Washington, DC 20540
Phone, 202-707-5000. Internet, http://www.loc.gov

Librarian Of Congress	CARLA D. HAYDEN
Deputy Librarian for Institutional Advancement	ROBERT R. NEWLEN
Chief of Staff	ELIZABETH C. MORRISON
Chief Operating Officer	EDWARD R. JABLONSKI
General Counsel	ELIZABETH PUGH
Inspector General	KURT W. HYDE
Chief Communications Officer	ROSWELL M. ENCINA
Director of Human Resources Services	RACHEL BOUMAN
Director of Congressional Research Service	MARY B. MAZANEC
Associate Librarian for Library Services	J. MARK SWEENEY
Director of National International Outreach	JANE MCAULIFFE
Law Librarian of Congress	JANE F. SÁNCHEZ
Acting Register of Copyrights	KARYN A. TEMPLE CLAGGETT

Library of Congress Trust Fund Board

CHAIR (Librarian of Congress)	CARLA D. HAYDEN
(Fiscal Assistant Secretary of the Treasury)	DAVID A. LEBRYK
(Chair, Joint Committee on the Library)	GREGG HARPER
(Vice Chair, Joint Committee on the Library)	RICHARD SHELBY
Member	KATHLEEN L. CASEY
Member	J. RICHARD FREDERICKS
Member	THOMAS GIRARDI
Member	CHRISTOPHER G. LONG
Member	SHEILA MARCELO
Member	GEORGE MARCUS
Member	JOHN MILLER
Member	(VACANCY)
Member	(VACANCY)
Member	(VACANCY)

The Library of Congress is the national library of the United States, offering diverse materials for research, including the world's most extensive collections in areas such as American history, music, and law.

The Library of Congress was established by Act of April 24, 1800 (2 Stat. 56), appropriating $5,000 "for the purchase of such books as may be necessary for the use of Congress . . . ." The Library's scope of responsibility has been widened by subsequent legislation (2 U.S.C. 131-168d). The Librarian, appointed by the President with the advice and consent of the Senate, directs the Library.

The Library's first responsibility is service to Congress. Its Congressional Research Service provides Congress with legislative research and analysis that is authoritative, confidential, objective, and timely during all stages of the legislative process. The Library's Congress.gov Web site serves as a source of legislative information for both Congress and the general public. https://www.congress.gov

As the Library has developed, its range of service has expanded to include the entire governmental establishment and the public at large. The Library serves as a national library for the United States, and its online presence makes it a global resource. https://www.loc.gov/about

Activities

Collections The Library's extensive collections are universal in scope. They include books, serials, and pamphlets on every subject and in more than 470 languages, and research materials in many formats, including maps, photographs, manuscripts, motion pictures, and sound recordings. Among them are the most comprehensive collections of books outside Asia and the former Soviet Union; the largest collection of published aeronautical literature; and the most extensive collection of books in the Western Hemisphere.

The manuscript collections relate to various aspects of American history and civilization and include the personal papers of most of the Presidents from George Washington to Calvin Coolidge. The music collections contain volumes and pieces—manuscript and published—from classic works to the newest popular compositions. Other materials available for research include maps and views; photographic records; recordings, prints, drawings, and posters; government documents, newspapers, and periodicals; and motion pictures, microforms, audio and video tapes, and digital and online materials. https://www.loc.gov/discover

Reference Resources Admission to the various research facilities of the Library is free. The Library's reading rooms are open to persons age 16 and older. Readers must register by presenting valid photo identification with a current address. For some collections, there are additional requirements. While priority is given to inquiries about special materials or to unique resources, the Library provides helpful responses to all inquirers. Online reference service is also available through the "Ask a Librarian" Web page. http://www.loc.gov/rr

Copyrights With the enactment of the second general revision of the U.S. copyright law by Act of July 8, 1870 (16 Stat. 212–217), all activities relating to copyright, including deposit and registration, were centralized in the Library of Congress. The Copyright Act of 1976 (90 Stat. 2541) brought all forms of copyrightable authorship, both published and unpublished, under a single statutory system which gives authors protection upon creation of their works. Exclusive rights granted to authors under the statute include the right to reproduce and prepare derivative works, distribute copies or phonorecords, perform and display the work publicly, and in the case of sound recordings, to perform the work publicly by means of a digital audio transmission. Works eligible for copyright include literary works (books and periodicals), musical works, dramatic works, pantomimes and choreographic works, pictorial, graphic, and sculptural works, motion pictures, sound recordings, vessel hull designs, mask works, and architectural works.

The Copyright Office serves as a National registry for creative works, registering more than 500,000 claims annually. It is also a major source of acquisitions for the Library's collections. Most paper information is also accessible on its Web site. http://www.copyright.gov

Extension of Service The Library offers duplication services; the sale of sound recordings, cataloging data and tools; the exchange of duplicates with other institutions; development of classification schemes; preparation of bibliographic lists for Government and research; maintenance and publication of cooperative publications; and publication of catalogs, bibliographic guides, and lists, and texts of original manuscripts and rare books. It has items for circulation in traveling exhibitions; books in Braille, as well as "talking books on the Internet, and books on tape. The Library distributes electronic materials and provides research and analytical services for a fee. The Library also manages the following programs: centralized and cooperative cataloging; cataloging-in-publication for unpublished books; interlibrary loan system; and the U.S. International Standard Serial Number (ISSN) Center.

Furthermore, the Library provides for the following: the preparation of bibliographical lists responsive to the needs of Government and research; the maintenance and the publication of cooperative publications; the publication of catalogs, bibliographical guides, and lists, and of texts of original manuscripts and rare books in the Library of Congress; the circulation in traveling exhibitions of items from the Library's collections; the provision of books in Braille, electronic access to Braille books on the Internet, "talking books," and books on tape for the blind and the physically handicapped through more than 100 cooperating libraries throughout the Nation; the distribution of its electronic materials via the Internet; and the provision of research and analytical services on a fee-for-service basis to agencies in the executive and judicial branches. https://www.loc.gov/services

American Folklife Center   The American Folklife Center was established in the Library of Congress by Act of January 2, 1976 (20 U.S.C. 2102 et seq.). It supports, preserves, and presents American folklife by receiving and maintaining folklife collections, scholarly research, field projects, performances, exhibitions, festivals, workshops, publications, and audiovisual presentations. The Center administers the Veterans History Project, which records and preserves the first-person accounts of war veterans. It collaborates with the Smithsonian Institution's National Museum of African American History and Culture to maintain the Civil Rights History Project and its resulting collection of interviews with leaders and participants in the Civil Rights movement. The Center also maintains and administers the American Folklife Center Archive, which is an extensive multi-format collection of ethnographic materials from this country and around the world, and serves as the national repository for folk-related field recordings, manuscripts, and other unpublished materials. The Archive also contains the collections of StoryCorps, a program to record and collect oral histories from people from all walks of life.

The Center's reading room contains over 4,000 books and periodicals; a sizable collection of magazines, newsletters, unpublished theses, and dissertations; field notes; and many textual and some musical transcriptions and recordings. Information on the Center's blog, social media, publications, and collections is available online. https://www.loc.gov/folklife

For further information, call 202-707-5510.

Center for the Book   The Center was established in the Library of Congress by an Act of October 13, 1977 (2 U.S.C. 171 et seq.), to stimulate public interest in books, reading, and libraries, and to encourage the study of books and print culture. The Center promotes and explores the vital role of books, reading, and libraries, nationally and internationally. As a partnership between the Government and the private sector, the Center for the Book depends on tax-deductible contributions from individuals and corporations to support its programs.

The Center's activities are directed toward the general public and scholars. The overall program includes reading promotion projects with television and radio networks, symposia, lectures, exhibitions, special events, and publications. More than 80 national education and civic organizations participate in the Center's annual reading promotion campaign.

The Center provides leadership for 52 affiliated State—including the District of Columbia and the Virgin Islands—centers for the book and nonprofit reading-promotion partners. It oversees the Library's read. gov Web site, administers the Library's

Young Readers Center and its Poetry and Literature Center, and plays a key role in the Library's annual National Book Festival. The Center also administers the position of Poet Laureate Consultant in Poetry, as well as, in collaboration with the Children's Book Council, the position of the National Ambassador for Young People's Literature. http://www.read.gov/cfb | Email: cfbook@loc.gov

For further information, contact the Center for the Book. Phone, 202-707-5221. Fax, 202-707-0269.

National Film Preservation Board   The National Film Preservation Board, established by the National Film Preservation Act of 1988 (102 Stat. 1785) and reauthorized by the National Film Preservation Act of 2005 (2 U.S.C. 179l note), serves as a public advisory group to the Librarian of Congress. The Board works to ensure the survival, conservation, and increased public availability of America's film heritage, including advising the Librarian on the annual selection of films to the National Film Registry and counseling the Librarian on development and implementation of the national film preservation plan. https://www.loc.gov/programs/national-film-preservation-board/about-this-program

For further information, call 202-707-5912.

National Sound Recording Preservation Board   The National Recording Preservation Board, established by the National Recording Preservation Act of 2000 (2 U.S.C. 1701 note) reviews nominated sound recordings for inclusion in the National Recording Registry and advises the Librarian on the inclusion of such recordings in the Registry to preserve sound recordings that are culturally, historically, or aesthetically significant. The Board comprises three major components: a National Recording Preservation Advisory Board, which brings together experts in the field; a National Recording Registry; and a fundraising foundation, all of which are conducted under the auspices of the Library of Congress. The Board implements a national plan for the long-term preservation and accessibility of the Nation's audio heritage. The national recording preservation program

sets standards for future private and public preservation efforts in conjunction with the Library's National Audio-Visual Conservation Center in Culpeper, VA. https://www.loc.gov/programs/national-recording-preservation-board/about-this-program

For further information, call 202-707-5856.

Preservation   The Library provides technical information related to the preservation of library and archival material. The Library's Preservation Directorate includes three preservation science laboratories, a Center for the Library's Analytical Science Samples, and a Collections Recovery Room. Information on publications and various preservation and conservation topics is available online. http://www.loc.gov/rr/askalib/ask-preserv.html

For further information, call 202-707-1840.

Sources of Information

Books for the Blind and Physically Handicapped   Braille and talking books and magazines, including music materials, are distributed through more than 100 regional and subregional libraries to residents of the United States and its territories who are blind or have a physical disability. Eligible Americans living abroad are also able to participate. Users may also register for the Braille and Audio Reading Download (BARD) online service, enabling them to use the BARD mobile app to read on smart devices. Information is available from the National Library Service for the Blind and Physically Handicapped, Library of Congress, 1291 Taylor Street NW., Washington, DC 20542-4960. Phone, 202-707-5100 or 1-888-NLS-READ (1-888-657-7323). http://www.loc.gov/ThatAllMayRead | Email: nls@loc.gov

Business Opportunities   To learn about business opportunities, visit the "Doing Business With the Library" Web page. http://www.loc.gov/about/doing-business-with-the-library

Cataloging Distribution Services   Cataloging and bibliographic information in the form of microfiche catalogs, book catalogs, magnetic tapes, CD-ROM cataloging tools, bibliographies, and other technical publications is distributed to libraries and other institutions. Information about ordering materials is available from the Cataloging Distribution Service, Library of Congress, Washington, DC 20541-4910. Phone, 202-707-6100. TDD, 202-707-0012. Fax, 202-707-1334. Email, cdsinfo@mail.loc. gov. Card numbers for new publications and Electronic Preassigned Control Numbers for publishers are available from the Cataloging in Publication Division, Library of Congress, Washington, DC 20541-4910. Phone, 202-707-6345.

Copyright Services   Information about the copyright law (title 17 of the U.S. Code), the method of securing copyright, and copyright registration procedures may be obtained by writing to the Copyright Office, Library of Congress, 101 Independence Avenue SE., Washington, DC 20559-6000. Phone, 202-707-3000. Registration application forms may be ordered by calling the forms hotline at 202-707-9100. Copyright records may be researched and reported by the Copyright Office for a fee; for an estimate, call 202-707-6850. Members of the public may use the copyright card catalog in the Copyright Office without charge. The database of Copyright Office records cataloged from January 1, 1978, to the present is available online at http://cocatalog.loc.gov/. The Copyright Information Office is located in Room LM-401, James Madison Memorial Building, 101 Independence Avenue SE., Washington, DC 20559-6000. It is open to the public Monday through Friday, 8:30 a.m. to 5 p.m., except for Federal holidays. http://www.loc.gov/copyright

Employment   The Library offers many opportunities for those seeking employment, fellowships or internships, or volunteer positions. Job vacancy announcements and application information are posted online and also available from the Employment Office, Room LM-107, 101 Independence Avenue SE., Washington, DC 20540. Phone, 202-707-4315. http://www.loc.gov/hr/employment

Duplication Services   Copies of manuscripts, prints, photographs, maps, and book material not subject to copyright and other restrictions are available for a fee. Order forms for photo reproduction and price schedules are available from Duplication Services, Library of Congress, 101 Independence Avenue SE., Washington, DC 20540-4570. Phone, 202-707-5640. http://www.loc.gov/duplicationservices

Exhibitions   Throughout the year, the Library offers free exhibitions featuring items from its collections. Library exhibitions may be viewed Monday through Saturday, 8:30 a.m. to 4:30 p.m., in the Thomas Jefferson Building. For more information, call 202-707-4604. To view current and past exhibitions online, use the link below. http://www.loc.gov/exhibits

Federal Agency Research Services   Federal agencies can procure research and analytical products on foreign and domestic topics using the collections of the Library of Congress through the Federal Research Division. Science, technology, humanities, and social science research are conducted by staff specialists exclusively on behalf of Federal agencies on a fee-for-service basis. Research requests should be directed to the Federal Research Division, Marketing Office, Library of Congress, Washington, DC 20540-4840. Phone, 202-707-9133. Fax, 202-707-3920. https://www.loc.gov/rr/frd

Publications   Library of Congress publications are available online. The Library of Congress Magazine (LCM) is published 6 times a year and may be viewed online at http://www.loc.gov/lcm/. The calendar of public events is also available online at www.loc.gov/loc/events and is available by mail to persons within 100 miles of Washington, DC. To be added to the calendar mailing list, send a request to Office Systems Services, Mail and Distribution Management Section, Library of Congress, 101 Independence Avenue SE., Washington, DC 20540-9441 or send an email to pao@loc.gov. http://www.loc.gov/visit/shopping

Reference and Bibliographic Services   Guidance is offered to readers in identifying and using the material in the Library's collections, and reference service is provided to those with inquiries who have exhausted local, State, and regional resources. Persons requiring services that cannot be performed by the Library staff can be supplied with names of private researchers who work on a fee-for-service basis. Requests for information should be directed to the Reference Referral Service, Library of Congress, 101 Independence Avenue SE., Washington, DC 20540-4720. Phone, 202-707-5522. Fax, 202-707-1389. Questions may also be submitted online at the "Ask a Librarian" Web site. http://www.loc.gov/rr/askalib

Research and Reference Services in Science and Technology Requests for reference services should be directed to the Science, Technology, and Business Division, Library of Congress, Science Reference Section, 101 Independence Avenue SE., Washington, DC 20540-4750. Phone, 202-707-5639. http://www.loc.gov/rr/scitech

Tours Guided tours of the Library are available on weekdays, 10:30 a.m.–3:30 p.m., and on Saturdays at 10:30 and 11:30 a.m. and at 1:30 and 2:30 p.m. For more information on scheduling a tour for a group of 10 or more, contact the Visitor Services Office. Phone, 202-707-0919. https://www.loc.gov/visit/tours. http://www.loc.gov | Email: pao@loc.gov

For further information, contact the Public Affairs Office, Library of Congress, 101 Independence Avenue SE., Washington, DC 20540-8610. Phone, 202-707-2905. Fax, 202-707-2905. Fax, 202-707-9199.

Congressional Research Service

101 Independence Avenue SE., Washington, DC 20540
Phone, 202-707-5000

Director, Congressional Research Service	MARY B. MAZANEC

The Congressional Research Service (CRS) provides comprehensive research and analysis on all legislative and oversight issues of interest to Congress. The CRS assists Congress by responding to specific questions and by preparing reports on legislative topics in anticipation of questions and emerging issues. The CRS works with Members, committees, and congressional staff to identify and clarify policy problems and assess the implications of proposed policy alternatives. CRS experts play a role in every stage of the legislative process. http://www.loc.gov/crsinfo/about

Sources of Information

Employment Current vacancies and entry-level opportunities are posted online, as well as information on internship programs. http://www.loc.gov/crsinfo/opportunities. http://www.loc.gov/crsinfo/contact

For further information, call 202-707-5700.

United States Botanic Garden

Office of Executive Director, 245 First Street SW., Washington, DC 20024
Phone, 202-226-8333. Internet, http://www.usbg.gov

Conservatory, , 100 Maryland Avenue SW., Washington, DC 20001

Production Facility, 4700 Shepherd Parkway SW., Washington, DC 20032

Phone, 202-226-4780

Acting Director	STEPHEN T. AYERS
Executive Director	SUSAN K. PELL, ACTING

The above list of key personnel was updated 09–2017.

The United States Botanic Garden informs visitors of the importance and value of plants to humankind and to Earth's ecosystems.

The U.S. Botanic Garden (USBG) has a long history that reaches back to the Founding Fathers. In October of 1796, President George Washington suggested that "a Botanic Garden would be a good appendage" to a Federal university. Twenty-four years later, President James Madison helped establish a botanic garden in the U.S. Capital under the auspices of the Columbian Institute, a society dedicated to promoting the arts and sciences. This early botanic collection served as the cornerstone of what would become the Nation's future botanic garden.

Congress also supported establishing a national botanic garden. By an act of August 26, 1842, it made provision for the safekeeping and arrangement of dried and living specimens that Lieutenant Charles Wilkes's expedition had collected while exploring the Pacific Rim. Congress placed the enlarged collection under the stewardship of its Joint Committee on the Library.

When the old Patent Office was expanded in 1849, a new location for the plants and greenhouse had to be found. Congress again intervened and, by an act of May 15, 1850, funded the construction of a new greenhouse and the collection's relocation. The Joint Committee on the Library, with assistance from the Commissioner of Public Buildings, managed the project. A new national botanic garden opened on the National Mall, at the west end of the Capitol Grounds, later that year.

By 1856—the collection had been named officially the United States Botanic Garden, Congress was providing an annual appropriation for its upkeep, and the Joint Committee on the Library had assumed responsibility for both its direction and maintenance. To satisfy the McMillan Commission's plan for a large, open mall, the USBG was moved in 1933, one block south, to its present site. The Joint Committee on the Library maintains oversight of the USBG through the Architect of the Capitol, who holds the title of Acting Director. https://www.usbg.gov/brief-history-us-botanic-garden

Activities

The USBG highlights botanical diversity worldwide, as well as the aesthetic, cultural,

ecological, economic, and therapeutic significance of plants. The agency promotes appreciation of plants and stimulates interest in botany through artistic plant displays, education programs, exhibits, and curation of a large plant collection. It supports conservation by serving as a repository for endangered plant species. It also encourages the exchange of ideas and disseminates mission-relevant information to national and international visitors and policymakers. https://www.usbg.gov/about-us

Three USBG sites are open year-round to the public: the Conservatory, the National Garden, and Bartholdi Park. The production facility is periodically open for public programs and tours. https://www.usbg.gov/hours-and-location-0

Sources of Information

America's Agricultural Experience   Based on a meeting that the U.S. Botanic Garden helped to organize of the Nation's leading agricultural and botanical educators, "Agriculture and the Future of Food: The Role of Botanic Gardens" presents a series of educational narratives that promote the reconnection of people and plants through the American agricultural experience. The document is available on the USBG Web site in Portable Document Format (PDF). https://www.usbg.gov/sites/default/files/attachments/agriculture_and_the_future_of_food_-_the_role_of_botanic_gardens.pdf

Calendar of Events   The USBG offers children and family programs, lectures, special tours, and workshops, as well as free theater, concerts, cooking demonstrations, and more. An events calendar is posted on the "Programs and Events" page, and a Portable Document Format (PDF) version is available for downloading. https://www.usbg.gov/programs-and-events

Career Opportunities   Information on career and volunteer opportunities is available online. https://www.usbg.gov/opportunities-us-botanic-garden

Exhibits   The USBG creates exhibits that not only delight and educate visitors, but that inspire them to become more active and better stewards of the plants supporting life on Earth. It posts Information on current and upcoming exhibits online. https://www.usbg.gov/exhibits

Factsheets Gardening factsheets are available on the USBG's Web site. https://www.usbg.gov/gardening-fact-sheets-0

Kids The USBG is a child-friendly living plant museum. https://www.usbg.gov/kids-are-welcome-us-botanic-garden

Land Development and Management An interdisciplinary partnership led by the USBG, American Society of Landscape Architects, and the Lady Bird Johnson Wildflower Center, the Sustainable Sites Initiative™ improves land development and management practices with a voluntary rating system for sustainable land design, construction, and maintenance practices. Architects, designers, developers, engineers, landscape architects, policymakers, and others use SITES to align land development and management with sustainable design. SITES supports the creation of ecologically resilient communities, and it benefits property owners, local and regional communities and their economies, as well as the environment. Certification covers development projects on land where buildings are absent or present. http://www.sustainablesites.org

Landscaping A collaboration between the USBG and the Lady Bird Johnson Wildflower Center, Landscape For Life™ promotes an approach to landscaping that respects nature. Irrespective of location—downtown, suburbia, or the farm—every landscape or garden can protect and even restore the environment, without sacrificing visual appeal. The Landscape for Life Web site contains a trove of information—getting started, materials, human health, plants, soil, and water—for transforming an environmentally ambivalent landscape into a healthy, sustainable one. http://landscapeforlife.org

Living Collections Database An online tool is available to search the USBG's living collections database. https://www.usbg.gov/search-collection

Native Plant Recommendations The USBG posts lists of selected plants to grow in the garden. The lists are available in Portable Document Format (PDF) for downloading. https://www.usbg.gov/national-garden-native-plant-recommendations

Plant Hotline Questions about a garden plant? Call the Plant Hotline. Phone, 202-226-4785.

Pollinators Learn about the role birds and bees, as well as other creatures like bats, beetles, butterflies, flies, moths, and even wasps, play in the life cycle of plants. https://www.usbg.gov/pollinator-information

Production Facility The production facility opens periodically for public programs and tours. An annual open house allows visitors to meet the gardeners, ask questions, and explore the facility. https://www.usbg.gov/us-botanic-garden-production-facility

Rare and Endangered Plants USBG experts bank seeds of rare plants, introduce rare plants to the horticultural trade, maintain live specimens, and study wild plants at risk of endangerment or extinction. The Web site features a gallery of plants with vulnerable, threatened, and endangered threat levels. https://www.usbg.gov/gardens/rare-and-endangered-plants-gallery

Site Map The Web site map allows visitors to look for specific topics or to browse content that aligns with their interests. https://www.usbg.gov/sitemap

Social Media The USBG has a Facebook account. https://www.facebook.com/usbotanicgarden. https://www.usbg.gov/contact-us-botanic-garden | Email: usbg@aoc.gov

For further information concerning the United States Botanic Garden, contact the Public Program Division, 245 First Street SW., Washington, DC 20515. Phone, 202-225-8333.

Judicial Branch

JUDICIAL BRANCH

The Supreme Court of the United States

United States Supreme Court Building, One First Street NE., Washington, DC 20543
Phone, 202-479-3000. Internet, http://www.supremecourt.gov

Members

Chief Justice of the United States	JOHN G. ROBERTS, JR.
Associate Justice	ANTHONY M. KENNEDY
Associate Justice	CLARENCE THOMAS
Associate Justice	RUTH BADER GINSBURG
Associate Justice	STEPHEN G. BREYER
Associate Justice	SAMUEL A. ALITO, JR.
Associate Justice	SONIA SOTOMAYOR
Associate Justice	ELENA KAGAN
Associate Justice	NEIL M. GORSUCH

Officers

Counselor To The Chief Justice	JEFFREY P. MINEAR
Clerk	SCOTT S. HARRIS
Court Counsel	ETHAN V. TORREY
Curator	CATHERINE E. FITTS
Director of Information Technology	ROBERT J. HAWKINS
Librarian	LINDA MASLOW
Marshal	PAMELA TALKIN
Public Information Officer	KATHLEEN L. ARBERG
Reporter of Decisions	CHRISTINE L. FALLON

Article III, section 1, of the Constitution of the United States provides that "[t]he judicial Power of the United States, shall be vested in one supreme Court, and in such inferior Courts as the Congress may from time to time ordain and establish."

The Supreme Court of the United States was created in accordance with this provision and by authority of the Judiciary Act of September 24, 1789 (1 Stat. 73). It was organized on February 2, 1790. Article III, section 2, of the Constitution defines the jurisdiction of the Supreme Court.

The Supreme Court comprises the Chief Justice of the United States and such number of Associate Justices as may be fixed by Congress, which is currently fixed at eight (28 U.S.C. 1). The President nominates the Justices with the advice and consent of the Senate. Article III, section 1, of the Constitution further provides that "[t]he Judges, both of the supreme and inferior Courts, shall hold their Offices during good Behaviour, and shall, at stated Times, receive for their Services, a Compensation, which shall not be diminished during their Continuance in Office."

Court officers assist the Court in the performance of its functions. They include: the Counselor to the Chief Justice, the Clerk,

71

the Court Counsel, the Curator, the Director of Information Technology, the Librarian, the Marshal, the Public Information Officer, and the Reporter of Decisions. Internet, http://www.supremecourt.gov/about/briefoverview.aspx

Appellate Jurisdiction   Various statutes, derived from the authority that the Constitution has given to Congress, confer appellate jurisdiction upon the Supreme Court. The basic statute effective at this time in conferring and controlling jurisdiction of the Supreme Court may be found in 28 U.S.C. 1251, 1253, 1254, 1257-1259, and various special statutes. Congress has no authority to change the original jurisdiction of this Court.

Court Term   The term of the Court begins on the first Monday in October and lasts until the first Monday in October of the next year. Over the course of a term, approximately 10,000 petitions are filed for cases to be briefed before the Court. Moreover, each year, about 1,200 applications that can be acted upon by a single Justice while serving in the capacity of a Circuit Justice are filed. Internet, http://www.supremecourt.gov/about/procedures.aspx

Rulemaking   From time to time, Congress has conferred upon the Supreme Court power to prescribe rules of procedure to be followed by the lower courts of the United States.

Sources of Information

Exhibitions   The Office of the Curator develops exhibitions to highlight the work of the Nation's highest Court, the lives of individual Justices, and the architecture of the Supreme Court building. Internet, http://www.supremecourt.gov/visiting/exhibition.aspx

News Media   Media advisories, press releases, speeches, and Year-End Reports on the Federal judiciary are accessible online. Information on the requirements and procedures for issuing Supreme Court press credentials is also available. Internet, http://www.supremecourt.gov/publicinfo/publicinfo.aspx

Public Access   The Supreme Court is open to the public from 9 a.m. to 4:30 p.m., weekdays, except on Federal holidays. Unless the Court or Chief Justice orders otherwise, the Clerk's office is open from 9 a.m. to 5 p.m., weekdays, except on Federal holidays. The library is open to members of the bar of the Court, attorneys for the various Federal departments and agencies, and Members of Congress. Internet, http://www.supremecourt.gov/visiting/visiting.aspx. http://www.supremecourt.gov/contact/contactus.aspx

For further information concerning the Supreme Court, contact the Public Information Office, United States Supreme Court Building, One First Street NE., Washington, DC 20543. Phone, 202-479-3211.

Lower Courts

Article III of the Constitution declares, in section 1, that the judicial power of the United States shall be invested in one Supreme Court and in "such inferior Courts as the Congress may from time to time ordain and establish." The Supreme Court has held that these constitutional courts ". . . share in the exercise of the judicial power defined in that section, can be invested with no other jurisdiction, and have judges who hold office during good behavior, with no power in Congress to provide otherwise."

United States Courts of Appeals

The courts of appeals are intermediate appellate courts created by act of March 3, 1891 (28 U.S.C. ch. 3), to relieve the Supreme Court of considering all appeals in cases originally decided by the Federal trial courts. They are empowered to review all final decisions and certain interlocutory decisions (18 U.S.C. 3731; 28 U.S.C. 1291, 1292) of district courts. They also are empowered to review and enforce orders of many Federal administrative bodies. The decisions of the courts of appeals are final except as they are subject to review on writ of certiorari by the Supreme Court.

The United States is divided geographically into 12 judicial circuits, including the District of Columbia. Each circuit has a court of appeals (28 U.S.C. 41, 1294). Each of the 50 States is assigned to one of the circuits. The territories and the Commonwealth of Puerto Rico are assigned variously to the first, third, and ninth circuits. There is also a Court of Appeals for the Federal Circuit, which has nationwide jurisdiction defined by subject matter. At present each court of appeals has from 6 to 28 permanent circuit judgeships (179 in all), depending upon the amount of judicial work in the circuit. Circuit judges hold their offices during good behavior as provided by Article III, section 1, of the Constitution. The judge senior in commission who is under 70 years of age (65 at inception of term), has been in office at least 1 year, and has not previously been chief judge, serves as the chief judge of the circuit for a 7-year term. One of the Justices of the Supreme Court is assigned as circuit justice for each of the 13 judicial circuits. Each court of appeals normally hears cases in panels consisting of three judges but may sit en banc with all judges present.

The judges of each circuit (except the Federal Circuit) by vote determine the size of the judicial council for the circuit, which consists of the chief judge and an equal number of circuit and district judges. The council considers the state of Federal judicial business in the circuit and may "make all necessary and appropriate orders for [its] effective and expeditious administration . . ." (28 U.S.C. 332).

The chief judge of each circuit may summon periodically a judicial conference of all judges of the circuit, including members of the bar, to discuss the business of the Federal courts of the circuit (28 U.S.C. 333). The chief judge of each circuit and a district judge elected from each of the 12 geographical circuits, together with the chief judge of the Court of International Trade, serve as members of the Judicial Conference of the United States, over which the Chief Justice of the United States presides. This is the governing body for the administration of the Federal judicial system as a whole (28 U.S.C. 331).

To obtain a complete list of judges, court officials, and official stations of the United States Courts of Appeals for the Federal Circuit, as well as information on opinions and cases before the court, consult the Judicial Circuit Web sites listed below.

List of Judicial Circuit Web Sites—United States Courts of Appeals

Circuit	URL
District of Columbia Circuit	http://www.cadc.uscourts.gov
First Circuit	http://www.ca1.uscourts.gov
Second Circuit	http://www.ca2.uscourts.gov
Third Circuit	http://www.ca3.uscourts.gov
Fourth Circuit	http://www.ca4.uscourts.gov
Fifth Circuit	http://www.ca5.uscourts.gov
Sixth Circuit	http://www.ca6.uscourts.gov
Seventh Circuit	http://www.ca7.uscourts.gov
Eighth Circuit	http://www.ca8.uscourts.gov
Ninth Circuit	http://www.ca9.uscourts.gov
Tenth Circuit	http://www.ca10.uscourts.gov
Eleventh Circuit	http://www.ca11.uscourts.gov

United States Court of Appeals for the Federal Circuit

This court was established under Article III of the Constitution pursuant to the Federal Courts Improvement Act of 1982 (28 U.S.C. 41, 44, 48), as successor to the former United States Court of Customs and Patent Appeals and the United States Court of Claims. The jurisdiction of the court is nationwide (as provided by 28 U.S.C. 1295) and includes appeals from the district courts in patent cases; appeals from the district courts in contract, and certain other civil actions in which the United States is a defendant; and appeals from final decisions of the U.S. Court of International Trade, the U.S. Court of Federal Claims, and the U.S. Court of Appeals for Veterans Claims. The jurisdiction of the court also includes the review of administrative rulings by the Patent and Trademark Office, U.S. International Trade Commission, Secretary of Commerce, agency boards of contract appeals, and the Merit Systems Protection Board, as well as rulemaking of the Department of Veterans Affairs; review of decisions of the U.S. Senate Committee on Ethics concerning discrimination claims of Senate employees; and review of a final order of an entity to be designated by the President concerning discrimination claims of Presidential appointees.

The court consists of 12 circuit judges. It sits in panels of three or more on each case and may also hear or rehear a case en banc. The court sits principally in Washington, DC, and may hold court wherever any court of appeals sits (28 U.S.C. 48). Internet, http://www.cafc.uscourts.gov

---

United States District Courts

The Nation's district courts are the trial courts of general Federal jurisdiction. These courts resolve disputes by determining the facts and applying legal principles to decide which party is right. Each State has at least one district court, and large States have as many as four. There are 89 district courts in the 50 States, plus one in the District of Columbia and another in the Commonwealth of Puerto Rico. Three other U.S. Territories also have courts that hear Federal cases: Guam and the Northern Mariana and Virgin Islands.

At present, each district court has from 2 to 28 Federal district judgeships, depending upon the amount of judicial work within its territory. Only one judge is usually required to hear and decide a case in a district court, but in some limited cases it is required that three judges be called together to comprise the court (28 U.S.C. 2284). The judge senior in commission who is under 70 years of age (65 at inception of term), has been in office for at least 1 year, and has not previously been chief judge, serves as chief judge for a 7-year term. There are 645 permanent district judgeships in the 50 States and 15 in the District of Columbia. There are seven district judgeships in Puerto Rico. District judges hold their offices during good behavior as provided by Article III, section 1, of the Constitution. However, Congress may temporary judgeships for a court with the provision that when a future vacancy occurs in that district, such vacancy shall not be filled. Each district court has one or more United States magistrate judges and bankruptcy judges, a clerk, a United States attorney, a United States marshal, probation officers, court reporters, and their staffs. The jurisdiction of the district courts is set forth in title 28, chapter 85, of the United States Code and at 18 U.S.C. 3231.

Cases from the district courts are reviewable on appeal by the applicable court of appeals. Internet, http://www.uscourts.gov/about-federal-courts/court-role-and-structure

Territorial Courts

Pursuant to its authority to govern the Territories (Art. IV, sec. 3, clause 2, of the Constitution), Congress has established district courts in the territories of Guam and the Virgin Islands. The District Court of the Canal Zone was abolished on April 1, 1982, pursuant to the Panama Canal Act of 1979 (22 U.S.C. 3601 note). Congress has also established a district court in the Northern Mariana Islands, which is administered by the United States under a trusteeship agreement with the United Nations. These Territorial courts have jurisdiction not only over the subjects described in the judicial article of the Constitution, but also over many local matters that, within the States, are decided in State courts. The District Court of Puerto Rico, by contrast, is established under Article III, is classified like other "district courts," and is called a "court of the United States" (28 U.S.C. 451). There is one judge each in Guam and the Northern Mariana Islands, and two in the Virgin Islands. The judges in these courts are appointed for terms of 10 years. Internet, http://www.uscourts.gov/about-federal-courts/court-role-and-structure

For further information concerning the lower courts, contact the Administrative Office of the United States Courts, Thurgood Marshall Federal Judiciary Building, One Columbus Circle NE., Washington, DC 20544. Phone, 202-502-2600.

United States Court of International Trade

This court was originally established as the Board of United States General Appraisers by act of June 10, 1890, which conferred upon it jurisdiction theretofore held by the district and circuit courts in actions arising under the tariff acts (19 U.S.C. ch. 4). The act of May 28, 1926 (19 U.S.C. 405a), created the United States Customs Court to supersede the Board; by acts of August 7, 1939, and June 25, 1948 (28 U.S.C. 1582, 1583), the court was integrated into the United States court structure, organization, and procedure. The act of July 14, 1956 (28 U.S.C. 251), established the court as a court of record of the United States under Article III of the Constitution. The Customs Court Act of 1980 (28 U.S.C. 251) constituted the court as the United States Court of International Trade.

The Court of International Trade has jurisdiction over any civil action against the United States arising from Federal laws governing import transactions. This includes classification and valuation cases, as well as authority to review certain agency determinations under the Trade Agreements Act of 1979 (19 U.S.C. 2501) involving antidumping and countervailing duty matters. In addition, it has exclusive jurisdiction of civil actions to review determinations as to the eligibility of workers, firms, and communities for adjustment assistance under the Trade Act of 1974 (19 U.S.C. 2101). Civil actions commenced by the United States to recover customs duties, to recover on a customs bond, or for certain civil penalties alleging fraud or negligence are also within the exclusive jurisdiction of the court.

The court is composed of a chief judge and eight judges, not more than five of whom may belong to any one political party. Any of its judges may be temporarily designated and assigned by the Chief Justice of the United States to sit as a court of appeals or district court judge in any circuit or district. The court has a clerk and deputy clerks, a librarian, court reporters, and other supporting personnel. Cases before the court may be tried before a jury. Under the Federal Courts Improvement Act of 1982 (28 U.S.C. 1295), appeals are taken to the U.S. Court of Appeals for the Federal Circuit, and ultimately review may be sought in appropriate cases in the Supreme Court of the United States.

The principal offices are located in New York, NY, but the court is empowered to hear and determine cases arising at any port or place within the jurisdiction of the United States. Internet, http://www.cit.uscourts.gov

For further information, contact the Clerk, United States Court of International Trade, One Federal Plaza, New York, NY 10278-0001. Phone, 212-264-2814.

Judicial Panel on Multidistrict Litigation

The Panel, created by act of April 29, 1968 (28 U.S.C. 1407), and consisting of seven Federal judges designated by the Chief Justice from the courts of appeals and district courts, is authorized to temporarily transfer to a single district, for coordinated or consolidated pretrial proceedings, civil actions pending in different districts that involve one or more common questions of fact. Internet, http://www.jpml.uscourts.gov

For further information, contact the Clerk, Judicial Panel on Multidistrict Litigation, Room G–255, Thurgood Marshall Federal Judiciary Building, One Columbus Circle NE., Washington, DC 20002-8041. Phone, 202-502-2800.

SPECIAL COURTS
United States Court of Appeals for the Armed Forces

450 E Street NW., Washington, DC 20442-0001

Phone, 202-761-1448. Fax, 202-761-4672. http://www.armfor.uscourts.gov

This court was established under Article I of the Constitution of the United States pursuant to act of May 5, 1950, as amended (10 U.S.C. 867). Subject only to certiorari review by the Supreme Court of the United States in a limited number of cases, the court serves as the final appellate tribunal to review court-martial convictions of all the Armed Forces. It is exclusively an appellate criminal court, consisting of five civilian judges who are appointed for 15-year terms by the President with the advice and consent of the Senate.

The court is called upon to exercise jurisdiction to review the record in all cases extending to death; certified to the court by a Judge Advocate General of one of the Armed Forces; or petitioned by accused who have received a sentence of confinement for 1 year or more and/or a punitive discharge.

The court also exercises authority under the All Writs Act (28 U.S.C. 1651(a)).

In addition, the judges of the court are required by law to work jointly with the senior uniformed lawyer from each of the Armed Forces and two members of the public appointed by the Secretary of Defense to make an annual comprehensive survey, to report annually to the Congress on the operation and progress of the military justice system under the Uniform Code of Military Justice, and to recommend improvements wherever necessary.

Sources of Information

Career Opportunities   Job openings and available clerkships are posted online. Internet, http://www.armfor.uscourts.gov/ newcaaf/employment.htm. http://www. armfor.uscourts.gov/newcaaf/contact.htm

For further information, contact the Clerk, United States Court of Appeals for the Armed Forces, 450 E Street NW., Washington, DC 20442-0001. Phone, 202-761-1448. Fax, 202-761-4672.

United States Court of Appeals for Veterans Claims

Suite 900, 625 Indiana Avenue NW., Washington, DC 20004-2950
Phone, 202-501-5970. Fax 202-501-5848. Internet, http://www.uscourts.cavc.gov

The United States Court of Appeals for Veterans Claims, a court of record under Article I of the Constitution, was established on November 18, 1988 (38 U.S.C. 7251) and given exclusive jurisdiction to review decisions of the Board of Veterans' Appeals. Appeals concern veteran disability benefits, dependent educational assistance, survivor benefits, and pension benefits claims. In addition to its review authority, the Court has contempt authority, as well as the authority to compel action by the Secretary of Veterans Affairs, the authority to grant a petition for extraordinary relief under the All Writs Act (28 U.S.C. 1651), and the authority to make attorney fee determinations under the Equal Access to Justice Act (28 U.S.C. 2412). Decisions of the Court of Appeals for Veterans Claims are subject to review by the United States Court of Appeals for the Federal Circuit on questions of law and on writ of certiorari by the United States Supreme Court.

The Court consists of nine judges whom the President appoints with the advice and consent of the Senate for 15-year terms. One of the judges serves as chief judge.

The Chief Judge generally conducts a judicial conference every 2 years. The primary purpose of the conference, which involves the active participation of members of the legal community, attorneys, and practitioners admitted to practice before the Court, is to consider the business of the Court and to recommend means of improving the administration of justice within the Court's jurisdiction.

The Court is located in Washington, DC, but it is a court of national jurisdiction and may sit at any location within the United States.

Opinions issued by the Court, case information, and a current list of judges and officials of the United States Court of Appeals for Veterans Claims are available online.

Sources of Information

Employment Job opportunities are posted online. Internet, http://www.uscourts.cavc. gov/employment.php. http://www.uscourts. cavc.gov/contact.php

For further information, contact the Clerk, United States Court of Appeals for Veterans Claims, Suite 900, 625 Indiana Avenue NW., Washington, DC 20004-2950. Phone, 202-501-5970. Fax, 202-501-5848

United States Court of Federal Claims

717 Madison Place NW., Washington, DC 20439

Phone, 202-357-6400. Internet, http://www.uscfc.uscourts.gov

The United States Court of Federal Claims has jurisdiction over claims seeking money judgments against the United States. A claim must be founded upon the Constitution, an act of Congress, an Executive order, a contract with the United States, or Federal regulations. Judges are appointed by the President for 15-year terms, subject to Senate confirmation. Appeals are to the U.S. Court of Appeals for the Federal Circuit.

Sources of Information

Career Opportunities Information on job opportunities and internships is available online. Internet, http://www.uscfc.uscourts. gov/job-opportunitiesemployment. http:// www.uscfc.uscourts.gov/court-directory

For further information, contact the Clerk's Office, United States Court of Federal Claims, 717 Madison Place NW., Washington, DC 20439. Phone, 202-357-6400.

United States Tax Court

400 Second Street NW., Washington, DC 20217-0002
Phone, 202-521-0700. Internet, http://www.ustaxcourt.gov

The United States Tax Court is a court of record under Article I of the Constitution of the United States (26 U.S.C. 7441). The court was created as the United States Board of Tax Appeals by the Revenue Act of 1924 (43 Stat. 336). The name was changed to the Tax Court of the United States by the Revenue Act of 1942 (56 Stat. 957). The Tax Reform Act of 1969 (83 Stat. 730) established the court under Article I and then changed its name to the United States Tax Court.

The court comprises 19 judges who are appointed by the President to 15-year terms and subject to Senate confirmation. The court also has varying numbers of both senior judges (who may be recalled by the chief judge to perform further judicial duties) and special trial judges (who are appointed by the chief judge and may hear and decide a variety of cases). The court's jurisdiction is set forth in various sections of title 26 of the U.S. Code.

The offices of the court and its judges are in Washington, DC. However, the court has national jurisdiction and schedules trial sessions in more than 70 cities in the United States. Each trial session is conducted by one judge, senior judge, or special trial judge. Court proceedings are open to the public and are conducted in accordance with the court's rules of practice and procedure and the rules of evidence applicable in trials without a jury in the U.S. District Court for the District of Columbia. A fee of $60 is charged for the filing of a petition. Practice before the court is limited to practitioners admitted under the court's rules of practice and procedure.

Decisions entered by the court, other than decisions in small tax cases, may be appealed to the regional courts of appeals and, thereafter, upon the granting of a writ of certiorari, to the Supreme Court of the United States. At the option of petitioners, simplified procedures may be used in small tax cases. Small tax cases are final and not subject to review by any court. Internet, http://www.ustaxcourt.gov/about.htm

Sources of Information

Career Opportunities   Vacancy announcements and information on the court's law clerk program are available online. Internet, http://www.ustaxcourt.gov/employment.htm
Forms   Applications, certificates, notices, and other forms can be completed online and then printed. Internet, http://www.ustaxcourt.gov/forms.htm
Taxpayer Information   An online guide provides information—not legal advice—that may be helpful for those representing themselves before the Tax Court. It answers frequent questions that taxpayers ask and explains the process of filing a petition to begin a Tax Court case and things that occur before, during, and after trial. It also features a glossary. Internet, http://www.ustaxcourt.gov/taxpayer_info_intro.htm | Email: info@ustaxcourt.gov. Internet, http://www.ustaxcourt.gov/phone.htm

For further information, contact the Office of the Clerk of the Court, United States Tax Court, 400 Second Street NW., Washington, DC 20217-0002. Phone, 202-521-0700.

Administrative Office of the United States Courts

One Columbus Circle NE., Washington, DC 20544
Phone, 202-502-2600. Internet, http://www.uscourts.gov

Director	JAMES C. DUFF
Deputy Director	LEE ANN BENNETT

Associate Directors

Department of Administrative Services	JAMES R. BAUGHER

Department of Program Services	LAURA C. MINOR
Department of Technology Services	JOSEPH R. PETERS, JR.
General Counsel	SHERYL L. WALTER
Judicial Conference Secretariat Officer	KATHERINE H. SIMON
Legislative Affairs Officer	CORDIA A. STROM
Public Affairs Officer	DAVID A. SELLERS

The Administrative Office of the United States Courts supports and serves the nonjudicial, administrative business of the United States Courts.

The Administrative Office of the United States Courts was created by act of August 7, 1939 (28 U.S.C. 601). It was established on November 6, 1939. The Chief Justice of the United States, after consultation with the Judicial Conference, appoints the Director and Deputy Director of the Administrative Office.

Administering the Courts   The Director is the administrative officer of the courts of the United States—except of the Supreme Court. Under the guidance of the Judicial Conference of the United States, the Director supervises all administrative matters relating to the offices of clerks and other clerical and administrative personnel of the courts; examines the state of the dockets of the courts, secures information as to the courts' need of assistance, and prepares statistical data and reports each quarter and transmits them to the chief judges of the circuits; submits an activities report of the Administrative Office and the courts' state of business to the annual meeting of the Judicial Conference of the United States; fixes the compensation of court employees whose compensation is not otherwise fixed by law; regulates and pays annuities to widows and surviving dependent children of judges; disburses moneys appropriated for the maintenance and operation of the courts; examines accounts of court officers; regulates travel of judicial personnel; provides accommodations and supplies for the courts and their clerical and administrative personnel; establishes and maintains programs for the certification and utilization of court interpreters and the provision of special interpretation services in the courts; and performs such other duties as may be assigned by the Supreme Court or the Judicial Conference of the United States.

The Director also prepares and submits the budget of the courts, which the Office of Management and Budget transmits to Congress without change. Internet, http://www.uscourts.gov/about-federal-courts/judicial-administration

Probation Officers   The Administrative Office exercises general supervision of the accounts and practices of the Federal probation offices, which are subject to primary control by the respective district courts that they serve. The Administrative Office publishes, in cooperation with the Department of Justice's Bureau of Prisons, the "Federal Probation Journal." This online, quarterly publication presents current thought, research, and practice in corrections, community supervision, and criminal justice.

In accordance with the Pretrial Services Act of 1982 (18 U.S.C. 3152), the Director establishes pretrial services in the district courts. The offices of these district courts report information on pretrial release of persons charged with Federal offenses and supervise such persons who are released to their custody. Internet, http://www.uscourts.gov/services-forms/probation-and-pretrial-services

Bankruptcy   According to the Bankruptcy Amendments and Federal Judgeship Act of 1984 (28 U.S.C. 151), the bankruptcy judges for each judicial district constitute a unit of the district court known as the bankruptcy court. The courts of appeals appoint bankruptcy judges in such numbers as authorized by Congress. These judges serve for a term of 14 years as judicial officers of the district courts.

This act placed jurisdiction in the district courts over all cases under title 11, United States Code, and all proceedings arising in or related to cases under that title (28 U.S.C.

1334). The district court may refer such cases and proceedings to its bankruptcy judges (as authorized by 28 U.S.C. 157).

The Director of the Administrative Office recommends to the Judicial Conference the duty stations of bankruptcy judges and the places they hold court, surveys the need for additional bankruptcy judgeships to be recommended to Congress, and determines the staff needs of bankruptcy judges and the clerks of the bankruptcy courts. Internet, http://www.uscourts.gov/services-forms/bankruptcy

Federal Magistrate Judges   The Director of the Administrative Office exercises general supervision over administrative matters in offices of U.S. magistrate judges, compiles and evaluates statistical data relating to such offices, and submits reports thereon to the Judicial Conference. The Director reports annually to Congress on the business that has come before U.S. magistrate judges and also prepares legal and administrative manuals for the magistrate judges. In compliance with the act, the Administrative Office conducts surveys of the conditions in the judicial districts to make recommendations as to the number, location, and salaries of magistrate judges. The Judicial Conference then determines their number, location, and salaries, subject to the availability of appropriated funds.

Federal Defenders   The Criminal Justice Act (18 U.S.C. 3006A) establishes the procedure for the appointment of private panel attorneys in Federal criminal cases for individuals who are unable to afford adequate representation, under plans adopted by each district court. The act also permits the establishment of Federal public defender or Federal community defender organizations by the district courts in districts where at least 200 persons annually require the appointment of counsel. Two adjacent districts may be combined to reach this total.

Each defender organization submits to the Director of the Administrative Office an annual report of its activities along with a proposed budget or, in the case of community defender organizations, a proposed grant for the coming year. The Director is responsible for the submission of the proposed budgets and grants to the Judicial Conference for approval. The Director also makes payments to the defender organizations out of appropriations in accordance with the approved budgets and grants, as well as compensating private counsel appointed to defend criminal cases in the United States courts. Internet, http://www.uscourts.gov/services-forms/defender-services

Sources of Information

Budget, Accounting, and Procurement   Phone, 202-502-2000. Internet, http://www.uscourts.gov/services-forms/business-opportunities
Court Services   Phone, 202-502-1500.
Defender Services   Phone, 202-502-3030. Internet, http://www.uscourts.gov/services-forms/defender-services
Educational Resources   Learning resources for students are available online. Internet, http://www.uscourts.gov/about-federal-courts/educational-resources
Electronic Filing   Attorneys and others may submit files online using the Federal courts' Case Management and Electronic Case Files system. Internet, http://www.uscourts.gov/courtrecords/electronic-filing-cmecf
Frequently Asked Questions (FAQs)   Answers to FAQs on the Federal Judiciary are available online. Internet, http://www.uscourts.gov/frequently-asked-questions-faqs
General Counsel   Phone, 202-502-1100.
Glossary   A glossary of legal terms is available online. Internet, http://www.uscourts.gov/glossary
Human Resources   Phone, 202-502-3100.
Judicial Conference Executive Secretariat   Phone, 202-502-2400. Internet, http://www.uscourts.gov/about-federal-courts/governance-judicial-conference/about-judicial-conference
Judicial Services   Phone, 202-502-1800.
Judiciary Reporting and Analysis   Phone, 202-502-1440.
Legislative Affairs   Phone, 202-502-1700.
Probation and Pretrial Services   Phone, 202-502-1600. Internet, http://www.uscourts.gov/services-forms/probation-and-pretrial-services
Public Affairs   Phone, 202-502-2600.

Publications The Federal judiciary and Administrative Office produce publications for the Congress, the public, and others to educate and inform about the work of the courts. Internet, http://www.uscourts.gov/statistics-reports/publications

Statistical Data Statistical data on the business of the Federal Judiciary are available online. Internet, http://www.uscourts.gov/statistics-reports/caseload-statistics-data-tables. http://www.uscourts.gov/contact-us

For further information, contact the Administrative Office of the United States Courts, Thurgood Marshall Federal Judiciary Building, One Columbus Circle NE., Washington, DC 20544. Phone, 202-502-2600.

Federal Judicial Center

Thurgood Marshall Federal Judiciary Building, One Columbus Circle NE., Washington, DC 20002-8003 Phone, 202-502-4000. Internet, http://www.fjc.gov

Director	JEREMY D. FOGEL
Deputy Director	JOHN S. COOKE
Director, Editorial and Information Services Office	JOHN S. COOKE
Director, Education Division	DANA K. CHIPMAN
Director, Federal Judicial History Office	CLARA ALTMAN
Director, Information Technology Office	ESTHER DEVRIES
Director, International Judicial Relations Office	MIRA GUR-ARIE
Director, Office of Administration	NANCY PAYNE
Director, Research Division	JAMES B. EAGLIN

The Federal Judicial Center is the judicial branch's agency for policy research and continuing education.

The Federal Judicial Center was created by act of December 20, 1967 (28 U.S.C. 620), to further the development and adoption of improved judicial administration in the courts of the United States.

The Center's basic policies and activities are determined by its Board, which is composed of the Chief Justice of the United States, who is permanent Chair of the Board by statute, and two judges of the U.S. courts of appeals, three judges of the U.S. district courts, one bankruptcy judge, and one magistrate judge, all of whom are elected for 4-year terms by the Judicial Conference of the United States. The Director of the Administrative Office of the United States Courts is also a permanent member of the Board.

The organization of the Center reflects its primary statutory mandates. The Education Division plans education and produces training—including curriculum packages for in-district training, in-person programs, publications, video programs, and web-based programs and resources—for judges and court staff. The Research Division examines and evaluates current

and alternative Federal court practices and policies. Its research assists Judicial Conference committees in developing policy recommendations. The research also contributes substantially to the Center's educational programs. The Federal Judicial History Office helps courts and others study and preserve Federal judicial history. The International Judicial Relations Office provides information to judicial and legal officials from foreign countries and informs Federal judicial personnel of developments in international law and other court systems that may affect their work. Two units of the Director's Office—the Information Technology Office and the Editorial and Information Services Office—support the agency's mission through editorial and design assistance, organization and dissemination of Center resources, and technology.

Sources of Information

Annual Reports Annual Reports, from 1969 to the present, are available to download as Portable Document Format (PDF) files. Internet, https://www.fjc.gov/content/annual-reports

Educational Materials   Materials that the Center produces as part of its educational programs for judges and court employees are accessible online. Internet, https://www.fjc.gov/education

Career Opportunities   The Center posts job openings online. Contact the Human Resources Office for more information. Phone, 202-502-4165. Internet, https://www.fjc.gov/about/job-vacancies

History   Questions about the history of the Federal judiciary? Submit them to the experts at the Federal Judicial History Office. Phone, 202-502-4180. Fax, 202-502-4077. Internet, https://www.fjc.gov/history | Email: history@fjc.gov

Nearly 600 images of historic Federal courthouses and other buildings that have served as the meeting places of Federal courts are available online. Internet, https://www.fjc.gov/history/courthouses

Publications   Single copies of most Federal Judicial Center publications that are printed in hard copy are available free of charge. Phone, 202-502-4153. Fax, 202-502-4077. Internet, https://www.fjc.gov/publications

Site Map   The Web site map allows visitors to look for specific topics or to browse content that aligns with their interests. Internet, https://www.fjc.gov/sitemap

Teaching Resources   Teaching and civic outreach resources are available online. Internet, https://www.fjc.gov/education/civic-education-about-courts

Visiting Foreign Judicial Fellows   Foreign judges, court officials, and scholars may apply for the opportunity to conduct research at the Center on topics concerning the administration of justice in the United States. Internet, https://www.fjc.gov/content/visiting-foreign-judicial-fellows-program. http://www.fjc.gov/public/home.nsf

For further information, contact the Federal Judicial Center, Thurgood Marshall Federal Judiciary Building, One Columbus Circle NE., Washington, DC 20002-8003. Phone, 202-502-4000.

United States Sentencing Commission

Suite 2-500, One Columbus Circle NE., Washington, DC 20002-8002
Phone, 202-502-4500. Internet, http://www.ussc.gov

Chair	WILLIAM H. PRYOR, JR., ACTING
Vice Chair	(VACANCY)
Vice Chair	(VACANCY)
Vice Chair	(VACANCY)
Commissioner	CHARLES R. BREYER
Commissioner	RACHEL E. BARKOW
Commissioner	DANNY C. REEVES
Commissioner	WIILIAM H. PRYOR, JR.
Commissioner (ex officio)	JONATHAN WROBLEWSKI
Commissioner (ex officio)	J. PATRICIA WILSON SMOOT
Staff Director	KENNETH P. COHEN
Director, Office of Administration and Planning	SUSAN M. BRAZEL
Director, Office of Education and Sentencing Practice	RAQUEL WILSON
Director, Office of Legislative and Public Affairs	CHRISTINE M. LEONARD
Director, Office of Research and Data	GLENN R. SCHMITT
General Counsel	KATHLEEN C. GRILLI

The United States Sentencing Commission develops sentencing guidelines and policies for the Federal court system.

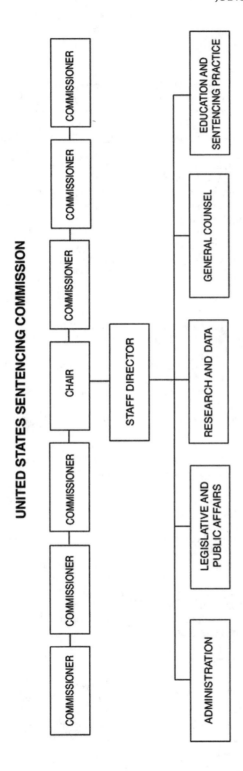

UNITED STATES SENTENCING COMMISSION

The United States Sentencing Commission was established as an independent agency in the judicial branch of the Federal Government by the Sentencing Reform Act of 1984 (28 U.S.C. 991 et seq. and 18 U.S.C. 3551 et seq.). The Commission establishes sentencing guidelines and policies for the Federal courts, advising them of the appropriate form and severity of punishment for offenders convicted of Federal crimes.

The Commission comprises seven voting members and two nonvoting members. The President appoints the voting members with the advice and consent of the Senate for 6-year terms. The President also appoints one of the voting members as the Chair and designates three others as Vice Chairs.

The Commission evaluates the effects of the sentencing guidelines on the criminal justice system, advises Congress on the modification or enactment of statutes pertaining to criminal law and sentencing matters, establishes a research and development program on sentencing issues, and performs other related duties.

In executing its duties, the Commission promulgates and distributes to Federal courts and to the U.S. probation system guidelines for determining sentences to be imposed in criminal cases, general policy statements regarding the application of guidelines, and policy statements on the appropriate use of probation and supervised release revocation provisions. These sentencing guidelines and policy statements are intended to support the principles of just punishment, deterrence, incapacitation, and rehabilitation; provide fairness in meeting the purposes of sentencing; avoid unwarranted disparity; and reflect advancement in the knowledge of human behavior as it relates to the criminal justice process.

The Commission also provides training, conducts research on sentencing-related issues, and serves as an information resource for Congress, criminal justice practitioners, and the public. Internet, http://www.ussc.gov/about

Sources of Information

Education   The Commission offers courses that fulfill continuing legal education requirements in several jurisdictions. Internet, http://www.ussc.gov/education/training-resources/continuing-legal-education

Career Opportunities   The Commission posts job announcements on its Web site. Internet, http://www.ussc.gov/employment

Guidelines Manual   The current "USSC Guidelines Manual" is available in Portable Document Format on the Commission's Web site. An electronic archive of the yearly manual starts with the year 1987. Internet, http://www.ussc.gov/guidelines/2015-guidelines-manual/archive

Helpline   Attorneys, judges, and probation officers who have questions may call the Commission's helpline for assistance. The helpline also handles data requests. Its hours of operations are 8:30 a.m.–5 p.m., eastern standard time, Monday–Friday, excluding Federal holidays. Phone, 202-502-4545.

News   Press releases are available on the Commission's Web site. Internet, http://www.ussc.gov/about/news/press-releases

The Commission also posts amicus curiae briefs, reports, speeches, statements, and testimonies online. Internet, http://www.ussc.gov/about/news/testimony-speeches/speeches-and-submissions

Publications   A topical index of publications is available online. Internet, http://www.ussc.gov/research/topical-index-publications

Reports   The Commission posts reports to the Congress on its Web site. Internet, http://www.ussc.gov/research/reports-congress

Annual overviews of Federal criminal cases are available online. Internet, http://www.ussc.gov/topic/year-review

The Office of Research and Data publishes periodic reports on Federal sentencing practices. The reports include information on the types of crimes committed, offenders who commit those crimes, the punishments imposed, and the manner in which the sentencing guidelines were applied. Internet, http://www.ussc.gov/topic/data-reports

Site Map   The Web site map allows visitors to look for specific topics or to browse content that aligns with their interests. Internet, http://www.ussc.gov/sitemap

Updates An online subscription form is available to sign up for regular email updates from the USSC. Internet, http://www.ussc. gov/sign-regular-updates. http://www.ussc. gov | Email: pubaffairs@ussc.gov

For further information, contact the Office of Legislative and Public Affairs, U.S. Sentencing Commission, Suite 2–500, One Columbus Circle NE., Washington, DC 20002-8002. Phone, 202-502-4500.

Executive Branch

EXECUTIVE BRANCH: THE PRESIDENT

THE PRESIDENT

The President of the United States	DONALD J. TRUMP

Article II, section 1, of the Constitution provides that "[t]he executive Power shall be vested in a President of the United States of America. He shall hold his Office during the Term of four Years, . . . together with the Vice President, chosen for the same Term . . . ." In addition to the powers set forth in the Constitution, the statutes have conferred upon the President specific authority and responsibility covering a wide range of matters (United States Code Index).

The President is the administrative head of the executive branch of the Government, which includes numerous agencies, both temporary and permanent, as well as the 15 executive departments.

The Cabinet   The Cabinet, a creation of custom and tradition dating back to George Washington's administration, functions at the pleasure of the President. Its purpose is to advise the President upon any subject, relating to the duties of the respective offices, on which he requests information (pursuant to Article II, section 2, of the Constitution).

The Cabinet is composed of the Vice President and the heads of the 15 executive departments--the Secretaries of Agriculture, Commerce, Defense, Education, Energy, Health and Human Services, Homeland Security, Housing and Urban Development, Interior, Labor, State, Transportation, Treasury, and Veterans Affairs, and the Attorney General. Additionally, in the Obama administration, Cabinet-level rank has been accorded to the Chief of Staff to the President; the Administrator, Environmental Protection Agency; the Chair, Council of Economic Advisers; the Director, Office of Management and Budget; the U.S. Permanent Representative to the United Nations; and the U.S. Trade Representative.

THE VICE PRESIDENT

The Vice President	MICHAEL R. PENCE

Article II, section 1, of the Constitution provides that the President "shall hold his Office during the Term of four Years, . . . together with the Vice President . . . ." In addition to his role as President of the Senate, the Vice President is empowered to succeed to the Presidency, pursuant to Article II and the 20th and 25th amendments to the Constitution.

The executive functions of the Vice President include participation in Cabinet meetings and, by statute, membership on the National Security Council and the Board of Regents of the Smithsonian Institution.

THE EXECUTIVE OFFICE OF THE PRESIDENT

Under authority of the Reorganization Act of 1939 (5 U.S.C. 133-133r, 133t note), various agencies were transferred to the Executive Office of the President by the President's Reorganization Plans I and II of 1939 (5 U.S.C. app.), effective July 1, 1939. Executive Order 8248 of September 8, 1939, established the divisions of the Executive Office and defined their functions. Subsequently, Presidents have used Executive orders, reorganization plans, and legislative initiatives to reorganize the Executive Office to make its composition compatible with the goals of their administrations.

White House Office

1600 Pennsylvania Avenue NW., Washington, DC 20500
Phone, 202-456-1414. Internet, http://www.whitehouse.gov.

Assistants to the President

Chief of Staff	Gen. John F. Kelly, USMC (retired)
Chief of Staff to the First Lady	Lindsay Reynolds
Counsel to the President	Donald F. McGahn II
Deputy Chief of Staff for Implementation	Rick Dearborn
Deputy Chief of Staff for Operations	Joe Hagin
Deputy National Security Adviser	Maj. Gen. Ricky Waddell, USA (retired)
Director of the White House Military Office	(vacancy)
Director of Communications	Hope C. Hicks
Director of Presidential Personnel	John DeStefano
Director of Scheduling and Advance	(vacancy)
National Security Adviser	Lt. General H.R. McMasters, USA
Press Secretary	Sarah H. Sanders
Assistant to the President for Homeland Security and Counterterrorism	Thomas Bossert
Counselor to the President	Kellyanne Conway

Senior Advisors

Assistant to the President for Climate, Conservation and Energy Policy	Brian C. Deese
Assistant to the President for Intergovernmental Affairs and Public Engagement	Valerie B. Jarrett
Assistant to the President for Strategy and Communications	Shailagh Murray

The above list of key personnel was updated 10–2017.

The White House Office serves the President in the performance of the many detailed activities incident to his immediate office.

The President's staff facilitates and maintains communication with the Congress, the heads of executive agencies, the press and other information media, and the general public. The various Assistants to the President aid the President in such matters as he may direct.

Office of the Vice President

Eisenhower Executive Office Building, Washington, DC 20501
Phone, 202-456-7549. Internet, http://https://www.whitehouse.gov/administration/vice-president-biden.

Chief of Staff to the Vice President	NICK AYERS
Chief of Staff to Karen Pence	KRISTAN KING NEVINS
Special Assistant to the Vice President	ZACH BAUER
Counsel / Assistant to the Vice President	MARK PAOLETTA
Deputy Chief of Staff to Karen Pence / Special Assistant to the President	ANTHONY BERNAL

Directors

Administration / Deputy Assistant to the Vice President	MIKE BOISVENUE
Advance / Deputy Assistant to the Vice President	ROBERT PEEDE
Communications	JARED AGEN
Public Engagement and Intergovernmental Affairs / Special Assistant to the President	ANDELIZ CASTILLO
Legislative Affairs / Assistant to the Vice President	JONATHAN HILAR
Scheduling / Deputy Assistant to the Vice President	MEGAN PATENAUDE
Speechwriting / Special Assistant to the President	STEPHEN FORD
National Security Advisor	ANDREA THOMPSON

The Office of the Vice President serves the Vice President in the performance of the many activities incident to his immediate office.

Council of Economic Advisers

Seventeenth and Pennsylvania Avenue NW., Washington, DC 20502
Phone, 202-456-4779. Internet, http://www.whitehouse.gov/cea.

Chair	KEVIN A. HASSETT
Members	TOMAS J. PHILIPSON
Members	RICHARD V. BURKHAUSER

The Council of Economic Advisers analyzes and appraises the national economy to make policy recommendations to the President.

The Council of Economic Advisers (CEA) was established in the Executive Office of the President by the Employment Act of 1946 (15 U.S.C. 1023). It now functions under that statute and Reorganization Plan No. 9 of 1953 (5 U.S.C. app.), effective August 1, 1953.

The Chair and the two members govern the Council. The President appoints the Chair, whom the Senate must confirm, and the two members.

The Council analyzes the national economy and its various segments; advises the President on economic developments; appraises the economic programs and policies of the Federal Government; recommends policies for economic growth and stability to the President; assists in the preparation of the President's economic reports to the Congress; and prepares the Annual Report of the Council of Economic Advisers.

Sources of Information

Career Opportunities   To learn about career opportunities, visit the "Jobs and Internships" Web page. https://www.whitehouse.gov/administration/eop/cea/jobs

History   Photographs and brief professional bios of former Council Chairs, beginning with Edwin G. Nourse, who served as the Chair from 1946 to 1949, are available online. https://www.whitehouse.gov/administration/eop/cea/about/former-chairs

Brief professional bios of former Council members, beginning with John D. Clark, who served as a member from 1946 to 1950 and then as the Vice Chair, are available online. https://www.whitehouse.gov/administration/eop/cea/about/Former-Members

Publications   Reports and briefs are available in Portable Document Format (PDF) on the Council's Web site. https://www.whitehouse.gov/administration/eop/cea/factsheets-reports

A monthly publication prepared by the Council for the Joint Economic Committee, "Economic Indicators" provides Congress and the public with information on business activity; credit, money, and prices; Federal finance; gross domestic product;

employment, income, and production; international statistics; and security markets. https://www.whitehouse.gov/administration/eop/cea/economic-indicators

A yearly report written by the Council's Chair, the "Economic Report of the President" presents the administration's domestic and international economic policies. The report surveys the Nation's economic progress with text and data appendices. The full report and individual chapters are accessible in Portable Document Format (PDF) for download on the Council's Web site. Statistical tables are also available for download in Portable Document and Excel formats. https://www.whitehouse.gov/administration/eop/cea/economic-report-of-the-President

Speeches / Testimony   The Council posts Op-Ed pieces, prepared testimonies for congressional hearings, and speeches on its Web site. https://www.whitehouse.gov/administration/eop/cea/speeches-testimony. http://www.whitehouse.gov/cea

For further information, contact the Council of Economic Advisers, Seventeenth and Pennsylvania Avenue NW., Washington, DC 20502. Phone, 202-456-4779.

Council on Environmental Quality

722 Jackson Place NW., Washington, DC 20503
Phone, 202-395-5750 or 202-456-6224. Fax, 202-456-2710. Internet, http://www.whitehouse.gov/administration/eop/ceq.

Chair	(VACANCY)
Chief of Staff	CHRISTOPHER ADAMO

Associate Directors

Climate Preparedness	JAINEY BAVISHI
Communications	NOREEN NIELSON
Conservation and Wildlife	TIMOTHY MALE
Energy and Climate Change	RICHARD DUKE
Lands and Water Ecosystems	MICHAEL DEGNAN
Legislative Affairs	STEPHENNE HARDING
NEPA Oversight	EDWARD BOLING
Ocean and Coastal Policy	WHITLEY SAUMWEBER

Deputy Associate Director, Public Engagement and Communications	MARK ANTONIEWICZ
General Counsel	BRENDA MALLORY
Managing Director	CHRISTINA GOLDFUSS

The Council on Environmental Quality formulates and recommends national policies and initiatives for improving the environment.

The Council on Environmental Quality (CEQ) was established within the Executive Office of the President by the National Environmental Policy Act of 1969 (NEPA) (42 U.S.C. 4321 et seq.). The Environmental Quality Improvement Act of 1970 (42 U.S.C. 4371 et seq.) established the Office of Environmental Quality (OEQ) to provide professional and administrative support for the Council. The CEQ and OEQ are referred to, collectively, as the Council on Environmental Quality. The CEQ Chair, whom the President appoints and the Senate confirms, serves as Director of the OEQ.

The Council develops policies that bring together the Nation's economic, social, and environmental priorities to improve Federal decisionmaking. As required by NEPA, the CEQ also evaluates, coordinates, and mediates Federal activities. It advises and assists the President on both national and international environmental policy matters. It oversees Federal agency and departmental implementation of NEPA. https://www.whitehouse.gov/administration/eop/ceq/initiatives

Sources of Information

Blog The CEQ Web site features a blog. https://www.whitehouse.gov/administration/eop/ceq/blog

Freedom of Information Act (FOIA) Requests may be submitted by email (without an attachment) or fax or sent by postal mail to the Freedom of Information Officer, Council on Environmental Quality, 722 Jackson Place NW., Washington, DC 20503. Fax, 202-456-0753. https://www.whitehouse.gov/administration/eop/ceq/foia | Email: efoia@ceq.eop.gov

Internships Most interns work a semester-based schedule (May–August, September–December, or January–April). A position may be customized, however, to accommodate applicant availability and project needs. Application deadlines are February 1 for the summer, June 13 for the fall, and October 1 for the spring. https://www.whitehouse.gov/administration/eop/ceq/internships | Email: internships@ceq.eop.gov

Open Government The CEQ supports the Open Government initiative by promoting the principles of collaboration, participation, and transparency. https://www.whitehouse.gov/administration/eop/ceq/open

Participation The CEQ maintains a social media presence on Twitter and Facebook. An online subscription form is available to sign up for email updates from the CEQ and opportunities to get involved. https://www.whitehouse.gov/administration/eop/ceq/stay-connected

Press Releases The CEQ posts announcements, factsheets, memoranda, statements, and other newsworthy items on its Web site. https://www.whitehouse.gov/administration/eop/ceq/press_releases. http://www.whitehouse.gov/administration/eop/ceq

For further information, contact the Information Office, Council on Environmental Quality, 722 Jackson Place NW., Washington, DC 20503. Phone, 202-395-5750. Fax, 202-456-2710.

National Security Council

Eisenhower Executive Office Building, Washington, DC 20504
Phone, 202-456-1414. Internet, http://www.whitehouse.gov.

Members

The President	Donald J. Trump
The Vice President	Michael R. Pence
Secretary of State	Rex Tillerson
Secretary of Defense	Gen. James Mattis, USMC (retired)

Statutory Advisers

Director of National Intelligence	Dan Coats
Chairman, Joint Chiefs of Staff	Gen. Joseph F. Dunford, Jr., USMC

Standing Participants

Secretary of the Treasury	STEVEN MNUCHIN
Chief of Staff to the President	GEN. JOHN KELLY, USMC (RETIRED)
Counsel to the President	DONALD F. MCGAHN, II
National Security Adviser	LT. GEN. H.R. MCMASTERS, USA (RETIRED)
Director of the National Economic Council	GARY D. COHN

Officials

National Security Adviser	LT. GEN. H.R. MCMASTERS, USA (RETIRED)
Deputy National Security Adviser	MAJ. GEN. RICKY WADDELL, USA (RETIRED)

The National Security Council was established by the National Security Act of 1947, as amended (50 U.S.C. 402). The Council was placed in the Executive Office of the President by Reorganization Plan No. 4 of 1949 (5 U.S.C. app.).

The President chairs the National Security Council. Its statutory members, in addition to the President, are the Vice President and the Secretaries of State and Defense. The Chairman of the Joint Chiefs of Staff is the statutory military adviser to the Council, and the Director of National Intelligence serves as its intelligence adviser. The Secretary of the Treasury, the U.S. Representative to the United Nations, the Assistant to the President for National Security Affairs, the Assistant to the President for Economic Policy, and the Chief of Staff to the President are invited to all meetings of the Council. The Attorney General and the Director of National Drug Control Policy are invited to attend meetings pertaining to their jurisdictions, and other officials are invited, as appropriate.

The Council advises and assists the President in integrating all aspects of national security policy as it affects the United States—domestic, foreign, military, intelligence, and economic—in conjunction with the National Economic Council. http://www.whitehouse.gov/nsc

For further information, contact the National Security Council, Eisenhower Executive Office Building, Washington, DC 20504. Phone, 202-456-1414.

Office of Administration

Eisenhower Executive Office Building, 1650 Pennsylvania Avenue, NW., Washington, DC 20503 Phone, 202-456-2861. Internet, http://www.whitehouse.gov/oa

Director / Deputy Assistant to the President	(VACANCY)
Chief Administrative Officer	(VACANCY)
Chief Financial Officer	FAISAL AMIN
Chief Logistics Officer	STEPHEN E. PEARSON, ACTING
General Counsel	HUGH L. BRADY

The Office of Administration was formally established within the Executive Office of the President by Executive Order 12028 of December 12, 1977. https://www.whitehouse.gov/administration/eop/oa/history

The Office is exclusively dedicated to assisting the President in providing uniform administrative support services to all units within the Executive Office of the President. The services provided include facilities, information, personnel, technology, and financial management; digital solutions, library, and research services; security; legislative liaisons; and general office operations such as mail, messenger, printing, procurement, and supply services. https://www.whitehouse.gov/administration/eop/oa

Sources of Information

Career Opportunities   The Office of Administration relies on professionals who come from diverse backgrounds and posses a rare blend of education, experience, and skill. The Office announces job vacancies on USAJobs.gov. https://www.whitehouse.gov/administration/eop/oa/jobs

Photo Gallery   The Office of Administration contributes to the architectural and historic preservation of the properties associated with the Executive Office of the President. Images of current and past preservation projects are available online. https://www.whitehouse.gov/administration/eop/oa/preservation/projects. http://www.whitehouse.gov/oa

For further information, contact the Office of the Director, Office of Administration, Washington, DC 20503. Phone, 202-456-2861.

Office of Management and Budget
New Executive Office Building, Washington, DC 20503
Phone, 202-395-3080. Internet, http://www.whitehouse.gov/omb.

Director	MICK MULVANEY
Deputy Director	THOMAS M. REILLY, ACTING
Controller, Office of Federal Financial Management	(VACANCY)
Deputy Director, Management	DUSTIN S. BROWN, ACTING
Executive Associate Director	(VACANCY)
General Counsel	(VACANCY)
Intellectual Property Enforcement Coordinator	(VACANCY)

Administrators

Office of Federal Procurement Policy	(VACANCY)
Office of Information and Regulatory Affairs	DOMINIC J. MANCINI, ACTING

DIRECTORS
Assistant Directors

Budget	KELLY A. KINNEEN, ACTING
Legislative Reference	MATTHEW J. VAETH
Management and Operations	SARAH W. SPOONER

Associate Directors

Communications	JOHN S. CZWARTACKI
Economic Policy	(VACANCY)
Education, Income Maintenance and Labor	JOHN W. GRAY
General Government Programs	KATHLEEN L. KRANINGER
Health	JOSEPH L. GROGAN
Information Technology and E–Government	(VACANCY)
Legislative Affairs	JONATHAN A. SLEMROD
National Security Programs	ROBERT B. BLAIR
Natural Resource Programs	JAMES P. HERZ
Performance Management	(VACANCY)

The Office of Management and Budget evaluates, formulates, and coordinates management procedures and program objectives within and among Federal departments and agencies. It also controls the administration of the Federal budget, while routinely providing the President with recommendations regarding budget proposals and relevant legislative enactments.

The Office of Management and Budget (OMB), formerly the Bureau of the Budget, was established in the Executive Office of the President pursuant to Reorganization Plan No. 1 of 1939 (5 U.S.C. app.).

The Office's primary functions are diverse and many: to assist the President in developing and maintaining effective government by reviewing the organizational structure and management procedures of the executive branch to ensure that the intended results are achieved; to assist in developing efficient coordinating mechanisms to implement Government activities and to expand interagency cooperation; to assist the President in preparing the budget and in formulating the Government's fiscal program; to supervise and control the administration of the budget; to assist the President by clearing and coordinating departmental advice on proposed legislation and by making recommendations effecting Presidential action on legislative enactments, in accordance with past practice; to assist in developing regulatory reform proposals and programs for paperwork reduction, especially reporting burdens of the public; to assist in considering, clearing, and, where necessary, preparing proposed Executive orders and proclamations; to plan and develop information systems that provide the President with program performance data; to plan, conduct, and promote evaluation efforts that assist the President in assessing program objectives, performance, and efficiency; to keep the President informed of the progress of activities by Government agencies with respect to work proposed, initiated, and completed, together with the relative timing of work between the several agencies of the Government, all to the end that the work programs of the several agencies of the executive branch of the Government may be coordinated and that the moneys appropriated by the Congress may be expended in the most economical manner, barring overlapping and duplication of effort; and to improve the efficiency and effectiveness of the procurement processes by providing overall direction of procurement policies, regulations, procedures, and forms. https://www.whitehouse.gov/omb/organization_mission

Sources of Information

Career Opportunities   The "Join OMB" Web page has links to learn more about career and detail opportunities, student internships, and applying for OMB positions. Questions may be addressed to the Human Resources Division, Office of Administration, Washington, DC 20500. Phone, 202-395-1088. https://www.whitehouse.gov/omb/recruitment_default

Freedom of Information Act (FOIA)   Information on how to submit a FOIA request is available online. The OMB's FOIA Request Service Center also provides assistance. Phone, 202-395-3642. https://www.whitehouse.gov/omb/foia_default#reading | Email: OMBFOIA@omb.eop.gov

Publications   A copy of the "Budget of the United States Government" may be downloaded from the OMB Web site or purchased from the Government Publishing Office bookstore. Phone, 202-512-0132. https://www.whitehouse.gov/omb/budget/Overview. https://bookstore.gpo.gov/catalog/budget-economy | Email: mainbks@gpo.gov. https://www.whitehouse.gov/omb/contact

For further information, contact the Office of Management and Budget, New Executive Office Building, Washington, DC 20503. Phone, 202-395-3080.

Office of Management and Budget

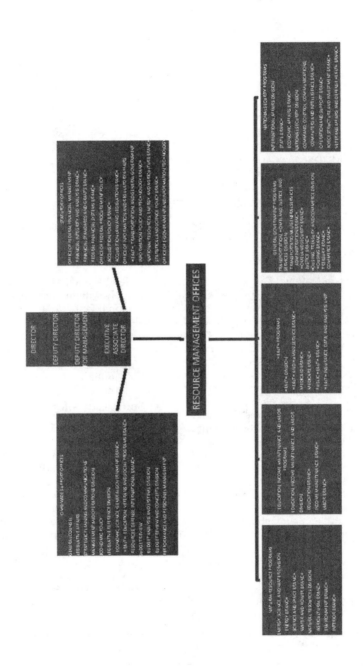

Office of National Drug Control Policy

Executive Office of the President, Washington, DC 20503
Phone, 202-395-6700. Fax, 202-395-6708. Internet, http://www.ondcp.gov.

Director	RICHARD J. BAUM, Acting
Chief of Staff	LAWRENCE L. MUIR, Acting
Deputy Director, Office of Policy, Research and Budget	(VACANCY)
General Counsel	LAWRENCE L. MUIR
Associate Directors	
Office of Intelligence	GERARD K. BURNS
Office of Intergovernmental Public Liaison	(VACANCY)
Office of Legislative Affairs	(VACANCY)
Office of Management and Administration	MICHELE C. MARX
Office of Public Affairs	(VACANCY)
Office of Research / Data Analysis	(VACANCY)

The Office of National Drug Control Policy helps the President establish his National Drug Control Strategy objectives, priorities, and policies and makes budget, program, and policy recommendations affecting National Drug Control Program agencies.

The Office of National Drug Control Policy (ONDCP) was established by the National Narcotics Leadership Act of 1988 (21 U.S.C. 1501 et seq.), effective January 29, 1989, reauthorized through the Office of National Drug Control Policy Reauthorization Act of 1988 (21 U.S.C. 1701 et seq.), and again reauthorized through the Office of National Drug Control Policy Reauthorization Act of 2006 (21 U.S.C. 1701 et seq.).

The President appoints the Director of National Drug Control Policy with the advice and consent of the Senate.

The Director establishes policies, objectives, priorities, and performance measurements for the National Drug Control Program. Each year, the Director promulgates the President's National Drug Control Strategy, other related drug control strategies, supporting reports, and a program budget that the President submits to Congress. The Director advises the President on necessary changes in the organization, management, budgeting, and personnel allocation of Federal agencies that monitor drug activities. The Director also notifies Federal agencies if their policies do not comply with their responsibilities under the National Drug Control Strategy. The ONDCP also has direct programmatic responsibility for the Drug-Free Communities Support and the High Intensity Drug Trafficking Areas programs. https://www.whitehouse.gov/ondcp/office-descriptions

Sources of Information

Career Opportunities Contact the Personnel Section, Office of National Drug Control Policy. Phone, 202-395-6695. Information on student opportunities is available on the "Working at ONDCP" Web page. https://www.whitehouse.gov/ondcp/working-at-ondcp

Publications To receive publications on drugs and crime control policies, to access specific drug-related data, to access customized bibliographic searches, and to learn more about data availability and other resources, visit the ONDCP Web site. https://www.whitehouse.gov/ondcp/news-releases. http://www.whitehouse.gov/ondcp

For further information, contact the Office of National Drug Control Policy, Executive Office of the President, Washington, DC 20503. Phone, 202-395-6700. Fax, 202-395-6708.

Office of Policy Development

The Office of Policy Development comprises the Domestic Policy and the National Economic Councils, which advise and assist the President in the formulation, coordination, and implementation of domestic and economic policy. The Office of Policy Development also supports other policy development and implementation activities as directed by the President.

Domestic Policy Council
Room 469, Eisenhower Executive Office Building, Washington, DC 20502
Phone, 202-456-5594. Internet, https://www.whitehouse.gov/administration/eop/dpc.

Domestic Policy Council
Director / Domestic Policy Advisor to the President   CECILIA MUÑOZ

The Domestic Policy Council was established August 16, 1993, by Executive Order 12859. The Council oversees development and implementation of the President's domestic policy agenda and ensures coordination and communication among the heads of relevant Federal offices and agencies.

National Economic Council
Room 235, Eisenhower Executive Office Building, Washington, DC 20502
Phone, 202-456-2800. Internet, https://www.whitehouse.gov/administration/eop/nec.

National Economic Council
Director / Assistant to the President for Economic Policy   JEFFREY D. ZIENTS

The National Economic Council was created January 25, 1993, by Executive Order 12835, to coordinate the economic policymaking process and advise the President on economic policy. The Council also ensures that economic policy decisions and programs remain consistent with the President's stated goals and monitors the implementation of the President's economic goals.

Office of Science and Technology Policy
Eisenhower Executive Office Building, 1650 Pennsylvania Avenue NW., Washington, DC 20502
Phone, 202-456-4444. Fax, 202-456-6021. Internet, http://www.ostp.gov.

Director	JOHN P. HOLDREN
Chief of Staff	CRISTIN DORGELO
Assistant Director, Federal Research and Development	KEI KOIZUMI
Assistant Director, Legislative Affairs	DONNA PIGNATELLI
Communications Director / Senior Policy Analyst	KRISTIN LEE
Deputy Chief of Staff / Assistant Director	TED M. WACKLER
General Counsel	RACHAEL LEONARD

Office of the Chief Technology Officer
Chief Technology Officer	MEGAN SMITH
Deputy Chief Technology Officer	ALEXANDER MACGILLIVRAY

Deputy Chief Technology Officer	CORINNA ZAREK
Deputy Chief Technology Officer	EDWARD W. FELTEN
Deputy Chief Technology Officer, Data Policy / Chief Data Scientist	DHANURAY PATIL

Environment and Energy Division

Associate Director	(VACANCY)
Assistant Director, Clean Energy and Transportation	AUSTIN BROWN
Assistant Director, Climate Adaptation and Ecosystems	LAURA PETES
Assistant Director, Climate Resilience and Information	AMY LUERS
Assistant Director, Climate Resilience and Land Use	RICH POUYAT
Assistant Director, Climate Science	DONALD WUEBBLES
Assistant Director, Earth Observations	DAVID HERMRECK
Assistant Director, Environmental Health	BRUCE RODAN
Assistant Director, Natural Disaster Resilience	JACQUELINE MESZAROS
Assistant Director, Polar Sciences	MARTIN JEFFRIES
Assistant Director, Space Weather	WILLIAM MURTAGH
Principal Assistant Director, Environment and Energy	TAMARA DICKINSON

National Security and International Affairs Division

Associate Director	(VACANCY)
Assistant Director, Biosecurity and Emerging Technologies	GERALD EPSTEIN
Assistant Director, Cybersecurity	TIMOTHY POLK
Assistant Director, Cybersecurity Strategy	GREGORY SHANNON
Assistant Director, Defense Programs	CHRIS FALL
Assistant Director, Global Security	MATTHEW J. HEAVNER
Assistant Director, Special Programs	MARK LEBLANC
Principal Assistant Director, National Security and International Affairs	STEVE FETTER

Science Division

Associate Director	JO EMILY HANDELSMAN
Assistant Director, Bioethics and Privacy	MELISSA GOLDSTEIN
Assistant Director, Broadening Participation	WANDA WARD
Assistant Director, Education and Learning Science	DANIELLE CARNIVAL
Assistant Director, Education and Physical Sciences	MEREDITH DROSBACK
Assistant Director, Research Infrastructure	ALTAF CARIM
Assistant Director, Scientific Data and Information	JERRY SHEEHAN

Technology and Innovation Division

Associate Director	(VACANCY)
Assistant Director, Behavioral Science	MAYA SHANKAR
Assistant Director, Biological Innovation	ROBBIE BARBERO
Assistant Director, Civil and Commercial Space	BENJAMIN ROBERTS
Assistant Director, Education and Telecommunications Innovation	AADIL GINWALA
Assistant Director, Entrepreneurship	DOUGLAS RAND
Assistant Director, Innovation for Growth	JENNIFER ERICKSON
Assistant Director, Learning and Innovation	KUMAR GARG
Assistant Director, Nanotechnology and Advanced Materials	LLOYD WHITMAN
Assistant Director, Open Innovation	CHRISTOFER NELSON
Deputy Director for Technology and Innovation	THOMAS KALIL

Budget and Administration

Operations Manager and Security Officer	STACY MURPHY

Councils

President's Council of Advisors on Science and Technology Executive Director	ASHLEY PREDITH

National Science and Technology Council

Executive Director	AFUA BRUCE
Director, National Nanotechnology Coordination Office	MICHAEL MEADOR
Director, Networking and Information Technology Research and Development National Coordination Office	BRYAN BIEGEL
Director, U.S. Global Change Research Program National Coordination Office	MICHAEL KUPERBERG
Director, U.S. Group on Earth Observation Program	TIMOTHY STRYKER

The Office of Science and Technology Policy (OSTP) was established within the Executive Office of the President by the National Science and Technology Policy, Organization, and Priorities Act of 1976 (42 U.S.C. 6611).

The Office supports the President by serving as a source of engineering, scientific, and technological analysis and judgment on plans, policies, and programs of the Federal Government. OSTP experts advise the President on scientific and technological matters that affect areas of national concern like the economy, environment, foreign relations, health, and national security; evaluate the effectiveness, quality, and scale of the Federal effort in science and technology; advise and assist the President, the Office of Management and Budget, and Federal agencies throughout the Federal budget development process; and help the President with leading and coordinating the Federal Government's research and development programs. https://www. whitehouse.gov/administration/eop/ostp/about

Sources of Information

Blog The OSTP's Web site features a blog. https://www.whitehouse.gov/administration/eop/ostp/blog

Freedom of Information Act (FOIA) Instructions for submitting a FOIA request are available online. https://www. whitehouse.gov/administration/eop/ostp/library/foia

Internships Internships offer a unique opportunity to work with senior White House officials and science and technology policy analysts in the OSTP's topic-based divisions or on the OSTP legal team. Applicants may apply for one of three terms: Fall, Spring, or Summer. Each term lasts no more than 90 days; interns receive no remuneration; and students may be eligible to receive academic credit. https://www. whitehouse.gov/administration/eop/ostp/about/student

Library The OSTP's resource library is an expanding collection of agency materials that includes compliance guidelines, documents, presentations, reports, speeches, and testimonies. An archival section contains materials from past administrations. https:// www.whitehouse.gov/administration/eop/ostp/library

Press Room White House factsheets and science and technology-related remarks, statements, weekly addresses, and other Presidential items are available on the OSTP's Web site. https://www.whitehouse. gov/administration/eop/ostp/pressroom. https://www.whitehouse.gov/administration/eop/ostp/contactus

For further information, contact the Office of Science and Technology Policy, Eisenhower Executive Office Building, 1650 Pennsylvania Avenue NW., Washington, DC 20502. Phone, 202-456-4444. Fax, 202-456-6021.

Office of the United States Trade Representative

600 Seventeenth Street NW., Washington, DC 20508
Phone, 202-395-3230. Internet, http://www.ustr.gov.

Office of the U.S. Trade Representative

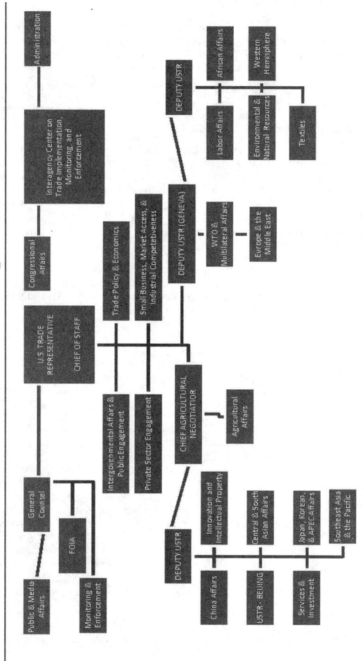

United States Trade Representative	Robert E. Lighthizer
Deputy U.S. Trade Representative–Geneva	(VACANCY)
Deputy U.S. Trade Representative–Washington	(VACANCY)
Deputy U.S. Trade Representative–Washington	(VACANCY)
Chief Agricultural Negotiator	(VACANCY)
Chief of Staff	Jamieson L. Greer
Director, Interagency Center on Trade Implementation, Monitoring and Enforcement	(VACANCY)
General Counsel	Stephen Vaughn

Assistant U.S. Trade Representatives

Administration	Fed Ames
African Affairs	(VACANCY)
Agricultural Affairs	Sharon Bomer Lauritsen
South and Central Asian Affairs	Mark Linscott
China Affairs	Terrence J. McCartin, Acting
Congressional Affairs	Christopher Jackson
Environment and Natural Resources	Jennifer Prescott
Europe and Middle East Affairs	L. Daniel Mullaney
Innovation and Intellectual Property	(VACANCY)
Intergovernmental Affairs and Public Engagement	(VACANCY)
Japan, Korea, and Asia Pacific Economic Cooperation (APEC) Affairs	Michael Beeman
Labor	Lewis Karesh
Monitoring and Enforcement	Juan Millan
Private Sector Engagement	(VACANCY)
Public and Media Affairs	(VACANCY)
Services and Investment	Daniel Bahar
Small Business, Market Access and Industrial Competitiveness	James Sanford
Southeast Asia and Pacific Affairs	Barbara Weisel
Textiles	William Jackson
Trade Policy and Economic Affairs	Edward Gresser
Western Hemisphere	John Melle
World Trade Organization (WTO) and Multilateral Affairs	Dawn Shackleford

The United States Trade Representative formulates trade policy for and directs all trade negotiations of the United States.

The Office of the U.S. Trade Representative was created as the Office of the Special Representative for Trade Negotiations by Executive Order 11075 of January 15, 1963. The Trade Act of 1974 (19 U.S.C. 2171) established the Office as an agency of the Executive Office of the President charged with administering the trade agreements program. https://ustr.gov/about-us/history

The Office sets and administers overall trade policy. The U.S. Trade Representative heads the Office and serves as the President's principal adviser, negotiator, and spokesperson on international trade and investment issues. The Representative acts as the chief representative of the United States in all General Agreement on Tariffs and Trade activities; in Organization for Economic Cooperation and Development discussions, meetings, and negotiations that deal primarily with commodity issues and trade; in U.N. Conference on Trade and Development negotiations and other multilateral institution negotiations that deal primarily with commodity issues and trade; in other bilateral and multilateral negotiations that deal primarily with commodities or trade, including East-West trade; in negotiations under sections 704 and 734 of the Tariff Act of 1930 (19 U.S.C. 1671c and 1673c); and in negotiations on direct investment incentives and disincentives and on bilateral investment issues concerning barriers to investment.

The Omnibus Trade and Competitiveness Act of 1988 codified these authorities and added additional authority, including the implementation of section 301 actions that enforce U.S. rights under international trade agreements.

The U.S. Trade Representative serves as a Cabinet-level official with the rank of Ambassador and reports directly to the President. The Chief Agricultural Negotiator and three Deputy U.S. Trade Representatives also hold the rank of Ambassador—two of the deputies are located in Washington, DC, and the other serves in Geneva, Switzerland.

The U.S. Trade Representative is also an ex officio member on the boards of directors of the Export-Import Bank and the Overseas Private Investment Corporation. The Representative also serves on the National Advisory Council on International Monetary and Financial Policy. https://ustr.gov/about-us

Sources of Information

Blog "Tradewinds" is the official blog of the U.S. Trade Representative. https://ustr.gov/tradewinds

Factsheets The U.S. Trade Representative releases factsheets on trade issues. https://ustr.gov/about-us/policy-offices/press-office/fact-sheets

Freedom of Information Act (FOIA) Requests must be made in writing: Freedom of Information Officer, Office of the U.S. Trade Representative, 1724 F Street NW., Washington, DC 20508. Security procedures can slow down mail receipt and processing. Sending a request by email or fax avoids security-related delays. To facilitate finding the desired information, a record description must contain key details—author, date, recipient, subject matter, title or name. The Office of the U.S. Trade Representative operates a FOIA requestor service center. Phone, 202-395-3419. Fax, 202-395-9458. https://ustr.gov/about-us/reading-room/freedom-information-act-foia | Email: FOIA@ustr.eop.gov

The electronic reading room contains information that is made available on a routine basis to the public. It also features documents that are frequently requested under the FOIA. This collection of online documents continues to grow as records in which the public expresses an interest are added. https://ustr.gov/about-us/reading-room/freedom-information-act-foia/electronic-reading-room

History In 1963, President John F. Kennedy created a new Office of the Special Trade Representative in the Executive Office of the President and designated two new Deputies, one in the Nation's capital and the other in Geneva, Switzerland. The rest of the story is available on the Web site of the Office of the U.S. Trade Representative. https://ustr.gov/about-us/history

The Office of the U.S. Trade Representative posted "Facts About Trade" to commemorate its 50th anniversary. https://ustr.gov/50/facts

Key Issues The Office of the U.S. Trade Representative focuses it's trade policy on 14 issue areas: agriculture, economy and trade, enforcement, environment, government procurement, industry and manufacturing, intellectual property, labor, preference programs, services and investment, small business, textiles and apparel, trade and development, and trade organizations. https://ustr.gov/issue-areas

Map The United States has trade relations with more than 75 countries worldwide. https://ustr.gov/countries-regions

North American Free Trade Agreement (NAFTA) The Web site of the Office of the U.S. Trade Representative features facts on the NAFTA. https://ustr.gov/trade-agreements/free-trade-agreements/north-american-free-trade-agreement-nafta

Open Government The Office of the U.S. Trade Representative supports the Open Government initiative by promoting the principles of collaboration, participation, and transparency. https://www.whitehouse.gov/open/around/eop/ustr

Press Releases The Office of the U.S. Trade Representative posts press releases on its Web site. https://ustr.gov/about-us/policy-offices/press-office/press-releases

Reports / Publications The Office of the U.S. Trade Representative posts reports and publications on its Web site. https://ustr.gov/about-us/policy-offices/press-office/reports-and-publications

Social Media The U.S. Trade Representative tweets announcements and other newsworthy items on Twitter. https://twitter.com/USTradeRep

The Office of the U.S. Trade Representative has a Facebook account. https://www.facebook.com/USTradeRep

Speeches / Transcripts The Office of the U.S. Trade Representative posts transcriptions of public remarks made by its senior staff. https://ustr.gov/about-us/policy-offices/press-office/speeches

Transatlantic Trade and Investment Partnership (T–TIP) The Web site of the Office of the U.S. Trade Representative features a T–TIP issue-by-issue information center. https://ustr.gov/trade-agreements/free-trade-agreements/transatlantic-trade-and-investment-partnership-t-tip/t-tip

Trans-Pacific Partnership (TPP) The Office of the U.S Trade Representative has answered frequently asked questions regarding the TPP on its Web site. https://ustr.gov/tpp/#facts. https://ustr.gov/about-us/policy-offices/press-office

For further information, contact the Office of Public and Media Affairs, Office of the U.S. Trade Representative, 600 Seventeenth Street NW., Washington, DC 20508. Phone, 202-395-3230.

EXECUTIVE BRANCH: DEPARTMENTS

DEPARTMENT OF AGRICULTURE

1400 Independence Avenue SW., Washington, DC 20250
Phone, 202-720-2791. Internet, http://www.usda.gov

Secretary Of Agriculture	GEORGE E. PERDUE III
Deputy Secretary	MICHAEL L. YOUNG, ACTING

AGENCY HEADS

Farm and Foreign Agricultural Services

Deputy Under Secretary	JASON HAFEMEISTER, ACTING
Administrator, Foreign Agricultural Service	HOLLY HIGGINS, ACTING
Administrator, Farm Service Agency	CHRIS BEYERHELM, ACTING
Administrator, Risk Management Agency	HEATHER MANZANO, ACTING

Food, Nutrition and Consumer Services

Deputy Under Secretary	YVETTE JACKSON, ACTING
Administrator, Food and Nutrition Service	JESSICA SHAHIN, ACTING
Director, Center for Nutrition Policy and Promotion	JACKIE HAVEN, ACTING

Food Safety

Deputy Under Secretary for Food Safety	ALFRED V. ALMANZA, ACTING
Administrator, Food Safety and Inspection Service	ALFRED V. ALMANZA

Marketing and Regulatory Programs

Deputy Under Secretary	KEVIN SHEA, ACTING
Administrator, Agricultural Marketing Service	BRUCE SUMMERS, ACTING
Administrator, Animal and Plant Health Inspection Service	(VACANCY)
Administrator, Grain Inspection, Packers and Stockyards Administration	RANDALL JONES, ACTING

Natural Resources and Environment

Deputy Under Secretary	DANIEL JIRON, ACTING
Chief, Forest Service	THOMAS TIDWELL
Chief, Natural Resources Conservation Service	LEONARD JORDAN

Research, Education and Economics

Under Secretary	ANN BARTUSKA, ACTING
Administrator, Agricultural Research Service	CHAVONDA JACOBS-YOUNG
Administrator, Economic Research Service	MARY BOHMAN
Administrator, National Agricultural Statistics Service	HUBERT HAMER, JR.
Director, National Institute of Food and Agriculture	SONNY RAMASWAMY

Rural Development

Deputy Under Secretary	ROGER GLENDENNING, ACTING
Administrator, Rural Business-Cooperative Service	CHADWICK O. PARKER, ACTING
Administrator, Rural Housing Service	RICHARD A. DAVIS, ACTING
Administrator, Rural Utilities Service	CHRIS MCLEAN, ACTING

Office Heads

Assistant Secretary for Administration	MALCOM SHORTER, ACTING, ACTING
Assistant Secretary for Civil Rights	(VACANCY)
Chief Economist	ROBERT JOHANSSON
Chief Financial Officer	LYNN M. MOANEY, ACTING
Chief Information Officer	JONATHAN ALBOUM
Deputy Assistant Secretary for Congressional Relations	ABBEY FRETZ, ACTING
Deputy Assistant Secretary for External and Intergovernmental Affairs	DOUG CRANDALL, ACTING
Director, Advocacy and Outreach	CAROLYN PARKER
Director, Budget and Program Analysis	MICHAEL L. YOUNG
Director, Communications	TIMOTHY M. MURTAUGH
Director, National Appeals Division	STEVEN C. SILVERMAN
General Counsel	STEPHEN A. VADEN, ACTING
Inspector General	PHYLLIS K. FONG

[For the Department of Agriculture statement of organization, see the Code of Federal Regulations, Title 7, Part 2]

The above list of key personnel was updated 06–2017.

The Department of Agriculture develops agricultural markets, fights hunger and malnutrition, conserves natural resources, and ensures food quality standards.

The Department of Agriculture (USDA) was created by an act of Congress on May 15, 1862 (7 U.S.C. 2201). In carrying out its work in the program mission areas, the USDA relies on the support of departmental administration staff, as well as on the Offices of Communications, Congressional Relations, the Chief Economist, the Chief Financial Officer, the Chief Information Officer, the General Counsel, and the Inspector General. http://www.usda.gov/wps/portal/usda/usdahome?navid=USDA150

Farm and Foreign Agricultural Services

This mission area centers on helping America's farmers and ranchers deal with the unpredictable nature of weather and markets. These services deliver commodity, conservation, credit, disaster, and emergency assistance programs to strengthen and stabilize the agricultural economy. http://www.usda.gov/wps/portal/usda/usdahome?navid=USDA_MISSION_AREAS

Farm Service Agency (FSA)   The Farm Service Agency administers farm commodity, disaster, and conservation programs for farmers and ranchers. It also makes and guarantees farm emergency, ownership, and operating loans through a network of State and county offices. http://www.fsa.usda.gov/index

Commodity Credit Corporation   The Commodity Credit Corporation, an agency and instrumentality of the United States within the USDA, is under the supervision of the Secretary of Agriculture. The Corporation does not have any employees, but relies on various Federal agencies, principally those in the USDA, to conduct its operations. It carries out a wide array of functions as authorized by the Commodity Credit Corporation Charter Act and as specifically authorized by the Congress in numerous statutes. Corporation funds are used to offer marketing assistance loans to producers of certain commodities, fund conservation programs to protect or enhance natural resources, support the export of agricultural commodities, provide humanitarian assistance abroad, and further economic progress in developing countries. http://www.fsa.usda.gov/about-fsa/structure-and-organization/commodity-credit-corporation/index

Commodity Operations   FSA facilitates the purchase, storage, transportation, and disposition of U.S.-origin commodities acquired as a result of commodity loan forfeiture or through procurement for humanitarian food aid programs. FSA administers the United States Warehouse Act, which authorizes the Secretary of Agriculture to license warehouse operators who store agricultural products. The FSA also enters into agreements with warehouse operators to store commodities owned by the Commodity Credit Corporation or pledged by farmers as security for Commodity Credit Corporation marketing assistance loans. http://www.fsa.usda. gov/about-fsa/structure-and-organization/ commodity-operations/index

Conservation Programs FSA's conservation programs include the Conservation Reserve Program, which is the Federal Government's largest environmental improvement program on private lands. It safeguards millions of acres of topsoil from erosion, improves air quality, increases wildlife habitat, and reduces water runoff and sedimentation. In return for planting a protective cover of grass or trees on environmentally sensitive land, participants receive an annual rental payment. Cost-share payments are available to help establish conservation practices such as the planting of native grass, trees, windbreaks, or plants that improve water quality and give shelter and food to wildlife. http://www.fsa.usda.gov/FSA/bapp?area=ho me&subject=copr&topic=landing

Farm Commodity Programs FSA manages farm safety net programs for America's farmers and ranchers. Its Commodity Credit Corporation stabilizes, supports, and protects farm income and prices; helps maintain balanced and adequate supplies of agricultural commodities; and aids in their orderly distribution. http://www.fsa.usda. gov/about-fsa/structure-and-organization/ commodity-credit-corporation/index

Farm Loan Programs FSA makes and guarantees loans to family farmers and ranchers to purchase farmland and finance agricultural production. These programs offer credit on reasonable rates and terms to farmers—those who have suffered financial setbacks from natural disasters, those with limited resources for establishing and maintaining profitable farming operations, and beginners. http://www.fsa.usda.gov/ programs-and-services/farm-loan-programs/ index

Noninsured Crop Disaster Assistance Program The Noninsured Crop Disaster Assistance Program gives financial assistance to producers of noninsurable crops when yields are low, inventory is lost, or natural disasters prevent planting. http://www.fsa. usda.gov/programs-and-services/disaster-assistance-program/noninsured-crop-disaster-assistance/index

Other Emergency Assistance In counties that are declared disaster areas, low-interest loans for eligible farmers help cover physical and production losses. Eligible producers can be compensated for crop losses, livestock feed losses, tree damage, and for the cost of rehabilitating certain farmlands damaged by natural disaster. http://www. fsa.usda.gov/programs-and-services/disaster-assistance-program/index

For further information, contact the Office of External Affairs, Farm Service Agency, Department of Agriculture, Stop 0506, 1400 Independence Avenue SW., Washington, DC 20250. Phone, 202-720-7807. Or, contact the Information Division, Foreign Agricultural Service, Department of Agriculture, Stop 1004, 1400 Independence Avenue SW., Washington, DC 20250. Phone, 202-720-7115. Fax, 202-720-1727.

Foreign Agricultural Service (FAS) The Foreign Agricultural Service improves foreign market access for U.S. products, builds new markets, improves the competitive position of U.S. agriculture in the global marketplace, and provides food aid and technical assistance to foreign countries.

FAS has the primary responsibility for USDA's activities in the areas of international marketing, trade agreements and negotiations, and the collection and analysis of international statistics and market information. It also administers the USDA's export credit guarantee and food aid programs. FAS helps increase income and food availability in developing nations by mobilizing expertise for agriculturally led economic growth.

FAS also enhances U.S. agricultural competitiveness through a global network of agricultural economists, marketing experts, negotiators, and other specialists. FAS agricultural counselors, attaches, trade officers, and locally employed staff are stationed in over 93 countries to support U.S. agricultural interests and cover 171 countries.

In addition to agricultural affairs offices in U.S. embassies, trade offices operate in a number of key foreign markets. They function as service centers for U.S. exporters and foreign buyers seeking market information.

Reports prepared by FAS overseas offices cover changes in policies and other developments that could affect U.S. agricultural exports. FAS staff in U.S.

embassies worldwide assess U.S. export marketing opportunities and respond to the daily informational needs of those who develop, initiate, monitor, and evaluate U.S. food and agricultural policies and programs.

The Service also maintains a worldwide agricultural reporting system based on information from U.S. agricultural traders, remote sensing systems, and other sources. Analysts in Washington, DC, prepare production forecasts, assess export marketing opportunities, and track changes in policies affecting U.S. agricultural exports and imports.

FAS programs help U.S. exporters develop and maintain markets for hundreds of food and agricultural products, from bulk commodities to brand-name items. Formal market promotion activities are carried out chiefly in cooperation with agricultural trade associations, State-regional trade groups, small businesses, and cooperatives that plan, manage, and contribute human and financial resources to these efforts. The Service also advises exporters on locating buyers and provides assistance through a variety of other methods, including supporting U.S. participation in trade shows and single-industry exhibitions each year. http://www.fas.usda.gov

For further information, contact the Public Affairs Division, Foreign Agricultural Service, Stop 1004, 1400 Independence Avenue SW., Department of Agriculture, Washington, DC 20250-1004. Phone, 202-720-7115. Fax, 202-720-1727.

Risk Management Agency (RMA)   The Risk Management Agency, on behalf of the Federal Crop Insurance Corporation (FCIC), oversees and administers the Federal crop insurance program under the Federal Crop Insurance Act.

Federal crop insurance is offered to qualifying producers through 16 private sector crop insurance companies. Under the Standard Reinsurance Agreement (SRA), RMA provides reinsurance, pays premium subsidies, reimburses insurers for administrative and operating expenses, and oversees the financial integrity and operational performance of the delivery system. RMA bears much of the noncommercial insurance risk under the SRA, allowing insurers to retain commercial

insurance risks or reinsure those risks in the private market.

In 2016, the Federal crop insurance program provided producers with more than $100 billion in protection. Twenty-five insurance plans are available, covering over 550 varieties of crops, 37 reinsured privately developed products, and 18 RMA-developed pilot programs in various stages of operation.

RMA also works closely with the private sector to find innovative ways to expand coverage. The expansion affects risk protection for specialty crops, livestock and forage, and rangeland and pasture. Thus, RMA is able to reduce the need for ad hoc disaster assistance, while providing coverage for production declines that result from adverse weather in many areas.

Additional information is available on the RMA Web site, which features agency news, State profiles, publications, and announcements on current issues. It also has summaries of insurance sales, pilot programs, downloadable crop policies, and agency-sponsored events. Online tools, calculators, and applications are also part of the Web site. http://www.rma.usda.gov

For further information, contact the Office of the Administrator, Risk Management Agency, Department of Agriculture, Stop 0801, 1400 Independence Avenue SW., Washington, DC 20250. Phone, 202-690-2803.

Food, Nutrition and Consumer Services

The mission area of the food, nutrition, and consumer services centers on harnessing the Nation's agricultural abundance to reduce hunger and improve health in the United States. Its agencies administer Federal domestic nutrition assistance programs and the Center for Nutrition Policy and Promotion, which links scientific research to the nutrition needs of consumers through science-based dietary guidance, nutrition policy coordination, and nutrition education. http://www.usda.gov/wps/portal/usda/ usdahome?navid=USDA_MISSION_AREAS

Center for Nutrition Policy and Promotion (CNPP)   The Center for Nutrition Policy and Promotion improves the health and well-being of Americans by developing and promoting dietary guidance that links the latest evidence-based scientific research to consumers' nutrition needs. Initiatives range from setting Federal dietary guidance to consumer-based nutrition education (MyPlate), to cutting-edge personalized electronic tools (SuperTracker), to "report cards" on the status of the American diet. https://www.choosemyplate.gov. https://www.supertracker.usda.gov. http://www.cnpp.usda.gov

For further information, contact the Office of Public Information, Center for Nutrition Policy and Promotion, Suite 200, 1120 20th Street NW., Washington, DC 20036-3406. Phone, 202-418-2312.

Food and Nutrition Service (FNS) The Food and Nutrition Service administers the USDA domestic nutrition assistance programs, serving one in four Americans in the course of a year. The FNS works in partnership with States and local agencies to increase food security and reduce hunger by providing children and low-income people with access to food, a healthy diet, and nutrition education. http://www.fns.usda.gov

FNS administers the following nutrition assistance programs:

The Supplemental Nutrition Assistance Program (SNAP) gives nutrition assistance to millions of eligible low-income individuals and families, and it provides economic benefits to communities. SNAP is the largest program in the domestic hunger safety net. FNS also works with State partners and the retail community to improve program administration and ensure program integrity. http://www.fns.usda.gov/snap/supplemental-nutrition-assistance-program-snap

The Special Supplemental Nutrition Program for Women, Infants, and Children (WIC) provides Federal grants to States for supplemental foods, health care referrals, and nutrition education for low-income pregnant, breastfeeding, and nonbreastfeeding postpartum women, and to infants and children up to age 5 who are found to be at nutritional risk. WIC and the Seniors' Farmers' Market Nutrition Programs provide WIC participants and senior citizens with increased access to fresh produce through coupons to purchase fresh fruits and vegetables from authorized farmers. http://www.fns.usda.gov/wic/women-infants-and-children-wic

The Farmers' Market Nutrition Program is linked to WIC, which provides supplemental foods, health care referrals, and nutrition education at no cost to low-income pregnant, breastfeeding, and nonbreastfeeding post partum women, and to infants and children who are up to 5 years of age and found to be at nutritional risk. http://www.fns.usda.gov/fmnp/wic-farmers-market-nutrition-program-fmnp

The Senior Farmers' Market Nutrition Program awards grants to States, U.S. Territories, and federally recognized Indian tribal governments for coupons that low-income seniors can use to purchase eligible foods at farmers' markets, roadside stands, and community-supported agriculture programs. http://www.fns.usda.gov/sfmnp/senior-farmers-market-nutrition-program-sfmnp

The Commodity Supplemental Food Program improves the health of low-income pregnant and breastfeeding women, nonbreastfeeding mothers up to 1 year postpartum, infants, and children up to age 6. The program supplements their diets with nutritious USDA commodity foods. It also provides food and administrative funds to States to supplement the diets of these groups. http://www.fns.usda.gov/csfp/commodity-supplemental-food-program-csfp

School districts and independent schools that choose to take part in the National School Lunch Program receive cash subsidies and donated commodities from the USDA. In return, they must serve lunches that meet Federal requirements and must offer free or reduced-price lunches to eligible children. School food authorities can also be reimbursed for snacks served to children through age 18 in afterschool educational or enrichment programs. http://www.fns.usda.gov/nslp/national-school-lunch-program-nslp

The School Breakfast Program operates like the National School Lunch Program. School districts and independent schools that choose to take part in the breakfast program receive cash subsidies from the USDA for each meal they serve. In return, they must serve breakfasts that meet Federal requirements and must offer free or reduced-price breakfasts to eligible children. http://www.fns.usda.gov/sbp/school-breakfast-program-sbp

The Special Milk Program provides milk to schoolchildren and children in childcare institutions who do not participate in other Federal meal service programs. The program reimburses schools for the milk that they serve. Schools in the National School Lunch or School Breakfast Programs may participate so that milk is available to prekindergarten and kindergarten children who may not have access to school meal programs. http://www.fns.usda.gov/smp/special-milk-program

The Child and Adult Care Food Program helps child and adult care institutions and family or group day care homes provide nutritious foods to promote the health and wellness of young children, older adults, and chronically impaired disabled persons. http://www.fns.usda.gov/cacfp/child-and-adult-care-food-program

The Summer Food Service Program ensures that low-income children receive nutritious meals when they are not attending school. http://www.fns.usda.gov/sfsp/summer-food-service-program-sfsp

The Emergency Food Assistance Program helps low-income and elderly Americans access free emergency food and nutrition assistance. The program provides food and administrative funds to States to supplement the diets of these groups. http://www.fns.usda.gov/tefap/emergency-food-assistance-program-tefap

The Food Distribution Program on Indian Reservations helps low-income households—including the elderly living on Indian reservations—and Native American families residing in designated areas in Oklahoma and near reservations elsewhere to access USDA foods. http://www.fns.usda.gov/fdpir/food-distribution-program-indian-reservations-fdpir

The Fresh Fruit and Vegetable Program helps make fruits and vegetables available to students free of charge, during the schoolday, in participating elementary schools. The program is a tool for reducing childhood obesity: It exposes schoolchildren to fresh produce that they otherwise might not have the opportunity to sample. http://www.fns.usda.gov/ffvp/fresh-fruit-and-vegetable-program

For further information, contact the Public Information Officer, Food and Nutrition Service, Department of Agriculture, 3101 Park Center Drive, Alexandria, VA 22302. Phone, 703-305-2286.

Food Safety

This mission area centers on the labeling and packaging, safety, and wholesomeness of the Nation's commercial supply of egg, poultry, and meat. It also contributes significantly to the President's Council on Food Safety and has helped coordinate a nationwide food safety strategic plan. http://www.usda.gov/wps/portal/usda/usdahome?navid=USDA_MISSION_AREAS

Food Safety and Inspection Service (FSIS)   The Food Safety and Inspection Service was established by the Secretary of Agriculture on June 17, 1981, pursuant to authority contained in 5 U.S.C. 301 and Reorganization Plan No. 2 of 1953 (5 U.S.C. app.). FSIS monitors the Nation's commercial supply of meat, poultry, and processed egg products. http://www.fsis.usda.gov/wps/portal/fsis/home

Meat, Poultry, and Processed Egg Products Inspection   FSIS is the public health regulatory agency in the U.S. Department of Agriculture that ensures commercial meat, poultry, and processed egg products are safe, wholesome, accurately labeled, and properly packaged. FSIS enforces the Federal Meat Inspection Act (FMIA), the Poultry Products Inspection Act (PPIA), and the Egg Products Inspection Act (EPIA), which require Federal inspection and regulation of meat, poultry, and processed egg products prepared for distribution in commerce for use as human food. FSIS is also responsible for administering the Humane Methods of Slaughter Act, which requires that livestock are handled and slaughtered humanely at the FSIS-inspected establishment.

FSIS administers FMIA, PPIA, and EPIA by developing and implementing data-driven regulations, including inspection, testing, and enforcement activities for the products under FSIS's jurisdiction. In addition to mandatory inspection of meat, poultry, and processed egg products, FSIS tests samples of these products for microbial and chemical residues to monitor trends for enforcement purposes and to understand, predict, and prevent contamination. FSIS also ensures that only meat, poultry, and processed egg products that meet U.S. requirements are imported into the United States, and it certifies meat, poultry, and processed egg products for export.

FSIS also monitors meat, poultry, and processed egg products throughout storage, distribution, and retail channels, and it ensures regulatory compliance to protect the public, including detention of products, voluntary product recalls, court-ordered seizures of products, administrative suspension and withdrawal of inspection, and referral of violations for criminal and civil prosecution. To protect against intentional contamination, the Agency conducts food defense activities, as well.

FSIS maintains a toll-free Meat and Poultry Hotline (phone, 888-674-6854; TTY, 800-256-7072) and chat feature to answer questions in English and Spanish about the safe handling of meat, poultry, and egg products. The Hotline's hours are weekdays, from 10 a.m. to 4 p.m., EST, year round. An extensive selection of food safety messages in English and Spanish is available at the same number at all hours of the day. Questions can also be submitted anytime to MPHotline.fsis@usda.gov.

"Ask Karen," an online virtual representative, provides answers to consumer questions on preventing foodborne illness, safe food handling and storage, and safe preparation of meat, poultry, and egg products (http://www.fsis.usda.gov/wps/portal/informational/askkaren). http://www.fsis.usda.gov

For further information, contact the Assistant Administrator, Office of Public Affairs and Consumer Education, Department of Agriculture, 1400 Independence Avenue SW., Washington, DC 20250. Phone, 202-720-3884.

Marketing and Regulatory Programs

The scope of the marketing and regulatory mission area includes marketing and regulatory programs other than those concerned with food safety. http://www.usda.gov/wps/portal/usda/usdahome?navid=USDA_MISSION_AREAS

Agricultural Marketing Service (AMS) The Agricultural Marketing Service was established by the Secretary of Agriculture on April 2, 1972, under the authority of Reorganization Plan No. 2 of 1953 (5 U.S.C. app.) and other authorities. The Service facilitates the fair and efficient marketing of U.S. agricultural products. It supports agriculture through a variety of programs: cotton and tobacco; dairy; fruit and vegetable; livestock, poultry, and seed; organic products; transportation and marketing, and science and technology. The Service's activities support American agriculture in the global marketplace and help ensure the availability of wholesome food. http://www.ams.usda.gov

Audit and Accreditation Services AMS audit and accreditation programs give producers and suppliers of agricultural products the opportunity to assure customers of their ability to provide consistent quality products and services. The AMS verifies their documented programs through independent, third-party audits. AMS audit and accreditation programs are voluntary and paid through hourly user-fees. http://www.ams.usda.gov/services/auditing

Commodity Purchasing The AMS purchases a variety of domestically produced and processed commodity food products through a competitive process involving approved vendors. The purchasing supports American agriculture by providing an outlet for surplus products and encouraging domestic consumption of domestic foods. The wholesome, high quality products, collectively called USDA Foods, are delivered to schools, food banks, and households across the country and constitute a vital component of the Nation's food safety net. http://www.ams.usda.gov/selling-food

Farmers Markets / Direct-to-Consumer Marketing The AMS regularly collects data and analyzes farmers market operations and other direct-to-consumer marketing outlets—Community Supported Agriculture, food hubs, on-farm markets—to help market managers, planners, and researchers better understand the effect of these outlets on food access and local economic development, and to help the public find sources of fresh, local food. http://www.ams.usda.gov/services/local-regional

Grades / Standards USDA grade shields, official seals, and labels are symbols of the quality and integrity of American agricultural products. Large-volume buyers such as grocery stores, military institutions, restaurants, and foreign governments benfit from the quality grades and standards because they serve as as a common "language" that simplifies business transactions. http://www.ams.usda.gov/AMSv1.0/standards

Grant Programs The AMS administers a series of grant programs that make over $100 million available to support a variety of agricultural activities, including the specialty crop industry and local and regional food system expansion. These grant programs improve domestic and international opportunities for growers and producers and help support rural America. http://www.ams.usda.gov/services/grants

Laboratory Testing and Approval Services The AMS oversees the National Science Laboratories (NSL), a fee-for-service lab network. NSL scientists and technicians conduct chemical, microbiological, and biomolecular analyses on food and agricultural commodities. The network provides testing services for AMS commodity programs, other USDA agencies, Federal and State agencies, research institutions, private sector food and agricultural industries, and the U.S. military. The AMS also approves or accredits labs to perform testing services in support of domestic and international trade. At the request of industry, other Federal agencies, or foreign governments, it develops and administers laboratory approval programs to verify that the analysis of food and agricultural products meet country or customer-specified requirements. http://www.ams.usda.gov/services/lab-testing

Marketing Agreements and Orders Marketing agreements and orders are initiated by industry to stabilize markets for dairy products, fruits, vegetables, and specialty crops. An agreement is binding only for handlers who sign the agreement. Marketing orders are a binding regulation for the entire industry in the specified geographical area, once the producers and the Secretary of Agriculture have approved it. http://www.ams.usda.gov/rules-regulations/moa

Market News Market News issues thousands of reports each year, providing the agricultural industry with important wholesale, retail, and shipping data. The reports give farmers, producers, and other agricultural businesses the information they need to evaluate market conditions, identify trends, make purchasing decisions, monitor price patterns, evaluate transportation equipment needs, and accurately assess movement. http://www.ams.usda.gov/market-news

National Organic Program The National Organic Program is a regulatory program housed within the AMS. It develops national standards for organically-produced agricultural products. The "USDA ORGANIC" seal means that a product met consistent and uniform standards. USDA organic regulations do not address food safety or nutrition. Organic production integrates cultural, biological, and mechanical practices to increase cycling of resources, biodiversity, and ecological balance. http://www.ams.usda.gov/about-ams/programs-offices/national-organic-program

Pesticide Data Program The Pesticide Data Program (PDP) monitors pesticide residue nationwide. It produces the most comprehensive pesticide residue database in the Nation. The PDP administers the sampling, testing, and reporting of pesticide residues on agricultural commodities in the U.S. food supply—with an emphasis on those commodities regularly consumed by infants and children. The AMS implements the program in cooperation with State agriculture departments and other Federal agencies. The Environmental Protection Agency relies on PDP data to assess dietary exposure, and Food and Drug Administration and other government experts use them for making informed decisions. http://www.ams.usda.gov/datasets/pdp

Plant Variety Protection Program The Plant Variety Protection Office protects the intellectual property of breeders of new seed and tuber varieties. Implementing the Plant Variety Protection Act, the Office examines new applications and grants certificates that protect varieties for 20 or 25 years. Certificate owners have exclusive rights to market and sell their varieties, manage the use of their varieties by other breeders, and benefit from legal protection of their work.

http://www.ams.usda.gov/services/plant-variety-protection

Regulatory Programs   The AMS administers several regulatory programs designed to protect producers, handlers, and consumers of agricultural commodities from financial loss or personal injury resulting from careless, deceptive, or fraudulent marketing practices. These regulatory programs encourage fair trading practices in the marketing of fruits and vegetables, and they require accuracy in seed labeling and in advertising. The AMS also enforces the Country of Origin Labeling law, which requires retailers— full-line grocery stores, supermarkets, club warehouse stores—to notify their customers with information regarding the source of certain foods. http://www.ams.usda.gov/rules-regulations

Research and Promotion Programs   The AMS monitors certain industry-sponsored research, promotion, and information programs authorized by Federal laws. These programs give farmers and processors a means to finance and operate various research, promotion, and information activities for agricultural products. http://www.ams.usda.gov/rules-regulations/research-promotion

Quality Grading / Inspections   Nearly 600 grade standards have been established for some 230 agricultural commodities to help buyers and sellers trade on agreed-upon quality levels. Standards are developed with assistance from individuals outside the Department, particularly from those involved with the industries directly affected. The AMS also participates in developing international commodity standards to facilitate trade. Grading and classing services are provided to certify the grade and quality of products. These grading services are provided to buyers and sellers of live cattle, swine, sheep, meat, poultry, eggs, rabbits, fruits, vegetables, tree nuts, peanuts, dairy products, tobacco, and other miscellaneous food products. Classing services are provided to buyers and sellers of cotton and cotton products. These services are mainly voluntary and are provided upon request and for a fee. The AMS is also responsible for testing seed. http://www.ams.usda.gov/services/grading

Transportation Research and Analysis   The Transportation Services Division (TSD) of the AMS serves as the definitive source for economic analysis of agricultural transportation. TSD experts support domestic and international agribusinesses by giving technical assistance and releasing reports and offering analysis. They track developments in truck, rail, barge, and ocean transportation and provide information on and analysis of these modes of moving food from farm to table, from port to market. http://www.ams.usda.gov/services/transportation-analysis

For further information, contact the Public Affairs Staff, Agricultural Marketing Service, Department of Agriculture, Room 3933, South Agriculture Building, Stop 0273, 1400 Independence Ave, SW., Washington, DC 20250. Phone, 202-720-8998.

Animal and Plant Health Inspection Service (APHIS)   [For the Animal and Plant Health Inspection Service statement of organization, see the Code of Federal Regulations, Title 7, Part 371]

The Animal and Plant Health Inspection Service was originally established in 1972 and reestablished by the Secretary of Agriculture on March 14, 1977, pursuant to authority contained in 5 U.S.C. 301 and Reorganization Plan No. 2 of 1953 (5 U.S.C. app.). The APHIS was established to conduct regulatory and control programs to protect and improve animal and plant health for the benefit of agriculture and the environment. In cooperation with State governments, industry stakeholders, and other Federal agencies, the APHIS works to prevent the entry and establishment of foreign animal and plant pests and diseases. It also regulates certain genetically engineered organisms and supports healthy international agricultural trade and exports of U.S. agricultural products. The agency also works to ensure the humane treatment of certain animals and carries out research and operational activities to mitigate damage caused by birds, rodents, and other wildlife. https://www.aphis.usda.gov/wps/portal/aphis/home

Animal Care   Animal Care upholds and enforces the Animal Welfare Act and the Horse Protection Act. The Animal Welfare Act requires that federally established standards of care and treatment be provided for certain warmblooded animals bred for commercial sale, used in research, transported commercially, or publicly exhibited. The Horse Protection Act seeks to end soring by preventing sored horses from participating in auctions, exhibitions, sales, and shows. The Center for Animal Welfare collaborates with other animal welfare entities to help the USDA build partnerships domestically and internationally, improve regulatory practices, and develop outreach, training, and educational resources. Animal Care's emergency response component provides national leadership on the safety and well-being of pets during disasters—supporting animal safety during emergencies is a significant factor in ensuring the well-being of pet owners. https://www.aphis.usda.gov/wps/portal/aphis/ourfocus/animalwelfare

Biotechnology Regulatory Services   To protect plant health, Biotechnology Regulatory Services implements APHIS regulations affecting the importation, movement, and field release of genetically engineered plants and certain other genetically engineered organisms that may pose a risk to plant health. The APHIS coordinates these responsibilities along with the other designated Federal agencies as part of the Federal coordinated framework for the regulation of biotechnology. https://www.aphis.usda.gov/wps/portal/aphis/ourfocus/biotechnology

International Services   APHIS protects the health and value of American agriculture and natural resources. Its International Services supports this mission in an international environment. The Services collaborate with foreign partners to control pests and diseases, facilitate safe agricultural trade, ensure effective and efficient management of internationally-based programs, and invest in international capacity-building with foreign counterparts to build technical and regulatory skills that prevent diseases and pests from spreading. https://www.aphis.usda.gov/wps/portal/aphis/ourfocus/internationalservices

Plant Protection and Quarantine   APHIS oversees Plant Protection and Quarantine. The program protects U.S. agriculture and natural resources against the entry, establishment, and spread of economically and environmentally significant pests. It also facilitates the safe trade of agricultural products. https://www.aphis.usda.gov/wps/portal/aphis/ourfocus/planthealth

Veterinary Services   Veterinary Services supports APHIS' efforts to protect and improve the health, quality, and marketability of the Nation's animals, animal products, and veterinary biologics. The Service is organized strategically into four sections: surveillance, preparedness, and response; national import export services; science, technology, and analysis; and program support services. https://www.aphis.usda.gov/wps/portal/aphis/ourfocus/animalhealth

Wildlife Services   Wildlife Services provides Federal leadership and expertise for resolving conflicts between wildlife and people to allow coexistence. It conducts program delivery, research, and other activities through regional and State offices, the National Wildlife Research Center and field stations, as well as through national programs. Contact the APHIS customer service call center for more information. Phone, 844-820-2234. https://www.aphis.usda.gov/wps/portal/aphis/ourfocus/wildlifedamage

For further information, contact Legislative and Public Affairs, Animal and Plant Health Inspection Service, Department of Agriculture, 1400 Independence Avenue SW., Washington, DC 20250. Phone, 202-799-7030.

Grain Inspection, Packers and Stockyards Administration (GIPSA)   The Grain Inspection, Packers and Stockyards Administration was established in 1994 to facilitate the marketing of livestock, poultry, meat, cereals, oilseeds, and related agricultural products, and to promote fair and competitive trading practices for the overall benefit of consumers and American agriculture. The Packers and Stockyards Program protects fair trade practices, financial integrity, and competitive markets for livestock, meat, and poultry. The Federal Grain Inspection Service facilitates the marketing of U.S. grains, oilseeds, and related agricultural products through its grain inspection and weighing system. The Service also maintains the integrity of the grain marketing system by developing unbiased grading standards and methods for assessing grain quality. http://www.gipsa.usda.gov

Inspection The United States Grain Standards Act requires most U.S. export grain to be inspected. At export port locations, GIPSA or State agencies that have been delegated authority by the Administrator carry out inspections. For domestic grain marketed at inland locations, the Administrator designates private and State agencies to provide official inspection services upon request. Both export and domestic services are provided on a fee-for-service basis. http://www.gipsa.usda.gov/fgis/inspectionservices.aspx

Methods Development GIPSA's methods development activities include applied research or tests to produce new or improved techniques for measuring grain quality. Examples include knowledge gained through the study of how to establish real-time grain inspection, develop reference methods in order to maintain consistency and standardization in the grain inspection system, as well as the comparison of different techniques for evaluation of end-use quality in wheat.

Packers and Stockyards Activities GIPSA prohibits deceptive, discriminatory, and unfair practices by market agencies, dealers, stockyards, packers, swine contractors, and live poultry dealers in the livestock, meat packing, and poultry industries. According to the provisions of the Packers and Stockyards Act, it fosters fair competition and ensures payment protection for growers and farmers through regulatory activities: investigating alleged violations of the act, auditing regulated entities, verifying the accuracy of scales, and monitoring industry trends to protect consumers and members of the livestock, meat, and poultry industries. The Administration also has certain responsibilities derived from the Truth-in-Lending and the Fair Credit Reporting Acts. GIPSA carries out the Secretary's responsibilities under section 1324 of the Food Security Act of 1985 pertaining to State-established central filing systems to prenotify buyers, commission merchants, and selling agents of security interests against farm products. GIPSA administers the section of the act commonly referred to as the "Clear Title" provision and certifies qualifying State systems. http://www.gipsa.usda.gov/psp/psp.aspx

Standardization Official inspections of grains, oilseeds, and other agricultural and processed commodities are based on established official U.S. standards. The inspections also rely on sound, proven, and standardized procedures, techniques, and equipment. The official standards and accompanying procedures, techniques, and equipment produce consistent test results and services, from elevator to elevator and State to State. http://www.gipsa.usda.gov/fgis/standardprocedures.aspx

Weighing GIPSA or State agencies that have been delegated authority the Administrator officially weigh U.S. export grain at port locations. For domestic grain marketed at inland locations, GIPSA or designated private or State agencies provide the weighing services. Weighing services are provided on a fee-for-service basis. http://www.gipsa.usda.gov/fgis/weighingservices.aspx

For further information, contact the Grain Inspection, Packers, and Stockyards Administration, Department of Agriculture, 1400 Independence Avenue SW., Washington, DC 20250. Phone, 202-720-0219.

Natural Resources and Environment

This mission area centers on stewardship of 75 percent of the Nation's total land area. The USDA's operating philosophy in this mission area places a premium on collaboration with diverse partners and on the health and sustainability of ecosystems to maximize stewardship of the Nation's natural resources. This approach ensures that the necessary requirements for maintaining healthy and sustainable systems are in balance with people's priorities and the products and services that they desire. http://www.usda.gov/wps/portal/usda/usdahome?navid=USDA_MISSION_AREAS

Forest Service (FS) [For the Forest Service statement of organization, see the Code of Federal Regulations, Title 36, Part 200.1]

In 1876, Congress created the Office of Special Agent in the Department of Agriculture to assess the condition of the forests in the United States. The Forest Service was created decades later by the Transfer Act of February 1, 1905 (16 U.S.C. 472), which transferred the Federal forest reserves and the responsibility for their management to the USDA from the Department of the Interior. The mission of the Forest Service is to achieve quality land management under the sustainable, multiple-use management concept to meet the diverse needs of people. The Service advocates a conservation ethic in promoting the health, productivity, diversity, and beauty of forests and associated lands; listens to people and responds to their diverse needs in making decisions; protects and manages the National Forests and Grasslands to best demonstrate the sustainable, multiple-use management concept; provides technical and financial assistance to State, tribal, and private forest landowners, encouraging them to become better stewards and quality land managers; helps cities and communities improve their natural environment by planting trees and caring for their forests; provides international technical assistance and scientific exchanges to sustain and enhance global resources and to encourage quality land management; assists States and communities in using the forests wisely to promote rural economic development and a quality rural environment; develops and disseminates scientific and technical knowledge that helps protect, manage, and improve use of forests and rangelands; and offers employment, training, and educational opportunities to the unemployed, underemployed, disadvantaged, elderly, and youth. http://www.fs.fed.us

Forest Research   The Service performs basic and applied research to develop the scientific information and technology needed to protect, manage, use, and sustain the natural resources of the Nation's forests and rangelands, including those on private and tribal lands. Its forest research strategy focuses on three major program components: understanding the structure and functions of forest and range ecosystems; understanding how people perceive and value the protection, management, and use of natural resources; and determining which protection, management, and utilization practices are most suitable for sustainable production and use of natural resources worldwide. http://www.fs.fed.us/research/research-topics

National Forest System   Using the principles of multiple-use and sustained

yield, the Service manages 154 National Forests, 20 National Grasslands, 1 tall grass prairie, and 8 national monuments on approximately 193 million acres of land in 44 States, the U.S. Virgin Islands, and Puerto Rico. The Nation's need for wood and paper products must be balanced against the other vital, renewable resources or benefits that the National Forests and Grasslands provide: recreation and natural beauty, wildlife habitat, livestock forage, and water supplies. As a guiding principle, the Service tries to achieve greatest good for the greatest number in the long run.

These lands are managed to promote resiliency against catastrophic wildfire, epidemics of disease and insect pests, erosion, and other threats. Burned areas receive emergency seeding treatment to prevent massive erosion and stream siltation. Roads and trails are built where needed to give the public access to outdoor recreation areas and provide scenic drives and hikes. Picnic, camping, skiing, water sport and other recreational areas feature facilities for public convenience and enjoyment. Vegetative management methods protect the land and streams, ensure rapid renewal of the forest, provide food and cover for wildlife and fish, and mitigate human impact on scenic and recreation assets. Local communities benefit from activities on National Forest lands. These lands also provide needed oil, gas, and minerals. Millions of livestock and game animals benefit from improved rangelands. The National Forests serve as a refuge for many species of endangered birds, animals, and fish. Some 34.6 million acres are set aside as wilderness and 175,000 acres as primitive areas where timber will not be harvested. http://www.fs.fed.us/managing-land/national-forests-grasslands

State and Private Forestry   The State and Private Forestry organization of the Forest Service reaches across the boundaries of National Forests to States, tribes, communities, and nonindustrial private landowners. The organization is the Federal leader in giving technical and financial assistance to landowners and resource managers to help sustain the Nation's forests and protect communities and the environment from wildland fires.

National priorities for State and private forestry promote four core actions: conserving and managing working forest landscapes for multiple values and uses, protecting forests from threats, enhancing public benefits from trees and forests, and increasing organizational effectiveness. The State and Private Forestry organization supports sustainable stewardship of non-Federal forest land nationwide, including 423 million acres of private forest land, 69 million acres of State forest land, 18 million acres of tribal forests, and over 130 million acres of urban and community forests. The organization offers leadership in wildland fire management, operations, methods development, risk mapping, forest products utilization, and advanced survey and monitoring, as well as geospatial technologies. http://www.fs.fed.us/spf

Natural Resources Conservation Service (NRCS) [For the Natural Resources Conservation Service statement of organization, see the Code of Federal Regulations, Title 7, Parts 600 and 601]

The Natural Resources Conservation Service, formerly known as the Soil Conservation Service, helps America's farmers, ranchers, and other private landowners develop and implement voluntary efforts to conserve and protect the Nation's natural resources. http://www.nrcs. usda.gov/wps/portal/nrcs/site/national/home

Agricultural Conservation Easement Program The Agricultural Conservation Easement Program helps conserve agricultural lands and wetlands by offering financial and technical assistance. Under the program's Agricultural Land Easements component, NRCS supports Indian tribes, State and local governments, and nongovernmental organizations in their efforts to protect working agricultural lands and to limit agricultural land use for nonagricultural purposes. Under the program's Wetlands Reserve Easements component, NRCS supports efforts to restore, protect, and enhance enrolled wetlands. http://www.nrcs.usda.gov/wps/portal/nrcs/main/national/programs/easements/acep

Agricultural Management Assistance Agricultural Management Assistance, by giving financial and technical assistance to agricultural producers, encourages them to incorporate conversation practices into their farming operations to improve water management and quality, to reduce erosion, and to mitigate risk through production diversification. The assistance supports producers' in their efforts to plant trees for windbreaks, construct irrigation structures, use integrated pest management, and transition to organic farming. NRCS administers the program's conservation components, while AMS and RMA handle the others. http://www.nrcs.usda.gov/wps/portal/nrcs/main/national/programs/financial/ama

Conservation Stewardship Program The Conservation Stewardship Program helps agricultural producers maintain and improve their existing conservation systems and adopt additional conservation practices that address resource concerns of high priority. Participants earn program payments for conservation performance: Payments are directly proportional to performance. The program offers two types of payments through 5-year contracts: annual payments for adopting new conservation practices and maintaining current ones, and supplemental payments for initiating a resource-conserving crop rotation. Producers may be able to renew a contract if they met the obligations of the initial contract and agree to achieve additional conservation goals. http://www.nrcs.usda.gov/wps/portal/nrcs/main/national/programs/financial/csp

Conservation Technical Assistance Conservation Technical Assistance makes conservation technology and the delivery system needed to achieve the benefits of a healthy and productive landscape available to land users. The program reduces the loss of soil from erosion; offers solutions for agricultural waste management, air quality, soil, and water conservation and quality problems; mitigates potential water, sedimentation, or drought damage; improves fish and wildlife habitat; assists others in facilitating changes in land use for natural resource protection and sustainability; and increases the long term sustainability of all lands—cropland, forestland, grazing lands, coastal lands, and developing or developed lands. Technical Assistance supports clients in their efforts to address concerns and problems and explore opportunities related to the use of natural resources. NRCS staff and the employees of other agencies or entities under the technical supervision of NRCS provide the assistance. http://www.nrcs.usda.gov/wps/portal/nrcs/main/national/programs/technical/cta

Emergency Watershed Protection Program The Emergency Watershed Protection Program safeguards lives and property in jeopardy due to sudden watershed impairment caused by natural disasters. Emergency assistance includes quickly establishing a protective plant cover on denuded land and stream banks, opening dangerously restricted channels, and repairing diversions and levees. To be eligible for assistance under this program, an emergency area does not need to be declared a national disaster area. NRCS may bear up to 75 percent of the construction cost of emergency measures. The remaining cost must come from local sources. Funding is subject to Congressional approval. http://www.nrcs.usda.gov/wps/portal/nrcs/main/national/programs/landscape/ewpp

Environmental Quality Incentives Program The Environmental Quality Incentives Program assists agricultural producers by offering contracts up to a maximum term of 10 years in length. These contracts provide financial assistance for planning and implementing conservation practices that address natural resource concerns and for improving air, animal, plant, soil, water, and related resources on agricultural land and nonindustrial private forestland. Sixty percent of the available funds are for conservation activities related to livestock production. The program also helps producers meet Federal, State, tribal and local environmental regulations. http://www.nrcs.usda.gov/wps/portal/nrcs/main/national/programs/financial/eqip

Healthy Forests Reserve Program The Healthy Forests Reserve Program helps landowners restore, enhance, and protect forestland resources on private lands through easements, 30-year contracts, and 10-year cost-share agreements. The program supports the efforts of landowners to promote the recovery of endangered or threatened species, increase plant and animal biodiversity, and improve carbon sequestration. http://www.nrcs.usda.gov/wps/portal/nrcs/main/national/programs/easements/forests

National Cooperative Soil Survey The National Cooperative Soil Survey, a nationwide partnership of Federal, State, regional, and local agencies and private entities and institutions, works cooperatively to investigate, inventory, document, classify, interpret, disseminate, and publish soil information. It informs the public about the uses and capabilities of local soils. The published survey for a county or other designated area includes maps and interpretations that are essential for farm planning, other private land use decisions, and governmental policy development and resource planning. http://www.nrcs.usda.gov/wps/portal/nrcs/main/soils/survey/partnership/ncss

Plant Materials Program The Plant Materials Program selects conservation plants and develops innovative planting technology for addressing natural resource challenges and maintaining healthy and productive farms and ranches. It focuses on using plants as a natural solution for conservation issues and reestablishing ecosystem function; collects, selects, and releases grasses, legumes, wildflowers, trees and shrubs, working with commercial, private, public, and tribal partners and land managers to apply new plant-based conservation methods; provides plant materials and new applied technologies for national initiatives; offers plant solutions to fight invasive species, heal lands damaged by natural disasters, reduce drought effects, promote air and water quality, and produce alternative energy; and assists Native American tribes with producing and protecting culturally significant plants. http://www.nrcs.usda.gov/wps/portal/nrcs/main/plantmaterials/about

Regional Conservation Partnership Program The Regional Conservation Partnership Program promotes coordination between NRCS and its partners for the delivery of conservation assistance to producers and landowners. NRCS assists producers through partnership agreements and program contracts or easement agreements. The program combines the authorities of four previous programs: the Cooperative Conservation

Partnership Initiative, the Agricultural Water Enhancement, the Chesapeake Bay Watershed, and the Great Lakes Basin Programs. http://www.nrcs.usda.gov/wps/portal/nrcs/main/national/programs/farmbill/rcpp

Small Watershed Program   The Small Watershed Program relies on local government sponsors to help participants solve natural resource and related economic problems on a watershed basis. Projects include efforts to protect watersheds, prevent floods, control erosion and sedimentation, improve water supply and quality, enhance fish and wildlife habitat, create and restore wetlands, and support public recreation in watersheds of 250,000 or fewer acres. The program offers both financial and technical assistance. Through the Small Watershed Program, NRCS maps flood hazard areas, solves local flooding problems, evaluates potential greenbelts along streams, develops guidelines for erosion control and runoff management, helps farmers control erosion in high priority watersheds, and improves the water quality of ground water and water bodies. http://www.nrcs.usda.gov/wps/portal/nrcs/detail/nd/programs/?cid=nrcs141p2_001682

Snow Survey and Water Supply Forecasts   The Snow Survey is conducted by NRCS to make information on future water supplies available to residents of Alaska and Western States. At more than 1,800 mountain sites, NRCS personnel collect and analyze data on snowpack depth and its water equivalent to estimate annual water availability, spring runoff, and summer streamflows. Federal and State agencies, organizations, and individuals rely on these forecasts for agricultural production, fish and wildlife management, municipal and industrial water supply, urban development, flood control, recreation power generation, and water quality management. The National Weather Service includes the forecasts in their river forecasting function. http://www.nrcs.usda.gov/wps/portal/nrcs/main/national/water/snowsurvey

Watershed Surveys and Planning   The Watershed Surveys and Planning program supports Federal, State, and local agencies and tribal governments in their efforts to protect watersheds from damage caused by erosion, floodwater, and sediment and to conserve and develop water and land resources. The program addresses a number of resource concerns: agricultural drought problems, municipal and industrial water needs, rural development, upstream flood damages, water quality and conservation, wetland and water storage capacity, and water needs for fish, wildlife, and forest-based industries. http://www.nrcs.usda.gov/wps/portal/nrcs/main/national/programs/landscape/wsp

Research, Education and Economics

This mission area centers on creating, applying, and transferring knowledge and technology to make available affordable food and fiber, ensure food safety and nutrition, and support rural development and people's natural resource needs. The creation, application, and transfer of this knowledge and technology are achieved by conducting integrated national and international research and by providing information, education, and statistical programs and services. http://www.usda.gov/wps/portal/usda/usdahome?navid=USDA_MISSION_AREAS

Agricultural Research Service (ARS)   The Agricultural Research Service conducts research on agricultural problems of high national priority. It provides information access and dissemination to ensure high-quality, safe food and other agricultural products; to assess the nutritional needs of Americans; to sustain a competitive agricultural economy; to enhance the natural resource base and the environment; and to promote economic opportunities for rural citizens, communities, and society as a whole.

Research activities are carried out at 96 domestic locations, including Puerto Rico and the U.S. Virgin Islands, and five overseas locations. ARS conducts much of this research in cooperation with partners in State universities and experiment stations, other Federal agencies, and private organizations. National Programs, headquartered in Beltsville, MD, plans and coordinates the research programs, and five area offices carry out the day-to-day management of the respective programs for specific field locations.

The National Agricultural Library, the primary resource in the United States for information on food, agriculture, and natural resources, serves as an electronic gateway to a widening array of scientific literature, printed text, and agricultural images. The library supports the USDA and a broad customer base of policymakers, agricultural specialists, research scientists, and the general public. It works with other agricultural libraries and institutions to advance open and democratic access specifically to the Nation's agricultural knowledge and to agricultural information in general. http://www.nal.usda.gov

For further information, contact the Agricultural Research Service, Department of Agriculture, 1400 Independence Avenue SW., Washington, DC 20250. Phone, 202-720-3656. Fax, 202-720-5427.

The National Institute of Food and Agriculture (NIFA)   The National Institute of Food and Agriculture invests in and advances agricultural education, extension, and research to address societal challenges. The Institute works with academic institutions, land-grant universities, and other science organizations nationwide. With its partners and customers, NIFA promotes a global system of research, extension, and higher education in the food and agricultural sciences and related environmental and human sciences for the good of people, communities, and the Nation.

The Institute collaborates with scientists, policymakers, experts, and educators in organizations worldwide to find innovative solutions to pressing local and global problems. Scientific discovery and application advance the competitiveness of American agriculture, strengthen the U.S. economy, make the Nation's food supply safer, improve the nutrition and well-being of American citizens, sustain natural resources and the environment, and build energy independence. Partnering with other Federal science agencies, NIFA also makes important contributions to science policy decisionmaking. http://nifa.usda.gov

For further information, contact the Communications Staff, The National Institute of Food and Agriculture , Department of Agriculture, 1400 Independence Avenue SW., Washington, DC 20250-2207. Phone, 202-720-4651. Fax, 202-690-0289.

Economic Research Service (ERS)   The Service informs and strengthens public and private decisionmaking on economic and policy issues affecting agriculture, food, rural development, and the environment. ERS also serves as a primary source of economic information and research in the USDA.

Using a variety of means, ERS disseminates economic information and research results. It produces agency-published research reports, economic briefs, data products, and market analysis and outlook reports. "Amber Waves," its award-winning online magazine features articles on the economics of food, farming, natural resources, and rural America (www.ers. usda.gov/amber-waves). The ERS Web site allows access to all agency products, and it connects users directly with ERS analysts. The agency delivers oral briefings, written staff analyses, and congressionally mandated studies to executive and legislative branch policymakers and program administrators. Its experts also write articles for professional journals and present papers at academic conferences and meetings. http://www.ers. usda.gov

For further information, contact the Information Services Division, Economic Research Service, Department of Agriculture, 1400 Independence Avenue SW., Washington, DC 20250. Phone, 202-694-5100. Fax, 202-245-4781.

National Agricultural Statistics Service (NASS)   The National Agricultural Statistics Service prepares estimates and reports on production, supply, price, chemical use, and other items necessary for the orderly operation of the U.S. agricultural economy.

NAAS reports include statistics on field crops, fruits and vegetables, dairy, cattle, hogs, sheep, poultry, aquaculture, and related commodities or processed products. Estimates concern farm numbers, farm production expenditures, agricultural chemical use, prices received by farmers for products sold, prices paid for commodities and services, indexes of prices received and paid, parity prices, farm employment, and farm wage rates.

NASS prepares these estimates through a complex system of sample surveys of producers, processors, buyers, and others associated with agriculture. Information is gathered by mail, electronic data reporting, telephone, and personal interviews.

The Service conducts the Census of Agriculture, which is taken every 5 years and provides comprehensive data on the agricultural economy down to the county level. It also conducts follow-on studies on aquaculture, irrigation, horticultural energy, and organic agriculture.

NASS performs reimbursable survey work and statistical consulting services for other Federal and State agencies. It also helps other countries develop agricultural data systems by offering technical assistance. http://www.nass.usda.gov

For further information, contact the Customer Service Center, National Agricultural Statistics Service, Department of Agriculture, 1400 Independence Avenue SW., Washington, DC 20250-2000. Phone, 202-720-3878.

Rural Development

The rural development mission area centers on increasing the economic opportunities of rural Americans and improving their quality of life. To achieve these goals, the USDA creates and fosters cooperative relationships among Government, industry, and communities. As a capital investment bank, the USDA provides financing for rural housing and community facilities, business and cooperative development, telephone and high-speed Internet access, and electric, water, and sewer infrastructure. Approximately 3,400 employees in 47 State offices and 477 field offices administer rural development loan and grant programs at the local level. http://www.usda.gov/wps/portal/usda/usdahome?navid=USDA_MISSION_AREAS

Advanced Biofuel Repayment Program   The program provides payments to producers to support and expand production of advanced biofuels refined from sources other than corn kernel starch. http://www.rd.usda.gov/programs-services/advanced-biofuel-payment-program

Biorefinery, Renewable Chemical, and Biobased Product Manufacturing Assistance Program   This program assists in the development, construction, and retrofitting of new and emerging technologies for developing advanced biofuels, renewable chemicals, and biobased product manufacturing by giving loan guarantees. http://www.rd.usda.gov/programs-services/biorefinery-renewable-chemical-and-biobased-product-manufacturing-assistance

Business and Industry Guaranteed Loan Program   This program creates jobs and stimulates the rural economy by financially backing rural businesses. It bolsters the existing private credit structure through the guaranteeing of loans for rural businesses, allowing private lenders to increase the credit that they extend. Borrowers use loan proceeds for working capital, machinery and equipment, buildings, real estate, and certain types of debt refinancing. A borrower may be a cooperative organization, corporation, partnership, nonprofit corporation, Native American tribe, federally recognized tribal group, public body, or individual. http://www.rd.usda.gov/programs-services/business-industry-loan-guarantees

Cooperative Programs   USDA Cooperative Programs is the Nation's major source for information on cooperatives. Its library of more than 150 co-op publications—many of which are available in hardcopy, as well as online—range from co-op primers, such as "Co-ops 101," to reports on technical topics, such as "Tax Law for Cooperatives," to reports focusing on co-op economic theory, such as "The Nature of the Cooperative." These publications may be accessed on the "Publications for Cooperatives" Web page. http://www.rd.usda.gov/programs-services/all-programs/cooperative-programs

Delta Health Care Services Grant Program   This program provides financial assistance to meet ongoing health needs in the Delta Region through cooperation among health care professionals, institutions of higher education, research institutions, and others in the Delta Region. http://www.rd.usda.gov/programs-services/delta-health-care-services-grants

Intermediary Relending Program   This program provides capital to rural areas through low-interest and direct loans made to nonprofit corporations, public agencies, Native American groups, and certain corporations (intermediaries). These intermediaries establish revolving loan funds so they can relend the money to businesses in economically and socially disadvantaged rural communities. The process creates a source of capital that promotes job growth and economic development. http://www.rd.usda.gov/programs-services/intermediary-relending-program

Repowering Assistance Program This program funds up to 50 percent of the total eligible costs for biorefineries to install renewable biomass systems for heating and power or to produce new energy from renewable biomass. http://www.rd.usda.gov/programs-services/repowering-assistance-program

Rural Business Development Grant Program This program provides grants for rural projects that promote small and emerging business development, business incubators, employment, and related adult education programs. It also provides grants for sustainable economic development in rural communities with exceptional needs. Recipients use the grants to fund community- and technology-based economic development projects, feasibility studies, leadership and entrepreneur training, rural business incubators, and long-term business strategic planning. Eligible organizations include Native American tribes, nonprofit corporations, and rural public entities. http://www.rd.usda.gov/programs-services/rural-business-development-grants

Rural Business-Cooperative Service To meet business credit needs in underserved rural areas, USDA's Rural Business-Cooperative Service provides loan guarantees, direct loans, and grants to rural businesses, cooperatives, farmers, and ranchers, often in partnership with private sector lenders. The following is a list and description of USDA's Rural Development business and cooperative programs. http://www.rd.usda.gov/about-rd/agencies/rural-business-cooperative-service

Rural Cooperative Development Grant Program This program improves rural economic conditions by assisting individuals and businesses in the startup, expansion or operational improvement of rural cooperatives and other mutually-owned businesses through Cooperative Development Centers. http://www.rd.usda.gov/programs-services/rural-cooperative-development-grant-program

Rural Economic Development (RED) Loan and Grant Program The RED Loan and Grant programs provide funding to rural projects through local utility organizations. Under the loan program, USDA gives zero-interest loans that local utilities pass through to local businesses for projects that create and retain employment in rural areas. Under the grant program, USDA gives grant funds to local utility organizations that use them to establish revolving loan funds. http://www.rd.usda.gov/programs-services/rural-economic-development-loan-grant-program

Rural Energy for America Program Grant recipients assist rural small businesses and agricultural producers by conducting and promoting energy audits and assisting in the development of renewable energy. http://www.rd.usda.gov/programs-services/rural-energy-america-program-energy-audit-renewable-energy-development-assistance

Rural Housing Programs USDA Rural Development improves the quality of life in rural America. Its Rural Housing Service offers loans, grants, and loan guarantees to support essential services such as housing, economic development, health care, first-responder equipment and personnel, and water, electric and communications infrastructure. It also helps rural residents buy or rent safe and affordable housing, and make home repairs to improve safety and to create healthier living environments. http://www.rd.usda.gov/about-rd/agencies/rural-housing-service

Rural Microentrepreneur Assistance Program This program makes loans and gives grants to Microenterprise Development Organizations. These organizations then provide microloans for microenterprise startups and growth through a rural microloan revolving fund. They also offer training and technical assistance to microloan borrowers and microentrepreneurs. http://www.rd.usda.gov/programs-services/rural-microentrepreneur-assistance-program

Rural Utilities Programs USDA Rural Development strengthens rural economies and makes life better for Americans living in rural areas. Its Rural Utilities Service administers programs that provide infrastructure or infrastructure improvements to nonurban communities. These programs include water and waste treatment and electric power and telecommunications services. Utilities programs connect residents to the global community and its economy by increasing access to broadband and 21st-century telecommunications services, funding sustainable renewable energy development and conservation, financing reliable and affordable electric systems, working to integrate electric smart grid technologies, and developing reliable and affordable rural water and wastewater systems. http://www.rd.usda.gov/about-rd/agencies/rural-utilities-service

Socially-Disadvantaged Groups Grant Program   This program gives technical assistance to small socially-disadvantaged agricultural producers in rural areas. http://www.rd.usda.gov/programs-services/socially-disadvantaged-groups-grant

Value-Added Producer Grant Program   This program helps agricultural producers engage in value-added activities related to the processing and marketing of bio-based, value-added products. The program is designed to generate new products, create and expand marketing opportunities, and increase producer income. http://www.rd.usda.gov/programs-services/value-added-producer-grants

For further information, contact the Rural Development Legislative and Public Affairs Staff, Department of Agriculture, Stop 0705, 1400 Independence Avenue SW., Washington, DC 20250-0320. Phone, 202-690-0498.

Sources of Information

Ask the Expert   This tool helps Web site visitors locate the answers to their USDA-related questions. http://www.usda.gov/wps/portal/usda/usdahome?navid=ASK_EXPERT2

A–Z Index   The USDA Web site has a topical index that is arranged in alphabetical order. http://www.usda.gov/wps/portal/usda/usdahome?navid=AZ_INDEX

Blog   The USDA Web site features a blog that includes contributions on conservation, energy, food and nutrition, forestry, knowing your farmer and your food, rural development, and other topics. http://blogs.usda.gov

Business Opportunities   Marketing to the USDA can be a daunting task. To assist

businessmen and women who seek to sell their products and services to the agency, the USDA has collected all of the necessary information and packaged it in one place—in the "Doing Business with USDA Kit" (2005 edition). http://www.dm.usda.gov/procurement/business/index.htm

The USDA awards over 50 percent of eligible contracting dollars to small businesses nationwide. Information on contracting or subcontracting opportunities, attending small business outreach events, or how to do business with the USDA is available on the "Office of Small and Disadvantaged Business Utilization" Web site. Phone, 202-720-7117. http://www.dm.usda.gov/smallbus/index.php

Career Opportunities   For information on vacant positions within the USDA and opportunities for students, recent graduates, and veterans, visit the "Careers and Jobs" Web page. http://www.usda.gov/wps/portal/usda/usdahome?navid=CAREERS

In 2016, the USDA ranked 9th among 18 large agencies in the Partnership for Public Service's Best Places To Work Agency Rankings. http://bestplacestowork.org/BPTW/rankings/detail/AG00

Freedom of Information Act (FOIA)   Departmental Management oversees the USDA's FOIA program. Twenty-one USDA FOIA officers at the mission area and agency levels work to increase Government transparency through proactive disclosures and the use of technology. http://www.dm.usda.gov/foia

Agency reading rooms are updated frequently and contain commonly requested records. Information seekers should visit the relevant reading rooms before submitting a FOIA request. http://www.dm.usda.gov/foia/agencyfoia.htm

The FOIA public access link (PAL) is a web portal that allows information seekers to create and submit a FOIA request and to check its status. Registration, which requires creating a user name and password, is the first step for using PAL. https://efoia-pal.usda.gov/palMain.aspx

Glossary   The USDA maintains a glossary of agency acronyms. http://www.usda.gov/wps/portal/usda/usdahome?navid=glossary#top

Newsroom   Announcements, factsheets, reports, and statements are accessible online. http://www.usda.gov/wps/portal/usda/usdahome?navid=NEWSROOM

Open Government   The USDA supports the Open Government initiative by promoting the principles of collaboration, participation, and transparency. http://www.usda.gov/wps/portal/usda/usdahome?navid=USDA_OPEN

Organic Agriculture   The USDA is committed to increasing organic agriculture. It operates many programs that serve the growing organic sector. The USDA Organic Seal, which has been in use nearly 15 years, is a leading global standard. Visit the "Organic Agriculture" Web pages to learn more. http://www.usda.gov/wps/portal/usda/usdahome?navid=organic-agriculture

Instructions for becoming a certified organic operation are available online. https://www.ams.usda.gov/services/organic-certification/faq-becoming-certified

To receive "USDA Organic Insider" updates via email, use the online subscription form. https://visitor.r20.constantcontact.com/manage/optin/ea?v=001tanuLSmJHqsq1D840Z7eyw%3D%3D

Organizational Chart   The USDA's organizational chart is available in Portable Document Format (PDF) for viewing and downloading. https://www.usda.gov/sites/default/files/documents/usda-organization-chart.pdf

Plain Language   In support of the Plain Writing Act of 2010, USDA editors and writers strive to provide the public with information that is clear, understandable, and useful in forms, instructions, letters, notices, and publications. If a USDA document or content on the Department's Web site is unclear or difficult to understand, contact the USDA via email. http://www.usda.gov/wps/portal/usda/usdahome?navid=PLAIN_WRITING | Email: plainlanguage@osec.usda.gov

Program Discrimination   The Office of the Assistant Secretary for Civil Rights investigates and resolves complaints of discrimination in programs operated or assisted by the USDA. Information on what to include in a letter of complaint is available online. For information on the discrimination complaint process, contact the information research service in the Office of the Assistant Secretary. Phone, 202-260-1026 or 866-632-9992. Federal Relay Service, 800-877-8339 (English) or 800-845-6136 (Spanish). https://www.ascr.usda.gov/filing-program-discrimination-complaint-usda-customer | Email: CR-INFO@ascr.usda.gov

Reports   Agency reports, data, and forecasts and outlooks are accessible online. http://www.usda.gov/wps/portal/usda/usdahome?navid=AGENCY_REPORTS

Site Map   The Web site map allows visitors to look for specific topics or to browse for topics that align with their interests. http://www.usda.gov/wps/portal/usda/usdahome?navtype=FT&navid=SITE_MAP

Snarge   Birds and other animals occasionally collide with airborne aircraft and planes moving on the ground. These collisions are called wildlife strikes, and snarge is the remaining residue after impact. To learn about efforts to reduce wildlife strikes, visit the Animal and Plant Health Inspection Service's (APHIS) wildlife strike Web page. https://www.aphis.usda.gov/aphis/ourfocus/wildlifedamage/programs/SA_Airport/CT_Wildlife_strike

Watch the USDA's video to see how bird parts and snarge are collected, reported, shipped, and identified. https://www.youtube.com/watch?v=_OhJXexmmTg&list=PLF1BE3AC34367E99E

Social Media   The USDA tweets announcements, events, and other newsworthy items on Twitter. https://twitter.com/usda

Speakers   Contact the nearest USDA office or county extension agent. In the District of Columbia, contact the Office of Communications, U.S. Department of Agriculture, 1400 Independence Avenue SW., Washington, DC 20250. Phone, 202-720-4623. http://www.usda.gov/wps/portal/usda/usdahome?navid=OC_MEDIA_COMMS

Whistleblower Hotline   To file a complaint of alleged improprieties—employee misconduct, conflicts of interest, criminal activity, mismanagement or wasteful use of funds, workplace violence—visit the "OIG Hotline" Web page and use the "Submit a Complaint" feature. Or, contact a regional office or the Office of the Inspector General, U.S. Department of Agriculture, P.O. Box 23399, Washington, DC 20026. Phone, 800-424-9121 or 202-690-1622.

TDD, 202-690-1202. Fax, 202-690-2474. http://www.usda.gov/oig/hotline.htm. http://www.usda.gov/wps/portal/usda/usdahome?navid=CONTACT_US

For further information concerning the Department of Agriculture, contact the Office of Communications, Department of Agriculture, 1400 Independence Avenue SW., Washington, DC 20250. Phone, 202-720-4623.

DEPARTMENT OF COMMERCE

Fourteenth Street and Constitution Avenue NW., Washington, DC 20230
Phone, 202-482-2000. Internet, http://www.doc.gov

Secretary of Commerce	WILBUR ROSS
Deputy Secretary	BRUCE H. ANDREWS
Assistant Secretary, Administration / Chief Financial Officer	ELLEN HERBST
Assistant Secretary, Legislative and Intergovernmental Affairs	STEVEN M. HARO
Chief Information Officer	STEVE COOPER
Director, Office of Business Liaison	THEODORE JOHNSTON
Director, Office of Policy and Strategic Planning	JOHN RATLIFF
Director, Office of Public Affairs	MARNI GOLDBERG
Director, Office of the Executive Secretariat	JAMES SLATTERY
Director, Office of White House Liaison	LAUREN LEONARD
General Counsel	KELLY R. WELSH
Inspector General	TODD J. ZINSER

The Department of Commerce promotes the Nation's domestic and international trade, economic growth, and technological advancement by fostering free enterprise worldwide, supporting fair trade, compiling social and economic statistics, protecting Earth's physical resources, granting patents and registering trademarks, and assisting small and minority-owned businesses.

The Department of Commerce was designated as such by act of March 4, 1913 (15 U.S.C. 1501). The act reorganized the Department of Commerce and Labor, created by act of February 14, 1903 (15 U.S.C. 1501), by transferring labor activities into a new, separate Department of Labor.

Office of the Secretary

Secretary   The Secretary is responsible for the administration of all functions and authorities assigned to the Department of Commerce and for advising the President on Federal policy and programs affecting the industrial and commercial segments of the national economy. The Secretary is served by the offices of Deputy Secretary, Inspector General, General Counsel, and the Assistant Secretaries of Administration, Legislative and Intergovernmental Affairs, and Public Affairs. Other offices whose public purposes are widely administered are detailed below. https://www.commerce.gov/office-secretary

Business Liaison   The Office of Business Liaison directs the business community to the offices and policy experts who can best respond to their needs by promoting proactive, responsive, and effective outreach programs and relationships with the business community. It also informs the Secretary and Department officials of the critical issues facing the business community, informs the business community of Department and administration initiatives and priorities, as well as information regarding Department resources, policies, and programs, and provides general assistance to the business community. https://www.commerce.gov/os/office-business-liaison

For further information, call 202-482-1360.

Sources of Information

Business Opportunities   Contact the Office of Small and Disadvantaged Business Utilization. Phone, 202-482-1472. http://www.osec.doc.gov/osdbu

DEPARTMENT OF COMMERCE

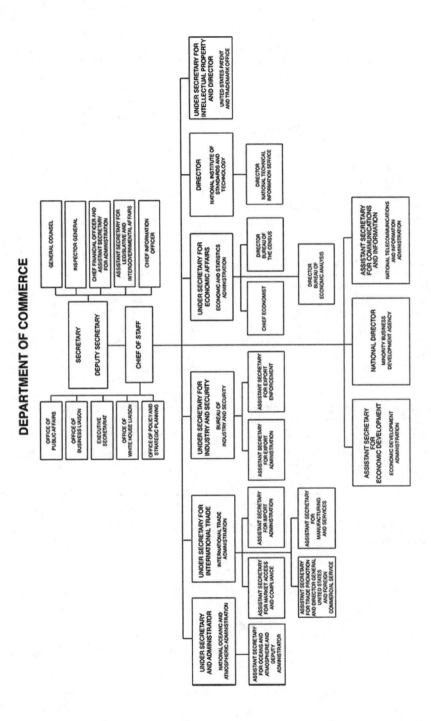

Data Age and sex and citizenship data are available online and from the Personal Census Search Unit, Bureau of the Census, National Processing Center, P.O. Box 1545, Jeffersonville, IN 47131. Phone, 812-218-3046. https://www.census.gov/population/age. https://www.census.gov/programs-surveys/acs/library/keywords/citizenship.html?cssp=SERP

Economic Development Information The Economic Development Administration maintains a clearinghouse for economic development information on its Web site. http://www.eda.gov

Career Opportunities For information on internships and career opportunities throughout the Department, visit the "Career Opportunities and Internships" Web page. https://www.commerce.gov/page/career-opportunities-and-internships

Environment The National Oceanic and Atmospheric Administration conducts research and gathers data on the atmosphere, oceans, space, and Sun, and it applies this knowledge to science and public service: warning of dangerous weather, charting seas and skies, guiding the use and protection of ocean and coastal resources, and improving stewardship of the environment. For more information, contact the Office of Communications, National Oceanic and Atmospheric Administration, Room 6013, Fourteenth Street and Constitution Avenue NW., Washington, DC 20230. Phone, 202-482-6090. Fax, 202-482-3154. http://www.noaa.gov

Inspector General Hotline The Office of Inspector General promotes economy, efficiency, and effectiveness and prevents and detects fraud, waste, abuse, and mismanagement in departmental programs and operations. To file a complaint, contact the Hotline, Inspector General, Complaint Intake Unit, Mail Stop 7886, 1401 Constitution Avenue, NW., Washington, DC 20230. Phone, 202-482-2495 or 800-424-5197. TTD, 202-482-5923 or 856-860-6950. Fax, 855-569-9235. http://www.oig.doc.gov | Email: hotline@oig.doc.gov

Publications The Department's "Find Data" Web page features recent releases of key economic indicators and the "Commerce Data Hub," which allows the general public to access an abundance of data. The titles of selected publications are noted in the appropriate sections below dealing with the operating units responsible for their issuance. These publications and others are announced in the weekly "Business Service Checklist": Contact the Government Publishing Office's Superintendent of Documents. Phone, 202-512-1800. https://www.commerce.gov/economicindicators. https://www.commerce.gov/os/office-public-affairs | Email: publicaffairs@doc.gov

For further information concerning the Department of Commerce, contact the Office of Public Affairs, Department of Commerce, Fourteenth Street and Constitution Avenue NW., Room 5040, Washington, DC 20230. Phone, 202-482-3263.

Bureau of Industry and Security

Department of Commerce, Washington, DC 20230
Phone, 202-482-2721. Internet, http://www.bis.doc.gov.

Under Secretary, Industry and Security	ERIC L. HIRSCHHORN
Deputy Under Secretary, Industry and Security	DANIEL O. HILL
Assistant Secretary, Export Administration	KEVIN J. WOLF
Assistant Secretary, Export Enforcement	DAVID W. MILLS

[For the Bureau of Industry and Security statement of organization, see the Federal Registers of June 7, 1988, 53 FR 20881, and April 26, 2002, 67 FR 20630]

The Bureau of Industry and Security (BIS) advances U.S. national security, foreign policy, and economic objectives by ensuring an effective export control and treaty compliance system and promoting continued U.S. strategic technology leadership. BIS activities include regulating the export of sensitive goods and technologies in an effective and efficient manner; enforcing export control, antiboycott, and public safety laws; cooperating with and assisting other countries on export control and strategic trade issues; assisting U.S. industry to comply with international arms control agreements; monitoring the viability of the U.S. defense industrial base; evaluating the effects on national security of foreign investments in U.S. companies; and supporting continued U.S. technology leadership in industries that are essential to national security. http://www.bis.doc.gov/index.php/about-bis

Export Administration   The Office of the Assistant Secretary for Export Administration is responsible for export licenses, treaty compliance, treaty obligations relating to weapons of mass destruction, and the defense industrial and technology base. The Office regulates the export of dual-use items requiring licenses for national security, nonproliferation, foreign policy, and short supply; ensures that approval or denial of license applications is consistent with economic and security concerns; promotes an understanding of export control regulations within the business community; represents the Department in interagency and international forums relating to export controls, particularly in multilateral regimes; monitors the availability of industrial resources of national defense; analyzes the impact of export controls on strategic industries; and assesses the security consequences of certain foreign investments. http://www.bis.doc.gov/index.php/regulations/export-administration-regulations-ear

Export Enforcement   The Office of the Assistant Secretary for Export Enforcement enforces dual-use export controls. This enables exporters to take advantage of legal export opportunities while ensuring that illegal exports will be detected and either prevented or investigated and sanctioned. The Office also ensures prompt, aggressive action against restrictive trade practices; and conducts cooperative enforcement activities on an international basis. Export Enforcement also enforces U.S. antiboycott laws and regulations by advising U.S. exporters on potential prohibited requests contained in foreign contracts; investigating violations such as the furnishing of boycott-related information, refusing to deal with blacklisted businesses; and pursuing criminal and administrative sanctions for violations.

Contact information for the nine export enforcement field offices is available on the "Investigations" Web page. http://www.bis.doc.gov/index.php/enforcement/oee/investigations

Management and Policy Coordination   The Management and Policy Coordination (MPC) unit establishes and evaluates the Bureau's overall policy agenda, priorities, goals, unit objectives, and key metrics. MPC performs oversight of program operations and expenditures; executes or supervises the President's Management Agenda; and adjudicates appeals of licensing and enforcement decisions as part of an extended legal process involving administrative law judges and the Office of General Counsel. MPC provides guidance and coordination for the Bureau's participation in the Export Control and Related Border Security Assistance Program, which provides technical assistance to strengthen the export and transit control systems of nations that are identified as potential locations for the exporting of weapons of mass destruction, missile delivery systems, or the commodities, technologies, and equipment that can be used to design and build them.

Sources of Information

Business Information   U.S. business information—export news, updates to Export Administration Regulations, export license and enforcement information, compliance and training information, Bureau program information, e-FOIA information, export seminar event schedules, and Denied Persons List information—is available on the Bureau's Web site. http://www.bis.doc.gov/index.php/about-bis/newsroom

Employment   BIS career opportunities are posted on USAJobs, a free web-based job board that serves as the Federal Government's official source of Federal

job listings and employment opportunity information. https://my.usajobs.gov
Enforcement   For enforcement-related questions, contact the partnership-in-security hotline. Phone, 800-424-2980. http://www.bis.doc.gov/index.php/component/rsform/form/14-reporting-violations-form?task=forms.edit
Outreach / Education   The Outreach and Educational Services Division has offices in Washington, DC (phone, 202-482-4811); Irvine, CA (phone, 949-660-0144); and San Jose, CA (phone, 408-998-8806). http://www.bis.doc.gov/index.php/program-offices
Publications   Publications available on the Bureau's Web site include the BIS's Annual Report to Congress, the guidance on the Commerce Department's Reexport Controls, and the Exporter User Manual and Licensing FAQ. http://www.bis.doc.gov/index.php/about-bis/newsroom/publications. http://www.bis.doc.gov/index.php/about-bis/newsroom
Rules   Subscribers to the Export Administration Regulations can stay informed of the latest rules. Subscriptions typically cost $199 per year. Phone, 301-208-0700 (ext. 112). http://www.bis.doc.gov/index.php/regulations/order-a-hard-copy-of-the-ear | Email: pubs@ocr-inc.com. http://www.bis.doc.gov/index.php/about-bis/contact-bis

For further information, contact the Bureau of Industry and Security, Office of Public Affairs, Room 3895, Fourteenth Street and Constitution Avenue NW., Washington, DC 20230. Phone, 202-482-2721.

Economic Development Administration
Department of Commerce, Washington, DC 20230
Phone, 202-482-5081. Internet, http://www.eda.gov

Assistant Secretary, Economic Development	JAY WILLIAMS
Deputy Assistant Secretary, Economic Development	MATTHEW ERSKINE

The Economic Development Administration (EDA) was created in 1965 under the Public Works and Economic Development Act (42 U.S.C. 3121) as part of an effort to target Federal resources to economically distressed areas and to help develop local economies in the United States. It was mandated to assist rural and urban communities that were outside the mainstream economy and that lagged in economic development, industrial growth, and personal income.

EDA provides grants to States, regions, and communities nationwide to generate wealth and minimize poverty by promoting an attractive business environment for private capital investment and higher skill, higher wage jobs through capacity building, planning, infrastructure, research grants, and strategic initiatives. Through its grant program, EDA uses public sector resources to cultivate an environment where the private sector risks capital and job opportunities are created. https://www.eda.gov/about

Sources of Information

Employment   For information on career opportunities, visit the "EDA Job Opportunities" Web page. http://www.eda.gov/careers
Newsroom   The online newsroom features blog posts, press releases, an archive of newsletters, and the latest media. https://www.eda.gov/news
Regional Offices   Contact information for the Administration's six regional offices—Atlanta, Austin, Chicago, Denver, Philadelphia, Seattle—is available on the "Contact" Web page. http://www.eda.gov/contact. https://www.eda.gov

For further information, contact the Economic Development Administration, Department of Commerce, Washington, DC 20230. Phone, 202-482-5081. Fax, 202-273-4781.

Economics and Statistics Administration

Department of Commerce, Washington, DC 20230
Phone, 202-482-3727. Internet, http://www.esa.doc.gov.

Under Secretary, Economic Affairs	JUSTIN ANTONIPILLAI
Deputy Under Secretary, Economic Affairs	KENNETH A. ARNOLD
Chief Economist	ELLEN HUGHES-CROMWICK
Director, Bureau of Economic Analysis	BRIAN C. MOYER
Director, Bureau of the Census	JOHN H. THOMPSON

The Economics and Statistics Administration (ESA), headed by the Under Secretary for Economic Affairs, has three principal components: the Office of the Chief Economist, the Bureau of the Census, and the Bureau of Economic Analysis. ESA develops policy options, analyzes economic developments, manages economic data systems, and produces a major share of U.S. economic and demographic statistics, including the national economic indicators. The Under Secretary is the chief economic adviser to the Secretary and provides leadership and executive management for the Office of the Chief Economist and the Bureaus of Economic Analysis and of the Census. http://www.esa.gov/content/about-economics-statistics-administration

Bureau of Economic Analysis

[For the Bureau of Economic Analysis statement of organization, see the Federal Register of Dec. 29, 1980, 45 FR 85496]

The Bureau of Economic Analysis (BEA) provides the most accurate, relevant, and timely economic accounts data in an objective and cost-effective manner. BEA's economic statistics offer a comprehensive picture of the U.S. economy. BEA prepares national, regional, industry, and international accounts that present essential information on such issues in the world economy.

BEA's national economic statistics provide a comprehensive look at U.S. production, consumption, investment, exports and imports, and income and saving. The international transactions accounts provide information on trade in goods and services (including the balance of payments and trade), investment income, and government and private finances. In addition, the accounts measure the value of U.S.

international assets and liabilities and direct investment by multinational companies.

The regional accounts provide data on total and per capita personal income by region, State, metropolitan area, and county, and on gross State product. The industry economic account provides a detailed view of the interrelationships between U.S. producers and users and the contribution to production across industries. http://www.bea.gov | Email: customerservice@bea.gov

For further information, contact the Public Information Office, Bureau of Economic Analysis, Department of Commerce, Washington, DC 20230. Phone, 202-606-9900. Fax, 202-606-5310.

Bureau of the Census

[For the Bureau of the Census statement of organization, see the Federal Register of Sept. 16, 1975, 40 FR 42765]

The Bureau of the Census was established as a permanent office by act of March 6, 1902 (32 Stat. 51). The major functions of the Census Bureau are authorized by the Constitution, which provides that a census of population shall be taken every 10 years, and by laws codified as title 13 of the United States Code. The law also provides that the information collected by the Census Bureau from individual persons, households, or establishments be kept strictly confidential and be used only for statistical purposes.

The Census Bureau is responsible for the decennial censuses of population and housing; the quinquennial censuses of State and local governments, manufacturers, mineral industries, distributive trades, construction industries, and transportation; current surveys that provide information on many of the subjects covered in the censuses at monthly, quarterly, annual, or other intervals; compilation of current statistics on U.S. foreign trade, including data on imports, exports, and shipping; special censuses at the request and expense of State and local government units; publication of estimates and projections of the population; publication of current data on population and housing characteristics; and current reports on manufacturing, retail and wholesale trade, services, construction, imports and exports, State and local government finances and employment, and other subjects.

The Census Bureau makes available statistical results of its censuses, surveys, and other programs to the public through the Internet, mobile applications, and other media. The Bureau also prepares special tabulations sponsored and paid for by data users. It also produces statistical compendia, catalogs, guides, and directories that are useful in locating information on specific subjects. Upon request, the Bureau makes searches of decennial census records and furnishes certificates to individuals for use as evidence of age, relationship, or place of birth. A fee is charged for searches. http://www.census.gov | Email: PIO@census.gov

For further information, contact the Public Information Office, Bureau of the Census, Department of Commerce, Washington, DC 20233. Phone, 301-763-3030. Fax, 301-763-3762.

Office of the Chief Economist

The economists and analysts of the Office of the Chief Economist analyze domestic and international economic developments and produce in-depth reports, factsheets, briefings, and social media postings. These tools cover policy issues and current economic events, as well as economic and demographic trends. Department of Commerce and White House policymakers, American businessmen, State and local governments, and news organizations worldwide rely on these tools. http://www.esa.gov/content/chief-economist

Sources of Information

Data   Monthly and quarterly economic indicators are posted online. To receive the most current economic indicators by email, subscribe using the online form. http://www.esa.gov/content/indicators. https://service.govdelivery.com/accounts/USESAEI/subscriber/new

Employment   For information on employment opportunities at the Bureaus of Economic Analysis or the Census, visit the "Working at BEA" or "Census Careers" Web page. http://www.bea.gov/jobs/index.htm. http://www.census.gov/about/census-careers.html

Publications   The BEA posts research papers, its customer guide, and the monthly journal "Survey of Current Business" under the "Publications" section on its Web site. The Census Bureau's most recently released publications are part of its online library. http://www.bea.gov/scb/index.htm. https://www.census.gov/library/publications.html

Regional Offices   Contact information for the Census Bureau's six regional offices— Atlanta, Chicago, Denver, Los Angeles, New York, Philadelphia—is available on its "Regional Offices" Web page. http://www.census.gov/regions. http://www.esa.gov | Email: ESAwebmaster@doc.gov

For further information, contact the Economics and Statistics Administration, Department of Commerce, Washington, DC 20230. Phone, 202-482-6607.

International Trade Administration

Department of Commerce, Washington, DC 20230
Phone, 202-482-3917. Internet, http://www.trade.gov.

Under Secretary, International Trade	KENNETH E. HYATT, ACTING
Deputy Under Secretary, International Trade	THOMAS MCGINTY, ACTING
Assistant Secretary, Enforcement and Compliance	PAUL PIQUADO

Assistant Secretary, Global Markets / Director General   ARUN M. KUMAR
of the U.S. And Foreign Commercial Service
Assistant Secretary, Industry and Analysis   MARCUS D. JADOTTE

[For the International Trade Administration statement of organization, see the Federal Register of Jan. 25, 1980, 45 FR 6148]

The International Trade Administration (ITA) was established on January 2, 1980, by the Secretary of Commerce to promote world trade and to strengthen the international trade and investment position of the United States.

The International Trade Administration (ITA) was established on January 2, 1980, by the Secretary of Commerce to promote world trade and to strengthen the international trade and investment position of the United States. The Under Secretary for International Trade heads the ITA, coordinating all issues concerning trade promotion, international commercial policy, market access, and trade law enforcement. The Administration is responsible for U.S. Government nonagricultural trade operations, and it supports the U.S. Trade Representative's efforts to negotiate trade policy. http://www.trade.gov/about.asp

Enforcement / Compliance   The Office of Enforcement and Compliance defends American industry against injurious and unfair trade practices by administering U.S. antidumping and countervailing duty trade laws. The Office also ensures the proper administration of foreign trade zones and advises the Secretary on establishment of new ones; oversees the administration of the Department's textiles program; and administers programs governing watch assemblies and other statutory import programs. http://www.trade.gov/enforcement

Global Markets   The Global Markets unit assists and advocates for U.S. businesses in international markets. Relying on a network of trade promotion and policy professionals located in over 70 countries and 100 U.S. locations, the unit promotes U.S. exports, especially those of small and medium-sized enterprises; advances and protects U.S. commercial interests overseas; and attracts investment from abroad into the United States. http://www.trade.gov/markets

Industry / Analysis   The Manufacturing and Services unit advises on domestic and international trade and investment policies affecting the competitiveness of U.S. industry. It also researches and analyzes manufacturing and services. Based on this analysis and interaction with U.S. industry, the unit Secretary develops strategies, policies, and programs to strengthen U.S. industry competitiveness domestically and globally. The unit manages an integrated program that includes industry and economic analysis, trade policy development and multilateral, regional, and bilateral trade agreements for manufactured goods and services; administers trade arrangements with foreign governments in product and service areas; and develops and provides business information and assistance to the United States on its rights and opportunities under multilateral and other agreements. http://www.trade.gov/industry

Sources of Information

Data   Trade data and export and import statistics are available online. http://www.trade.gov/data.asp

Employment   For information on career opportunities, visit the "Jobs" Web page. http://www.trade.gov/jobs

Publications   The ITA has an online bookstore. http://www.trade.gov/publications. http://www.trade.gov/contact.asp

For further information, contact the International Trade Administration, Department of Commerce, Washington, DC 20230. Phone, 202-482-3917.

Minority Business Development Agency

Department of Commerce, Washington, DC 20230
Phone, 202-482-2332. Internet, http://www.mbda.gov.

National Director	ALEJANDRA Y. CASTILLO
National Deputy Director	ALBERT K. SHEN

[For the Minority Business Development Agency statement of organization, see the Federal Register of Mar. 17, 1972, 37 FR 5650, as amended]

The Minority Business Development Agency was established by Executive order in 1969. The Agency develops and coordinates a national program for minority business enterprise.

The Agency was created to help minority businesses achieve effective and equitable participation in the American free enterprise system and overcome social and economic disadvantages that limited past participation. The Agency provides policies and leadership supporting a partnership of business, industry, and government with the Nation's minority businesses.

Business development services are provided to the minority business community through three vehicles: the minority business opportunity committees, which disseminate information on business opportunities; the minority business development centers, which provide management and technical assistance and other business development services; and electronic commerce, which includes a Web site that shows how to start a business and use the service to find contract opportunities.

The Agency promotes and coordinates the efforts of other Federal agencies in assisting or providing market opportunities for minority business. It coordinates opportunities for minority firms in the private sector. Through such public and private cooperative activities, the Agency promotes the participation of Federal, State, and local governments, and business and industry in directing resources for the development of strong minority businesses. http://www.mbda.gov/main/who-mbda/about-minority-business-development-agency

Sources of Information

Internships   Information on student eligibility and how to apply is available online. http://www.mbda.gov/main/intern-program
Library   An online research library serves as a repository for factsheets, reports, statistical data, and other publications. http://www.mbda.gov/pressroom/research-library
Newsletter   A free, monthly newsletter is accessible online. http://www.mbda.gov/newsletter
Speakers   For information on scheduling a speaker for an organized event, visit the "Speaker Request Form" Web page. http://www.mbda.gov/main/mbda-speaker-request-form. http://www.mbda.gov/contact

For further information, contact the Office of the National Director, Minority Business Development Agency, Department of Commerce, Washington, DC 20230. Phone, 202-482-2332.

National Oceanic and Atmospheric Administration

Department of Commerce, Washington, DC 20230
Phone, 202-482-2985. Internet, http://www.noaa.gov.

Under Secretary, Oceans and Atmosphere / Administrator	KATHRYN D. SULLIVAN
Assistant Secretary, Conservation and Management / Deputy Administrator	CHRISTINE BLACKBURN, ACTING

Assistant Secretary, Environmental Observation
  and Prediction / Deputy Administrator
Chief Scientist

Manson K. Brown

Richard W. Spinrad

[For the National Oceanic and Atmospheric Administration statement of organization, see the Federal Register of Feb. 13, 1978, 43 FR 6128]

The National Oceanic and Atmospheric Administration (NOAA) was formed on October 3, 1970, by Reorganization Plan No. 4 of 1970 (5 U.S.C. app.).

NOAA's mission centers on environmental assessment, prediction, and stewardship. It monitors and assesses the state of the environment to make accurate and timely forecasts to protect life, property, and natural resources; to promote the Nation's economic health; and to enhance its environmental security. The agency protects America's ocean, coastal, and living marine resources while promoting sustainable economic development. http://www.noaa.gov/our-mission-and-vision

National Environmental Satellite, Data, and Information Service The National Environmental Satellite, Data, and Information Service operates the Nation's civilian geostationary and polar-orbiting environmental satellites. It also manages the largest collection of atmospheric, climatic, geophysical, and oceanographic data in the world. The Service develops and provides, through various media, environmental data for forecasts, national security, and weather warnings to protect life and property. These data are also used for energy distribution, global food supplies development, natural resources management, and rescuing downed pilots and mariners in distress. http://www.nesdis.noaa.gov/about_nesdis.html

For further information, contact the National Environmental Satellite, Data, and Information Service, 1335 East-West Highway, Silver Spring, MD 20910-3283. Phone, 301-713-3578. Fax, 301-713-1249.

National Marine Fisheries Service The National Marine Fisheries Service supports the management, conservation, and sustainable development of domestic and international living marine resources and the protection and restoration of ecosystems. The Service helps assess the stock of the Nation's multi-billion-dollar marine fisheries,

protect marine mammals and threatened species, conserve habitats, assist trade and industry, and conduct fishery enforcement activities. http://www.nmfs.noaa.gov

For further information, contact the National Marine Fisheries Service, 1315 East-West Highway, Silver Spring, MD 20910. Phone, 301-713-2239. Fax, 301-713-1940.

National Ocean Service The National Ocean Service helps balance the Nation's use of coastal resources through research, management, and policy. The Service monitors the health of U.S. coasts by examining how human use and natural events affect coastal ecosystems. Coastal communities rely on the Service for information on natural hazards so they can reduce or eliminate destructive effects of coastal hazards. The Service assesses the damage caused by hazardous material spills and tries to restore or replace the affected coastal resources. The Service also protects beaches, water quality, wetlands, and wildlife. It provides a wide range of navigational products and data that help vessels move safely through U.S. waters, and it supplies the basic information for establishing the latitude, longitude, and elevation framework necessary for the Nation's mapping, navigation, positioning, and surveying activities. http://www.nos.noaa.gov

For further information, contact the National Ocean Service, Room 13231, SSMC 4, 1305 East-West Highway, Silver Spring, MD 20910. Phone, 301-713-3074. Fax, 301-713-4307.

National Weather Service The National Weather Service (NWS) provides weather, water, and climate warnings and forecasts and data for the United States, its territories, and adjacent waters and ocean areas. Government agencies, the private sector, the general public, and the global community rely on NWS data and products to protect life and property. Working with partners in Government, academic and research institutions, and private industry, the Service responds to the needs of the American public through its products and services. NWS data and information support aviation, maritime activities, and other sectors of the economy, as well as wildfire suppression. The Service also helps national security efforts with long- and short-range forecasts, air quality and cloud dispersion forecasts, and broadcasts of warnings and critical information over the 800-station NOAA Weather Radio network. http://www.weather.gov

For further information, contact the National Weather Service–Executive Affairs, 1325 East-West Highway, Silver Spring, MD 20910-3283. Phone, 301-713-0675. Fax, 301-713-0049.

Office of Marine and Aviation Operations
The Office of Marine and Aviation Operations manages the aviation safety, the small boat, and the NOAA diving programs. It also operates a fleet of specialized ships and aircraft that collect data and carry out research to support NOAA's mission, the Global Earth Observation System, and the Integrated Ocean Observing System—including flying "hurricane hunter" aircraft into the most turbulent storms to collect data critical for research. http://www.omao.noaa.gov/about.html

For further information, contact Office of Marine and Aviation Operations, Suite 500, 8403 Colesville Rd., Silver Spring, MD 20910. Phone, 301-713-7600. Fax, 301-713-1541.

Office of Oceanic and Atmospheric Research
The Office of Oceanic and Atmospheric Research conducts research on air quality and composition, climate variability and change, weather, and coastal, marine, and Great Lakes ecosystems. The Office uses its own laboratories and offices to run research programs in atmospheric, coastal, marine, and space sciences, as well as relying on networks of university-based programs across the country. http://www.oar.noaa.gov

For further information, contact the Office of Oceanic and Atmospheric Research, Room 11458, 1315 East-West Highway, Silver Spring, MD 20910. Phone, 301-713-2458. Fax, 301-713-0163.

Sources of Information

Employment For information on career and volunteer opportunities, contracting and partnering, and grants, visit the "Working with NOAA" Web page. http://www.noaa.gov/opportunities.html

Facilities Information on NOAA facilities, programs, and activities nationwide is available on the "NOAA in Your State and Territory" Web page. http://www.legislative.noaa.gov/NIYS/index.html

News News and features—explainers, stories, and videos—are available online. http://www.noaa.gov/news-features

Weather The NOAA Weather Radio All Hazards network broadcasts continuous weather information nationwide from the nearest National Weather Service office. The network broadcasts official Weather Service forecasts, warnings, watches, and other hazard information around the clock every day. http://www.nws.noaa.gov/nwr. http://www.noaa.gov/media.html

For further information, contact the Office of Communications and External Affairs, National Oceanic and Atmospheric Administration, Department of Commerce, Washington, DC 20230. Phone, 202-482-6090. Fax, 202-482-3154.

National Telecommunications and Information Administration

Department of Commerce, Washington, DC 20230
Phone, 202-428-1840. Internet, http://www.ntia.doc.gov.

Assistant Secretary, Communications and Information / Administrator	LAWRENCE E. STRICKLING
Deputy Assistant Secretary, Communications and Information	ANGELA SIMPSON

[For the National Telecommunications and Information Administration statement of organization, see the Federal Register of June 5, 1978, 43 FR 24348]

The National Telecommunications and Information Administration (NTIA) was established in 1978 by Reorganization Plan No. 1 of 1977 (5 U.S.C. app.) and Executive Order 12046 of March 27, 1978 (3 CFR, 1978 Comp., p. 158), by combining the Office of Telecommunications Policy of the Executive Office of the President and the Office of Telecommunications of the Department of Commerce to form a new agency reporting to the Secretary of Commerce. NTIA operates under the authority of the National Telecommunications and Information Administration Organization Act (47 U.S.C. 901).

NTIA serves as the principal executive branch adviser to the President on telecommunications and information policy; develops and presents U.S. plans and policies at international communications conferences and related meetings; prescribes policies for and manages Federal use of the radio frequency spectrum; serves as the principal Federal telecommunications research and engineering laboratory— NTIA's Institute for Telecommunication Sciences; promotes broadband deployment and adoption through BroadbandUSA (www2.ntia.doc.gov); and assists the First Responder Network Authority (www.firstnet. gov) develop and operate a nationwide broadband network dedicated to public safety. https://www.ntia.doc.gov/about

Sources of Information

Employment To see current NTIA career opportunities on USAJobs, click on the link below, scroll down, and select "NTIA Jobs." https://www.ntia.doc.gov/about

Publications Since 1954, NTIA and its predecessors have published several hundred technical reports and memoranda, special publications, contractor reports, and other information products. For more information, call the Office of Spectrum Management in Washington, DC, at 202-482-1850. Or, contact the publications officer at the Institute for Telecommunication Sciences–Department of Commerce, 325 Broadway, MC ITS.D, Boulder, CO 80305. Phone, 303-497-3572. https://www.ntia.doc. gov/publications

Speakers A speaker request form is available online. https://www.ntia.doc.gov/ webform/speaker-request

Telecommunications Research For information on telecommunications research and engineering services, visit the "Institute for Telecommunication Sciences" Web page. Phone, 303-497-3571. http://www.its. bldrdoc.gov | Email: info@its.bldrdoc.gov. https://www.ntia.doc.gov/contact

For further information, contact the National Telecommunications and Information Administration, Department of Commerce, Washington, DC 20230. Phone, 202-482-1551.

National Institute of Standards and Technology

100 Bureau Drive, Gaithersburg, MD 20899
Phone, 301-975-2000. Internet, http://www.nist.gov.

Under Secretary, Standards and Technology / Director   WILLIE E. MAY

The National Institute of Standards and Technology (NIST) operates under the authority of the National Institute of Standards and Technology Act (15 U.S.C. 271), which amends the Organic Act of March 3, 1901 (ch. 872), which created the National Bureau of Standards (NBS) in 1901. In 1988, the Congress renamed NBS as NIST and expanded its activities and responsibilities. http://www.nist.gov/ timeline.cfm

NIST is a nonregulatory Federal agency within the Department of Commerce. To carry out its mission, NIST relies on research laboratories, user facilities, innovative manufacturing programs, and its participation in collaborative institutes and centers. NIST research laboratories conduct world-class research to advance the Nation's technological infrastructure and help U.S. companies improve products and services. The Baldrige Performance Excellence Program (www.nist.gov/baldrige) also helps them and other organizations increase operational performance and quality. NIST user facilities include the Center for Nanoscale Science and Technology (www.nist.gov/cnst) and NIST Center for Neutron Research (www.ncnr.nist.gov). http://www.nist.gov/programs-projects.cfm

Sources of Information

Employment For information on career opportunities, visit the "Careers at NIST" Web page. http://www.nist.gov/ohrm/careers.cfm

Publications The "Journal of Research of the National Institute of Standards and Technology" and other publications are available online. http://www.nist.gov/nvl/nist_publications.cfm http://www.nist.gov/public_affairs/contact.cfm | Email: inquiries@nist.gov

For further information, contact the National Institute of Standards and Technology, 100 Bureau Drive, Mail Stop 1070, Gaithersburg, MD 20899-1070. Phone, 301-975-6478. Fax, 301-926-1630.

National Technical Information Service

5301 Shawnee Road, Alexandria, VA 22312
Phone, 703-605-6050. Fax, 888-584-8332. Internet, http://www.ntis.gov.

Director	AVI BENDER

The National Technical Information Service (NTIS) is the largest central resource for business-related, engineering, Government-funded, scientific, and technical information available. For more than 60 years, the Service has assured businesses, Government, universities, and the public timely access to approximately 3 million publications covering over 350 subject areas. The Service supports the Department of Commerce's mission by providing access to information that stimulates innovation and discovery. The Service receives no appropriations and recovers its costs through fees charged for products and services.

The NTIS promotes economic growth, progress, and science and information. On behalf of the Secretary of Commerce, the Service operates a permanent clearinghouse of scientific and technical information and makes it readily available to industry, business, and the general public—codified as chapter 23 of Title 15 of the United States Code (15 U.S.C. 1151-1157). The Service collects scientific and technical information; catalogs, abstracts, indexes, and permanently archives the information; disseminates information through electronic and other media; and provides information processing services to other Federal agencies.

NTIS also provides information management services to other Federal agencies to help them interact with and better serve the information needs of their own constituents. It develops, plans, evaluates, and implements business strategies for information management and dissemination services and Internet-based service business opportunities for Federal agencies; uses new and existing technologies to ensure optimal access to Government online information services; and manages service projects using in-house capabilities and through joint public-private partnerships. NTIS provides eTraining and Knowledge Management, Web services and cloud computing, distribution and fulfillment, digitization and scanning services for Federal Government agencies. http://www.ntis.gov/about

Sources of Information

Employment Approximately 150 NTIS employees work in Northern Virginia. The Service hires professionals with skills in administration, information technology, and program management. https://www.usajobs.gov

Freedom of Information Act (FOIA) The Office of Director handles Freedom of

Information Act (FOIA) requests. The FOIA contact reviews, coordinates, and responds to requests within 20 days under the requirements of the Freedom of Information Act. http://www.ntis.gov/about/FOIA
Products For general information or to place a telephone order, call the Customer Contact Center, 8 a.m.–6 p.m., eastern standard time. Phone, 800-553-6847. TDD, 703-487-4639. Fax, 703-605-6900. http://www.ntis.gov/products | Email: info@ntis.gov

Services To learn more about NTIS information services for Federal agencies, call the Office of Federal Services at 703-605-6800. http://www.ntis.gov/services | Email: obdinfo@ntis.gov. http://www.ntis.gov/about/contact

For further information, contact the National Technical Information Service, 5301 Shawnee Road, Alexandria, VA 22312. Phone, 703-605-6000 or 800-553-6847.

United States Patent and Trademark Office

600 Dulany Street, Alexandria, VA 22314
Phone, 571-272-8700. Internet, http://www.uspto.gov.

Under Secretary, Intellectual Property / Director	MICHELLE K. LEE
Deputy Under Secretary, Intellectual Property / Deputy Director	RUSSELL D. SLIFER

[For the Patent and Trademark Office statement of organization, see the Federal Register of Apr. 14, 1975, 40 FR 16707]

The United States Patent and Trademark Office (USPTO) was established by the act of July 19, 1952 (35 U.S.C. 1) "to promote the progress of science and useful arts, by securing for limited times to authors and inventors the exclusive right to their respective writings and discoveries" (U.S. Constitution Art. I, sec. 8). The commerce clause provides the constitutional basis for the registration of trademarks.

USPTO examines and issues patents. There are three major patent categories: utility patents, design patents, and plant patents. USPTO also issues statutory invention registrations and processes international patent applications.

Through the registration of trademarks, USPTO assists businessmen and women in protecting their investments, promoting goods and services, and safeguarding consumers against confusion and deception in the marketplace. A trademark includes any distinctive word, name, symbol, device, or any combination thereof adopted and used or intended to be used by a manufacturer or merchant to identify his or her goods or services and distinguish them from those manufactured or sold by others. Trademarks are examined by the Office for compliance with various statutory requirements to prevent unfair competition and consumer deception.

In addition to the examination of patent and trademark applications, issuance of patents, and registration of trademarks, USPTO advises and assists government agencies and officials in matters involving all domestic and global aspects of intellectual property. USPTO also promotes an understanding of intellectual property protection.

USPTO provides public access to patent, trademark, and related scientific and technical information. Patents and trademarks may be reviewed and searched online or at designated Patent and Trademark Depository Libraries. There are 80 Patent and Trademark Depository Libraries located within the United States and Puerto Rico. Additionally, USPTO's Scientific and Technical Information Center in Alexandria, VA, houses over 120,000 volumes of scientific and technical books in various languages; 90,000 bound volumes of periodicals devoted to science and technology; the official journals of 77 foreign patent organizations; and over 40 million foreign patents on paper, microfilm, microfiche, and CD–ROM. http://www.uspto.gov/about-us

Sources of Information

Data Monthly summaries for patents data and quarterly summaries for trademark data are available online. http://www.uspto.gov/learning-and-resources/statistics

Employment Information on employment opportunities is available on the "Careers" Web page. http://careers.uspto.gov

Patents Information on getting started and applying for and maintaining a patent is available online. http://www.uspto.gov/patent

Publications The "Official Gazette" journal, "Inventors Eye" newsletter, and other publications are accessible online. http://www.uspto.gov/learning-and-resources/official-gazette. http://www.uspto.gov/learning-and-resources/newsletter-archives. http://www.uspto.gov/about-us/news-updates

Speakers A speaker request form is available online. http://www.uspto.gov/about-us/organizational-offices/office-chief-communications-officer/speaker-request-form

Trademarks Information on getting started and applying for and maintaining a trademark is available online. http://www.uspto.gov/trademark. http://www.uspto.gov/about-us/organizational-offices/office-chief-communications-officer

For further information, contact the Office of the Chief Communications Officer, United States Patent and Trademark Office, 600 Dulany Street, Alexandria, VA 22314. Phone, 571-272-8400.

DEPARTMENT OF DEFENSE

Office of the Secretary, The Pentagon, Washington, DC 20301-1155
Phone, 703-545-6700. Internet, http://www.defense.gov.

Secretary of Defense	JAMES M. MATTIS
Deputy Secretary of Defense	PATRICK M. SHANAHAN
Under Secretary of Defense for Acquisition, Technology and Logistics	JAMES MacSTRAVIC, ACTING
Under Secretary of Defense Comptroller / Chief Financial Officer	DAVID L. NORQUIST
Under Secretary of Defense for Intelligence	KARI BINGEN, ACTING
Under Secretary of Defense for Personnel and Readiness	ANTHONY M. KURTA, ACTING
Under Secretary of Defense for Policy	ROBERT KAREM, ACTING
Principal Deputy Under Secretary of Defense Comptroller / DOD Chief Financial Officer	JOHN ZANGARDI, ACTING
Principal Deputy Under Secretary of Defense for Acquisition, Technology and Logistics	(VACANCY)
Principal Under Secretary of Defense for Intelligence	TODD LOWERY, ACTING
Principal Under Secretary of Defense for Personnel and Readiness	(VACANCY)
Principal Under Secretary of Defense for Policy	THERESA WHELAN, ACTING
Assistant Secretary of Defense for Acquisition	DYKE WEATHERINGTON, ACTING
Assistant Secretary of Defense for Asian and Pacific Security Affairs	DAVID HELVY, ACTING
Assistant Secretary of Defense for Health Affairs	DAVID SMITH, ACTING
Assistant Secretary of Defense for Homeland Defense and Global Security	KENNETH RAPUANO
Assistant Secretary of Defense for International Security Affairs	ROBERT KAREM
Assistant Secretary of Defense for Legislative Affairs	PETE GIAMBASTIANI, ACTING
Assistant Secretary of Defense for Logistics and Materiel Readiness	KRISTIN FRENCH, ACTING
Assistant Secretary of Defense for Manpower and Reserve Affairs	STEPHANIE BARNA, ACTING
Assistant Secretary of Defense for Nuclear, Chemical, and Biological Defense Programs	TOM HOPKINS, ACTING
Assistant Secretary of Defense for Operational Energy Plans and Programs	THOMAS E. MOREHOUSE, ACTING
Assistant Secretary of Defense for Personnel and Readiness	ELIZABETH VAN WINKLE, ACTING
Assistant Secretary of Defense for Research and Engineering	MARY MILLER, ACTING
Assistant Secretary of Defense for Special Operations/Low-Intensity Conflict	CARYN HOLLIS, ACTING
Chief Information Officer	JOHN A. ZANGARDI, ACTING

Chief Operating Officer	STEVEN L. SCHLEIEN
Director, Administration and Management	MICHAEL L. RHODES
Director, Cost Assessment and Program Evaluation	SCOTT COMES, ACTING
Director, Operational Test and Evaluation	DAVID DUMA, ACTING
General Counsel	PAUL S. KOFFSKY, ACTING
Inspector General	GLENN A. FINE, ACTING
Assistant to the Secretary of Defense for Public Affairs	DANA W. WHITE
Deputy Chief Management Officer	DAVID TILLOTSON III, ACTING

Joint Chiefs of Staff

CHAIR	GEN. JOSEPH F. DUNFORD, JR., USMC
Vice Chair	GEN. PAUL J. SELVA, USAF
Senior Enlisted Advisor to the Chair	CSM JOHN W. TROXWELL, USMC
Chief of Naval Operations	ADM. JOHN RICHARDSON, USN
Chief of Staff, Air Force	GEN. DAVID L. GOLDFEIN, USAF
Chief of Staff, Army	GEN. MARK A. MILLEY, USA
Chief of the National Guard Bureau	GEN. JOSEPH L. LENGYEL, USAF
Commandant of the Marine Corps	GEN. ROBERT B. NELLER, USMC

[For the Department of Defense statement of organization, see the Code of Federal Regulations, Title 32, Chapter I, Subchapter R]

The Department of Defense provides the military forces needed to deter war and protect national security. Under the President, the Secretary of Defense directs and exercises authority and control over the separately organized Departments of the Air Force, the Army, and the Navy; over the Joint Chiefs of Staff; over the combatant commands; and over defense agencies and field activities.

The National Security Act Amendments of 1949 redesignated the National Military Establishment as the Department of Defense (DOD) and established it as an executive department (10 U.S.C. 111) headed by the Secretary of Defense.

Structure   The Department of Defense is composed of the Office of the Secretary of Defense; the military departments and the military services within those departments; the Chairman of the Joint Chiefs of Staff and the Joint Staff; the combatant commands; the defense agencies; DOD field activities; and such other offices, agencies, activities, and commands as may be established or designated by law or by the President or the Secretary of Defense.

Each military department is separately organized under its own Secretary and functions under the authority, direction, and control of the Secretary of Defense. The Secretary of each military department is responsible to the Secretary of Defense for the operation and efficiency of his department. Orders to the military departments are issued through the Secretaries of these departments or their designees, by the Secretary of Defense, or under authority specifically delegated in writing by the Secretary of Defense or provided by law.

The commanders of the combatant commands are responsible to the President and the Secretary of Defense for accomplishing the military missions assigned to them and exercising command authority over forces assigned to them. The operational chain of command runs from the President to the Secretary of Defense, to the commanders of the combatant commands. The Chairman of the Joint Chiefs of Staff functions within the chain of command by transmitting the orders of the President or the Secretary of Defense to the commanders of the combatant commands.

Office of the Secretary of Defense

Secretary of Defense   The Secretary of Defense is the principal defense policy adviser to the President and is responsible for the formulation of general defense

DEPARTMENT OF DEFENSE

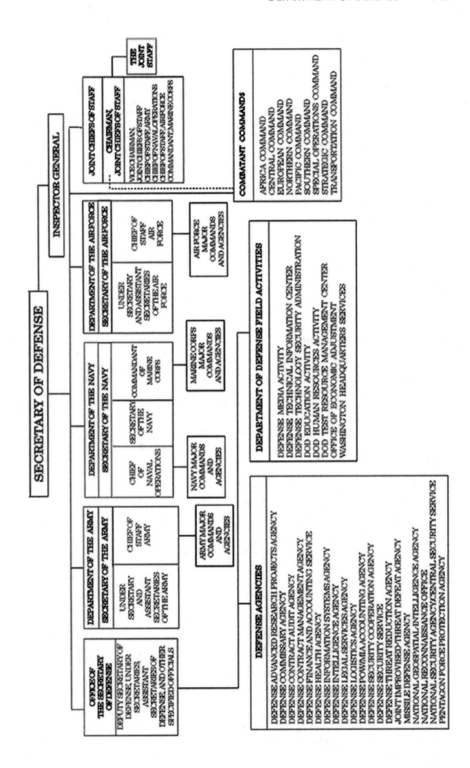

SECRETARY OF DEFENSE

INSPECTOR GENERAL

JOINT CHIEFS OF STAFF

CHAIRMAN, JOINT CHIEFS OF STAFF

VICE CHAIRMAN, JOINT CHIEFS OF STAFF
CHIEF OF STAFF, ARMY
CHIEF OF NAVAL OPERATIONS
CHIEF OF STAFF, AIR FORCE
COMMANDANT, MARINE CORPS

THE JOINT STAFF

COMBATANT COMMANDS

AFRICA COMMAND
CENTRAL COMMAND
EUROPEAN COMMAND
NORTHERN COMMAND
PACIFIC COMMAND
SOUTHERN COMMAND
SPECIAL OPERATIONS COMMAND
STRATEGIC COMMAND
TRANSPORTATION COMMAND

OFFICE OF THE SECRETARY OF DEFENSE

DEPUTY SECRETARY OF DEFENSE, UNDER SECRETARIES, ASSISTANT SECRETARIES OF DEFENSE, AND OTHER SPECIFIED OFFICIALS

DEPARTMENT OF THE ARMY

SECRETARY OF THE ARMY

UNDER SECRETARY AND ASSISTANT SECRETARIES OF THE ARMY

CHIEF OF STAFF ARMY

ARMY MAJOR COMMANDS AND AGENCIES

DEPARTMENT OF THE NAVY

SECRETARY OF THE NAVY

CHIEF OF NAVAL OPERATIONS

COMMANDANT OF MARINE CORPS

NAVY MAJOR COMMANDS AND AGENCIES

MARINE CORPS MAJOR COMMANDS AND AGENCIES

DEPARTMENT OF THE AIR FORCE

SECRETARY OF THE AIR FORCE

UNDER SECRETARY AND ASSISTANT SECRETARIES OF THE AIR FORCE

CHIEF OF STAFF AIR FORCE

AIR FORCE MAJOR COMMANDS AND AGENCIES

DEFENSE AGENCIES

DEFENSE ADVANCED RESEARCH PROJECTS AGENCY
DEFENSE COMMISSARY AGENCY
DEFENSE CONTRACT AUDIT AGENCY
DEFENSE CONTRACT MANAGEMENT AGENCY
DEFENSE FINANCE AND ACCOUNTING SERVICE
DEFENSE HEALTH AGENCY
DEFENSE INFORMATION SYSTEMS AGENCY
DEFENSE INTELLIGENCE AGENCY
DEFENSE LEGAL SERVICES AGENCY
DEFENSE LOGISTICS AGENCY
DEFENSE POW/MIA ACCOUNTING AGENCY
DEFENSE SECURITY COOPERATION AGENCY
DEFENSE SECURITY SERVICE
DEFENSE THREAT REDUCTION AGENCY
JOINT IMPROVISED-THREAT DEFEAT AGENCY
MISSILE DEFENSE AGENCY
NATIONAL GEOSPATIAL-INTELLIGENCE AGENCY
NATIONAL RECONNAISSANCE OFFICE
NATIONAL SECURITY AGENCY/CENTRAL SECURITY SERVICE
PENTAGON FORCE PROTECTION AGENCY

DEPARTMENT OF DEFENSE FIELD ACTIVITIES

DEFENSE MEDIA ACTIVITY
DEFENSE TECHNICAL INFORMATION CENTER
DEFENSE TECHNOLOGY SECURITY ADMINISTRATION
DOD EDUCATION ACTIVITY
DOD HUMAN RESOURCES ACTIVITY
DOD TEST RESOURCE MANAGEMENT CENTER
OFFICE OF ECONOMIC ADJUSTMENT
WASHINGTON HEADQUARTERS SERVICES

policy and policy related to DOD and for the execution of approved policy. Under the direction of the President, the Secretary exercises authority, direction, and control over the Department of Defense. http://www.defense.gov/osd

Acquisition, Technology and Logistics   The Under Secretary of Defense for Acquisition, Technology and Logistics is the principal staff assistant and adviser to the Secretary of Defense for all matters relating to the DOD Acquisition System; research and development; modeling and simulation; systems engineering; advanced technology; developmental test and evaluation; production; systems integration; logistics; installation management; military construction; procurement; environment, safety, and occupational health management; utilities and energy management; business management modernization; document services; and nuclear, chemical, and biological defense programs. http://www.acq.osd.mil

Intelligence   The Under Secretary of Defense for Intelligence is the principal staff assistant and adviser to the Secretary and Deputy Secretary of Defense for intelligence, intelligence-related matters, counterintelligence, and security. The Under Secretary of Defense for Intelligence supervises all intelligence and intelligence-related affairs of DOD.

Networks and Information Integration   The Assistant Secretary of Defense for Networks and Information Integration is the principal staff assistant and adviser to the Secretary and Deputy Secretary of Defense for achieving and maintaining information superiority in support of DOD missions, while exploiting or denying an adversary's ability to do the same. The Assistant Secretary of Defense for Networks and Information Integration also serves as the Chief Information Officer. http://dodcio.defense.gov

Personnel and Readiness   The Under Secretary of Defense for Personnel and Readiness is the principal staff assistant and adviser to the Secretary of Defense for policy matters relating to the structure and readiness of the total force. Functional areas include readiness; civilian and military personnel policies, programs, and systems; civilian and military equal opportunity programs; health policies, programs, and activities;

Reserve component programs, policies, and activities; family policy, dependents' education, and personnel support programs; mobilization planning and requirements; language capabilities and programs; and the Federal Voting Assistance Program. The Under Secretary of Defense for Personnel and Readiness also serves as the Chief Human Capital Officer. http://prhome.defense.gov

Policy   The Under Secretary of Defense for Policy is the principal staff assistant and adviser to the Secretary of Defense for policy matters relating to overall international security policy and political-military affairs and represents the Department at the National Security Council and other external agencies involved with national security policy. The Under Secretary's areas of activity include homeland defense; NATO affairs; foreign military sales; arms limitation agreements; international trade and technology security; regional security affairs; special operations and low-intensity conflict; stability operations; integration of departmental plans and policies with overall national security objectives; drug control policy, requirements, priorities, systems, resources, and programs; and issuance of policy guidance affecting departmental programs. http://policy.defense.gov

Special Staff   A special staff assists the Secretary and Deputy Secretary of Defense. This special staff of assistants includes the Assistant Secretaries of Defense for Legislative Affairs and for Public Affairs; the Under Secretary of Defense (Comptroller), who also functions as the Chief Financial Officer; the General Counsel; the Inspector General; the Assistant to the Secretary of Defense for Intelligence Oversight; the Directors of Administration and Management, of Operational Test and Evaluation, of Business Transformation, of Net Assessment, of Program Analysis and Evaluation; and other officers whom the Secretary of Defense determines are necessary to help carry out his or her duties and responsibilities. http://www.defense.gov/About-DoD/Leaders

Joint Chiefs of Staff

The Joint Chiefs of Staff consist of the Chairman, the Vice Chairman, the Chief of Staff of the Army, the Chief of Naval Operations, the Chief of Staff of the Air Force, and the Commandant of the Marine Corps. The Chairman of the Joint Chiefs of Staff is the principal military adviser to the President, the National Security Council, and the Secretary of Defense. The other members of the Joint Chiefs of Staff are military advisers who may provide additional information upon request from the President, the National Security Council, or the Secretary of Defense. They may also submit their advice when it does not agree with that of the Chairman. Subject to the authority of the President and the Secretary of Defense, the Chairman of the Joint Chiefs of Staff is responsible for assisting the President and the Secretary of Defense in providing strategic direction and planning for the Armed Forces; making recommendations for the assignment of responsibilities within the Armed Forces; comparing the capabilities of American and allied Armed Forces with those of potential adversaries; preparing and reviewing contingency plans that conform to policy guidance; preparing joint logistic and mobility plans; and recommending assignment of logistic and mobility responsibilities.

The Chairman, while so serving, holds the grade of general or admiral and outranks all other officers of the Armed Forces.

The Vice Chairman of the Joint Chiefs performs duties assigned by the Chairman, with the approval of the Secretary of Defense. The Vice Chairman acts as Chairman when there is a vacancy in the office of the Chairman or in the absence or disability of the Chairman. The Vice Chairman, while so serving, holds the grade of general or admiral and outranks all other officers of the Armed Forces except the Chairman of the Joint Chiefs of Staff. http://www.jcs.mil

Joint Staff   The Joint Staff, under the Chairman of the Joint Chiefs of Staff, assists the Chairman and the other members of the Joint Chiefs of Staff in carrying out their responsibilities.

The Joint Staff is headed by a Director who is selected by the Chairman in consultation with the other members of the Joint Chiefs of Staff and with the approval of the Secretary of Defense. Officers assigned to serve on the Joint Staff are selected by the Chairman in approximately equal numbers from the Army, Navy, Marine Corps, and Air Force. http://www.jcs.mil/About.aspx

Combatant Commands

The combatant commands are military commands with broad continuing missions maintaining the security and defense of the United States against attack; supporting and advancing the national policies and interests of the United States and discharging U.S. military responsibilities in their assigned areas; and preparing plans, conducting operations, and coordinating activities of the forces assigned to them in accordance with the directives of higher authority. The operational chain of command runs from the President to the Secretary of Defense, to the commanders of the combatant commands. The Chairman of the Joint Chiefs of Staff serves as the spokesman for the commanders of the combatant commands, especially on the administrative requirements of their commands. http://www.defense.gov/Sites/Unified-Combatant-Commands

Field Activities

Counterintelligence Field Activity   The DOD Counterintelligence Field Activity was established in 2002 to build a Defense counterintelligence (CI) system that is informed by national goals and objectives and supports the protection of DOD personnel and critical assets from foreign intelligence services, foreign terrorists, and other clandestine or covert threats. The desired end is a transformed Defense CI system that integrates and synchronizes the counterintelligence activities of the military departments, defense agencies, Joint Staff, and combatant commands.

Defense Health Agency   The Defense Health Agency (DHA) manages the activities of the Military Health System. It is also the market manager for the National Capital Region enhanced Multi-Service Market, which includes Walter Reed National Military Medical Center and Fort Belvoir Community Hospital. http://www.dha.mil

Defense Media Activity   Defense Media Activity (DMA) gathers Defense news and information from all departmental levels and reports that news and information to DOD audiences worldwide through American Forces Network online, radio, television, and through publications. DMA reports news on individual airmen, marines, sailors, soldiers, and DOD civilian employees to the American public through the Hometown News Service. DMA provides World Wide Web infrastructure and services for DOD organizations. It collects, processes, and stores DOD imagery products created by the Department and makes them available to the American public. It trains the Department's public affairs and visual information military and civilian professionals. DMA also operates Stars and Stripes, a news and information organization, free of Government editorial control and censorship, for military audiences overseas. http://www.dma.mil

Defense Prisoner of War / Missing in Action Accounting Agency The Defense POW / MIA Accounting Agency (DPAA) provides centralized management of prisoner of war and missing personnel affairs within the DOD. DPAA's primary responsibilities include leadership for and policy oversight over all efforts to account for Americans still missing from past conflicts and the recovery of and accounting for those who may become isolated in hostile territory in future conflicts. DPAA also provides administrative and logistical support to the U.S.-Russia Joint Commission on POW / MIAs, conducts research and analysis to help resolve cases of those unaccounted for, examines DOD documents for possible public disclosure, and maintains viable channels of communications on POW / MIA matters between the DOD and Congress, the families of the missing, and the American public. http://www.dpaa.mil

Defense Technical Information Center The Defense Technical Information Center (DTIC) is a field activity in the Office of the Under Secretary of Defense for Acquisition, Technology and Logistics. It operates under the authority, direction, and control of the Director of Defense Research and Engineering. DTIC provides defense scientific and technical information, offers controlled access to defense information, and designs and hosts more than 100 DOD Web sites. DTIC's collections include technical reports, summaries of research in progress, independent research and development material, defense technology transfer agreements, and DOD planning

documents. http://www.dtic.mil/dtic/about/about.html

Defense Technology Security Administration The Defense Technology Security Administration (DTSA) is the central DOD point of contact for development and implementation of technology security policies governing defense articles and services and dual-use commodities. DTSA administers the development and implementation of DOD technology security policies on international transfers of defense-related goods, services, and technologies. It does so to ensure that critical U.S. military technological advantages are preserved, transfers that could prove detrimental to U.S. security interests are controlled and limited, weapons of mass destruction and their means of delivery do not proliferate, diversion of defense-related goods to terrorists is prevented, legitimate defense cooperation with foreign friends and allies is supported, and the health of the defense industrial base is assured. http://www.dtsa.mil/SitePages/default.aspx

Education Activity The Department of Defense Education Activity (DODEA) was established in 1992. It consists of two subordinate organizational entities: the Department of Defense Dependents Schools (DODDS) and the Department of Defense Domestic Dependent Elementary and Secondary Schools (DDESS). DODEA formulates, develops, and implements policies, technical guidance, and standards for the effective management of Defense dependents education activities and programs. It also plans, directs, coordinates, and manages the education programs for eligible dependents of U.S. military and civilian personnel stationed overseas and stateside; evaluates the programmatic and operational policies and procedures for DODDS and DDESS; and provides education activity representation at meetings and deliberations of educational panels and advisory groups. http://www.dodea.edu/Americas

Human Resources Field Activity The Department of Defense Human Resources Activity (DODHRA) enhances the operational effectiveness and efficiency of a host of dynamic and diverse programs supporting the Office of the Under Secretary of Defense for Personnel and Readiness. The Field Activity supports policy development, performs cutting-edge research and expert analysis, supports readiness and reengineering efforts, manages the largest automated personnel data repositories in the world, prepares tomorrow's leaders through robust developmental programs, supports recruiting and retaining the best and brightest, and delivers both benefits and critical services to warfighters and their families. http://www.dhra.mil/website/index.shtml

Office of Economic Adjustment The Office of Economic Adjustment (OEA) assists communities that are adversely affected by base closures, expansions, or realignments and Defense contract or program cancellations. OEA provides technical and financial assistance to those communities and coordinates other Federal agencies' involvement through the Defense Economic Adjustment Program. http://www.oea.gov

Test Resource Management The Test Resource Management Center (TRMC) is a DOD Field Activity under the authority, direction, and control of the Under Secretary of Defense for Acquisition, Technology and Logistics. The Center develops policy, plans for, and assesses the adequacy of the major range and test facility base to provide adequate testing in support of development, acquisition, fielding, and sustainment of defense systems. TRMC develops and maintains the test and evaluation resources strategic plan, reviews the proposed DOD test and evaluation budgets, and certifies the adequacy of the proposed budgets and whether they provide balanced support of the strategic plan. TRMC manages the Central Test and Evaluation Investment Program, the Test and Evaluation Science and Technology Program, and the Joint Mission Environment Test Capability Program. http://www.acq.osd.mil/dte-trmc

Washington Headquarters Services Washington Headquarters Services (WHS), established as a DOD Field Activity on October 1, 1977, is under the authority and control of the Deputy Chief Management Officer. WHS provides a range of administrative and operational services to the Office of the Secretary of Defense, specified DOD components, the general public, and for Federal Government activities. WHS services include contracting and procurement; data systems and information technology support; Defense facilities, directives and records, and financial management; enterprise information technology infrastructure, human resource, legal, library, and personnel security services; evaluation and planning functions; Pentagon renovation and construction; and support for advisory boards and commissions. http://www.whs.mil

Sources of Information

Budget Data The Defense Technical Information Center (DTIC) sponsors a Web site that features congressional budget data pertaining to the DOD. The DTIC posts data from each budget report once it is filed and made available on the Library of Congress' Web site. The data are accessible in Portable Document Format (PDF) and Excel spreadsheet format. http://www.dtic.mil/congressional_budget

Business Opportunities Information on and resources for acquisition, business, contracting, and subcontracting opportunities are available on the DOD's Web site. http://www.defense.gov/Resources/Contract-Resources

The Office of Small Business Programs supports the participation of small businesses in the acquisition of goods and services for the DOD. http://www.acq.osd.mil/osbp

Career Opportunities The DOD employs over 718,000 civilian personnel. For additional information on applying for DOD job opportunities, contact Washington Headquarters Services–Human Resources Servicing Team. Phone, 614-692-0252. https://dod.usajobs.gov

Dictionary The Defense Technical Information Center's Web site features the "DOD Dictionary of Military and Associated Terms," which is commonly called the "DOD Dictionary." The dictionary facilitates communication and mutual understanding within the DOD, with external Federal agencies, and between the United States and its international partners by standardizing

military and associated terminology. http://
www.dtic.mil/doctrine/dod_dictionary
**Freedom of Information Act
(FOIA)**   Approved by President Lyndon
B. Johnson in 1966, the statute generally
provides that any person has the right to
request access to Federal agency information
or records. Upon receiving a written
request, the Federal agency holding the
desired document or record must disclose
it. Some records, however, are shielded
from disclosure by one of the FOIA's nine
exemptions or three exclusions. http://open.
defense.gov/Transparency/FOIA.aspx
History   A short history of the Pentagon,
from construction to completion, is available
on the Pentagon Tours Office's Web site.
https://pentagontours.osd.mil/Tours/
construction.jsp
Joint Chiefs of Staff   The Joint Chiefs of Staff
maintain a Web site. http://www.jcs.mil
News   The DOD posts news releases on
its Web site. http://www.defense.gov/News/
News-Releases
Plain Language   The DOD aims to write
documents in readable English by adhering
to Federal plain language guidelines. http://
www.dtic.mil/whs/directives/plainlanguage.
html
Popular Resources   A page of popular
DOD resources is available on the DOD
Web site. http://www.defense.gov/Resources
Social Media   The DOD tweets
announcements and other newsworthy items
on Twitter. https://twitter.com/DeptofDefense
   The DOD has a Facebook account. https://
www.facebook.com/DeptofDefense

The DOD posts videos on its YouTube
channel. https://www.youtube.com/user/
DODvClips/featured
Site Index   The Web site index allows
visitors to look for specific topics or to
browse content that aligns with their
interests. http://www.defense.gov/Site-Index
Speakers   Civilian and military officials
from the DOD are available to speak to
public and private sector groups interested
in defense-related topics, including the
global war on terrorism. Requests for
speakers should be addressed to the Director
for Community Relations and Public Liaison,
1400 Defense Pentagon, Room 2C546,
Washington, DC 20310-1400.
Today in the DOD   The "Today in the
Department of Defense" Web page features
contracts, news and casualty releases,
photos, press advisories, speeches, and
transcripts on a daily basis. http://www.
defense.gov/Today-in-DoD
Tours   For information on guided tours
of the Pentagon, contact the Pentagon
Tours Office. Phone, 703-697-1776.
http://pentagontours.osd.mil | Email: osd.
pentagon.pa.mbx.pentagon-tours-schedule@
mail.mil
Web Sites   A list of DOD Web site links is
available online. http://www.defense.gov/
Military-Services/DoD-Websites
   An A–Z list of DOD Web site links is
available online. http://www.defense.gov/
Military-Services/A-Z-List. http://www.
defense.gov/Contact

For further information concerning the Department of Defense, contact the Director, Directorate for Public Inquiry
and Analysis, Office of the Assistant Secretary of Defense for Public Affairs, 1400 Defense Pentagon, Washington, DC
20301-1400. Phone, 703- 697-9312.

Department of the Air Force

1690 Air Force Pentagon, Washington, DC 20330-1670
Phone, 703-697-6061. Internet, http://www.af.mil.

Air Force Secretariat

Secretary of the Air Force	Dr. Heather A. Wilson
Under Secretary of the Air Force	Lisa S. Disbrow
Administrative Assistant	Patricia J. Zarodkiewicz
Auditor General	Daniel F. McMillin
General Counsel	Joseph M. McDade, Jr.

Information Dominance and Chief Information Officer (A6) — LT. GEN. WILLIAM J. BENDER
Inspector General — LT. GEN. ANTHONY J. ROCK
Legislative Liaison — MAJ. GEN. STEVEN L. BASHAM

Assistant Secretary, Acquisition — DARLENE COSTELLO
Assistant Secretary, Financial Management and Comptroller — DOUG BENNETT
Assistant Secretary, Installations, Environment, and Energy — RICHARD K. HARTLEY
Assistant Secretary, Manpower and Reserve Affairs — DANIEL R. SITTERLY

Deputy Under Secretary for Management — MARILYN M. THOMAS
Deputy Under Secretary, International Affairs — HEIDI H. GRANT
Deputy Under Secretary, Space — WINSTON BEAUCHAMP
Director, Air Force Small Business Programs — MARK S. TESKEY
Director, Public Affairs — BRIG. GEN. EDWARD W. THOMAS, JR.

Air Staff
Chief of Staff — GEN. DAVID L. GOLDFEIN
Vice Chief of Staff — GEN. STEPHEN W. WILSON
Chief Master Sergeant of the Air Force — CMSAF KALETH O. WRIGHT

Assistant Vice Chief of Staff — LT. GEN. STAYCE D. HARRIS
Judge Advocate General — LT. GEN. CHRISTOPHER F. BURNE
Surgeon General — LT. GEN. MARK A. EDIGER

Chief of Air Force Reserve — LT. GEN. MARYANNE MILLER
Chief of Chaplains — MAJ. GEN. DONDI CONSTIN
Chief of Safety — MAJ. GEN. ANDREW MUELLER
Chief of Staff, Strategic Deterrence and Nuclear Integration (A10) — LT. GEN. JACK WEINSTEIN
Chief Scientist — GREG L. ZACHARIAS

Deputy Chief of Staff, Intelligence, Surveillance and Reconnaissance (A2) — LT. GEN. VERALINN JAMIESON
Deputy Chief of Staff, Logistics, Engineering and Force Protection (A4) — LT. GEN. JOHN B. COOPER
Deputy Chief of Staff, Manpower, Personnel and Services (A1) — LT. GEN. GINA GROSSO
Deputy Chief of Staff, Operations, Plans and Requirements (A3) — LT. GEN. MARK C. NOWLAND
Deputy Chief of Staff, Strategic Plans and Programs (A5/8) — LT. GEN. JERRY D. HARRIS, JR.

Director, Air Force Sexual Assault Prevention and Response — MAJ. GEN. JAMES C. JOHNSON
Director, Air National Guard — LT. GEN. L. SCOTT RICE
Director, History and Museums Policies and Programs — WALTER A. GRUDZINSKAS
Director, Studies and Analyses, Assessments (A9) — KEVIN E. WILLIAMS
Director, Test and Evaluation — DEVIN CATE

Major Commands
Air Combat Command — GEN. JAMES M. HOLMES
Air Education and Training Command — LT. GEN. DARRYL L. ROBERSON
Air Force Global Strike Command — GEN. ROBIN RAND

Air Force Materiel Command	GEN. ELLEN M. PAWLIKOWSKI
Air Force Reserve Command	LT. GEN. MARYANNE MILLER
Air Force Space Command	GEN. JOHN W. RAYMOND
Air Force Special Operations Command	LT. GEN. MARSHALL B. WEBB
Air Mobility Command	GEN. CARLTON D. EVERHART II
Pacific Air Forces	GEN. TERRENCE J. O'SHAUGHNESSY
U.S. Air Forces in Europe	GEN. TOD D. WOLTERS

The Department of the Air Force defends the United States by providing air, space, and cyberspace capabilities.

The Department of the Air Force (USAF) was established as part of the National Military Establishment by the National Security Act of 1947 (61 Stat. 502) and came into being on September 18, 1947. The National Security Act Amendments of 1949 redesignated the National Military Establishment as the Department of Defense, established it as an executive department, and made the Department of the Air Force a military department within the Department of Defense (63 Stat. 578). The Department of the Air Force is separately organized under the Secretary of the Air Force. It operates under the authority, direction, and control of the Secretary of Defense (10 U.S.C. 8010). The Department comprises the Office of the Secretary of the Air Force, the Air Staff, and field organizations.

Secretary   The Secretary and Secretariat Staff oversee matters of organization, training, logistical support, maintenance, welfare of personnel, administrative, recruiting, research and development, and other activities that the President or Secretary of Defense prescribes. http://www.af.mil/AboutUs/AirForceSeniorLeaders/SECAF.aspx

Air Staff   The Air Staff assists the Secretary, the Under Secretary, the Assistant Secretaries, and the Chief of Staff in carrying out their responsibilities.

Field Organizations   The major commands, field operating agencies, and direct reporting units constitute the field organizations of the Air Force. They are organized primarily on a functional basis in the United States and on a geographic basis overseas. These commands are responsible for accomplishing certain phases of the Air Force's worldwide activities. They also organize, administer, equip, and train subordinate elements to accomplish assigned missions.

Major Commands: Continental U.S. Commands

Air Combat Command   The Air Combat Command operates CONUS-based, combat-coded fighter and attack aircraft. It organizes, trains, equips, and maintains combat-ready forces for rapid deployment and employment while ensuring strategic air defense forces are ready to meet the challenges of peacetime air sovereignty and wartime air defense. http://www.acc.af.mil

Air Education and Training Command   The Air Education and Training Command recruits, assesses, commissions, educates, and trains Air Force enlisted and officer personnel. It provides basic military training, initial and advanced technical training, flying training, and professional military and post-secondary education. The Command also conducts Air Force security assistance, joint, medical service, and readiness training. http://www.aetc.af.mil

Air Force Global Strike Command   The Air Force Global Strike Command is responsible for the Nation's three intercontinental ballistic missile wings; the Air Force's bomber force, including the B–1, B–2, and B–52 wings; the Long Range Strike Bomber program; and operational and maintenance support to organizations within the nuclear enterprise. http://www.afgsc.af.mil

Air Force Materiel Command   The Air Force Materiel Command delivers expeditionary capabilities through research, development, test, evaluation, acquisition, modernization, and sustainment of aerospace weapon systems throughout their life cycles. Those weapon systems include Air Force fighter, bomber, cargo, and attack fleets and armament. They also include net-centric command and control assets; intelligence, surveillance,

Department of the Air Force

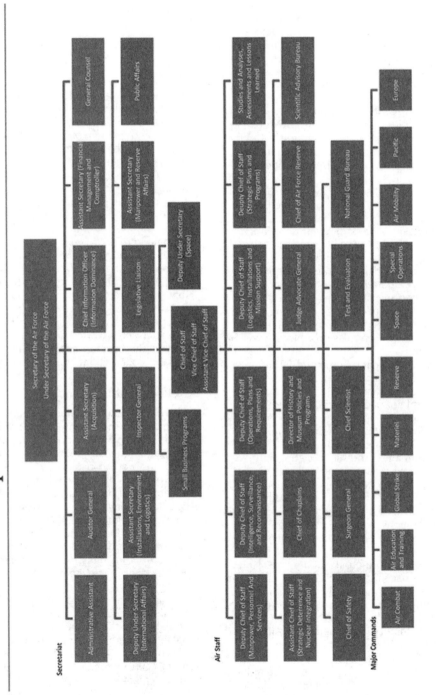

and reconnaissance assets; and combat support information systems. The command oversees basic research and development that support air, space, and cyberspace capabilities. The command relies on an integrated, efficient life cycle management approach to ensure the best possible support to warfighters. http://www.afmc.af.mil

Air Force Reserve Command   The Air Force Reserve Command provides the Air Force with approximately 14 percent of the total force and approximately 4 percent of the manpower budget. Reservists support air, space, and cyberspace superiority; command and control; global integrated intelligence surveillance reconnaissance; global precision attack; nuclear deterrence operations; special operations; rapid global mobility; and personnel recovery. They also perform aircraft flight testing, space operations, and aerial port operations, as well as communications, civil engineer, military training, mobility support, security forces, services, and transportation missions. http://www.afrc.af.mil

Air Force Space Command   The Air Force Space Command provides space and cyberspace capabilities such as missile warning, space control, spacelift, satellite operations, and designated cyberspace activities. http://www.afspc.af.mil

Air Force Special Operations Command   The Air Force Special Operations Command provides the air component of U.S. Special Operations Command. The command deploys specialized air power and delivers special operations combat power wherever and whenever needed. It provides agile combat support, combat search and rescue, information warfare, precision aerospace fires, psychological operations, and specialized aerospace mobility and refueling to unified commands. http://www.afsoc.af.mil

Air Mobility Command   The Air Mobility Command provides airlift, air refueling, special air missions, and aeromedical evacuation for U.S. forces. It also airlifts forces to theater commands to support wartime tasking. http://www.amc.af.mil

Major Commands: Overseas Commands

Pacific Air Forces   The Pacific Air Forces deliver rapid and precise air, space, and cyberspace capabilities to protect the United States, its territories, and its allies and partners; provide integrated air and missile warning and defense; promote interoperability throughout the Pacific area of responsibility; maintain strategic access and freedom of movement across all domains; and posture to respond across the full spectrum of military contingencies to restore regional security. http://www.pacaf.af.mil

U.S. Air Forces in Europe   The U.S. Air Forces in Europe (USAFE) execute the Air Force, European Command, and Africa Command missions with forward-based air power and infrastructure to conduct and enable theater and global operations. The USAFE direct air operations in a theater that spans three continents, covers more than 19 million square miles, contains 104 independent states, produces more than a quarter of the world's gross domestic product, and comprises more than a quarter of Earth's population. http://www.usafe.af.mil

Field Operating Agencies

Air Force Agency for Modeling and Simulation   The Air Force Agency for Modeling and Simulation provides seamless integration of cross-functional live, virtual, and constructive operational training environments that allow war fighters to maximize performance and optimize decisionmaking. The agency works with combatant commands, major commands, the Air Force Reserve Command, the Air National Guard, the Air Force headquarters, direct reporting units, and field operating agencies to provide the necessary development and implementation standards for common access and interoperability within the live, virtual, and constructive domains for efficient and secure global operations. http://www.afams.af.mil

Air Force Audit Agency   The Air Force Audit Agency provides all levels of Air Force management with independent, objective, and quality audit services by reviewing and promoting operational economy, effectiveness, and efficiency; evaluating programs and activities to achieve intended results; and assessing and improving financial reporting. http://www.afaa.af.mil

Air Force Cost Analysis Agency The Air Force Cost Analysis Agency performs nonadvocate cost analyses for major space, aircraft, and information system programs. The agency supports the departmentwide cost analysis program by developing and maintaining cost-estimating tools, techniques, and infrastructure. It provides guidance, analytical support, quantitative risk analyses, and special studies to improve long-range planning, force structure, analysis of alternatives, and lifecycle cost analyses.

Air Force Flight Standards Agency The Air Force Flight Standards Agency performs worldwide inspection of airfields, navigation systems, and instrument approaches. It provides flight standards to develop Air Force instrument requirements and certifies procedures and directives for cockpit display and navigation systems. It also provides air traffic control and airlift procedures and evaluates air traffic control systems and airspace management procedures.

Air Force Historical Research Agency The Air Force Historical Research Agency serves as a repository for Air Force historical records and maintains research facilities for scholars and the general public. http://www.afhra.af.mil/index.asp

Air Force Inspection Agency The Air Force Inspection Agency provides independent inspection, evaluation, oversight, training and analysis to improve the effectiveness and efficiency of the Air Force. http://www.af.mil/AboutUs/FactSheets/Display/tabid/224/Article/104564/air-force-inspection-agency.aspx

Air Force Legal Operations Agency The Air Force Legal Operations Agency includes all senior defense, senior trial, appellate defense, and Government counsel in the Air Force, as well as all Air Force civil litigators who defend the Air Force against civil lawsuits that claim damages and seek other remedies in contracts, environmental, labor, and tort litigation.

Air Force Manpower Analysis Agency The Air Force Manpower Analysis Agency provides analysis and develops tools for helping Air Force and Department of Defense senior leaders make decisions affecting total force manpower requirements. The agency supports the Under Secretary of the Air Force for Management's efforts to improve processes and carries out departmentwide transformation initiatives. It also oversees human capital planning and training to develop and sustain manpower-specific capabilities at adequate levels. http://www.af.mil/AboutUs/FactSheets/Display/tabid/224/Article/104598/air-force-manpower-agency.aspx

Air Force Medical Operations Agency The Air Force Medical Operations Agency assists the Air Force Surgeon General in developing plans, programs, and policies for aerospace medicine, bioenvironmental engineering, clinical investigations, family advocacy, health promotion, military public health, quality assurance, radioactive material management, and the medical service. http://www.airforcemedicine.af.mil/afmoa

Air Force Medical Support Agency The Air Force Medical Support Agency provides consultative support and policy development for the Air Force Surgeon General in medical force management. It also supports ground and air expeditionary medical capabilities used in global, homeland security, and force health protection, as well as all aspects of medical and dental services, aerospace medicine operations, and medical support functions.

Air Force Mortuary Affairs Operations The Air Force Mortuary Affairs Operations, a field operating agency of the Deputy Chief of Staff for Manpower, Personnel and Services, works to support the entire Department of Defense and other Federal entities ensuring dignity, honor and respect to the fallen, and care, service, and support to their families. http://www.mortuary.af.mil

Air Force Office of Special Investigations The Air Force Office of Special Investigations identifies, exploits, and neutralizes criminal, terrorist, and intelligence threats to the U.S. Air Force, Department of Defense, and U.S. Government. Its primary responsibilities are criminal investigations and counterintelligence services. It also protects critical technologies and information, detects and mitigates threats, provides global specialized services, conducts major criminal investigations, and offensively engages foreign adversaries and threats. http://www.osi.af.mil

Air Force Operations Group   The Air Force Operations Group collects, processes, analyzes, and communicates information, enabling situational awareness of USAF operations worldwide. This awareness facilitates timely, responsive, and effective decisionmaking by senior USAF leaders and combatant commanders.

Air Force Personnel Center   The Air Force Personnel Center ensures that commanders around the world have enough skilled Air Force personnel to carry out the mission. The center also runs programs affecting the entire life cycle of military and civilian Air Force personnel from accession through retirement. http://www.af.mil/AboutUs/FactSheets/Display/tabid/224/Article/104554/air-force-personnel-center.aspx

Air Force Program Executive Offices   The Air Force Program Executive Offices (PEOs) oversee the execution of a program throughout its entire lifecycle. While the PEOs are not part of USAF headquarters, they report on acquisition and program-specific issues directly to the Air Force Service Acquisition Executive and the Assistant Secretary of the Air Force for Acquisition. Air Force PEOs are currently responsible for diverse programs in a range of areas: aircraft, command and control and combat support systems, Joint Strike Fighter, and weapons. http://ww3.safaq.hq.af.mil/organizations/index.asp

Air Force Public Affairs Agency   The Air Force Public Affairs Agency manages the Air Force media center. The center collects, archives, and distributes Air Force imagery; manages licensing and branding of Air Force trademarks; provides policy guidance and oversight for the Air Force's Web site and social media programs; operates the Air Force's official social media program; composes original musical arrangements for Air Force regional bands; and develops training curricula and requirements for the Air Force's nearly 6,000 public affairs practitioners. http://www.publicaffairs.af.mil

Air Force Review Boards Agency   The Air Force Review Boards Agency manages various military and civilian appellate processes for the Secretary of the Air Force. http://www.af.mil/AboutUs/FactSheets/Display/tabid/224/Article/104511/air-force-review-boards-agency.aspx

Air Force Safety Center   The Air Force Safety Center promotes safety to reduce the number and severity of mishaps. It also supports combat readiness by developing, implementing, executing, and evaluating Air Force aviation, ground, weapons, nuclear surety, space, and system programs. http://www.safety.af.mil

Air National Guard Readiness Center   The Air National Guard Readiness Center performs the operational and technical tasks associated with manning, equipping, and training Air National Guard units to meet required readiness levels. http://www.angrc.ang.af.mil

National Air and Space Intelligence Center   The National Air and Space Intelligence Center (NASIC) assesses foreign air and space threats. It creates integrated, predictive intelligence in the domains of air, space, and cyberspace to support military operations, force modernization, and policymaking. NASIC analyzes data on foreign aerospace forces and weapons systems to determine performance characteristics, capabilities, vulnerabilities, and intentions. These assessments are used to shape national security and defense policies. NASIC personnel also play a role in weapons treaty negotiations and verification. http://www.nasic.af.mil

Direct Reporting Units

Air Force District of Washington   The Air Force District of Washington supports Headquarters Air Force and other Air Force units in the National Capital Region. http://www.afdw.af.mil

Air Force Operational Test and Evaluation Center   The Air Force Operational Test and Evaluation Center plans and conducts test and evaluation procedures to determine operational effectiveness and suitability of new or modified USAF systems and their capacity to meet mission needs. http://www.afotec.af.mil

U.S. Air Force Academy The U.S. Air Force Academy provides academic and military instruction and experience to prepare future USAF career officers. The Academy offers Bachelor of Science degrees in 31 academic majors, and upon completion, graduates receive commissions as second lieutenants. http://www.usafa.af.mil

Sources of Information

Employment Members of the Air Force civilian service work side by side with active duty airmen. They are a diverse group of professionals: contract specialists, engineers, human resources specialists, intelligence experts, mechanics, scientists, teachers, and more. https://afciviliancareers.com/content/home-air-force-civilian-service

Factsheets Factsheets contain current information and statistics on Air Force careers, organizations, inventory, and equipment—including aircraft and weapons. http://www.af.mil/AboutUs/FactSheets.aspx | Email: DMAPublicAffairs@mail.mil

Freedom of Information Act (FOIA) The Freedom of Information and Privacy Act Office manages the policy and procedural guidance for the Freedom of Information Act (FOIA), Privacy Act (PA) and Quality of Information (QIP) programs in accordance with applicable laws. http://www.foia.af.mil/Welcome.aspx

Links to FOIA requester service centers are available online. The service centers are grouped, by base and command, in two lists. http://www.foia.af.mil/Offices

Frequently Asked Questions (FAQs) The Air Force provides answers to FAQs on its web-site. http://www.af.mil/Questions.aspx

History For over a century, the Air Force has relied on the bravery and skill of American airmen to protect the United States in the air, space, and cyberspace. An overview of that history is available online. https://www.airforce.com/mission/history

Inspector General (IG) The IG receives and investigates complaints of abuse, fraud, and waste involving Air Force personnel or programs. http://www.af.mil/InspectorGeneralComplaints.aspx | Email: usaf.ighotline@mail.mil

Intelligence, Surveillance, and Reconnaissance (ISR) The Air Force's web-site features a section dedicated to ISR activities and news. http://www.af.mil/ISR.aspx

Joining the Air Force To learn about its mission, how to join, and about educational, training, and career opportunities that enlistment offers, visit the Air Force's recruitment Web site. https://www.airforce.com/how-to-join

Medal of Honor Members of the Air Force and its predecessor organizations have earned Medals of Honor. The medal is awarded for conspicuous gallantry and intrepidity at the risk of life above and beyond the call of duty. http://www.af.mil/MedalofHonor.aspx

News The Air Force posts announcements, art, commentaries, news items, and photos on its Web site. Air Force TV and radio news are also accessible online. http://www.af.mil/News.aspx | Email: DMAPublicAffairs@mail.mil

"Air Force Magazine" is posted online. Beginning in January 2013, full issues are available. Beginning in November 2015, HTML5 versions are available. http://www.airforcemag.com/MagazineArchive/Pages/default.aspx

Reading List The Air Force Chief of Staff's annual reading list (2016) is available on the Department's Web site. An archives of the reading list, starting with the year 2007, is also available online. http://static.dma.mil/usaf/csafreadinglist/01_books.html

Sexual Assault The "Sexual Assault Prevention and Response" (SAPR) Web page has information, policies, and reports on sexual assault, as well as links leading to additional resources within the Department of Defense (DOD) community and to external resources. http://www.af.mil/SAPR.aspx

The "SAPR" Web page also provides access to the Safe Helpline—an anonymous, confidential, and free crisis support service for DOD community members who have been affected by sexual assault. Phone, 877-995-5247. https://www.safehelpline.org/about-dod-safe-helpline

Social Media The Air Force has a blog and maintains a social media presence on Facebook, Flickr, Instagram, Twitter, and YouTube. The Web site provides shortcuts to the different platforms as well as social media resources. http://www.af.mil/AFSites/SocialMediaSites.aspx

Strategic Documents   The site contains various "CSAF Focus Area", and other strategic documents in Portable Document Format (PDF). http://www.af.mil/Airpower4America.aspx

Suicide Prevention   The "Suicide Prevention" Web page promotes resources like the ACE (Ask, Care, and Escort) Card and provides access, by phone or confidential online chat, to the Military Crisis Line. Phone, 800-273-8255. http://www.af.mil/SuicidePrevention.aspx

Web sites   A directory of all registered Air Force Web sites is available online. http://www.af.mil/ContactUs.aspx

For further information concerning the Department of the Air Force, contact the Office of the Director of Public Affairs, Department of the Air Force, 1690 Air Force Pentagon, Washington, DC 20330-1670. Phone, 703-697-6061.

Department of the Army

The Pentagon, Washington, DC 20310
Phone, 703-695-6518. Internet, http://www.army.mil.

Executive Office

Secretary of The Army	ROBERT SPEER, ACTING
Under Secretary of the Army	KARL F. SCHNEIDER, ACTING
Administrative Assistant to the Secretary of the Army	GERALD B. O'KEEFE
Auditor General	ANNE L. RICHARDS
Deputy Under Secretary of the Army	THOMAS E. HAWLEY
Director, Small Business Programs	TOMMY L. MARKS
Executive Director, Army National Military Cemeteries	PATRICK K. HALLINAN
General Counsel	(VACANCY)
Inspector General	LT. GEN. DAVID E. QUANTOCK
Assistant Secretary of the Army, Acquisition, Logistics and Technology	STEFFANIE EASTER
Assistant Secretary of the Army, Civil Works	JO-ELLEN DARCY
Assistant Secretary of the Army, Financial Management / Comptroller	ROBERT M. SPEER
Assistant Secretary of the Army, Installations, Energy and Environment	KATHERINE G. HAMMACK
Assistant Secretary of the Army, Manpower and Reserve Affairs	DEBRA S. WADA
Chief Information Officer (G–6)	MAJ. GEN. BRUCE T. CRAWFORD
Chief of Legislative Liaison	MAJ. GEN. LAURA E. RICHARDSON
Chief of Public Affairs	BRIG. GEN. OMAR J. JONES IV

Office of the Chief of Staff

Chief of Staff of the Army	GEN. MARK A. MILLEY
Vice Chief of Staff of the Army	GEN. DANIEL B. ALLYN
Director of the Army Staff	LT. GEN. GARY H. CHEEK
Vice Director of the Army Staff	STEVEN J. REDMANN

Army Staff

Sergeant Major of the Army	SMA DANIEL A. DAILEY
Chief of the National Guard Bureau	GEN. JOSEPH LENGYEL
Assistant Chief of Staff, Installation Management	LT. GEN. GWEN BINGHAM
Chief of Army Reserve	LT. GEN. CHARLES D. LUCKEY

Chief of Chaplains	Maj. Gen. Paul K. Hurley
Chief of Engineers	Lt. Gen. Todd T. Semonite
Director, Army National Guard	Lt. Gen. Timothy J. Kadavy
Judge Advocate General	Lt. Gen. Flora D. Darpino
Provost Marshal General	Maj. Gen. Mark S. Inch
Surgeon General	Lt. Gen. Nadja Y. West

Deputy Chiefs of Staff

Financial Management (G–8)	Lt. Gen. John M. Murray
Intelligence (G–2)	Lt. Gen. Robert P. Ashley, Jr.
Logistics (G–4)	Lt. Gen. Gustave F. Perna
Operations (G–3/5/7)	Lt. Gen. Joseph Anderson
Personnel (G–1)	Lt. Gen. James C. McConville

Commands
Commanding Generals

U.S. Army Forces Command	Gen. Robert B. Abrams
U.S. Army Materiel Command	Gen. Gustave F. Perna
U.S. Army Training and Doctrine Command	Gen. David G. Perkins

Army Service Component Commands
Commanding Generals

U.S. Army Africa / Southern European Task Force	Maj. Gen. Joseph P. Harrington
U.S. Army Central	Lt. Gen. Michael X. Garrett
U.S. Army Europe	Lt. Gen. Ben Hodges
U.S. Army North	Lt. Gen. Jeffrey S. Buchanan
U.S. Army Pacific	Gen. Robert B. Brown
U.S. Army South	Maj. Gen. Clarence K.K. Chinn
U.S. Army Military Surface Deployment and Distribution Command	Maj. Gen. Susan A. Davidson
U.S. Army Space and Missile Defense Command/Army Strategic Command	Lt. Gen. David L. Mann
U.S. Army Special Operations Command	Lt. Gen. Kenneth E. Tovo

Direct Reporting Units

Commandant, U.S. Army War College	Maj. Gen. William E. Rapp
Commander, Second Army	Lt. Gen. Edward C. Cardon
Commander, U.S. Army Accessions Support Brigade	Col. Janet R. Holliday
Director, U.S. Army Acquisition Support Center	Craig A. Spisak
Executive Director, Arlington National Cemetery	Patrick K. Hallinan
Superintendent, U.S. Military Academy	Lt. Gen. Robert L. Caslen, Jr.

Commanding Generals

U.S. Army Corps of Engineers	Lt. Gen. Todd T. Semonite
U.S. Army Criminal Investigation Command	Maj. Gen. Mark S. Inch
U.S. Army Installation Management Command	Lt. Gen. Kenneth R. Dahl
U.S. Army Intelligence and Security Command	Maj. Gen. Christopher S. Ballard
U.S. Army Medical Command	Lt. Gen. Nadja Y. West
U.S. Army Military District of Washington	Maj. Gen. Bradley A. Becker
U.S. Army Reserve Command	Lt. Gen. Charles D. Luckey
U.S. Army Test and Evaluation Command	Maj. Gen. Daniel L. Karbler

---

The Department of the Army equips, organizes, and trains active duty and reserve forces to maintain peace and security and to defend the Nation; administers programs to mitigate erosion and flooding, to develop water resources, to improve waterway navigation, and to protect the environment; and provides military and natural disaster relief assistance to Federal, State, and local government agencies.

DEPARTMENT OF THE ARMY

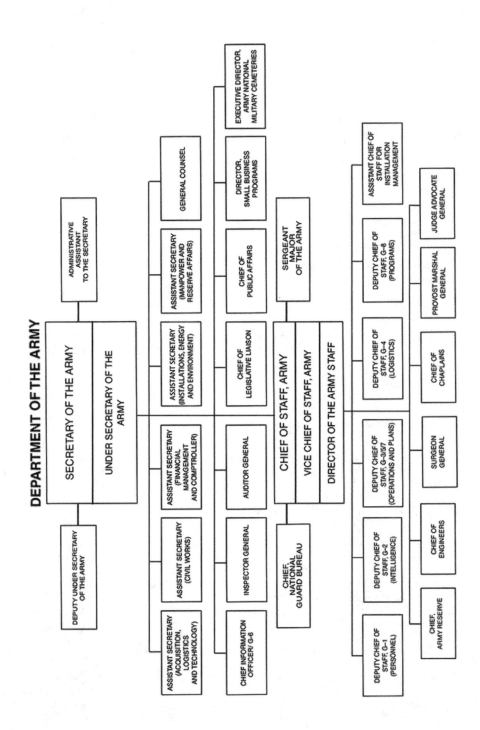

The Continental Congress established the American Continental Army, now called the United States Army, on June 14, 1775, more than a year before the Declaration of Independence. The Department of War was established as an executive department at the seat of Government by act approved August 7, 1789 (1 Stat. 49). The Secretary of War was established as its head. The National Security Act of 1947 (50 U.S.C. 401) created the National Military Establishment, and the Department of War was designated the Department of the Army. The title of its Secretary became Secretary of the Army (5 U.S.C. 171). The National Security Act Amendments of 1949 (63 Stat. 578) provided that the Department of the Army be a military department within the Department of Defense.

Secretary

The Secretary of the Army is the senior official of the Department of the Army. Subject to the direction, authority, and control of the President as Commander in Chief and of the Secretary of Defense, the Secretary of the Army is responsible for and has the authority to conduct all affairs of the Department of the Army, including its organization, administration, operation, efficiency, and such other activities as may be prescribed by the President or the Secretary of Defense as authorized by law. https://www.army.mil/leaders/sa

For further information, call 703-695-2422.

Army Staff

The Army Staff is the Secretary of the Army's military staff. It makes preparations for deploying the Army, including recruiting, organizing, supplying, equipping, training, mobilizing, and demobilizing it, to support the Secretary or the Chief of Staff in his or her executive capacity; investigates and reports on the efficiency of the Army and its preparation for military operations; acts as the agent of the Secretary of the Army and the Chief of Staff in coordinating the action of all organizations of the Department of the Army; and performs other nonstatutory duties that the Secretary of the Army may prescribe.

Program Areas

Civil Functions Civil functions of the Department of the Army include the administration of Arlington and the U.S. Soldiers' and Airmen's Home National Cemeteries and the Civil Works Program— the Nation's principal Federal water resources development activity involving dams, reservoirs, levees, harbors, waterways, locks, and other engineering structures. http://www.army.mil/asacw

History This area includes advisory and coordination service provided to the Army Secretariat and staff on all historical matters: the formulation and execution of the Army historical program, the maintenance of the organizational history of Army units, the preparation and publication of histories that the Army requires, and historical properties. http://www.history.army.mil | Email: usarmy.mcnair.cmh.mbx.answers@mail.mil

Installations This area consists of policies, procedures, and resources for the management of installations to ensure the availability of efficient and affordable base services and infrastructure in support of military missions. It includes the identification and validation of resource requirements, the review of facilities requirements and stationing, and program and budget development and justification. Other activities include support for base operations; base realignment and closure; competitive sourcing; energy security and sustainability; environmental programs; housing; military construction; morale, recreation, and welfare; and real property maintenance and repair. https://www.army.mil/info/organization/unitsandcommands/commandstructure/imcom

Intelligence This area includes management of Army intelligence with responsibility for policy formulation, planning, programming, budgeting, evaluation, and oversight of intelligence activities. The Army Staff is responsible for monitoring relevant foreign intelligence developments and foreign disclosure; imagery, signals, human, open-source, measurement, and signatures intelligence; counterintelligence; threat models and simulations; and security countermeasures. https://www.army.mil/inscom/?from=org

Medical   This area includes management of health services for the Army and as directed for other services, agencies, and organizations; health standards for Army personnel; health professional education and training; career management authority over commissioned and warrant officer personnel of the Army Medical Department; medical research, materiel development, testing, and evaluation; policies concerning health aspects of Army environmental programs and prevention of disease; and planning, programming, and budgeting for Armywide health services. https://www.army.mil/armymedicine/?from=org

Military Operations and Plans   This includes Army forces strategy formation; mid-range, long-range, and regional strategy application; arms control, negotiation, and disarmament; national security affairs; joint service matters; net assessment; politico-military affairs; force mobilization, demobilization, and planning; programming structuring, development, analysis, requirements, and management; operational readiness; overall roles and missions; collective security; individual and unit training; psychological operations; information operations; unconventional warfare; counterterrorism; operations security; signal security; special plans; equipment development and approval; nuclear and chemical matters; civil affairs; military support of civil defense; civil disturbance; domestic actions; command and control; automation and communications programs and activities; management of the program for law enforcement, correction, and crime prevention for military members of the Army; special operations forces; foreign language and distance learning; and physical security.

Reserve Components   This area includes management of individual and unit readiness and mobilization for Reserve Components, which consist of the Army National Guard and U.S. Army Reserve. https://www.army.mil/reserve/?from=org

Religious   This area includes departmentwide management of religious and moral leadership and chaplain support activities; religious ministrations, religious education, pastoral care, and counseling for Army military personnel; liaison with ecclesiastical agencies; chapel construction requirements and design approval; and career management of clergymen serving in the Chaplains Corps. http://www.army.mil/chaplaincorps

Army Commands

U.S. Army Forces Command   Headquartered at Fort Bragg, NC, U.S. Army Forces Command (FORSCOM) prepares conventional forces to provide a sustained flow of trained and ready land power to combatant commanders in defense of the Nation at home and abroad. https://www.army.mil/info/organization/unitsandcommands/commandstructure/forscom/?from=org

For further information, contact the FORSCOM Public Affairs Office. Phone, 910-570-7200.

U.S. Army Materiel Command   U.S. Army Materiel Command (AMC) is the Army's premier provider of materiel readiness—technology, acquisition support, materiel development, logistics power projection, and sustainment—to the total force across the spectrum of joint military operations. Headquartered at Redstone Arsenal, Alabama, AMC's missions include the development of weapon systems, advanced research on future technologies, and maintenance and distribution of spare parts and equipment. AMC works closely with program executive offices, industry, academia, and other Military Services and Government agencies to develop, test, and acquire equipment that soldiers and units need to accomplish their missions. https://www.army.mil/info/organization/unitsandcommands/commandstructure/amc/?from=org

For further information, contact the AMC Public Affairs Office. Phone, 256-450-7978.

U.S. Army Training and Doctrine Command   Headquartered in Fort Eustis, VA, U.S. Army Training and Doctrine Command (TRADOC) develops, educates, and trains soldiers, civilians, and leaders; supports unit training; and designs, builds, and integrates a versatile mix of capabilities, formations, and equipment to strengthen the U.S. Army as a force of decisive action. https://www.army.mil/tradoc/?from=org

For further information, contact the TRADOC Public Affairs Office. Phone, 757-501-5876.

Army Service Component Commands

U.S. Army Africa / Southern European Task Force

U.S. Army Africa (USARAF) / Southern European Task Force (SETAF) is the Army service component command for U.S. Africa Command. It supports U.S. Africa Command operations, employs Army forces as partners, builds sustainable capacity, and supports the joint force to disrupt transnational threats and promote regional security in Africa. http://www.usaraf.army.mil

For further information, contact the USARAF / SETAF Public Affairs Office. Phone, 011-39-0444-71-8341 or 8342.

U.S. Army Central

U.S. Army Central (ARCENT) shapes the U.S. Central Command area of responsibility in 20 countries through forward land power presence and security cooperation engagements that ensure access, build partner capacity, and develop relationships. ARCENT also provides flexible options and strategic depth to the U.S. combatant commander and sets the conditions for improved regional security and stability. http://www.arcent.army.mil | Email: usarmy.shaw.usarcent.mbx.public-affairs@mail.mil

For further information, contact the USARCENT Public Affairs Office. Phone, 803-885-8266.

U.S. Army Europe

U.S. Army Europe (USAREUR) provides the principal land component for U.S. European Command throughout a 51-country area. As the U.S. Army's largest forward-deployed expeditionary force, USAREUR supports NATO and U.S. bilateral, multinational, and unilateral objectives. It supports U.S. Army forces in the European Command area; receives and assists in the reception, staging, and onward movement and integration of U.S. forces; establishes, operates, and expands operational lines of communication; ensures regional security, access, and stability through presence and security cooperation; and supports U.S. combatant commanders and joint and combined commanders. http://www.eur.army.mil

For further information, contact the USAREUR Public Affairs Office. Phone, 011-49-611-143-537-0005 or 0006.

U.S. Army North

U.S. Army North (USARNORTH) supports U.S. Northern Command, the unified command responsible for defending the U.S. homeland and coordinating defense support of civil authorities. USARNORTH helps maintain readiness to support homeland defense, civil support operations, and theater security cooperation activities. http://www.arnorth.army.mil | Email: usarmy.jbsa.arnorth.list.pao-owner@mail.mil

For further information, contact the USARNORTH Public Affairs Office. Phone, 210-221-0015.

U.S. Army South

U.S. Army South (ARSOUTH) is the Army service component command of U.S. Southern Command. ARSOUTH conducts security cooperation and responds to contingencies as part of a whole-of-government approach in conjunction with partner national armies in the U.S. Southern Command area of responsibility, which encompasses 31 countries and 15 areas of special sovereignty in Central and South America and the Caribbean. These activities counter transnational threats and strengthen regional security in defense of the homeland. ARSOUTH maintains a deployable headquarters at Fort Sam Houston, Texas, where it conducts strategic and operational planning. http://www.arsouth.army.mil | Email: usarmy.jbsa.arsouth.mbx.pao@mail.mil

For further information, contact the ARSOUTH Public Affairs Office. Phone, 210-295-6739.

U.S. Army Pacific

U.S. Army Pacific (USARPAC) prepares the force for unified land operations, responds to threats, sustains and protects the force, and builds military relationships that develop partner defense capacity to contribute to the stability and security of the U.S. Pacific Command area of responsibility. USARPAC commands soldiers in an area spanning from the Northwest

Coast and Alaska to the Asia-Pacific region, including Japan. Since September 11, 2001, USARPAC soldiers have played a vital role in homeland defense for Alaska and Hawaii, Guam, and Japan, as well as in supporting operations with our allies elsewhere in the region. https://www.army.mil/info/organization/unitsandcommands/commandstructure/usarpac/?from=org

For further information, contact USARPAC Public Affairs. Phone, 808-438-9761.

U.S. Army Military Surface Deployment and Distribution Command   U.S. Army Military Surface Deployment and Distribution Command (SDDC) delivers world-class, origin-to-destination distribution. It is the Army service component command of the U.S. Transportation Command and a subordinate command to the Army Materiel Command. This relationship links the Transportation Command's joint deployment and distribution enterprise with the Army Materiel Command's materiel enterprise. The SDDC also partners with the commercial transportation industry as the coordinating link between Department of Defense surface transportation requirements and the capability industry provides. http://www.sddc.army.mil

For further information, contact the SDDC Public Affairs Office. Phone, 618-220-6284.

U.S. Army Space and Missile Defense Command / Army Strategic Command   U.S. Army Space and Missile Defense Command (SMDC / ARSTRAT) conducts space and missile defense operations and provides planning, integration, control, and coordination of Army forces and capabilities in support of U.S. Strategic Command missions. SMDC / ARSTRAT also supports space, high-altitude, and global missile defense modernization efforts; serves as the Army operational integrator for global missile defense; and conducts mission-related research and development to support the Army's statutory responsibilities. http://www.army.mil/info/organization/unitsandcommands/commandstructure/smdc

For further information, contact the SMDC Public Affairs Office. Phone, 256-955-3887.

U.S. Army Special Operations Command   U.S. Army Special Operations Command (USASOC) administers, deploys, educates, equips, funds, mans, mobilizes, organizes, sustains, and trains Army special operations forces to carry out missions worldwide, as directed. These special and diverse military operations support regional combatant commanders, American ambassadors, and other agencies. https://www.army.mil/usasoc/?from=org. http://www.soc.mil | Email: pao@soc.mil

For further information, contact the USASOC Public Affairs Office. Phone, 910-432-6005.

Sources of Information

Business Opportunities   For information on contract procurement policies and procedures, contact the Deputy Assistant Secretary of the Army, Procurement. Phone, 703-695-2488. http://www.micc.army.mil/contracting-offices.asp

Assistance for small businesses and minority educational institutions to increase participation in the Army contracting program is available through the Office of Small Business Programs. Phone, 703-697-2868. Fax, 703-693-3898. http://www.micc.army.mil/small-business.asp

Cemeteries   Arlington National Cemetery is one of the two national military cemeteries that the Army maintains. This cemetery is the final resting place for more than 400,000 active duty servicemembers, veterans, and their families. For more information, visit its Web site or contact the cemetery. Phone, 877-907-8585. http://www.arlingtoncemetery.mil

The U.S. Soldiers' and Airmen's Home National Cemetery is one of the two national military cemeteries that the Army maintains. This cemetery is the final resting place for more than 14,000 veterans, including those that fought in the Civil War. For more information, visit its Web site or contact the Superintendent. Phone, 877-907-8585. http://www.nps.gov/nr/travel/national_cemeteries/district_of_columbia/us_soldiers_and_airmens_home_national_cemetery.html

Environment   Information is available from the U.S. Army Environmental Command. https://aec.army.mil

Information is also available from the Office of the Deputy Assistant Secretary of the Army for Environment, Safety and Occupational Health. http://www.asaie.army.mil/Public/ESOH

The Army Environmental Policy Institute posts publications on its Web site. "Army Water Security Strategy" (DEC 2011), the results of the first comprehensive study of Army water security management, is available in Portable Document Format (PDF). "Quantifying the Army Supply Chain Water Bootprint" (DEC 2011), an initial step to quantify the amount of water used by suppliers to produce the goods and services that the Army procures through the supply chain, is also available in PDF. http://www.aepi.army.mil

Employment   More than 330,000 Army civilians work in a wide range of diverse professions. These professionals are not active duty military, but serve as an integral part of the Army team to support the defense of the Nation. http://armycivilianservice.com

Films   Address loan requests for Army-produced films to the Visual Information Support Centers of Army installations. Unclassified Army productions are available for sale from the National Audiovisual Center, National Technical Information Service, 5301 Shawnee Road, Alexandria, VA 22312. Phone, 800-553-6847. http://www.ntis.gov/Index.aspx | Email: orders@ntis.gov

Freedom of Information Act (FOIA)   Contact the appropriate information management officer associated with the Army installation or activity managing the desired information. Information is also available on the Records Management and Declassification Agency's Web site. https://www.rmda.army.mil

Frequently Asked Questions (FAQs)   The Army posts answers to FAQs on its Web site. https://www.army.mil/faq

Gold Star Survivors   All Gold Star family members have made a sacrifice to the Nation. The Army recognizes that no one gives more for the Nation than a family member of the fallen. Gold Star Mother's and Family's Day is the last Sunday of September, and Gold Star Spouses Day is April 5. https://www.army.mil/goldstar

History   "Army History" magazine, the professional bulletin of Army history, is available online in Portable Document Format (PDF). http://www.history.army.mil/news/2016/160900a_armyHistoryMag.html

A directory of Army museums is available on the Center of Military History's Web site. http://www.history.army.mil/museums/directory.html

The Office of Historic Properties and Partnerships raises awareness of and explores and tests creative uses for the Army's historic buildings. Its staff also promotes partnerships between the Army and nonprofit organizations, public or private, to preserve, renovate, and restore. http://www.asaie.army.mil/Public/IH/OHP/ohp.htm

Joining the Army   Information on Army life, assignments, benefits, pay, and enlisting or joining in other capacities is available online. Phone, 888-550-2769. http://www.goarmy.com

National Guard   The National Guard responds to domestic emergencies, counterdrug efforts, overseas combat missions, reconstruction missions, and more. The President or a State governor can call on the Guard in a moment's notice. Guard soldiers hold civilian jobs or attend college while maintaining their military training on a part-time basis, and their primary area of operation is their home state. https://www.nationalguard.com

Public Affairs / Community Relations   For official Army and community relations information, contact the Office of the Chief of Public Affairs. Phone, 703-695-0616. Automated assistance is available after normal work hours. Phone, 201-590-6575. http://www.army.mil/info/institution/publicAffairs

Publications   To request a publication, contact either the proponent listed on the title page of the document or the information management officer of the Army activity that publishes the desired publication. If the requester does not know which Army activity published the document, contact the Publishing Division, Army Publishing Directorate. Phone, 703-693-1557. http://www.army.mil/media/publications

Official texts published by Headquarters, Department of the Army, are available from the National Technical Information Service. Phone, 888-584-8332. http://www.ntis.gov

Ranks Descriptions of officer, warrant officer, and enlisted ranks are available on the Army Web site. https://www.army.mil/symbols/armyranks.html

Reading List The U.S. Army Chief of Staff's professional reading list comprises three categories—Armies at war: battles and campaigns; the Army profession; and strategy and the strategic environment—and is accessible online. http://www.history.army.mil/html/books/105/105-1-1/index.html

Research The Research, Development and Engineering Command is the Army's technology leader and largest technology developer. Its Web site features news on and resources related to long-range research and development plans for materiel requirements and objectives. Phone, 443-395-4006 (Public Affairs) or 3922 (Media Relations). http://www.army.mil/info/organization/unitsandcommands/commandstructure/rdecom

Reserve Officers' Training Corps (ROTC) Available at over 1,100 colleges and universities nationwide, the ROTC offers merit-based scholarships that can cover the full cost of tuition and open educational opportunities. http://www.goarmy.com/rotc.html

Site Index The Army's Web site features an A–Z index. https://www.army.mil/info/a-z

Specialized Careers Information on how to become an Army chaplain, the chaplain candidate program, and chaplain corps careers and jobs is available online and from the U.S. Army Recruiting Command. Phone, 877-437-6572. http://www.goarmy.com/chaplain

Health care professionals serving as officers in the Army's medical department benefit from a wide range of opportunities and financial incentives. http://www.goarmy.com/amedd.html

Members of the Army Judge Advocate General's corps often represent soldiers during courts-martial; however, they also engage in a wider range of legal activities that include civil litigation, international law, labor law, and tort claims. For more information, contact the Army Judge Advocate Recruiting Office. Phone, 866-276-9524. http://www.goarmy.com/jag

The Army relies on talented musicians to assist with military ceremonies, boost morale, and provide entertainment. http://www.goarmy.com/band.html

Speakers The Public Affairs Office nearest the event can help provide local Army speakers. The Office of the Chief of Public Affairs can assist with scheduling a general officer to address Army matters at public forums. To request a general officer speaker, writer to the Office of the Chief of Public Affairs, ATTN: Community Relations, Division (Speaker Request), 1500 Army Pentagon, Washington, DC 20310-1500. A lead time of at least 60–90 days is required. Phone, 703-614-1107. http://www.army.mil/comrel/assetrequests

U. S. Military Academy West Point has been educating, training, and inspiring U.S. Army leaders for more than 200 years. The academy offers a 47-month leader-development program of academic rigor, military discipline, and physical challenges with adherence to a code of honor. http://www.usma.edu | Email: admissions-info@usma.edu. http://www.army.mil/info/institution/publicAffairs

For further information concerning the Department of the Army, contact U.S. Army Public Affairs, Community Relations Division, Office of the Chief of Public Affairs, 1500 Army Pentagon, Washington, DC 20310-1500.

Department of the Navy

The Pentagon, Washington, DC 20350
Phone, 703-697-7391. Internet, http://www.navy.mil.

Secretary of the Navy	SEAN J. STACKLEY, ACTING
Under Secretary of the Navy	THOMAS P. DEE, ACTING
Assistant Secretaries	
Energy, Installations and Environment	STEVEN R. ISELIN, ACTING
Financial Management / Comptroller	JOSEPH B. MARSHALL JR., ACTING
Manpower and Reserve Affairs	ROBERT L. WOODS, ACTING
Research, Development and Acquisition	ALLISON F. STILLER
Auditor General	DONJETTE L. GILMORE, ACTING
Chief Information Officer	ROBERT FOSTER
Chief of Information	REAR ADM. DAWN CUTLER, ACTING
Chief of Legislative Affairs	REAR ADM. CRAIG S. FALLER
Chief of Naval Research	REAR ADM. DAVID J. HAHN
Director, Naval Criminal Investigative Service	ANDREW L. TRAVER
General Counsel	ANNE M. BRENNAN, ACTING
Judge Advocate General	VICE ADM. JAMES W. CRAWFORD III
Naval Inspector General	VICE ADM. HERMAN SHELANSKI
Deputy Under Secretary of the Navy (Management)	SCOTT W. LUTTERLOH
Director, Sexual Assault Prevention and Response Office	JILL VINES LOFTUS
Chief of Naval Operations	ADMIRAL JOHN M. RICHARDSON
Vice Chief of Naval Operations	ADMIRAL BILL MORAN
Master Chief Petty Officer of the Navy	STEVEN S. GIORDANO

Naval Operations

Chief of Naval Operations	ADM. JOHN M. RICHARDSON
Vice Chief of Naval Operations	ADM. WILLIAM F. MORAN
Deputy Chiefs of Naval Operations	
Fleet Readiness and Logistics	VICE ADM. DIXON SMITH
Information Dominance	VICE ADM. JAN TIGHE
Integration of Capabilities and Resources	VICE ADM. WILLIAM LESCHER
Manpower, Personnel, Training Education	VICE ADM. ROBERT P. BURKE
Operations, Plans and Strategy	VICE ADM. JOHN C. AQUILINO
Directors	
Naval Intelligence	VICE ADM. JAN TIGHE
Naval Nuclear Propulsion Program	ADM. JAMES F. CALDWELL
Navy Staff	VICE ADM. JAMES G. FOGGO
Test and Evaluation and Technology Requirements / Chief of Naval Research	REAR ADM. DAVID J. HAHN
Chief of Chaplains of the Navy	REAR ADM. MARGARET G. KIBBEN
Chief of Naval Reserve	VICE ADM. LUKE MCCOLLUM
Master Chief Petty Officer of the Navy	STEVEN GIORDANO
Oceanographer of the Navy / Navigator of the Navy	REAR ADM. TIMOTHY C. GALLAUDET
Surgeon General of the Navy	VICE ADM. C. FORREST FAISON III

Shore Establishment

Chief of Naval Operations	ADM. JOHN M. RICHARDSON
Commanders	
Naval Air Systems Command	VICE ADM. PAUL GROSKLAGS

Naval Education and Training Command	Rear Adm. Michael S. White
Naval Facilities Engineering Command	Rear Adm. Kate L. Gregory
Naval Legal Service Command	Rear Adm. John G. Hannink
Naval Meteorology and Oceanography	Rear Adm. Timothy C. Galludet
Naval Network Warfare Command	Capt. John W. Chandler
Naval Sea Systems Command	Vice Adm. Thomas Moore
Naval Supply Systems Command	Rear Adm. Jonathan A. Yuen
Naval Warfare Development Command	Rear Adm. Bret C. Batchelder
Navy Installations Command	Vice Adm. Dixon Smith
Space and Naval Warfare Systems Command	Rear Adm. David H. Lewis
Chief, Bureau of Medicine and Surgery	Vice Adm. C. Forrest Faison III
Chief, Naval Personnel	Vice Adm. Robert P. Burke
Director, National Maritime Intelligence-Integration Office / Commander, Office of Naval Intelligence	Rear Adm. Elizabeth L. Train
Director, Strategic Systems Program	Rear Adm. Terry J. Benedict
Superintendent, U.S. Naval Academy	Vice Adm. Walter E. Carter, Jr.

Operating Forces
Commanders

U.S. Fleet Forces Command	Adm. Philip S. Davidson
Pacific Fleet	Adm. Scott H. Swift
Military Sealift Command	Rear Adm. Dee L. Mewbourne
Naval Forces Central Command	Vice Adm. Kevin M. Donegan
Naval Forces Europe	Adm. Michelle J. Howard
Naval Reserve Forces Command	Rear Adm. Thomas W. Luscher
Naval Special Warfare Command	Rear Adm. Timothy Szymanski
Operational Test and Evaluation Force	Rear Adm. Jeffrey R. Penfield

[For the Department of the Navy statement of organization, see the Code of Federal Regulations, Title 32, Part 700]

The Department of the Navy protects the United States and its interests by the prosecution of war at sea, including the seizure or defense of advanced naval bases with the assistance of its Marine Corps component; supports the forces of all military departments of the United States; and safeguards freedom of the seas.

The United States Navy was founded on October 13, 1775, when Congress enacted the first legislation creating the Continental Navy of the American Revolution. The Department of the Navy and the Office of Secretary of the Navy were established by act of April 30, 1798 (10 U.S.C. 5011, 5031). For 9 years prior to that date, by act of August 7, 1789 (1 Stat. 49), the Secretary of War oversaw the conduct of naval affairs.

The National Security Act Amendments of 1949 provided that the Department of the Navy be a military department within the Department of Defense (63 Stat. 578).

The President appoints the Secretary of the Navy as the head of the Department of the Navy. The Secretary is responsible to the Secretary of Defense for the operation and efficiency of the Navy (10 U.S.C. 5031).

The Department of the Navy includes the U.S. Coast Guard when it is operating as a Service in the Navy.

Secretary   The Secretary of the Navy is the head of the Department of the Navy, responsible for the policies and control of the Department of the Navy, including its organization, administration, functioning, and efficiency. The members of the Secretary's executive administration assist in the discharge of the responsibilities of the Secretary of the Navy. http://www.navy.mil/secnav

Legal   The Office of the Judge Advocate General provides all legal advice and related services throughout the Department of the Navy, except for the advice and services provided by the General Counsel. It also provides legal and policy advice

DEPARTMENT OF THE NAVY

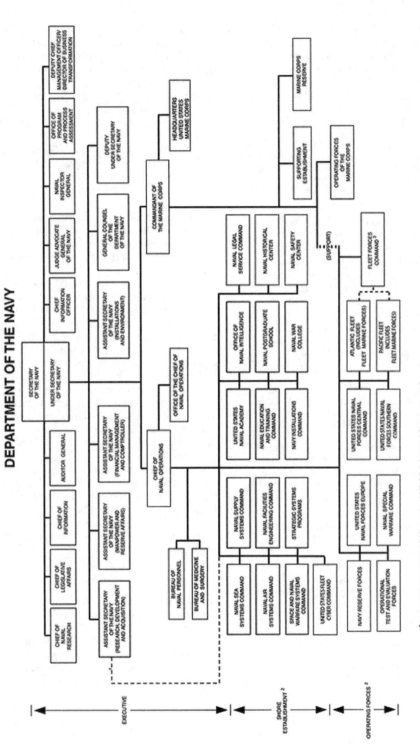

1 Systems commands and SSP report to ASN (RDA) for acquisition matters only.
2 Also includes other Echelon 2 commands and subordinate activities under the command or supervision of the designated organizations.
3 For Interdeployment Training Cycle purposes, Commander, Fleet Forces Command Controls LANFLT and PACFLT assets.

EXECUTIVE

SHORE ESTABLISHMENT 2

OPERATING FORCES 2

to the Secretary of the Navy on military justice, ethics, administrative law, claims, environmental law, operational and international law and treaty interpretation, and litigation involving these issues. The Judge Advocate General provides technical supervision for the Naval Justice School at Newport, RI. http://www.navy.mil/local/jag/index.asp

For further information, contact the Office of the Judge Advocate General, Department of the Navy, Washington Navy Yard, Suite 3000, 1322 Patterson Avenue SE., Washington Navy Yard, DC 20374-5066. Phone, 202-685-5190.

Criminal Investigations   The Naval Criminal Investigative Service investigates and neutralizes criminal, terrorist, and foreign intelligence threats to the United States Navy and Marine Corps. To carry out its mission, the Service relies on the professionalism and law enforcement expertise of administrative support personnel, forensic specialists, intelligence analysts, investigators, military personnel, security specialists, special agents, and technical investigative specialists. http://www.ncis.navy.mil

For further information, contact the Naval Criminal Investigative Service, 27130 Telegraph Road, Quantico, VA 22134. Phone, 877-579-3648.

Research   The Office of Naval Research initiates, coordinates, plans, and promotes naval research, including the coordination of research and development conducted by other agencies and offices in the Department of the Navy. The Office researches, develops, and delivers decisive naval capabilities by investing in a balanced portfolio of promising scientific research, innovative technology, and talent. It also manages and controls activities within the Department concerning copyrights, inventions, manufacturing technology, patents, royalty payments, small businesses, and trademarks. http://www.onr.navy.mil | Email: onrpublicaffairs@navy.mil

For further information, contact the Public Affairs Office, Office of Naval Research, One Liberty Center, 875 North Randolph Street, Arlington, VA 22203-1995. Phone, 703-696-5031.

Operating Forces   Operating forces carry out operations that enable the Navy to meet its responsibility to uphold and advance the national policies and interests of the United States. These forces include the several fleets; seagoing, fleet marine, and other assigned Marine Corps forces; the Military Sealift Command; Naval Reserve forces; and other forces and activities that the President or the Secretary of the Navy may assign. The Chief of Naval Operations administers and commands the operating forces of the Navy.

The Atlantic Fleet is composed of ships, submarines, and aircraft that operate throughout the Atlantic Ocean and Mediterranean Sea.

The Naval Forces Europe includes forces assigned by the Chief of Naval Operations or made available from either the Pacific or Atlantic Fleet to operate in the European theater.

The Pacific Fleet is composed of ships, submarines, and aircraft operating throughout the Pacific and Indian Oceans.

The Military Sealift Command provides ocean transportation for personnel and cargo of all components of the Department of Defense and, as authorized, for other Federal agencies; operates and maintains underway replenishment ships and other vessels providing mobile logistic support to elements of the combatant fleets; and operates ships in support of scientific projects and other programs for Federal agencies.

Other major commands of the operating forces of the Navy are the Naval Forces Central Command, Operational Test and Evaluation Force, Naval Special Warfare Command, and Naval Reserve Force. http://www.navy.mil/navydata/organization/orgopfor.asp

Activities

Air Systems   The Naval Air Systems Command provides full life-cycle support of naval aviation aircraft, weapons, and systems operated by Sailors and Marines. This support includes research, design, development, and systems engineering; acquisition; test and evaluation; training facilities and equipment; repair and modification; and in-service engineering and logistics support. The Command comprises eight "competencies" or communities of practice: program management, contracts, research and engineering, test and evaluation, logistics and industrial operations, corporate operations, comptroller, and counsel. The Command also supports the affiliated naval aviation program executive officer and the assigned program managers, who are responsible for meeting the cost, schedule, and performance requirements of their assigned programs. It is the principal provider for the Naval Aviation Enterprise, while contributing to every warfare enterprise in the interest of national security. http://www.navair.navy.mil

For further information, contact the Commander, Naval Air Systems Command, 47123 Buse Road, Building 2272, Suite 540, Patuxent River, MD 20670-1547. Phone, 301-757-7825.

Coast Guard The Commandant of the Coast Guard reports to the Secretary of the Navy and the Chief of Naval Operations when the Coast Guard is operating as a service in the Navy and represents the Coast Guard before the Joint Chiefs of Staff. During such service, Coast Guard operations are integrated and uniform with Department of the Navy operations to the maximum extent possible. The Commandant of the Coast Guard organizes, trains, prepares, and maintains the readiness of the Coast Guard for the performance of national defense missions as directed. The Commandant also maintains a security capability; enforces Federal laws and regulations on and under the high seas and waters subject to the jurisdiction of the United States; and develops, establishes, maintains, and operates aids to maritime navigation, as well as ice-breaking and rescue facilities, with due regard to the requirements of national defense. http://www.uscg.mil

Computers and Telecommunications Naval Network Warfare Command operates the Navy's networks to achieve effective command and control through optimal alignment, common architecture, mature processes, and functions and standard terminology. The command enhances the Navy's network security posture and improves IT services through standardized enterprise-level management, network information assurance compliance, enterprise management, and root cause

and trend analysis. Naval Network Warfare Command also delivers enhanced space products to operating forces by leveraging Department of Defense, national, commercial, and international space capabilities. The command serves as the Navy's commercial satellite operations manager; it executes tactical-level command and control of Navy networks and leverages Joint Space capabilities for Navy and Joint Operations. http://www.public.navy.mil/fcc-c10f/nnwc/Pages/default.aspx

For further information, contact Public Affairs, Naval Network Warfare Command, 112 Lake View Parkway, Suffolk, VA 23435. Phone, 757-203-0205.

Education and Training The Naval Education and Training Command provides shore-based education and training for Navy, certain Marine Corps, and other personnel; develops specifically designated education and training afloat programs for the fleet; provides voluntary and dependents education; and participates with research and development activities in the development and implementation of the most effective teaching and training systems and devices for optimal education and training. http://www.navy.mil/local/cnet/ | Email: pnsc.netc.pao@navy.mil

For further information, contact the NETC Office of Public Affairs, 250 Dallas Street, Pensacola, FL 32508-5220. Phone, 850-452-4858.

Facilities The Naval Facilities Engineering Command provides material and technical support to the Navy and Marine Corps for shore facilities, real property and utilities, fixed ocean systems and structures, transportation and construction equipment, energy, environmental and natural resources management, and support of the naval construction forces. http://www.navy.mil/local/navfachq

For further information, contact the Commander, Naval Facilities Engineering Command and Chief of Civil Engineers, Washington Navy Yard, 1322 Patterson Avenue SE., Suite 1000, Washington, DC 20374-5065. Phone, 202-685-1423.

Intelligence The Office of Naval Intelligence ensures the fulfillment of the intelligence requirements and responsibilities of the Department of the Navy. http://www.oni.navy.mil | Email: pao@nmic.navy.mil

For further information, contact the Office of Public Affairs, Office of Naval Intelligence, Department of the Navy, 4251 Suitland Road, Washington, DC 20395-5720. Phone, 301-669-5670.

Manpower   The Bureau of Naval Personnel directs the procurement, distribution, administration, and career motivation of the military personnel of the regular and reserve components of the U.S. Navy to meet the quantitative and qualitative manpower requirements determined by the Chief of Naval Operations. http://www.navy.mil/cnp/index.asp

For further information, contact the Bureau of Naval Personnel, Department of the Navy, Federal Office Building 2, Washington, DC 20370-5000. Phone, 703-614-2000.

Medicine   The Bureau of Medicine and Surgery directs the medical and dental services for Navy and Marine Corps personnel and their dependents; administers the implementation of contingency support plans and programs to effect medical and dental readiness capability; provides medical and dental services to the fleet, fleet marine force, and shore activities of the Navy; and ensures cooperation with civil authorities in matters of public health disasters and other emergencies. http://www.med.navy.mil

For further information, contact the Bureau of Medicine and Surgery, Department of the Navy, 2300 E Street NW., Washington, DC 20373-5300. Phone, 202-762-3211.

Oceanography   The Naval Meteorology and Oceanography Command and the Naval Observatory are responsible for the science, technology, and engineering operations that are essential to explore the ocean and the atmosphere and to provide astronomical data and time for naval and related national objectives. To that end, the naval oceanographic program studies astrometry, hydrography, meteorology, oceanography, and precise time. http://www.usno.navy.mil/USNO

For further information, contact the Commander, Naval Meteorology and Oceanography Command, 1100 Balch Boulevard, Stennis Space Center, MS 39529-5005. Phone, 228-688-4384. Internet, http://www.navmetoccom.navy.mil. Or, contact the Oceanographer of the Navy, U.S. Naval Observatory, 3450 Massachusetts Avenue NW., Washington, DC 20392-1800. Phone, 202-762-1026.

Sea Systems   The Naval Sea Systems Command provides material support to the Navy and Marine Corps and to the Departments of Defense and Transportation for ships, submarines, and other sea platforms, shipboard combat systems and components, other surface and undersea warfare and weapons systems, and ordnance expendables not specifically assigned to other system commands. http://www.navsea.navy.mil | Email: nssc_public_affairs@navy.mil

For further information, contact the Office of Public Affairs, Naval Sea Systems Command, 1333 Isaac Hull Avenue SE., Washington Navy Yard, DC 20376-1010. Phone, 202-781-4123.

Space and Naval Warfare   The Space and Naval Warfare Systems Command develops, delivers, and sustains advanced cyber capabilities for naval warfighters. It helps provide the hardware and software needed to executive Navy missions. With nearly 10,000 active military and civilian professionals worldwide, the Command is at the forefront of research, engineering, and acquisition relevant for keeping U.S. military forces connected around the globe. http://www.spawar.navy.mil

For further information, contact the Commander, Space and Naval Warfare Systems Command, 4301 Pacific Highway, San Diego, CA 92110-3127. Phone, 619-524-3428.

Strategic Systems   The Office of Strategic Systems Programs provides development, production, and material support to the Navy for fleet ballistic missile and strategic weapons systems, security, training of personnel, and the installation and direction of necessary supporting facilities. http://www.ssp.navy.mil

For further information, contact the Director, Strategic Systems Programs, Department of the Navy, Nebraska Avenue Complex, 287 Somers Court NW., Suite 10041, Washington, DC 20393-5446. Phone, 202-764-1608.

Supply Systems   The Naval Supply Systems Command provides supply management policies and methods and administers related support service systems for the Navy and Marine Corps. http://www.navy.mil/local/navsup | Email: navsuphqQuestions@navy.mil

For further information, contact the Commander, Naval Supply Systems Command, 5450 Carlisle Pike, P.O. Box 2050, Mechanicsburg, PA 17055-0791. Phone, 717-605-3565.

Warfare Development The Navy Warfare Development Command plans and coordinates experiments employing emerging operational concepts; represents the Department of the Navy in joint and other service laboratories and facilities and tactical development commands; and publishes and disseminates naval doctrine. http://www.navy.mil/local/nwdc

For further information, contact the Commander, Navy Warfare Development Command, 686 Cushing Road, Sims Hall, Newport, RI 02841. Phone, 401-841-2833.

Sources of Information

Business Opportunities "Open for Business," a short video that gives an overview of the Navy's buying activities and small business programs, is available online. For more information, contact the Office of Small Business Programs. Phone, 202-685-6485. http://www.secnav.navy.mil/smallbusiness/Pages/video-openforbusiness.aspx | Email: osbp.info@navy.mil

Civilian Employment The possibilities of a civilian career at the Department of the Navy are many and diverse. They include a full range of occupations: from aircraft mechanic to pipefitter, from electrician to engineer, from zoologist to physician, and more. The Navy offers hundreds of different occupations nationwide and around the world. http://www.secnav.navy.mil/donhr/Pages/Default.aspx | Email: donhrfaq@navy.mil

Environment For information on Navy and Marine Corps environmental protection and natural resources management programs, contact the Deputy Assistant Secretary–Environment, 1000 Navy Pentagon, Room 4A674, Washington, DC 20350-1000. Phone, 703-614-5493. http://www.secnav.navy.mil/eie/Pages/Environment.aspx

The "U.S. Navy Climate Change Roadmap" (April 2010) is available in Portable Document Format (PDF) online. http://www.navy.mil/navydata/documents/CCR.pdf

The Navy has posted its environmental goals and descriptions of its strategies to achieve them. http://greenfleet.dodlive.mil/environment

Glossary The origins of Navy terminology section explains nautical terminology that has become a part of everyday English. http://www.navy.mil/navydata/traditions/html/navyterm.html

Joining the Navy Unparalleled opportunities, challenges, and experiences motivate bright and skilled people to join. America's Navy offers careers and jobs that match many backgrounds and interests. Hundreds of distinct roles in dozens of professional fields are part of what the Navy has to offer. http://www.navy.com/joining.html

Naval Oceanography Portal The U.S. Naval Meteorology and Oceanography Command provides information from the ocean depths to the distant reaches of space to meet the needs of civilian and the military and scientific communities. http://www.usno.navy.mil

The U.S. Naval Observatory offers a wide range of astronomical data and products, and it serves as the official source of time for the Department of Defense and as the official source of a standard of time for the entire United States. http://www.usno.navy.mil/USNO

"The Sky This Week" is a weekly set of pictures and descriptions of the planets, sky, and stars. http://www.usno.navy.mil/USNO/tours-events/sky-this-week/the-sky-this-week

News The Navy posts recent headline news stories on its Web site. http://www.navy.mil/listStories.asp?x=2

An online subscription form is available to sign up for updates from the Navy news service. https://service.govdelivery.com/accounts/USNAVYDMA/subscriber/new

"All Hands" magazine is an electronic publication for sailors by sailors. It features articles, imagery, information, and videos that are relevant to sailors and their families. http://www.navy.mil/ah_online

Research Programs Research programs of the Office of Naval Research cover a broad spectrum of scientific fields. The research is primarily for the needs of the Navy and Marine Corps, but some of these programs conduct research that has relevance for the general public. For information on specific research programs, contact the Office of Naval Research–Public Affairs, One Liberty Center 875 N. Randolph Street, Arlington, VA 22203-1995. Phone, 703-696-5031. http://www.onr.navy.mil

Ships   The Navy operates and relies on many types of ships to carry out its mission.

Descriptions of these different ships—aircraft carriers, amphibious assault ships, cruisers, destroyers, littoral combat ships, and submarines—are available online. http://www.navy.mil/navydata/our_ships.asp

Site Index   An A–Z information index is available on the Navy's Web site. http://www.navy.mil/navydata/infoIndex.asp?id=A. http://www.navy.mil/submit/contacts.asp

For further information concerning the Navy, contact the Office of Information, Department of the Navy, 1200 Navy Pentagon, Washington, DC 20350-1200. For press inquiries, phone 703-697-7391 or 703-697-5342.

United States Marine Corps
Commandant of the Marine Corps, Headquarters, U.S. Marine Corps, 3000 Pentagon, Washington, DC 20380-1775
Phone, 703-614-1034. Internet, http://www.usmc.mil.

Commandant of the Marine Corps	Gen. Robert B. Neller
Assistant Commandant of the Marine Corps	Gen. Glenn M. Wa
Sergeant Major of the Marine Corps	Sgt. Maj. Ronald L. Green

The Continental Congress established the United States Marine Corps by resolution on November 10, 1775. Marine Corps composition and functions are detailed in 10 U.S.C. 5063.

The Marine Corps, which is part of the Department of the Navy, is the smallest of the Nation's combat forces. It also is the only service that the Congress has tasked specifically to be able to fight in the air, on land, and at sea. Although Marines fight in each of these dimensions, they are primarily a maritime force linked with the Navy, moving from the sea to fight on land.

The Marine Corps conducts entry-level training for its enlisted marines at two bases: Marine Corps Recruit Depot, Parris Island, SC; and Marine Corps Recruit Depot, San Diego, CA. Officer candidates are evaluated at Officer Candidate School, Marine Corps Combat Development Command, Quantico, VA. Marines train to be first on the scene to respond to attacks on the United States or its interests and to acts of political violence against Americans abroad, to provide disaster relief and humanitarian assistance, and to evacuate Americans from foreign countries.

Sources of Information

DSTRESS Line   The DSTRESS Line offers an around-the-clock anonymous phone, live chat, and referral service. The call center is staffed with veteran Marines, Fleet Marine Force Navy Corpsmen who were previously attached to the Marine Corps, Marine spouses and other family members, and licensed behavioral health counselors trained in Marine Corps culture. DSTRESS Line is designed to help callers improve overall fitness and to develop the necessary skills for coping with the challenges of life in the Marine Corps. Phone, 877-476-7734. http://www.usmc-mccs.org/index.cfm/services/support/dstress-line | Email: dstressline@usmc.mil

Electronic Publications   Authentic and current digital versions of publications issued by Headquarters Marine Corps staff agencies, major commands, and other Department of Defense and Federal agencies are available online. http://www.marines.mil/News/Publications

Freedom of Information Act (FOIA)   Procedures for requesting records that the U.S. Marine Corps controls are available online. Phone, 703-614-4008.

http://www.hqmc.marines.mil/Agencies/
USMC-FOIA | Email: hqmcfoia@usmc.mil
Marine Corps Bands   Marine Corps bands
perform at ceremonies, concerts, festivals,
parades, professional sporting events, and
other public events. Marine Corps bands
perform six types of ensembles: brass/
woodwind quintet, bugler, ceremonial
band, concert band, jazz combo, and jazz/
show band. Phone, 504-697-8184. http://
www.marines.mil/Community-Relations/
Asset-Requests/Band | Email: smb.mfr.pao.
comrel@usmc.mil
News   The Marine Corps posts press
releases on its Web site. http://www.marines.
mil/News/Press-Releases

Marines TV is accessible via the Marine
Corps Web site. http://www.marines.mil/
News/Marines-TV
Reading List   The Commandant's
professional reading list is available online.
http://guides.grc.usmcu.edu/content.
php?pid=408059&sid=3340387 |
Email: Reading@usmc.mil
Sexual Assault   The Marine Corps' Sexual
Assault Prevention and Response program
lowers the incidence of sexual assault
through preventative strategies and provides
care to victims of the crime. http://www.
usmc-mccs.org/index.cfm/services/support/
sexual-assault-prevention

The Safe Helpline provides anonymous
and confidential support for sexual assault
survivors in the military. Phone, 877-995-
5247. https://safehelpline.org
Silent Drill Platoon   The Marine Corps
Silent Drill Platoon is a 24-Marine rifle
platoon that performs a precision drill
exhibition. This disciplined platoon
exemplifies the professionalism associated
with the U.S. Marine Corps. It first performed
in the Sunset Parades of 1948 and received
such a favorable response that it became

a regular part of the parades at Marine
Barracks, Washington, DC. Performance
requests for the Silent Drill Platoon should
be made 30–90 days prior to the event.
Phone, 504-697-8184. http://www.marines.
mil/Community-Relations/Asset-Requests/
Silent-Drill-Platoon | Email: smb.mfr.pao.
comrel@usmc.mil
Site Map   The Web site map allows visitors
to look for specific topics or to browse
content that aligns with their interests.
http://www.marines.mil/Home/SiteMap.aspx
Social Media   The Marine Corps maintains
a social media presence and supports online
communities where people can go to share
and collect information and stories. http://
www.marines.mil/News/Social-Media
Speakers   The Marine Corps supports
speaking engagements for community
events nationwide, ranging from small-
town civic organizations to big-city
national conventions. The Marine Corps
In the Community program helps business
executives, educators, members of civic
organizations, conference organizers, and
others make contact with a Marine Corps
public speaker. Phone, 504-697-8184.
http://www.marines.mil/Community-
Relations/Asset-Requests/Speakers |
Email: smb.mfr.pao.comrel@usmc.mil
Tattoo Regulations   The Marine Corps
tattoo policy seeks to balance personal
taste with the high standards of professional
military appearance and heritage. The
Marine Corps Bulletin 1020 (June 2016)
explains the current tattoo policy, which
replaces previous guidance on the subject.
http://www.marines.mil/Tattoos.aspx
Unit Directory   A complete list of Marine
Corps units with links to their respective
web pages is available online. http://www.
marines.mil/Units.aspx. http://www.marines.
mil/Contact-Us

For further information regarding the Marine Corps, contact the Director of Public Affairs, Headquarters, U.S. Marine Corps, 2 Navy Annex–Pentagon 5D773, Washington, DC 20380-1775. Phone, 703-614-1492.

United States Naval Academy
Annapolis, MD 21402-5018
Phone, 410-293-1500. Internet, http://www.usna.edu.

Superintendent	VICE ADM. WALTER E. CARTER, JR., USN
Commandant of Midshipmen	COL. STEPHEN E. LISZEWSKI, USMC

The U.S. Naval Academy is the undergraduate college of the Naval Service. Through its comprehensive 4-year program, which stresses excellence in academics, physical education, professional training, conduct, and honor, the Academy prepares young men and women morally, mentally, and physically to be professional officers in the Navy and Marine Corps. All graduates receive a Bachelor of Science degree in 1 of 19 majors. https://www.usna.edu/About/index.php

Sources of Information

Armel-Leftwich Visitor Center   From March to December, the visitor center is open daily, 9 a.m.–5 p.m. During January and February, the visitor center is open on weekdays, 9 a.m.–4 p.m. The gift shop, however, is open on the weekends, 9 a.m.–5 p.m. http://www.usnabsd.com/for-visitors | Email: tourinfo@usna.edu

A–Z Index   The Naval Academy's Web site has an alphabetical index to help visitors search for information or browse topics of interest. https://www.usna.edu/TOC/index.php

Career Opportunities   Six sources of employment are associated with the Naval Academy and its supporting organizations. https://www.usna.edu/Employment

Naval Academy Preparatory School   The Naval Academy Preparatory School prepares midshipman candidates for success at the U.S. Naval Academy. The 10-month course of instruction, August–May, centers on preparation in Chemistry, English Composition, Information Technology, Mathematics, and Physics. Phone, 401-841-6966 (administration). Phone, 401-841-2947 (academics). https://www.usna.edu/NAPS

Naval Academy Store   All Profits support the brigade of midshipmen. http://navyonline.com

Nimitz Library   An online tool is available to search the library's collection of articles, books, ebooks, and journals. Phone, 410-293-6945. https://www.usna.edu/Library | Email: askref@usna.edu. https://www.usna.edu/Contact

For further information concerning the U.S. Naval Academy, contact the Superintendent, U.S. Naval Academy, 121 Blake Road, Annapolis, MD 21402-5018.

DEFENSE AGENCIES

The Defense Agencies' personnel tables were updated 09–2017.

Defense Advanced Research Projects Agency

675 North Randolph Street, Arlington, VA 22203-2114
Phone, 703-526-6630. Internet, http://www.darpa.mil.

Director	STEVEN H. WALKER, ACTING
Deputy Director	STEFANIE TOMPKINS, ACTING

The Defense Advanced Research Projects Agency is a separately organized agency within the Department of Defense and is under the authority, direction, and control of the Under Secretary of Defense (Acquisition, Technology and Logistics). The Agency serves as the central research and development organization of the Department of Defense with a primary responsibility to maintain U.S. technological superiority over potential adversaries. It pursues imaginative and innovative research and development projects, and conducts demonstration projects that represent technology appropriate for joint programs, programs in support of deployed forces, or selected programs of the military departments. To this end, the Agency arranges, manages, and directs the performance of work connected with assigned advanced projects by the military departments, other Government agencies, individuals, private business entities, and educational or research institutions, as appropriate. http://www.darpa.mil

For further information, contact the Defense Advanced Research Projects Agency, 675 North Randolph Street, Arlington, VA 22203-2114. Phone, 703-526-6630.

Defense Commissary Agency

1300 E Avenue, Fort Lee, VA 23801-1800
Phone, 804-734-8720. Internet, http://www.commissaries.com

Director and Chief Executive Officer	MICHAEL J. DOWLING, ACTING
Deputy Director/Chief Operating Officer	MICHAEL J. DOWLING

The Defense Commissary Agency (DeCA) was established in 1990 and is under the authority, direction, and control of the Under Secretary of Defense for Personnel and Readiness and the operational supervision of the Defense Commissary Agency Board of Directors.

DeCA provides an efficient and effective worldwide system of commissaries that sell quality groceries and household supplies at low prices to members of the Armed Services community. This benefit satisfies customer demand for quality products and delivers exceptional savings while enhancing the military community's quality of life. DeCA works closely with its employees, customers, and civilian business partners to satisfy its customers and to promote the commissary benefit. The benefit fosters recruitment, retention, and readiness of skilled and trained personnel.

Sources of Information

Employment information is available at www.commissaries.com or by calling the following telephone numbers: employment (703-603-1600); small business activities (804-734-8000, extension 4-8015/4-8529); contracting for resale items (804-734-8000, extension 4-8884/4-8885); and contracting for operations support and equipment (804-734-8000, extension 4-8391/4-8830). http://www.commissaries.com

For further information, contact the Defense Commissary Agency, 1300 E Avenue, Fort Lee, VA 23801-1800. Phone, 804-734-8720

Defense Contract Audit Agency

8725 John J. Kingman Road, Suite 2135, Fort Belvoir, VA 22060-6219
Phone, 703-767-3265. Email, dcaaweb@dcaa.mil. Internet, http://www.dcaa.mil.

Director	ANITA F. BALES
Deputy Director	KENNETH J. SACCOCCIA

The Defense Contract Audit Agency (DCAA) was established in 1965 and is under the authority, direction, and control of the Under Secretary of Defense (Comptroller)/Chief Financial Officer. DCAA performs all necessary contract audit functions for

DOD and provides accounting and financial advisory services to all Defense components responsible for procurement and contract administration. These services are provided in connection with the negotiation, administration, and settlement of contracts and subcontracts to ensure taxpayer dollars are spent on fair and reasonable contract prices. They include evaluating the acceptability of costs claimed or proposed by contractors and reviewing the efficiency and economy of contractor operations. Other Government agencies may request the DCAA's services under appropriate arrangements.

DCAA manages its operations through five regional offices responsible for approximately 104 field audit offices throughout the United States and overseas. Each region is responsible for the contract auditing function in its assigned area. Point of contact information for DCAA regional offices is available at www.dcaa.mil. http://www.dcaa.mil | Email: dcaaweb@dcaa.mil

For further information, contact the Executive Officer, Defense Contract Audit Agency, 8725 John J. Kingman Road, Suite 2135, Fort Belvoir, VA 22060-6219. Phone, 703-767-3265.

Defense Contract Management Agency
3901 A Avenue, Fort Lee, VA 23801
Phone, 804-734-0814. Internet, http://www.dcma.mil

Director	Vice Adm. David H. Lewis, USN
Deputy Director	(vacancy)

The Defense Contract Management Agency (DCMA) was established by the Deputy Secretary of Defense in 2000 and is under the authority, direction, and control of the Under Secretary of Defense (Acquisition, Technology, and Logistics). DCMA is responsible for DOD contract management in support of the military departments, other DOD components, the National Aeronautics and Space Administration, other designated Federal and State agencies, foreign governments, and international organizations, as appropriate. http://www.dcma.mil

For further information, contact the Office of General Counsel, Defense Contract Management Agency, 3901 A Avenue, Fort Lee, VA 23801. Phone, 804-734-0814.

Defense Finance and Accounting Service
4800 Mark Center Drive, Suite 08J25-01, Alexandria, VA 22350-3000
571-372-7883 http://www.dfas.mil

Director	Teresa A. McKay
Principal Deputy Director	Audrey Y. Davis

The Defense Finance and Accounting Service (DFAS) was established in 1991 under the authority, direction, and control of the Under Secretary of Defense (Comptroller)/Chief Financial Officer to strengthen and reduce costs of financial management and operations within DOD. DFAS is responsible for all payments to servicemembers, employees, vendors, and contractors. It provides business intelligence and finance and accounting information to DOD decisionmakers. DFAS is also responsible for preparing annual financial statements and the consolidation, standardization, and modernization of finance and accounting requirements, functions, processes, operations, and systems for DOD. http://www.dfas.mil

For further information, contact Defense Finance and Accounting Service Corporate Communications, 4800 Mark Center Drive, Suite 08J25-01, Alexandria, VA 22350-3000. Phone, 571-372-7883.

Defense Information Systems Agency

P.O. Box 549, Command Building, Fort Meade, MD 20755
Phone, 301-225-6000. Internet, http://www.disa.mil | Email: dia-pao@dia.mil.

Director	LT. GEN. ALAN R. LYNN, USAF
Vice Director	REAR ADM. NANCY A. NORTON, USN

The Defense Information Systems Agency (DISA), established originally as the Defense Communications Agency in 1960, is under the authority, direction, and control of the Assistant Secretary of Defense (Networks and Information Integration). DISA is a combat support agency responsible for planning, engineering, acquiring, fielding, operating, and supporting global net-centric solutions to serve the needs of the President, Vice President, Secretary of Defense, and other DOD components. http://www.disa.mil | Email: dia-pao@dia.mil

For further information, contact the Public Affairs Office, Defense Information Systems Agency, P.O. Box 549, Command Building, Fort Meade, MD 20755. Phone, 301-225-6000.

Defense Intelligence Agency

200 MacDill Boulevard, Washington DC 20340-5100
Phone, 202-231-0800. Internet, http://www.dia.mil | Email: dia-pao@dia.mil

Director	LT. GEN. VINCENT R. STEWART, USMC
Deputy Director	MELISSA A. DRISKO

The Defense Intelligence Agency (DIA) was established in 1961 and is under the authority, direction, and control of the Under Secretary of Defense for Intelligence. DIA provides timely, objective, and cogent military intelligence to warfighters, force planners, as well as defense and national security policymakers. DIA obtains and reports information through its field sites worldwide and the Defense Attache System; provides timely intelligence analysis; directs Defense Human Intelligence programs; operates the Joint Intelligence Task Force for Combating Terrorism and the Joint Military Intelligence College; coordinates and facilitates Measurement and Signature Intelligence activities; manages and plans collections from specialized technical sources; manages secure DOD intelligence networks; and coordinates required intelligence support for the Secretary of Defense, Joint Chiefs of Staff, Combatant Commanders, and Joint Task Forces. http://www.dia.mil | Email: dia-pao@dia.mil

For further information, contact the Public Affairs Office, Defense Intelligence Agency, 200 MacDill Boulevard, Washington DC 20340-5100. Phone, 202-231-0800.

Defense Legal Services Agency

The Pentagon, Washington, DC 20301-1600
Phone, 703-695-3341. Internet, http://www.dod.mil/dodgc

Director / General Counsel of The Department of Defense	WILLIAM S. CASTLE, ACTING
Principal Deputy General Counsel of the Department of Defense	WILLIAM S. CASTLE

The Defense Legal Services Agency (DLSA) was established in 1981 and is under the authority, direction, and control of the General Counsel of the Department of Defense, who also serves as its Director. DLSA provides legal advice and services for specified DOD components and adjudication of personnel security cases for DOD and other assigned Federal agencies and departments. It also provides technical support and assistance for development of the Department's legislative program; coordinates positions on legislation and Presidential Executive orders; provides a centralized legislative and congressional document reference and distribution point for the Department; maintains the Department's historical legislative files; and administers programs governing standards of conduct and alternative dispute resolution. http://www.dod.mil/dodgc

For further information, contact the Administrative Office, Defense Legal Services Agency, Room 3A734, Washington, DC 20301-1600. Phone, 703-697-8343.

Defense Logistics Agency

8725 John J. Kingman Road, Suite 2533, Fort Belvoir, VA 22060-6221
Phone, 703-767-5264. Internet, http://www.dla.mil

Director	LT. GEN. DARRELL K. WILLIAMS, USA
Vice Director	EDWARD J. CASE

The Defense Logistics Agency (DLA) is under the authority, direction, and control of the Under Secretary of Defense for Acquisition, Technology, and Logistics. DLA supports both the logistics requirements of the military services and their acquisition of weapons and other materiel. It provides logistics support and technical services to all branches of the military and to a number of Federal agencies. DLA supply centers consolidate the requirements of the military services and procure the supplies in sufficient quantities to meet their projected needs. DLA manages supplies in eight commodity areas: fuel, food, clothing, construction material, electronic supplies, general supplies, industrial supplies, and medical supplies. Information on DLA's field activities and regional commands is available at www.dla.mil/ataglance.aspx.

Sources of Information

Career Opportunities For the Washington, DC, metropolitan area, all inquiries and applications concerning job recruitment programs should be addressed to Human Resources, Customer Support Office, 3990 East Broad Street, Building 11, Section 3, Columbus, OH, 43213-0919. Phone, 877-352-4762. http://www.dla.mil/Careers.aspx

Environmental Program For information on the environmental program, contact the Staff Director, Environmental and Safety, Defense Logistics Agency, Attn: DSS-E, 8725 John J. Kingman Road, Fort Belvoir, VA 22060-6221. Phone, 703-767-6278.

Procurement / Small Business Activities For information on procurement and small business activities, contact the Director, Small and Disadvantaged Business Utilization, Defense Logistics

Agency, Attn: DB, 8725 John J. Kingman Road, Fort Belvoir, VA 22060-6221. Phone, 703-767-0192. http://www.dla.mil/ DoingBusinessWithDLA.aspx
Surplus Sales Program   Questions concerning this program should be addressed to DOD Surplus Sales, International Sales Office, 74 Washington Avenue North, Battle Creek, MI 49017-3092. Phone, 877-352-2255. http:// dispositionservices.dla.mil/sales/Pages/ default.aspx. http://www.dla.mil

For further information, contact the Defense Logistics Agency, 8725 John J. Kingman Road, Fort Belvoir, VA 22060-6221. Phone, 703-767-5264.

Defense Security Cooperation Agency

201 Twelfth Street South, Suite 203, Arlington, VA 22202-5408
Phone, 703-604-6605. Internet, http://www.dsca.mil

Director	Lt. Gen. Charles Hooper, USA
Deputy Director	Gregory M. Kausner

The Defense Security Cooperation Agency (DSCA) was established in 1971 and is under the authority, direction, and control of the Under Secretary of Defense (Policy). DSCA provides traditional security assistance functions such as military assistance, international military education and training, and foreign military sales. DSCA also has program management responsibilities for humanitarian assistance, demining, and other DOD programs. http://www.dsca.mil | Email: info@dsca.mil

For further information, contact the Defense Security Cooperation Agency, 201 Twelfth Street South, Suite 203, Arlington, VA 22202-5408. Phone, 703-604-6605.

Defense Security Service

27130 Telegraph Road, Quantico, VA 22134
Phone, 703-617-2352. Internet, http://www.dss.mil

Director	Daniel E. Payne
Deputy Director	James J. Kren

The Defense Security Service (DSS) is under the authority, direction, and control of the Under Secretary of Defense for Intelligence. DSS ensures the safeguarding of classified information used by contractors on behalf of the DOD and 22 other executive branch agencies under the National Industrial Security Program. It oversees the protection of conventional arms, munitions, and explosives in the custody of DOD contractors; evaluates the protection of selected private sector critical assets and infrastructures (physical and cyber-based systems) and recommends measures needed to maintain operations identified as vital to DOD. DSS makes clearance determinations for industry and provides support services for DOD Central Adjudicative Facilities. It provides security education, training, and proactive awareness programs for military, civilian, and cleared industry to enhance their proficiency and awareness of DOD security policies and procedures. DSS also has a counterintelligence office to integrate counterintelligence principles into security countermeasures missions and to support the national counterintelligence strategy. Information on DSS operating locations and centers is available at www.dss.mil/isp/ dss_oper_loc.html.

For further information, contact the Defense Security Service, Office of Public Affairs, 27130 Telegraph Road, Quantico, VA 22134. Phone, 703-617-2352.

Defense Threat Reduction Agency

8725 John J. Kingman Road, MS 6201, Fort Belvoir, VA 22060-6201
Phone, 703-767-7594. Internet, http://www.dtra.mil

Director	VAYL S. OXFORD
Deputy Director	REAR ADM. SCOTT JERABEK, USN

The Defense Threat Reduction Agency (DTRA) was established in 1998 and is under the authority, direction, and control of the Under Secretary of Defense for Acquisition, Technology, and Logistics. DTRA's mission is to reduce the threat posed by weapons of mass destruction (WMD). DTRA covers the full range of WMD threats (chemical, biological, nuclear, radiological, and high explosive), bridges the gap between the warfighters and the technical community, sustains the nuclear deterrent, and provides both offensive and defensive technology and operational concepts to warfighters. DTRA reduces the threat of WMD by implementing arms control treaties and executing the Cooperative Threat Reduction Program. It uses combat support, technology development, and chemical-biological defense to deter the use and reduce the impact of such weapons. DTRA also prepares for future threats by developing the technology and concepts needed to counter new WMD threats and adversaris. http://www.dtra.mil

For further information, contact the Public Affairs Office, Defense Threat Reduction Agency, 8725 John J. Kingman Road, MS 6201, Fort Belvoir, VA 22060-5916. Phone, 703-767-7594. Email, dtra.publicaffairs@dtra.mil.

Missile Defense Agency

5700 Eighteenth Street, Bldg 245, Fort Belvoir, VA 22060-5573
Phone, 703-695-6420. Internet, Email: mda.info@mda.mil

Director	LT. GEN. SAMUEL A. GREAVES, USAF
Deputy Director	REAR ADM. JON A. HILL, USN

[For the Missile Defense Agency statement of organization, see the Code of Federal Regulations, Title 32, Part 388]

The Missile Defense Agency's (MDA) mission is to establish and deploy a layered ballistic missile defense system to intercept missiles in all phases of their flight and against all ranges of threats. This capability will provide a defense of the United States, deployed forces, and allies. MDA is under the authority, direction, and control of the Under Secretary of Defense for Acquisition, Technology, and Logistics. MDA manages and directs DOD's ballistic missile defense acquisition programs and enables the Services to field elements of the overall system as soon as practicable. MDA develops and tests technologies and, if necessary, uses prototype and test assets to provide early capability. Additionally, MDA improves the effectiveness of deployed capabilities by implementing new technologies as they become available or when the threat warrants an accelerated capability. https://www.mda.mil | Email: mda.info@mda.mil

For further information, contact the Human Resources Directorate, Missile Defense Agency, 5700 Eighteenth Street, Bldg 245, Fort Belvoir, VA 22060-5573. Phone, 703-695-6420. Email, mda.info@mda.mil.

National Geospatial-Intelligence Agency

7500 Geoint Drive, MS N73-OCCAE, Springfield, Virginia 22150
Phone, 571-557-7300. Internet, http://www.nga.mil.

Director	ROBERT CARDILLO
Deputy Director	JUSTIN POOLE

The National Geospatial-Intelligence Agency (NGA), formerly the National Imagery and Mapping Agency, was established in 1996 and is under the authority, direction, and control of the Under Secretary of Defense for Intelligence. NGA is a DOD combat support agency and a member of the national intelligence community. NGA's mission is to provide timely, relevant, and accurate geospatial intelligence in support of our national security. Geospatial intelligence means the use and analysis of imagery to describe, assess, and visually depict physical features and geographically referenced activities on the Earth. Headquartered in Bethesda, MD, NGA has major facilities in the Washington, DC, Northern Virginia, and St. Louis, MO, areas with NGA support teams worldwide.http://www.nga.mil | Email: publicaffairs@nga.mil

For further information, contact the Public Affairs Office, National Geospatial-Intelligence Agency,. 7500 Geoint Drive, MS N73-OCCAE, Springfield, Virginia 22150. Phone, 571-557-7300.

National Security Agency / Central Security Service

Fort Meade, MD 20755-6248
Phone, 301-688-6524. Fax, 301-688-6198. Internet, http://www.nsa.gov.

Director	ADM. MICHAEL S. ROGERS, USN
Deputy Director	GEORGE C. BARNES

The National Security Agency (NSA) was established in 1952 and the Central Security Service (CSS) was established in 1972. NSA/CSS is under the authority, direction, and control of the Under Secretary of Defense for Intelligence. As the Nation's cryptologic organization, NSA/CSS employs the Nation's premier codemakers and codebreakers. It ensures an informed, alert, and secure environment for U.S. warfighters and policymakers. The cryptologic resources of NSA/CSS unite to provide U.S. policymakers with intelligence information derived from America's adversaries while protecting U.S. Government signals and information systems from exploitation by those same adversaries. http://www.nsa.gov | Email: nsapao@nsa.gov

For further information, contact the Public Affairs Office, National Security Agency/Central Security Service, Fort Meade, MD 20755-6248. Phone, 301-688-6524. Fax, 301-688-6198.

Pentagon Force Protection Agency

9000 Defense Pentagon, Washington, DC 20301
Phone, 703-697-1001. Internet, http://www.pfpa.mil.

Director	JONATHAN H. COFER
Principal Deputy Director	DANIEL P. WALSH, ACTING

The Pentagon Force Protection Agency (PFPA) was established in May 2002 in response to the events of September 11, 2001, and subsequent terrorist threats facing the DOD workforce and facilities in the National Capital Region (NCR). PFPA is under the authority, direction, and control of the Director, Administration and Management, in the Office of the Secretary of Defense. PFPA provides force protection, security, and law enforcement for the people, facilities, infrastructure, and other resources at the Pentagon and for DOD activities and facilities within the NCR that are not under the jurisdiction of a military department. Consistent with the national strategy on combating terrorism, PFPA addresses threats, including chemical, biological, and radiological agents, through a strategy of prevention, preparedness, detection, and response to ensure that the DOD workforce and facilities in the NCR are secure and protected. http://www.pfpa.mil

For further information, contact the Pentagon Force Protection Agency, 9000 Defense Pentagon, Washington, DC 20301. Phone, 703-697-1001.

Joint Service Schools
Defense Acquisition University

9820 Belvoir Road, Fort Belvoir, VA 22060-5565
Phone, 703-805-2764. Internet, http://www.dau.mil.

President   JAMES P. WOOSLEY

The Defense Acquisition University (DAU), established pursuant to the Defense Acquisition Workforce Improvement Act of 1990 (10 U.S.C. 1701 note), serves as the DOD center for acquisition, technology, and logistics training; performance support; continuous learning; and knowledge sharing. DAU is a unified structure with five regional campuses and the Defense Systems Management College-School of Program Managers, which provides executive and international acquisition training. DAU's mission is to provide the training, career management, and services that enable the acquisition, technology, and logistics community to make smart business decisions and deliver timely and affordable capabilities to warfighters. http://www.dau.mil

For further information, contact the Director, Operations Support Group, Defense Acquisition University, 9820 Belvoir Road, Fort Belvoir, VA 22060-5565. Phone, 800-845-7606.

National Intelligence University

Defense Intelligence Analysis Center, Washington, DC 20340-5100
Phone, 202-231-5466. Internet, http://www.ni-u.edu.

President   J. SCOTT CAMERON

The National Intelligence University, formerly the Joint Military Intelligence College, was established in 1962. The College is a joint service interagency educational institution serving the intelligence community and operates under the authority of the Director, Defense Intelligence Agency. Its mission is to educate military and civilian intelligence professionals, conduct and disseminate relevant intelligence research, and perform academic outreach regarding intelligence matters. The College is authorized by Congress to award the bachelor of science in intelligence, master of science and technology intelligence, and master of science of strategic intelligence. Courses are offered to full-time students in a traditional daytime format and for part-time students in the evening, on Saturday, and in an executive format (one weekend per month and a 2-week intensive summer period). http://www.ni-u.edu

For further information, contact the Admissions Office, National Intelligence University, 200 MacDill Blvd (MCA-2), Washington, DC 20340-5100. Phone, 202-231-5466 or 202-231-3319.

National Defense University

300 Fifth Avenue, Building 62, Fort McNair, DC 20319-5066
Phone, 202-685-2649. Internet, http://www.ndu.edu.
College of International Security Affairs: 260 Fifth Avenue, Building 64, Fort McNair, DC 20319-5066
Phone, 202-685-3870. Internet, http://cisa.ndu.edu.
Dwight D. Eisenhower School for National Security and Resource Strategy: 408 Fourth Avenue,
Building 59, Fort McNair, DC 20319-5062
Phone, 202-685-4333. Internet, http://es.ndu.edu/Home.aspx.
Information Resources Management College: 300 Fifth Avenue, Building 62, Fort McNair,
DC 20319-5066
Phone, 202-685-6300. Internet, http://icollege.ndu.edu.
Joint Forces Staff College: 7800 Hampton Boulevard, Norfolk, VA 23511-1702
Phone, 757-443-6124. Internet, http://jfsc.ndu.edu.
National War College: 300 D Street SW., Building 61, Fort McNair, DC 20319-5078
Phone, 202-685-3674. Fax, 202-685-6461. Internet, http://nwc.ndu.edu.

President	MAJ. GEN. FREDERICK M. PADILLA, USMC
Senior Vice President	DONALD YAMAMOTO
Commandant, Dwight D. Eisenhower School for National Security and Resource Strategy	BRIG. GEN. JOHN JANSEN, USMC
Commandant, Joint Forces Staff College	REAR ADM. JEFFREY RUTH, USN
Commandant, National War College	BRIG. GEN. DARREN E. HARTFORD, USAF
Chancellor, College of International Security Affairs	COL. MICHAEL S. BELL, USA (RETIRED)
Chancellor, Information Resources Management College	REAR ADM. JANICE HAMBY, USN (RETIRED)

National Defense University

The mission of the National Defense University is to prepare military and civilian leaders from the United States and other countries to evaluate national and international security challenges through multidisciplinary educational and research programs, professional exchanges, and outreach.

The National Defense University was established in 1976 and comprises the following colleges and programs: the Dwight D. Eisenhower School for National Security and Resource Strategy, National War College, Joint Forces Staff College, Information Resources Management College, College of International Security Affairs, Institute for National Strategic Studies, Center for the Study of Weapons of Mass Destruction, Center for Technology and National Security Policy, International Student Management Office, Joint Reserve Affairs Center, CAPSTONE, Security of Defense Corporate Fellows Program, NATO Education Center, Institute for National Security Ethics and Leadership, Center for Joint Strategic Logistics Excellence, Center for Applied Strategic Leaders, and Center for Complex Operations. http://www.ndu.edu

For further information, contact the Human Resources
Directorate, National Defense University, 300 Fifth
Avenue, Building 62, Fort McNair, DC 20319-5066.
Phone, 202-685-2169.

College of International Security
Affairs   The College of International
Security Affairs (CISA) is one of NDU's
five colleges. CISA educates students
from across the international, interagency,
and interservice communities. CISA's
primary areas of concentration include
counterterrorism, conflict management of
stability of operations, homeland security,
and defense and international security
studies. CISA is also home to NDU's
International Counterterrorism Fellowship
Program. http://cisa.ndu.edu

For further information, contact the Office of Academic
Affairs, College of International Security Affairs, 260
Fifth Avenue, Building 64, Fort McNair, DC 20319-5066.
Phone, 202-685-7774.

Dwight D. Eisenhower School for National
Security and Resource Strategy   The
Dwight D. Eisenhower School for
National Security and Resource Strategy
provides graduate level education to
senior members of the U.S. Armed Forces,
Government civilians, foreign nationals,
and professionals from the private industrial
sector. The School prepares students to
contribute to national security strategy
and policy, emphasizing the evaluation,
marshaling, and managing of national
resources. Students who fulfill the degree
requirements receive a Master of Science
degree in national resource strategy. http://
es.ndu.edu/Home.aspx

For further information, contact the Director of
Operations, Dwight D. Eisenhower School for National
Security and Resource Strategy, 408 Fourth Avenue,
Building 59, Fort McNair, DC 20319-5062. Phone, 202-
685-4333.

Information Resources Management
College   The Information Resources
Management College provides graduate-
level courses in information resources
management. The College prepares leaders
to direct the information component of
national power by leveraging information
and information technology for strategic
advantage. The College's primary areas
of concentration include policy, strategic
planning, leadership/management, process

improvement, capital planning and
investment, performance- and results-based
management, technology assessment,
architecture, information assurance and
security, acquisition, domestic preparedness,
transformation, e-Government, and
information operations. http://icollege.ndu.
edu

For further information, contact the Office of Student
Services, Information Resources Management College,
300 Fifth Avenue, Building 62, Fort McNair, DC 20319-
5066. Phone, 202-685-6300.

Joint Forces Staff College   The Joint Forces
Staff College (JFSC) is an intermediate- and
senior-level joint college in the professional
military education system dedicated to
the study of the principles, perspectives,
and techniques of joint operational-level
planning and warfare. The mission of JFSC
is to educate national security professionals
in the planning and execution of joint,
multinational, and interagency operations
in order to instill a primary commitment
to joint, multinational, and interagency
teamwork, attitudes, and perspectives. The
College accomplishes this mission through
four schools: the Joint Advanced Warfighters
School, the Joint and Combined Warfighting
School, the Joint Continuing and Distance
Education School, and the Joint Command,
Control, and Information Operations School.
http://jfsc.ndu.edu

For further information, contact the Public Affairs
Officer, Joint Forces Staff College, 7800 Hampton
Boulevard, Norfolk, VA 23511-1702. Phone, 757-443-
6212. Fax, 757-443-6210.

National War College   The National War
College provides education in national
security policy to selected military officers
and career civil service employees
of Federal departments and agencies
concerned with national security. It is
the only senior service college with the
primary mission of offering a course of
study that emphasizes national security
policy formulation and the planning and
implementation of national strategy. Its
10-month academic program is an issue-
centered study in U.S. national security.
The elective program is designed to permit
each student to tailor his or her academic
experience to meet individual professional
development needs. http://nwc.ndu.edu

For further information, contact the Office of Administration, National War College, 300 D Street SW., Building 61, Fort McNair, DC 20319-5078. Phone, 202-685-3674.

Uniformed Services University of the Health Sciences
4301 Jones Bridge Road, Bethesda, MD 20814-4799
Phone, 301-295-3190. Internet, http://www.usuhs.mil.

President	MAJ. GEN. RICHARD W. THOMAS, USA (RETIRED)

Authorized by act of September 21, 1972 (10 U.S.C. 2112), the Uniformed Services University of the Health Sciences was established to educate career-oriented medical officers for the Military Departments and the Public Health Service. The University currently incorporates the F. Edward Hebert School of Medicine (including graduate and continuing education programs) and the Graduate School of Nursing.

Students are selected by procedures recommended by the Board of Regents and prescribed by the Secretary of Defense. The actual selection is carried out by a faculty committee on admissions and is based upon motivation and dedication to a career in the uniformed services and an overall appraisal of the personal and intellectual characteristics of the candidates without regard to sex, race, religion, or national origin. Applicants must be U.S. citizens.

Medical school matriculants will be commissioned officers in one of the uniformed services. They must meet the physical and personal qualifications for such a commission and must give evidence of a strong commitment to serving as a uniformed medical officer. The graduating medical student is required to serve a period of obligation of not less than 7 years, excluding graduate medical education.

Students of the Graduate School of Nursing must be commissioned officers of the Army, Navy, Air Force, or Public Health Service prior to application. Graduate nursing students must serve a commitment determined by their respective service. http://www.usuhs.mil

For further information, contact the President, Uniformed Services University of the Health Sciences, 4301 Jones Bridge Road, Bethesda, MD 20814-4799. Phone, 301-295-3013.

DEPARTMENT OF EDUCATION

400 Maryland Avenue SW., Washington, DC 20202
Phone, 202-401-2000. TTY, 800-437-0833. Internet, http://www.ed.gov.

Secretary of Education	BETSY DEVOS
Deputy Secretary	(VACANCY)
Under Secretary	JAMES MANNING, ACTING

Office of the Secretary

Assistant Deputy Secretary and Director, Office of English Language Acquisition	JOSE VIANA
Assistant Deputy Secretary, Office of Innovation and Improvement	MARGO ANDERSON, ACTING
Assistant Secretary, Office for Civil Rights	CANDICE JACKSON, ACTING
Assistant Secretary, Office of Communication and Outreach	(VACANCY)
Assistant Secretary, Office of Elementary and Secondary Education	JASON BOTEL, ACTING
Assistant Secretary, Office of Legislation and Congressional Affairs	PETER OPPENHEIM
Assistant Secretary, Office of Planning, Evaluation and Policy Development	JENNIFER BELL-ELLWANGER, ACTING
Assistant Secretary, Office of Special Education and Rehabilitative Services	RUTH RYDER, ACTING
Chief of Staff	JOSHUA VENABLE
Director, International Affairs Office	MAUREEN A. MCLAUGHLIN
Director, Institute of Education Sciences	SUE BETKA, ACTING
Inspector General	KATHLEEN S. TIGHE

Office of the Deputy Secretary

Assistant Secretary, Office of Management	HOLLY HAM
Chief Financial Officer	TIM SOLTIS, ACTING
Chief Information Officer	JASON K. GRAY
Director, Office of Educational Technology	JOSEPH SMITH
General Counsel	STEVEN MENASHI, ACTING

Office of the Under Secretary

Assistant Secretary, Office of Career, Technical, and Adult Education	KIM FORD, ACTING
Assistant Secretary, Office of Postsecondary Education	KATHLEEN SMITH, ACTING
Chief Operating Officer for Federal Student Aid	DR. A. WAYNE JOHNSON
Director, Center for Faith-Based and Neighborhood Partnerships	(VACANCY)
Executive Director, White House Initiative on American Indian and Alaska Native Education	(VACANCY)
Executive Director, White House Initiative on Asian Americans and Pacific Islanders	(VACANCY)
Executive Director, White House Initiative on Educational Excellence for African Americans	(VACANCY)

Executive Director, White House Initiative on   (VACANCY)
  Educational Excellence for Hispanic Americans
Executive Director, White House Initiative on Historically   (VACANCY)
  Black Colleges and Universities

The Department of Education ensures equal access to education; promotes educational excellence; and administers, coordinates, and makes policy for most Federal assistance to education with the aim of raising levels of student achievement and readiness for the global future.

The Department of Education was created by the Department of Education Organization Act (20 U.S.C. 3411) and is administered under the supervision and direction of the Secretary of Education. http://www2.ed.gov/about/landing.jhtml?src=ln
Secretary   The Secretary of Education advises the President on education plans, policies, and programs of the Federal Government and serves as the chief executive officer of the Department, supervising all Department activities, providing support to States and localities, and focusing resources to ensure equal access to educational excellence throughout the Nation. http://www2.ed.gov/about/offices/list/os/index.html?src=oc

Activities

Career, Technical, and Adult Education   The Office of Career, Technical, and Adult Education (OCTAE) administers grant, contract, and technical assistance programs for vocational-technical education and for adult education and literacy. It promotes programs that enable adults to acquire the basic literacy skills necessary to function in today's society. The Office also helps students acquire challenging academic and technical skills and prepare for high-skill, high-wage, and high-demand occupations in the 21st-century global economy. OCTAE provides national leadership and works to strengthen the role of community colleges in expanding access to postsecondary education for youth and adults in advancing workforce development. http://www2.ed.gov/about/offices/list/ovae/index.html
Education Sciences   The Institute of Education Sciences was formally established by the Education Sciences Reform Act of 2002 (20 U.S.C. 9501 note). The Institute

includes national education centers focused on research, special education, statistics, and evaluation and is the mechanism through which the Department supports the research activities needed to improve education policy and practice. https://ies.ed.gov
Elementary and Secondary Education   The Office of Elementary and Secondary Education directs, coordinates, and formulates policy relating to early childhood, elementary, and secondary education. Included are grants and contracts to State educational agencies and local school districts, postsecondary schools, and nonprofit organizations for disadvantaged, migrant, and Indian children; enhancement of State student achievement assessment systems; improvement of reading instruction; economic impact aid; technology; safe and healthy schools; and after-school learning programs. The Office also focuses on improving K–12 education, providing children with language and cognitive development, early reading, and other readiness skills, and improving the quality of teachers and other instructional staff. http://www2.ed.gov/about/offices/list/oese/index.html
English Language Acquisition   The Office of English Language Acquisition helps children who are limited in their English, including immigrant children and youth, attain English proficiency, develop high levels of academic attainment in English, and meet the same challenging State academic content and student academic achievement standards that all children are expected to meet. http://www2.ed.gov/about/offices/list/oela/index.html
Federal Student Aid   Federal Student Aid partners with postsecondary schools and financial institutions to deliver programs and services that help students finance their

DEPARTMENT OF EDUCATION

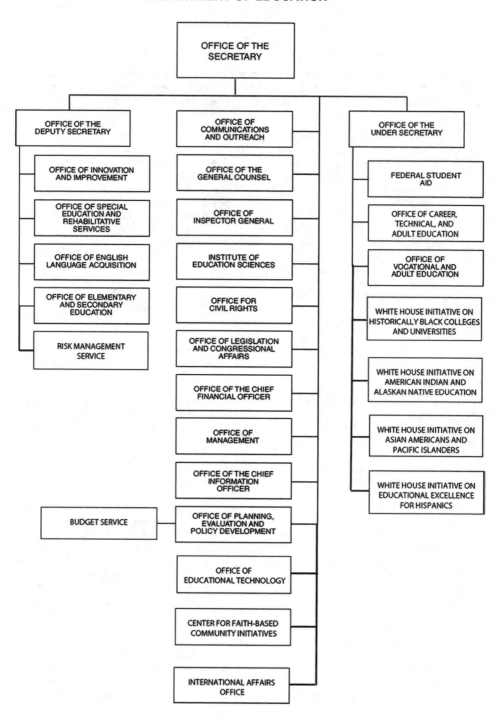

education beyond high school. This includes administering postsecondary student financial assistance programs authorized under Title IV of the Higher Education Act of 1965, as amended. https://studentaid.ed.gov

Innovation and Improvement The Office of Innovation and Improvement (OII) oversees competitive grant programs that support innovations in the educational system and disseminates the lessons learned from these innovative practices. OII administers, coordinates, and recommends programs and policy for improving the quality of activities designed to support and test innovations throughout the K–12 system in areas such as parental choice, teacher quality, use of technology in education, and arts in education. OII encourages the establishment of charter schools through planning, start-up funding, and approaches to credit enhancement for charter school facilities. OII also serves as the Department's liaison and resource to the nonpublic education community. http://innovation.ed.gov

Postsecondary Education The Office of Postsecondary Education (OPE) formulates Federal postsecondary education policy and administers programs that address critical national needs in support of the mission to increase access to quality postsecondary education. OPE develops policy for Federal student financial programs and support programs that reach out to low-income, first-generation college students and communities. OPE also supports programs that strengthen the capacity of colleges and universities serving a high percentage of disadvantaged students and improve teacher quality. OPE recognizes accrediting agencies that monitor academic quality, promote innovation in higher education, and expand American educational resources for international studies and services. http://www2.ed.gov/about/offices/list/ope/index.html

Special Education and Rehabilitative Services The Office of Special Education and Rehabilitative Services (OSERS) provides leadership and resources to help ensure that people with disabilities have equal opportunities to learn, work, and live as fully integrated and contributing members of society. OSERS has three components: The Office of Special Education Programs administers the Individuals with Disabilities Education Act legislation, which helps States meet the early intervention and educational needs of infants, toddlers, children, and youth with disabilities. The Rehabilitation Services Administration supports State vocational rehabilitation, independent living, and assistive technology programs that provide people with disabilities the services, technology, and job training and placement assistance they need to gain meaningful employment and lead independent lives. The National Institute on Disability and Rehabilitation Research supports research and development programs that improve the ability of individuals with disabilities to work and live in a barrier-free, inclusive society. OSERS also supports Gallaudet University, the National Technical Institute for the Deaf, the American Printing House for the Blind, and the Helen Keller National Center. http://www2.ed.gov/about/offices/list/osers/index.html

Sources of Information

Blog "Homeroom" is the official blog of the Department of Education. http://blog.ed.gov

Business Opportunities Contact the Office of Small and Disadvantaged Business Utilization. Phone, 202-245-6301. http://www.ed.gov/fund/contract-opportunities.html

College Scorecard The Department of Education's Web site features a tool to help college bound students find colleges and universities based upon their location, size, and the programs and degrees that they offer. https://collegescorecard.ed.gov

Data / Statistics Information on school accreditation and data on the academic achievement of U.S. students are available on the "Data and Research" Web page. The National Center for Education Statistics collects and analyzes data related to education. Phone, 202-403-5551. http://www2.ed.gov/rschstat/landing.jhtml?src=pn. http://nces.ed.gov

Career Opportunities For information on employment and the college recruitment program, contact Human Capital and Client Services. Phone, 202-401-0553. http://www.ed.gov/jobs

Freedom of Information Act (FOIA)   The FOIA generally provides that any person has the right to request access to Federal agency records or information; all agencies of the Government are required to disclose records upon receiving a written request for them; nine exemptions to the FOIA protect certain records from disclosure; and three special protection provisions or record exclusions authorize Federal law enforcement agencies, under exceptional circumstances, to exclude records from FIOA requirements. The Federal FOIA does not provide access to records held by State or local government agencies, or by private businesses or individuals. http://www2.ed.gov/policy/gen/leg/foia/foiatoc.html?src=ft

Before submitting a request, browse the electronic FOIA Library and search the Department of Education's Web site. The desired records and information may be immediately available online and not require a FOIA request to access them. http://www2.ed.gov/policy/gen/leg/foia/readingroom.html

Frequently Asked Questions (FAQs)   The Department of Education provides answers to FAQs on its Web site. https://answers.ed.gov/ics/support/default.asp?deptID=28025&_referrer=http://www.ed.gov/&src=ft

Glossaries   The Department of Education's Web site features a glossary of reading terms. https://lincs.ed.gov/research/Glossary.html

The Department of Education's Web site features a glossary of terms related to Federal student aid. https://studentaid.ed.gov/sa/glossary

The Department of Education's Web site features a glossary of terms related to education research. http://www.ies.ed.gov/ncee/wwc/Glossary

The Department of Education's Web site features a glossary of terms related to education statistical standards. http://nces.ed.gov/statprog/2002/glossary.asp

Language Assistance   Education resources for Spanish speakers are available on the Department's Web site. http://www2.ed.gov/espanol/bienvenidos/es/index.html?src=ft

Free language assistance services—Chinese, Korean, Spanish, Vietnamese,

Tagalog—are available to the public. Phone, 800-872-5327. http://www.ed.gov/notices/english-la | Email: Ed.Language.Assistance@ed.gov

News   The Department of Education posts media advisories, press releases, and speeches on its Web site. http://www.ed.gov/news

Press releases in Spanish are also available on the Department's Web site. http://www2.ed.gov/espanol/news/pressreleases/index.html

Open Government   The Department of Education supports the Open Government initiative by promoting the principles of collaboration, participation, and transparency. http://www2.ed.gov/about/open.html | Email: opengov@ed.gov

Plain Language   Department of Education writers and editors are committed to using Federal plain language guidelines. Publishing clear, useful information on programs and services is a priority and an ongoing effort. To comment on the clarity of a written product or to offer a suggestion for improvement, please communicate via email. http://www.ed.gov/plain-language | Email: plainwriting@ed.gov

Regional Offices   Each regional office serves as a center for the dissemination of information and provides technical assistance to State and local educational agencies and other institutions and individuals interested in Federal educational activities. Offices are located in Boston, MA; New York, NY; Philadelphia, PA; Atlanta, GA; Chicago, IL; Cleveland, OH; Dallas, TX; Kansas City, MO; Denver, CO; San Francisco, CA; and Seattle, WA. http://www2.ed.gov/about/contacts/gen/regions.html

Site Map   The Web site map allows visitors to look for specific topics or to browse content that aligns with their interests. http://www2.ed.gov/help/site/map/sitemap.jsp

Student Loans   Information on student loans is available online. http://www2.ed.gov/fund/grants-college.html?src=pn. http://www2.ed.gov/about/contacts/gen/index.html

For further information, contact the Information Resources Center, Department of Education, Room 5E248 (FB–6), 400 Maryland Avenue SW., Washington, DC 20202. Phone, 800-872-5327.

Federally Aided Corporations
American Printing House for the Blind

P.O. Box 6085, Louisville, KY 40206
Phone, 502-895-2405. Internet, http://www.aph.org.

President	CRAIG MEADOR
Chairman of the Board	JANE HARDY

Founded in 1858 as a nonprofit organization, the American Printing House for the Blind (APH) received its Federal charter in 1879 when Congress passed the Act to Promote Education of the Blind. This Act designates APH as the official supplier of educational materials adapted for students who are legally blind and who are enrolled in formal educational programs below the college level. Materials produced and distributed by APH include textbooks in Braille and large type, educational tools such as Braille typewriters and computer software and hardware, teaching aides such as tests and performance measures, and other special supplies. The materials are distributed through allotments to the States to programs serving individuals who are blind. http://www.aph.org/about

Sources of Information

Business Opportunities Requests for proposals are posted online. http://www.aph.org/rfp
Employment The APH is the world's largest manufacturer of products for people who are blind and visually impaired. It is a drug-free workplace: New hires must pass a drug screening test and background check. http://www.aph.org/careers. http://www.aph.org/contact

For further information, contact the American Printing House for the Blind, P.O. Box 6085, Louisville, KY 40206. Phone, 502-895-2405.

Gallaudet University

800 Florida Avenue NE., Washington, DC 20002
Phone, 202-651-5000. Internet, http://www.gallaudet.edu.

President, Gallaudet University	T. ALAN HURWITZ
Chair, Board of Trustees	HEATHER HARKER

Gallaudet University received its Federal charter in 1864 and is currently authorized by the Education of the Deaf Act of 1986, as amended. Gallaudet is a private, nonprofit educational institution providing elementary, secondary, undergraduate, and continuing education programs for persons who are deaf. The University offers a traditional liberal arts curriculum for students who are deaf and graduate programs in fields related to deafness for students who are deaf and students who are hearing. Gallaudet also conducts a wide variety of basic and applied deafness research and provides public service programs for persons who are deaf and for professionals who work with persons who are deaf.

Gallaudet University is accredited by a number of organizations, among which are the Middle States Association of Colleges and Secondary Schools, the National Council for Accreditation of Teacher Education, and the Conference of Educational Administrators of Schools and Programs for the Deaf. http://www2.gallaudet.edu/attend-gallaudet/about-gallaudet
Laurent Clerc National Deaf Education Center Gallaudet's Laurent Clerc National Deaf Education Center operates elementary

and secondary education programs on the main campus of the University. These programs are authorized by the Education of the Deaf Act of 1986 (20 U.S.C. 4304, as amended) for the primary purpose of developing, evaluating, and disseminating model curricula, instructional strategies, and materials in order to serve individuals who are deaf or hard of hearing. The Education of the Deaf Act requires the programs to include students preparing for postsecondary opportunities other than college and students with a broad spectrum of needs, such as students who are academically challenged, come from non-English-speaking homes, have secondary disabilities, are members of minority groups, or are from rural areas. http://www.gallaudet.edu/clerc-center.html

Model Secondary School for the Deaf   The school was established by act of October 15, 1966, which was superseded by the Education of the Deaf Act of 1986. The school provides day and residential facilities for secondary-age students from across the United States from grades 9 to 12, inclusively. http://www.gallaudet.edu/mssd.html

Kendall Demonstration Elementary School   The school became the Nation's first demonstration elementary school for the deaf by the act of December 24, 1970 (20 U.S.C. 695), which was also later superseded by the Education of the Deaf Act of 1986. The school is a day program for students from the Washington, DC, metropolitan area from the age of onset of deafness to age 15, inclusively, but not beyond the eighth grade or its equivalent. http://www.gallaudet.edu/kdes.html

Sources of Information

Campus Tour   A virtual tour of the University's campus is available online. http://www.gallaudet.edu/visitors-center/virtual-tour.html

Employment   Serving deaf and hard of hearing students from many different backgrounds, Gallaudet University seeks to develop a workforce that reflects its diversity. The University is an equal employment opportunity and affirmative action employer, and it encourages members of traditionally underrepresented groups, persons with disabilities, veterans, and women to apply for vacancies. http://www.gallaudet.edu/hrs/employment-opportunities.html. http://www.gallaudet.edu/about-gallaudet/contact-us.html

For further information, contact the Public Relations Office, Gallaudet University, 800 Florida Avenue NE., Washington, DC 20002. Phone, 202-651-5505.

Howard University

2400 Sixth Street NW., Washington, DC 20059
Phone, 202-806-6100. Internet, http://www.howard.edu.

President   WAYNE A.I. FREDERICK

Howard University was established by Congress by the act of March 2, 1867 (14 Stat. 438). It offers instruction in 12 schools and colleges, as follows: the colleges of arts and sciences; dentistry; engineering, architecture, and computer sciences; medicine; pharmacy, nursing, and allied health sciences; the graduate school; the schools of business; communications; divinity; education; law; and social work. In addition, Howard University has research institutes, centers, and special programs in the following areas: cancer, child development, computational science and engineering, international affairs, sickle cell disease, and the national human genome project. https://www2.howard.edu/about/howard-glance

Sources of Information

Employment   Information is available on the "Career Opportunities" Web page. https://www2.howard.edu/about/careers

Libraries   The Howard University Libraries are accessible online. http://library.howard.edu/library. https://www2.howard.edu/contact

For further information, contact the Office of University Communications, Howard University, 2400 Sixth Street NW., Washington, DC 20059. Phone, 202-806-0970.

National Technical Institute for the Deaf / Rochester Institute of Technology

52 Lomb Memorial Drive, Rochester, NY 14623
Phone, 585-475-6317. Internet, http://www.ntid.rit.edu.

President, Rochester Institute of Technology	WILLIAM W. DESTLER
President, National Technical Institute for the Deaf / Vice President, Rochester Institute of Technology	GERARD J. BUCKLEY

The National Technical Institute for the Deaf (NTID) was established by act of June 8, 1965 (20 U.S.C. 681) to promote the employment of persons who are deaf by providing technical and professional education. The National Technical Institute for the Deaf Act was superseded by the Education of the Deaf Act of 1986 (20 U.S.C. 4431, as amended). The U.S. Department of Education contracts with the Rochester Institute of Technology (RIT) for the operation of a residential facility for postsecondary technical training and education for individuals who are deaf. The purpose of the special relationship with the host institution is to give NTID's faculty and students access to more facilities, institutional services, and career preparation options than could be provided otherwise by a national technical institute for the deaf operating independently.

NTID offers a variety of technical programs at the certificate, diploma, and associate degree levels. Degree programs include majors in business, engineering, science, and visual communications. In addition, NTID students may participate in approximately 200 educational programs available through RIT.

NTID also conducts applied research in occupational- and employment-related aspects of deafness, communication assessment, demographics of NTID's target population, and learning processes in postsecondary education. In addition, NTID conducts training workshops and seminars related to deafness. These workshops and seminars are offered nationwide to professionals who employ, work with, teach, or serve persons who are deaf. http://www.ntid.rit.edu/about

Sources of Information

Campus Tour   A virtual tour of the college's campus is available online. http://www.ntid.rit.edu/virtual-tour. http://www.ntid.rit.edu/contact

For further information, contact the Rochester Institute of Technology, National Technical Institute for the Deaf, Department of Recruitment and Admissions, Lyndon Baines Johnson Building, 52 Lomb Memorial Drive, Rochester, NY 14623-5604. Phone, 716-475-6700.

DEPARTMENT OF ENERGY

1000 Independence Avenue SW., Washington, DC 20585
Phone, 202-586-5000. Internet, http://www.energy.gov.

Office of the Secretary

Secretary of Energy	RICHARD PERRY
Deputy Secretary / Chief Operating Officer	VACANT
Associate Deputy Secretary	VACANT
Chief of Staff	BRIAN MCCORMACK
Inspector General	APRIL STEPHENSON, ACTING
Administrator, U.S. Energy Information Administration	HOWARD GRUENSPECHT, ACTING
Assistant Secretary, Congressional and Intergovernmental Affairs	SHARI DAVENPORT, ACTING
Assistant Secretary, International Affairs	ANDREA LOCKWOOD, ACTING
Chief Financial Officer	ALISON DOONE, ACTING
Director, Advanced Research Projects Agency–Energy	ERIC ROHLFING, ACTING
Director, Energy Policy and System Analysis	CAROL BATTERSHELL, ACTING
Director, Enterprise Assessment	GLENN S. PODONSKY
Director, Intelligence and Counterintelligence	STEVEN BLACK
Director, Public Affairs	ROBERT HAUS
Director, Small and Disadvantaged Business Utilization	CHRISTY JACKIEWICZ, ACTING
Executive Director, Loan Programs Office	JOHN SNEED
General Counsel	JOHN LUCAS, DESIGNATED BY POTUS
Ombudsman	RITA FRANKLIN

Office of the Under Secretary for Management and Performance

Assistant Secretary, Environmental Management	SUSAN CANGE, ACTING
Under Secretary	MATTHEW MOURY, ACTING
Deputy Under Secretary	VACANT
Associate Under Secretary, Environment, Health, Safety and Security	ANDREW LAWRENCE, ACTING
Chief Human Capital Officer	TONYA MACKEY, ACTING
Chief Information Officer	STEPHEN EVERETT
Director, Economic Impact and Diversity	ANDRE SAYLES, ACTING
Director, Hearing and Appeals	POLI MARMOLEJOS
Director, Legacy Management	CARMELO MELENDEZ
Director, Management	INGRID KOLB
Director, Project Management Oversight and Assessment	PAUL BOSCO

Office of the Under Secretary for Science and Energy

Under Secretary	PATRICIA A. HOFFMAN, DESIGNATED BY POTUS
Deputy Under Secretary	VACANT
Assistant Secretary, Electricity Delivery and Energy Reliability	PATRICIA A. HOFFMAN, ACTING
Assistant Secretary, Energy Efficiency and Renewable Energy	DANIEL SIMMONS, ACTING
Assistant Secretary, Fossil Energy	DOUGLAS HOLLETT, ACTING
Assistant Secretary, Nuclear Energy	EDWARD MCGINNIS, ACTING
Director, Indian Energy Policy and Programs	WILLIAM BRADFORD

Director, Science	STEVE BINKLEY, ACTING
Director, Technology Transitions	ROCHELLE BLAUSTEIN, ACTING

Office of the Under Secretary for Nuclear Security / National Nuclear Security Administration

Under Secretary, Nuclear Security / Administrator, National Nuclear Security Administration	LT. GENERAL FRANK G. KLOTZ, USAF (RETIRED)
Principal Deputy Administrator, National Nuclear Security	WILLIAM WHITE, DESIGNATED BY POTUS
Deputy Under Secretary, Counterterrorism and Counterproliferation	JAY TILDEN
Deputy Administrator, Defense Nuclear Nonproliferation	DAVID HUIZENGA, ACTING
Deputy Administrator, Defense Programs	PHILIP CALBOS, ACTING
Deputy Administrator, Naval Reactors	ADM. JAMES F. CALDWELL, JR., USN
Associate Administrator, Emergency Operations	ERIC SMITH, ACTING
Associate Administrator, Defense Nuclear Security	JEFFREY JOHNSON
Associate Administrator Safety, Infrastructure and Operations	JAMES MCCONNELL
Associate Administrator, Counterterrorism and Counterproliferation	JAY TILDEN

The Department of Energy addresses the Nation's energy, environmental, and nuclear challenges, using transformative science and technology to ensure national security and prosperity.

The Department of Energy (DOE) was established by the Department of Energy Organization Act (42 U.S.C. 7131), effective October 1, 1977, pursuant to Executive Order 12009 of September 13, 1977. The act consolidated the major Federal energy functions into one Cabinet-level department. http://www.energy.gov/management/office-management/operational-management/history/brief-history-department-energy

Secretary The Secretary decides major energy policy and planning issues; acts as the principal spokesperson for the Department; and ensures effective communication and working relationships with the public and with Federal, State, local, and tribal governments. The Secretary also serves as the President's principal adviser on energy policies, plans, and programs. http://www.energy.gov/leadership

Enterprise Assessments The Office of Enterprise Assessments functions as an autonomous organization that assesses nuclear and industrial safety performance, cyber and physical security performance, and other critical functions as directed by the Secretary and his or her leadership team. The Office implements congressionally-mandated enforcement functions, manages the National Training Center, serves as an important check-and-balance that meets the DOE's self-regulating responsibilities. http://www.energy.gov/ea/about-us

For further information, contact the Office of Resources, Communications and Congressional Affairs. Phone, 301-903-3272.

Environment, Health, Safety, and Security The Office of the Associate Under Secretary for Environment, Health, Safety and Security increases the effectiveness and efficiency of DOE primary mission-support organizations and initiates enterprisewide responses to common, widespread challenges. The Office serves as the central organization responsible for health, safety, environment, and security and for coordinating and integrating these vital programs. It develops policy and assists with technical matters, provides safety analysis, and oversees corporate safety and security programs. http://www.energy.gov/ehss/about-us

For further information, contact the Office of Resources Management. Phone, 301-903-5139.

Intelligence and Counterintelligence The Office of Intelligence and Counterintelligence safeguards national security information and technologies that comprise intellectual property of incalculable value. The Office has the ability to leverage the Department's scientific and technological expertise to assist policymakers, as well as national security missions in cyber, energy, and homeland security, and in defense and intelligence. http://www.energy.gov/office-intelligence-and-counterintelligence

For further information, contact the Office of Intelligence and Counterintelligence. Phone, 202-586-2610.

Operations, Field, and Site Offices   The Administration of Government-owned, contractor-operated facility contracts is the principal responsibility of the operations, field, and site offices. Contractors who operate Government-owned facilities do most of the DOE's energy and physical research and development, environmental restoration, and waste management.

Department operations offices act as a formal link between Department headquarters and the field laboratories and other operating facilities. They manage programs and projects that the lead headquarters program offices assign. The appropriate assistant secretary, office director, or program officer provides daily, specific program direction for the operations offices. He or she also provides management guidance and coordination for and oversight of them and the field and site offices. http://www.energy.gov/offices

Project Management Oversight and Assessments   The Office of Project Management Oversight and Assessments is the Department of Energy's central management organization providing leadership and assistance in developing and implementing departmentwide policies, procedures, programs, and management systems pertaining to project management, and independently monitors, assesses, and reports on project execution performance. http://www.energy.gov/projectmanagement/about_us

Energy Programs

Advanced Research Projects Agency–Energy   The Advanced Research Projects Agency–Energy (ARPA–E) advances high-potential, high-impact energy technologies before they attract private-sector investment. ARPA-E awardees pursue new ways of generating, storing, and using energy. The Agency focuses on transformational energy projects that can be advanced with a small investment over a defined period of time. A streamlined awards process allows quick action to stimulate cutting-edge energy research. http://arpa-e.energy.gov/?q=arpa-e-site-page/about

For further information, contact the Office of the Director. Phone, 202-287-1004.

Efficiency and Renewable Energy   The Office of Energy Efficiency and Renewable Energy leads the Department's efforts to develop and deliver market-driven solutions for sustainable transportation, renewable electricity generation, and energy-saving homes, buildings, and manufacturing. It supports research and development and technology transfer activities to improve energy efficiency in the transportation, building, industrial, and utility sectors. The Office also administers programs providing financial assistance for State energy planning, weatherizing homes owned by the poor and disadvantaged, implementing State and local energy conservation initiatives, and promoting energy efficient construction and renovation of Federal facilities. http://www.energy.gov/eere/office-energy-efficiency-renewable-energy

For further information, contact the Director of Information and Business Management Systems. Phone, 202-586-7241.

Electricity Delivery and Energy Reliability   The Office of Electricity Delivery and Energy Reliability comprises five divisions: Advanced Grid Integration, Energy Infrastructure Modeling and Analysis, Infrastructure Security and Energy Restoration, National Electricity Delivery, and Power Systems Engineering Research and Development. It promotes electric grid modernization and energy infrastructure resiliency and leads the Department's efforts to ensure a resilient, reliable, and flexible electricity system. http://www.energy.gov/oe/about-office-electricity-delivery-and-energy-reliability

For further information, contact the Office of the Director. Phone, 202-586-1411.

Energy Information   The Energy Information Administration collects, processes, and disseminates data on energy consumption, demand, distribution, production, resource reserves, and technology. It also helps government and nongovernment energy users understand trends by offering analyses of the data. http://www.eia.gov/about

For further information, contact the Director, National Energy Information Center. Phone, 202-586-6537.

Fossil Energy   The Office of Fossil Energy is responsible for Federal research, development, and demonstration efforts on advanced carbon capture and storage (CCS) technologies, as well as the development of technological solutions for the prudent and sustainable development of our unconventional oil and gas domestic resources. It also manages the nation's Strategic Petroleum Reserve and Northeast Home Heating Oil Reserve, both key emergency response tools available to the President to protect Americans from energy supply disruptions. http://www.energy.gov/fe/about

For further information, contact the Office of Communications. Phone, 202-586-6803.

Indian Energy Policy and Programs   The Office of Indian Energy Policy and Programs coordinates, directs, fosters, and implements energy planning, education, management, and programs to assist Tribes with energy development, capacity building, energy infrastructure, energy costs, and electrification of Indian lands and homes. The Office works within the Department, across Government agencies, and with tribes and organizations to promote Indian energy policies and initiatives. https://www.energy.gov/indianenergy/about-us-0

For further information, contact the Director. Phone, 202-586-1272.

Loan Programs Office   The Loan Programs Office accelerates the domestic commercial deployment of innovative and advanced clean energy technologies at a scale that contributes significantly to achieving national clean energy objectives: enhanced American global economic competitiveness, job creation, reduced dependency on foreign oil, and an improved environmental legacy. It fulfills this mission by guaranteeing loans to eligible clean energy projects and by providing direct loans to eligible manufacturers of advanced technology vehicles and components. http://www.energy.gov/lpo/about-us-home | Email: lgprogram@hq.doe.gov

For further information, contact Loan Programs Office. Phone, 202-586-8335.

Nuclear Energy   The Office of Nuclear Energy advances nuclear power as a resource capable of meeting the Nation's energy, environmental, and national security needs. It relies on research, development, and demonstration to resolve barriers of cost, proliferation resistance, safety, security, and technology. Four research objectives guide the Office's efforts: developing technologies and other solutions to improve the reliability, maintain the safety, and extend the life of current reactors; making new reactors more affordable so that nuclear energy can play a bigger role in meeting energy security and climate change goals; developing sustainable fuel cycles; and understanding and minimizing the risks of nuclear proliferation and terrorism. http://www.energy.gov/ne/about-us

For further information, contact the Director, Corporate Communications and External Affairs. Phone, 301-903-1636.

Science   The Office of Science delivers scientific discoveries and tools to transform our understanding of nature and to advance national security, including the Nation's economic and energy security. The Office is the lead Federal agency supporting fundamental scientific research for energy and the Nation's largest supporter of basic research in the physical sciences. It supports scientific research and the development, construction, and operation of open-access, state-of-the-art facilities for researchers. For example, it supports research in all 50 States and the District of Columbia—at DOE laboratories and more than 300 universities and institutions of higher learning nationwide. http://science.energy.gov/about

For further information, contact the Director of Human Resources. Phone, 202-586-5430

Technology Transitions   The Office of Technology Transitions oversees and advances the DOE's mission by expanding the commercial impact of its portfolio of research, development, demonstration, and deployment activities in the short, medium, and long term. The Office develops the Department's policy and vision for expanding the commercial results of its research investments, and it streamlines information and access to DOE's national labs and sites to foster partnerships that will move innovations from the labs into the marketplace. http://www.energy.gov/technologytransitions/about-us

Environmental Quality Programs

Environmental Management   The Office of Environmental Management completes the safe cleanup of the environmental legacy after decades of nuclear weapons development and Government-sponsored nuclear energy research. The Office adheres to a mission philosophy based on reducing risk and reducing environmental liability. Current activities include fulfilling commitments to lower risk and complete cleanup across all sites; constructing and operating facilities treating radioactive liquid tank waste in a safe, stable form; securing and storing nuclear material in a safe, stable manner in secure locations; transporting and disposing transuranic and low-level wastes in a safe, cost-effective way; decontaminating and decommissioning facilities without further value; remediating soil and ground water containing radioactive and hazardous contaminants; and planning a facility to manage and store mercury. http://www.energy.gov/em/mission

For further information, contact the Director of Communication/External Affairs. Phone, 202-287-5591.

Legacy Management   The Office of Legacy Management manages DOE post-closure responsibilities and ensures the future protection of human health and the environment. The Office has control and custody for legacy land, structures, and facilities that it maintains at levels consistent with DOE long-term plans. Its activities include protecting human health

and the environment through long-term surveillance and maintenance; preserving, protecting, and making accessible legacy records and information; supporting a workforce structured to accomplish DOE missions; implementing departmental policy affecting continuity of worker pension and medical benefits; managing legacy land and assets with an emphasis on safety, reuse, and disposition; mitigating community impacts from the cleanup of legacy waste and changing departmental missions; and coordinating policy issues with appropriate departmental organizations. http://www.energy.gov/lm/mission

For further information, contact the Director of Business Operations. Phone, 202-586-7388.

Nuclear Security Programs

Defense Programs   The Office of Defense Programs ensures that the U.S. nuclear arsenal meets national security requirements and continues to serve as a deterrent. In partnership with the Department of Defense, the Office provides the research, development, secure transportation, and production activities necessary to support the U.S. nuclear weapons stockpile. http://www.nnsa.energy.gov/aboutus/ourprograms/defenseprograms

For further information, contact the Associate Administrator for Management and Budget. Phone, 202-586-5753.

Naval Nuclear Propulsion   The Naval Reactors Office administers the Naval Nuclear Propulsion Program, which provides militarily effective nuclear propulsion plants and maintains their operational safety, reliability, and longevity. This program relies on trained U.S. Navy personnel, fast and stealthy ships, and supply-chain independence to carry out its mission. http://www.nnsa.energy.gov/aboutus/ourprograms/powernavy2

For further information, contact the Deputy Administrator for Naval Reactors. Phone, 202-781-6174.

Nuclear Nonproliferation   The Office of Defense Nuclear Nonproliferation works closely with a range of international partners, U.S. Federal agencies, the U.S. national laboratories, and the private sector.

It secures and safeguards or disposes of dangerous nuclear and radiological material and monitors and controls the proliferation of weapons-of-mass-destruction technology and expertise. http://nnsa.energy.gov/aboutus/ourprograms/nonproliferation-0

For further information, contact the Associate Administrator for Management and Budget. Phone, 202-586-5753.

Nuclear Security Administration The National Nuclear Security Administration (NNSA) was created by Congress through the National Defense Authorization Act for Fiscal Year 2000 (113 Stat. 512) to bring focus to the management of the Nation's defense nuclear security programs. Three existing organizations within the Department of Energy—Defense Programs, Defense Nuclear Nonproliferation, and Naval Reactors—were combined into a new, separately managed agency, headed by an Administrator who reports to the Secretary of Energy. The NNSA seeks to strengthen national security through military application of nuclear energy and by reducing the global threat from terrorism and weapons of mass destruction.

The Administration's service center and eight site offices provide operations oversight and contract administration for NNSA site activities. Federally-run site offices oversee the management and operating contractors for each of NNSA's eight sites. These offices provide the necessary communication between Federal and contractor employees as well as oversight to improve management procedures. http://www.nnsa.energy.gov/ourmission

For further information, contact the Associate Administrator for Management and Budget. Phone, 202-586-5753.

Power Administrations

The Department's four Power Administrations market and transmit electric power produced at Federal hydroelectric projects and reservoirs. The Deputy Secretary provides management oversight of the Power Administrations.

Bonneville Power Administration The Bonneville Power Administration is a nonprofit federal power marketing administration based in the Pacific Northwest. Although BPA is part of the U.S. Department of Energy, it is self-funding and covers its costs by selling its products and services. BPA markets wholesale electrical power from 31 federal hydroelectric projects in the Northwest, one nonfederal nuclear plant and several small nonfederal power plants. BPA promotes energy efficiency, renewable resources and new technologies that improve its ability to deliver on its mission. It also funds regional efforts to protect and rebuild fish and wildlife populations affected by hydropower development in the Columbia River Basin. BPA is committed to public service and makes its decisions with input from all stakeholders. BPA dedicates itself to providing high system reliability, low rates consistent with sound business principles, environmental stewardship, and accountability. http://www.bpa.gov/Pages/home.aspx

For further information, contact the Bonneville Power Administration, 905 Eleventh Avenue NE., Portland, OR 97232-4169. Phone, 503-230-3000 or 800-282-3713.

Southeastern Power Administration This Administration transmits and disposes of surplus electric power and energy generated at reservoir projects in Alabama, Florida, Georgia, Kentucky, Mississippi, North and South Carolina, Tennessee, Virginia, and West Virginia.

It sets the lowest possible rates for consumers consistent with sound business practices and gives preference to public entities. http://www.energy.gov/sepa/about-us

For further information, contact the Southeastern Power Administration, 1166 Athens Tech Road, Elberton, GA 30635-4578. Phone, 706-213-3800.

Southwestern Power Administration This Administration sells and disposes of electric power and energy in Arkansas, Kansas, Louisiana, Missouri, Oklahoma, and Texas.

It transmits and disposes of the electric power and energy generated at Federal reservoir projects, supplemented by power purchased from public and private utilities, in such a manner as to encourage the most widespread and economical use. It sets the lowest possible rates for consumers consistent with sound business practices and gives preference to public entities. It also conducts and participates in the comprehensive planning of water resource development in the Southwest. http://www.swpa.gov/agency.aspx

For further information, contact the Southwestern Power Administration, Suite 1600, Williams Center Tower One, One West Third Street, Tulsa, OK 74103-3532. Phone, 918-595-6600.

Western Area Power Administration WAPA markets and transmits wholesale electricity from multi-use water projects. Its service area encompasses a 15-state region of the central and western U.S. where more than 17,000 circuit mile transmission system carries electricity from 56 hydropower plants operated by the Bureau of Reclamation, U.S. Army Corps of Engineers and the International Boundary and Water Commission. WAPA also markets power from the Navajo Generating Station coal-fired plant near Page, Ariz. Together, these plants have an installed capacity of 10,504 megawatts. WAPA sells power to preference customers such as Federal and state agencies, cities and towns, rural electric cooperatives, public utility districts, irrigation districts and Native American tribes. In turn, they provide retail electric service to millions of consumers in the West. http://www.wapa.gov/About/Pages/about.aspx

For further information, contact the Western Area Power Administration, 12155 West Alameda Parkway, Lakewood, CO 80228-1213. Phone, 720-962-7000.

Sources of Information

Business Opportunities To learn about the Office of Small and Disadvantaged Business Utilization and its mission or to find information on the services that it offers and its programs, visit the Office's Web site. Phone, 202-586-7377. http://www.energy.gov/osdbu/office-small-and-disadvantaged-business-utilization | Email: smallbusiness@hq.doe.gov

Useful external links for small businesses are available on the Office of Small and Disadvantaged Business Utilization's Web site. http://www.energy.gov/osdbu/small-business-services/useful-links-small-businesses

Employment The DOE offers career opportunities that span a broad, diverse range of professions: accounting and contracting, administration, business, communications and information technology, computer science, engineering, mathematics, national security and international affairs, public affairs, science and technology, and more. Most Federal jobs require U.S. citizenship; however, noncitizens may apply for some opportunities at the National Laboratories. http://www.energy.gov/jobs/jobs

Information on opportunities for students and recent graduates, veterans, and those with disabilities is available on the DOE Web site. For more information, contact the Chief Human Capital Officer. Phone, 202-586-1234. http://www.energy.gov/jobs/services/students-recent-graduates

Energy Saver Energy Saver is the DOE's consumer resource on saving energy and using renewable energy technologies at home. http://www.energy.gov/energysaver/energy-saver

When deciding whether or not to invest in more energy efficiency, consumers can benefit from knowing electricity usages and the associated costs. The online energy use calculator estimates annual energy use and costs associated with operating appliances and home electronics. http://energy.gov/energysaver/estimating-appliance-and-home-electronic-energy-use

Energy Simulation Software EnergyPlus is cross-platform, free, and open-source software that runs on the Windows, Mac OS X, and Linux operating systems. It is a whole building energy simulation program that architects, engineers, and researchers use to model energy consumption and water use in buildings. The DOE's Building Technologies Office funded the development of EnergyPlus, and the National Renewable Energy Laboratory manages it. http://apps1.eere.energy.gov/buildings/energyplus

Freedom of Information Act (FOIA) The Office of Information Resources administers policies, procedures, and programs to ensure DOE compliance with the FOIA. The DOE provides resources on its Web site to assist information seekers with finding answers to questions about DOE programs and with locating information that is already publicly available and does not require a

FOIA request to access. Information seekers should use these resources before submitting a FOIA request for DOE records. http://www.energy.gov/management/office-management/operational-management/freedom-information-act

Contact information for FOIA requester service centers and FOIA public liaisons and officers is available online. http://www.energy.gov/management/office-management/operational-management/freedom-information-act/foia-contacts | Email: foia-central@hq.doe.gov

The DOE Web site features an electronic FOIA request form. http://www.energy.gov/doe-headquarters-foia-request-form

Glossaries   The Bioenergy Technologies Office maintains an online biomass glossary. Its short descriptions are intended to help students and researchers understand biomass terminology. http://www.energy.gov/eere/bioenergy/glossary

The waterpower program maintains an online hydropower glossary. It is intended to help readers understand terminology associated with hydroturbine and hydropower plant components. http://www.energy.gov/eere/water/glossary-hydropower-terms

History   The DOE history timeline provides the public with easy access to information on the Department's history and its predecessor agencies. The timeline includes links to press releases, reports, speeches, and other documentation. http://energy.gov/management/office-management/operational-management/history/doe-history-timeline

Maps   The DOE Web site features maps depicting a variety of energy-related topics and trends: alternative fueling stations, carbon capture, climate vulnerabilities, per capita energy expenditure, renewable energy production, solar energy potential, and more. http://www.energy.gov/maps

National Laboratories   For more than 60 years, these Laboratories have been leading institutions for scientific innovation in the United States. To learn more about the Ames Laboratory, Princeton Plasma Physics Laboratory, Thomas Jefferson National Accelerator Facility, and the other 14 National Laboratories, visit the DOE's "About the National Labs" Web page. http://energy.gov/about-national-labs

News   The DOE posts news stories, photos, speeches, and videos on its Web site, which also features a blog. http://www.energy.gov/news-blog

The DOE's online photo galleries are diverse and extensive, as well as captivating for browsers who have an interest in America's energy future. https://www.energy.gov/photos

An online subscription form is available to sign up for DOE advisories and press releases. http://onlinepressroom.net/doe

Office of Inspector General (OIG)   The OIG maintains electronic and telephone hotlines to facilitate the reporting of allegations of abuse, fraud, mismanagement, or waste in DOE programs or operations. Phone, 202-586-4073 or 800-541-1625. http://www.energy.gov/ig/office-inspector-general | Email: ighotline@hq.doe.gov

An online complaint form for reporting allegations is also available on the OIG Web site. http://www.energy.gov/ig/complaint-form

The early alert system is a distribution list used to inform subscribers of significant press releases, publications, and reports the moment that the OIG posts them online. Subscription is free and available to anyone who has an email address and an interest in the OIG's work. http://www.energy.gov/ig/subscription-information | Email: ignewmedia@hq.doe.gov

Open Government   The DOE supports the Open Government initiative to create a more open and transparent Government by promoting the principles of collaboration, participation, and transparency. http://www.energy.gov/open-government | Email: open@hq.doe.gov

Phonebook   A departmentwide phonebook with a text box for entering search requests is available on the DOE Web site. http://www.energy.gov/phonebook

Program and Staff Offices   The "Offices" Web page features links to the program and staff offices' Web sites. It also includes links to the Web sites of the laboratories and technology centers, power marketing administrations, field sites, and Energy Information and National Nuclear Security Administrations. http://www.energy.gov/offices

Renewable Energy The steady expansion of the U.S. renewable energy sector indicates that a clean energy revolution is underway nationwide. The DOE Web site features charts that graphically illustrates trends that will shape America's energy future. http://energy.gov/science-innovation/energy-sources/renewable-energy

Scientific and Technical Information The Office of Scientific and Technical Information (OSTI) advances science and sustains technological creativity by making research and development findings available to and useful for DOE researchers and the public. The OSTI Web site provides access to DOE science resources and to U.S. Federal science (Science.gov) and global science (WorldWideScience.org) information. https://www.osti.gov/home/2014-catalogue-collections

Social Media The DOE tweets announcements and other newsworthy items on Twitter. https://twitter.com/energy

The DOE has a Facebook page. https://www.facebook.com/energygov. http://www.energy.gov/contact-us

For further information, contact the Office of Public Affairs, Department of Energy, 1000 Independence Avenue SW., Washington, DC 20585. Phone, 202-586-4940.

Federal Energy Regulatory Commission

888 First Street NE., Washington, DC 20426
Phone, 202-502-8004. Internet, http://www.ferc.gov.

Chair	CHERYL A. LeFLEUR, ACTING
Commissioner	(VACANCY)
Commissioner	(VACANCY)
Commissioner	(VACANCY)
Commissioner	(VACANCY)

The Federal Energy Regulatory Commission helps consumers obtain efficient, reliable, and sustainable energy services at fair and reasonable rates through regulatory and market means.

The Federal Energy Regulatory Commission (FERC) is an independent agency within the Department of Energy that regulates the interstate transmission of electricity, natural gas, and oil. The Commission comprises five members whom the President appoints with the advice and consent of the Senate. FERC Commissioners serve 5-year terms and have an equal vote on regulatory matters. The President designates one member to serve as both the Commission's Chair and its administrative head.

Under the authority of the Federal Power, the Natural Gas, and the Interstate Commerce Acts, the FERC regulates the interstate transmission of electricity, natural gas, and oil. That authority also includes review of proposals to build interstate natural gas pipelines, natural gas storage facilities, and liquefied natural gas terminals, and licensing of nonfederal hydropower dams.

The FERC enforces regulatory requirements by imposing civil penalties and other means, monitors and investigates energy markets, and protects the reliability of the high voltage interstate transmission system through mandatory reliability standards. http://www.ferc.gov/about/ferc-does.asp

Sources of Information

Critical Energy Infrastructure Information (CEII) The FERC protects energy facilities by restricting public access to CEII. An electronic CEII request form is available on the Commission's Web site. http://www.ferc.gov/legal/ceii-foia/ceii/eceii.asp

Employment Information on college recruitment and internship programs, reasons for pursuing career opportunities at the FERC, and a list of job vacancies are available online. http://ferc.gov/careers/careers.asp

In 2016, the FERC was ranked as the #4 best midsize agencies at which to work in the Federal Government, and #1 in Work-Life Balance for three years running. http://bestplacestowork.org/BPTW/rankings/detail/DR00

FERC Online FERC Online serves as a portal to documents and dockets and provides an easy and efficient way to communicate and do business with the Commission. http://www.ferc.gov/docs-filing/ferconline.asp

Freedom of Information Act (FOIA) An electronic FOIA request form is available on the Commission's Web site. http://www.ferc.gov/legal/ceii-foia/foia/foia-new-form/FOIARequest.aspx

Frequently Asked Questions (FAQs) A topical list of FAQs is available on the Commission's Web site. http://www.ferc.gov/resources/faqs.asp

Glossary The FERC maintains a glossary and list of acronyms on its Web site. http://www.ferc.gov/resources/glossary.asp. http://www.ferc.gov/resources/acronyms.asp

Media The Commission posts headlines, news releases, photographs, and statements, as well as informational videos and podcasts, congressional testimony, speeches, and interviews. http://www.ferc.gov/media/media.asp

Open Government The FERC supports the principles of collaboration, participation, and transparency to expand the openness of the Federal Government. https://www.ferc.gov/open.asp

Phone Book The employee phone directory is available online in Portable Document Form (PDF). http://www.ferc.gov/contact-us/tel-num/phone.pdf

Plain Language The Commission is committed to the Plain Writing Act of 2010 and adheres to Federal plain language guidelines. Please let FERC editors and writers know if a document or section of the Web site is difficult to understand. https://www.ferc.gov/open/plain-language.asp | Email: customer@ferc.gov

Public Participation Citizens who may be affected by a proposed natural gas or hydroelectric project that the Commission regulates have certain rights. These rights range from being able to look at project correspondence to becoming an intervener and being able to appeal FERC decisions in Federal court. http://www.ferc.gov/resources/get-involved.asp

Speakers An online form is available to initiate a request for a FERC representative to serve as a speaker at an organized event. http://ferc.gov/contact-us/speak-req.asp. http://www.ferc.gov/contact-us/tel-num.asp

For further information, contact the Office of External Affairs. Phone, 202-502-8004 or 866-208-3372. Fax, 202-208-2106.

Editorial Note

The Department of Health and Human Services did not meet the publication deadline for submitting updated information of its activities, functions, and sources of information as required by the automatic disclosure provisions of the Freedom of Information Act (5 U.S.C. 552(a)(1)(A)).

DEPARTMENT OF HEALTH AND HUMAN SERVICES

200 Independence Avenue SW., Washington, DC 20201
Phone, 202-690-6343. Internet, http://www.hhs.gov.

Secretary of Health and Human Services	THOMAS E. PRICE
Deputy Secretary	MARY K. WAKEFIELD, ACTING
Chief of Staff	ALASTAIR M. FITZPAYNE
Chair, Departmental Appeals Board	CONSTANCE B. TOBIAS
Chief Administrative Law Judge, Office of Medicare Hearings and Appeals	NANCY J. GRISWOLD
Executive Secretary	MADHURA VALVERDE
General Counsel	PEGGY DOTZEL, ACTING
Inspector General	DANIEL R. LEVINSON
National Coordinator for Health Information Technology	KAREN B. DESALVO
Surgeon General	VIVEK H. MURTHY

Assistant Secretaries

Administration	COLLEEN BARROS, ACTING
Financial Resources	ELLEN G. MURRAY
Global Affairs	JIMMY KOLKER
Health	KAREN B. DESALVO, ACTING
Legislation	JIM R. ESQUEA
Planning and Evaluation	KATHRYN MARTIN, ACTING
Preparedness and Response	NICOLE LURIE
Public Affairs	KEVIN GRIFFIS

Directors

Center for Faith-Based and Neighborhood Partnerships	ACACIA BAMBERG SALATTI
Office for Civil Rights	JOCELYN SAMUELS
Office of Health Reform	MEENA SESHAMANI
Office of Intergovernmental and External Affairs	EMILY BARSON

The Department of Health and Human Services strengthens the public health and welfare of the American people by making affordable and quality health care and childcare accessible, ensuring the safety of food products, preparing for public health emergencies, and advancing the diagnosis, treatment, and curing of life-threatening illnesses.

The Department of Health and Human Services (HHS) was created as the Department of Health, Education, and Welfare on April 11, 1953 (5 U.S.C. app.).
Secretary The Secretary of Health and Human Services advises the President on health, welfare, and income security plans, policies, and programs of the Federal Government and directs Department staff in carrying out the programs and activities of the Department and promotes general public understanding of the Department's goals,

programs, and objectives. http://www.hhs. gov/about/leadership/index.html#secretary
Office of Intergovernmental and External Affairs The Office of Intergovernmental and External Affairs (IEA) supports the Secretary by serving as the primary liaison between the Department and external stakeholders and governments at the State, local, territorial, and tribal levels. The Office facilitates communication regarding HHS initiatives as they relate to external stakeholders and governments at the State,

206

DEPARTMENT OF HEALTH AND HUMAN SERVICES

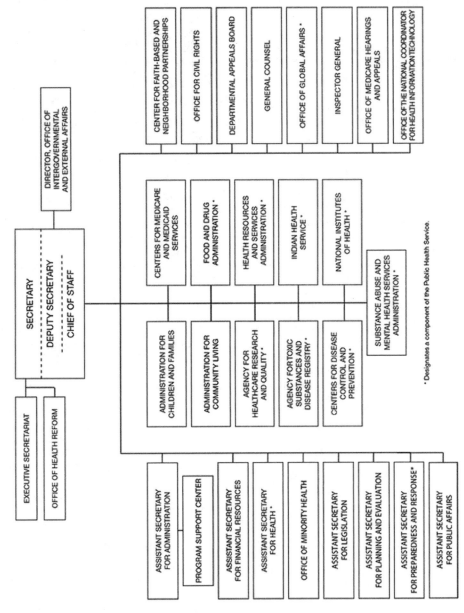

SECRETARY
DEPUTY SECRETARY
CHIEF OF STAFF

DIRECTOR, OFFICE OF INTERGOVERNMENTAL AND EXTERNAL AFFAIRS

EXECUTIVE SECRETARIAT

OFFICE OF HEALTH REFORM

CENTER FOR FAITH-BASED AND NEIGHBORHOOD PARTNERSHIPS

OFFICE FOR CIVIL RIGHTS

DEPARTMENTAL APPEALS BOARD

GENERAL COUNSEL

OFFICE OF GLOBAL AFFAIRS *

INSPECTOR GENERAL

OFFICE OF MEDICARE HEARINGS AND APPEALS

OFFICE OF THE NATIONAL COORDINATOR FOR HEALTH INFORMATION TECHNOLOGY

CENTERS FOR MEDICARE AND MEDICAID SERVICES

FOOD AND DRUG ADMINISTRATION *

HEALTH RESOURCES AND SERVICES ADMINISTRATION *

INDIAN HEALTH SERVICE *

NATIONAL INSTITUTES OF HEALTH *

ADMINISTRATION FOR CHILDREN AND FAMILIES

ADMINISTRATION FOR COMMUNITY LIVING

AGENCY FOR HEALTHCARE RESEARCH AND QUALITY *

AGENCY FOR TOXIC SUBSTANCES AND DISEASE REGISTRY *

CENTERS FOR DISEASE CONTROL AND PREVENTION *

SUBSTANCE ABUSE AND MENTAL HEALTH SERVICES ADMINISTRATION *

* Designates a component of the Public Health Service.

ASSISTANT SECRETARY FOR ADMINISTRATION

PROGRAM SUPPORT CENTER

ASSISTANT SECRETARY FOR FINANCIAL RESOURCES

ASSISTANT SECRETARY FOR HEALTH *

OFFICE OF MINORITY HEALTH

ASSISTANT SECRETARY FOR LEGISLATION

ASSISTANT SECRETARY FOR PLANNING AND EVALUATION

ASSISTANT SECRETARY FOR PREPAREDNESS AND RESPONSE *

ASSISTANT SECRETARY FOR PUBLIC AFFAIRS

local, territorial, and tribal levels. The IEA both represents the State, territorial, and tribal perspective in the process of Federal policymaking and clarifies the Federal perspective to State, territorial and tribal representatives. http://www.hhs.gov/intergovernmental

For further information, contact the Office of Intergovernmental and External Affairs. Phone, 202-690-6060.

Office of the Assistant Secretary for Preparedness and Response

The Office of the Assistant Secretary for Preparedness and Response (ASPR) provides national leadership in the prevention of, preparation for, and response to the adverse health effects of public health emergencies and disasters. It acts as the primary advisor to the HHS Secretary on bioterrorism and other public health emergency matters, strengthens the Nation's health and response systems, and enhances national health security. The ASPR leads a collaborative policy approach to the Department's preparedness, response, and recovery portfolio. It works with partners across Federal, State, local, tribal, and international bodies, in communities, and in the private sector to promote a unified and strategic approach to the challenges of public health and medical preparedness, response, and recovery through programs like the Hospital Preparedness Program. The ASPR coordinates public health and medical support available from across the Federal Government to help prepare communities and to augment local capabilities of overwhelmed communities during and after disasters, which includes providing medical professionals through the ASPR's National Disaster Medical System and the Medical Reserve Corps. The ASPR provides an integrated, systematic approach to the advanced development and acquisition of the necessary vaccines, drugs, therapies, and diagnostic tools for public health medical emergencies. It also coordinates within the Department and among Federal partners on the policy, prioritization, funding, acquisition, and distribution of these medical countermeasures. In addition,

offices within the ASPR coordinate within the division, within the Department and with Federal, State, local, territorial, tribal and international bodies on emergency communications, science preparedness, and administrative management to support decisionmakers in emergencies. http://www.phe.gov/preparedness/pages/default.aspx

For further information, contact the Office of the Assistant Secretary for Preparedness and Response. Phone, 202-205-2882.

Office of the Assistant Secretary for Health

The Office of the Assistant Secretary for Health (ASH) comprises 12 offices and 10 Presidential and secretarial advisory committees. The Assistant Secretary for Health heads the Office and serves as the Secretary's senior public health advisor. ASH provides assistance in implementing and coordinating secretarial decisions for the Public Health Service and coordination of population-based health clinical divisions; provides oversight of research conducted or supported by the Department; implements programs that provide population-based public health services; and provides direction and policy oversight, through the Office of the Surgeon General, for the Public Health Service Commissioned Corps. ASH administers a wide array of interdisciplinary programs related to disease prevention, health promotion, the reduction of health disparities, women's health, HIV/AIDS, vaccine programs, physical fitness and sports, bioethics, population affairs, blood supply, research integrity, and human research protections. http://www.hhs.gov/ash

For further information, contact the Office of the Assistant Secretary for Health. Phone, 202-690-7694.

Sources of Information

A–Z Index   The HHS Web site features an alphabetical index to help visitors search for specific topics or browse content that aligns with their interests. http://www.hhs.gov/az/a/index.html

Bullying   The HHS manages StopBullying.gov, a Web site that provides resources for defining, preventing, and responding to bullying, and for identifying who may be at risk. The Web site also features sections for children and teens, educators, parents, and communities. https://www.stopbullying.gov

Information on identifying, preventing, and reporting cyberbullying is also available on the Web site. https://www.stopbullying.gov/cyberbullying/index.html

Business Opportunities The HHS relies on its contractors and grantees to help protect the health of Americans and provide essential human services. http://www.hhs.gov/grants/index.html#contract

The Office of Small and Disadvantaged Business Utilization helps develop and implement outreach programs to raise awareness of HHS contracting opportunities within the small business community. For information on programs, contact the Office of Small and Disadvantaged Business Utilization. Phone, 202-690-7300. http://www.hhs.gov/asfr/ogapa/osbdu

Civil Rights The Office for Civil Rights improves people's health and well-being, ensures equal access to health care and services without discrimination, and protects the privacy and security of people's health information. For information on enforcement of civil rights laws, contact the Director, Office for Civil Rights, 200 Independence Avenue SW.,Room 515–F Washington, DC 20201. Phone, 800-368-1019. TDD, 800-537-7697. http://www.hhs.gov/ocr/civilrights

Departmental Appeals Board For information, contact the Departmental Appeals Board Immediate Office, MS 6127, Wilbur J. Cohen Building, 330 Independence Avenue SW., Room G–644, Washington, DC 20201. Phone, 202-565-0200. http://www.hhs.gov/dab

Career Opportunities For information on training opportunities and opportunities for recent graduates and students or to view current job openings, visit the "Why a Career at HHS?" Web page. http://www.hhs.gov/about/careers/index.html

Freedom of Information Act (FOIA) The FOIA allows individuals to request access to Federal agency records. The statute contains, however, nine exemptions that exempt some records or portions of them from disclosure. The Assistant Secretary for Public Affairs also serves as the Agency Chief FOIA Officer.

http://www.hhs.gov/foia | Email: hhs.acfo@hhs.gov

Frequently Asked Questions (FAQs) The HHS posts answers to FAQs on its Web site. http://www.hhs.gov/answers

Glossary In the world of organ donation and transplantation, terms are used and topics discussed that many may not recognize. The OrganDonor.gov Web site features a glossary of organ donation terms. http://www.organdonor.gov/about/facts-terms/terms.html

Inspector General Contact the Office of Inspector General, Wilbur J. Cohen Building, 330 Independence Avenue SW., Washington, DC 20201. http://oig.hhs.gov

To report fraud, waste, or abuse in Department programs, contact the Office of Inspector General, OIG Hotline Operations, P.O. Box 23489, L'Enfant Plaza Station, Washington, DC 20026-3489. TIPS Line, 800-447-8477. OIG Fugitive Line, 888-476-4453. TTY, 800-377-4950. Fax, 800-223-8164. https://forms.oig.hhs.gov/hotlineoperations

Medicare Hearings / Appeals For information on Medicare hearings before administrative law judges, regarding Medicare coverage and payment determinations that Medicare contractors, Medicare Advantage Organizations, or Part D plan sponsors have made, as well as information on determinations related to Medicare beneficiary eligibility and entitlement, Part B late enrollment penalties, and income-related monthly adjustment amounts that the Social Security Administration has made, contact the Office of Medicare Hearings and Appeals. Phone, 703-235-0635 or 855-556-8475. http://www.hhs.gov/omha | Email: medicare.appeals@hhs.gov

Open Government The HHS supports the Open Government initiative by promoting the principles of collaboration, participation, and transparency. http://www.hhs.gov/open/index.html

Privacy Rights For information on the HIPAA privacy, security, and breach notification rules or the Patient Safety Act, contact the Office for Civil Rights. Phone, 800-368-1019. TDD, 800-537-7697. http://www.hhs.gov/ocr/privacy

Public Health Service Commissioned Corps Officer Program   Information on the Commissioned Corps Officer programs is available at the Public Health Service Commissioned Corps Officer Web site. http://www.usphs.gov
Regional Offices   Visit the "Regional Offices" Web page for contact information. http://www.hhs.gov/about/agencies/regional-offices
Support Services (Fee-for-Service Activities)   The Program Support Center provides support services to all components of the Department and Federal agencies worldwide. For information concerning fee-for-service activities in the areas of acquisitions, occupational health, information technology support and security, human resource systems, financial management, and administrative operations, contact the Program Support Center, 5600 Fishers Lane, Rockville, MD 20857. Phone, 301-443-0034. http://www.psc.gov
Surgeon General   For information on the benefits of active living, healthy eating, mental and emotional well-being, and tobacco-free living, visit the "Surgeon General" Web site. Phone, 240-276-8853. http://www.surgeongeneral.gov. http://www.hhs.gov/contactus.html

For further information, contact the U.S. Department of Health and Human Services, 200 Independence Avenue SW., Washington, DC 20201. Phone, 877-696-6775.

Administration for Children and Families

330 C Street SW., Washington, DC 20201
Phone, 202-401-9200. Internet, http://www.acf.hhs.gov.

Assistant Secretary For Children and Families	Mark Greenberg, Acting
Chief of Staff	S. Jeffrey Hild

The Administration for Children and Families administers programs and provides advice to the Secretary on issues relevant to children, youth, and families; child support enforcement; community services; developmental disabilities; family assistance; Native American assistance; and refugee resettlement. http://www.acf.hhs.gov/about/what-we-do

Sources of Information

Career Opportunities   The Administration employs professionals with diverse academic and social backgrounds in a broad range of career fields and positions. http://www.acf.hhs.gov/about/jobs-contracts
History   The Administration for Children and Families was created on April 15, 1991. A short history of the Administration is available on its Web site. http://www.acf.hhs.gov
Homelessness   The Administration's Web site features information on its programs and services for the homeless and for those at risk of becoming homeless. http://www.acf.hhs.gov/program-topics/homelessness

Hotlines   The Administration supports nationwide crisis hotlines for child abuse, domestic violence, human trafficking, and runaways. The Health Insurance Marketplace Call Center assists callers with choosing coverage that provides the best protection and benefits for them and family members, as well as for their businesses. http://www.acf.hhs.gov/acf-hotlines
Lesbian, Gay, Bisexual, and Transgender (LGBT) Assistance   The Administration's Web site features information on its programs and services for the LGBT community, especially for LGBT families and youth. http://www.acf.hhs.gov/program-topics/lgbt-0
News   The Administration posts press releases on its Web site. http://www.acf.hhs.gov/media/press
Programs / Services   The Administration's Web site features a page showcasing by topic the programs and services that it provides to support families, children, individuals, and communities. Topics include children and youth, communities, emergency response and recovery, families, financial security, global populations,

Hispanic outreach, homelessness, human trafficking, LGBT, Native Americans and tribes, and unaccompanied children. http://www.acf.hhs.gov/program-topics. http://www.acf.hhs.gov/media/program-contacts

For further information, contact the Administration for Children and Families, 330 C Street SW., Washington, DC 20201. Phone, 202-401-9200.

Administration for Community Living

330 C Street SW., Washington, DC 20201
Phone, 202-401-4634. TTY, internet, 800-877-8339. Internet, http://www.acl.gov.

Administrator	MARY LAZARE, ACTING
Principal Deputy Administrator	MARY LAZARE, ACTING

The Administration for Community Living administers programs and advises the Secretary on issues relevant to people with disabilities, their families and caregivers, and the independence, well-being, and health of older adults. https://acl.gov/About_ACL/Index.aspx

Sources of Information

Blog The Administration's Blog presents diverse perspectives on trends and issues related to older adults and people with disabilities. https://acl.gov/NewsRoom/blog/Index.aspx
Data / Statistics Data and statistics on older adults, as well as on persons with intellectual, physical, and developmental disabilities, are available on the Administration's Web site. https://acl.gov/Data_Outcomes/Index.aspx

Elder Care Services The elder care locator is a public service that provides information on services for older adults and their families. Online chat with an information specialist is also available Monday–Friday, 9 a.m.–8 p.m., eastern time. Phone, 800-677-1116. http://www.eldercare.gov/Eldercare.NET/Public/Index.aspx
Employment For information on employment opportunities, visit the "Career Opportunities" Web page. http://www.acl.gov/About_ACL/CareerOpportunities/Index.aspx
Help / Resources The Administration's Web site features resources for connecting caregivers, families, older adults, people with disabilities, and professionals to Federal, national, and local programs and information. https://acl.gov/Get_Help/Index.aspx. http://www.acl.gov

For further information, contact the Administration for Community Living, 330 C Street SW., Washington, DC 20201. Phone, 202-401-4634. TTY, 800-877-8339.

Agency for Healthcare Research and Quality

5600 Fishers Lane, Rockville, MD 20857
Phone, 301-427-1364. Internet, http://www.ahrq.gov.

Director	ANDREW BINDMAN
Deputy Director	SHARON B. ARNOLD

The Agency for Healthcare Research and Quality produces evidence to make health care affordable, equitable, more accessible, of a higher quality, and safer. It also works within the Department of Health and Human Services and with other partners to ensure that the evidence is understood and used. http://www.ahrq.gov/cpi/about/profile/index.html

Sources of Information

Data   Statistical portraits of health care delivery in the United States are available on the Agency's Web site. http://www.ahrq.gov/research/data/index.html

Career Opportunities   For information on employment opportunities, visit the "Job Opportunities" Web page. http://www.ahrq.gov/cpi/about/careers/index.html

Frequently Asked Questions (FAQs)   The Agency posts answers to FAQs on is Web site. https://info.ahrq.gov

Site Map   The Web site map allows visitors to look for specific topics or to browse content that aligns with their interests. http://www.ahrq.gov/sitemap.html. http://www.ahrq.gov

For further information, contact the Agency for Healthcare Research and Quality, 5600 Fishers Lane, Rockville, MD 20857. Phone, 301-427-1364.

Agency for Toxic Substances and Disease Registry

MS E–61, 4770 Buford Highway NE., Atlanta, GA 30341
Phone, 770-488-0604. Internet, http://www.atsdr.cdc.gov.

Administrator	BRENDA FITZGERALD

The Agency for Toxic Substances and Disease Registry (ATSDR), as part of the Public Health Service, tries to prevent exposure to toxic substances—exposure to substances from wastesites, unplanned releases, and other pollution sources present in the environment—which produces adverse health effects and diminishes the quality of life. https://www.atsdr.cdc.gov/about/index.html

Sources of Information

A–Z Index   The Agency's Web site features an alphabetical index to help visitors search for specific topics or browse content that aligns with their interests. https://www.atsdr.cdc.gov/az/a.html

ATSDR in 60 Seconds   The ATSDR protects people from the health effects of chemical exposures. The Agency's Web site features the 60-second video "Dangerous Discovery" that communicates the importance of its mission. https://www.atsdr.cdc.gov/videos/ATSDR_DangerousDiscovery_h264.mp4

Internships / Training   Information on internships and educational and training opportunities is available on the ATSDR Web site. http://www.atsdr.cdc.gov/environmentaleducation.html

Toxic Frequently Asked Questions (ToxFAQs)   ToxFAQs features a series of summaries on hazardous substances that the Agency's Division of Toxicology developed. ATSDR toxicological profiles and public health statements are the sources of information on which the series relies. Each factsheet serves as a guide that is quick to read and easy to understand. ToxFAQs also answers FAQs on exposure to hazardous substances that are encountered near wastesites and their effects on human health. https://www.atsdr.cdc.gov/toxfaqs/index.asp

Toxic Substances Portal   The portal offers convenient access to the most relevant information on toxic substances and their effects on human health. The portal's Web pages feature an alphabetical ordering of documents on specific substances, toxicological information by health effect or chemical class, and toxicological information for specific audiences (community members, emergency responders, toxicological and health professionals, and health care providers). https://www.atsdr.cdc.gov/substances/index.asp. http://www.atsdr.cdc.gov

For further information, contact the Agency for Toxic Substances and Disease Registry, 4770 Buford Highway NE., Atlanta, GA 30341. Phone, 770-488-0604.

Centers for Disease Control and Prevention

1600 Clifton Road, Atlanta, GA 30333
Phone, 800-232-4636. Internet, http://www.cdc.gov.

Director	BRENDA FITZGERALD
Principal Deputy Director	ANNE SCHUCHAT

The Centers for Disease Control and Prevention (CDC), as part of the Public Health Service, protect the public health of the Nation by providing leadership and direction in the prevention and control of diseases and other preventable conditions and by responding to public health emergencies. Within the CDC, the following seven centers, institutes, and offices lead prevention, diagnosis, and treatment efforts for public health concerns. http://www.cdc.gov/about/default.htm

Center for Global Health The Center leads the CDC global health strategy, working in partnership with foreign governments and international organizations to help countries worldwide evaluate, manage, and plan global health care programs. The Center works to eradicate chronic diseases and life-threatening injuries, expanding global health care programs to address the leading causes of disability, morbidity, and mortality. http://www.cdc.gov/globalhealth/index.html

National Institute for Occupational Safety and Health The Institute coordinates, directs, and plans a national program to develop and establish recommended occupational safety and health standards and to conduct research and training, offer technical assistance, and engage in related activities to assure safe and healthy work conditions for every working person. http://www.cdc.gov/NIOSH

Office of Infectious Diseases The Office facilitates research, programs, and policies to reduce the national and international burden of infectious diseases. The Office includes the following organizational components: the National Center for HIV/AIDS, Viral Hepatitis, STD and TB Prevention; the National Center for Immunization and Respiratory Diseases; and the National Center for Emerging and Zoonotic Infectious Diseases. http://www.cdc.gov/oid

Office of Noncommunicable Diseases, Injury, and Environmental Health The Office provides strategic direction and leadership for the prevention of noncommunicable diseases, injuries, disabilities, and environmental health hazards. The Office includes the following organizational components: the National Center on Birth Defects and Developmental Disabilities; the National Center for Chronic Disease Prevention and Health Promotion; the National Center for Environmental Health; and the National Center for Injury Prevention and Control. http://www.cdc.gov/maso/pdf/ONDIEHfs.pdf

Office of Public Health Preparedness and Response The Office helps the Nation prepare for and respond to urgent public health threats by providing strategic direction, coordination, and support for CDC's terrorism preparedness and emergency response activities. http://www.cdc.gov/phpr

Office of Public Health Scientific Services The Office provides scientific services, knowledge, and resources to promote public health, prepare for potential health threats, and prevent disease, disability, and injury. It includes the following organizational components: the National Center for Health Statistics and the Center for Surveillance, Epidemiology, and Laboratory Services. http://www.cdc.gov/ophss

Office of State, Tribal, Local, and Territorial Support The Office provides guidance, strategic direction, oversight, and leadership in support of State, local, territorial, and tribal public health agencies, initiatives, and priorities to improve the capacity and performance of a comprehensive public health system. http://www.cdc.gov/stltpublichealth

Sources of Information

Disease of the Week The "Disease of the Week" Web page features key facts on, prevention tips for, and a quiz to test one's knowledge of common, serious diseases. http://www.cdc.gov/dotw

Career Opportunities   The CDC is the leading national public health protection agency in the United States. It relies on professionals with scientific and nonscientific expertise to protect Earth's human population from the threat of deadly diseases like Ebola, HIV/AIDS, influenza, malaria, and tuberculosis. Most scientific and technical positions at the CDC are filled through the Commissioned Corps of the Public Health Service, a uniformed service of the U.S. Government. http://jobs.cdc.gov

Freedom of Information Act (FOIA)   The CDC posts answers to frequently asked FOIA questions on its Web site. http://www.cdc.gov/od/foia/faqs/index.htm | Email: FOIARequests@cdc.gov

The CDC posts frequently requested agency records in its electronic reading room. http://www.cdc.gov/od/foia/reading/records/index.htm

Influenza (Flu)   The CDC Web site features of trove of influenza information and resources. https://www.cdc.gov/flu/index.htm

Library   The Stephen B. Thacker CDC Library helps the advancement of science and public health and safety through information. It provides a full range of information services and products to support public health research, policy, and action. The Library, which comprises the headquarters library in Atlanta and six branches, serves CDC employees nationwide, as well as employees working in international locations. http://www.cdc.gov/library

Museum   The David J. Sencer CDC Museum features award-winning permanent and changing exhibitions that focus on public health topics, as well as on the history of the CDC. The museum is located in Atlanta, GA, and admission is free. It is open to the public on weekdays, excluding Federal holidays. Phone, 404-639-0830. http://www.cdc.gov/museum/index.htm

Podcasts   CDC podcasts provide reliable health and safety information. https://www2c.cdc.gov/podcasts

Publications   Many publications are accessible on the CDC's Web site. https://www.cdc.gov/publications

Reports   The monthly report "CDC Vital Signs" is released on the first Tuesday of every month. Past editions have addressed topics like colorectal and breast cancer screening, obesity, alcohol and tobacco use, HIV testing, motor vehicle safety, cardiovascular disease, teen pregnancy and infections associated with health care, foodborne disease, and more. The report is also available in Spanish. http://www.cdc.gov/vitalsigns

The CDC prepares the "Morbidity and Mortality Weekly Report," which it uses for scientific publication of accurate, authoritative, objective, reliable, timely, and useful public health information and recommendations. Educators, epidemiologists and other scientists, physicians and nurses, public health practitioners, and researchers and laboratorians regularly read the report. https://www.cdc.gov/mmwr/index.html | Email: mmwrq@cdc.gov

Social Media   CDC uses social media to provide users with access to credible, science-based health information https://www.cdc.gov/socialmedia/

Stress   The CDC's Web site provides information on managing stress after a traumatic event. https://www.cdc.gov/features/copingwithstress/index.html

Travel Health Notices   The CDC posts travel health notices on its Web site. http://wwwnc.cdc.gov/travel/notices. http://www.cdc.gov

For further information, contact the Centers for Disease Control and Prevention, 1600 Clifton Road, Atlanta, GA 30333. Phone, 800-232-4636. TTY, 888-232-6348.

Centers for Medicare and Medicaid Services

7500 Security Boulevard, Baltimore, MD 21244
Phone, 410-786-3000. Internet, http://www.cms.gov.

Administrator	ANDREW SLAVITT, ACTING
Principal Deputy Administrator	PATRICK H. CONWAY, ACTING
Chief Operating Officer / Chief of Staff	MANDY COHEN

The Centers for Medicare and Medicaid Services (CMS) provides health coverage to more than 100 million people through Medicare, Medicaid, the Children's Health Insurance Program, and the Health Insurance Marketplace. The CMS seeks to strengthen and modernize the Nation's health care system, to provide access to high quality care and improved health at lower costs. https://www.cms.gov/About-CMS/About-CMS.html

Sources of Information

Blog   The CMS maintains an official blog on its Web site. https://blog.cms.gov

Career Opportunities   For information on career opportunities, visit the "Careers at CMS" Web page. https://www.cms.gov/About-CMS/Career-Information/CareersatCMS/index.html

Forms   Many CMS forms are accessible on the agency's Web site. https://www.cms.gov/Medicare/CMS-Forms/CMS-Forms/CMS-Forms-List.html

Frequently Asked Questions (FAQs)   The CMS posts answers to FAQs on its Web site. https://questions.cms.gov

Glossary   The CMS maintains a glossary that explains terms found on its Web site. https://www.cms.gov/apps/glossary

History   The CMS Web site features the agency's program history. https://www.cms.gov/About-CMS/Agency-Information/History/index.html

Medicaid   The CMS manages the Medicaid.gov Web site. https://www.medicaid.gov

Medicare   The CMS manages the Medicare.gov Web site. https://www.medicare.gov

The Medicare Coverage Database contains all national coverage determinations and local coverage determinations, local articles, and proposed national coverage determination decisions. The database also includes several other types of national coverage policy-related documents, including national coverage analyses, coding analyses for labs, Medicare Evidence Development and Coverage Advisory Committee proceedings, and Medicare coverage guidance documents. https://www.cms.gov/medicare-coverage-database

The CMS manages the "STOP Medicare Fraud" Web site. To report Medicare fraud, call 800-447-8477. TTY, 800-377-4950. https://www.stopmedicarefraud.gov/index.html

Newsroom   The CMS posts news items on its Web site. https://www.cms.gov/Newsroom/Newsroom-Center.html

Social Media   The CMS tweets announcements and other newsworthy items on Twitter. https://twitter.com/cmsgov

The CMS posts videos on its YouTube channel. https://www.youtube.com/user/CMSHHSgov. http://www.cms.gov

For further information, contact the Centers for Medicare and Medicaid Services, Department of Health and Human Services, 7500 Security Boulevard, Baltimore, MD 21244. Phone, 410-786-3000.

Food and Drug Administration

10903 New Hampshire Avenue, Silver Spring, MD 20993
Phone, 888-463-6332. Internet, http://www.fda.gov.

Commissioner	Scott Gottlieb
Chief of Staff	Lauren Silvis

The Food and Drug Administration (FDA) protects the public health by ensuring the safety, security, and efficacy of human and veterinary drugs, biological products, medical devices, the Nation's food supply, cosmetics, and products that emit radiation. The FDA also advances the public health by accelerating innovations to make medicines more effective and by providing the public with accurate, science-based information on medicines and food to improve health. The agency plays a significant role in the Nation's counterterrorism capability by ensuring the security of the food supply. http://www.fda.gov/AboutFDA/default.htm

Sources of Information

Animal and Veterinary Recalls The FDA posts animal and veterinary recall information—brand name, date of recall, company name, product description, and the reason or problem—on its Web site. http://www.fda.gov/AnimalVeterinary/SafetyHealth/RecallsWithdrawals/default.htm

A–Z Index The FDA's Web site features an alphabetical index to help visitors search for specific topics or browse content that aligns with their interests. http://www.fda.gov/SiteIndex/default.htm

Career Opportunities The FDA relies on attorneys, biologists, chemists, consumer safety officers, engineers, information technology specialists, medical officers, microbiologists, pharmacists, pharmacologists, statisticians, and other professionals to carry out its mission. http://www.fda.gov/AboutFDA/WorkingatFDA/default.htm

Cigarettes The FDA describes cigarettes with three words: attractive, addictive, and deadly. Cigarettes are designed to be attractive and addictive. The FDA's infographic "How a Cigarette is Engineered" explains the role design plays in attraction and addiction. http://www.fda.gov/TobaccoProducts/NewsEvents/ucm529397.htm

Cosmetics The FDA posts answers to the questions that consumers frequently ask about cosmetic safety and regulation. http://www.fda.gov/Cosmetics/ResourcesForYou/Consumers/ucm2005206.htm

Foodborne Illnesses The FDA regulates human and animal food. It posts information on recent foodborne illness outbreaks on its Web site. http://www.fda.gov/Food/RecallsOutbreaksEmergencies/Outbreaks/default.htm

Recalls / Safety Alerts Information gathered from press releases and other public notices on certain recalls of FDA-regulated products is available online. http://www.fda.gov/Safety/Recalls/default.htm. http://www.fda.gov

For further information contact the Food and Drug Administration, 10903 New Hampshire Avenue, Silver Spring, MD 20993. Phone, 888-463-6332.

Health Resources and Services Administration

5600 Fishers Lane, Rockville, MD 20857
Phone, 301-443-3376. Internet, http://www.hrsa.gov.

Administrator	George Sigounas
Deputy Administrator	Diana Espinosa

The Health Resources and Services Administration (HRSA) improves access to health care by strengthening the health care workforce, building healthy communities, and achieving health equity. HRSA programs make health care accessible to people who are geographically isolated or economically or medically vulnerable. It supports the training of health professionals, the distribution of providers to areas where they are needed most, and improvements in health care delivery. The agency also oversees organ, bone marrow, and cord blood donations; compensates individuals harmed by vaccination; and maintains databases that protect against health care abuse, fraud, malpractice, and waste. https://www.hrsa.gov/about/index.html

Sources of Information

Data   The HRSA maintains an online data warehouse. https://datawarehouse.hrsa.gov
Career Opportunities   The HRSA posts career opportunities on its Web site. https://www.hrsa.gov/hr/

Freedom of Information Act (FOIA)   The FOIA requires the HRSA to disclose documents or records that any person properly requests in writing. Certain documents or records, or parts of them, may be protected, however, from disclosure by one of the nine exemptions contained in the statute. https://www.hrsa.gov/foia/index.html
Organ Donation and Transplantation   The HRSA manages the OrganDonor.gov Web site, which provides the public with U.S. Government information on organ donation and transplantation. http://organdonor.gov/index.html
Social Media   The HRSA tweets announcements and other newsworthy items on Twitter. https://twitter.com/HRSAgov
The HRSA has a Facebook account. https://www.facebook.com/HRSAgov
The HRSA posts videos on its YouTube channel. https://www.youtube.com/user/HRSAtube/videos. http://www.hrsa.gov/about/contact

For further information, contact the Office of Communications, Health Resources and Services Administration, 5600 Fishers Lane, Rockville, MD 20857. Phone, 301-443-3376.

Indian Health Service

5600 Fishers Lane Rockville, MD 20857
Phone, 301-443-3593. Internet, http://www.ihs.gov.

Director	(VACANCY)
Principal Deputy Director	MICHAEL WEAHKEE
Deputy Director	CHRISTOPHER BUCHANAN

The Indian Health Service, as part of the Public Health Service, provides a comprehensive health services delivery system for American Indians and Alaska Natives. It helps Native American tribes develop their health programs; facilitates and assists tribes in coordinating health planning and obtaining and utilizing health resources available through Federal, State, and local programs, in operating comprehensive health programs and evaluating them; and provides comprehensive health care services, including hospital and ambulatory medical care, preventive and rehabilitative services,

and development of community sanitation facilities. https://www.ihs.gov/aboutihs

Sources of Information

A–Z Index   The Indian Health Service's Web site features an alphabetical index to help visitors search for specific topics or browse content that aligns with their interests. https://www.ihs.gov/atoz/a/
Career Opportunities   For information on employment, visit the "Career Opportunities" Web page. https://www.ihs.gov/careeropps

Freedom of Information Act (FOIA)   The Indian Health Service's Web site features an electronic FOIA requester center. https://www.ihs.gov/FOIA
Newsroom   The Newsroom features announcements, congressional testimony, factsheets, press releases, and speeches. https://www.ihs.gov/newsroom | Email: newsroom@ihs.gov

Social Media   The Indian Health Service has a Facebook account. https://www.facebook.com/IndianHealthService
The Indian Health Service posts videos on its YouTube channel. https://www.youtube.com/user/IHSgov/feed. http://www.ihs.gov/contact

For further information, contact the Management Policy and Internal Control Staff, Indian Health Service, 5600 Fishers Lane Rockville, MD 20857. Phone, 301-443-3593.

National Institutes of Health

1 Center Drive, Bethesda, MD 20892
Phone, 301-496-4000. Internet, http://www.nih.gov.

Director	FRANCIS S. COLLINS
Principal Deputy Director	LAWRENCE A. TABAK

The National Institutes of Health (NIH) support biomedical and behavioral research domestically and abroad, conduct research in NIH laboratories and clinics, train research scientists, and develop and disseminate credible, science-based health information to the public. https://www.nih.gov/about-nih/what-we-do

Aging   The National Institute on Aging (NIA) conducts and supports research on the aging process, age-related diseases, and other special problems and needs of older people. It is also the lead NIH Institute for research on age-related cognitive change and Alzheimer's disease. The NIA provides information on aging to the scientific community, health care providers, and the public. http://www.nia.nih.gov

For further information, contact the National Institute on Aging. Phone, 301-496-1752.

Alcohol Abuse and Alcoholism   The National Institute on Alcohol Abuse and Alcoholism leads the national effort to reduce alcohol-related problems by conducting and supporting biomedical and behavioral research into the causes, consequences, prevention, and treatment of alcohol-use disorders. http://www.niaaa.nih.gov

For further information, contact the National Institute on Alcohol Abuse and Alcoholism. Phone, 301-443-3885.

Allergy and Infectious Diseases   The National Institute of Allergy and Infectious Diseases conducts and supports research to study the causes of infectious diseases and immune-mediated diseases and to develop better means of preventing, diagnosing, and treating these diseases. http://www.niaid.nih.gov

For further information, contact the National Institute of Allergy and Infectious Diseases. Phone, 866-284-4107 or 301-496-5717.

Arthritis and Musculoskeletal and Skin Diseases   The National Institute of Arthritis and Musculoskeletal and Skin Diseases supports research on the causes, treatment, and prevention of arthritis and musculoskeletal and skin diseases; the basic and clinical training of scientists to carry out this research; and the dissemination of information on research progress. http://www.niams.nih.gov

For further information, contact the National Institute of Arthritis and Musculoskeletal and Skin Diseases. Phone, 877-226-4267 or 301-496-8190.

Behavioral and Social Sciences Research   The Office of Behavioral and Social Sciences Research supports and coordinates health-related behavioral and social sciences research that the NIH conducts or supports, and it integrates these sciences within the larger NIH research enterprise. It also communicates and disseminates research findings to stakeholders within and outside the Federal Government, thereby increasing understanding and improving treatment and prevention of disease. https://obssr.od.nih.gov

For further information, contact the Office of Behavioral and Social Sciences Research. Phone, 301-402-1146.

Biomedical Imaging and Bioengineering

The National Institute of Biomedical Imaging and Bioengineering supports research, training, and the dissemination of research advances for accelerating the development and application of biomedical technologies to improve the detection, treatment, and prevention of disease. It integrates the physical and engineering sciences with the life sciences to advance basic research and medical care. http://www.nibib.nih.gov

For further information, contact the National Institute of Biomedical Imaging and Bioengineering. Phone, 301-496-3500.

Cancer

The National Cancer Institute (NCI) is the Federal Government's principal agency for cancer research and training. It coordinates the National Cancer Program, which conducts and supports research, training, health information dissemination, and other activities associated with diagnosing, preventing, treating, and finding the cause of cancer and with the continuing care of cancer patients and their families. http://www.cancer.gov

For further information, contact the Cancer Information Service. Phone, 800-422-6237.

Center for Information Technology

The Center for Information Technology provides, coordinates, and manages information technology to advance computational science. http://www.cit.nih.gov

For further information, contact the Center for Information Technology. Phone, 301-496-5703.

Child Health and Human Development

The Eunice Kennedy Shriver National Institute of Child Health and Human Development conducts and supports basic, clinical, and epidemiological research on the reproductive, rehabilitative, neurobiological, developmental, and behavioral processes that determine the health of children, adults, families, and communities. http://www.nichd.nih.gov

For further information, contact the Eunice Kennedy Shriver National Institute of Child Health and Human Development. Phone, 800-370-2943.

Clinical Center

The Clinical Center is the clinical research hospital for the NIH. By doing clinical research, investigators translate laboratory discoveries into better treatments, therapies, and interventions to improve the Nation's health. The Center conducts clinical and laboratory research and trains future clinical investigators. Nearly 500,000 volunteers from across the Nation have participated in clinical research studies since the Center opened in 1953. About 1,500 clinical research studies are currently in progress. http://clinicalcenter.nih.gov

For further information, contact the Clinical Center. Phone, 301-496-4000.

Communications

The Office of Communications and Public Liaison communicates information on consumer health, scientific results, and NIH accomplishments, issues, and research and training programs to the public, media, scientific and medical communities, and other interested groups. http://www.nih.gov/institutes-nih/nih-office-director/office-communications-public-liaison

For further information, contact the Office of Communications and Public Liaison. Phone, 301-496-5787

Complementary and Integrative Health

The National Center for Complementary and Integrative Health defines the utility and safety of complementary and integrative health interventions and their roles in improving health and health care. This science-based information helps the public, health care professionals, and health policymakers make decisions on the use and integration of complementary and integrative health approaches. https://nccih.nih.gov

For further information, contact the National Center for Complementary and Integrative Health. Phone, 888-644-6226.

Deafness and Other Communication Disorders   The National Institute on Deafness and Other Communication Disorders conducts and supports biomedical and behavioral research and training on normal and disordered processes of hearing, balance, taste, smell, voice, speech, and language. The Institute also makes science-based health information publicly available, and it supports efforts to create devices that substitute for lost or impaired sensory and communication function. http://www.nidcd. nih.gov | Email: NIDCDinfo@nidcd.nih.gov

For further information, contact the National Institute on Deafness and Other Communication Disorders. Phone, 800-241-1044. TTY, 800-241-1055.

Dental and Craniofacial Research   The National Institute of Dental and Craniofacial Research funds research on dental, oral, and craniofacial health and disorders. It also conducts research in its own laboratories and clinic, supports research training, and promotes the timely transfer of research-based knowledge and its implications for health to researchers, to health professionals, to patients, and to the general public. http://www.nidcr.nih.gov

For further information, contact the National Institute of Dental and Craniofacial Research. Phone, 301-496-4261.

Diabetes and Digestive and Kidney Diseases   The National Institute of Diabetes and Digestive and Kidney Diseases conducts, supports, and coordinates research and research training. It also offers science-based information on diabetes and other endocrine and metabolic diseases; on digestive diseases, nutritional disorders, weight control, and obesity; and on kidney, urologic and blood diseases. https://www.niddk.nih.gov

For further information, contact the National Institute of Diabetes and Digestive and Kidney Diseases. Phone, 301-496-3583.

Drug Abuse   The National Institute on Drug Abuse supports and conducts basic and clinical research on drug use, its consequences, and the underlying neurobiological, behavioral, and social mechanisms. The Institute also ensures effective translation and dissemination of scientific findings to improve the prevention and treatment of substance-use disorders, and it works at raising the public's awareness that addiction is a type of brain disorder. http://www.drugabuse.gov

For further information, contact the National Institute on Drug Abuse. Phone, 877-643-2644.

Environmental Health Sciences   The National Institute of Environmental Health Sciences supports research that explores how the environment affects people's health. Its research centers on environmental exposures and understanding their effects on human biology and health with an emphasis on disease and disability prevention. The Institute also houses the national toxicology program, a cross-agency organization that coordinates toxicity testing across the Federal Government. http://www.niehs.nih. gov

For further information, contact the National Institute of Environmental Health Sciences. Phone, 919-541-3345.

Eye and Vision Diseases   The National Eye Institute conducts, fosters, and supports research on the causes, natural history, prevention, diagnosis, and treatment of disorders of the eye and visual system. It also directs the National Eye Health Education Program. http://www.nei.nih.gov

For further information, contact the National Eye Institute. Phone, 301-496-5248.

Fogarty International Center   The Fogarty International Center addresses global health challenges through innovative and collaborative research and training programs. It also supports and advances the NIH mission through international partnerships. http://www.fic.nih.gov

For further information, contact the Fogarty International Center. Phone, 301-496-2075.

General Medical Sciences   The National Institute of General Medical Sciences (NIGMS) supports basic research that increases understanding of biological processes and lays the foundation for advances in disease diagnosis, treatment, and prevention. NIGMS-funded scientists investigate how living systems work at a range of levels, from molecules and cells to tissues, to whole organisms and populations. The Institute also supports research in clinical areas, primarily those that affect multiple organ systems. To assure the vitality and productivity of the research enterprise, the NIGMS provides leadership in training the next generation of scientists, in diversifying the scientific workforce, and in developing research capacities throughout the country. http://www.nigms.nih.gov

For further information, contact the National Institute of General Medical Sciences. Phone, 301-496-7301.

Heart, Lung, and Blood Diseases   The National Heart, Lung, and Blood Institute provides leadership for a global program in sleep disorders, blood resources, and diseases of the heart, blood vessels, blood, and lungs. It conducts, fosters, and supports a comprehensive program of basic research, clinical investigations and trials, observational and implementation science studies, as well as demonstration and education projects. http://www.nhlbi.nih.gov

For further information, contact the National Heart, Lung, and Blood Institute. Phone, 301-592-8573.

Human Genome Research   The National Human Genome Research Institute supports research to uncover the role that the genome plays in human health and disease; studies on the ethical, legal, and social implications of genomics research for individuals, families, and communities; and the application of genomics research to medical care. http://www.genome.gov

For further information, contact the National Human Genome Research Institute. Phone, 301-402-0911.

Library of Medicine   The National Library of Medicine, the world's largest biomedical library, serves as the Nation's principal medical information source, providing medical library services and extensive online information resources to scientists, practitioners, and the general public. It conducts, fosters, and supports research and training in biomedical informatics and supports development and dissemination of clinical terminology standards. http://www.nlm.nih.gov

For further information, contact the National Library of Medicine. Phone, 301-496-6308.

Mental Health   The National Institute of Mental Health works to transform the understanding and treatment of mental illnesses. Through basic and clinical research, it advances the prevention, recovery, and cure of mental conditions that disable many Americans. http://www.nimh.nih.gov

For further information, contact the National Institute of Mental Health. Phone, 866-615-6464.

Minority Health and Health Disparities   The National Institute on Minority Health and Health Disparities leads scientific research to improve minority health and eliminate health disparities. The Institute plans, reviews, coordinates, and evaluates all minority health and health disparities research and activities of the NIH; conducts and supports research on minority health and health disparities; promotes and supports the training of a diverse research workforce; translates and disseminates research information; and fosters innovative collaborations and partnerships. http://www.nimhd.nih.gov

For further information, contact the National Institute on Minority Health and Health Disparities. Phone, 301-402-1366.

Neurological Disorders and Stroke   The National Institute of Neurological Disorders and Stroke works to better understand the brain and spinal cord and to use that knowledge to mitigate the effects of neurological disease. It conducts, promotes, coordinates, and guides research and training on the causes, prevention, diagnosis, and treatment of neurological disorders and stroke. It also supports basic, translational, and clinical research in related scientific areas. http://www.ninds.nih.gov

For further information, contact the National Institute of Neurological Disorders and Stroke. Phone, 301-496-5751.

Nursing Research   The National Institute of Nursing Research supports clinical and basic research and research training to build the scientific foundation for clinical practice, to prevent disease and disability, to manage and eliminate symptoms caused by illness, to enhance end-of-life and palliative care, and to train the next generation of nurse scientists. http://www.ninr.nih.gov

For further information, contact the National Institute of Nursing Research. Phone, 301-496-0207.

Program Coordination, Planning, and Strategic Initiatives   The Division of Program Coordination, Planning, and Strategic Initiatives coordinates trans-NIH programs, planning, and strategic scientific initiatives in the Office of the NIH Director. The Division includes major programmatic offices that coordinate and support research and research infrastructure. The Division also serves as a portfolio analysis resource, coordinates evaluation reporting and agency activities under the Government Performance and Results Act, and supports science education partnership awards. http://dpcpsi.nih.gov

For further information, contact the Division of Program Coordination, Planning, and Strategic Initiatives. Phone, 301-402-9852.

Scientific Review   The Center for Scientific Review (CSR) organizes the peer review groups that evaluate the majority of grant applications submitted to the NIH. These groups include experienced and respected researchers from across the country and abroad. Since 1946, CSR has ensured that NIH grant applications receive fair, independent, expert, and timely reviews— free from inappropriate influences—so the NIH can fund the most promising research. CSR also receives all incoming applications and assigns them to the appropriate Centers and Institutes that fund grants. http://public.csr.nih.gov

For further information, contact the Center for Scientific Review. Phone, 301-435-1111.

Translational Sciences   The National Center for Advancing Translational Sciences focuses on what is common across diseases and the translational process. The Center emphasizes innovation and deliverables, relying on data and new technologies to develop, demonstrate, and disseminate advances in translational science that tangibly improve human health. https://ncats.nih.gov

For further information, contact the National Center for Advancing Translational Sciences. Phone, 301-435-0888.

Sources of Information

Employment   For information on employment opportunities, visit the "Jobs at NIH" Web page. http://www.jobs.nih.gov

Events   The NIH posts upcoming events on its Web site. https://www.nih.gov/news-events/events

Freedom of Information Act (FOIA)   The FOIA gives a right to access documents or records in the possession of the Federal Government to any person. The Government may withhold, however, information pursuant to the statute's nine exemptions and three exclusions. For more information, contact the NIH FOIA Office. Phone, 301-496-5633. Fax, 301-402-4541. https://www.nih.gov/institutes-nih/nih-office-director/office-communications-public-liaison/freedom-information-act-office | Email: nihfoia@mail.nih.gov

Frequently Asked Questions (FAQs)   The NIH posts answers to FAQs on its Web site. https://www.nih.gov/about-nih/frequently-asked-questions

History   The story of the agency begins in 1887, and a brief retelling of it is available online. https://www.nih.gov/about-nih/who-we-are/history

The DeWitt Stetten, Jr., Museum of Medical Research, also known as the NIH Stetten Museum, preserves and interprets the material culture of the NIH's scientific work through physical and virtual exhibits. https://history.nih.gov/museum/index.html

News   The NIH posts news releases on its Web site. https://www.nih.gov/news-events/news-releases

The monthly newsletter "NIH News In Health" features practical consumer health news and information that is based on NIH research. https://newsinhealth.nih.gov

Social Media   The NIH tweets announcements and other newsworthy items on Twitter. https://twitter.com/NIH

The NIH has a Facebook account. https://www.facebook.com/nih.gov

The NIH posts videos on its YouTube channel. https://www.youtube.com/user/nihod

Spanish   Important health information is available in Spanish. https://salud.nih.gov

Staff Directory   The NIH enterprise directory allows users to search for staff members by email address, name, or phone number. https://ned.nih.gov/search

Visitor Information   Maps and information on access and security, parking, tours, the campus shuttle, and more are available on the NIH Web site. https://www.nih.gov/about-nih/visitor-information

Weight Management The National Institute of Diabetes and Digestive and Kidney Diseases' Web site has a trove of weight management information and resources. https://www.niddk.nih.gov/health-information/weight-management

The online body weight planner allows users to make personalized calorie and physical activity plans for reaching a target weight within a specific time period—and for maintaining it afterwards. https://www.niddk.nih.gov/health-information/health-topics/weight-control/body-weight-planner/Pages/bwp.aspx. https://www.nih.gov/about-nih/contact-us

For further information, contact the National Institutes of Health, 1 Center Drive, Bethesda, MD 20892. Phone, 301-496-4000.

Substance Abuse and Mental Health Services Administration

5600 Fishers Lane Rockville, MD 20857
Phone, 240-276-2130. Internet, http://www.samhsa.gov.

Administrator	KANA ENOMOTO, ACTING
Chief of Staff	TOM CODERRE

The Substance Abuse and Mental Health Services Administration mitigates the effects of substance abuse and mental illness on communities nationwide. It provides national leadership, serving as a voice for behavioral health; funds State and local service agencies through grants and formulas; collects data and makes available surveillance reports on the effect of behavioral health on Americans; leads efforts to offer public education on mental illness and substance abuse prevention, treatment, and recovery; regulates and oversees national behavioral health programs; and promotes practice improvement in community-based, primary, and specialty care settings. http://www.samhsa.gov/about-us

Sources of Information

Blog The Administration's Web site features a blog. https://blog.samhsa.gov

Data The Administration maintains five collections of data: Center for Behavioral Health Statistics and Quality reports, client level data, mental health facilities data, population data, and substance abuse facilities data. http://www.samhsa.gov/data

Career Opportunities For information on career opportunities, visit the "Jobs and Internships" Web page. http://www.samhsa.gov/about-us/jobs-internships

Help / Treatment Resources for help and treatment are available on the Administration's Web site. http://www.samhsa.gov/find-help

KSOC–TV KSOC–TV is a web-based technical assistance program featuring behavioral health experts discussing leading issues in children's mental health. http://www.samhsa.gov/children/multimedia

Newsroom Press announcements, quarterly newsletters, and media highlights of initiatives and other activities are available in the newsroom. http://www.samhsa.gov/newsroom

Offices / Centers The agency's offices and centers provide leadership and assistance for quality behavioral health services, as well as support States, territories, tribes, communities, and local organizations through grants and contract awards. Contact information for these offices and centers is available online. http://www.samhsa.gov/about-us/who-we-are/offices-centers

Publications Hundreds of publications are available on the Administration's Web site. http://store.samhsa.gov

Site Map The Web site map allows visitors to look for specific topics or to browse content that aligns with their interests. http://www.samhsa.gov/sitemap

Social Media The Administration uses various forms of social media to connect with the Internet community and engage people. http://www.samhsa.gov/social-media/social-media-accounts

Suicide Prevention The Administration funds the National Suicide Prevention Lifeline. Phone, 800-273-8255. http://suicidepreventionlifeline.org/?WT_ac=AD20110315NSPL#

Treatment Services Locator The behavioral health treatment services locator is a confidential and anonymous source of information for persons seeking treatment facilities in the United States or U.S. Territories for substance abuse, addiction, mental health problems, or a combination of the three. Phone, 800-662-4357. TDD, 800-487-4889. https://findtreatment.samhsa.gov

Underage Drinking Underage drinking accounts for 11 percent of all the alcohol consumed in the United States. Alcohol is the most widely misused substance among America's youth. The Administration disseminates information on the dangers of underage drinking and offers prevention tips. http://www.samhsa.gov/underage-drinking-topic. http://www.samhsa.gov/about-us/contact-us

For further information, contact the Substance Abuse and Mental Health Services Administration, 5600 Fishers Lane Rockville, MD 20857, Rockville, MD 20857. Phone, 240-276-2130.

DEPARTMENT OF HOMELAND SECURITY

Washington, DC 20528
Phone, 202-282-8000. Internet, http://www.dhs.gov.

Secretary of Homeland Security	JOHN F. KELLY
Deputy Secretary	ELAINE C. DUKE
Chief of Staff	KIRSTKEN NIELSEN
Executive Secretary	SCOTT KRAUSE
General Counsel	JOSEPH B. MAHER (ACTING)
Under Secretary, Management	CHIP FULGHUM (ACTING)
Under Secretary, National Protection and Programs Directorate	DAVID HESS (ACTING)
Under Secretary, Science and Technology	ROBERT GRIFFIN (ACTING)
Under Secretary, Intelligence and Analysis	PATRICIA F.S. COGSWELL (ACTING)
Under Secretary for Strategy, Policy, and Plans	(VACANCY)
Assistant Secretary, Partnership and Engagement	JOHN BARSA (ACTING)
Director, U.S. Citizenship and Immigration Services	JAMES MCCAMENT, ACTING
Commandant, United States Coast Guard	ADM. PAUL F. ZUKUNFT
Commissioner, U.S. Customs and Border Protection	KEVIN MCALEENAN (ACTING)
Director, U.S. Immigration and Customs Enforcement	THOMAS D. HOMAN (ACTING)
Administrator, Federal Emergency Management Agency	ROBERT J. FENTON (ACTING)
Director, United States Secret Service	RANDOLPH D. ALLES
Administrator, Transportation Security Administration	HUBAN A. GOWADIA (ACTING)
Ombudsman, Citizenship and Immigration Services	JULIE KIRCHNER
Officer, Civil Rights and Civil Liberties	VERONICA VENTURE (ACTING)
Director, Domestic Nuclear Detection Office	L. WAYNE BRASURE, ACTING
Director, Federal Law Enforcement Training Centers	CONNIE L. PATRICK
Assistant Secretary, Health Affairs / Chief Medical Officer	LARRY D. FLUTY (ACTING)
Inspector General	JOHN ROTH
Assistant Secretary, Legislative Affairs	BENJAMIN CASSIDY
Director, Operations Coordination	RICHARD CHÁVEZ
Chief Privacy Officer	JONATHAN CANTOR (ACTING)
Assistant Secretary, Public Affairs	JONATHAN R. HOFFMANN
Chief Financial Officer	STACY MARCOTT (ACTING)

The Department of Homeland Security prevents terrorism and enhances security, secures and manages the Nation's borders, enforces and administers its immigration laws, safeguards and secures cyberspace, and ensures resilience to disasters.

The Department of Homeland Security (DHS) was established by the Homeland Security Act of 2002 (6 U.S.C. 101 note). The Department came into existence on January 24, 2003, and is administered under the supervision and direction of the Secretary of Homeland Security.

Office of the Secretary

The Office of the Secretary oversees activities in collaboration with other Federal, State, local, and private entities to carry out the Department's overall mission. The Office of the Secretary comprises 10 smaller offices that support the Secretary in fulfilling his or her responsibilities. http://www.dhs.gov/office-secretary

Secretary   The Secretary is responsible for developing and coordinating a comprehensive national strategy to protect the United States against terrorist attacks. The Secretary advises the President on how to: strengthen and manage U.S. borders; safeguard and secure cyberspace; enforce and administer immigration laws, provide for intelligence analysis and infrastructure protection; improve the use of science and technology to counter weapons of mass destruction; and ensure resilience to disasters. http://www.dhs.gov/leadership

Office for Civil Rights and Civil Liberties   The Office for Civil Rights and Civil Liberties ensures that Department of Homeland Security secures the Nation while preserving individual liberty, fairness, and equality under the law by: promoting respect for civil rights and civil liberties in policy creation and implementation; advising Department leadership and personnel, and state and local partners; communicating with individuals and communities whose civil rights and civil liberties may be affected by Department activities, informing them about policies and avenues of redress, and bringing appropriate attention within the Department to their experiences and concerns; investigating civil rights and civil liberties complaints filed by the public regarding Department policies or activities, or actions taken by Department personnel; and leading the Department's equal employment opportunity (EEO) programs and promoting workforce diversity and merit system principles. http://www.dhs.gov/office-civil-rights-and-civil-liberties

Office of General Counsel   The Office of General Counsel (OGC) is responsible for ensuring that departmental activities comply with applicable legal requirements. OGC provides legal advice on areas such as national security, immigration, litigation, international law, maritime safety and security, transportation security, border security law, cybersecurity, fiscal and appropriations law, environmental law, and many others. It also ensures that the Department's efforts to secure the Nation are consistent with the civil rights and civil liberties of its citizens and follow the rule of law. OGC also provides legal services in several areas where the law intersects with the achievement of mission goals, such as the coordination of the Department's rulemaking activities, managing interdepartmental clearance of proposed legislation, and providing legal training for law enforcement officers. http://www.dhs.gov/office-general-counsel

Office of Inspector General   The Office of Inspector General (OIG) conducts and supervises audits, investigations, and inspections relating to the Department's programs and operations. The OIG examines, evaluates, and where necessary, critiques these operations and activities, recommending ways for DHS to carry out its responsibilities in the most economical, efficient, and effective manner possible. The OIG also reviews recommendations regarding existing and proposed legislation and regulations relating to the Department's programs and operations. https://www.oig.dhs.gov

Office of Legislative Affairs   The Office of Legislative Affairs (OLA) serves as the Department's primary liaison to Congress. It advocates for the policy interests of the administration and the Secretary. OLA also ensures that all DHS components are actively engaged with Congress in their specific areas of responsibility. The Office articulates views on behalf of DHS components and their legislative initiatives. It responds to requests and inquiries from congressional committees, individual Members of Congress, and their staffs. OLA also participates in the Senate confirmation process for each DHS Presidential nominee. http://www.dhs.gov/about-office-legislative-affairs

Office of Partnership and Engagement   The Office of Partnership and Engagement includes the following offices and programs: the Office for State and Local Law Enforcement, Private Sector Office, Office of Academic Engagement, Committee Management Office, Homeland Security Advisory Council, Homeland Security Academic Advisory Council, Blue Campaign,, and the "If You See Something, Say Something" public awareness campaign. The Office comprises stakeholder engagement offices that communicate with State, local, tribal, and territorial governments, and with law enforcement, the private sector, academia and Federal advisory committees. These offices also coordinate DHS programs and policies with these same stakeholders. The Office also serves as the liaison between these stakeholders and the Office of the Secretary. It promotes an integrated national approach to homeland security by coordinating and advancing Federal interaction with external stakeholders, and it is responsible for continuing the homeland security dialogue with those partners and with the national associations that represent them. http://www.dhs.gov/partnership-engagement

Office of Public Affairs   The Office of Public Affairs (OPA) manages all of the Department's external (media) and internal (employee) communications. OPA also oversees and coordinates all public affairs activities for the Department's components and offices. OPA is the primary point of contact for news media, policies, procedures, statistics and services. OPA also assists the Secretary on all public affairs, as well as incident, strategic and internal communications matters. http://www.dhs.gov/office-public-affairs

Office of the Chief Financial Officer   The Office of the Chief Financial Officer (OCFO) is responsible for the fiscal management, integrity, and accountability of DHS. The OCFO provides guidance and oversight of the Department's budget, financial management, financial operations for all Departmental management and operations, the DHS Working Capital Fund, grants and assistance awards, and resource management systems to obtain, allocate, and expend funds for DHS's mission in accordance with the Department's priorities and relevant law and policies. http://www.dhs.gov/office-chief-financial-officer

Office of the Citizenship and Immigration Services Ombudsman   The Office of the Citizenship and Immigration Services Ombudsman (CISOMB) helps individuals and employers resolve problems with the delivery of immigration services and benefits issued by U.S. Citizenship and Immigration Services. The CISOMB identifies trends and proposes changes to mitigate problems and improve the delivery of immigration services. It is a confidential, independent, and neutral office where stakeholders can submit requests for assistance and provide feedback. The CISOMB delivers an annual report directly to Congress each year. http://www.dhs.gov/topic/cis-ombudsman

Office of the Executive Secretary   The Office of the Executive Secretary (ESEC) provides analytical and administrative support to the Office of the Secretary and the Office of the Deputy Secretary. ESEC manages the Secretary's internal and external correspondence, prepares classified and unclassified briefing materials, and oversees development of departmental testimony, questions for the record, and congressional reports. ESEC also facilitates departmental communications with Federal departments and agencies, the National Security Council, and other White House executive offices. http://www.dhs.gov/office-executive-secretary

Office of the Military Advisor   The Senior Military Advisor provides counsel to the Secretary and DHS Components relating to the facilitation, coordination, and execution of policy, procedures, and preparedness activities and operations between DHS and the Department of Defense. http://www.dhs.gov/about-office-military-advisor

Privacy Office   The Privacy Office protects the collection, use, and disclosure of personally identifiable information and departmental information. It ensures that appropriate access to information is consistent with the vision, strategic mission, and core values of DHS. The Office also implements the policies of the Department to defend and protect the individual rights, liberties, and information interests of our citizens. The Office has oversight of all privacy and disclosure policy matters, including compliance with the Privacy Act of 1974, the Freedom of Information Act, and the completion of privacy impact statements on all new programs and systems, as required by the E-Government Act of 2002 and Section 222 of the Homeland Security Act. http://www.dhs.gov/privacy-office

Operational And Support Components

Directorate for Management   The Directorate for Management is responsible for accounting and finance, appropriations, budget, expenditure of funds, and procurement; equipment, facilities, property, and other material resources; human resources, personnel, and their security; identification and tracking of performance measurements relating to the responsibilities of the Department, and information technology and communication systems.

The Directorate for Management ensures that the Department's employees have well-defined responsibilities and that managers and their employees have effective means of communicating with one another, with other governmental and nongovernmental bodies, and with the public they serve. http://www.dhs.gov/directorate-management

Directorate for Science and Technology   The Science and Technology Directorate is the primary research and development arm of the Department. The Directorate provides Federal, State, and local officials with the technology and capabilities to protect the homeland. Its strategic objectives are to develop and deploy systems to prevent, detect, and mitigate the consequences of chemical, biological, radiological, nuclear, and explosive attacks; develop equipment, protocols, and training procedures for response to and recovery from those attacks; enhance the Department's and other Federal, State, local, and tribal agencies' technical capabilities to fulfill their homeland security-related functions; and develop technical standards and establish certified laboratories to evaluate homeland security and emergency responder technologies for SAFETY Act certification. http://www.dhs.gov/science-and-technology/our-work

Domestic Nuclear Detection Office   The Domestic Nuclear Detection Office focuses solely on preventing nuclear terrorism, by continuously improving the nation's ability to deter, detect, respond to, and attribute attacks, in coordination with domestic and international partners. DNDO coordinates development of the global nuclear detection architecture with partners from local, state, federal, and international governments, and the private sector. The Office is responsible for developing, acquiring, and supporting the deployment of mechanisms to detect and report attempts to import, possess, store, transport, develop, or use unauthorized nuclear and other radioactive material in the United States. It also improves that domestic system over time.

DNDO further serves as steward of an enduring national technical nuclear forensics capability and leads efforts to improve national nuclear forensics expertise. Working with the international community, the Office promotes the development of nuclear detection architectures and nuclear forensics guidance. http://www.dhs.gov/domestic-nuclear-detection-office

Federal Emergency Management Agency   Federal Emergency Management Agency (FEMA) leads and supports the Nation in a risk-based, comprehensive emergency management system of preparedness, protection, response, recovery, and mitigation to reduce the loss of life and property, and protect the Nation from all hazards, including natural disasters, acts of terrorism, and other man-made disasters. FEMA coordinates programs to improve the effectiveness of emergency response providers at all levels of the government, initiates proactive mitigation activities, and manages the National Flood Insurance Program and U.S. Fire Administration. FEMA also leads government continuity planning, guidance, and operations for the Federal Executive Branch to minimize the disruption of essential operations and guarantee an enduring Constitutional government. http://www.fema.gov

Federal Law Enforcement Training Centers   The Federal Law Enforcement Training Centers (FLETC) provides career-long training to law enforcement professionals to help them fulfill their responsibilities safely and proficiently. Under a collaborative training model, FLETC's federal partner organizations deliver training unique to their missions, while FLETC provides training in areas common to all law enforcement officers, such as firearms, driving, tactics, investigations, and legal training. To train all those who protect the homeland, its audience also includes state, local, and tribal departments throughout the U.S., as well as international training and capacity-building activities. https://www.fletc.gov

National Protection and Programs Directorate   The National Protection and Programs Directorate executes the DHS operational mission of securing the Nation's infrastructure and enhancing its resilience against cyber and physical threats. Secure and resilient infrastructure advances public health and safety, promotes economic vitality, and safeguards national security. The National Protection and Programs Directorate collaborates with Federal, State, local, tribal, and territorial, as well as international and private-sector entities, to maintain situational awareness of both physical and cyber events, to share information about risks that may disrupt critical infrastructure, and to build capabilities to reduce those risks. http://www.dhs.gov/national-protection-and-programs-directorate

Office of Health Affairs   The Office of Health Affairs (OHA) serves as the principal adviser to the Secretary on medical and public health issues. OHA leads the Department's workforce health protection and medical support activities. The Office also manages and coordinates the Department's biological and chemical defense programs and provides medical and scientific expertise to support DHS preparedness and response efforts. http://www.dhs.gov/office-health-affairs

Office of Intelligence and Analysis   The Office of Intelligence and Analysis, as a member of the U.S. Intelligence Community, is the nexus between the Nation's intelligence apparatus and DHS components and other State, local, and private sector partners. The Office ensures that information is gathered from all relevant DHS field operations and other State, local, and private sector partners and that this information is shared with appropriate stakeholders to produce accurate, timely, and actionable analytical intelligence products and services. https://www.dhs.gov/office-intelligence-and-analysis

Office of Operations Coordination   The Office of Operations Coordination provides decision support and enables the Secretary's execution of responsibilities across the homeland security enterprise by promoting situational awareness and information sharing, integrating and synchronizing strategic operations, and administering the DHS continuity program. At the strategic level, the Office provides a joint operations coordination capability to support DHS operational decision making, departmental leadership, and participation in interagency operations throughout the homeland security enterprise and across all mission areas. http://www.dhs.gov/office-operations-coordination

Office of Strategy, Policy, and Plans   The Office of Strategy, Policy, and Plans develops and coordinates department-wide policies, strategies, and plans to ensure consistency. The Office leads and coordinates both DHS interagency and foreign engagement. http://www.dhs.gov/office-policy

Transportation Security Administration   The Transportation Security Administration protects the Nation's transportation systems to ensure freedom of movement for people and commerce. https://www.tsa.gov

United States Citizenship and Immigration Services   The Unites States Citizenship and Immigration Services (USCIS) administers our Nation's legal immigration system. Operating primarily by fee funding, it ensures that information and decisions on citizenship and immigration benefits are provided to applications and petitioners in a timely, accurate, consistent, courteous, and professional manner consistent with national security. USCIS is also enhances the integrity of our country's legal immigration system by deterring, detecting, and pursuing immigration-related fraud, combating the unauthorized practice of immigration law, and helping to combat unauthorized employment in the workplace. http://www.uscis.gov

United States Coast Guard   The U.S. Coast Guard protects those on the sea, protects the Nation from seaborne threats, and ensures the safety, security, and stewardship of the Nation's ports, waterways, coasts, and far-reaching maritime regions of economic and national security interest. The Coast Guard manages six major operational mission programs: Maritime Law Enforcement, Maritime Response, Maritime Prevention, Maritime Transportation System Management, Maritime Security Operations, and Defense Operations. http://www.uscg. mil

U.S. Customs and Border Protection   The U.S. Customs and Border Protection secures America's borders to protect the public from terrorists and terrorist weapons, while enabling legitimate trade and travel to enhance the Nation's global economic competitiveness. http://www.cbp.gov

U.S. Immigration and Customs Enforcement   U.S. Immigration and Customs Enforcement (ICE) is the principal investigative arm of DHS. ICE's primary mission is to promote homeland security and public safety through the criminal and civil enforcement of Federal laws governing border control, customs, trade, and immigration. https://www.ice.gov

United States Secret Service   The U.S. Secret Service carries out a dual mission of protection and investigation. It protects the President, Vice President, and their families; major Presidential and Vice Presidential candidates; visiting heads of state and government; and National Special Security Events, as well as the White House and other designated buildings within the Washington, DC, area. The Secret Service also safeguards the Nation's financial infrastructure and payments systems to preserve the integrity of the economy. http:// www.secretservice.gov

Sources of Information

Blog   The DHS maintains a blog on its Web site. https://www.dhs.gov/news-releases/ blog?field_news_type_tid=588

Data   The DHS and its components provide Internet access to statistical reports and datasets: Coast Guard maritime information, Customs and Border Protection intellectual property rights recordations, Federal Emergency Management Agency disaster declarations, immigration data, and more. https://www.dhs.gov/topic/data

Employment   To search DHS job postings and to learn how to apply, visit the "Careers" Web page. https://www.dhs.gov/homeland-security-careers

Flood Insurance Rate Maps (FIRMs)   Flooding can occur anywhere in the United States; however, certain areas are prone to serious flooding. To help communities understand their risk, flood maps or FIRMs have been created to show the locations of high-risk, moderate-to-low risk, and undetermined-risk areas. Banks, citizens, insurance agents, and all levels of government rely on FIRMs to determine whether flood insurance is required. https:// msc.fema.gov/portal

Freedom of Information Act (FOIA)   The FOIA provides for the full disclosure of agency records and information to the public as long as those records and information are not exempted under clearly delineated statutory language. Instructions for submitting a FOIA request, filing a Privacy Act request, and information on other FOIA-related matters are available on the DHS Web site. https://www.dhs.gov/ how-submit-foia-request

The DHS maintains a FOIA library on its Web site. Information seekers should use the library's online resources to determine if the desired document or record is immediately available and, therefore, does not require a FOIA request to access it. https://www.dhs. gov/foia-library

Green Card   A person may obtain authorization to live and work in the United States on a permanent basis in several ways: A family member or employer in the United States may sponsor the Green Card applicant; refugee or asylee status and other humanitarian programs offer additional pathways; and, in some cases, a person may be eligible to file on his or her own initiative for permanent residency. https://www.dhs. gov/how-do-i/get-green-card

How Do I?   The DHS Web site features a comprehensive section that organizes answers to "how do I" questions according to audience: DHS employees, businessmen and women, travelers, and the general public. Entrepreneurs can learn how to apply for grants, find forms for exporting and importing, and verify employment eligibility; travelers can learn how to check wait times at airports and border crossings; and members of the public can learn how to adopt a child internationally, become a citizen, check the status of an immigration case, prepare for a disaster, and report cyber incidents and suspicious activity. https://www.dhs.gov/how-do-i

Keywords   The DHS Web site features a long list of keywords that are linked to pages containing information on the DHS, its components, and its mission. https://www.dhs.gov/keywords

Multilingual Resources   The Office of Civil Rights and Civil Liberties identifies documents containing information that is particularly important to diverse communities of limited English proficiency. These documents are often translated into Arabic, Chinese, French, Haitian-Creole, Portuguese, Russian, Somali, Spanish, and Vietnamese. https://www.dhs.gov/dhs-multilingual-resources

Naturalization   In the Immigration and Nationality Act, Congress established the requirements that a foreign citizen or national must fulfill to receive U.S. citizenship. The process of being granted citizenship is known as naturalization. The U.S. Citizenship and Immigration Services' Web site offers resources for those seeking citizenship through naturalization. These resources include citizenship and naturalization guidance; a guide to help permanent residents apply for citizenship; the application for naturalization (Form N–400) in Portable Document Format (PDF) and instructions for completing it; educational materials to prepare for the civics, history, and English sections of the naturalization test; and links that lead to Web pages with additional relevant information. https://www.uscis.gov/us-citizenship/citizenship-through-naturalization

News   The DHS posts audio items, congressional testimony, factsheets, photos and videos, press releases, and speeches on its Web site. It also posts news items on national security in Spanish. https://www.dhs.gov/news

Open Government   The DHS supports the Open Government initiative by promoting the principles of collaboration, participation, and transparency. https://www.dhs.gov/open-government

Operational Components   The DHS comprises nine operational components: the U.S. Department of Homeland Security, U.S. Customs and Border Protection, Federal Emergency Management Agency, Federal Law Enforcement Training Center, U.S. Immigration and Customs Enforcement, U.S. Secret Service, Transportation Security Administration, U.S. Coast Guard, and U.S. Citizenship and Immigration Services. The DHS Web site offers easy access to all of their home pages. https://www.dhs.gov/dhs-component-websites

Publications   The DHS publications library contains brochures, guidance and policy papers, guidelines, program regulations, reports, strategies, and more. https://www.dhs.gov/publications

Report Cyber Incidents   To protect the Nation's cybersecurity, the DHS has organizations dedicated to collecting information and reporting on cyber incidents, phishing, malware, and other vulnerabilities. https://www.dhs.gov/how-do-i/report-cyber-incidents

Site Map   The Web site map allows visitors to look for specific topics or to browse content that aligns with their interests. https://www.dhs.gov/sitemap

The DHS Web site features an A–Z index to help visitors navigate its content. https://www.dhs.gov/dhsgov-z-index

Social Media   The DHS maintains accounts on Facebook, Flickr, Instagram, and Twitter. An online subscription form also is available to sign up for email updates. https://www.dhs.gov/social-media-directory

Terrorist Threats   The National Terrorism Advisory System provides detailed, timely information on terrorist threats to the American public. https://www.dhs.gov/national-terrorism-advisory-system

Transportation Security   The "Transportation Security" Web page provides information on transportation and travel: aviation security, cargo screening, domestic travel, electronic passports, visas, and more. https://www.dhs.gov/topic/transportation-security

Travel Alerts   The DHS Web site offers convenient access to alerts and wait times: airport security checkpoint wait times from the Transportation Security Administration, airport wait times from the U.S. Customs and Border Protection, international travel warnings from the Department of State, and health alerts from the Centers for Disease Control and Prevention. https://www.dhs.gov/travel-alerts. http://www.dhs.gov/office-public-affairs

For further information, contact the Office of Public Affairs, Department of Homeland Security, Washington, DC 20528. Phone, 202-282-8010.

DEPARTMENT OF HOUSING AND URBAN DEVELOPMENT

451 Seventh Street SW., Washington, DC 20410
Phone, 202-708-1422. Internet, http://www.hud.gov.

Secretary of Housing and Urban Development	BENJAMIN S. CARSON, SR.
Deputy Secretary	JANET GOLRICK, ACTING
Assistant Secretary, Congressional and Intergovernmental Relations	(VACANCY)
Assistant Secretary, Field Policy and Management	(VACANCY)
Assistant Secretary, Fair Housing and Equal Opportunity	(VACANCY)
Assistant Secretary, Policy Development and Research	(VACANCY)
Assistant Secretary, Public Affairs	(VACANCY)
Chief Administrative Officer / Executive Secretary	HELEN GOFF FOSTER
Chief Human Capital Officer	TOWANDA BROOKS
Chief Information Officer	(VACANCY)
Chief of Staff	SHEILA GREENWOOD
Chief Procurement Officer	KEITH W. SURBER
Deputy Chief Financial Officer	COURTNEY B. TIMBERLAKE
Director, Office of Departmental Equal Employment Opportunity	JOHN P. BENISON
Director, Office of Lead Hazard Control and Healthy Homes	MICHELLE MILLER, ACTING
Director, Office of Strategic Planning and Management	HENRY HENSLEY
General Counsel	LINDA CRUCIANI, ACTING
Inspector General	DAVID A. MONTOYA
President, Government National Mortgage Association–Ginnie Mae	(VACANCY)
Principal Deputy Assistant Secretary, Community Planning and Development	(VACANCY)
Principal Deputy Assistant Secretary, Office of Housing	(VACANCY)
Principal Deputy Assistant Secretary, Office of Public and Indian Housing	(VACANCY)

The Department of Housing and Urban Development oversees housing needs nationwide, ensures fair housing opportunities, and creates strong, sustainable, and inclusive communities.

The Department of Housing and Urban Development (HUD) was established in 1965 by the Department of Housing and Urban Development Act (42 U.S.C. 3532–3537). It was created to administer the principal programs that provide assistance for housing and the development of communities; to promote finding solutions to housing and community development problems through States and localities; and to maximize contributions of the homebuilding and mortgage lending industries to housing, community development, and the national economy.

HUD administers many programs; however, it has six core functions: insuring mortgages for single-family and multifamily dwellings and extending loans for home improvement and for the purchasing of mobile homes; channeling funds from investors to the mortgage industry through the Government National Mortgage Association–Ginnie Mae; making direct loans for construction or rehabilitation of housing projects that benefit the elderly and handicapped; providing Federal housing subsidies for low- and moderate-income families; giving community development

DEPARTMENT OF HOUSING AND URBAN DEVELOPMENT

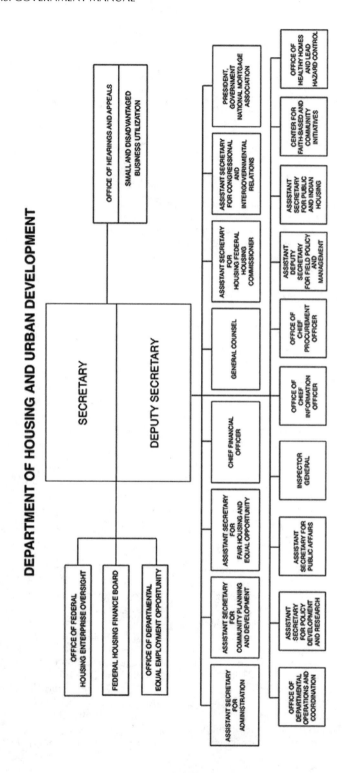

grants to States and communities; and promoting and enforcing fair housing and equal housing opportunity.

Secretary   The Secretary formulates policy recommendations affecting housing and community development; encourages the participation of private enterprise in housing and community development; promotes the growth of cities and States and the efficient and effective use of housing and community and economic development resources by stimulating private sector initiatives, public-private sector partnerships, and public entrepreneurship; ensures equal access to housing and affirmatively prevents housing discrimination; and oversees the Federal National Mortgage Association–Fannie Mae.

To learn more about the powers of the Secretary, visit HUD's Web site: http://portal. hud.gov/hudportal/HUD?src=/about/hud_ secretary/powersec

Program Areas

Community Planning and Development   The Office of Community and Planning Development administers grant programs to help communities plan and finance growth and development, to increase their governing capacity, and to shelter and provide services for the homeless. The Office is responsible for implementing Community Development Block Grant (CDBG) programs for entitlement communities; the State- and HUD-administered Small Cities Program; community development loan guarantees; special purpose grants for insular areas and historically black colleges and universities; Appalachian Regional Commission grants; the Home Investment in Affordable Housing Program, which provides Federal assistance for housing rehabilitation, tenant-based assistance, first-time homebuyers, and new construction when a jurisdiction is determined to need new rental housing; the Department's programs to address homelessness; the John Heinz Neighborhood Development Program; community outreach partnerships; the joint community development plan that assists institutions of higher education working in concert with State and local governments to undertake activities under the CDBG program; community adjustment

and economic diversification planning grants; empowerment zones and enterprise communities; efforts to improve the environment; and community planning and development efforts of other departments and agencies, public and private organizations, private industry, financial markets, and international organizations. http://portal.hud.gov/hudportal/HUD?src=/ program_offices/comm_planning

For further information, contact the Office of Community Planning and Development. Phone, 202-708-2690.

Fair Housing and Equal Opportunity   The Office of Fair Housing and Equal Opportunity administers fair housing laws and regulations prohibiting discrimination in public and private housing; equal opportunity laws and regulations prohibiting discrimination in HUD-assisted housing and community development programs; the fair housing assistance grants program to provide financial and technical assistance to State and local government agencies to implement local fair housing laws and ordinances; and the Community Housing Resources Boards program to provide grants for fair housing activities, including outreach and education, identification of institutional barriers to fair housing, and telephone hotlines for complaints. http://portal.hud. gov/hudportal/HUD?src=/program_offices/ fair_housing_equal_opp

For further information, contact the Office of Fair Housing and Equal Opportunity. Phone, 202-708-4252.

Government National Mortgage Association–Ginnie Mae   This Government corporation supports expanded affordable housing by providing an efficient, Government-guaranteed secondary market vehicle to link the capital markets with Federal housing markets. Ginnie Mae guarantees mortgage-backed securities composed of FHA-insured or VA-guaranteed mortgage loans that private lenders issued and Ginnie Mae guaranteed with the full faith and credit of the United States. These programs allow Ginnie Mae to increase the overall supply of credit available for housing by providing a vehicle for channeling funds from the securities market into the mortgage market. http://www.ginniemae.gov/pages/ default.aspx

For further information, contact the Government National Mortgage Association. Phone, 202-708-0926.

Housing   The Office of Housing oversees aid for construction and financing of new and rehabilitated housing and for preservation of existing housing. The Office underwrites single-family, multifamily, property improvement, and manufactured home loans; administers special purpose programs designed for the elderly, handicapped, and chronically mentally ill; administers housing assistance programs for low-income families having difficulties affording standard housing; administers grants to fund resident ownership of multifamily house properties; and protects consumers against fraudulent land development and promotional practices. http://portal.hud.gov/hudportal/HUD?src=/ program_offices/housing

For further information, contact the Office of Housing. Phone, 202-708-3600.

Lead Hazard Control and Healthy Homes   The Office of Lead Hazard Control and Healthy Homes is responsible for lead hazard control policy development, abatement, training, regulations, and research. Activities of the Office include increasing public and building-industry awareness of the dangers of lead-based paint poisoning and the options for detection, risk reduction, and abatement; encouraging the development of safer, more effective, and less costly methods for detection, risk reduction, and abatement; and encouraging State and local governments to develop lead-based paint programs covering contractor certification, hazard reduction, financing, enforcement, and primary prevention, including public education. http://portal. hud.gov/hudportal/HUD?src=/program_ offices/healthy_homes

For further information, contact the Office of Lead Hazard Control and Healthy Homes. Phone, 202-755-1785.

Public and Indian Housing   The Office of Public and Indian Housing administers public and Indian housing programs; assists technically and financially with planning, developing, and managing low-income projects; subsidizes the operations of public housing agencies (PHAs) and Indian housing authorities (IHAs) and provides procedures for reviewing the management of public housing agencies; administers the comprehensive improvement assistance and comprehensive grant programs for modernizing low-income housing projects; administers programs for resident participation, resident management, home ownership, economic development and supportive services, and drug-free neighborhood programs; protects low-income tenants from lead-based paint poisoning by requiring PHAs and IHAs to comply with HUD regulations for the testing and removal of lead-based paint; implements and monitors program requirements related to program eligibility and admission of families to public and assisted housing, as well as tenant income and rent requirements for continued occupancy; administers the HOPE VI and vacancy reduction programs; administers voucher and certificate programs and the Moderate Rehabilitation Program; coordinates all departmental housing and community development programs for Indian and Alaskan Natives; and awards grants to PHAs and IHAs for the construction, acquisition, and operation of public and Indian housing projects. http://portal.hud.gov/hudportal/HUD?src=/ program_offices/public_indian_housing/ih

For further information, contact the Office of Public and Indian Housing. Phone, 202-708-0950.

Sources of Information

A–Z Index   An alphabetical index is available on the HUD Web site to help visitors search for specific topics or browse content that aligns with their interests. https://portal.hud.gov/hudportal/HUD?src=/ siteindex/quicklinks

Business Opportunities   To learn about contracting opportunities, programs, and resources, use the link below. The Office of the Chief Procurement Officer can provide additional information. Phone, 202-708-1290. TDD, 202-708-1455. http://portal.hud.gov/ hudportal/HUD?src=/program_offices/cpo

Career Opportunities   Information on career opportunities—including opportunities for veterans, students, and people with disabilities—is available online. Information is also available from the Personnel Division at the nearest regional office and from the

Office of Human Resources in Washington, DC. Phone, 202-708-0408. http://portal.hud.gov/hudportal/HUD?src=/program_offices/administration/careers

Data / Research   The Office of Policy Development and Research posts datasets, publications, research, and information on initiatives on its "HUD User" Web site. http://www.huduser.org/portal/home.html

Directory Locator   To locate a HUD employee or to send a HUD employee an email, visit the "Search for HUD Employees" Web page. An automated phone locator service is also available. Phone, 202-708-1112. TDD, 202-708-1455. http://peoplesearch.hud.gov/po/i/netlocator

Field Offices   Visit HUD's online local office directory to find contact information for its field offices. http://portal.hud.gov/hudportal/HUD?src=/program_offices/field_policy_mgt/localoffices

Freedom of Information Act (FOIA)   Many HUD documents are available online. Before submitting a written request, see the "Frequently Requested Materials" and "E–FOIA Reading Room" links on HUD's FOIA Web page. Send written requests to the Director, Executive Secretariat, Department of Housing and Urban Development, Room 10139, 451 Seventh Street SW., Washington, DC 20410. For information on inspecting documents or records, contact the Freedom of Information Officer. Phone, 202-708-3054. http://portal.hud.gov/hudportal/HUD?src=/program_offices/administration/foia

Frequently Asked Questions (FAQs)   Answers to FAQs are posted online. https://portal.hud.gov/hudportal/HUD?src=/faqs

Good Stories   To learn about the positive things that HUD funding helps support, see the Department's online collection of good stories and feature stories. https://archives.hud.gov/library/goodstories/index.cfm

History   In the aftermath of assassination that outraged communities of color and sparked protest and violence in American cities, President Lyndon B. Johnson approved Title VIII of the Civil Rights Act of 1968, commonly referred to as the Fair Housing Act. Signing "into law the promises of a century" was his description of that moment. The promises of this legislation included outlawing most housing discrimination and giving enforcement responsibility to HUD. To learn more about HUD's history of overseeing and coordinating Federal housing programs and enforcing fair housing practices, visit the "HUD History" Web page. https://portal.hud.gov/hudportal/HUD?src=/about/hud_history

Hotline   The Office of the Inspector General maintains the Hotline to report fraud, mismanagement, and waste. Phone, 202-708-4200 or 800-347-3735. TDD, 202-708-2451. http://www.hudoig.gov/hotline | Email: hotline@hudoig.gov

Library   The library is located at HUD headquarters in Washington, DC. Visitors must schedule an appointment to use the library. It is open weekdays, except Federal holidays, from 9:30 a.m. to 5 p.m. Phone, 202-402-2680.

Property Disposition   For single-family properties, contact the Chief Property Officer at the nearest HUD regional office or the Property Disposition Division. Phone, 202-708-0614. For multifamily properties, contact the Regional Housing Director at the nearest HUD regional office or the Property Disposition Division. Phone, 202-708-0614. http://portal.hud.gov/hudportal/HUD?src=/topics/homes_for_sale

Site Map   The Web site map allows visitors to look for specific topics or to browse content that aligns with their interests. https://portal.hud.gov/hudportal/HUD?src=/siteindex

Social Media   HUD's social media directory provides links to all of its official blogs and social media platforms on Facebook, Flickr, Instagram, Twitter, and YouTube. https://portal.hud.gov/hudportal/HUD?src=/program_offices/public_affairs/socialmedia. http://portal.hud.gov/hudportal/HUD?src=/contact

For further information, contact the Office of Public Affairs, Department of Housing and Urban Development, 451 Seventh Street SW., Washington, DC 20410. Phone, 202-708-0980.

Editorial Note

The Department of Justice did not meet the publication deadline for submitting updated information of its activities, functions, and sources of information as required by the automatic disclosure provisions of the Freedom of Information Act (5 U.S.C. 552(a)(1)(A))

DEPARTMENT OF JUSTICE

950 Pennsylvania Avenue NW., Washington, DC 20530
Phone, 202-514-2000. Internet, http://www.justice.gov.

Attorney General	JEFF SESSIONS
Deputy Attorney General	ROD J. ROSENSTEIN
Associate Attorney General	RACHEL L. BRAND
Counsel, Office of Professional Responsibility	ROBIN C. ASHTON
Inspector General	MICHAEL E. HOROWITZ
Pardon Attorney	LAWRENCE KUPERS, ACTING
Solicitor General	JEFF WALL, ACTING

Assistant Attorneys General

Criminal Division	LESLIE RAGON CALDWELL
Environment and Natural Resources Division	JOHN C. CRUDEN
Justice Management Division / Chief Financial Officer	LEE J. LOFTHUS
National Security Division	JOHN P. CARLIN
Office of Legislative Affairs	PETER J. KADZIK
Tax Division	CAROLINE D. CIRAOLO, ACTING

Directors

Community Relations Service	PAUL MONTEIRO, ACTING
Executive Office for Organized Crime and Drug Enforcement Task Force	BRUCE G. OHR
Executive Office for U.S. Attorneys	MONTY WILKINSON
Executive Office for U.S. Trustees	CLIFFORD J. WHITE III
Office for Access to Justice	LISA FOSTER
Office of Information Policy	MELANIE ANN PUSTAY
Office of Public Affairs	SARAH ISGUR FLORES
Office of Tribal Justice and Safety	TRACY TOULOU
Professional Responsibility Advisory Office	STACY LUDWIG

Principal Deputy Assistant Attorneys General

Antitrust Division	ANDREW C. FINCH, ACTING
Civil Division	CHAD A. READLER, ACTING
Civil Rights Division	JOHN M. GORE, ACTING
Office of Legal Counsel	CURTIS E. GANNON, ACTING
Office of Legal Policy	RYAN NEWMAN, ACTING

The Department of Justice serves as counsel for U.S citizens and represents them by enforcing the law in the public interest. It deters criminality and subversion, ensures healthy business competition, safeguards consumers, and enforces drug, immigration, and naturalization laws.

The Department of Justice was established by act of June 22, 1870 (28 U.S.C. 501, 503, 509 note), with the Attorney General as its head. The affairs and activities of the Department of Justice are generally directed by the Attorney General.

Attorney General The Attorney General represents the United States in legal matters generally and gives advice and opinions to the President and to the heads of the executive departments of the Government when so requested. The Attorney General

238

U.S. Department of Justice

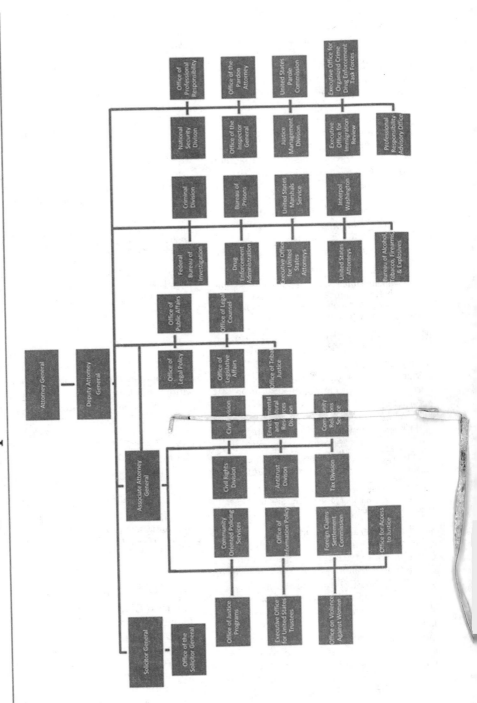

appears in person to represent the Government before the U.S. Supreme Court in cases of exceptional gravity or importance.

Community Relations Service The Service offers assistance to communities in resolving disputes relating to race, color, or national origin and facilitates the development of viable agreements as alternatives to coercion, violence, or litigation. It also assists and supports communities in developing local mechanisms as proactive measures to prevent or reduce ethnic and racial tensions.

A list of Community Relations Service regional offices—including contact information—is available online. http://www.justice.gov/crs/about-crs/regional-and-field-offices. http://www.justice.gov/crs/contact-office

For further information, contact any regional office or the Director, Community Relations Service, Department of Justice, Suite 2000, 600 E Street NW., Washington, DC 20530. Phone, 202-305-2935.

Pardon Attorney The Office of the Pardon Attorney assists the President in the exercise of his pardon power under the Constitution. Generally, all requests for pardon or other forms of executive clemency, including commutation of sentences, are directed to the Pardon Attorney for investigation and review. The Pardon Attorney prepares the Department's recommendation to the President for final disposition of each application. http://www.justice.gov/pardon

For further information, contact the Office of the Pardon Attorney, Department of Justice, Suite 5E–508, 145 N Street NE., Washington, DC 20530. Phone, 202-616-6070.

Solicitor General The Office of the Solicitor General represents the U.S. Government in cases before the Supreme Court. It decides what cases the Government should ask the Supreme Court to review and what position the Government should take in cases before the Court. It also supervises the preparation of the Government's Supreme Court briefs and other legal documents and the conduct of the oral arguments in the Court. The Solicitor General also decides whether the United States should appeal in cases that it loses before the lower courts. http://www.justice.gov/osg

For further information, contact the Executive Officer, Office of the Solicitor General, Room 5142, 950 Pennsylvania Avenue NW., RFK Justice Building (Main), Washington, DC 20530-0001.

U.S. Attorneys The Executive Office for U.S. Attorneys was created on April 6, 1953, to provide liaison between the Department of Justice in Washington, DC, and the U.S. attorneys. It gives general executive assistance to the 94 offices of the U.S. attorneys and coordinates the relationship between the U.S. attorneys and the organization components of the Department of Justice and other Federal agencies. http://www.justice.gov/usao/eousa

For further information, contact the Executive Office for U.S. Attorneys, Department of Justice, Room 2261, 950 Pennsylvania Avenue NW., Washington, DC 20530. Phone, 202-514-1020.

U.S. Trustee Program The Program was established by the Bankruptcy Reform Act of 1978 (11 U.S.C. 101 et seq.) as a pilot effort in 10 regions comprising 18 Federal judicial districts to promote the efficiency and protect the integrity of the bankruptcy system by identifying and helping to investigate bankruptcy fraud and abuse. It now operates nationwide except in Alabama and North Carolina. The Bankruptcy Abuse Prevention and Consumer Protection Act of 2005 (11 U.S.C. 101 note) significantly expanded the Program's responsibilities and provided additional tools to fight bankruptcy fraud and abuse. The Executive Office for U.S. Trustees provides day-to-day policy and legal direction, coordination, and control. http://www.justice.gov/ust

For further information, contact the Executive Office for U.S. Trustees, Department of Justice, Suite 6150, 441 G Street NW., Washington, DC 20530. Phone, 202-307-1391.

Divisions

Antitrust Division The Assistant Attorney General in charge of the Antitrust Division is responsible for promoting and maintaining competitive markets by enforcing the Federal antitrust laws. This involves investigating possible antitrust violations, conducting grand jury proceedings, reviewing proposed mergers and acquisitions, preparing and trying antitrust cases, prosecuting appeals, and negotiating and enforcing final judgments. The Division prosecutes serious and willful violations of antitrust laws by filing criminal suits that can lead to large fines and jail sentences. Where criminal prosecution is not appropriate, the Division seeks a court order forbidding future violations of the law and requiring steps by the defendant to remedy the anticompetitive effects of past violations.

The Division also is responsible for acting as an advocate of competition within the Federal Government as well as internationally. This involves formal appearances in Federal administrative agency proceedings, development of legislative initiatives to promote deregulation and eliminate unjustifiable exemptions from the antitrust laws, and participation on executive branch policy task forces and in multilateral international organizations. The Division provides formal advice to other agencies on the competitive implications of proposed transactions requiring Federal approval, such as mergers of financial institutions. http://www.justice. gov/atr

For further information, contact the Office of the Assistant Attorney General, Antitrust Division, Department of Justice, 950 Pennsylvania Avenue NW., Washington, DC 20530. Phone, 202-514-2401.

Civil Division   The Civil Division represents the United States, its departments and agencies, Members of Congress, Cabinet officers, and other Federal employees. Its litigation reflects the diversity of Government activities involving, for example, the defense of challenges to Presidential actions; national security issues; benefit programs; energy policies; commercial issues such as contract disputes, banking, insurance, fraud, and debt collection; all manner of accident and liability claims; and violations of the immigration and consumer protection laws. The Division confronts significant policy issues, which often rise to constitutional dimensions, in defending and enforcing various Federal programs and actions. Each year, Division attorneys handle thousands of cases that collectively involve billions of dollars in claims and recoveries.

The Division litigates cases in the following areas:

Commercial litigation, litigation associated with the Government's diverse financial involvements including all monetary suits involving contracts, express or implied; actions to foreclose on Government mortgages and liens; bankruptcy and insolvency proceedings; suits against guarantors and sureties; actions involving fraud against the Government, including false or fraudulent claims for Federal insurance, loans, subsidies, and other benefits such as Medicare, false or fraudulent claims for payment under Federal contracts, whistleblower suits, and Government corruption; patent, copyright, and trademark cases and suits arising out of construction, procurement, service contracts, and claims associated with contract terminations; claims for just compensation under the Fifth Amendment; claims for salary or retirement by civilian and military personnel; cases assigned by congressional reference or special legislation; and litigation involving interests of the United States in any foreign court, whether civil or criminal in nature.

Consumer litigation, including civil and criminal litigation and related matters arising under various consumer protection and public health statutes.

Federal programs, including constitutional challenges to statutes, suits to overturn Government policies and programs, challenges to the legality of Government decisions, allegations that the President has violated the Constitution or Federal law, suits to enforce regulatory statutes and to remedy or prevent statutory or regulatory violations.

The areas of litigation include:

Suits against the heads of Federal departments and agencies and other Government officials to enjoin official actions, as well as suits for judicial review of administrative decisions, orders, and regulations; suits involving national security, including suits to protect sensitive intelligence sources and materials; suits to prevent interference with Government operations; litigation concerning the constitutionality of Federal laws; and suits raising employment discrimination claims and Government personnel issues.

Immigration litigation, involving civil litigation under the Immigration and

Nationality Act and related laws; district court litigation, habeas corpus review and general advice; petitions for removal order review and immigration-related appellate matters; cases pertaining to the issuance of visas and passports; and litigation arising under the legalization and employer sanction provisions of the immigration laws.

Torts, including the broad range of tort litigation arising from the operation of the Federal Government, constitutional tort claims against Federal Government officials throughout the Government, aviation disasters, environmental and occupational disease, and radiation and toxic substance exposure. It defends petitions filed pursuant to the Vaccine Injury Compensation Program and is responsible for administering the Radiation Exposure Compensation Program. It also handles maritime litigation and suits that seek personal monetary judgments against individual officers or employees.

Appellate, having primary responsibility for the litigation of Civil Division cases in the courts of appeal, and on occasion, State appeal courts. The Appellate Staff prepares Government briefs and presents oral arguments for these cases. Additionally, the Appellate Staff works with the Solicitor General's office to prepare documents filed for these cases in the Supreme Court, including briefs on the merits, petitions for certiorari, and jurisdictional statements. The Appellate Staff also works with the Solicitor General's office to obtain authorization for appellate review. http://www.justice.gov/civil

For further information, contact the Office of the Assistant Attorney General, Civil Division, Department of Justice, Tenth Street and Pennsylvania Avenue NW., Washington, DC 20530. Phone, 202-514-3301.

Civil Rights Division   The Civil Rights Division, headed by an Assistant Attorney General, was established in 1957 to secure effective Federal enforcement of civil rights. The Division is the primary institution within the Federal Government responsible for enforcing Federal statutes prohibiting discrimination on the basis of race, sex, disability, religion, citizenship, and national origin. The Division has responsibilities in the following areas:

Coordination and review of various civil rights statutes that prohibit discrimination on the basis of race, color, national origin, sex, and religion in programs and activities that receive Federal financial assistance by Federal agencies.

Criminal cases involving conspiracies to interfere with federally protected rights; deprivation of rights under color of law; the use of force or threat of force to injure or intimidate someone in their enjoyment of specific rights (such as voting, housing, employment, education, public facilities, and accommodations); interference with the free exercise of religious beliefs or damage to religious property; the holding of a worker in a condition of slavery or involuntary servitude; and interference with persons seeking to obtain or provide reproductive services.

Disability rights cases, achieving equal opportunity for people with disabilities in the United States by implementing the Americans with Disabilities Act (ADA). ADA mandates are carried out through enforcement, certification, regulatory, coordination, and technical assistance activities, combined with an innovative mediation program and a technical assistance grant program. The Division also carries out responsibilities under sections 504 and 508 of the Rehabilitation Act, the Help America Vote Act of 2002, the Small Business Regulatory Enforcement Fairness Act, and Executive Order 12250.

Educational opportunities litigation, involving title IV of the Civil Rights Act of 1964, the Equal Educational Opportunities Act of 1974, and title III of the Americans with Disabilities Act. In addition, the Division is responsible for enforcing other statutes such as title VI of the Civil Rights Act of 1964, title IX of the Education Amendments of 1972, section 504 of the Rehabilitation Act of 1973, title II of the Americans with Disabilities Act, and the Individuals with Disabilities Education Act upon referral from other governmental agencies.

Employment litigation enforcing against State and local government employers the provisions of title VII of the Civil Rights Act of 1964, as amended, and other Federal laws prohibiting employment practices that discriminate on grounds of race, sex, religion, and national origin. The Division also enforces against State and local government and private employers the provisions of the Uniformed Services Employment and Reemployment Rights Act of 1994, which prohibits employers from discriminating or retaliating against an employee or applicant for employment because of such person's past, current, or future military obligation.

Housing and Civil Enforcement statutes enforcing the Fair Housing Act, which prohibits discrimination in housing; the Equal Credit Opportunity Act, which prohibits discrimination in credit; title II of the Civil Rights Act of 1964, which prohibits discrimination in certain places of public accommodation, such as hotels, restaurants, nightclubs and theaters; title III of the Civil Rights Act of 1964, which prohibits discrimination in public facilities; and the Religious Land Use and Institutionalized Persons Act, which prohibits local governments from adopting or enforcing land use regulations that discriminate against religious assemblies and institutions or which unjustifiably burden religious exercise.

Immigration-related unfair employment practices enforcing the antidiscrimination provisions of the Immigration and Nationality Act, which protect U.S. citizens and legal immigrants from employment discrimination based upon citizenship or immigration status and national origin, unfair documentary practices relating to the employment eligibility verification process, and retaliation.

Special litigation protecting the constitutional and statutory rights of persons confined in certain institutions owned or operated by State or local governments, including facilities for individuals with mental and developmental disabilities, nursing homes, prisons, jails, and juvenile detention facilities where a pattern or practice of violations exist; civil enforcement of statutes prohibiting a pattern or practice of conduct by law enforcement agencies that violates Federal law; and protection against a threat of force and physical obstruction that injures, intimidates, or interferes with a person seeking to obtain or provide reproductive health services, or to exercise

the first amendment right of religious freedom at a place of worship.

Voting cases enforcing the Voting Rights Act, the Help America Vote Act of 2002, the National Voter Registration Act, the Voting Accessibility for the Elderly and Handicapped Act, the Uniformed and Overseas Citizens Absentee Voting Act, and other Federal statutes designed to safeguard citizens' rights to vote. This includes racial and language minorities, illiterate persons, individuals with disabilities, overseas citizens, persons who change their residence shortly before a Presidential election, and persons 18 to 20 years of age. http://www.justice.gov/crt

For further information, contact the Executive Officer, Civil Rights Division, Department of Justice, 950 Pennsylvania Avenue NW., Washington, DC 20035. Phone, 202-514-4224.

Criminal Division The Criminal Division develops, enforces, and supervises the application of all Federal criminal laws, except those specifically assigned to other divisions. In addition to its direct litigation responsibilities, the Division formulates and implements criminal enforcement policy and provides advice and assistance, including representing the United States before the United States Courts of Appeal. The Division engages in and coordinates a wide range of criminal investigations and prosecutions, such as those targeting individuals and organizations that engage in international and national drug trafficking and money laundering systems or organizations and organized crime groups. The Division also approves or monitors sensitive areas of law enforcement such as participation in the Witness Security Program and the use of electronic surveillance; advises the Attorney General, Congress, the Office of Management and Budget, and the White House on matters of criminal law; provides legal advice, assistance, and training to Federal, State, and local prosecutors and investigative agencies; provides leadership for coordinating international and national law enforcement matters; and provides training and development assistance to foreign criminal justice systems. Areas of responsibility include the following:

Asset forfeiture and money laundering, including the prosecution of complex, sensitive, multidistrict, and international cases; formulating policy and conducting training in the money laundering and forfeiture areas; developing legislation and regulations; ensuring the uniform application of forfeiture and money laundering statutes; participating in bilateral and multilateral initiatives to develop international forfeiture and money laundering policy and promote international cooperation; adjudicating petitions for remission or mitigation of forfeited assets; distributing forfeited funds and properties to appropriate domestic and foreign law enforcement agencies and community groups within the United States; and ensuring that such agencies comply with proper usage of received funds.

Child exploitation and obscenity, including the prosecution of sexual predators, sex trafficking of children, U.S. citizens and resident aliens who travel abroad to sexually abuse foreign children (sex tourism), and the enforcement of sex offender registration laws; providing forensic assistance to Federal prosecutors and law enforcement agents in investigating and prosecuting child exploitation: coordinating nationwide operations targeting child predators; and developing policy and legislative proposals related to these issues.

Computer and intellectual property crimes, including cyberattacks on critical information systems (cyberterrorism); strengthening, domestic and international laws prosecute computer crimes; and directing multidistrict and transnational cyberinvestigations and prosecutions.

Enforcement, including the review of all Federal electronic surveillance requests and requests to apply for court orders permitting the use video surveillance; authorizing or denying the entry of applicants into the Federal Witness Security Program (WSP) and coordinating and administering its program components; reviewing requests for witness immunity ; transfer of prisoners to and from foreign countries to serve the remainder of their prison sentences; attorney and press subpoenas; applications for S-visa status; and disclosure of grand jury information.

Fraud, including the investigation and prosecution of white-collar crimes (corporate, securities, and investment fraud), government program and procurement fraud, and international criminal violations including the bribery of foreign government officials in violation of the Foreign Corrupt Practices Act.

International affairs, including making requests for international extradition and foreign evidence on behalf of Federal, State, and local prosecutors and investigators, fulfilling foreign requests for fugitives and evidence, and negotiating and implementing law enforcement treaties.

Narcotics and dangerous drugs, including domestic and international drug trafficking and narco-terrorism; enforcing laws that criminalize the extraterritorial manufacture or distribution of certain controlled substances; prosecuting drug traffickers who support a person or organization that engages in terrorist activity; and providing targeted intelligence support to the DEA and other law enforcement agencies worldwide.

Organized crime, including combining the resources and expertise of several Federal agencies in cooperation with the Tax Division, U.S. attorneys offices, and State and local law enforcement to identify, disrupt, and dismantle major drug supply and money laundering organizations through coordinated, nationwide investigations targeting the entire infrastructure of these enterprises.

Assistance to foreign law enforcement institutions, including the creation of new and reforming existing police forces in other countries and international peacekeeping operations; enhancing the capabilities of existing police forces in emerging democracies; and assisting nations that are combating terrorism.

Overseas prosecutorial development, assistance, and training for prosecutors and judicial personnel in other countries to develop and sustain democratic criminal justice institutions.

Policy and legislation, developing legislative proposals and reviewing pending legislation affecting the Federal criminal justice system; reviewing and developing proposed changes to the Federal sentencing guidelines and rules; and analyzing crime policy and program issues.

Public integrity efforts to combat corruption of elected and appointed public officials at all levels of government.

Human rights and special prosecutions, investigating and prosecuting human rights violations, international violent crime, immigration violations, and war crimes.

Appellate work, including drafting briefs and certiorari petitions for the Solicitor General for filing in the U.S. Supreme Court; making recommendations to the Solicitor General as to whether further review is warranted on adverse decisions in the district courts and courts of appeals; and preparing briefs and arguing cases in the courts of appeals.

Counterterrorism, including in conjunction with the National Security Division, investigating and prosecuting terrorist financing and material support cases; establishing and maintaining an essential communication network between the Department of Justice and United States Attorneys' Offices for the rapid transmission of information on terrorism threats and investigative activity; providing and serving as trusted liaisons to the intelligence, defense, and immigration communities as well as to foreign government partners on counterterrorism issues and cases. http://www.justice.gov/criminal

For further information, contact the Office of the Assistant Attorney General, Criminal Division, Department of Justice, Tenth Street and Pennsylvania Avenue NW., Washington, DC 20530. Phone, 202-514-2601.

Environment and Natural Resources Division

The Environment and Natural Resources Division is the Nation's environmental lawyer. The Division's responsibilities include enforcing civil and criminal environmental laws that protect America's health and environment. It also defends environmental challenges to Government activities and programs and ensures that environmental laws are implemented in a fair and consistent manner nationwide. It also represents the United States in all matters concerning the protection, use, and development of the Nation's natural resources and public lands, wildlife protection, Indian rights and claims, and the acquisition of Federal property. To carry out this broad mission, the Division litigates in the following areas:

Environmental crimes, prosecuting individuals and corporate entities violating laws designed to protect the environment.

Civil environmental enforcement, on behalf of EPA; claims for damages to natural resources filed on behalf of the Departments of the Interior, Commerce, and Agriculture; claims for contribution against private parties for contamination of public land; and recoupment of money spent to clean up certain oil spills on behalf of the U.S. Coast Guard.

Environmental defense, representing the United States in suits challenging the Government's administration of Federal environmental laws including claims that regulations are too strict or lenient and claims alleging that Federal agencies are not complying with environmental standards.

Wildlife and marine resources protection, including prosecution of smugglers and black-market dealers in protected wildlife.

Use and protection of federally owned public lands and natural resources across a broad spectrum of laws.

Indian resources protection, including establishing water rights, establishing and protecting hunting and fishing rights, collecting damages for trespass on Indian lands, and establishing reservation boundaries and rights to land.

Land acquisition for use by the Federal Government for purposes ranging from establishing public parks to building Federal courthouses. http://justice.gov/enrd

For further information, contact the Office of the Assistant Attorney General, Environment and Natural Resources Division, Department of Justice, Tenth Street and Pennsylvania Avenue NW., Washington, DC 20530. Phone, 202-514-2701.

National Security Division

The National Security Division (NSD) develops, enforces, and supervises the application of all Federal criminal laws related to the national counterterrorism and counterespionage enforcement programs, except those specifically assigned to other divisions. NSD litigates and coordinates a wide range of prosecutions and criminal investigations involving terrorism and violations of the espionage, export control, and foreign agents registration laws. It administers the

Foreign Intelligence Surveillance Act and other legal authorities for national security activities; approves and monitors the use of electronic surveillance; provides legal and policy advice regarding the classification of and access to national security information; performs prepublication review of materials written by present and former DOJ employees; trains the law enforcement and intelligence communities; and advises the Department and legislative and executive branches on all areas of national security law. NSD also serves as the Department's representative on interdepartmental boards, committees, and entities dealing with issues related to national security.

NSD also has some additional counterterrorism, counterespionage, and intelligence oversight responsibilities as follows: to promote and oversee national counterterrorism enforcement programs; develop and implement counterterrorism strategies, legislation, and initiatives; facilitate information sharing between and among the Department and other Federal agencies on terrorism threats; share information with international law enforcement officials to assist with international threat information and litigation initiatives; liaison with the intelligence, defense, and immigration communities and foreign governments on counterterrorism issues and cases; supervise the investigation and prosecution of cases involving national security, foreign relations, the export of military and strategic commodities and technology, espionage, sabotage, neutrality, and atomic energy; coordinate cases involving the application for the Classified Information Procedures Act; enforce the Foreign Agents Registration Act of 1938 and related disclosure laws; supervise the preparation of certifications and applications for orders under the Foreign Intelligence Surveillance Act (FISA); represent the United States before the Foreign Intelligence Surveillance Court; participate in the development, implementation, and review of United States intelligence policies; evaluate existing and proposed national security-related activities to determine their consistency with relevant policies and law; monitor intelligence and counterintelligence activities of other agencies to ensure

conformity with Department objectives; prepare reports evaluating domestic and foreign intelligence and counterintelligence activities; and process requests to use FISA-derived information in criminal, civil, and immigration proceedings and to disseminate that information to foreign governments. http://www.justice.gov/nsd

For further information, contact the Office of the Assistant Attorney General, National Security Division, Department of Justice, Tenth Street and Pennsylvania Avenue NW., Washington, DC 20530. Phone, 202-514-5600.

Tax Division   Tax Division ensures the uniform and fair enforcement of Federal tax laws in Federal and State courts. The Division conducts enforcement activities to deter specific taxpayers, as well as the taxpaying public at large, from conduct that deprives the Federal Government of its tax-related revenue. It represents the United States and its officers in all civil and criminal litigation arising under the internal revenue laws, other than proceedings in the U.S. Tax Court. Tax Division attorneys frequently join with assistant U.S. attorneys in prosecuting tax cases. Some criminal tax grand jury investigations and prosecutions are handled solely by Tax Division prosecutors, while others are delegated to assistant U.S. attorneys. Division attorneys evaluate requests by the Internal Revenue Service or U.S. attorneys to initiate grand jury investigations or prosecutions of tax crimes.

The Division handles a wide array of civil tax litigation, including the following: suits to enjoin the promotion of abusive tax shelters and to enjoin activities relating to aiding and abetting the understatement of tax liabilities of others; suits to enforce Internal Revenue Service administrative summonses that seek information essential to determine and collect taxpayers' liabilities, including summonses for records of corporate tax shelters and offshore transactions; suits brought by the United States to set aside fraudulent conveyances and to collect assets held by nominees and egos; tax refund suits challenging the Internal Revenue Service's determination of taxpayers' Federal income, employment, excise, and estate liabilities; bankruptcy litigation raising issues of the validity, dischargeability, and priority of Federal tax claims, and the feasibility of reorganization plans; suits brought by taxpayers challenging determinations made in the collection due process proceedings before the Internal Revenue Service's Office of Appeals; and suits against the United States for damages for the unauthorized disclosure of tax return information or for damages claimed because of alleged injuries caused by Internal Revenue Service employees in the performance of their official duties.

The Division also collects judgments in tax cases. To this end, the Division directs collection efforts and coordinates with, monitors the efforts of, and provides assistance to the various U.S. attorneys' offices in collecting outstanding judgments in tax cases. The Division also works with the Internal Revenue Service, U.S. attorneys, and other Government agencies on policy and legislative proposals to enhance tax administration and handling tax cases assigned to those offices. http://www.justice. gov/tax

For further information, contact the Office of the Assistant Attorney General, Tax Division, Department of Justice, Tenth Street and Pennsylvania Avenue NW., Washington, DC 20530. Phone, 202-514-2901.

Sources of Information

Americans with Disabilities The Civil Rights Division maintains an Americans with disabilities hotline. Phone, 800-514-0301. TDD, 800-514-0383. http://www.usdoj.gov/crt/ada/adahom1.htm

Business Opportunities / Grants For information on business opportunities, grants, and small and disadvantaged business utilization, visit the "Business and Grants" Web page. http://www.justice.gov/business

Career Opportunities For general information on career opportunities, visit the "Careers" Web page. http://www.justice.gov/careers

The "Legal Careers" Web page provides information that is of interest to experienced and entry-level attorneys and law students. http://www.justice.gov/legal-careers

Component Agencies A single Web page contains a convenient collection of links leading to the Web sites of the Department's

component agencies. https://www.justice. gov/agencies

Drugs / Crime The Bureau of Justice Statistics' Web page includes criminal justice statistics on drugs and crime. http://www.bjs.gov/index.cfm?ty=tp&tid=35

Forms The Department's Web site features a forms list that can be sorted by form number, form title, or agency. This list does not include Federal Bureau of Prisons forms because they are available on the Bureau's Web site. https://www.justice.gov/forms

Freedom of Information Act (FOIA) The Department manages the Web site FOIA.gov to make information on the FOIA accessible, interactive, and understandable. https://www.foia.gov/index.html

Instructions for properly submitting a FOIA request to the Department are available online. https://www.justice.gov/oip/make-foia-request-doj

History Historical information on the Attorneys General of the United States, the Department's motto and seal, and the art and architecture of the Robert F. Kennedy Department of Justice Building is available online. https://www.justice.gov/about/history

Housing Discrimination Contact the Civil Rights Division's housing and civil enforcement section. Phone, 800-896-7743. http://www.justice.gov/crt/housing-and-civil-enforcement-section

Immigration-Related Employment Matters The Civil Rights Division maintains a worker hotline. Phone, 800-255-7688. TDD, 800-237-2515. It also offers information for employers. Phone, 800-255-8155. TDD, 800-362-2735. http://www.justice.gov/crt/hotline-technical-assistance-referral-agencies

Open Government The Department supports the Open Government initiative by promoting the principles of collaboration, participation, and transparency. https://www.justice.gov/open

Plain Language The Department supports the Plain Writing Act of 2010. Online visitors who find a document lacking in clarity, should contact the Department via email and include the relevant page title and Uniform Resources Locator (URL). https://www.justice.gov/open/plain-writing-act | Email: DOJPlainWriting@usdoj.gov

Publications   Department of Justice reports and publications are accessible and arranged alphabetically online. https://www.justice.gov/publications/usdoj-resources-publications-alphabetical-list

Each year, the Department publishes the U.S. Attorney General's annual report and posts it online. http://www.justice.gov/ag/publications.htm

Textbooks on citizenship—teacher manuals and student textbooks at various reading levels—are distributed free to public schools for citizenship applicants. Others may purchase them from the Superintendent of Documents, Government Publishing Office, Washington, DC 20402. Public schools or organizations under the supervision of public schools that are entitled to free textbooks should make their requests to the appropriate Immigration and Naturalization Service regional office.

Reading Rooms   Reading rooms are located in Washington, DC, at the Department of Justice, Tenth Street and Constitution Avenue NW., and at the National Institute of Justice, 633 Indiana Avenue NW., and in Falls Church, VA, at the Board of Immigration Appeals, 5107 Leesburg Pike. Phone, 202-514-3775. http://www.justice.gov/contact-us

For further information, contact the Office of Public Affairs, Department of Justice, Tenth Street and Constitution Avenue NW., Washington, DC 20530. Phone, 202-514-2007. TDD, 202-786-5731.

BUREAUS
Bureau of Alcohol, Tobacco, Firearms and Explosives

99 New York Avenue NE., Washington, DC 20226
Phone, 202-648-8500. Internet, http://www.atf.gov.

Director	THOMAS E. BRANDON, ACTING
Associate Deputy Director/Chief Operating Officer	RONALD B. TURK

The Bureau of Alcohol, Tobacco, Firearms and Explosives (ATF) is responsible for enforcing Federal criminal laws and regulating the firearms and explosives industries. ATF, formerly known as the Bureau of Alcohol, Tobacco, and Firearms, was initially established by Department of Treasury Order No. 221, effective July 1, 1972, which transferred the functions, powers, and duties arising under laws relating to alcohol, tobacco, firearms, and explosives from the Internal Revenue Service to ATF. The Homeland Security Act of 2002 (6 U.S.C. 531) transferred certain functions and authorities of ATF to the Department of Justice and established it under its current name. Directly and through partnerships, ATF investigates and deters violent crime involving arson, firearms and explosives, and trafficking of alcohol and tobacco products. The Bureau provides training and support to its Federal, State, local, and international law enforcement partners and works primarily in 25 field divisions across the 50 States, Puerto Rico, the U.S. Virgin Islands, and Guam. It also has foreign offices in Canada, Colombia, France, and Mexico.

Sources of Information

Employment   Information on career opportunities is available online. https://www.atf.gov/careers

Publications   FOIA and regulations libraries and factsheets are accessible online. https://www.atf.gov/resource-center/publications-library. https://www.atf.gov/contact

For further information, contact the Office of Public Affairs, Bureau of Alcohol, Tobacco, Firearms and Explosives, Department of Justice, 99 New York Avenue NE., Suite 10W.121, Washington, DC 20530. Phone, 202-648-8500.

Bureau of Prisons

320 First Street NW., Washington, DC 20534
Phone, 202-307-3198. Internet, http://www.bop.gov.

Director	THOMAS R. KANE, ACTING
Deputy Director Federal Bureau Of Prisons	JUDI SIMON GARRETT, ACTING

The BOP was established in 1930 to provide more progressive and humane care for Federal inmates, to professionalize the prison service, and to ensure consistent and centralized administration of the 11 Federal prisons in operation at that time. Today, the Bureau comprises more than 100 institutions and 6 regional offices. The Bureau has its headquarters, also known as Central Office, in Washington, DC. The Central Office is divided into 10 divisions, including the National Institute of Corrections.

The Correctional Programs Division (CPD) is responsible for inmate classification and programming, including psychology and religious services, substance abuse treatment, case management, and programs for special needs offenders. CPD provides policy direction and daily operational oversight of institution security, emergency preparedness, intelligence gathering, inmate discipline, inmate sentence computations, receiving and discharge, and inmate transportation, as well as coordinating international treaty transfers and overseeing the special security needs of inmates placed in the Federal Witness Protection Program. CPD administers contracts and intergovernmental agreements for the confinement of offenders in community-based programs, community corrections centers, and other facilities, including privately managed facilities. CPD staff is also involved in the Bureau's privatization efforts.

The Industries, Education, and Vocational Training Division oversees Federal Prison Industries, or UNICOR, which is a wholly owned Government corporation that provides employment and training opportunities for inmates confined in Federal correctional facilities. Additionally, it is responsible for oversight of educational, occupational, and vocational training and leisure-time programs, as well as those related to inmate release preparation.

The National Institute of Corrections (NIC) provides technical assistance, training, and information to State and local corrections agencies throughout the country, as well as the Bureau. It also provides research assistance and documents through the NIC Information Center. https://www.bop.gov/about/agency

Sources of Information

Business Opportunities   Information is available on the "Let's Do Business" Web page. http://www.bop.gov/business

Career Opportunities   Job openings are posted online. For additional career-related information, contact any regional or field office or the Central Office, 320 First Street NW., Washington, DC 20534. Phone, 202-307-3082. http://www.bop.gov/jobs

Find an Inmate   The Department's Web site features a search tool for locating Federal inmates who were incarcerated after 1981. https://www.bop.gov/inmateloc

Locations   The "Our Locations" Web page features a list of locations, a search tool that requires the facility's name, and location maps (national, regional, type of facility). https://www.bop.gov/locations

Population Statistics   Federal inmate population statistics are online. https://www.bop.gov/about/statistics/population_statistics.jsp

Reading Room   The reading room is located at the Bureau of Prisons, 320 First Street NW., Washington, DC 20534. Phone, 202-307-3029.

Resources by Audience   Resources to help Bureau of Prisons staff and their families access frequently used services are online. https://www.bop.gov/resources/employee_resources.jsp

Resources to help former inmates make the transition from incarceration to normal life within a community are online. https://www.bop.gov/resources/former_inmate_resources.jsp

The Attorney General and the Secretary of Health and Human Services provide health management guidelines for infectious disease prevention, detection, and treatment of inmates and correctional employees who are exposed to infectious diseases in correctional facilities. https://www.bop.gov/resources/health_care_mngmt.jsp

Resources to help qualified media representatives visit institutions and gather information on programs and activities or conduct interviews are online. https://www.bop.gov/resources/media_resources.jsp

Resources to help victims or witnesses of Federal crimes find information on complaint procedures, notifications, and payments are online. https://www.bop.gov/resources/victim_resources.jsp. http://www.bop.gov/contact

For further information, contact the Public Information Office, Bureau of Prisons, 320 First Street NW., Washington, DC 20534. Phone, 202-514-6551.

Drug Enforcement Administration

8701 Morrissette Drive, Springfield, VA 22152
Phone, 202-307-1000. Internet, http://www.dea.gov/index.shtml.

Administrator	CHARLES ROSENBERG, ACTING

The Drug Enforcement Administration (DEA) is the lead Federal agency in enforcing narcotics and controlled substances laws and regulations. The DEA also enforces the Federal money laundering and bulk currency smuggling statutes when the funds involved in the transactions or smuggling are derived from the sale of narcotics. It was created in July 1973 by Reorganization Plan No. 2 of 1973 (5 U.S.C. app.).

The DEA enforces the provisions of the controlled substances and chemical diversion and trafficking laws and regulations of the United States, operating on a worldwide basis. It presents cases to the criminal and civil justice systems of the United States—or any other competent jurisdiction—on those significant organizations and their members involved in cultivation, production, smuggling, distribution, laundering of proceeds, or diversion of controlled substances appearing in or destined for illegal traffic in the United States. The DEA disrupts and dismantles these organizations by arresting their members, confiscating their drugs, and seizing their assets; and it creates, manages, and supports enforcement-related programs—domestically and internationally—to reduce the availability of and demand for illicit controlled substances.

The DEA's responsibilities include: investigation of major narcotic, chemical, drug-money laundering, and bulk currency smuggling violators who operate at interstate and international levels; seizure and forfeiture of assets derived from, traceable to, or intended to be used for illicit drug trafficking; seizure and forfeiture of assets derived from or traceable to drug-money laundering or the smuggling of bulk currency derived from illegal drugs; enforcement of regulations governing the legal manufacture, distribution, and dispensing of controlled substances; management of an intelligence program that supports drug investigations, initiatives, and operations worldwide; coordination with Federal, State, and local law enforcement authorities and cooperation with counterpart agencies abroad; assistance to State and local law enforcement agencies in addressing their most significant drug and drug-related violence problems; leadership and influence over international counterdrug and chemical policy and support for institution building in host nations; training, scientific research, and information exchange in support of drug traffic prevention and control; and education and assistance to the public community on the prevention, treatment, and dangers of drugs.

The DEA maintains liaison with the United Nations, INTERPOL, and other organizations on matters relating to international narcotics control programs. It has 222 offices in 21 divisions throughout the United States and 86 foreign offices located in 67 countries.

Sources of Information

Controlled Substances Act Registration For information on registration under the Controlled Substances Act, contact the Office of Diversion Control, 8701 Morrissette Drive, Springfield, VA 22152. Phone: 800-882-9539. http://www. deadiversion.usdoj.gov/drugreg/index.html | Email: DEA.Registration.Help@usdoj.gov
Employment For career information, contact the nearest DEA field division recruitment office. To learn about searching for job vacancies online and applying, visit the "How To Apply" Web page. http://www. dea.gov/careers/how-to-apply.shtml
Publications A limited selection of pamphlets and brochures is available. The most frequently requested publication is "Drugs of Abuse," an identification manual intended for professional use. Single copies are free. http://www.dea.gov/docs/drugs_ of_abuse_2011.pdf. http://www.dea.gov/ contact.shtml

For further information, contact the Public Affairs Section, Drug Enforcement Administration, 8701 Morrissette Drive Springfield, VA 22152. Phone, 202-307-7977.

Federal Bureau of Investigation

935 Pennsylvania Avenue NW., Washington, DC 20535
Phone, 202-324-3000. Internet, http://www.fbi.gov.

Director	CHRISTOPHER WRAY

The Federal Bureau of Investigation (FBI) is the Department of Justice's principal investigative arm. It is primarily charged with gathering and reporting facts, locating witnesses, and compiling evidence in cases involving Federal jurisdiction. It also provides law enforcement leadership and assistance to State and international law enforcement agencies.

The FBI was established in 1908 by the Attorney General, who directed that Department of Justice investigations be handled by its own staff. The Bureau is charged with investigating all violations of Federal law except those that have been assigned by legislative enactment or otherwise to another Federal agency. Its jurisdiction includes a wide range of responsibilities in the national security, criminal, and civil fields. Priority has been assigned to areas such as counterterrorism, counterintelligence, cybercrimes, internationally and nationally organized crime and drug-related activities, and financial crimes.

The FBI also offers cooperative services to local, State, and international law enforcement agencies. These services include fingerprint identification, laboratory examination, police training, the Law Enforcement Online communication and information service for use by the law enforcement community, the National Crime Information Center, and the National Center for the Analysis of Violent Crime.

Sources of Information

Employment The FBI relies on professionals with diverse expertise and skills to analyze data for the intelligence community, safeguard national security, and support the structure of the Bureau. Information on career opportunities, including student internships, is available online. https://www.fbijobs.gov
Publications The "FBI Law Enforcement Bulletin," reports, and other publications are available online. https://leb.fbi.gov. https:// www.fbi.gov/stats-services/publications. https://www.fbi.gov/contact-us

For further information, contact the Office of Public Affairs, Federal Bureau of Investigation, J. Edgar Hoover FBI Building, 935 Pennsylvania Avenue NW., Washington, DC 20535. Phone, 202-317-2727.

International Criminal Police Organization (INTERPOL)–Washington

Department of Justice, Washington, DC 20530
Phone, 202-616-9000. Fax, 202-616-8400. Internet, http://www.justice.gov/interpol-washington.

Director	WAYNE SALZGABER, ACTING

INTERPOL–Washington is a separate component under the supervision of the Deputy Attorney General and comanaged with the Department of Homeland Security. It provides an essential communications link between the U.S. police community and their counterparts in the foreign member countries.

INTERPOL is an association of 190 countries that promotes mutual assistance among law enforcement authorities to prevent and suppress international crime. With no police force of its own, INTERPOL has no powers of arrest or search and seizure and, therefore, relies on the law enforcement authorities of its member countries. Each member country is required to have a national central bureau, such as INTERPOL–Washington, to act as the primary point of contact for police affairs. INTERPOL serves as a channel of communication for its member countries to cooperate in the investigation and prosecution of crime; provides a forum for discussions, working group meetings, and symposia to help police focus on specific areas of criminal activity affecting their countries; and issues information and maintains databases—supplied and used by member countries—on crime, fugitives, humanitarian concerns, missing persons, and stolen passports and vehicles.

INTERPOL–Washington has permanent staff and detailed special agents from numerous Federal law enforcement agencies. It is organized into seven divisions: the Alien and Fugitive, Counterterrorism, Drug, Economic Crimes, Human Trafficking and Child Protection, State and Local Police Liaison, and Violent Crimes Divisions.

Sources of Information

Employment   Information on career opportunities is available online. http://www.justice.gov/interpol-washington/employment. http://www.justice.gov/interpol-washington

For further information, contact the INTERPOL–Washington, Department of Justice, Washington, DC 20530. Phone, 202-616-9000.

Office of Justice Programs

810 Seventh Street NW., Washington, DC 20531
Phone, 202-307-0703. Internet, http://www.ojp.gov | Email: askojp@ojp.usdoj.gov.

Assistant Attorney General	ANDREW C. FINCH, ACTING

The Office of Justice Programs (OJP) was established by the Justice Assistance Act of 1984 (42 U.S.C. 3711) and reauthorized in 1994 and 2005 to provide Federal leadership, coordination, and assistance needed to make the Nation's justice system more efficient and effective in preventing and controlling crime. OJP is responsible for collecting statistical data and conducting analyses; identifying emerging criminal justice issues; developing and testing promising approaches to address these issues; evaluating program results; and disseminating these findings and other information to State and local governments.

The OJP is comprised of the following bureaus and offices: the Bureau of Justice Assistance provides funding, training, and technical assistance to State and local governments to combat violent and drug-related crime and help improve the criminal justice system; the Bureau of Justice Statistics is responsible for collecting and analyzing data on crime, criminal offenders, crime victims, and the operations of justice systems at all levels of government; the National Institute of Justice sponsors research and development programs, conducts demonstrations of innovative approaches to improve criminal justice, and develops new criminal justice technologies; the Office of Juvenile Justice and Delinquency Prevention provides grants and contracts to States to help them improve their juvenile justice systems and sponsors innovative research, demonstration, evaluation, statistics, replication, technical assistance, and training programs to increase the Nation's understanding of and improve its response to juvenile violence and delinquency; the Office for Victims of Crime administers victim compensation and assistance grant programs and provides funding, training, and technical assistance to victim service organizations, criminal justice agencies, and other professionals to improve the Nation's response to crime victims; and the Office of Sex Offender Sentencing, Monitoring, Apprehending, Registering, and Tracking (SMART) maintains the standards of the Sex Offender Registration and Notification Act as defined by the Adam Walsh Act. The SMART Office also provides technical assistance and supports innovative and best practices in the field of sex offender management.

Sources of Information

Employment   For employment information, contact the Human Resources Division, 810 Seventh Street NW., Washington, DC 20531. Phone, 202-307-0730. http://www.ojp.usdoj.gov/about/jobs.htm. http://ojp.gov/home/contactus.htm | Email: askojp@ojp.usdoj.gov

For further information, contact the Department of Justice Response Center. Phone, 800-421-6770.

United States Marshals Service

Department of Justice, Washington, DC 20530
Phone, 703-740-1699. Internet, http://www.usmarshals.gov.

Director	DAVID HARLOW, ACTING
Deputy Director	DAVID HARLOW

The United States Marshals Service is the Nation's oldest Federal law enforcement agency, having served as a vital link between the executive and judicial branches of the Government since 1789. The Marshals Service performs tasks that are essential to the operation of virtually every aspect of the Federal justice system.

The Marshals Service has these responsibilities: providing support and protection for the Federal courts, including security for 800 judicial facilities and nearly 2,000 judges and magistrates, as well as countless other trial participants such as jurors and attorneys; apprehending the majority of Federal fugitives; operating the Federal Witness Security Program and ensuring the safety of endangered Government witnesses; maintaining custody of and transporting thousands of Federal prisoners annually; executing court orders and arrest warrants; managing and selling seized property forfeited to the Government by drug traffickers and other criminals and assisting the Justice Department's asset forfeiture program; responding to emergency circumstances, including civil disturbances, terrorist incidents, and other crisis situations through its Special Operations Group; restoring order in riot and mob-violence situations; providing housing, transportation, and medical care of federal detainees; and operating the U.S. Marshals Service Training Academy.

Sources of Information

Business Opportunities The Marshals Service posts online products and services that it purchases. https://www.usmarshals. gov/business/products.html

Employment The Marshals Service hires administrative staff, aviation and detention enforcement officers, Deputy U.S. Marshals, and other types of professionals. Information on Deputy U.S. Marshal hiring programs is available online. https://www.usmarshals. gov/careers/index.html. http://www. usmarshals.gov/contacts/index.html

For further information, contact the Office of Public Affairs, U.S. Marshals Service, Department of Justice, Washington, DC 20530. Phone, 703-740-1699.

Offices and Boards
Executive Office for Immigration Review

Falls Church, VA 22041
Phone, 703-305-0289. Internet, http://www.usdoj.gov/eoir.

Director	JAMES MCHENRY, ACTING

The Executive Office for Immigration Review (EOIR), under a delegation of authority from the Attorney General, is charged with adjudicating matters brought under various immigration statutes before its three administrative tribunals: the Office of the Chief Immigration Judge, the Board of Immigration Appeals, and the Office of the Chief Administrative Hearing Officer.

The Office of the Chief Immigration Judge provides overall direction for more than 300 immigration judges located in 58 immigration courts throughout the Nation. Immigration judges are responsible for conducting formal administrative proceedings and act independently in their decision-making capacity. Their decisions are administratively final, unless appealed or certified to the BIA.

In removal proceedings, an immigration judge determines whether an alien should be removed or allowed to remain in the United States. Judges are located throughout the United States, and each judge has jurisdiction to consider various forms of relief available under the law.

The Board of Immigration Appeals (BIA) has nationwide jurisdiction to hear appeals from certain decisions made by immigration judges and by district directors of the Department of Homeland Security (DHS). In addition, the BIA is responsible for hearing appeals involving disciplinary actions against attorneys and representatives before DHS and EOIR.

Decisions of the BIA are binding on all DHS officers and immigration judges unless modified or overruled by the Attorney General or a Federal court. All BIA decisions are subject to judicial review in Federal court. The majority of appeals reaching the BIA involve orders of removal and applications for relief from removal. Other cases before the BIA include petitions to classify the status of alien relatives for the issuance of preference immigrant visas, fines imposed upon carriers for the violation of the immigration laws, and motions for reopening or reconsideration of decisions previously rendered.

The Office of the Chief Administrative Hearing Officer (OCAHO) is headed by a Chief Administrative Hearing Officer (CAHO), who is responsible for the general supervision and management of administrative law judges (ALJs). OCAHO ALJs preside at hearings that are mandated by provisions of immigration law concerning allegations of unlawful employment of aliens, employment eligibility verification violations ("employer sanctions), unfair immigration-related employment practices, and immigration document fraud. ALJ decisions in employer sanctions and document fraud cases may be reviewed by the CAHO and the Attorney General, and all OCAHO cases may be appealed to the appropriate U.S. Circuit Court of Appeals.

Sources of Information

Library   A virtual law library that serves as a complement to the Law Library and Immigration Research Center is available online. http://www.justice.gov/eoir/virtual-law-library

Statistics and Publications   Agency decisions and plans, instructions and manuals, meeting notes, and reports and updates are available on the "Statistics and Publications" Web page. http://www.justice. gov/eoir/statistics-and-publications#Top

For further information, contact the Office of Communications and Legislative and Public Affairs, Executive Office for Immigration Review, Department of Justice, 5107 Leesburg Pike, Suite 1902, Falls Church, VA 22041. Phone, 703-305-0289. Fax, 703-605-0365.

Foreign Claims Settlement Commission of the United States

Suite 6002, 600 E Street NW., Washington, DC 20579
Phone, 202-616-6975. Fax, 202-616-6993. Internet, http://www.justice.gov/fcsc.

Commissioners	Anuj C. Desai,
	Sylvia M. Becker

The Foreign Claims Settlement Commission of the United States is a quasi-judicial, independent agency within the Department of Justice, which adjudicates claims of U.S. nationals against foreign governments, either under specific jurisdiction conferred by Congress or the Department of State or pursuant to international claims settlement agreements. The decisions of the Commission are final and are not reviewable under any standard by any court or other authority. Funds for payment of the Commission's awards are derived from congressional appropriations, international claims settlements, or the liquidation of foreign assets in the United States by the Departments of Justice and the Treasury.

The Commission also has authority to receive, determine the validity and amount, and provide for the payment of claims by members of the U.S. Armed Services and civilians held as prisoners of war or interned by a hostile force in Southeast Asia during the Vietnam conflict or by the survivors of such servicemembers and civilians.

The Commission is also responsible for maintaining records and responding to inquiries related to the various claims programs it has conducted against the Governments of Albania, Bulgaria, China, Cuba, Czechoslovakia, Egypt, Ethiopia, the Federal Republic of Germany, the German Democratic Republic, Hungary, Iran, Italy, Panama, Poland, Romania, the Soviet Union, Vietnam, and Yugoslavia, as well as those authorized under the War Claims Act of 1948 and other statutes.

Sources of Information

Employment   General information on career opportunities is available on the Department of Justice's "Careers" Web page. For additional information on attorney positions, contact the Office of the Chief Counsel, 600 E Street NW., Suite 6002, Washington, DC 20579. Phone, 202-616-6975. http://www.justice.gov/careers

Publications   Annual reports, starting with the year 2008, are available on the "Publications" Web page. http://www.justice.gov/fcsc/publications

Reading Room   The reading room is located at 600 E Street NW., Washington, DC 20579. Phone, 202-616-6975. http://www.justice.gov/fcsc/contact-commission

For further information, contact the Office of the Chairman, Foreign Claims Settlement Commission of the United States, Department of Justice, Suite 6002, 600 E Street NW., Washington, DC 20579. Phone, 202-616-6975. Fax, 202-616-6993.

Office of Community Oriented Policing Services

935 N. Street NE., Washington, DC 20530
Phone, 202-514-2058. Internet, http://www.cops.usdoj.gov.

Director	RONALD L. DAVIS

The Office of Community Oriented Policing Services (COPS) was established to assist law enforcement agencies in enhancing public safety through the implementation of community policing strategies. The Office gives assistance by providing training to enhance law enforcement officers' problem-solving and community interaction skills and helping law enforcement and community members develop initiatives to prevent crime; increasing the number of law enforcement officers directly interacting with communities; and supporting the development of new technologies to shift law enforcement's focus to preventing crime and disorder within communities.

Sources of Information

Employment   To sign up to receive email updates on COPS employment opportunities, visit the "Careers" Web page. http://www.cops.usdoj.gov/careers
Grants and Funding   COPS grants and funding opportunities support State, local, and tribal law enforcement efforts to advance community policing. Current applicant and grantee information— announcements, fiscal year grant programs, current funding opportunities, and resources for grantees—is available online. http://www.cops.usdoj.gov/grants. http://www.cops.usdoj.gov/contact

For further information, contact the Office of Community Oriented Policing Services (COPS), Department of Justice, 935 N Street NE., Washington, DC 20530. Phone, 202-514-2058.

Office on Violence Against Women

145 N Street NE., Suite 10W–121, Washington, DC 20530
Phone: 202-307-6026. Internet, http://www.justice.gov/ovw.

Director	NADINE M. NEUFVILLE, ACTING

The Office on Violence Against Women (OVW) was established in 1995 to reduce violence against women through the implementation of the Violence Against Women Act. The Office administers financial and technical assistance to communities that are developing programs, policies, and practices to end domestic and dating violence, sexual assault, and stalking.

Sources of Information

Employment   Information on employment and internship opportunities is available online. http://www.justice.gov/ovw/careers
Publications   Portable Document Format (PDF) files of selected publications are available online. http://www.justice.gov/ovw/selected-publications. http://www.justice.gov/ovw/contact-office | Email: ovw.info@usdoj.gov

For further information, contact the Office on Violence Against Women, 145 N Street NE., Suite 10W–121, Washington, DC, 20530. Phone, 202-307-6026.

United States Parole Commission

90 K Street NE., Washington, DC 20530
Phone, 202-346-7000. Internet, http://www.usdoj.gov/uspc.

Chair	J. Patricia Wilson Smoot

The U.S. Parole Commission (USPC) makes parole release decisions for eligible Federal and District of Columbia prisoners; authorizes methods of release and conditions under which release occurs; prescribes, modifies, and monitors compliance with the terms and conditions governing offenders' behavior while on parole or mandatory or supervised release; issues warrants for violation of supervision; determines probable cause for the revocation process; revokes parole, mandatory, or supervised release; releases from supervision those offenders who are no longer a risk to public safety; and promulgates the rules, regulations, and guidelines for the exercise of USPC's authority and the implementation of a national parole policy.

USPC has sole jurisdiction over the following: Federal offenders who committed offenses before November 1, 1987; DC Code offenders who committed offenses before August 5, 2000; DC Code offenders sentenced to a term of supervised release; Uniform Code of Military Justice offenders who are in Bureau of Prison's custody; transfer treaty cases; and State probationers and parolees in the Federal Witness Protection Program.

Sources of Information

Freedom of Information Act (FOIA)   The Commission maintains an online FOIA library. Information on Freedom of Information Act requests is available online. http://www.justice.gov/uspc/freedom-information-act-foia/foia-library. http://www.justice.gov/uspc/freedom-information-act-foia | Email: USPC.FOIA@usdoj.gov
Reading Room   The reading room is located at 90 K Street NE., Washington, DC 20530. Phone, 202-346-7000. http://www.justice.gov/uspc/contact-commission

For further information, contact the U.S. Parole Commission, Department of Justice, 90 K Street NE., Washington, DC 20530. Phone, 202-346-7000.

DEPARTMENT OF LABOR

200 Constitution Avenue NW., Washington, DC 20210
Phone, 202-693-6000. Internet, http://www.dol.gov.

Secretary of Labor	R. ALEXANDER ACOSTA
Deputy Secretary	VACANT
Chief Economist	VACANT
Chief of Staff	WAYNE PALMER
Executive Secretariat Director	ELIZABETH WAY, ACTING

Agencies

Administrator, Wage and Hour Division	VACANT
Chief Administrative Law Judge	STEPHEN R. HENLEY
Chief Financial Officer	GEOFFREY KENYON, ACTING
Commissioner, Bureau of Labor Statistics	WILLIAM WIATROWSKI, ACTING
Deputy Undersecretary, Bureau of International Labor Affairs	MARK MITTELHAUSER, ACTING
Inspector General	SCOTT S. DAHL
Ombudsman, Energy Employee Occupational Illness Compensation Program	MALCOLM NELSON
Solicitor of Labor	NICHOLAS GEALE, ACTING

Assistant Secretaries

Employee Benefits Security Administration	TIMOTHY HAUSER, ACTING
Employment and Training Administration	BYRON ZUIDEMA, ACTING
Mine Safety and Health Administration	PATRICIA SILVEY, ACTING
Occupational Safety and Health Administration	THOMAS GALASSI, ACTING
Office of Congressional and Intergovernmental Affairs	VACANT
Office of Disability Employment Policy	JENNIFER SHEEHY, ACTING
Office of Public Affairs	VACANT
Office of the Assistant Secretary, Administration and Management	EDWARD C. HUGLER, ACTING
Office of the Assistant Secretary, Policy	VACANT
Veterans' Employment and Training Services	SAM SHELLENBERGER, ACTING

Chief Judges / Chairs

Administrative Review Board	PAUL M. IGASAKI
Benefits Review Board	BETTY JEAN HALL
Employees' Compensation Appeals Board	CHRISTOPHER GODFREY

Directors

Center for Faith-Based and Neighborhood Partnerships	VACANT
Office of Workers' Compensation Programs	GARY STEINBERG, ACTING
Office of Federal Contract Compliance Programs	THOMAS DOWD, ACTING
Office of Labor-Management Standards	ANDREW AUERBACH, ACTING
Office of Public Engagement	VACANT
Women's Bureau	JOAN HARRIGAN-FARRELLY, ACTING

The Department of Labor promotes the welfare of job seekers, wage earners, and retirees by improving working conditions, advancing opportunities for profitable employment, protecting retirement and health care benefits, matching workers to employers, strengthening free collective bargaining, and tracking changes in economic indicators on a national scale.

258

DEPARTMENT OF LABOR

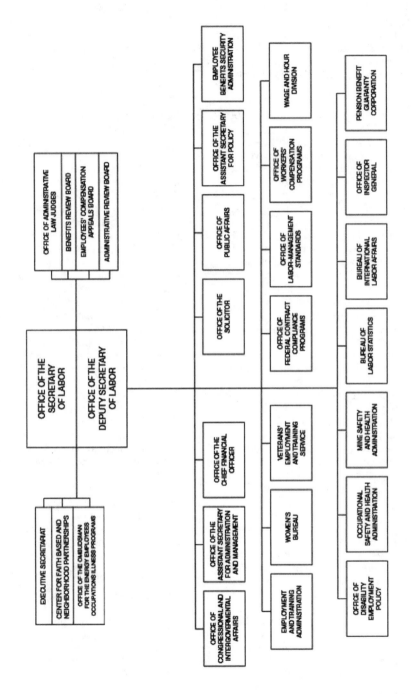

The Department of Labor (DOL) was created by act of March 4, 1913 (29 U.S.C. 551). Congress first created a Bureau of Labor in the Interior Department by act of June 24, 1884. The Bureau of Labor later became independent as a Department of Labor without executive rank by act of June 13, 1888. It returned to bureau status in the Department of Commerce and Labor, which was created by act of February 14, 1903 (15 U.S.C. 1501; 29 U.S.C. 1 note).

The Department administers a variety of Federal labor laws to guarantee workers' rights to fair, safe, and healthy working conditions, including minimum hourly wage and overtime pay, protection against employment discrimination, and unemployment insurance.

Secretary   The Secretary is the principal adviser to the President on the development and execution of policies and the administration and enforcement of laws relating to wage earners, their working conditions, and their employment opportunities. http://www.dol.gov/_sec

Administrative Law   Administrative law judges from the Office of Administrative Law Judges preside over formal adversarial hearings involving labor-related matters: the Longshore and Harbor Workers' Compensation, the Defense Base, the Black Lung Benefits, the McNamara O'Hara Service Contract, and the Davis Bacon Act; environmental, transportation, and securities whistleblower protection laws; permanent and temporary immigration; child labor law violations; employment discrimination; training; seasonal and migrant workers; and Federal construction and service contracts. The Office is comprised of headquarters in Washington, D.C. and seven district offices. Its judges are nonpolitical appointees: They are appointed under and guaranteed decisional independence by the Administrative Procedure Act. The Administrative Review Board or Benefits Review Board typically reviews appeals of the decisions made by the Office's judges. Depending upon the statute at issue, appeals then go to Federal district or appellate courts and, ultimately, may go to the U.S. Supreme Court. http://www.oalj.dol.gov

For further information, call 202-693-7300.

Administration and Management   The Office of the Assistant Secretary for Administration and Management is responsible for the development and promulgation of policies, standards, procedures, systems, and materials related to the resource and administrative management of the Department and for the execution of such policies and directives at Headquarters and in the field. http://www.dol.gov/oasam

For more information, call 202-693-4040.

Audits / Investigations   The Office of Inspector General (OIG) conducts audits to review the economy, effectiveness, efficiency, and integrity of all DOL programs and operations, including those performed by its contractors and grantees. The Inspector General works to answer the following types of questions: Do Department programs and operations comply with the applicable laws and regulations; are departmental resources being utilized efficiently and economically; and are DOL programs achieving their intended results? The Office also conducts administrative, civil, and criminal investigations relating to violations of Federal laws, regulations, or rules—including violations committed by DOL contractors and grantees—as well as investigations of allegations of misconduct on the part of DOL employees. In addition, the OIG has an "external" program function to conduct criminal investigations to combat the influence of labor racketeering and organized crime in the nation's labor unions. The OIG conducts labor racketeering investigations in three areas: employee benefit plans, labor-management relations, and internal union affairs. The OIG also works with other law enforcement partners on human trafficking matters. http://www.oig.dol.gov

For further information, call 202-693-5100.

Communications / Public Affairs   The Office of Public Affairs (OPA) directs and coordinates all public and employee communications activities. The Assistant Secretary of the Office acts as the chief adviser to the Secretary of Labor and his or her Deputy Secretary and to the agency heads and departmental staff for developing and implementing strategies that engage and connect with the public and educate it about the work and mission of the Department.

The Assistant Secretary also acts as the Secretary's chief adviser on crisis communications. The OPA serves as the first point of contact for news media inquiries, as the clearance and dissemination point for DOL public-facing materials, and it develops and maintains the Department's Web-based, audiovisual, and contact center communications. The OPA also administers "lock ups" when sensitive economic data are released to the press under an embargo. https://www.dol.gov/general/contact/media-contact

For further information, call 202-693-4676.

Disability Employment Policy The Office of Disability Employment Policy (ODEP) is the only non-regulatory federal agency that promotes policies and coordinates with employers and all levels of government to increase workplace success for people with disabilities. ODEP helps employers foster inclusive workplaces where all employees can contribute and succeed, and works to improve government workforce systems so people with disabilities can secure good jobs and excel in the workplace. http://www.dol.gov/odep

For further information, call 202-693-7880. TTY, 202-693-7881.

Energy Employees Occupational Illness Compensation The Office of the Ombudsman for the Energy Employees Occupational Illness Compensation Program was established in 2004 under Part E of the Energy Employees Occupational Illness Compensation Program Act (EEOICPA), as amended (42 U.S.C. 7385s-15). The EEOICPA is a system of Federal payments to compensate certain nuclear workers for occupational illnesses caused by exposure to toxic substances. This small and independent Office is headed by the Ombudsman, whom the Secretary of Labor appoints. It provides information to claimants on the benefits available under Parts B and E of the EEOICPA and issues annual reports to Congress detailing the complaints, grievances, and requests for assistance that the Office receives. http://www.dol.gov/eeombd

For further information, call 202-693-5890.

Federal Contract Compliance The Office of Federal Contract Compliance Programs administers and enforces three equal employment opportunity laws: Executive Order 11246, Section 503 of the Rehabilitation Act of 1973, and the Vietnam Era Veterans' Readjustment Assistance Act of 1974. As amended, these laws prohibit Federal contractors and subcontractors from discriminating based on race, color, religion, sex, sexual orientation, gender identity, national origin, disability, or status as a protected veteran. Executive Order 11246 prohibits Federal contractors and subcontractors, with limited exceptions, from taking adverse employment actions against applicants and employees for asking about, discussing, or sharing information on their pay or the pay of their coworkers. These laws also require Federal contractors and subcontractors to take affirmative action to ensure equal employment opportunity. http://www.dol.gov/ofccp | Email: OFCCP-Public@dol.gov

For further information, call 800-397-6251.

Labor-Management Standards The Office of Labor-Management Standards (OLMS) administers and enforces most provisions of the Labor-Management Reporting and Disclosure Act of 1959 (LMRDA). The LMRDA primarily promotes union democracy and financial integrity in private sector labor unions through standards for union officer elections and union trusteeships and safeguards for union assets. Additionally, the LMRDA promotes labor union and labor-management transparency through reporting and disclosure requirements for labor unions and their officials, employers, labor relations consultants, and surety companies.

OLMS also administers provisions of the Civil Service Reform Act of 1978 and the Foreign Service Act of 1980, which extend comparable protections to Federal labor unions. OLMS does not have jurisdiction over unions representing solely state, county, or municipal employees. In addition, the Division of Statutory Programs (DSP) administers DOL responsibilities under the Federal Transit Act by ensuring that fair and equitable arrangements protecting mass transit employees are in place before the release of Federal transit grant funds. http://www.dol.gov/olms

For further information, call 202-693-0123.

Legal Services   The Office of the Solicitor of Labor (SOL) provides comprehensive legal services to help the Department achieve its mission. More specifically, the Solicitor serves dual roles in the Department. The Solicitor is the Department's chief enforcement officer, pursuing affirmative litigation on behalf of the Secretary before administrative law judges, review boards and commissions, and in the Federal district courts and courts of appeals. The Solicitor is also the Department's general counsel, assisting in the development of regulations, standards, and legislative proposals; providing legal opinions and advice on all of the Department's activities; advising the Solicitor General on Supreme Court litigation; and coordinating with the Department of Justice, as appropriate, to defend the Department in litigation. http://www.dol.gov/sol

For further information, call 202-693-5260.

Policy and Rulemaking   The Office of the Assistant Secretary for Policy advises and assists the Secretary, Deputy Secretary, and Department on policy development, policy evaluation, regulation, and legislation that improve the lives of workers, retirees, and their families. The Office also serves as the DOL's regulatory policy officer and regulatory reform officer to ensure that the Department complies with the regulatory and guidance development requirements of Executive Order 12866, as amended, Executive Order 13777, and any other related Office of Management and Budget circular or bulletin. The Office leads special initiatives and manages department-wide and interdepartmental activities. In its capacity as the DOL's policy innovation arm, it invests in research and analysis of current and emerging labor issues. https://www.dol.gov/asp

For further information, call 202-693-5959.

Workers' Compensation   The Office of Workers' Compensation Programs (OWCP) protects workers who are injured or become ill on the job by making decisions on claims, paying benefits, and helping workers return to their jobs. OWCP administers eight major disability compensation statutes: the Federal Employees' Compensation Act; the Longshore and Harbor Workers' Compensation Act; the Defense Base Act (DBA); the Nonappropriated Fund Instrumentalities Act; the Outer Continental Shelf Lands Act; the War Hazards Compensation Act; the Black Lung Benefits Act; and the Energy Employees Occupational Illness Compensation Act. OWCP serves specific employee groups that are covered under the relevant statutes and regulations by mitigating the financial burden resulting from workplace injury or illness and promoting return to work when appropriate. Dependents or survivors may also be eligible for benefits. http://www.dol.gov/owcp

For further information, call 202-343-5580.

Boards

Administrative Review   The Administrative Review Board (ARB) consists of five members appointed by the Secretary. It issues final agency decisions for appeals cases under a wide range of worker protection laws, including the Service Contract Act (SCA) and the Davis Bacon Act (DBA). The appeals cases primarily address environmental, transportation, and securities whistleblower protection; H-1B immigration provisions; child labor law violations; employment discrimination; job training; seasonal and migrant workers. The Board's cases generally arise upon appeal from decisions of Department of Labor Administrative Law Judges (OALJ) or the Administrator of the Department's Wage and Hour Division (WHD). Depending upon the statute at issue, the parties may appeal the Board's decisions to Federal district or appellate courts and, ultimately, to the U.S. Supreme Court. http://www.dol.gov/arb/welcome.html

For further information, call 202-693-6234.

Benefits Review   The Benefits Review Board (BRB) consists of five members appointed by the Secretary. In 1972, Congress created the Board to review and issue decisions on appeals of workers'

compensation cases arising under the Longshore and Harbor Workers' Compensation Act, and its extensions, and the Black Lung Benefits amendments to the Federal Coal Mine Safety Act of 1969. Board decisions may be appealed to the U.S. Courts of Appeals and to the U.S. Supreme Court. http://www.dol.gov/brb/welcome. html

For further information, call 202-693-6234.

Employees' Compensation Appeals   The Employees' Compensation Appeals Board (ECAB) is a five-member quasi-judicial body appointed by the Secretary and delegated exclusive jurisdiction by Congress to hear and make final decisions on appeals filed by Federal workers arising under the Federal Employees' Compensation Act (FECA). The Board was created by Reorganization Plan No. 2 of 1946 (60 Stat. 1095). The Board's decisions are not reviewable and are binding upon the Office of Workers' Compensation Programs (OWCP). http://www.dol.gov/ecab/welcome.html

For further information, call 202-693-6234.

Sources of Information

Agencies / Programs   The DOL carries out its mission through a number of offices and agencies, which are organized into major program areas. An Assistant Secretary, Director, or other official oversees each of these offices and agencies. https://www.dol.gov/agencies. https://www.dol.gov/general/dol-agencies

A–Z Index   The DOL Web site features an alphabetical index to help visitors search for information or browse topics of interest. https://www.dol.gov/general/siteindex

Business Opportunities   The Office of Procurement Services is the primary procurement office for the DOL national office. It carries out most contracting, grants, and related activities. The Office procures a variety of goods and services on a recurring basis: auditors, expert witnesses, moving services, printing and graphics, support services, technical studies, and video productions. It also acts as the central procurement center for the Department's information technology needs. Phone, 202-

693-4570. http://www.dol.gov/oasam/boc/ops/index.htm

The Office of Small and Disadvantaged Business Utilization administers the DOL's small business program in accordance with the Small Business Act. It seeks to ensure a fair share of procurement opportunities for small businesses, as well as for Historically Underutilized Business Zone (HUBZone) certified, service-disabled veteran-owned, small disadvantaged, and woman-owned small businesses. Phone, 202-603-7299. https://www.dol.gov/oasam/boc/osdbu/index.htm

Employment   Detailed information on job opportunities with the DOL—including the addresses and telephone numbers of personnel offices in the regions and in Washington, DC—is available online. http://www.dol.gov/dol/jobs.htm

Find It!   The "Find It" Web page allows Internet visitors to look for information by audience or by topic. It also contains the following internal links: A–Z index, DOL agencies, DOL forms, DOL services by location, and top 20 requested items. https://www.dol.gov/general/findit

Freedom of Information Act (FOIA)   The FOIA provides that anyone can request access to Federal agency records or information. The DOL must disclose records that are properly requested in writing by any person. Pursuant, however, to one or more of nine exemptions and three exclusions contained in the law, a Federal agency may withhold information. The FOIA applies only to Federal agencies and does not create a right of access to records held by Congress, the courts, State or local government agencies, and private entities. https://www.dol.gov/general/foia

Frequently Asked Questions (FAQs)   Answers to many FAQs are posted on the DOL's Web site. http://webapps.dol.gov/dolfaq/dolfaq.asp

History   A historical timeline is available on the DOL's Web site. https://www.dol.gov/general/aboutdol/history

The history of the DOL in narrative form is available on its Web site. https://www.dol.gov/general/aboutdol/history/webannalspage

Library   The Wirtz Labor Library maintains an online card catalog of holdings added to the library after January of 1975. The online catalog also includes collections of historical significance: for example, the Folio and James Taylor Collections. The library is open to the public from 8:15 a.m. to 4:45 p.m. on weekdays, excluding Federal holidays. If the purpose of a visit is to access research material, contact the library in advance: Wirtz Labor Library, 200 Constitution Avenue NW., Frances Perkins Building, Room N–2445, Washington, DC 20210. Phone, 202-693-6600. http://www.dol.gov/oasam/wirtzlaborlibrary | Email: m-Library@dol.gov

Minimum Wage   The DOL Web site features a list of DOL Web pages that deal with the topic of minimum wage. The Wage and Hour Division administers and enforces the federal minimum wage law. https://www.dol.gov/general/topic/wages/minimumwage

Newsroom   The newsroom features the DOL newsletter, news releases, and press resources, including national media contact information. Phone, 202-693-4676. https://www.dol.gov/newsroom

Office of Inspector General (OIG)   To file a complaint of abuse, fraud, or waste, use the online complaint form, call the OIG Hotline, or write to the Office of Inspector General, Department of Labor, 200 Constitution Avenue NW., Room S–5506, Washington, DC 20210. Phone, 202-693-6999 or 800-347-3756. Fax, 202-693-7020. https://www.oig.dol.gov/hotline.htm

The OIG maintains a glossary of terms related to its activities and mission. https://www.oig.dol.gov/hotlineterms.htm

Open Government   The DOL has a comprehensive Open Government plan to support the making of a more accountable, responsive, and transparent Government. https://www.dol.gov/open

Plain Language   The DOL is committed to producing documents whose content complies with Federal plain language guidelines. It trains its employees and has adopted an oversight process to ensure the use of plain language in any document that is necessary for obtaining Federal Government benefits or services or filing taxes, provides information on Federal Government benefits or services, or explains to the public how to comply with a requirement that the Federal Government administers or enforces. https://www.dol.gov/general/plainwriting

Popular Topics   The DOL Web site features a topics page with links for convenient access to popular material. https://www.dol.gov/general/topic

Publications   The Office of Public Affairs distributes factsheets that describe the activities of the major agencies within the Department. See individual agency webpages for more information.

Public Disclosure   The Office of Labor-Management Standards maintains an online disclosure room where online visitors can search for union annual financial reports starting with the year 2000; view and print reports filed by unions, union officers and employees, employers, and labor relations consultants starting with the year 2000; and order copies of reports for the years prior to 2000. Certain collective bargaining agreements are also available. OLMS has public disclosure room: 200 Constitution Avenue NW., Room N–1519, Washington, DC 20210, which offers the same materials. http://www.unionreports.gov | Email: OLMS-Public@dol.gov

Spanish   The DOL supports the Hispanic workforce. An online list highlights some of the Department's Spanish resources. This list is intended for English-speakers who are looking for information in Spanish to share with the Hispanic community. https://www.dol.gov/general/topic/spanish-speakingtopic. http://www.dol.gov/dol/contact/media-contact-regional.htm

For further information concerning the Department of Labor, contact the Office of Public Affairs, Department of Labor, Room S–1032, 200 Constitution Avenue NW., Washington, DC 20210. Phone, 202-693-4650.

Bureau of International Labor Affairs

200 Constitution Avenue NW., Washington, DC 20210
Phone, 202-693-4770. Internet, http://www.dol.gov/ilab.

Deputy Under Secretary	VACANT
Associates Deputy Undersecretary	VACANT
Associate Deputy Undersecretary	MARK MITTELHAUSER

The Bureau of International Labor Affairs (ILAB) promotes a fair global playing field for workers and businesses in the United States by enforcing trade commitments; strengthening labor standards; and combating international child labor, forced labor, and human trafficking. ILAB combines trade and labor monitoring and enforcement, policy engagement, technical assistance, and research to carry out the international responsibilities of the Department. https://www.dol.gov/agencies/ilab/about-us/offices

Sources of Information

Contracts / Grants   The Bureau of International Labor Affairs partners with international organizations, non-governmental organizations, universities, research institutions, and others to advance workers' rights and livelihoods through technical assistance projects, research, and project evaluations. These activities are funded through grants, cooperative agreements, and contracts. https://www.dol.gov/agencies/ilab/resources/grants

Laws / Regulations   ILAB's work supports the President's and the Secretary of Labor's objectives related to labor and foreign policy and meets all applicable congressional mandates. The Bureau's Web site features a page of laws and regulations that are relevant to its work. https://www.dol.gov/agencies/ilab/about/laws

Newsroom   The Bureau posts news releases on its Web site. https://www.dol.gov/agencies/ilab/newsroom

Reports   Legislation and delegations from the President mandate that ILAB prepare a number of reports to inform policy deliberations and the public about certain trade and labor issues. ILAB publishes three reports on international child labor and forced labor that serve as valuable resources for research, advocacy, government action and corporate responsibility. These reports are The Department of Labor's Findings on the Worst Forms of Child Labor; the List of Goods Produced by Child Labor or Forced Labor; and the List of Products Produced by Forced or Indentured Child Labor. For each new trade agreement that the President submits to Congress, ILAB prepares reports on the potential employment impacts in the United States and on the labor rights situation in the proposed partner country or countries. https://www.dol.gov/ilab/reports

Research   ILAB conducts and funds rigorous research and evaluation projects and uses the results to inform the design and implementation of policy and programs. Our research programs cover the effects of trade on American workers, cross-country comparisons of labor markets, worker livelihoods, and worker rights and related enforcement issues, including with regard to child labor and forced labor around the world. https://www.dol.gov/ilab/research

Web-based Resources   The Bureau's Web sites features a toolkit to help responsible entrepreneurs reduce the chance that their products—and the raw materials from which they are made—are harvested, manufactured, or mined by children who should be in school or by workers who are locked in sweatshops or forced to work through threats or false promises. ILAB has also made available to the public a research app, Sweat & Toil: Child Labor, Forced Labor, and Human Trafficking Around the World. This app represents a comprehensive resource, developed by ILAB, documenting child labor and forced labor worldwide, with data and research from ILAB's three flagship reports on child labor and forced labor. https://www.dol.gov/ilab/child-forced-labor/index.htm. http://www.dol.gov/ilab

For further information, contact the Bureau of International Affairs, Department of Labor, Room C–2235, Washington, DC 20201. Phone, 202-693-4770.

Bureau of Labor Statistics

2 Massachusetts Avenue NE., Washington, DC 20212
Phone, 202-691-7800; 800-877-8339. (TDD). Internet, http://www.bls.gov.

Commissioner	ERICA L. GROSHEN
Deputy Commissioner	WILLIAM WIATROWSKI

The Bureau of Labor Statistics (BLS) was established, in the Department of the Interior, as the Bureau of Labor by the act of June 27, 1884 (23 Stat. 60). It was renamed the Bureau of Labor Statistics by the act of March 4, 1913 (37 Stat. 737). The BLS measures labor market activity, working conditions, and price changes in the economy. It also collects, analyzes, and disseminates essential economic information to support public and private decisionmaking.

The Bureau strives to have its data satisfy a number of criteria, including: relevance to current social and economic issues, timeliness in reflecting today's rapidly changing economic conditions, accuracy and consistently high statistical quality, and impartiality in both subject matter and presentation.

Basic data are issued in monthly, quarterly, and annual news releases; bulletins, reports, and special publications; and periodicals. Regional offices issue additional reports and releases that often contain content of local or regional relevance. http://www.bls.gov/bls/infohome.htm

Sources of Information

Data Tools Calculators, databases, and tables are available online. http://www.bls.gov/data
Employment Information on career opportunities is available online. http://bls.gov/jobs/home.htm
Frequently Asked Questions (FAQs) The BLS posts answers to FAQs on its Web site. http://www.bls.gov/bls/faqs.htm
Glossary The BLS maintains a glossary on its Web site. http://www.bls.gov/bls/glossary.htm
Green Jobs The BLS received funding to develop and implement the collection of new data on environmentally sustainable jobs. The Quarterly Census of Employment and Wages and Occupational Employment Statistics programs are involved in this effort. Information on the BLS green jobs initiative, the status of survey development, the BLS green jobs definition, as well as a link to career information for selected green jobs, and other information, are available on the "Measuring Green Jobs" Web page. https://www.bls.gov/green/home.htm

The BLS has defined the term "green jobs" for use in data collection and posted its green jobs definition online. https://www.bls.gov/green/home.htm#definition
Publications The BLS publishes bulletins and reports and economic news releases. Its major publications include "Beyond the Numbers," "Career Outlook," "Monthly Labor Review," "Occupational Outlook Handbook," "The Economics Daily", and "Spotlight on Statistics." These publications are available online. For more information, contact the Washington Information Office or one of the Bureau's regional offices. http://www.bls.gov/opub
Regional Information Economic statistics and data according to geographic areas are available on the "Regional Information Offices" Web page. http://www.bls.gov/bls/regnhome.htm
Resources by Audience The BLS Web site contains pages of useful information on the economy for the benefit of specific audiences: business leaders, consumers, developers, economists, investors, job seekers, media, public policymakers, students and teachers, and survey respondents. https://www.bls.gov/audience/home.htm
A–Z Index The BLS Web site features an alphabetical index to help visitors navigate its content. http://www.bls.gov/bls/topicsaz.htm
Unemployment / Employment A local area unemployment statistics map is available on the BLS Web site. http://data.bls.gov/map/MapToolServlet?survey=la

An overview of statistics on unemployment is available on the BLS Web site. http://www.bls.gov/bls/unemployment.htm

An overview of statistics on employment is available on the BLS Web site. http://www.bls.gov/bls/employment.htm

Updates The BLS Web site features an online subscription form to sign up for electronic updates. https://subscriptions.bls.gov/accounts/USDOLBLS/subscriber/new. http://www.bls.gov

For further information, contact the Bureau of Labor Statistics, Department of Labor, Room 4040, 2 Massachusetts Avenue NE., Washington, DC 20212. Phone, 202-691-7800.

Employee Benefits Security Administration

Department of Labor, Washington, DC 20210
Phone, 866-444-3272. Internet, http://www.dol.gov/ebsa.

Assistant Secretary	PHYLLIS C. BORZI
Deputy Assistant Secretary for Policy	JUDITH MARES
Deputy Assistant Secretary for Program Operations	TIMOTHY HAUSER

The Employee Benefits Security Administration (EBSA) promotes and protects the retirement, health, and other benefits of the over 141 million participants and beneficiaries in over 5 million private sector employee benefit plans. EBSA develops regulations; assists and educates workers, plan sponsors, fiduciaries, and service providers; and enforces the law. The Employee Retirement Income Security Act is enforced through 13 field offices nationwide and a national office in Washington, DC. https://www.dol.gov/agencies/ebsa/about-ebsa

Sources of Information

Ask EBSA EBSA's workers and families assistance Web page provides accessible information on programs and services, answers to questions, and assistance in cases where a health or retirement benefit has been denied inappropriately. https://www.dol.gov/agencies/ebsa/about-ebsa/ask-a-question/ask-ebsa

Key Topics The EBSA Web site features a page with links to key topics: health and other employee benefits, reporting and filing, and retirement. https://www.dol.gov/agencies/ebsa/key-topics

Offices A list of EBSA regional and district offices is available online. https://www.dol.gov/agencies/ebsa/about-ebsa/about-us/regional-offices#district-offices

Publications The EBSA distributes booklets, factsheets, and pamphlets on employer obligations and employee rights under the Employee Retirement Income Security Act. A list of publications is available online or from the Office of Outreach, Education, and Assistance. Phone, 866-444-3272. http://www.dol.gov/ebsa/publications/main.html

Reading Room The EBSA maintains a disclosure room at Room N–1513, 200 Constitution Avenue NW., Washington, DC 20210. Reports filed under the Employee Retirement Income Security Act may be examined in the public disclosure room and purchased for 15 cents per page. Phone, 202-693-8673. http://www.dol.gov/ebsa/foia/foia.html

Spanish Information is available in Spanish. https://www.dol.gov/es/agencies/ebsa/about-ebsa/our-activities/informacion-en-espanol. http://www.dol.gov/ebsa

For further information, contact the Employee Benefits Security Administration, Department of Labor, Room S-2524, Washington, DC 20210. Phone, 866-444-3272.

Employment and Training Administration

Department of Labor, Washington, DC 20520
Phone, 877-872-5627. Internet, http://www.doleta.gov.

Assistant Secretary	PORTIA Y. WU
Deputy Assistants Secretary	GERRI FIALA,
	ERIC SELEZNOW,
	BYRON ZUIDEMA

The Employment and Training Administration (ETA) provides quality job training, employment, labor market information, and income maintenance services, primarily through State and local workforce development systems. ETA also administers programs to enhance employment opportunities and business prosperity. https://www.doleta.gov/etainfo/mission.cfm

Apprenticeship Programs   The Office of Apprenticeship oversees the National Apprenticeship System, sets standards for apprenticeship, and assists States, industry, and labor in developing apprenticeship programs that meet required standards while promoting equal opportunity and safeguarding the welfare of apprentices. http://www.dol.gov/apprenticeship

For more information, call 202-693-2796.

Contracts Management   The Office of Contracts Management (OCM) provides leadership and direction to ensure acquisition excellence, integrity, accountability, and sound management of procurement resources to support Employment and Training Administration (ETA) and Job Corps goals and guiding principles for the acquisition of goods and services. Job Corps contracts account for 75 percent of the Department's contracting activity. Non-Job Corps contract activity supports ETA grant programs through technical assistance and long-term studies and evaluations. http://www.doleta.gov/contracts

For further information, contact the Office of Contracts Management, Department of Labor, Suite N-4643, Washington, DC 20210. Phone, 202-693-3701.

Financial Administration   The Office of Financial Administration (OFA) is responsible for managing all ETA fiscal resources for programs and activities for which funds are appropriated through its functions of accounting, budget, and financial system oversight. OFA provides critical budgetary, accounting, audit, and internal control management. It coordinates with the Departmental Budget Center and the Office of the Chief Financial Officer to provide financial management supporting the accomplishment of all aspects of ETA's mission. http://www.doleta.gov/budget

For further information, call 202-693-3162.

Foreign Labor Certification   The Office of Foreign Labor Certification (OFLC) carries out the delegated responsibility of the Secretary of Labor under the Immigration and Nationality Act, as amended, concerning the admission of foreign workers into the United States for employment.

In carrying out this responsibility, OFLC administers temporary nonimmigrant and permanent labor certification programs through ETA's National Processing Centers located, respectively, in Chicago and Atlanta.

OFLC also administers nationally the issuance of employer-requested prevailing wage determinations through ETA's National Prevailing Wage and Helpdesk Center located in Washington, DC. Prevailing wage determinations are issued for use in all nonagricultural temporary labor certification programs and the permanent labor certification program. http://www.foreignlaborcert.doleta.gov

For more information, call 202-693-3010.

Job Training   The Office of Job Corps (OJC) teaches young adults relevant skills they need to become employable and independent and helps them secure meaningful jobs or opportunities for further education. OJC has six regional offices responsible for monitoring and oversight of

Job Corps centers, outreach and admissions, and career transition services. http://www.jobcorps.gov/home.aspx

For further information, call 202-693-3000.

Management and Administrative Services

The Office of Management and Administrative Services (OMAS) is responsible for managing administrative and grant management programs for ETA. OMAS provides critical grant-making and human resources management, information technology services, controlled correspondence, emergency preparedness, Freedom of Information Act coordination, facilities management, and facilitates communication and coordination of activities providing strategic advice, counsel, and customer service to ETA's six regions. OMAS provides technological infrastructure and administrative support for critical ETA functions. https://www.doleta.gov/grants

For further information, call 202-693-2800.

Policy Development and Research

The Office of Policy Development and Research (OPDR) supports ETA policies and investments to improve the public workforce system by analyzing, formulating, and recommending legislative changes and options for policy initiatives, including budget justifications. OPDR coordinates ETA's legislative and regulatory activities and their interactions with international organizations and foreign countries. OPDR maintains ETA's portion of the Department's regulatory agenda and disseminates advisories and publications to the public workforce system. OPDR provides ETA with strategic approaches to improve performance and outcomes through research, demonstrations, and evaluation of its major programs. OPDR manages the Workforce Investment Act performance accountability reporting system; oversees the maintenance of wage record exchange systems for State and other grantees; coordinates the development of ETA's Operating Plan; and disseminates workforce program performance results. OPDR also provides policy guidance and technical assistance on the Worker Adjustment and Retraining Notification Act. http://www.doleta.gov/etainfo/opder

For further information, call 202-693-3700.

Trade Adjustment Assistance

The Office of Trade Adjustment Assistance (TAA) is responsible for administering a workers assistance program for those who have lost or may lose their jobs because of foreign trade. The TAA program provides reemployment services and allowances for eligible individuals. http://www.doleta.gov/tradeact

For further information, call 202-693-3560.

Unemployment Compensation

The Office of Unemployment Insurance (OUI) provides national leadership, oversight, policy guidance, and technical assistance to the Federal-State unemployment compensation system. OUI also interprets Federal legislative requirements. http://www.unemploymentinsurance.doleta.gov

For more information, call 202-693-3029.

Workforce Investment

The Office of Workforce Investment (OWI) is responsible for implementing an integrated national workforce investment system that supports economic growth and provides workers with the information, advice, job search assistance, supportive services, and training needed for employment. OWI also helps employers acquire skilled workers. http://www.doleta.gov/etainfo/WrkSys/WIOffice.cfm

For further information, call 202-693-3980.

Sources of Information

Advisories The ETA uses its advisory system to disseminate its interpretations of Federal laws; procedural, administrative, management, and program direction; and other information to the States, direct grant recipients, and other interested parties. https://wdr.doleta.gov/directives

Data Unemployment insurance data are available on the ETA Web site. http://www.ows.doleta.gov/unemploy/DataDashboard.asp

Program data from the Office of Foreign Labor Certification are available on the ETA Web site. https://www.foreignlaborcert.doleta.gov/performancedata.cfm

Statistics, charts, and other information used to analyze the Trade Adjustment Assistance for Workers program are available on the ETA Web site. https://www.doleta.gov/tradeact/StatMap2015.cfm

Job Corps   Answers to frequently asked questions are posted on the Job Corps Web site. http://www.jobcorps.gov/faq.aspx

The six Job Corps regional offices oversee Job Corps centers nationwide. Contact information for these regional offices is available on the Job Corps Web site. http://www.jobcorps.gov/contact.aspx#national

Job Corps trains more than 60,000 students at 125 centers nationwide. Contact information for these training centers is available on the Job Corps Web site. Phone, 800-733-5627. http://www.jobcorps.gov/centers.aspx

Library   A large repository of information is available online at the ETA Library. http://www.doleta.gov/reports

News   The ETA posts news releases on its Web site. https://www.doleta.gov/ETA_News_Releases

Regional Offices   Contact information for the ETA's six regional offices is available on its Web site. https://www.doleta.gov/regions/regoffices/Pages/eta_default.cfm?CFID=847134926&CFTOKEN=31628934

Research   The research publication database provides access to a collection of research and evaluation reports. The ETA commissioned the research and evaluation reports to help guide the workforce investment system in administering effective programs that enhance employment opportunity and business. https://wdr.doleta.gov/research/eta_default.cfm

Youth Services   The Division of Youth Services has a "Resources" Web page. https://www.doleta.gov/Youth_services/resources.cfm. https://www.doleta.gov/etainfo/ETA_Contacts.cfm

For further information, contact the Employment and Training Administration, Department of Labor, Washington, DC 20210. Phone, 877-872-5627.

Mine Safety and Health Administration

201 12th Street South, Suite 400, Arlington, Virginia 22202
Phone, 202-693-9400. Internet, http://www.msha.gov.

Assistant Secretary	JOSEPH A. MAIN
Deputy Assistant Secretary for Operations	PATRICIA W. SILVEY
Deputy Assistant Secretary for Policy	LAURA MCCLINTOCK

The Mine Safety and Health Administration (MSHA) was created in 1978, when the Federal Mine Safety and Health Act of 1977 transferred the Federal mine safety program from the Department of the Interior to the Department of Labor. https://www.msha.gov/about/history

The MSHA promotes safe and healthful workplaces for the Nation's miners. The MSHA develops and enforces safety and health rules for all U.S. mines. The MSHA also provides technical, educational, and other assistance to mine operators. https://www.msha.gov/about/mission

Sources of Information

Data   Mine safety and health data—information on accidents, air sampling, employment, injuries, illnesses, inspections, production totals, violations, and more—are available on the MSHA Web site. Compliance calculator tools that allow users to find a mine's history of key health and safety violations are also available the Web site. https://www.msha.gov/data-reports/data-sources-calculators

Summaries of MSHA data on annual fatality and injury statistics, most frequently cited standards, number of citations and orders issued, total dollar amount of penalties assessed, and more are available on the MSHA Web site. https://www.msha.gov/data-reports/statistics

Employment   Information on employment opportunities is available online. http://www.msha.gov/about/careers

The MSHA seeks motivated professionals committed to ensuring the health and safety of the Nation's miners. http://arlweb.msha.gov/inspectors/inspectorhiringprogram.asp

Frequently Asked Questions (FAQs)   The MSHA posts answers to FAQs on its Web site. https://www.msha.gov/training-education/frequently-asked-questions | Email: mshatraining@dol.gov

News / Media   The MSHA posts alerts and hazards, announcements, congressional testimonies, events, news releases, photographs and videos, and speeches on its Web site. https://www.msha.gov/news-media

Offices   A complete listing of MSHA district and field offices is available online. http://www.msha.gov/district/disthome.htm

Reports   Current and historical preliminary accident reports, fatalgrams, and fatal investigation reports for metal, nonmetal, and coal mines are accessible on the MSHA Web site. Quarterly and annual summaries of mining fatalities along with associated best practices and preventative recommendations are also accessible. https://www.msha.gov/data-reports/fatality-reports

Part 50 of Title 30 of the "Code of Federal Regulation" (30 CFR Part 50) requires mine operators to notify the MSHA of accidents, requires operators to investigate accidents, and restricts disturbance of accident related areas. This part also requires them to file reports with the MSHA pertaining to accidents, occupational injuries, and occupational illnesses, as well as employment and coal production data. These Data are summarized in quarterly and annual reports. https://www.msha.gov/data-reports/reports

Resources / Tools   Mine emergency operations information, miners' resources, and technical resources and reports are available on the MSHA Web site. https://www.msha.gov/support-resources/resources-tools

Spanish   In the top right corner of the MSHA's home page are an Español option and an Inglés option. Using these options, visitors to the Web site can toggle between content in Spanish or English. https://www.msha.gov. https://www.msha.gov/about/contact-msha | Email: AskMSHA@dol.gov

For further information, contact the Office of Program Education and Outreach Services, Mine Safety and Health Administration, Department of Labor, 201 12th Street South, Suite 400, Arlington, Virginia 22202. Phone, 202-693-9400.

Occupational Safety and Health Administration

Department of Labor, Washington, DC 20210
Phone, 800-321-6742. Internet, http://www.osha.gov.

Assistant Secretary	DAVID MICHAELS
Deputy Assistants Secretary	JORDAN BARAB,
Deputy Assistant Secretary	DOROTHY DOUGHERTY

The Occupational Safety and Health Administration (OSHA), created pursuant to the Occupational Safety and Health Act of 1970 (29 U.S.C. 651 et seq.), assures safe and healthful working conditions for men and women by promulgating common sense, protective health, and safety standards; enforcing workplace safety and health rules; providing training, outreach, education, and assistance to workers and employers in their efforts to control workplace hazards; prevent work-related injuries, illnesses, and fatalities; and partnering with States that run their own

OSHA-approved programs. https://www.osha.gov/about.html

Sources of Information

Enforcement Cases   The OSHA Web site features a nationwide map of enforcement cases with initial penalties above $40,000. https://www.osha.gov/topcases/bystate.html

File a Complaint   Information on how to file a safety and health complaint and an electronic complaint form are available on the OSHA Web site. Phone, 800-321-

6742. https://www.osha.gov/workers/file_complaint.html

Freedom of Information Act (FOIA) The OSHA is required to disclose records that are properly requested in writing by any person. An agency may withhold information pursuant to one or more of nine exemptions and three exclusions contained in the FOIA. The act applies only to Federal agencies and does not create a right of access to records held by Congress, the courts, State or local government agencies, and private entities. https://www.osha.gov/as/opa/foia/foia.html

Frequently Asked Questions (FAQs) The OSHA posts answers to FAQs on its Web site. https://www.osha.gov/OSHA_FAQs.html

Injury and Illness Data The OSHA Web site features a searchable, establishment-specific database for establishments that provided OSHA with valid data from 1996 through 2011. https://www.osha.gov/pls/odi/establishment_search.html

Workplace injury, illness, and fatality statistics are available on the OSHA Web site. https://www.osha.gov/oshstats/work.html

Make a Report Employers must notify OSHA when an employee is killed on the job or suffers a work-related amputation, hospitalization, or loss of an eye. A fatality must be reported within 8 hours; an amputation, in-patient hospitalization, or eye loss must be reported within 24 hours. An employer should be prepared to supply the name of the business, the names of employees who were affected, the location and time of the incident, a brief description of the incident, and a contact person and phone number. https://www.osha.gov/report.html

News The OSHA posts news releases, which can be sorted by subject, date, or region, on its Web site. https://www.osha.gov/newsrelease.html

The "What's New" Web page features news items that are organized chronologically. https://www.osha.gov/whatsnew.html

Offices A complete listing of OSHA regional and area offices is available online. http://www.osha.gov/html/RAmap.html

Publications OSHA publications are accessible online. https://www.osha.gov/pls/publications/publication.html

Site Index An A–Z index is available on the OSHA Web site. https://www.osha.gov/html/a-z-index.html

Spanish In the top right corner of the OSHA's home page are an Español option and an Inglés option. Using these options, visitors to the Web site can toggle between content in Spanish or English. https://www.osha.gov

Training / Education Stand-alone, interactive, Web-based training tools—eTools and the eMatrix—are available on the OSHA Web site. These tools are highly illustrated and utilize graphical menus. https://www.osha.gov/dts/osta/oshasoft/index.html

Prevention video training tools (v-tools) on construction hazards are available on the OSHA Web site. These videos show how workers can be injured suddenly or even killed on the job. The videos assist those who are in the construction industry with identifying, reducing, and eliminating hazards. The videos are presented in clear, accessible vocabulary; show common construction worksite activities; and most are 2–4 minutes long. https://www.osha.gov/dts/vtools/construction.html. https://www.osha.gov/html/Feed_Back.html

For further information, contact the Occupational Safety and Health Administration, Department of Labor, Washington, DC 20210. Phone, 202-693-2000 or 800-321-6742.

Veterans' Employment and Training Service

Department of Labor, Washington, DC 20210
Phone, 866-487-2365. Internet, http://www.dol.gov/vets.

Assistant Secretary	MIKE MICHAUD
Deputy Assistant Secretary for Policy	TERESA W. GERTON
Deputy Assistant Secretary for Operations and Management	SAM SHELLENBERGER

The Veterans' Employment and Training Service (VETS) is responsible for administering veterans' employment and training programs and compliance activities that help them and servicemembers succeed in their civilian careers. VETS also administers the Jobs for Veterans State Grant program, which provides grants to States to fund personnel dedicated to serving the employment needs of veterans. VETS field staff works closely with and provides technical assistance to State employment workforce agencies to ensure that veterans receive priority of service and gain meaningful employment. VETS has two competitive grants programs: the Homeless Veterans Reintegration Program, and the Incarcerated Veterans Transition Program. VETS also prepares separating servicemembers for the civilian labor market with its Transition Assistance Program Employment Workshop.

VETS has three distinct compliance programs: the Federal Contractor Program, Veterans' Preference in Federal hiring and the Uniformed Services Employment and Reemployment Rights Act of 1994 (USERRA). With respect to Federal contractors, VETS promulgates regulations and maintains oversight of the program by assisting contractors to comply with their affirmative action and reporting obligations. Although the Office of Personnel Management is responsible for administering and interpreting statutes and regulations governing veterans' preference in Federal hiring, VETS investigates allegations that veterans' preference rights have been violated. In addition, VETS preserves servicemembers' employment and reemployment rights through its administration and enforcement of the USERRA statute. VETS conducts thorough investigations of alleged violations and conducts an extensive USERRA outreach program. https://www.dol.gov/vets/aboutvets/aboutvets.htm

Sources of Information

Directories A national office directory is available online. https://www.dol.gov/vets/aboutvets/nationaloffice.htm

A regional and State directory is available online. https://www.dol.gov/vets/aboutvets/regionaloffices/map.htm

Freedom of Information Act (FOIA) Any person has the right to request access to Federal agency records or information. VETS is required to disclose records that are properly requested in writing by any person. An agency may withhold information pursuant to nine exemptions and three exclusions contained in the FOIA. The act applies only to Federal agencies and does not create a right of access to records held by Congress, the courts, or by State or local government agencies. A FOIA request should be submitted to the appropriate national or regional VETS office by email, fax, or mail. The subject line, cover page, or envelope should be clearly labeled "Freedom of Information Act Request." The content of the request should indicate that it is a FOIA request, and it should contain as much information as possible describing the record or records being sought. https://www.dol.gov/vets/foia

Frequently Asked Questions (FAQs) VETS posts answers to FAQs on its Web site. https://www.dol.gov/vets/resources/faqs.htm

Grants Information on grants and other opportunities is available online. http://www.dol.gov/vets/resources/grants.htm

Hire a Veteran Resources to help employers hire veterans are available online. https://www.dol.gov/vets/hire/index.htm

News / Media VETS posts news releases and public service announcements on its Web site. https://www.dol.gov/vets/news.htm

Updates / Reports The VETS Web site features updates and reports, as well as congressional testimonies, factsheets, and infographics. https://www.dol.gov/vets/updates/index.htm. http://www.dol.gov/vets

For further information, contact the Assistant Secretary for Veterans' Employment and Training, Department of Labor, Washington, DC 20210. Phone, 202-693-4700.

Wage and Hour Division

Department of Labor, Washington, DC 20210
Phone, 866-487-9243. Internet, http://www.dol.gov/whd.

Administrator	DAVID WEIL
Deputy Administrator	LAURA A. FORTMAN
Deputy Administrator for Program Operations	PATRICIA DAVIDSON

The Wage and Hour Division (WHD) enforces Federal minimum wage, overtime pay, recordkeeping, and child labor law requirements of the Fair Labor Standards Act. WHD also enforces the Migrant and Seasonal Agricultural Worker Protection Act, the Employee Polygraph Protection Act, the Family and Medical Leave Act, wage garnishment provisions of the Consumer Credit Protection Act, and a number of employment standards and worker protections as provided in several immigration-related statutes. Additionally, WHD administers and enforces the prevailing wage requirements of the Davis Bacon Act and the Service Contract Act and other statutes applicable to Federal contracts for construction and for the provision of goods and services. https://www.dol.gov/whd/about/mission/whdmiss.htm

Sources of Information

Evaluations / Studies The WHD posts evaluations and studies on its Web site in Portable Document Format (PDF). https://www.dol.gov/whd/resources/evaluations.htm
File a Complaint Instructions for filing a complaint are available online. Phone, 866-487-9243. https://www.dol.gov/wecanhelp/howtofilecomplaint.htm
Freedom of Information Act (FOIA) The WHD is required to disclose records that are properly requested in writing by any person. The WHD may withhold information pursuant to nine exemptions and three exclusions contained in the FOIA. The WHD does not require a special FOIA request form. A request must reasonably describe the desired record. Providing its name or title is not mandatory, but the more specific the record description, the more likely that WHD staff can locate it. A FOIA request must be made in writing and may be submitted by courier service, email, fax, or postal mail. https://www.dol.gov/whd/foia/index.htm
Frequently Asked Questions (FAQs) The WHD provides answers to FAQs on its Web site. https://www.dol.gov/wecanhelp/faq.htm
News The WHD posts national and State news releases on its Web site. https://www.dol.gov/whd/media/press/whdprssToc.asp
Offices Contact information for WHD area, district, and regional offices is available on the "WHD Local Offices" Web page. https://www.dol.gov/whd/america2.htm
Resources Resources for workers are available on the WHD Web site. https://www.dol.gov/whd/workers.htm
  Resources for employers are available on the WHD Web site. https://www.dol.gov/whd/foremployers.htm
  Resources for State and local governments are available on the WHD Web site. https://www.dol.gov/whd/forstatelocalgovernments.htm. https://www.dol.gov/whd/contact_us.htm

For further information, contact the Office of the Administrator, Wage and Hour Division, Department of Labor, Room S-3502, Washington, DC 20210. Phone, 202-693-0051.

Women's Bureau

Department of Labor, Washington, DC 20210
Phone, 202-693-6710. Internet, http://www.dol.gov/wb.

Director	LATIFA LYLES
Deputy Director	JOAN HARRIGAN-FARRELLY

The Women's Bureau develops policies and standards and conducts inquiries to safeguard the interests of working women, to advocate for their equality and the economic security of their families, and to promote quality work environments.

The Bureau identifies, researches, and analyzes topics that are relevant for working women; pioneers policies and programs to address those topics; and enhances public education and outreach efforts to raise awareness on key issues and developments affecting women in the workforce. http://www.dol.gov/wb/overview_14.htm

Sources of Information

Blog   The Bureau's Web site features a blog. https://www.dol.gov/wb/media/blog_posts.htm

Data / Statistics   Current and historical statistics on a broad range of topics and subpopulations of women in the labor force are available online. http://www.dol.gov/wb/stats/stats_data.htm

Regional Offices   A complete listing of Women's Bureau regional offices is available online. http://www.dol.gov/wb/info_about_wb/regions/regional_offices.htm

Resources   Resources for women in the labor force produced by or in collaboration with the Bureau are available on its Web site. https://www.dol.gov/wb/resources. https://www.dol.gov/wb/info_about_wb/contact_us.htm

For further information, contact the Women's Bureau, Department of Labor, Room S-3002, NW., Washington, DC 20210. Phone, 202-693-6710.

DEPARTMENT OF STATE

2201 C Street NW., Washington, DC 20520
Phone, 202-647-4000. Internet, http://www.state.gov.

Secretary of State	Rex Tillerson
Deputy Secretary of State	John Sullivan
Deputy Secretary of State for Management and Resources	Vacancy
Counselor of the Department	Vacancy
Director, Office of U.S. Foreign Assistance	Hari Sastry
Executive Secretary	Lisa D. Kenna
Under Secretary for Arms Control and International Security Affairs	Vacancy
Assistant Secretary for International Security and Nonproliferation	C.S. Eliot Kang, Acting
Assistant Secretary for Political-Military Affairs	Tina Kaidanow, Acting
Assistant Secretary for Arms Control, Verification and Compliance	Anita Friedt, Acting
Under Secretary for Civilian Security, Democracy, and Human Rights	Vacancy
Ambassador-at-Large for the Office to Monitor and Combat Trafficking in Persons	Susan Coppedge
Assistant Secretary for Conflict and Stabilization Operations	Thomas Hushek , Acting
Assistant Secretary for Democracy, Human Rights, and Labor	Virginia Bennett, Acting
Assistant Secretary for International Narcotics and Law Enforcement Affairs	William Brownfield
Assistant Secretary for Population, Refugees, and Migration	Simon Henshaw, Acting
Coordinator for Counterterrorism	Justin Siberell, Acting
Special Coordinator for the Office of Global Criminal Justice	Todd Buchwald
Under Secretary for Economic Growth, Energy, and the Environment	Vacancy
Assistant Secretary for Economic and Business Affairs	Patricia Haslach, Acting
Assistant Secretary for Energy Resources	Mary Warlick, Acting
Assistant Secretary for Oceans and International Environmental and Scientific Affairs	Judith Garber, Acting
Office of the Chief Economist	Keith Maskus
Under Secretary for Management	Vacancy
Assistant Secretary for Administration	Harry Maher, Acting
Assistant Secretary for Consular Affairs	David Donahue, Acting
Assistant Secretary for Diplomatic Security	Bill Miller, Acting
Assistant Secretary for Information Resource Management / Chief Information Officer	Frontis Wiggins
Comptroller, Bureau of the Comptroller and Global Financial Services	Christopher H. Flaggs

276

Director, Budget and Planning	DOUGLAS PITKIN
Director, Foreign Service Institute	MARK OSTFIELD, ACTING
Director, Human Resources / Director General of the Foreign Service	WILLIAM TODD, ACTING
Director, Office of Management Policy, Rightsizing and Innovation	PAUL WEDDERIEN
Director, Office of Medical Services	CHARLES ROSENFARB
Director, Overseas Buildings Operations	WILLIAM MOSER, ACTING
Under Secretary for Political Affairs	THOMAS SHANNON
Assistant Secretary for African Affairs	LINDA THOMAS-GREENFIELD
Assistant Secretary for East Asian and Pacific Affairs	PETER BARLERIN, ACTING
Assistant Secretary for European and Eurasian Affairs	JOHN HEFFERN, ACTING
Assistant Secretary for International Organization Affairs	TRACEY JACOBSON, ACTING
Assistant Secretary for Near Eastern Affairs	STUART JONES, ACTING
Assistant Secretary for South and Central Asian Affairs	ALICE G. WELLS, ACTING
Assistant Secretary for Western Hemisphere Affairs	FRANCISCO PALMIERI, ACTING
Under Secretary for Public Diplomacy and Public Affairs	BRUCE WHARTON, ACTING
Assistant Secretary for Educational and Cultural Affairs	MARK TAPLIN, ACTING
Assistant Secretary for Public Affairs	SUSAN STEVENSON, ACTING
Coordinator of International Information Programs	JONATHAN HENICK, ACTING
Assistant Secretary for Intelligence and Research	DANIEL SMITH
Assistant Secretary for Legislative Affairs	MARY K. WATERS, ACTING
Ambassador-at-Large of the Office of Global Women's Issues	VACANCY
Chief of Protocol	ROSEMARIE PAULI, ACTING
Coordinator, Office of U.S. Global AIDS	DEBORAH BIRX
Director, Office of Civil Rights	GREGORY B. SMITH
Director, Office of Policy Planning	DAVID HOOK
Inspector General	STEVE A. LINICK
Legal Adviser	RICHARD VISEK, ACTING

United States Mission to the United Nations

799 United Nations Plaza, New York, NY 10017

United States Permanent Representative to the United Nations and Representative in the Security Council	NIKKI HALEY
Deputy United States Representative to the United Nations	MICHELE SISSON
United States Alternate Representative for Special Political Affairs in the United Nations	AMY TACHCO, ACTING
United States Representative to the Economic and Social Council	STEFANIE AMADEO, ACTING
United States Representative for United Nations Management and Reform	ISOBEL COLEMAN

[For the Department of State statement of organization, see the U.S. Code of Federal Regulations, Title 22, Part 5.]

The Department of State advises the President on issues of foreign policy; supports democracy, freedom, and prosperity for all people; and fosters conditions that favor stability and progress worldwide.

The Department of State was established by act of July 27, 1789, as the Department of Foreign Affairs and was renamed Department of State by act of September 15, 1789 (22 U.S.C. 2651 note).

Secretary of State   The Secretary of State is responsible for the overall direction, coordination, and supervision of U.S. foreign relations and for the interdepartmental activities of the U.S. Government abroad. The Secretary is the first-ranking member of the Cabinet, is a member of the National Security Council, and is in charge of the operations of the Department, including the Foreign Service. http://www.state.gov/secretary

Regional Bureaus   Foreign affairs activities worldwide are handled by the geographic bureaus, which include the Bureaus of African Affairs, European and Eurasian Affairs, East Asian and Pacific Affairs, Near Eastern Affairs, South and Central Asian Affairs, and Western Hemisphere Affairs. http://www.state.gov/p

Administration   The Bureau of Administration provides support programs and services to Department of State operations worldwide, as well as programs and services to other U.S. Government agencies represented at U.S. Embassies and consulates. These functions include administrative policy; domestic emergency management; management of owned or leased facilities in the United States; procurement, supply, travel, and transportation support; classified pouch, unclassified pouch, and domestic mail distribution; official records, publishing, library, and foreign language interpreting and translating services; and support to the schools abroad that educate dependents of U.S. Government employees assigned to diplomatic and consular missions. Direct services to the public include authenticating documents used abroad for legal and business purposes; responding to requests under the Freedom of Information and Privacy Acts; providing the electronic reading room for public reference to State Department records; and determining use of the diplomatic reception rooms of the Harry S. Truman headquarters building in Washington, DC. http://www.state.gov/m/a

For further information, contact the Bureau of Administration. Phone, 202-485-7000.

Arms Control, Verification and Compliance   The Bureau of Arms Control, Verification and Compliance is responsible for ensuring and verifying compliance with international arms control, nonproliferation, and disarmament agreements and commitments. The Bureau also leads negotiation and implementation efforts with respect to strategic arms control, most recently the new START Treaty and conventional forces in Europe. The Bureau is the principal policy representative to the intelligence community with regard to verification and compliance matters and uses this role to promote, preserve, and enhance key collection and analytic capabilities and to ensure that intelligence verification, compliance, and implementation requirements are met. The Bureau staffs and manages treaty implementation commissions, creates negotiation and implementation policy for agreements and commitments, and develops policy for future arms control, nonproliferation, and disarmament arrangements. It also provides secure government-to-government communication linkages with foreign treaty partners. The Bureau is also responsible for preparing verifiability assessments on proposals and agreements, and reporting these to Congress as required. The Bureau also prepares the "President's Annual Report to Congress on Adherence to and Compliance With Arms Control, Nonproliferation, and Disarmament Agreements and Commitments," as well as the reports required by the Iran, North Korea, and Syria Nonproliferation Act. http://www.state.gov/t/avc

For further information, contact the Bureau of Arms Control, Verification and Compliance. Phone, 202-647-6830. Fax, 202-647-1321.

Budget and Planning   The Bureau of Budget and Planning manages budgeting and resource management for operation accounts. http://www.state.gov/s/d/rm

For further information, contact the Bureau of Budget and Planning. Phone, 202-647-8517.

Comptroller and Global Financial Services   The Bureau of the Comptroller and Global Financial Services, led by the Chief Financial Officer, integrates strategic planning, budgeting, and performance to secure departmental resources. The Bureau manages all departmental strategic and performance planning; global financial services, including accounting, disbursing, and payroll; issuance of financial statements and oversight of the Department's management control program; coordination of national security resources and remediation of vulnerabilities within the Department's global critical infrastructure; and management of the International Cooperative Administrative Support Services Program. http://www.state.gov/m/cgfs

For further information, contact the Bureau of the Comptroller and Global Financial Services. Phone, 703-875-4364.

Conflict and Stabilization Operations The Bureau of Conflict and Stabilization Operations advances U.S. national security by driving integrated, civilian-led efforts to prevent, respond to, and stabilize crises in priority states, setting conditions for long-term peace. The Bureau emphasizes sustainable solutions guided by local dynamics and actors and promotes unity of effort, strategic use of scarce resources, and burden sharing with international partners. http://www.state.gov/j/cso

For further information, contact the Bureau of Conflict Stabilization Operations. Phone, 202-663-0299.

Consular Affairs The Bureau of Consular Affairs is responsible for the protection and welfare of American citizens and interests abroad; the administration and enforcement of the provisions of the immigration and nationality laws insofar as they concern the Department of State and Foreign Service; the issuance of passports and visas; and related services. Approximately 18 million passports a year are issued by the Bureau's Office of Passport Services at the processing centers in Portsmouth, NH, and Charleston, SC, and the regional agencies in Boston, MA; Chicago, IL; Aurora, CO; Honolulu, HI; Houston, TX; Los Angeles, CA; Miami, FL; New Orleans, LA; New York, NY; Philadelphia, PA; San Francisco, CA; Seattle, WA; Norwalk, CT; Detroit, MI; Minneapolis, MN; and Washington, DC. In addition,

the Bureau helps secure America's borders against entry by terrorists or narcotraffickers, facilitates international adoptions, and supports parents whose children have been abducted abroad. http://travel.state.gov/content/travel/en.html

More information is available online at the Bureau of Consular Affairs.

Counterterrorism The Bureau of Counterterrorism leads the Department in the U.S. Government's effort to counter terrorism abroad and secure the United States against foreign terrorist threats. To carry out its mission, the Bureau develops and implements counterterrorism strategies, promotes international cooperation on counterterrorism issues, serves as the Department's key link on counterterrorism to the Department of Homeland Security, focuses efforts to counter violent extremism, and develops international partner counterterrorism capacity. http://www.state.gov/j/ct

For further information, contact CT's Office of Public Affairs. Phone, 202-647-1845.

Democracy, Human Rights, and Labor The Bureau of Democracy, Human Rights, and Labor (DRL) is responsible for developing and implementing U.S. policy on democracy, human rights, labor, religious freedom, monitoring and combating anti-Semitism, and advocating for inclusion of people with disabilities. DRL practices diplomatic engagement and advocacy to protect human rights and strengthen democratic institutions. Working with governments, civil society, and multilateral organizations to support democratic governance and human rights, the Bureau also participates in multi-stakeholder initiatives to encourage multinational corporations to adhere to human rights standards of conduct, including the elimination of child labor. DRL fulfills the USG reporting responsibilities on human rights and democracy, producing the annual "Country Reports on Human Rights Practices," the annual "International Religious Freedom" report, and the "Advancing Freedom and Democracy" report. Providing targeted program assistance through the Human Rights and

Democracy Fund and other funding streams, the Bureau works to protect human rights and strengthen democratic institutions around the world. DRL programs help prosecute war criminals, promote religious freedom, support workers' rights, encourage accountability in governance, as well as facilitate freedom of expression and freedom to access information on the Internet. The Bureau also has a Congressionally mandated responsibility to ensure that foreign military assistance and training is not provided to gross violators of human rights. DRL leads the Secretary of State's Task Force on Global Internet Freedom. http://www.state.gov/j/drl

For further information, contact the Bureau of Democracy, Human Rights, and Labor. Phone, 202-647-2126.

Diplomatic Security   The Bureau of Diplomatic Security provides a secure environment to promote U.S. interests at home and abroad. The Bureau's mission includes protecting the Secretary of State and other senior Government officials, resident and visiting foreign dignitaries, and foreign missions in the United States; conducting criminal, counterintelligence, and personnel security investigations; ensuring the integrity of international travel documents, sensitive information, classified processing equipment, and management information systems; the physical and technical protection of domestic and overseas facilities of the Department of State; providing professional law enforcement and security training to U.S. and foreign personnel; and a comprehensive, multifaceted overseas security program serving the needs of U.S. missions and resident U.S. citizens and business communities. Through the Office of Foreign Missions, the Bureau regulates the domestic activities of the foreign diplomatic community in the areas of taxation, real property acquisitions, motor vehicle operation, domestic travel, and customs processing. http://www.state.gov/m/ds

For further information, contact the Bureau of Diplomatic Security Office of Public Affairs. Phone, 571-345-2502.

Economic and Business Affairs   The Bureau of Economic and Business Affairs (EB) promotes international trade, investment,

economic development, and financial stability on behalf of the American people. EB works to build prosperity and economic security at home and abroad by implementing policy related to the promotion of U.S. trade, investment and exports, international development and reconstruction, intellectual property enforcement, terrorism financing and economic sanctions, international communications and information policy, and aviation and maritime affairs. EB formulates and carries out U.S. foreign economic policy and works to sustain a more democratic, secure, and prosperous world. http://www.state.gov/e/eb

For further information, contact the Bureau of Economic and Business Affairs. Phone, 202-647-9204.

Educational and Cultural Affairs   The Bureau of Educational and Cultural Affairs administers the principal provisions of the Mutual Educational and Cultural Exchange Act (the Fulbright-Hays Act), including U.S. international educational and cultural exchange programs. These programs include the prestigious Fulbright Program for students, scholars, and teachers; the International Visitor Leadership Program, which brings leaders and future leaders from other countries to the United States for consultation with their professional colleagues; and professional, youth, sports, and cultural exchanges. Programs are implemented through cooperative relationships with U.S. nongovernmental organizations that support the Bureau's mission. http://exchanges.state.gov

For further information, contact the Bureau of Educational and Cultural Affairs. Phone, 202-632-6445. Fax, 202-632-2701.

Energy Resources   The Bureau of Energy Resources (ENR) leads the State Department in the U.S. Government's promotion of U.S. and international energy policy. ENR works to ensure that international energy markets are secure and predictable in order to mitigate potential disruptions, while also working with international partners to diversify U.S. energy supplies. The Bureau also seeks to encourage the transformation of United States and world production and consumption of energy to confront the limits of a hydrocarbon-based society and rapid increases in energy demand. ENR works to promote good governance, transparency, and reform of energy sectors globally, which will help broaden energy access, further ensure stable energy supplies, and reduce political instability. http://www.state.gov/e/enr

For further information, contact the Bureau of Energy Resources. Phone, 202-647-3423.

Foreign Service   To a great extent, the future of our country depends on the relations we have with other countries, and those relations are conducted principally by the U.S. Foreign Service. Trained representatives stationed worldwide provide the President and the Secretary of State with much of the raw material from which foreign policy is made and with the recommendations that help shape it.

Ambassadors are the personal representatives of the President and report to the President through the Secretary of State. Ambassadors have full responsibility for implementation of U.S. foreign policy by any and all U.S. Government personnel within their country of assignment, except those under military commands. Their responsibilities include negotiating agreements between the United States and the host country, explaining and disseminating official U.S. policy, and maintaining cordial relations with that country's government and people.

For a complete listing of Foreign Service posts, including addresses, telephone numbers, and key officials, use the link below. http://www.usembassy.gov

Foreign Service Institute   The Foreign Service Institute of the Department of State is the Federal Government's primary foreign affairs-related training institution. In addition to the Department of State, the Institute provides training for more than 47 other Government agencies. The Institute has more than 700 courses, including some 70 foreign language courses, ranging in length from 1 day to 2 years. The courses are designed to promote successful performance in each professional assignment, to ease the adjustment to other countries and cultures, and to enhance the leadership and management capabilities of the foreign affairs community. http://www.state.gov/m/fsi

For further information, contact the Foreign Service Institute. Phone, 703-302-7144. Fax, 703-302-7152.

Information Resource Management   The Bureau of Information Resource Management (IRM) provides the Department with the information technology it needs to carry out U.S. diplomacy in the information age. The IRM Bureau is led by the Department's Chief Information Officer. IRM establishes effective information resource management planning and policies; ensures availability of information technology systems and operations, including information technology contingency planning, to support the Department's diplomatic, consular, and management operations; exercises management responsibility to ensure the Department's information resources meet the business requirements of the Department and provide an effective basis for knowledge sharing and collaboration within the Department and with other foreign affairs agencies and partners; exercises delegated approving authority for the Secretary of State for the development and administration of the Department's computer and information security programs and policies. http://www.state.gov/m/irm

For further information, contact the Bureau of Information Resource Management. Phone, 202-647-2977.

Inspector General   The Office of Inspector General (OIG) conducts independent audits, inspections, and investigations to promote effective management, accountability, and positive change in the Department of State, the Broadcasting Board of Governors (BBG), and the foreign affairs community. OIG provides leadership to promote integrity, efficiency, effectiveness, and economy; prevents and detects waste, fraud, abuse, and mismanagement; identifies vulnerabilities and recommends constructive solutions; offers expert assistance to improve Department and BBG operations; communicates timely, useful information that facilitates decision-making and achieves measurable gains; and keeps the Department, BBG, and Congress informed. http://www.oig.state.gov

For further information, contact the Office of Inspector General. Phone, 202-663-0340.

Intelligence and Research   The primary mission of the Bureau of Intelligence and Research (INR) is to harness intelligence to serve U.S. diplomacy. Drawing on all-source intelligence, INR provides value-added independent analysis of events to Department policymakers, ensures that intelligence activities support foreign policy and national security purposes, and serves as the focal point in the Department for ensuring policy review of sensitive counterintelligence and law enforcement activities. The Bureau also analyzes geographical and international boundary issues. INR is a member of the U.S. Intelligence Community and serves as the Community's Executive Agent for Analytical Outreach. http://www.state.gov/s/inr

For further information, contact the Bureau of Intelligence and Research. Phone, 202-647-1080.

International Information Programs   The Bureau of International Information Programs (IIP) informs, engages, and influences international audiences about U.S. policy and society to advance America's interests. IIP is a leader in developing and implementing public diplomacy strategies that measurably influence international audiences through quality programs and cutting-edge technologies. IIP provides localized contact for U.S. policies and messages, reaching millions worldwide in English, Arabic, Chinese, French, Persian, Russian, and Spanish. IIP delivers America's message to the world through a number of key products and services. These programs reach, and are created strictly for, key international audiences, such as U.S. diplomatic missions abroad, the media, government officials, opinion leaders, and the general public in more than 140 countries around the world. They include Web and print publications, in-person and telecommunications-based speaker programs, and information resource services. IIP orchestrates the State Department's efforts to counter anti-American disinformation/propaganda and serves as the Department's chief link with other agencies in coordinating international public diplomacy programs. http://www.state.gov/r/iip

For further information, contact the Bureau of International Information Programs. Phone, 202-632-9942.

International Narcotics and Law Enforcement   The Bureau of International Narcotics and Law Enforcement Affairs (INL) is responsible for developing policies and managing programs to combat and counter international narcotics production and trafficking, and for strengthening law enforcement and other rule of law institutional capabilities outside the United States. The Bureau also directs narcotics control coordinators at posts abroad and provides guidance on narcotics control, justice sector reform, and anticrime matters to the chiefs of missions. It supports the development of strong, sustainable criminal justice systems as well as training for police force and judicial officials. INL works closely with a broad range of other U.S. Government agencies. http://www.state.gov/j/inl

For further information, contact the Bureau of International Narcotics and Law Enforcement Affairs. Phone, 202-647-2545. Fax, 202-736-4045.

International Organizations   The Bureau of International Organization Affairs provides guidance and support for U.S. participation in international organizations and conferences and formulates and implements U.S. policy toward international organizations, with particular emphasis on those organizations which make up the United Nations system. It provides direction in the development, coordination, and implementation of U.S. multilateral policy. http://www.state.gov/p/io

For further information, contact the Bureau of International Organization Affairs. Phone, 202-647-9600. Fax, 202-736-4116.

International Security and Nonproliferation   The Bureau of International Security and Nonproliferation (ISN), is responsible for managing a broad range of nonproliferation, counterproliferation, and arms control functions. ISN leads U.S. efforts to prevent the spread of weapons of mass destruction (nuclear, radiological, chemical, and biological weapons) related materials, and their delivery systems. It is responsible for spearheading efforts to promote international consensus on weapons of mass destruction proliferation through bilateral and multilateral diplomacy; addressing weapons of mass destruction proliferation threats posed by nonstate actors and terrorist groups by improving physical security, using interdiction and sanctions, and actively participating in the Proliferation Security Initiative; coordinating the implementation of key international treaties and arrangements, working to make them relevant to today's security challenges; working closely with the U.N., the G–8, NATO, the Organization for the Prohibition of Chemical Weapons, the International Atomic Energy Agency, and other international institutions and organizations to reduce and eliminate the threat posed by weapons of mass destruction; and supporting efforts of foreign partners to prevent, protect against, and respond to the threat or use of weapons of mass destruction by terrorists. http://www.state.gov/t/isn

For further information, contact the Bureau of International Security and Nonproliferation. Phone, 202-647-9868. Fax, 202-736-4863.

Legal Adviser The Office of the Legal Adviser advises the Secretary of State and other Department officials on all domestic and international legal matters relating to the Department of State, Foreign Service, and diplomatic and consular posts abroad. The Office's lawyers draft, negotiate, and interpret treaties, international agreements, domestic statutes, departmental regulations, Executive orders, and other legal documents; provide guidance on international and domestic law; represent the United States in international organization, negotiation, and treaty commission meetings; work on domestic and foreign litigation affecting the Department's interests; and represent the United States before international tribunals, including the International Court of Justice. http://www.state.gov/s/l

For further information, contact the Office of the Legal Adviser. Phone, 202-647-9598.

Legislative Affairs The Bureau of Legislative Affairs coordinates legislative activity for the Department of State and advises the Secretary, the Deputy, as well as the Under Secretaries and Assistant Secretaries on legislative strategy. The Bureau facilitates effective communication between State Department officials and the Members of Congress and their staffs. Legislative Affairs works closely with the authorizing, appropriations, and oversight committees of the House and Senate, as well as with individual Members that have an interest in State Department or foreign policy issues. The Bureau also manages Department testimony before House and Senate hearings, organizes Member and staff briefings, facilitates congressional travel to overseas posts for Members and staff throughout the year, reviews proposed legislation, and coordinates Statements of Administration Policy on legislation affecting the conduct of U.S. foreign policy. The Legislative Affairs staff advises individual Bureaus of the Department on legislative and outreach strategies and coordinates those strategies with the Secretary's priorities. http://www.state.gov/s/h

For further information, contact the Bureau of Legislative Affairs. Phone, 202-647-1714.

Medical Services The Office of Medical Services (MED) develops, manages, and staffs a worldwide primary health care system for U.S. Government employees and their eligible dependents residing overseas. In support of its overseas operations, MED approves and monitors the medical evacuation of patients, conducts pre-employment and in-service physical clearance examinations, and provides clinical referral and advisory services. MED also provides for emergency medical response in the event of a crisis at an overseas post. http://www.state.gov/m/med

For further information, contact the Office of Medical Services. Phone, 202-663-1649. Fax, 202-663-1613.

Oceans and International Environmental and Scientific Affairs The Bureau of Oceans and International Environmental and Scientific Affairs (OES) serves as the foreign policy focal point for international oceans, as well as environmental and scientific efforts. OES projects, protects, and promotes U.S. global interests in these areas by articulating U.S. foreign policy, encouraging international cooperation, and negotiating treaties and other instruments of international law. The Bureau serves as the principal adviser to the Secretary of State on international environment, science, and technology matters and takes the lead in coordinating and brokering diverse interests in the interagency process, where the development of international policies or the negotiation and implementation of relevant international agreements are concerned. The Bureau seeks to promote the peaceful exploitation of outer space, develop and coordinate policy on international health issues, encourage government-to-government scientific cooperation, and prevent the destruction and degradation of the planet's natural resources and the global environment. http://www.state.gov/e/oes

For further information, contact the Bureau of Oceans and International Environmental and Scientific Affairs. Phone, 202-647-3004.

Overseas Buildings Operations The Bureau of Overseas Buildings Operations (OBO) directs the worldwide overseas buildings program for the Department of State and the U.S. Government community serving abroad under the authority of the chiefs of mission. Along with the input and support of other State Department bureaus, foreign affairs agencies, and Congress, OBO sets worldwide priorities for the design, construction, acquisition, maintenance, use, and sale of real properties and the use of sales proceeds. OBO also serves as the Single Real Property Manager of all overseas facilities under the authority of the chiefs of mission. http://overseasbuildings.state.gov

For further information, contact the Bureau of Overseas Buildings Operations. Phone, 703-875-4131. Fax, 703-875-5043.

Political-Military Affairs The Bureau of Political-Military Affairs is the principal link between the Departments of State and Defense and is the Department of State's lead on operational military matters. The Bureau provides policy direction in the areas of international security, security assistance, military operations, defense strategy and policy, counterpiracy measures, and defense trade. Its responsibilities include coordinating the U.S. Government's response to piracy in the waters off the Horn

of Africa, securing base access to support the deployment of U.S. military forces overseas, negotiating status of forces agreements, coordinating participation in coalition combat and stabilization forces, regulating arms transfers, directing military assistance to U.S. allies, combating illegal trafficking in small arms and light weapons, facilitating the education and training of international peacekeepers and foreign military personnel, managing humanitarian mine action programs, and assisting other countries in reducing the availability of man-portable air defense systems. http://www.state.gov/t/pm

For further information, contact the Bureau of Political-Military Affairs. Phone, 202-647-9022. Fax, 202-736-4413.

Population, Refugees, and Migration The Bureau of Population, Refugees, and Migration directs the Department's population, refugee, and migration policy development. It administers U.S. contributions to international organizations and nongovernmental organizations for humanitarian assistance- and protection-related programs on behalf of refugees, conflict victims, and internally displaced persons. The Bureau oversees the annual admissions of refugees to the United States for permanent resettlement, working closely with the Department of Homeland Security, the Department of Health and Human Services, and various State and private voluntary agencies. It coordinates U.S. international population policy and promotes its goals through bilateral and multilateral cooperation. It works closely with the U.S. Agency for International Development, which administers U.S. international population programs. The Bureau also coordinates the Department's international migration policy through bilateral and multilateral diplomacy. The Bureau oversees efforts to encourage greater participation in humanitarian assistance and refugee resettlement on the part of foreign governments and uses humanitarian diplomacy to increase access and assistance to those in need in the absence of political solutions. http://www.state.gov/j/prm

For further information, contact the Bureau of Population, Refugees, and Migration. Phone, 202-453-9339. Fax, 202-453-9394.

Protocol The Chief of Protocol is the principal adviser to the U.S. Government, the President, the Vice President, and the Secretary of State on matters of diplomatic procedure governed by law or international custom and practice. The Office is responsible for arranging visits of foreign chiefs of state, heads of government, and other high officials to the United States; organizing credential presentations of newly arrived Ambassadors, as presented to the President and to the Secretary of State; operating the President's guest house, Blair House; organizing delegations representing the President at official ceremonies abroad; conducting official ceremonial functions and public events; interpreting the official order of precedence; conducting outreach programs of cultural enrichment and substantive briefings of the Diplomatic Corps; accrediting of over 118,000 embassy, consular, international organization, and other foreign government personnel, members of their families, and domestics throughout the United States; determining entitlement to diplomatic or consular immunity; publishing of diplomatic and consular lists; resolving problems arising out of diplomatic or consular immunity, such as legal and police matters; and approving the opening of embassy and consular offices in conjunction with the Office of Foreign Missions. http://www.state.gov/s/cpr

For further information, contact the Office of the Chief of Protocol. Phone, 202-647-1735. Fax, 202-647-1560.

Public Affairs The Bureau of Public Affairs (PA) supports U.S. foreign policy goals and objectives, advances national interests, and enhances National security by informing and influencing domestic and global public opinion about American interaction with the rest of the world. In addition, PA works to help Americans understand the importance of foreign affairs by conducting press briefings for the domestic and foreign press, pursuing media outreach by other means, arranging townhall meetings and community speakers, and preparing historical studies on U.S. diplomacy and foreign affairs matters. http://www.state.gov/r/pa

For further information, contact the Bureau of Public Affairs. Phone, 202-647-6575.

Sources of Information

A–Z Index The Department of State's Web site features an alphabetical subject index that allows visitors to look for specific topics or to browse content that aligns with their interests. http://www.state.gov/r/pa/ei/subject/index.htm#x

Bureaus / Offices An alphabetical list of bureaus and offices is available online. https://www.state.gov/r/pa/ei/rls/dos/1718.htm

Business Opportunities The Department of State and U.S. Embassies overseas post contract opportunities on the Federal Government business opportunities (FedBizOpps.gov) and the commodities marketplace service (FedBid.com) Web sites. The Office of Acquisitions Management offers professional procurement and grant services—acquisition planning, contract negotiations and administration, and cost and price analysis—to customers worldwide. Phone, 703-516-1706. Fax, 703-875-6085. http://www.state.gov/m/a/c8020.htm

The Office of Small and Disadvantaged Business Utilization's Web site features information and resources that support businesses falling into one or more of the legislatively specified small business categories in their efforts to secure prime contracts and subcontracts. Phone, 703-875-6822. http://www.state.gov/s/dmr/sdbu/index.htm

Career Opportunities To learn about joining the Civil Service, becoming a Foreign Service Specialist, or the Consular Fellows Program, visit the "Careers" Web page. Information of interest to students, recent graduates, veterans, and persons with disabilities is also accessible online. State Department personnel are available to answer questions on Federal workdays, 8:30 a.m.–4:30 p.m., eastern standard time. Phone, 202-663-2176. http://www.careers.state.gov | Email: cspapps@state.gov

The "Intern" Web pages contain information for advisors, parents, and students. https://careers.state.gov/intern

The Department of State consistently ranks high among large agencies in the Partnership for Public Service's Best Places To Work Agency Rankings. http://bestplacestowork.org/BPTW/rankings/overall/large

Data   To support the Open Government Initiative, the Department of State publishes datasets online. http://www.state.gov/open

Diplomatic and Official Passports   Those inquiring about these types of passports should contact their respective travel offices. The U.S. Government only issues these types of passports to individuals traveling abroad in connection with official employment. Additional information is available online at Consular Affairs. http://travel.state.gov

Emergencies Abroad   For information on missing persons, emergencies, travel warnings, overseas voting, judicial assistance, and arrests or deaths of Americans abroad, contact the Office of American Citizens Services and Crisis Management, Department of State. Phone, 888-407-4747 or 202-501-4444 (international). Address correspondence to Overseas Citizens Services, Bureau of Consular Affairs, Department of State, SA–29, 2201 C Street NW., Washington, DC 20520. Inquiries regarding international parental child abduction should be directed to the Office of Children's Issues, Bureau of Consular Affairs, Department of State, SA–29, 2201 C Street NW., Washington, DC 20520-4818. Phone, 888-407-4747 or 202-501-4444 (international). http://travel.state.gov/content/passports/english/emergencies.html

Freedom of Information Act (FOIA)   To request records, write to the Director, Office of Information Programs and Services, A/GIS/IPS/RL, Department of State, SA–2, Washington, DC 20522-8100. For more information, contact the FOIA Requester Service Center. Phone, 202-261-8484. https://foia.state.gov/Default.aspx

The Department of State maintains a virtual reading room on its Web site. Before submitting a FOIA request, search the reading room to see if a desired document is already accessible. https://foia.state.gov/Search/Search.aspx

Frequently Asked Questions (FAQs)   The Department of State posts answers to FAQs on its Web site. https://register.state.gov/contactus

International Adoptions   For information on adoption of foreign children by private U.S. citizens, contact the Office of Children's Issues, Bureau of Consular Affairs, Department of State, SA–29, 2201 C Street NW., Washington, DC 20520-4818. Phone, 888-407-4747 or 202-501-4444 (international). http://travel.state.gov/content/adoptionsabroad/en.html

News   The Department of State maintains an online media center. http://www.state.gov/media

Open Government   The Department of State supports the Open Government initiative by promoting collaboration, participation, and transparency. https://www.state.gov/open/index.htm

Organizational Chart   The Department of State posts an organizational chart on its Web. https://www.state.gov/r/pa/ei/rls/dos/99484.htm

The Department's organizational chart is available in Portable Document Format (PDF) for viewing and downloading. https://www.state.gov/documents/organization/263637.pdf

Passports   Passport information, including where to apply, is available online at the Bureau of Consular Affairs. For passport questions, travel emergencies, or to make an appointment at any regional passport agency, call the National Passport Information Center. Phone, 877-487-2778. TDD/TTY, 888-874-7793. Passport information is available around the clock, 7 days a week; customer service representatives are available on weekdays, 8 a.m.–10 p.m., eastern standard time, excluding Federal holidays. Correspondence may be submitted online, or direct it to the appropriate regional agency (http://travel.state.gov/passport) or to the Correspondence Branch, Passport Services, Room 510, 1111 Nineteenth Street NW., Washington, DC 20524. http://travel.state.gov/content/travel/english.html | Email: NPIC@state.gov

Publications   Publications that are produced on a regular basis include "Background Notes" and the "Foreign Relations" series. The Bureau of Public Affairs also occasionally publishes brochures and other publications to inform the public of U.S. diplomatic efforts. http://www.state.gov/r/pa/ei/rls/dos/221.htm

Social Media   The Department of State tweets announcements and other newsworthy items on Twitter. https://twitter.com/StateDept

The Department of State has a Facebook account. https://www.facebook.com/usdos

The Department of State posts videos on its YouTube channel. https://www.youtube.com/user/statevideo

Telephone Directory   The Department's telephone directory can be accessed online. http://www.state.gov/m/a/gps/directory

Tips for U.S. Travelers   Information for Americans traveling abroad—including a traveler's checklist and tips on destinations, personal safety, health, and other topics—is available online from the Bureau of Consular Affairs. http://travel.state.gov/content/passports/english/go.html

Travel Alerts / Warnings   The Bureau of Consular Affairs Web site provides travel warnings and other information designed to help Americans travel safely abroad, as well as information on U.S. passports, visas, and downloadable applications. http://travel.state.gov/content/passports/en/alertswarnings.html

Visas   For information on visas for foreigners wishing to enter the United States, visit the Bureau of Consular Affairs online or call 603-334-0700. http://nvc.state.gov. http://www.state.gov/r/pa/pl/index.htm

For further information, contact the Office of Public Communication, Public Information Service, Bureau of Public Affairs, Department of State, Washington, DC 20520. Phone, 202-647-6575.

DEPARTMENT OF TRANSPORTATION

1200 New Jersey Avenue SE., Washington, DC 20590
Phone, 202-366-4000. Internet, http://www.dot.gov.

Secretary of Transportation	ELAINE L. CHAO
Deputy Secretary	JEFFREY ROSEN
Under Secretary of Transportation, Policy	MARIA LEFEVRE, ACTING
Chief of Staff	GEOFF BURR
General Counsel	JUDY KALETA, ACTING

Assistant Secretaries

Administration	G. BRYAN SLATER
Aviation and International Affairs	SUSAN MCDERMOTT, ACTING
Budget and Programs / Chief Financial Officer	LANA HURDLE, ACTING
Governmental Affairs	SEAN MCMASTER, ACTING
Transportation Policy	MARIA LEFEVRE, ACTING
Research and Technology	AUDREY FARLEY, ACTING

Directors

Departmental Office of Civil Rights	CHARLES JAMES
Executive Secretariat	RUTH DRINKARD KNOUSE
Office of Intelligence, Security and Emergency Response	MICHAEL W. LOWDER
Office of Small and Disadvantaged Business Utilization	WILLIS MORRIS
Office of the Chief Information Officer	KRISTEN BALDWIN, ACTING
Public Affairs	MARIANNE MCINERNEY

Inspector General	CALVIN L. SCOVEL III

[For the Department of Transportation statement of organization, see the Code of Federal Regulations, Title 49, Part 1, Subpart A]

The above list of key personnel was updated 06–2017.

The Department of Transportation establishes national transportation policy for highway planning and construction, motor carrier safety, urban mass transit, railroads, aviation, and the safety of waterways, ports, highways, and pipelines.

The Department of Transportation (DOT) was established by act of October 15, 1966, as amended (49 U.S.C. 102 and 102 note), "to assure the coordinated, effective administration of the transportation programs of the Federal Government" and to develop "national transportation policies and programs conducive to the provision of fast, safe, efficient, and convenient transportation at the lowest cost consistent therewith." It became operational in April 1967 and comprised elements transferred from eight other major departments and agencies.

Secretary The Secretary of Transportation, who serves as the principal adviser to the President in all Federal transportation program matters, administers the DOT. https://www.transportation.gov/office-of-secretary

Under Secretary The Under Secretary for Policy serves as a principal policy adviser to the Secretary and provides leadership in policy development for the DOT. https://www.transportation.gov/policy

Aviation and International Affairs

The Office of the Assistant Secretary for Aviation and International Affairs develops, reviews, and coordinates policy for international transportation and develops, coordinates, and implements policy on economic regulation of the airline industry. The Office licenses U.S. and foreign carriers to serve in international air transportation and conducts carrier fitness determinations for carriers serving the United States. The Office participates in negotiations with foreign governments to develop multilateral and bilateral aviation and maritime policies on international transportation and trade and to coordinate cooperative agreements for the exchange of scientific and technical information. The Office also resolves complaints of unfair competitive practices in domestic and international air transportation, establishes international and intra-Alaska mail rates, determines the disposition of requests for approval and immunization from the antitrust laws of international aviation agreements, and administers the essential air service program. https://www.transportation.gov/policy/assistant-secretary-aviation-international-affairs

For further information, contact the Office of the Assistant Secretary for Aviation and International Affairs. Phone, 202-366-8822.

Drug and Alcohol Policy and Compliance

The Office of Drug and Alcohol Policy and Compliance ensures that the Secretary's national and international drug and alcohol policies and goals are developed and implemented in a consistent, efficient, and effective manner within the transportation industry. Experts from the Office advise, counsel, and give recommendations on drugs and alcohol, as they pertain to the DOT and testing within the industry, to the Secretary. https://www.transportation.gov/odapc

For further information, contact the Office of Drug and Alcohol Policy and Compliance. Phone, 202-366-3784.

Intelligence, Security and Emergency Response

The Office of Intelligence, Security and Emergency Response ensures development, coordination, and execution of plans and procedures for the DOT to balance transportation security requirements with safety, mobility, and the Nation's economic needs. The Office monitors the Nation's transportation network on a continuous basis; advises the Secretary on incidents affecting transportation systems; leads on issues of national preparedness, response, and transportation security; briefs the Secretary on transportation-related intelligence; performs the DOT's National Response Framework Emergency Support Function responsibilities; coordinates departmental participation in emergency preparedness and response exercises under the National Training and Exercise Program; administers the DOT's Continuity of Government and Continuity of Operations programs; and serves as the DOT representative for emergency planning for civil aviation support to NATO and other allies. https://www.transportation.gov/mission/administrations/intelligence-security-emergency-response

For further information, contact the Office of Intelligence, Security and Emergency Response. Phone, 202-366-6525.

Transportation Policy

The Office of the Assistant Secretary for Transportation Policy analyzes, develops, articulates, and reviews policies and plans for all transportation modes. It also develops, coordinates, and evaluates public policy on safety, energy, and environmental initiatives that affect air, surface, marine, and pipeline transportation. It maintains policy and economic oversight of DOT regulatory programs and legislative initiatives. The Office also analyzes the economic and institutional implications of current and emerging transportation policy issues, transportation infrastructure finances, and new transportation technologies. https://www.transportation.gov/policy/assistant-secretary-transportation-policy

For further information, contact the Office of Transportation Policy. Phone, 202-366-8979.

Research and Technology

The Office of the Assistant Secretary for Research and Technology (OST–R)

was created by title I, division L, of the Department of Transportation Appropriations Act, 2014 (49 USC 112 note), which transferred the authorities, functions, personnel, and powers and duties of the former Research and Innovative Technology Administration to the OST–R. The Office coordinates, facilitates, and reviews DOT research and development programs and activities; performs transportation statistics research, analysis, and reporting; and promotes innovative technologies for improving transportation systems. The OST–R is composed of the staff from the Bureau of Transportation Statistics, the Volpe National Transportation Systems Center, the Transportation Safety Institute, and the Office of Research, Development, and Technology. http://www.rita.dot.gov/about_rita

Sources of Information

Administrations The "Our Administrations" Web page provides convenient Internet access to the home pages of the DOT's administrations. https://www.transportation.gov/administrations

Aviation Consumer Protection For information on air travelers' rights or for assistance in resolving consumer problems with providers of commercial air transportation services, contact the Consumer Affairs Division. Phone, 202-366-2220. https://www.transportation.gov/airconsumer

The Office of Aviation Enforcement and Proceedings produces the "Air Travel Consumer Report" each month. The report makes information on the quality of airline services accessible to consumers. Issues of the consumer report are posted on the DOT's Web site in Portable Document Format (PDF). Phone, 202-366-2220. TTY, 202-366-0511. https://www.transportation.gov/airconsumer/air-travel-consumer-reports

Blog "Fast Lane" is the DOT's official blog. https://www.transportation.gov/blog/fastlane

Business Opportunities Contact the Office of the Senior Procurement Executive. Phone, 202-366-4263. Information is also available on the "Small Business" Web page. https://www.transportation.gov/osdbu

Career Opportunities The DOT employs administrators and managers, air traffic controllers, aviation safety specialists, clerical staff, electronics maintenance technicians, and engineers—aeronautical, automotive, civil, electrical, highway, and general. For further information, contact the Office of the Secretary–Human Resource Operations, 1200 New Jersey Avenue SE., Room W75–340, Washington, DC 20590. Phone, 202-366-9391 or 800-525-2878. https://www.transportation.gov/careers

In 2016, the DOT ranked 8th among 18 large agencies in the Partnership for Public Service's Best Places To Work Agency Rankings. http://bestplacestowork.org/BPTW/rankings/detail/TD00

In 2016, the Office of the Inspector General ranked 13th among 305 agency subcomponents in the Partnership for Public Service's Best Places To Work Agency Rankings. http://bestplacestowork.org/BPTW/rankings/detail/TD12

Civil Rights For information on equal employment opportunity, nondiscrimination in DOT employment and transportation services, or the Department's disadvantaged business enterprise certification appeals program, contact the Director, Departmental Office of Civil Rights. Phone, 202-366-4648. https://www.civilrights.dot.gov

Freedom of Information Act (FOIA) The FOIA gives information seekers the right to access DOT records, unless the Departement reasonably foresees that the release of the information would harm an interest protected by one or more of the nine FOIA exemptions or the release is prohibited by law. The DOT's responsibility is to provide an information seeker with copies of the documents or records or the portions of them that he or she is entitled to receive under the law. https://www.transportation.gov/foia

Motor Vehicle Safety To report vehicle safety problems, get motor vehicle and highway safety information, or request consumer information publications, visit the National Highway Traffic Safety Administration's SafeCar.gov Web site or call its vehicle safety hotline. Phone, 888-327-4236. TTY, 800-424-9153. Complaints also can be filed online. http://www.safercar.gov

News The DOT posts press releases on its Web site. https://www.transportation.gov/press-releases

Office of Inspector General (OIG) To report abuse, fraud, or waste, contact the DOT Inspector General, 1200 New Jersey Avenue SE., West Building–7th floor, Washington, DC 20590. Phone, 202-366-1461 or 800-424-9071. https://www.oig.dot.gov/Hotline

Open Government The DOT supports the Open Government initiative by promoting the principles of collaboration, participation, and transparency. https://www.transportation.gov/mission/open/open-government

Organizational Chart The DOT's organizational chart is accessible online. https://www.transportation.gov/sites/dot.gov/files/DOT-Org-Chart-2017_.png

Plain Language The DOT seeks to comply with the Plain Writing Act of 2010. If a DOT document or Web page is difficult to understand, please contact the Department via email and point out the lack of clarity. https://www.transportation.gov/open/plain-language | Email: PlainLanguage@dot.gov

Policy Initiatives The DOT posts current policy initiatives on its Web site. https://www.transportation.gov/policy-initiatives

Publications The DOT and its operating agencies issue publications on a variety of subjects. Some of these publications are available from the issuing administration or from the Government Publishing Office. http://www.gpo.gov/customers/p-i-sales.htm

Other publications are available from the National Technical Information Service, 5285 Port Royal Road, Springfield, VA 22151. https://www.ntis.gov/index.html

Reading Rooms Contact the Public Docket, Room W12–140, 1200 New Jersey Avenue SE., Washington, DC 20590. Phone, 800-647-5527. DOT administrations and their regional offices maintain reading rooms for public use. Contact the appropriate administration at the address or phone number indicated in the relevant section above or below. Other reading rooms are located at the Technical and Law Libraries: Technical Library, Room 2200, 1200 New Jersey Avenue SE., Washington, DC 20590. Phone, 202-366-0745. Law Library, Room W12–300, 1200 New Jersey Avenue SE., Washington, DC 20590. Phone, 202-366-0746. http://ntl.bts.gov/about_ntl.html | Email: library@dot.gov

Social Media The DOT has a YouTube channel and maintains Facebook, Flickr, Instagram, LinkedIn, and Twitter accounts. https://www.transportation.gov/social. https://www.transportation.gov/briefingroom/administration-news

For further information, contact the Department of Transportation, Office of Public Affairs, 1200 New Jersey Avenue SE., Washington, DC 20590. Phone, 202-366-5580.

Federal Aviation Administration

800 Independence Avenue SW., Washington, DC 20591
Phone, 202-366-4000. Fax, 866-835-5322. Internet, http://www.faa.gov.

Administrator	MICHAEL P. HUERTA
Deputy Administrator	DANIEL K. ELWELL
Chief of Staff	CHRISTOPHER ROCHELEAU

The Federal Aviation Administration (FAA), formerly the Federal Aviation Agency, was established by the Federal Aviation Act of 1958 (72 Stat. 731). The Administration became a component of the Department of Transportation in 1967, pursuant to the Department of Transportation Act (49 U.S.C. 106). The FAA regulates civil aviation and U.S. commercial space transportation, maintains and operates air traffic control and navigation systems for civil and military aircraft, and develops and administers programs involving aviation safety and the National Airspace System.

Activities

Air Navigation Facilities The FAA locates and positions, constructs or installs, maintains, operates, and assures the quality of Federal air navigation electronic and visual aids. At flight service stations, airport traffic control towers, and air route traffic control centers, the Administration operates and maintains computer systems, radar facilities, and voice-data communications and visual display equipment. http://www.faa.gov/about/safety_efficiency

Airport Programs The Administration maintains a national plan of airport requirements, administers a grant program for development of public-use airports to assure and improve safety and to meet current and future airport capacity needs, evaluates the environmental effects of airport development, and administers an airport noise compatibility program. It also develops standards for and technical guidance on airport planning, design, operations, and safety and provides grants to assist public agencies in airport system and master planning and airport development and improvement. http://www.faa.gov/airports

Airspace and Air Traffic Management FAA activities center on the safe and efficient utilization of the navigable airspace. To achieve this goal, the Administration operates a network of airport traffic control towers, air route traffic control centers, and flight service stations. It develops air traffic rules and regulations and allocates airspace use. It also provides air traffic security control that meets national defense requirements. http://www.faa.gov/air_traffic

Civil Aviation Abroad Under the Federal Aviation Act of 1958 and the International Aviation Facilities Act (49 U.S.C. app. 1151), the FAA promotes aviation safety and supports civil aviation abroad. FAA experts exchange aeronautical information with foreign counterparts; certify foreign airmen, mechanics, and repair shops; provide technical aid and training; negotiate bilateral airworthiness agreements with other countries; and participate in international conferences. http://www.faa.gov/about/safety_efficiency

Commercial Space Transportation The Administration regulates and supports the U.S. commercial space transportation industry. It licenses commercial space launch facilities and private sector launches of space payloads on expendable vehicles. It also sets insurance requirements for the protection of persons and property and ensures that space transportation activities comply with U.S. domestic and foreign policy. http://www.faa.gov/about/office_org/headquarters_offices/ast/about

Registration The Aircraft Registry establishes and maintains the record of every U.S. civil aircraft. Buyers seeking information on aircraft they want to acquire, banks that finance aircraft purchases, aviation historians, and law enforcement and security agencies rely on the registry. An aircraft record contains information on the aircraft's registered owner, its airworthiness, and on recorded aircraft security interests. http://www.faa.gov/licenses_certificates/aircraft_certification/aircraft_registry/about_aircraft_records

Research, Engineering, and Development The research, engineering, and development activities of the FAA provide the systems, procedures, facilities, and devices needed for a safe and efficient air navigation and air traffic control system for civil aviation and air defense. The Administration also performs an aeromedical research function: It applies knowledge gained from its research program and the work of others to improve civil aviation safety and the safety, health, and efficiency of FAA employees. The Administration also supports the development and testing of aircraft and their parts. http://www.faa.gov/data_research/research

Safety Regulation The FAA issues and enforces regulations and minimum standards affecting the manufacture, operation, and maintenance of aircraft. It also certifies airmen and airports that serve air carriers. http://www.faa.gov/about/safety_efficiency

Test and Evaluation The FAA tests and evaluates specified items such as aviation systems, subsystems, equipment, devices, materials, concepts, or procedures at any phase in the cycle of their development from conception to acceptance, to implementation. At key decision points, it also carries out assigned independent testing.

Other Programs The FAA administers the Aviation Insurance Program, which provides insurance products to cover U.S. domestic air transportation industry needs that are not adequately met by the commercial insurance market. The Administration develops specifications for the preparation of aeronautical charts. It also publishes current information on airways and airport service; issues technical publications for the improvement of in-flight safety, airport planning and design, and other aeronautical activities; and serves as the executive administration for the operation and maintenance of the DOT automated payroll and personnel systems. http://www.faa.gov/about/office_org/headquarters_offices/apl/aviation_insurance. http://www.faa.gov/air_traffic/flight_info/aeronav

Sources of Information

A–Z Index   The FAA Web site features an alphabetical index to help visitors browse its content or search for information. https://www.faa.gov/quick_reference

Aircraft Registry   The FAA maintains a registry that allows users to search aircraft registration information online. https://www.faa.gov/licenses_certificates/aircraft_certification/aircraft_registry

Airlines   The Air Traffic Control System Command Center Web site features a list of links for the Web sites of airlines. http://www.fly.faa.gov/FAQ/Airline_Links/airline_links.jsp

Airmen Certification   The FAA posts answers to frequently asked questions dealing with airmen certification on its Web site. https://www.faa.gov/licenses_certificates/airmen_certification/airmen_FAQ

Business Opportunities   Registration with the System for Award Management is required for doing business with the FAA. https://faaco.faa.gov

The FAA's small business development program supports the procurement of goods and services from qualified small businesses. http://www.sbo.faa.gov/Home.cfm

Career Opportunities   The FAA offers civil aviation career opportunities in air traffic control, acquisition, contracts, engineering, information technology, safety and security, and other fields. https://www.faa.gov/jobs/career_fields

In 2016, the FAA ranked 165th among 305 agency subcomponents in the Partnership for Public Service's Best Places To Work Agency Rankings. http://bestplacestowork.org/BPTW/rankings/detail/TD03

Contact the FAA   Information for finding the appropriate point of contact or reporting an issue to the FAA is available online. https://www.faa.gov/contact

Data / Research   The FAA conducts research on commercial and general aviation. It posts information on how the research is carried out, the resulting data and statistics, and grant data and funding information. https://www.faa.gov/data_research

Field and Regional Offices   Contact information for field and regional offices is available on the FAA Web site. https://www.faa.gov/about/office_org

Flight Delays   The FAA's Air Traffic Control System Command Center provides status information, which is not flight specific, for general airport conditions nationwide. http://www.fly.faa.gov/flyfaa/usmap.jsp

Email, personal digital assistants (PDAs), pagers, phones, and wireless devices can be used to monitor the real-time operating status of the Nation's largest airports and receive delay information from the FAA. https://www.fly.faa.gov/ais/jsp/ais.jsp

Freedom of Information Act (FOIA)   The FOIA gives anybody the right to access information from the Federal Government. The law requires agencies to disclose information that is requested, unless that information is protected from public disclosure. https://www.faa.gov/foia

FAA posts a lot of information on its Web site. Before making a formal FOIA request, first look through what is immediately available, particularly through the contents of the FAA's electronic FOIA library. The desired information already may be accessible. https://www.faa.gov/foia/electronic_reading_room

Frequently Asked Questions (FAQs)   The FAA posts answers to FAQs on its Web site. https://faa.custhelp.com

Glossary   The Air Traffic Control System Command Center maintains a glossary of air traffic control management acronyms and terms. http://www.fly.faa.gov/FAQ/Acronyms/acronyms.jsp

History   The FAA's Web site features a timeline of aerospace history that starts on December 17, 1903, with Orville and Wilbur Wright's first self-propelled airplane flight. https://www.faa.gov/about/history/timeline

News   The FAA posts factsheets, news items and updates, press releases, speeches, and testimony on its Web site. https://www.faa.gov/news

NextGen   NextGen is a comprehensive suite of state-of-the-art technologies and procedures that enable aircraft to move more directly between two distant points. These technologies will help passengers reach their destinations on schedule and mitigate environmental damage by reducing fuel consumption. To learn more about NextGen and the improvements that it will bring to air travel in the United States, visit its Web site. https://www.faa.gov/nextgen

Social Media   The FAA has accounts on Facebook, Flickr, Instagram, LinkedIn, and Twitter, as well as a channel on YouTube. https://www.faa.gov/news/stay_connected

Wildlife Strikes   Aircraft and wildlife in the United States collide on occasion. Wildlife strikes almost always involve birds; however, the FAA also has received reports of alligator, bat, coyote, deer, skunk, and turtle strikes. The most frequently struck birds are gulls, but ducks and geese cause more damage per strike. The FAA's National Wildlife Strike Database contains the information needed for telling the full story of collisions involving aircraft and animals. http://wildlife.faa.gov

The wildlife strike reporting system helps the FAA collect the information used to build the National Wildlife Strike Database. An online form is available for submitting a strike report. http://wildlife.faa.gov/strikenew.aspx. https://www.faa.gov/about/office_org/headquarters_offices/aoc/contact

For further information, contact the Federal Aviation Administration, Office of Communications, 800 Independence Avenue SW., Washington, DC 20591. Phone, 202-267-3883. Fax, 202-267-5039.

Federal Highway Administration

1200 New Jersey Avenue SE., Washington, DC 20590
Phone, 202-366-0650. Internet, http://www.fhwa.dot.gov.

Administrator	(VACANCY)
Deputy Administrator	BRANDYE L. HENDRICKSON
Executive Director	WALTER C. WAIDELICH, JR.

The Federal Highway Administration (FHWA) was established as an agency of the Department of Transportation by the Department of Transportation Act (49 U.S.C. 104). Title 23 of the United States Code and other supporting legislation authorize the Administration's various activities.

The FHWA improves mobility on our Nation's highways through national leadership, innovation, and program delivery. The Administration works with Federal, State, and local agencies as well as with other stakeholders and partners to maintain and improve the National Highway System, which includes the Interstate System and other roads of importance for national defense and mobility. The FHWA works to increase the National Highway System's safety and to minimize its traffic congestion. The FHWA ensures that America's roads and highways

remain safe, technologically up-to-date, and environmentally friendly.

Through surface transportation programs, innovative and traditional financing mechanisms, and new types of pavement and operational technology, the FHWA helps people and goods move more efficiently throughout the Nation. The Administration also improves the efficiency of highway and road connections to other modes of transportation. The Federal-aid Highway Program's budget is primarily divided between Federal-aid funding and the Federal Lands Highway Program. http://www.fhwa.dot.gov/about

Activities

Federal-aid Highway Program   The Federal-Aid Highway Program supports State highway systems, providing financial assistance for the construction, maintenance and operations of the Nation's 3.9 million-mile highway network, which includes the Interstate Highway System, primary highways, and secondary local roads. The FHWA implements the Federal-aid Highway Program in cooperation with State and local governments. http://www.fhwa.dot.gov/federal-aidessentials/federalaid.cfm

Federal Lands Highway Program   The Office of Federal Lands Highway promotes effective, efficient, and reliable administration for a coordinated program of Federal public roads and bridges; protects and enhances the Nation's natural resources; and gives transportation access to Native Americans. The Office provides financial resources and engineering assistance for public roads that meet the transportation needs of Federal and Indian lands. These services are provided in all 50 States, Puerto Rico, U.S. Territories, and the District of Columbia through the Office's Headquarters and its eastern, central, and western Federal Lands Highway division offices. http://flh.fhwa.dot.gov/about

Sources of Information

All-American Roads / National Scenic Byways   America's Byways—which include the National Scenic Byways and All-American Roads—is an umbrella term referring to the collection of 150 roads that the Secretary of Transportation selects for inclusion based on distinctiveness and diverseness. http://www.fhwa.dot.gov/byways

Business Opportunities   FHWA programs generate a large number of contracting and procurement opportunities. http://www.fhwa.dot.gov/about/business.cfm

The Office of Acquisition and Grants Management manages most FHWA contracting opportunities. Phone, 202-366-4232. http://www.fhwa.dot.gov/aaa

Career Opportunities   The FHWA operates offices throughout the country and hires professionals with expertise in a variety of fields to carry out its mission. http://www.fhwa.dot.gov/careers

The FHWA consistently ranks high among agency subcomponents in the Partnership for Public Service's Best Places To Work Agency Rankings. http://bestplacestowork.org/BPTW/rankings/detail/TD04

Core Topics   The "Core Highway Topics" Web page features a topical, alphabetical list. The topics are categorized according to nine headings: environment, Federal and Indian lands, highway funding, international, research and technologies, road operations and congestion, roads and bridges, road users, and safety. http://www.fhwa.dot.gov/resources/topics

Environment   The "Air Quality and Climate Change Highlights" newsletter is available on the FHWA Web site. https://www.fhwa.dot.gov/environment/sustainability/newsletter/index.cfm

Federal-Aid Essentials   Federal-aid Essentials offers an online library of informational videos and resources for local public agencies. Each video addresses a single topic and condenses the complex regulations and requirements of the Federal-aid Highway Program into basic concepts and illustrated examples. http://www.fhwa.dot.gov/federal-aidessentials

Field and Division Offices   The FHWA comprises a headquarters office in Washington, DC; a Federal-aid division office in each State, Puerto Rico, and the District of Columbia; four metropolitan offices—Chicago, Los Angeles, New York City, Philadelphia—that serve as extensions of the corresponding Federal-aid division offices; and three Federal Lands Highway division offices. http://www.fhwa.dot.gov/about/field.cfm

Freedom of Information Act (FOIA)   The FOIA establishes a presumption that records in the possession of agencies and departments of the Federal Government's executive branch are available to the public. The statute sets standards for determining when Government records must be made available and which records may be withheld. It also gives information seekers specific legal rights and provides administrative and judicial remedies when access is denied. Most importantly, the FOIA requires that Federal agencies provide, to the fullest extent possible, access to and disclosure of information pertaining to the Government's business. http://www.fhwa.dot.gov/foia

The FHWA maintains an electronic FOIA reading room. It contains records that are often requested under the statute.http://www.fhwa.dot.gov/foia/err.cfm

Glossary   The FHWA Web site features a glossary of transportation planning terms and acronyms. https://www.fhwa.dot.gov/planning/glossary

History   The FHWA Web site features a general highway history. http://www.fhwa.dot.gov/infrastructure/history.cfm

Infrastructure   The FHWA's Web site offers a trove of information on the following infrastructure topics: asset management, bridges and structures, construction, design, Federal-aid Program administration, Federal-aid programs and special funding, geotechnical, hydraulics, pavement, preservation, and transportation performance management. http://www.fhwa.dot.gov/infrastructure

Libraries   The FHWA research library is located in the Turner-Fairbank Highway Research Center in McLean, VA. It is open on weekdays, excluding Federal holidays, 7:30–4 p.m. Phone, 202-493-3172. Fax, 202-493-3495. http://www.fhwa.dot.gov/research/library/ | Email: fhwalibrary@dot.gov

Each FHWA office maintains accessibility information that relates to its own program. The accessibility resource library supports the effort to organize information relating to the Americans with Disabilities Act and other accessibility resources that may affect FHWA projects. http://www.fhwa.dot.gov/accessibility

Newsroom   The FHWA posts press releases, as well as photos and videos, speeches and testimony, on its Web site and YouTube channel. http://www.fhwa.dot.gov/briefingroom

Resource Center / Technical Service Teams   The FHWA's technical service teams are organized into 12 activity areas: air quality, civil rights, construction and program management, environment and realty, finance services, geotechnical, hydraulics, operations, pavement and materials, planning, safety and design, and structures. Contact information for these teams and information on their activities, products, and services are available online in the Resource Center. http://www.fhwa.dot.gov/resourcecenter/index.cfm

Social Media   The FHWA tweets announcements and other newsworthy items on Twitter. https://twitter.com/USDOTFHWA

The FHWA maintains a page on Facebook. https://www.facebook.com/FederalHighwayAdmin

The FHWA posts videos on its YouTube channel. https://www.youtube.com/user/USDOTFHWA

Staff Directories   The headquarters organizational directory, key field personnel directory, and Washington headquarters fax numbers are available on the FHWA's Web site. http://www.fhwa.dot.gov/about/staff.cfm

Sustainability   The FHWA provides technical assistance to local, regional, and State transportation agencies to help them enhance sustainability, improve resilience, and reduce energy use and emissions on the Nation's highway system. https://www.fhwa.dot.gov/environment/sustainability/index.cfm. http://www.fhwa.dot.gov/contact

For further information, contact the Federal Highway Administration, Office of Public Affairs, 1200 New Jersey Avenue, SE., Washington, DC 20590. Phone, 202-366-0660.

Federal Motor Carrier Safety Administration

1200 New Jersey Avenue SE., Washington, DC 20590
Phone, 202-366-2519. Internet, http://www.fmcsa.dot.gov.

Administrator	(VACANCY)
Deputy Administrator	DAPHNE Y. JEFFERSON

The Federal Motor Carrier Safety Administration (FMCSA) was established within the Department of Transportation on January 1, 2000, pursuant to the Motor Carrier Safety Improvement Act of 1999 (49 U.S.C. 113).

Formerly a part of the Federal Highway Administration, the FMCSA reduces commercial motor vehicle-related fatalities and injuries. Administration activities increase the safety of motor carrier operations by enforcing safety regulations—targeting high-risk commercial drivers and carriers; improving safety information systems and commercial motor vehicle technologies; strengthening equipment and operating standards; and increasing safety awareness. When carrying out these activities, the Administration works with representatives of the motor carrier industry, labor safety interest groups, and Federal, State, and local enforcement agencies. https://www.fmcsa.dot.gov/mission/about-us

Activities

Commercial Licensing The FMCSA develops standards to test and license commercial motor vehicle drivers. https://www.fmcsa.dot.gov/registration/commercial-drivers-license

Data / Analysis The FMCSA collects and disseminates data on motor carrier safety and directs resources to improve motor carrier safety. https://www.fmcsa.dot.gov/safety/data-and-statistics/motor-carrier-safety-progress-reports

Regulatory Compliance / Enforcement The FMCSA operates a program to improve safety performance and remove high-risk carriers from the Nation's highways. https://www.fmcsa.dot.gov/regulations

Research / Technology The FMCSA coordinates research and development to improve the safety of motor carrier operations and commercial motor vehicles and drivers. https://www.fmcsa.dot.gov/safety/research-and-analysis/active-research-projects

Safety Assistance The FMCSA provides States with financial assistance for roadside inspections and other commercial motor vehicle safety programs. https://www.fmcsa.dot.gov/safety

Other Activities The FMCSA supports the development of unified motor carrier safety requirements and procedures throughout North America. It participates in international technical organizations and committees to help share best-practices

in motor carrier safety worldwide. It enforces regulations ensuring safe highway transportation of hazardous materials and maintains a task force to identify and investigate carriers of household goods that exhibit an unmistakable pattern of consumer abuse.

Sources of Information

Bicyclists / Pedestrians Bicyclists and pedestrians share roads with large trucks and buses. The FMCSA Web site features resources promoting safety issues affecting riders, walkers, and drivers. https://www.fmcsa.dot.gov/safety/resources-bicyclists-and-pedestrians

Career Opportunities The FMCSA posts job announcements on the USAJobs Web site. Application tips, information for students and recent graduates, and reasons for pursuing a career at the FMCSA are available on its Web site. Phone, 800-832-5660. https://www.fmcsa.dot.gov/careers

In 2016, the FMCSA ranked 69th among 305 agency subcomponents in the Partnership for Public Service's Best Places To Work Agency Rankings. http://bestplacestowork.org/BPTW/rankings/detail/TD17

Certified Medical Examiners Inclusion in the National Registry of Certified Medical Examiners is limited to medical professionals who complete training and pass an exam on the FMCSA's physical qualification standards. https://nationalregistry.fmcsa.dot.gov/NRPublicUI/home.seam

Commercial Carriers The FMCSA Web site features resources to help carrier companies with registration and safety and regulatory matters. https://www.fmcsa.dot.gov/resources-for-carrier-companies

The FMCSA Web site features resources—regulatory information and safety publications—to help passenger carriers comply with regulations and operate safely. https://www.fmcsa.dot.gov/safety/passenger-safety/safety-information-passenger-carriers

Commercial Drivers The FMCSA Web site features driver resources to promote safety and for registration and licensing. https://www.fmcsa.dot.gov/resources-for-drivers

Company Safety Records The FMCSA maintains Web sites that provide convenient access to safety-related information. To perform a search, a user must know a company's name, USDOT number, or motor carrier number. https://www.fmcsa.dot.gov/safety/company-safety-records

Data / Statistics   The annual "Pocket Guide to Large Truck and Bus Statistics" highlights the FMCSA's role in collecting and analyzing data on large trucks and buses. The pocket guide is a compilation of statistics from the overall state of the industry to enforcement activity, details on traffic violations and other incidents, the costs of crashes, and more. https://www.fmcsa.dot.gov/safety/data-and-statistics/commercial-motor-vehicle-facts

The Analysis Division compiles the information used for "Large Truck and Bus Crash Facts," an annual report containing descriptive statistics on fatal, injurious, and property-damage-only crashes involving large trucks and buses. https://www.fmcsa.dot.gov/safety/data-and-statistics/large-truck-and-bus-crash-facts

Freedom of Information Act (FOIA)   The FMCSA supports efforts to create a more open and transparent Federal Government, and it conscientiously carries out its FOIA responsibilities. The FMCSA ensures that nonexempt documents or records are accessible to anyone who properly files a FOIA request. Phone, 202-366-2960. Fax, 202-385-2335. https://www.fmcsa.dot.gov/foia | Email: foia@fmcsa.dot.gov

The FMCSA's electronic reading room contains frequently requested records, as well as final opinions and orders, policy statements, and staff manuals. https://www.fmcsa.dot.gov/foia/foia-electronic-reading-room

Frequently Asked Questions (FAQs)   The FMCSA provides answers to FAQs on its Web site. https://www.fmcsa.dot.gov/faq

Grants   State and local government agencies in the 50 States and the District of Columbia, as well as in American Samoa, Guam, Puerto Rico, and the Northern Mariana and the U.S. Virgin Islands may apply for safety grant funding. https://www.fmcsa.dot.gov/mission/grants

Look Before You Book   The FMCSA Web site features resources to assist travel planners or those chartering buses for sport events, field trips, or other group activities. Safety tips and information, software applications (apps) to research bus operators, and information on reporting safety violations are available on the "Look Before You Book" Web pages. https://www.fmcsa.dot.gov/safety/look-you-book/look-you-book

Bus travel safety kits for seniors, students, and those traveling to faith-based events are available on "Look Before You Book." https://www.fmcsa.dot.gov/safety/look-you-book/consumer-safety-resources

Newsroom   The FMCSA posts events, news releases, speeches, and testimony on its Web site. https://www.fmcsa.dot.gov/newsroom

Protect Your Move   The "Protect Your Move" Web pages feature a trove of information on and resources for planning a move, selecting a mover, and filing a moving fraud complaint. https://www.fmcsa.dot.gov/protect-your-move

Safety Violations   Safety, service, or discrimination issues involving a bus or truck or moving company or a cargo tank facility? If so, file a complaint on the National Consumer Complaint Database Web site or by phone on weekdays, 8 a.m.–8 p.m., eastern time. Phone, 888-368-7238. https://nccdb.fmcsa.dot.gov/nccdb/home.aspx

Service Centers / Field Offices   Contact information for service centers and field offices is available on the FMCSA Web site. Phone, 800-832-5660. https://www.fmcsa.dot.gov/mission/field-offices

Social Media   The FMCSA tweets announcements and other newsworthy items on Twitter. https://twitter.com/fmcsa

The FMCSA has a Facebook account. https://www.facebook.com/FMCSA

USDOT Numbers   The FMCSA Web site features an interactive tool that can determine whether or not a commercial vehicle requires a USDOT number. https://www.fmcsa.dot.gov/registration/do-i-need-usdot-number

Veterans   The FMCSA helps veterans find employment in the motor carrier industry. Several provisions in the Fixing America's Surface Transportation (FAST) Act support this effort. https://www.fmcsa.dot.gov/fastact/veteran-drivers. https://www.fmcsa.dot.gov/contact-us

For further information, contact the Federal Motor Carrier Safety Administration, 1200 New Jersey Avenue SE., Washington, DC 20590. Phone, 202-366-2519.

Federal Railroad Administration

1200 New Jersey Avenue, SE., West Building, Washington, DC 20590
Phone, 202-493-6014. Internet, http://www.fra.dot.gov.

Administrator	HEATH HALL, ACTING
Deputy Administrator	HEATH HALL
Executive Director	PATRICK T. WARREN

The Federal Railroad Administration (FRA) was created pursuant to section 3(e)(1) of the Department of Transportation Act of 1966 (49 U.S.C. 103). The Administration promulgates and enforces rail safety regulations, administers railroad financial assistance programs, conducts research and development to improve railroad safety and national rail transportation policy, provides for the rehabilitation of Northeast Corridor rail passenger service, and consolidates Government support of rail transportation activities. https://www.fra.dot.gov/Page/P0002

Activities

Passenger and Freight Services   The FRA's passenger rail activities include administering Federal grants and loans to Amtrak, Alaska Railroad, and high-speed rail; supporting the Secretary of Transportation in his or her role as a member of Amtrak's board of directors; providing guidance and analysis of intercity passenger rail services and high-speed rail. Its freight rail activities include supporting current freight rail market share and growth and developing strategies to attract 50 percent of all shipments 500 miles or more to intermodal rail. The Administration's Office of Railroad Policy and Development implements programs that provide financial support, research and development, and analysis and guidance for the freight rail industry and its stakeholders. https://www.fra.dot.gov/Page/P0247. https://www.fra.dot.gov/Page/P0528

Railroad Safety   The Administration administers and enforces the Federal laws and regulations that promote railroad safety, and it exercises jurisdiction over all areas of rail safety under the Rail Safety Act of 1970—track maintenance, inspection standards, equipment standards, operating

practices. Railroad and related industry equipment, facilities, and records are inspected and required reports are reviewed. The Administration also educates the public about safety at highway rail grade crossings and the danger of trespassing on rail property. https://www.fra.dot.gov/Page/P0010

Research and Development   The FRA's research and development program relies on basic and applied research and on the development of innovations and solutions to ensure the efficient, reliable, and safe movement of people and goods. Safety is the principal driver of the research and development program. https://www.fra.dot.gov/Page/P0019

Transportation Test Center   The Administration tests and evaluates conventional and advanced railroad systems and components at the Transportation Test Center, Inc. Private sector companies and the Governments of Canada, Japan, and the United States use the facility to study the operation of conventional and advanced systems under controlled conditions. Amtrak tests new high-speed locomotives and trains at the Center, and the Federal Transit Administration uses it for testing urban rapid transit vehicles. https://www.fra.dot.gov/Page/P0153. http://www.ttci.aar.com

Sources of Information

Business Opportunities   The FRA's Web site explains how to become eligible for doing business and how to identify business opportunities with the FRA. The Web site also features a database of small business vendors. https://www.fra.dot.gov/Page/P0009

Career Opportunities   The FRA relies heavily on railroad safety inspectors— hazardous materials, motive power and equipment, operating practices, signals and train control, and track inspectors—to carry out its mission. Safety inspectors inspect for compliance with Federal laws, regulations, rules, and standards; conduct accident investigations and report on their findings; and seek correction of unsafe conditions. They also testify as expert witnesses in civil suits. These jobs require skill in evaluation, factfinding, and report writing; comprehension and application of technical and regulatory standards; an ability to build rapport with individuals and organizations; and knowledge of methods used in installation, operation, and maintenance or manufacturing of railroad equipment and systems. https://www.fra.dot.gov/Page/P0008

In 2016, the FRA ranked 106th among 305 agency subcomponents in the Partnership for Public Service's Best Places To Work Agency Rankings. http://bestplacestowork.org/BPTW/rankings/detail/TD05

Electronic Library (E-library)   An e-library offers convenient access to all the documents that are found on the FRA's public Web site. https://www.fra.dot.gov/eLib/Find

Freedom of Information Act (FOIA)   Any person—U.S. citizens, foreign nationals, as well as those representing organizations, associations, and universities—can file a FOIA request. All FOIA requests must be submitted in writing and are processed in the Office of Chief Counsel at FRA headquarters in Washington, DC. https://www.fra.dot.gov/Page/P0386 | Email: FRAFOIA@dot.gov

To comply with the Electronic Freedom of Information Act (E–FOIA) Amendments of 1996, agencies must make some categories of records available to the public on an ongoing basis. https://www.fra.dot.gov/Page/P0388

Horn Noise   Noise from transportation systems, including rail operations, often produces adverse environmental effects. The FRA posts answers to frequently asked questions on horn noise. https://www.fra.dot.gov/Page/P0599

Maps   The FRA Web site features a Geographic Information System safety map. https://www.fra.dot.gov/Page/P0053

News   The FRA posts news items on its Web site. https://www.fra.dot.gov/Page/P0095

Railroad Crossings / Trespassing   FRA programs have helped to reduce the number of railroad crossing and trespassing fatalities by 60% over the last two decades. The Railroad Crossing Safety and Trespasser Prevention Division seeks to continue this trend. Information on and resources for railroad crossing safety and preventing trespassing along railroad rights-of-way are available online. https://www.fra.dot.gov/Page/P0841

Railroad Safety   The Office of Safety Analysis posts railroad safety information—data related to railroad accidents and incidents, including highway-rail grade crossing accidents, rail equipment accidents, and employee injuries and illnesses—on its Web site. http://safetydata.fra.dot.gov/OfficeofSafety/Default.aspx

The FRA monitors the occurrence of train accidents and incidents and investigates serious events to determine their cause and to assess compliance with safety laws and regulations. Detailed information on these investigations is available on the FRA's Web site. https://www.fra.dot.gov/Page/P0037

Regional Offices   A list of the Federal Railroad Administration's eight regional offices—California, Georgia, Illinois, Massachusetts, Missouri, Pennsylvania, Texas, and the District of Columbia —is available on the "Regional Offices" Web page. https://www.fra.dot.gov/Page/P0244

Research / Development   The Office of Research and Development is organized into four divisions and works in 10 program areas. An online table shows where the four divisions and 10 program areas intersect with the most frequent causes of railroad accidents and incidents. https://www.fra.dot.gov/Page/P0562

Social Media   The FRA posts photographs and tweets announcements and other newsworthy items on Twitter. https://twitter.com/USDOTFRA

The FRA has a Facebook page. https://www.facebook.com/USDOTFRA

The FRA posts videos on its YouTube channel. https://www.youtube.com/user/usdotfra. http://www.fra.dot.gov | Email: FRAPA@dot.gov

For further information, contact the Federal Railroad Administration, Office of Public Affairs, 1200 New Jersey Avenue SE., Washington, DC 20590. Phone, 202-493-6024. Fax, 202-493-6481.

Federal Transit Administration

1200 New Jersey Avenue SE., Washington, DC 20590
Phone, 202-366-4043. Internet, http://www.fta.dot.gov.

Administrator	K. JANE WILLIAMS, ACTING
Deputy Administrator	K. JANE WILLIAMS
Executive Director	MATTHEW J. WELBES

[For the Federal Transit Administration statement of organization, see the Code of Federal Regulations, Title 49, Part 601]

The Federal Transit Administration (FTA), formerly the Urban Mass Transportation Administration, was established as an operating administration of the U.S. Department of Transportation by section 1 of Reorganization Plan No. 2 of 1968 (5 U.S.C. app. 1), effective July 1, 1968. The FTA helps America's communities by developing improved public transportation and providing financial assistance to State and local governments to finance public transportation systems and carry out national transit goals and policy. https://www.transit.dot.gov/about-fta

Programs

Alternatives Analysis   The Alternatives Analysis program provides grants to help identify public transportation needs and the costs and benefits of various transportation strategies for a defined travel corridor. The results of these studies may be the selection of a locally preferred transportation alternative, which is the first step for developing viable projects for possible future funding under the New Starts and Small Starts program. http://www.fta.dot.gov/grants/13094_7395.html

For further information, call the Office of Program Management. Phone, 202-366-2053.

Capital Investment   The Capital Investment program helps finance the acquisition, construction, reconstruction, and improvement of facilities and equipment for public transportation service in urban areas. The Capital Investment program makes available three types of funds: fixed guideway modernization funds for rolling stock renewal, safety-related improvements, and signal and power modernization; new and small starts funds for construction of new fixed guideway systems or extensions to

existing fixed guideway systems or corridor based rapid bus systems; and bus and bus facilities funds for the acquisition of buses and rolling stock, ancillary equipment, and the construction of bus facilities. http://www.fta.dot.gov/12304.html

For further information, call the Office of Program Management. Phone, 202-366-2053.

Clean Fuels Grants   The Clean Fuels Grants program helps nonattainment and maintenance areas achieve or maintain the National Ambient Air Quality Standards for ozone and carbon monoxide, and it supports emerging clean fuel and advanced propulsion technologies for transit buses and markets for those technologies. The program funds purchasing or leasing clean fuel buses, including buses that employ a lightweight composite primary structure and vans for use in revenue service; constructing or leasing clean fuel bus facilities, including electrical recharging facilities and related equipment; and projects involving clean fuel, biodiesel, hybrid electric, or zero emissions technology buses. http://www.fta.dot.gov/cleanfuels

For further information, call the Office of Program Management. Phone, 202-366-2053.

Elderly Persons and Persons With Disabilities   The Transportation for Elderly Persons and Persons With Disabilities program provides financial assistance to private nonprofit agencies for the transportation needs of elderly persons and persons with disabilities in places where public services are unavailable, insufficient, or inappropriate; to public bodies approved by the State to coordinate services for elderly persons or persons with disabilities; and to public bodies that certify to the Governor that no nonprofit corporation or association is readily available in an area to provide the service. Funds are allocated by formula to the States. Local organizations apply for funding through a designated State agency. http://www.fta.dot.gov/grants/13093_3556.html

For further information, call the Office of Program Management. Phone, 202-366-2053.

Job Access and Reverse Commuting The Job Access and Reverse Commute program addresses the transportation challenges faced by welfare recipients and low-income persons seeking or maintaining employment. The program provides capital and planning and operating expenses for projects that transport low income individuals to and from jobs and employment-related activities and for projects that support reverse commuting. Many new entry level jobs are located in suburban areas: Low-income individuals have difficulty accessing these jobs from their inner city, urban, or rural neighborhoods. Many entry level-jobs also require working late or on weekends when conventional transit services are either reduced or nonexistent. Many employment related-trips also are complex, involving multiple destinations. http://www.fta.dot.gov/grants/13093_3550.html

For further information, call the Office of Program Management. Phone, 202-366-2053.

New Freedom The New Freedom formula grants program supports new public transportation services that surpass the requirements of the Americans with Disabilities Act (ADA) of 1990. The program makes capital and operating funding available to private nonprofit organizations, State and local governmental authorities, and operators of public transportation services, including private operators of public transportation services. Eligible projects must benefit individuals with disabilities: Projects must assist them with transportation—including transportation to and from jobs and employment services—and remove barriers to transportation. http://www.fta.dot.gov/grants/13093_3549.html

For further information, call the Office of Program Management. Phone, 202-366-2053.

Nonurban Area Assistance The Other Than Urbanized Areas formula grants program provides funding to States to support public transportation in rural areas—with populations under 50,000. The program enhances people's access in nonurbanized areas to health care, shopping, education, employment, public services, and recreation; assists in the maintenance, development, improvement, and use of public transportation systems in nonurbanized areas; encourages and facilitates the most efficient use of all transportation funds used to provide passenger transportation in nonurbanized areas through the coordination of programs and services; helps develop and support intercity bus transportation; and promotes the participation of private transportation providers in nonurbanized transportation. http://www.fta.dot.gov/grants/13093_3555.html

For further information, call the Office of Program Management. Phone, 202-366-2053.

Planning The Office of Planning and Environment supports the development of information that Federal, State, and local officials use to make transportation investment decisions. With FHWA partners, the Office co-administers a national planning program that provides funding, guidance, oversight, and technical support to State and local transportation agencies. The FTA's 10 region offices and FHWA's 52 division offices work to convey the program to State and local governments and other transportation agencies. http://www.fta.dot.gov/about/12347.html

For further information, call the Office of Planning and Environment. Phone, 202-366-4033.

Research and Technology The FTA conducts research, development, demonstration, deployment, and evaluation projects to improve public transportation services. The FTA administers the Bus Testing, International Public Transportation, National Research and Technology, and Transit Cooperative Research Programs. Through the Transit Investments for Greenhouse Gas and Energy Reduction (TIGGER) program, the Administration works with public transportation agencies to implement new strategies for lowering greenhouse gas emissions and to reduce energy use within transit operations. The

FTA has five priority research areas: bicycles and transit, bus rapid transit, environmental sustainability, livable and sustainable communities, and state of good repair. https://www.transit.dot.gov/about/research-innovation

For further information, call the Office of Research, Demonstration and Innovation. Phone, 202-366-4052.

Rural Transit Assistance   The Rural Transit Assistance Program provides a funding source to help design and implement training and technical assistance projects and other support services tailored to meet the needs of transit operators in nonurbanized areas. States, local governments, and providers of rural transit services can receive program funds. States may use the funds to support nonurbanized transit activities in four areas: training, technical assistance, research, and related support services. http://www.fta.dot.gov/grants/13093_3554.html

For further information, call the Office of Program Management. Phone, 202-366-2053.

Safety   The Office of Transit Safety and Oversight administers a national safety program and oversees compliance with it. Based on FTA legislative, policy, and regulatory requirements, the program helps further the nationwide provision of transit service that is equitable, reliable, and safe. http://www.fta.dot.gov/tso.html

For further information, call the Office of Transit Safety and Oversight. Phone, 202-366-1783.

Training and Technical Assistance   The Administration funds the National Transit Institute at Rutgers, The State University of New Jersey. Working with the Institute, the FTA develops and offers training courses on transit operations, planning, workforce performance, and productivity. Institute courses are offered at locations nationwide on a variety of subjects. Current course offerings are posted online. http://www.ntionline.com/courses/list.php

For further information, call the Office of Research, Demonstration and Innovation. Phone, 202-366-4052.

Transit in Parks   The Paul S. Sarbanes Transit in Parks Program provides funding for alternative transportation projects in and around National Parks and other Federal recreation areas. Alternative transportation includes bicycle, ferry, pedestrian trail, shuttle bus, and other forms of public or nonmotorized transportation. These projects reduce congestion, protect sensitive natural and cultural treasures, and enhance visitor experience. Funding is awarded through a competitive process to units of Federal land management agencies and to State, local and tribal government agencies. http://www.fta.dot.gov/transitinparks

For further information, call the Office of Program Management. Phone, 202-366-2053.

Sources of Information

Business Opportunities   Procurement-related information and resources are available on the FTA Web site. https://www.transit.dot.gov/funding/procurement/procurement

Career Opportunities   FTA fills vacancies in its Washington, DC, headquarters and regional offices. The FTA relies on attorneys, congressional relations specialists, engineers, environmental specialists, planners, program management specialists, research program specialists, and other professionals to carry out its mission. https://www.transit.dot.gov/about/jobs/jobs
    In 2016, the FTA ranked 228th among 305 agency subcomponents in the Partnership for Public Service's Best Places To Work Agency Rankings. http://bestplacestowork.org/BPTW/rankings/detail/TD09

Environmental Justice   The FTA posts answers to questions related to environmental justice on its Web site. https://www.transit.dot.gov/regulations-and-guidance/environmental-programs/environmental-justice/environmental-justice-faqs

Events   The FTA has a calendar of events on its Web site. https://www.transit.dot.gov/about/events

Freedom of Information Act (FOIA)   The FOIA grants public access to the content of certain records that are held by the offices, agencies, corporations, administrations, commissions, boards, and services of the Federal Government's executive branch. Some records that contain sensitive commercial, governmental, and personal information are protected from disclosure. https://www.transit.dot.gov/foia/foia-requests | Email: FTA.FOIA@dot.gov

The FTA maintains an electronic reading room. Before submitting a FOIA request, information seekers should search for the desired document or record in the reading room to determine whether it is accessible immediately, without charge. https://www.transit.dot.gov/foia/foia-electronic-reading-room

Glossary   The FTA maintains a National Transit Database glossary on its Web site. https://www.transit.dot.gov/ntd/national-transit-database-ntd-glossary

Grants   The FTA provides grants to local public transit systems. It invests billions of dollars each year to support and to expand public transit services. It provides annual formula grants to transit agencies nationwide, as well as discretionary funding in competitive processes. https://www.transit.dot.gov/funding/grants/grant-programs

History   A brief history of mass transit is available on the FTA Web site. https://www.transit.dot.gov/about/brief-history-mass-transit

National Transit Database   U.S. transit ridership has grown by more than 20 percent in the last decade. To keep track of the industry and provide public information and statistics as growth continues, the National Transit Database records the asset, financial, and operating conditions of transit systems. Phone, 888-252-0936. https://www.transit.dot.gov/ntd | Email: NTDhelp@dot.gov

News   The FTA posts news releases on its Web site. https://www.transit.dot.gov/about/news

Regional Offices   Contact information for the 10 regional offices is available on the FTA's Web site. https://www.transit.dot.gov/about/regional-offices/regional-offices

Research / Innovation   Research projects assess new operational processes, expand public-private partnerships, fund demonstration grants for low or no emissions buses, improve traveler experiences, and test systems that monitor safety. Research and innovation reports and publications are available on the FTA Web site. https://www.transit.dot.gov/research-innovation/research-innovation-reports-and-publications

Social Media   The FTA maintains a channel on YouTube, as well as accounts on Facebook, LinkedIn, and Twitter. https://www.transit.dot.gov/about/news/social-media

Updates   A subscription form is available on the FTA Web site to sign up for email updates. https://public.govdelivery.com/accounts/USDOTFTA/subscriber/new. http://www.fta.dot.gov/newsroom/13006.html

For further information, contact the Federal Transit Administration, Office of Communications and Congressional Affairs, 1200 New Jersey Avenue SE., Washington, DC 20590. Phone, 202-366-4043.

Maritime Administration

1200 New Jersey Avenue SE., Washington, DC 20590
Phone, 202-366-5807. Fax, 800-996-2723. Internet, http://www.marad.dot.gov.

Administrator	REAR ADM. MARK H. BUZBY, USN (RETIRED)
Deputy Administrator	(VACANCY)
Executive Director	JOEL SZABAT

The Maritime Administration was established by Reorganization Plan No. 21 of 1950 (5 U.S.C. app.). The Maritime Act of 1981 (46 U.S.C. 1601) transferred the Maritime Administration to the DOT. The Administration manages programs that help develop and promote the U.S. merchant marine and its operations. It also organizes and directs emergency merchant ship operations.

The Administration serves as the DOT's waterborne transportation agency. Its programs promote waterborne transportation use, the seamless integration of waterborne transportation with other parts of the transportation system, and U.S. merchant marine viability. The Administration's activities involve ships and shipping, shipbuilding, port operations, vessel operations, national security, safety, and the environment. It also maintains the health of the merchant marine—commercial mariners, vessels, and intermodal facilities contribute significantly to national security. The Administration, therefore, supports current mariners, helps educate future mariners, and informs Americans about the maritime industry and how it benefits them. Recently, the Administration realigned its functions to be more effective as an industry promoter and to focus more attention on the environment and safety.

The Administration administers the Maritime Security Program, which maintains a core fleet of U.S.-flag, privately-owned ships that operate in international commerce. Under agreement, these ships are available to provide needed capacity, during war and national emergencies, to meet Department of Defense requirements.

It also administers the Ready Reserve Force program to facilitate deployment of U.S. military forces—rapidly and worldwide. The Force primarily supports transport of Army and Marine Corps unit equipment and combat support equipment. The Force also supports initial resupply during the critical surge period before commercial ships become available. The program provides nearly one-half of the Government-owned surge sealift capability.

For information on the Administration's 10 Gateway Offices, visit the "Gateway Presence" Web page. http://www.marad.dot.gov/about-us/gateway-offices

Sources of Information

Business Opportunities   Links to business services are available on the Administration's Web site. http://www.marad.dot.gov/about-us/links-to-business-services

The Administration uses FedBizOpps.Gov for announcing solicitations and requests for comments. https://www.marad.dot.gov/about-us/office-of-acquisition

Career Opportunities   For information, visit the "Careers" Web page. http://www.marad.

dot.gov/about-us/maritime-administration-careers

In 2016, the Maritime Administration ranked 79th among 305 agency subcomponents in the Partnership for Public Service's Best Places To Work Agency Rankings. http://bestplacestowork.org/BPTW/rankings/detail/TD13

Data / Statistics   The Administration's Web site features an open data portal that provides access to maritime data and statistics. https://www.marad.dot.gov/resources/data-statistics

Educational Resources   The Adopt a Ship program allows a class of students to partner with a ship's crew. During the school year, the class and crew correspond and share experiences. The correspondence stimulates interest in English, geography, history, math, science, trade, and transportation. It gives children a unique opportunity for responding to their natural curiosity of the sea and introduces them to the men and women of the American Merchant Marine. https://www.marad.dot.gov/education/adopt-a-ship-program

A video archives is available on the Administration's Web site. https://www.marad.dot.gov/resources/multimedia-gallery

Exhibits / Virtual Tours   A shipbuilding exhibit and virtual tours inside cargo and crew spaces and engine rooms are part of the Administration's Web site. https://www.marad.dot.gov/about-us/maritime-administration-history-program/maritime-administrations-artifact-collection/exhibits

Freedom of Information Act (FOIA)   Instructions for submitting a FOIA request are available on the Administration's Web site. Fax, 202-366-7485. https://www.marad.dot.gov/about-us/foia | Email: FOIA.Marad@dot.gov

The Administration maintains an electronic reading room. Before submitting a FOIA request, an information seeker should search for the desired document or record in the reading room to determine whether it may be available immediately, without charge. https://www.marad.dot.gov/about-us/foia/electronic-reading-room

Frequently Asked Questions (FAQs)   The Administration posts answers to FAQs on its

Web site. https://www.marad.dot.gov/about-us/frequently-asked-questions
History Historical documents and resources are available on the Administration's Web site. https://www.marad.dot.gov/about-us/maritime-administration-history-program/historical-documents-and-resources
Newsroom News items and releases, as well as advisories, events, photographs, and speeches, are accessible in the newsroom. https://www.marad.dot.gov/newsroom
Ports Information on the importance of ports to the Nation's economy and the Strong Ports program is available on

the Administration's Web site. https://www.marad.dot.gov/ports/strongports | Email: StrongPorts@dot.gov
Publications Factsheets, policy papers, and reports are available on the Administration's Web site. http://www.marad.dot.gov/resources/maritime-publications
Ship Disposal The Administration's Web site provides information on four methods of ship disposal: artificial reefing, domestic recycling, ship donations, and naval sink at sea live-fire training exercises (SINKEX). https://www.marad.dot.gov/ships-and-shipping/ship-disposal. http://www.marad.dot.gov/about-us/contact-us

For further information, contact the Maritime Administration, Office of Congressional and Public Affairs, 1200 New Jersey Avenue SE., Washington, DC 20590. Phone, 202-366-5807.

National Highway Traffic Safety Administration

1200 New Jersey Avenue SE., Washington, DC 20590
Phone, 202-366-9550. Fax, 888-327-4236. Internet, http://www.nhtsa.gov.

Administrator	(VACANCY)
Deputy Administrator	JACK DANIELSON, ACTING
Executive Director	TERRY T. SHELTON, ACTING

[For the National Highway Traffic Safety Administration statement of organization, see the Code of Federal Regulations, Title 49, Part 501]

The National Highway Traffic Safety Administration (NHTSA) was established by the Highway Safety Act of 1970 (23 U.S.C. 401 note) to reduce the number of deaths, injuries, and economic losses resulting from motor vehicle crashes on the Nation's highways.

The Administration administers motor vehicle and related equipment safety performance programs; co-administers the State and community highway safety program; regulates the Corporate Average Fuel Economy program; issues Federal Motor Vehicle Safety Standards (FMVSS) that prescribe safety features and levels of safety-related performance for vehicles and vehicular equipment; rates the safety of passenger vehicles in the New Car Assessment Program; monitors and participates in international vehicle safety forums to harmonize the FMVSS where appropriate; investigates and prosecutes odometer fraud; administers the National

Driver Register Program; conducts studies and operates programs to reduce economic losses in motor vehicle crashes and repairs; performs studies, conducts demonstration projects, and issues regulations requiring manufacturers to provide motor vehicle consumer information; promotes programs to reduce impaired driving, to reduce risky driver behaviors, and to increase seat belt use; and issues theft prevention standards for passenger motor vehicles.

Activities

Research and Program Development The Administration helps develop motor vehicle and highway safety program standards. It analyzes data and researches, develops, tests, and evaluates motor vehicles, motor vehicle equipment, and advanced technologies, and it collects and analyzes crash data. NHTSA activities are broad in scope with respect to safety: The

Administration encourages industry to adopt advanced motor vehicle safety designs, increases public awareness of safety issues, and provides a base for vehicle safety information. http://www.nhtsa.gov/Research

Regional Operations and Program Delivery The NHTSA administers State highway safety grant programs that the Safe, Accountable, Flexible, Efficient Transportation Equity Act: A Legacy for Users authorized. The Highway Safety formula grant program provides funds to States, Indian nations, and the territories each year to support safety programs, particularly in the following priority areas: data and traffic records, emergency medical services, impaired driving, motorcycle safety, occupant protection, pedestrian and bicycle safety, police traffic services, roadway safety, and speed control. Incentive grants are also used to encourage States to implement effective data improvement, impaired driving, motorcycle safety, and occupant protection programs. https://www.nhtsa.gov/highway-safety-grants-program

Rulemaking The Administration issues FMVSS that prescribe safety features and levels of safety-related performance for vehicles and vehicular equipment. The Administration participates in the United Nations World Forum for the Harmonization of Vehicle Regulations (WP.29). It also oversees the New Car Assessment Program and the Government's Five Star Safety Rating Program, which evaluates the safety performance of light trucks, passenger cars, vans, and child seats (https://www.nhtsa.gov/ratings). These evaluations are highly publicized—star ratings must be visible on the price labels of new vehicles. The Administration also educates consumers on topics such as driving while distracted, as well as the proper use of vehicle safety features and child restraint seats. To promote fuel economy, it manages a program establishing and revising fleet average fuel economy standards for passenger car and light truck manufacturers (https://www.nhtsa.gov/laws-regulations/corporate-average-fuel-economy). The Administration also runs an antitheft program. Under this program the NHTSA issues rules requiring that certain passenger motor vehicles meet parts-marking requirements, and it calculates and publishes annual motor vehicle theft rates. https://www.nhtsa.gov/laws-regulations

Enforcement The Administration's Office of Enforcement assures that all new vehicles sold in the U.S. meet applicable FMVSS. Under its compliance program, the Office conducts random tests and collects consumer complaints to identify and investigate problems with motor vehicles and vehicular equipment. If a vehicle or equipment suffers from a safety-related defect or does not meet all applicable FMVSS, the Office seeks a recall, which requires manufacturers to notify owners and to remedy the defect free of charge. The Office monitors recalls to ensure that owners are notified in a timely manner and that the scope of the recall and the remedy are adequate. The Office also assures that all motor vehicles subject to the Corporate Average Fuel Economy (CAFE) regulations meet their respective targets, and it enforces violations of Federal odometer fraud regulations by criminally prosecuting offenders. https://www.nhtsa.gov/recalls

National Center for Statistics and Analysis The NHTSA maintains a collection of scientific and technical information on motor vehicle safety. It also operates the National Center for Statistics and Analysis, whose activities include the development and maintenance of national highway-crash data collection systems and related statistical and economic analyses. The public and the private sector and universities and Federal, State, and local agencies rely on these motor vehicle safety information resources for documentation. https://www.nhtsa.gov/research-data/national-center-statistics-and-analysis-ncsa

Communications and Consumer Information The Office of Communications and Consumer Information develops, directs, and implements communication strategies based on NHTSA policy and programs, including campaigns to support high visibility enforcement efforts. It promotes safety messages for NHTSA vehicle-related issues. The Office also manages NHTSA Web sites and the toll-free Vehicle Safety Hotline. Information received from calls to the hotline forms the basis of investigations, which can lead to recalls if safety-related defects are identified. http://www.trafficsafetymarketing.gov/ciot

Sources of Information

Car Seats   A car seat glossary is available on the Parents Central Web site. http://www.safercar.gov/parents/CarSeats/Car-Seat-Glossary-of-Terms.htm?view=full

The car seat finder is an online tool that uses date of birth, height, and weight to find a car seat type that properly fits a child. http://www.safercar.gov/cpsApp/crs/index.htm

Career Opportunities   Information on job openings is available on the "Jobs at NHTSA" Web page. http://www.nhtsa.gov/Jobs

In 2016, the NHTSA ranked 290th among 305 agency subcomponents in the Partnership for Public Service's Best Places To Work Agency Rankings. http://bestplacestowork.org/BPTW/rankings/detail/TD10

Data   The NHTSA posts factsheets, reports, research notes, statistics, and studies on its Web site. https://www.nhtsa.gov/research-data

Driving Safety   The NHTSA Web site features a trove of safety information and resources. Disabled, older, and teen drivers, as well as motorcyclists and others can find Web pages dedicated to improving their driving habits and addressing their safety needs. http://www.nhtsa.gov/Driving-Safety

Events   The NHTSA hosts meetings and forums to explore new approaches to highway safety. Information and materials from these event are available online. https://www.nhtsa.gov/events

Freedom of Information Act (FOIA)   The NHTSA is required to disclose records that are properly requested in writing by any person. A Government agency may withhold information pursuant to one or more of nine exemptions and three exclusions contained in the FOIA. The act applies only to Federal agencies and does not give a right of access to records held by Congress, the courts, State or local government agencies, and private entities. https://www.nhtsa.gov/about-nhtsa/foia

The NHTSA maintains an electronic reading room. Before submitting a FOIA request, an information seeker should search for the desired document or record in the reading room to determine whether it may be available immediately, without charge. The NHTSA also operates a service center for answering FOIA-related questions. Phone, 202-366-2870. https://www.nhtsa.gov/about-nhtsa/electronic-reading-room

News   The NHTSA posts press releases on its Web site. http://www.nhtsa.gov/About-NHTSA/Press-Releases

The NHTSA posts speeches, press events, and testimonies on its Web site. https://www.nhtsa.gov/speeches-presentations

Publications   The NHTSA disseminates information on traffic safety programs in "Traffic Techs." The publication, starting with the year 1995, is available online. Staring with the years 2005 and 2006, "Traffic Techs" becomes available in Portable Document Format (PDF). http://www.nhtsa.gov/About-NHTSA/Traffic-Techs | Email: TrafficTech@dot.gov

Recalls   The Recalls Spotlight monitors high-profile recalls and provides resources finding and addressing vehicle recalls. http://www.safercar.gov/rs/index.html

The NHTSA's Web site features a search tool that allows the user to enter a vehicle's identification number (VIN) to learn whether it has been repaired as part of a safety recall in the last 15 years. http://www-odi.nhtsa.dot.gov/owners/SearchSafetyIssues

Regional Offices   Contact information for the NHTSA's 10 regional offices is available on the "Regional Offices" Web page. http://www.nhtsa.gov/nhtsa/whatis/regions

Research   The Office of Vehicle Safety Research strategizes, plans, and implements research programs to reduce crashes, fatalities, and injuries. The NHTSA's Web site contains a trove of information related to these programs. http://www.nhtsa.gov/Research

Resources for Parents   The Parents Central Web site features resources to help parents protect their children and educate them on car and road safety and becoming responsible drivers. http://www.safercar.gov/parents/index.htm

Vehicle Safety   The NHTSA Web site features a trove of information on and resources for vehicle safety. Topics include defects and recalls, odometer fraud, theft protection, and tires. http://www.nhtsa.gov/ **Vehicle-Safety** To report suspected safety defects in vehicles, vehicle equipment, and child restraint seats, call the Vehicle Safety Hotline. English- and Spanish-speaking representatives are available on weekdays, excluding Federal holidays. Phone, 888-327-4236. TTY, 800-424-9153. https://www-odi. nhtsa.dot.gov/VehicleComplaint. https:// www.nhtsa.gov/about-nhtsa/contact-us

For further information, contact the National Highway Traffic Safety Administration, Office of Communications and Consumer Information, 1200 New Jersey Avenue SE., Washington, DC 20590. Phone, 202-366-9550.

Pipeline and Hazardous Materials Safety Administration

1200 New Jersey Avenue SE., Washington, DC 20590
Phone, 202-366-4433. Internet, http://www.phmsa.dot.gov.

Administrator	DRUE PEARCE, ACTING
Deputy Administrator	DRUE PEARCE
Executive Director	HOWARD MCMILLAN

The Pipeline and Hazardous Materials Safety Administration (PHMSA) was established on February 20, 2005. It is responsible for hazardous materials transportation and pipeline safety.

Hazardous Materials

The Office of Hazardous Materials Safety develops and issues regulations for the safe and secure transportation of hazardous materials by all modes, except bulk transportation by water. The regulations cover shipper and carrier operations, packaging and container specifications, and hazardous materials definitions. The Office provides training and outreach to help shippers and carriers meet hazardous material regulatory requirements. The Office enforces regulations other than those applicable to a single mode of transportation. It manages a fee-funded grant program to help States plan for hazardous materials emergencies and to assist them and Indian tribes with training for hazardous materials emergencies. The Office also maintains a national safety program to safeguard food and other products from contamination during motor or rail transportation. http://www.phmsa.dot.gov/ hazmat/info-center | Email: phmsa.hm-infocenter@dot.gov

For further information, call the Hazardous Materials Information Center. Phone, 800-467-4922.

Pipelines

The Office of Pipeline Safety (OPS) ensures the safety, security, and environmental protection of the Nation's pipeline transportation system. The Office establishes and enforces safety and environmental standards for pipeline transportation of gas and hazardous liquids. The Office analyzes data, educates and trains, promotes damage prevention, and conducts research and development for pipeline safety. Through OPS administered grants, States that voluntarily assume regulatory jurisdiction of pipelines can receive funding for up to 50 percent of the costs for their intrastate pipeline safety programs. OPS engineers inspect most interstate pipelines and other facilities not covered by State programs. In accordance with the Oil Pollution Act of 1990, the Office also approves and tests oil pipeline spill response plans. http://phmsa. dot.gov/pipeline

For further information, call the Pipeline Safety Information Center. Phone, 202-366-4595. Fax, 202-493-2311.

Sources of Information

Business Opportunities Information on the acquisition vehicles that the PHMSA uses to fulfill the requirements for goods and services of its program offices is available online. http://www.phmsa.dot.gov/doing-biz

Career Opportunities   The PHMSA relies on accident investigators, accountants, attorneys, auditors, budget analysts, economists, engineers, finance analysts, geographic information systems specialists, grant specialists, human resource specialists, information technology specialists, and other professionals to carry out its mission. http://www.phmsa.dot.gov/careers

In 2016, the PHMSA ranked 136th among 305 agency subcomponents in the Partnership for Public Service's Best Places To Work Agency Rankings. http://bestplacestowork.org/BPTW/rankings/detail/TD16

Data / Statistics   The Office of Pipeline Safety makes available data on federally regulated and State regulated natural gas pipelines, hazardous liquid pipelines, and liquefied natural gas plants. The operators of these pipeline facilities report this data in accordance with PHMSA pipeline safety regulations. The PHMSA provides downloads of the raw data, yearly summaries, multiyear trends of safety performance metrics, and inventories tracking the removal of aging and other higher-risk infrastructure. http://www.phmsa.dot.gov/pipeline/library/data-stats

Environmental Justice   The PHMSA Web site provides information for promoting environmental justice and ensuring nondiscrimination in communities. http://phmsa.dot.gov/org/civilrights/EnvironmentalJustice

Events   A calendar of PHMSA events is available online. http://www.phmsa.dot.gov/portal/site/PHMSA/menuitem.c078b89b7940f5f756f2cee62d9c8789/?vgnextoid=574ffed8df6ec410VgnVCM100000d2c97898RCRD&vgnextchannel=574ffed8df6ec410VgnVCM100000d2c97898RCRD&vgnextfmt=print

Freedom of Information Act (FOIA)   The FOIA establishes the public's right to obtain information from Federal Government agencies. Any person may file a FOIA request, including citizens and foreign nationals, as well as associations, organizations, and universities. http://www.phmsa.dot.gov/about/foia

Frequently Asked Questions (FAQs)   The PHMSA posts answers to FAQs on its Web site. http://www.phmsa.dot.gov/about/faq

Glossary   The PHMSA's Web site features an online glossary. http://www.phmsa.dot.gov/resources/glossary

History   Millions of miles of transportation pipelines deliver the energy products that the American public uses to keep homes and businesses running. While rare, pipeline incidents can be fatal and cost millions of dollars in property damage. The Office of Pipeline Safety participated in the investigations of major pipeline incidents in San Bruno, CA; Allentown, PA; and Marshall, MI. In its commitment to safety awareness and outreach, the Office offers a historical look at high-profile pipeline incidents. http://www.phmsa.dot.gov/pipeline/safety-awareness-and-outreach/pipeline-incidents

Library   The electronic library contains an accessible collection of public documents related to the safe transport of hazardous materials. http://www.phmsa.dot.gov/hazmat/library

The Pipeline Library is an online resource containing electronic files that stakeholders and pipeline safety industry professionals regularly use. These files include archives, forms, frequently asked questions, glossaries, and Freedom of Information Act information. http://www.phmsa.dot.gov/pipeline/library

Mapping System   The National Pipeline Mapping System public map viewer is a Web-based application designed to assist the general public with displaying and querying data related to gas transmission and hazardous liquid pipelines, liquefied natural gas plants, and breakout tanks under the jurisdiction of the PHMSA. https://www.npms.phmsa.dot.gov/Default.aspx

News   The PHMSA posts announcements, congressional testimony, events, press releases, speeches, videos, and more in its electronic briefing room. http://www.phmsa.dot.gov/media-congress

Site Map   The Web site map allows visitors to look for specific topics or to browse content that aligns with their interests. http://www.phmsa.dot.gov/about/sitemap. http://www.phmsa.dot.gov/about/contact

For further information, contact the Pipeline and Hazardous Materials Safety Administration, Office of Governmental, International and Public Affairs, 1200 New Jersey Avenue SE., East Building—2d Floor, Washington, DC 20590. Phone: 202-366-4831.

Saint Lawrence Seaway Development Corporation

55 M Street SE., Suite 930, Washington, DC 20003.
Phone, 202-366-0091, 202-366-7147. Internet, http://www.seaway.dot.gov.

Departmental Postal Address: Saint Lawrence Seaway Development Corporation, 1200 New Jersey Avenue SE., Washington, DC 20590.
Email: slsdc@dot.gov.

Postal and Physical Address: Saint Lawrence Seaway Development Corporation–Operations, 180 Andrews Street, Massena, NY 13662.
Phone, 315-764-3200, 315-764-3235

Policy Headquarters—Washington, DC

Administrator	(VACANCY)
Deputy Administrator	CRAIG H. MIDDLEBROOK

Operational Headquarters—Massena, NY

Associate Administrator, Seaway Operations	THOMAS A. LAVIGNE

The Saint Lawrence Seaway Development Corporation (SLSDC) was established by the Saint Lawrence Seaway Act of May 13, 1954 (33 U.S.C. 981-990) and became an operating administration of the DOT in 1966.

The SLSDC, working jointly with the Saint Lawrence Seaway Management Corporation (SLSMC) of Canada, operates and maintains a safe, reliable, and efficient deep draft waterway between the Great Lakes and the Atlantic Ocean. It ensures the safe transit of commercial and noncommercial vessels through the two U.S. locks and the navigation channels of the Saint Lawrence Seaway System and engages in economic and trade development activities to stimulate trade and employment in the eight States of the Great Lakes region. The SLSDC and SLSMC work together on all matters related to rules and regulations, overall operations, vessel inspections, traffic control, navigation aids, safety, operating dates, and trade development programs.

The Great Lakes-Saint Lawrence Seaway System extends from the Atlantic Ocean to the Lake Superior ports of Duluth and Superior, a distance of 2,342 miles. The Corporation's main customers are vessel owners and operators, Midwest States and Canadian Provinces, Great Lakes port communities, shippers and receivers of domestic and international cargo, and the maritime and related service industries of the Great Lakes and Saint Lawrence Seaway systems. https://www.seaway.dot.gov/about/what-does-slsdc-do

Sources of Information

Career Opportunities The SLSDC relies on professionals with expertise in administration, engineering, information technology, management, marine operations, public policy, and other fields. https://www.seaway.dot.gov/about/careers-slsdc

Freedom of Information Act (FOIA) Any person has the right to a copy of certain records possessed by the Government's executive administrations, agencies, boards, commissions, corporations, offices, and services. Some records, however, are protected from disclosure. https://www.seaway.dot.gov/publications/electronic-reading-room

Grants The SLSDC has an easy-to-use Federal grants toolkit that offers a snapshot of the essential information, resources, and tools needed to identify Federal agencies and processes offering financial assistance to maritime stakeholders seeking to carry out environmental, infrastructural, intermodal, and other development projects. https://www.seaway.dot.gov/publications/slsdc-federal-grants-toolkit

Map An interactive map of vessels transiting the Great Lakes-St. Lawrence Seaway System is available online. https://www.seaway.dot.gov/explore/interactive-shipping-map-and-shipping-schedule

News The SLSDC's quarterly newsletter "Seaway Compass" is available online. It features current information and recent news on the Great Lakes-St. Lawrence Seaway System. https://www.seaway.dot.gov/publications/seaway-compass

Publications The "Great Lakes-St. Lawrence Seaway System Directory" is a comprehensive publication on the ports and shipping-related businesses that are critical throughout the region and beyond. It features extensive photography and serves as an excellent resource for readers who are interested in the Great Lakes Seaway maritime industry. https://www.seaway.dot.gov/publications/seaway-system-directory

The SLSDC's marketing brochure offers comprehensive information on the waterway and its significance to the Great Lakes region. It is available online in Portable Document Format (PDF). https://www.seaway.dot.gov/publications/slsdc-marketing-brochure

Reports The SLSDC posts annual reports on its Web site. https://www.seaway.dot.gov/publications/annual-reports

The SLSDC posts Asset Renewal Program reports on its Web site. https://www.seaway.dot.gov/publications/asset-renewal-program-reports

Social Media The SLSDC maintains a Facebook account. https://www.facebook.com/USDOTSLSDC

Studies The "Environmental and Social Impacts of Marine Transport in the Great Lakes-St. Lawrence Seaway Region" study provides marine stakeholders, transportation planners, and government policymakers with an assessment of the potential environmental and social consequences that could occur if cargo carried by marine vessels on the Seaway navigation system shifted to rail and road modes of transport. https://www.seaway.dot.gov/publications/social-impact-study

Videos The SLSDC's Web site features a video gallery. https://www.seaway.dot.gov/explore/video-about-the-seaway

Visitors' Center The Seaway Visitors' Center at the Eisenhower Lock provides tourists and ship watchers with an observation deck where they can view commercial vessels and cruise ships transiting the lock. Each year, hundreds of ships from all over the globe make thousands of transits through the St. Lawrence Seaway. They carry a wide variety of cargoes: coal, grains, iron ore, steel, steel slabs, stone, and more. https://www.seaway.dot.gov/explore/visitors-center. https://www.seaway.dot.gov/about/contact-us

For further information, contact the Saint Lawrence Seaway Development Corporation, Director of Congressional and Public Relations, 1200 New Jersey Avenue SE., Washington, DC 20590. Phone, 202-366-0091. Fax, 202-366-7147.

DEPARTMENT OF VETERANS AFFAIRS

810 Vermont Avenue NW., Washington, DC 20420
Phone, 202-461-4800. Internet, http://www.va.gov.

Secretary of Veterans Affairs	DAVID J. SHULKIN
Deputy Secretary	SCOTT R. BLACKBURN, ACTING
Chair, Board of Veterans' Appeals	DAVID C. SPICKLER, ACTING
Chief of Staff	VIVIECA WRIGHT SIMPSON
Executive Director, Office of Acquisition, Logistics, and Construction	STELLA FIOTES, ACTING
General Counsel	MEGHAN K. FLANZ, ACTING
Inspector General	MICHAEL J. MISSAL

Under Secretaries

Benefits	THOMAS J. MURPHY, ACTING
Health	POONAM ALAIGH, ACTING
Memorial Affairs	RONALD E. WALTERS, ACTING

Assistant Secretaries

Congressional and Legislative Affairs	CHRISTOPHER E. O'CONNOR, ACTING
Human Resources and Administration	PAMELA S. MITCHELL, ACTING
Information and Technology / Chief Information Officer	ROB C. THOMAS II
Management / Chief Financial Officer	EDWARD MURRAY, ACTING
Operations, Security and Preparedness	KEVIN T. HANRETTA, ACTING
Enterprise Integration	DAT P. TRAN, ACTING
Public Affairs	JOHN ULLYOT
Chief Veterans Experience Officer	LYNDA DAVIS

The Department of Veterans Affairs operates programs benefiting Veterans and members of their families: It offers education opportunities and rehabilitation services and provides compensation payments for disabilities or death related to military service, home loan guaranties, pensions, burials, and health care that includes the services in clinics, medical centers, community living centers (which replace nursing home)s, and home- and community-based settings.

The Department of Veterans Affairs (VA) was established as an executive department by the Department of Veterans Affairs Act (38 U.S.C. 201 note). It is comprised of three organizations that administer Veterans programs: the Veterans Health Administration, the Veterans Benefits Administration, and the National Cemetery Administration. Each organization has field facilities and a central office component. Staff offices support the overall function of the Department and its Administrations. http://www.va.gov/landing2_about.htm

Activities

Advisory Committee Management Office The Advisory Committee Management Office (ACMO) provides administrative and management support to the Department's 29 Federal Advisory Committees (as of July 2017). VA's advisory committees solicit advice and recommendations from outside experts and the public concerning programs for which the Department is responsible for by law. http://www.va.gov/ADVISORY

Department of Veterans Affairs

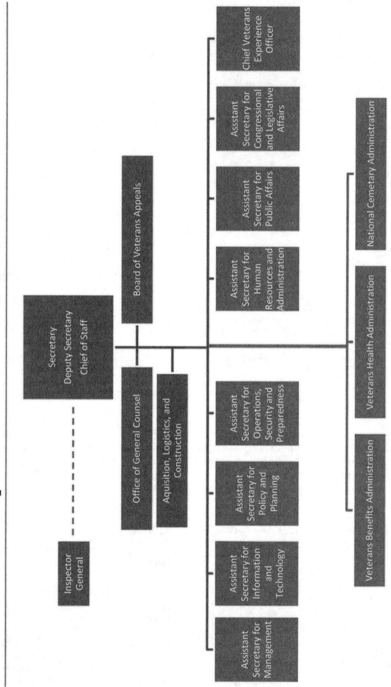

Office of Acquisition, Logistics, and Construction   The Office of Acquisition, Logistics, and Construction (OALC) is a multifunctional organization responsible for directing the acquisition, logistics, construction, and leasing functions within the VA. The Executive Director, OALC, is also the Chief Acquisition Officer for the VA. http://www.va.gov/OALC

Cemeteries   The National Cemetery Administration (NCA) is responsible for the management and oversight of 135 national cemeteries in the United States and Puerto Rico, as well as 33 soldiers' lots, Confederate cemeteries, and monument sites. Burial in a national cemetery is available to eligible veterans, certain members of reserve components, and their spouses and dependent children. At no cost to the family, a national cemetery burial includes the gravesite, graveliner, opening and closing of the grave, headstone or marker, and perpetual care as part of a national shrine. If an eligible veteran is buried in an unmarked grave in a private cemetery anywhere in the world, NCA will provide a headstone or marker. A Government-furnished headstone or marker may be provided for eligible Veterans who died on or after Nov. 1, 1990 and whose grave is marked with a privately purchased headstone. A Government-furnished medallion may be provided for eligible Veterans who served on or after Apr. 6, 1917 and whose grave is marked with a privately purchased headstone or marker. NCA's Veterans Cemetery Grants Program provides funds to State and tribal governments to establish, expand, or improve veterans' cemeteries. NCA issues Presidential Memorial Certificates to honor the memory of deceased veterans who are eligible for burial in a national cemetery. http://www.cem.va.gov

Center for Minority Veterans   The Center for Minority Veterans (CMV), established by the Veterans' Benefits Improvement Act of 1994, identifies barriers to benefits and health care access, promotes awareness of minority Veteran-related issues, develops strategies for improving minority Veterans' participation in existing VA programs, The CMV focuses on the unique and special needs of African Americans, Hispanics, Asian Americans, Pacific Islanders, and Native Americans, which include American Indians, Native Hawaiians, and Alaska Natives. http://www.va.gov/centerforminorityveterans

Center for Women Veterans   The Center for Women Veterans (CWV), established by the Veterans' Benefits Improvement Act of 1994, monitors and coordinates VA's health care, benefits, services, and programs for women Veterans. CWV advocates a cultural transformation within VA and the general public to recognize the service and contributions of women Veterans and women in the military, and raises awareness of the responsibility to treat women Veterans with dignity and respect. The CWV Director serves as the primary advisor to the SECVA on all matters related to policy, legislation, programs, issues, and initiatives affecting women Veterans. http://www.va.gov/WOMENVET

Health Services   The Veterans Health Administration (VHA) is the largest integrated health care system in the United States. It provides hospital, long-term services and support in community living centers (which replace nursing homes)- and home- and community- based settings, domiciliary, and outpatient medical and dental care and community care to eligible Veterans of the Armed Forces. In addition to providing health care, VHA performs research, and assists in the education and training of physicians, dentists, and many other health care professionals through its affiliations with educational institutions and organizations. As of March 2017, VHA treated over 8.76 million patients in over 1,700 sites of care. VHA has 1,247 health care facilities, including 170 VA Medical Centers and 1,067 outpatient sites of care of varying complexity (VHA outpatient clinics). In addition, VA purchases medical care when needed from community providers including long-term services and supports in community nursing homes, State Veterans Homes, and in home and community based settings. In 2016, VA hospitals had about 621,520 inpatient admissions and provided nearly 84 million outpatient visits. In addition to care delivered in the VA system, VA also delivers care to millions of Veterans in the community. The number of women Veterans receiving health care from VA more than tripled between 2000 and 2016, growing from 160,000 in 2000 to 475,000. VA hospitals provide more public data about quality and safety than any health care system in the world and held academic affiliations with more than 1,800 educational institutions. More than 123,552 health care students receive clinical training at a VA facility each year.

Historically, VHA has been at the forefront of medical research. The first electronic health record, cardiac pacemaker, bionic ankle, and successful liver transplant were all developed at VA. VA has also developed new drugs and treatments for acquired immune deficiency syndrome/human immunodeficiency virus, diabetes, Alzheimer's disease, and osteoporosis. Currently, VHA medical centers provide a wide range of services including traditional services such as primary care, surgery, critical care, mental health, orthopedics, pharmacy, radiology and physical therapy. Additional medical and surgical specialty services, including audiology & speech pathology, dermatology, dental, geriatrics, neurology, palliative medicine, oncology, podiatry, prosthetics, urology, vision care and extended care services; such as facility and community based long-term services and supports and hospice care are available. Some medical centers also offer advanced services such as organ transplants and plastic surgery. VA is also using Telehealth and Telemedicine to improve access to care, especially in remote areas. http://www.va.gov/HEALTH

Operations, Security, and Preparedness   The Office of the Operations, Security, and Preparedness provides executive oversight of VA's emergency management, preparedness, identity management, physical security, personnel security and suitability, law enforcement activity, organizational resource management, and federal legal and regulatory compliance to maintain continuity of performance of mission-essential functions across the full spectrum of threats. https://www.osp.va.gov/

Veterans Benefits   VBA provides information, advice, and assistance to Veterans, their dependents, beneficiaries, representatives, and others applying for VA benefits. It also cooperates with the Department of Labor and other Federal, State, and local agencies in developing employment opportunities for Veterans and referrals for assistance in resolving socioeconomic, housing, and other related problems.

VBA's Compensation and Pension and Fiduciary Services are responsible for adjudicating claims for disability compensation and pension, specially adapted housing, accrued benefits, adjusted compensation in death cases, reimbursement for headstones or markers, allowances for automobiles and special adaptive equipment, special clothing allowances, emergency officers' retirement pay, Survivors' claims for death compensation, dependency and indemnity compensation, death pension, burial and plot allowances, forfeiture determinations, and a benefits protection program for minors and incompetent adult beneficiaries.

VBA's Education Service administers VA education benefits to Veterans, Servicemembers, National Guard members, Selected Reserve members, and eligible dependents. These benefits provide financial assistance for attending institutions of higher learning, non-college degree programs, on-the-job and apprenticeship training, flight training, distance learning, correspondence training, national testing programs, licensing and certifications, entrepreneurship training, work-study programs, and co-op training. Education Service also performs compliance surveys to ensure that approved programs are compliant with pertinent laws. Additional information is available at www.benefits.va.gov/gibill.

VBA's Insurance Service operates for the benefit of Servicemembers, Veterans, and their beneficiaries. Customers can reach Insurance Service through the VA Insurance Center (phone, 800-669-8477). The Insurance Center performs a complete range of activities necessary to operate national life insurance programs. Activities include maintenance of individual accounts, underwriting functions, life and death insurance claims awards, and other insurance-related transactions for multiple insurance programs. The Insurance Center administers the Veterans Mortgage Life Insurance Program for those disabled Veterans who receive a VA grant for specially adapted housing, and the Service-Disabled Veterans Insurance program for Veterans who receive a service-connected disability rating. In addition, Insurance Service oversees the Servicemembers' Group Life Insurance (SGLI) and Veterans' Group Life Insurance Programs, as well as the Family Servicemembers' Group Life Insurance and SGLI Traumatic Injury Protection programs.

VBA's Loan Guaranty Service is responsible for administering operations that include establishing the eligibility of Veterans for the program; ensuring VA credit, income, and appraisal requirements are met; managing a panel of appraisers and establishing a property value; approving grants for specially adapted housing; supervising the construction of new residential properties; making direct loans to Native American Veterans to acquire a home on trust land; servicing and liquidating defaulted loans; and disposing of real estate acquired as the consequence of defaulted loans.

VBA's Vocational Rehabilitation and Employment Service (VR&E) program provides assistance to Veterans and Servicemembers with service-connected disabilities and an employment handicap, to prepare for, obtain, and maintain suitable employment. For those persons who are severely disabled and suitable employment is not an option, assistance may be provided to allow each person to live more independently. Through VA's VR&E program, individuals may benefit from individual support, vocational counseling, evaluation of interest, aptitudes and abilities, training, employment assistance, and other rehabilitation services. In some cases, rehabilitation services are available to spouses and children of totally and permanently disabled Veterans as well as Survivors of certain deceased Veterans.

Under 38 U.S.C. Chapter 18, VR&E provides vocational training and rehabilitation services to children with spina bifida having a parent who served in the Republic of Vietnam during the Vietnam era or who served in certain military units in or near the demilitarized zone in Korea between September 1, 1967 and August 31, 1971.

The Appeals Management Office assumes responsibility for and authority over all VBA appeals-related program policy, planning, budgeting, staffing, and other operational control as a separate entity under the VBA Principal Deputy Under Secretary for Benefits (PDUSB). This office works closely with the Board of Veterans Appeals to better service Veterans and their families. http://www.benefits.va.gov/benefits

Veterans' Appeals The Board of Veterans' Appeals (BVA) renders final decisions on behalf of the Secretary on appeals from decisions of local VA offices. The Board reviews all appeals for entitlement to Veterans' benefits, including claims for service connection, increased disability ratings, total disability ratings, pension, insurance benefits, educational benefits, home loan guaranties, vocational rehabilitation, dependency and indemnity compensation, health care delivery, and fiduciary matters. The Board has jurisdiction over appeals arising from the VA regional offices, VA medical centers, the National Cemetery Administration, and the Office of General Counsel. The Board's mission is to conduct hearings and issue timely, understandable, and quality decisions for Veterans and other appellants in compliance with the requirements of law. Final BVA decisions are appealable to the U.S. Court of Appeals for Veterans Claims. http://www.bva.va.gov

Field Facilities The Department's operations are handled through the following field facilities: cemeteries, medical centers, outpatient clinics, community living centers, domiciliaries, and regional offices. Cemeteries provide burial services to Veterans, their spouses, and dependent children. Medical centers provide eligible beneficiaries with medical and other health care services equivalent to those provided by private sector institutions, augmented in many instances by services to meet the special requirements of Veterans. Outpatient clinics provide the most common outpatient services, including health and wellness visits, without the hassle of visiting a larger medical center. Community Living Centers (CLC) are skilled nursing facilities, often referred to as nursing homes. Veterans with chronic stable conditions such as dementia, those requiring rehabilitation or those who need comfort and care at the end of life are served within one of our 135 Community Living Centers. Domiciliaries provide a variety of care to Veterans who suffer from a wide range of medical, psychiatric, vocational, educational, or social problems and illnesses in a safe, secure, homelike environment. VHA continues to expand the network of outpatient clinics to include more rural locations, putting access to care closer to home.

Regional offices grant benefits and services provided by law for Veterans, their dependents, and beneficiaries within an assigned territory; furnish information regarding VA benefits and services; adjudicate claims and make awards for disability compensation and pension; conduct outreach and information dissemination; provide support and assistance to various segments of the Veteran population to include former prisoners of war, minorities, the homeless, women, and elderly Veterans; supervise payment of VA benefits to incompetent beneficiaries; provide vocational rehabilitation and employment training; administer educational benefits; guarantee loans for purchase, construction, or alteration of homes; process grants for specially adapted housing; process death claims; and assist Veterans in exercising rights to benefits and services. https://www.va.gov/directory/guide/home. asp

Office of Survivors Assistance   Office of Survivors Assistance (OSA) provides support to survivors of Veterans by identifying and informing them of the benefits and services offered by VA. https://www.va.gov/survivors/

Center for Faith-Based and Neighborhood Partnerships   The mission of the Center for Faith-Based and Neighborhood Partnerships (CFBNP) is to develop partnerships with, provide relevant information to, and expand participation of faith-based, nonprofit, and community/neighborhood organizations in VA programs in order to better serve the needs of Veterans, their families, survivors, caregivers, and other beneficiaries. https://www.va.gov/cfbnpartnerships/

Congressional and Legislative Affairs   The mission of the Office of the Assistant Secretary for Congressional and Legislative Affairs (OCLA) is to improve the lives of Veterans and their families by advancing pro-Veteran legislation and maintaining responsive and effective communications with Congress. OCLA coordinates the Department's activities with Congress. It is the Department's focal point for interactions and engagements with Members of Congress, authorization committees, and personal staff. Additionally, the Office is the Department's liaison with the Government Accountability Office (GAO). https://www. va.gov/oca/

Office of Small and Disadvantaged Business Utilization (OSDBU)   The Office of Small and Disadvantaged Business Utilization (OSDBU) is the Department's principal liaison to the Small Business Administration (SBA), the Department of Commerce, the General Services Administration (GSA), and the Office of Federal Procurement Policy for matters dealing with small and disadvantaged business activities. OSDBU's mission is to enable Veterans to gain access to economic opportunity by leveraging the federal procurement system and expanding participation of procurement-ready small businesses.

Information for doing business with the VA is available on the Office of Acquisition and Logistics' Web. http://www.va.gov/osdbu

Sources of Information

Blog   "VAntage Point" is the VA's official blog. http://www.blogs.va.gov/VAntage | Email: blog.dalcbdt@va.gov

Business Opportunities   For information on small and Veteran-owned business programs, call 866-584-2344. More information is available from the Office of Small and Disadvantaged Business Utilization's Web https://www.vip.vetbiz. gov/Default.aspx. http://www.va.gov/oal/business/dbwva.asp | Email: dalcbdt@va.gov

For information on small and veteran-owned business programs, call 800-949-8387 or 202-461-4300. More information is available from the Office of Small and Disadvantaged Business Utilization's

Web pages. http://www.va.gov/osdbu | Email: osdbu@va.gov

Business Ownership Services The Center for Verification and Evaluation is a program office in the Office of Small and Disadvantaged Business Utilization. The center provides verification to Veteran-owned and service-disabled Veteran-owned small businesses. Phone, 866-584-2344. http://www.va.gov/osdbu/verification/assistance | Email: pages.osdbu@va.gov

Career Opportunities To provide exceptional health care and other services for our nation's Veterans and their loved ones, the Department of Veterans Affairs (VA) employs over 300,000 people in over 300 occupations. VA uses the traditional Title 5 competitive merit system and the Title 38 excepted merit system in recruiting medical, administrative, and support professionals. Under its Title 38 excepted merit system, VA hires numerous direct patient care professionals such as dentists, licensed nurses, licensed physical therapists, optometrists, occupational therapists, pharmacists, physician assistants, and physicians. These positions are excepted from traditional competitive hiring procedures. Under the Title 5 competitive merit system, VA fills various administrative, clerical, and technical occupations such as management analyst, secretary, and Veterans claims examiner. For information on employment, contact the human resources office at the nearest VA facility, or access VA's online, career-building resources at www.vacareers.gov. http://www.va.gov/jobs

Construction / Design Projects Major Construction projects in excess of $10 million are the responsibility of VA's Office of Construction & and Facilities Management (CFM). CFM is responsible for the oversight and the management for planning, design, construction and operation of facilities and infrastructure of the Department. Projects are advertised on the Federal Business Opportunities website (FedBizOpps.gov). Project-specific qualifications (SF 330) may be submitted to the Regional Directors, Acquisition Support located in Washington, DC, Silver Spring, MD, North Chicago, IL or Vallejo, CA as specified in the project specific advertisement. Additional information on

the selection process can be found on CFM's Web page at https://www.cfm.va.gov/. Construction projects for VA medical centers and other facilities that cost less than $10 million are managed and controlled by the Veterans Health Administration (VHA), Procurement and Logistics Office (P&LO). For information on specific projects visit the P&LO website at https://www.va.gov/plo/. http://www.cfm.va.gov

Data / Statistics The Web site of the National Center for Veterans Analysis and Statistics features reports, statistics, surveys, and other information. https://www.va.gov/vetdata | Email: vancvas@va.gov

Freedom of Information Act (FOIA) The Freedom of Information Act (FOIA) provides that federal agencies must disclose records requested unless they may be withheld in accordance with one or more of nine statutory exemptions (5 U.S.C. § 552(b)). A FOIA request should be addressed to one of the approximately 400 geographically dispersed components where the desired document or record is kept. Contacts are listed here: https://www.oprm.va.gov/docs/foia/VACO_FOIA_Offices_Contact_List.pdf. A request may be sent by email, fax, or postal mail. If the information seeker does not know which office or component maintains the desired document or record, he or she should contact the Director, FOIA Service, (005R1C), 810 Vermont Avenue NW., Washington, DC 20420. Phone, 877-750-3642. Fax 202-273-0487. http://www.va.gov/oig/foia

Health Benefits Glossary The VA Web site features a health benefits glossary. https://www.va.gov/HEALTHBENEFITS/resources/glossary.asp

Patient Safety Glossary The VA National Center for Patient Safety maintains an online glossary of patient safety terms. http://www.patientsafety.va.gov/professionals/publications/glossary.asp

Health Topics The items in the Veterans Health A-Z Index represent popular topics, frequent inquiries and areas of critical importance to Veterans and their caregivers. This navigational and informational tool is designed to help you quickly find and retrieve specific information. The A-Z Index is structured so that synonyms, acronyms, and cross-referencing provide multiple ways for you to access the topics and features on Veterans Health websites. The index will continue to evolve as additional topics are added. https://www.va.gov/health/topics

History The Department's Web site features a history of the VA. https://www.va.gov/about_va/vahistory.asp?

Homeless Veterans Information and resources to help a homeless Veteran find a home are available on the VA Web site. https://www.va.gov/homeless

Locations This page provides a facility locator that allows users to search for VHA facilities by state or territory, street address, type of facility, and distance. https://www.va.gov/directory/guide/division.asp?dnum=1

Media Room The VA posts news releases on its Web site. http://www.va.gov/opa/pressrel

The VA posts speeches on its Web site. http://www.va.gov/opa/speeches

National Gravesite Locator The National Cemetery Administration's Web site features a database of burial information that is updated each day. The online locator allows users to search for the burial locations of Veterans and their family members in VA National Cemeteries, State Veterans cemeteries, and various other military and Department of Interior cemeteries, as well as for the interment sites of Veterans who were buried in private cemeteries and whose graves are marked with Government grave markers. http://gravelocator.cem.va.gov/index.html

Our Doctors The Federation of State Medical Boards web site features an online directory that allows users to search for information about physicians. http://www.docinfo.org/#/search/query

Public Affairs / News Media Contact the nearest regional Office of Public Affairs: Atlanta (404-929-5880); Chicago (312-980-4235); Dallas (817-385-3720); Denver (303-914-5855); Los Angeles (310-268-4207); New York (212-807-3429); or Washington, DC (202-530-9360). Representatives of the national media may prefer contacting the Office of Public Affairs in the VA Central Office, 810 Vermont Avenue NW., Washington, DC 20420. Phone, 202-461-7400. http://www.va.gov/opa

Publications Information on books, factsheets, and other publications is available on the Office of Public and Intergovernmental Affairs Web. http://www.va.gov/opa/publications

Office of Inspector General (OIG) Public documents and information are available on the OIG's Web site. Complaints may be sent to the VA Inspector General (53E), P.O. Box 50410, Washington, DC 20091-0410. Hotline phone, 800-488-8244. http://www.va.gov/oig/default.asp | Email: page.vaoighotline@va.gov

Site Map The Web site map allows visitors to look for specific topics or to browse content that aligns with their interests. http://www.va.gov/site_map.htm

Social Media The VA tweets announcements and other newsworthy items on Twitter. https://twitter.com/DeptVetAffairs

The VA has a Facebook account. https://www.facebook.com/VeteransAffairs

The VA posts photos on Flickr. https://www.flickr.com/photos/VeteransAffairs

The VA posts videos on its YouTube channel. https://www.youtube.com/user/DeptVetAffairs

Veterans Service Organizations The VA's Web site features a directory of Veterans services organizations. For further information, contact the Office of Public and Intergovernmental Affairs, Department of Veterans Affairs, 810 Vermont Avenue NW., Washington, DC 20420. Phone, 202-273-6000. http://www.va.gov/vso. http://www.va.gov/opa

For further information, contact the Office of Public and Intergovernmental Affairs, Department of Veterans Affairs, 810 Vermont Avenue NW., Washington, DC 20420. Phone, 202-273-6000.

DEPARTMENT OF THE INTERIOR

1849 C Street NW., Washington, DC 20240
Phone, 202-208-3100. Internet, http://www.doi.gov.

Secretary of the Interior	RYAN K. ZINKE
Deputy Secretary	VACANT

Assistant Secretaries

Indian Affairs	VACANT
Insular Areas	VACANT
Land and Minerals Management	VACANT
Water and Science	VACANT
Fish and Wildlife and Parks	VACANT
Policy, Management and Budget	VACANT

Principal Deputy Assistant Secretaries

Fish and Wildlife and Parks	VIRGINIA JOHNSON
Water and Science	VACANT
Land and Minerals Management	KATHARINE MACGREGOR
Policy, Management and Budget	SCOTT CAMERON

Chief Information Officer	SYLVIA BURNS
Deputy Inspector General	MARY L. KENDALL
Solicitor	VACANT
Special Trustee for American Indians	VACANT

The Department of the Interior protects America's heritage and natural resources, honors its cultures and tribal communities, and supplies energy for powering its future.

The Department of the Interior was created by act of March 3, 1849 (43 U.S.C. 1451), which transferred the Office of Indian Affairs and the General Land, the Patent, and the Pension Offices to the new Department. It was reorganized by Reorganization Plan No. 3 of 1950, as amended (5 U.S.C. app.). https://www.doi.gov/whoweare

The Department manages the Nation's public lands and minerals, national parks, national wildlife refuges, and western water resources and upholds Federal trust responsibilities to Indian tribes and Alaska Natives. It is also responsible for endangered species and migratory wildlife conservation; historic preservation; surface-mined lands protection and restoration; mapping geological, hydrological, and biological science; and giving financial and technical assistance to the insular areas. https://www.doi.gov/ourpriorities

Secretary The Secretary of the Interior reports directly to the President and directs and supervises all operations and activities of the Department, which has over 70,000 employees and serves as steward of approximately onefifth of the Nation's lands. https://www.doi.gov/whoweare/secretary-ryan-zinke

Fish and Wildlife and Parks The Office of the Assistant Secretary for Fish and Wildlife and Parks oversees natural resources use, management, and conservation programs; National Park and National Refuge Systems lands and cultural facilities; and fish, wildlife, and habitat conservation and enhancement. The Office represents the Department in the coordination and oversight of ecosystems restoration and biological resources programs with States and tribes and other Federal agencies. It also exercises secretarial direction and

321

supervision over the U.S. Fish and Wildlife and the National Park Services.

Indian Affairs   The Office of the Assistant Secretary for Indian Affairs establishes and implements Indian policy and programs; maintains the Federaltribal Governmenttogovernment relationship; assists the Secretary of the Interior with carrying out the Department's Federal trust and treaty responsibilities; directs and supervises the Bureau of Indian Affairs and the Bureau of Indian Education; supervises the Offices of Federal Acknowledgement, of Self Governance, of Indian Gaming, of Indian Economic Development, and all administrative and financial resource management activities; and maintains liaison coordination between the Department and other Federal agencies that provide services or funding to the federally recognized tribes and to the eligible American Indians and Alaska Natives.

The Office of the Special Trustee for American Indians oversees departmentwide Indian trust reform efforts to increase the Secretary of the Interior's effectiveness at carrying out trust responsibilities to American Indian Tribes, individual American Indians, and Alaska Natives. The Office also has programmatic responsibility for the management of financial trust assets, appraisals, and fiduciary trust beneficiary services. https://www.doi.gov/ost

Insular Areas   The Office of the Assistant Secretary for Insular Areas gives financial and technical assistance to the territories of American Samoa, Guam, the U.S. Virgin Islands, and the Commonwealth of the Northern Mariana Islands to promote better governance. It plays a role in the management of relations between the United States and the insular areas by developing and promoting appropriate Federal policies. The Office also carries out the Secretary's responsibilities that are related to the three freely associated states (the Federated States of Micronesia, the Republic of the Marshall Islands, and the Republic of Palau), the Palmyra Atoll excluded areas, and Wake Atoll's residual administration. https://www.doi.gov/oia/who-we-are

Land and Minerals Management   The Office of the Assistant Secretary for Land and Minerals Management oversees the Bureaus of Land Management, of Ocean Energy Management, of Safety and Environmental Enforcement, and the Office of Surface Mining Reclamation and Enforcement. These bureaus run programs associated with public land management; operations management and leasing of public lands for energy resources and mineral extraction, including the Outer Continental Shelf to the outer limits of U.S. economic jurisdiction; mineral operations management on Indian lands; and surface mining reclamation and enforcement functions.

Water and Science   The Office of the Assistant Secretary for Water and Science oversees the U.S. Geological Survey, the Bureau of Reclamation, and the Central Utah Project Completion Act Office. It guides policy and oversees program areas dealing with water project operations, facility security, natural resource management, and research involving geology, hydrology, cartography, biology, and technology. It also guides the development of national water and science policies and supports environmental improvement. https://www.doi.gov/water

For further information, contact the Department of the Interior, 1849 C Street NW., Washington, DC 20240. Phone, 202-208-3186.

Sources of Information

Blog   The Department of the Interior has a blog. https://www.doi.gov/blog

Bureaus and Offices   The Department's Web site features a web page that provides easy access to the numerous bureau and office web sites. https://www.doi.gov/bureaus

Business Opportunities   The Department of the Interior is helping America establish a new foundation for economic prosperity by supporting the transition to a clean energy economy, stimulating local economic growth through stewardship, and procuring goods and services from American businesses. The Department relies on American businesses for bridge, irrigation system, office building, reservoir, road, school, and other types of maintenance.

Additional information is available from the Office of Acquisition and Property

Management, 1849 C Street NW., Rm. 4262, Washington, DC 20240. Phone, 2025137554. https://www.doi.gov/pam

Career Opportunities Information to assist persons with disabilities, students and recent graduates, veterans, and others interested in career opportunities is available on the Department's Web site. https://www.doi.gov/joinus

Information on voluntarism and service is available on the Department's Web site. https://www.doi.gov/volunteer

Climate Science The Department of the Interior posts news items from its Climate Science Centers on its Web site. https://nccwsc.usgs.gov

Diversity Inclusion A list of resources is available on the Department's Web site. https://www.doi.gov/pmb/eeo/resources

Freedom of Information Act (FOIA) Thirteen bureaus and offices support the Department's FOIA operations. The Department's Web site features a single web page that allows convenient access to those bureaus and offices and to their electronic FOIA libraries. From the same web page, an information seeker may file a request, track the status of a request, learn about the FOIA program's structure, and review FOIA-related guidance and resources. Please note: the Department and its bureaus and offices post a great deal of information online; therefore, an information seeker should visit the appropriate electronic libraries and search for the desired information before submitting a FOIA request. That information already may be accessible, immediately and without charge. https://www.doi.gov/foia

Library The Interior Library's holdings and its reference and research services support the mission of the Department and its agencies and bureaus. Its holdings cover American history, geology, law, national parks, Native American culture and history, nature, and public lands and wildlife management. The library offers subscription databases and other online data sources that give Interior employees and external researchers nationwide access. A holdings catalog and descriptions of educational programs and training opportunities are available on the library's Web site. Please note: A temporary library is now open

in Room 2262 of the Stewart Lee Udall Department of Interior Building. Phone, 202-208-5815. https://www.doi.gov/library | Email: library@ios.doi.gov

Wing 1 of the Stewart Lee Udall Department of the Interior Building is undergoing a 2-year modernization project. On May 30, 2014, the Interior Library closed its historic reading room and stack areas. More information is available online to help patrons understand how the modernization project will affect their access to library resources. https://www.doi.gov/library/about/modernization

Museum The Interior Museum offers exhibits on the history and mission of the Department. Programs highlight bureau management of cultural and natural resources. Museum guides conduct tours of the Interior Building's New Deal era art and architecture. Phone, 202-208-4743. https://www.doi.gov/interiormuseum

News The Department posts press releases online. https://www.doi.gov/pressreleases

Open Government The Department of the Interior supports the Open Government initiative by promoting the principles of collaboration, participation, and transparency. Beyond meeting Open Government requirements, the agency intends to create better relationships between citizens and their Government; to become better at understanding citizens' demands for services and more responsive to their needs; to accelerate the rate of innovation by leveraging public knowledge; to increase the Department's ability to carry out its mission more effectively and efficiently by transparently engaging the public in decisionmaking; and to encourage the development of Open Government programs. https://www.doi.gov/open | Email: open@ios.doi.gov

Site Map The Web site map allows visitors to look for specific topics or to browse content that aligns with their interests. https://www.doi.gov/sitemap

Sustainability Programs The Department of the Interior is dedicated to conserving and protecting the Nation's natural and cultural resources now and for future generations. Its employees are passionate about their stewardship responsibility for the resources and properties that they manage for the

American People. https://www.doi.gov/stewardship

Water Conservation   The WaterSMART program improves water conservation and helps water-resource managers make sound decisions about water use. It identifies strategies to ensure that this and future generations will have sufficient supplies

of clean water for drinking, economic activities, ecosystem health, and recreation. The program also identifies adaptive measures to address climate change and its effect on future water demands. https://www.doi.gov/watersmart. https://www.doi.gov/contact-us

For further information, contact the Department of the Interior, 1849 C Street NW., Washington, DC 20240. Phone, 202-208-3100.

Bureau of Indian Affairs

Department of the Interior, 1849 C Street NW., Washington, DC 20240
Phone, 202-208-3710. Internet, http://www.bia.gov.

Director	Weldon "Bruce" Loudermilk

The Bureau of Indian Affairs (BIA) was created as part of the War Department in 1824 and transferred to the Department of the Interior when the latter was established in 1849. The BIA's mission is to fulfill its trust responsibilities and promote self-determination on behalf of federally recognized tribal governments, American Indians, and Alaska Natives. The Bureau provides services directly or through contracts, grants, and compacts to members of 566 federally recognized Indian tribes in the 48 contiguous United States and Alaska—approximately 1.9 million American Indians and Alaska Natives.

BIA programs cover the entire range of State and local government services. These programs, administered by either tribes or the Bureau, support the following activities: managing natural resources on 55 million acres of trust land, providing fire protection and emergency natural disaster relief, developing economically isolated and depressed areas of the United States, law enforcement and administrating tribal courts and detention centers, implementing land and water claim settlements, building and repairing and maintaining roads and bridges, repairing and maintaining high-hazard dams, and managing irrigation systems and agriculture on Federal Indian lands.

The BIA works with American Indian and Alaska Native tribal governments and organizations, other Federal agencies, State

and local governments, and other groups to develop programs and implement them effectively. https://www.bia.gov/WhatWeDo/index.htm

Sources of Information

Career Opportunities   BIA job opportunities, common job documents, and hiring information for American Indian and Alaska Native veterans are available online. https://www.bia.gov/Jobs/index.htm

The BIA tweets Indian Affairs job opportunities on Twitter. https://twitter.com/USIAJobs

Climate Change   The Tribal Climate Resilience program mainstreams climate considerations at the project level through leadership engagement, delivery of data and tools, training, and tribal capacity building. Mainstreaming climate change considerations into all BIA activities is a high priority. Climate change will bring new challenges to Indian Country and Alaska Native Villages. The BIA serves as the lead agency to support tribes as they address changes in the climate. https://www.bia.gov/WhoWeAre/BIA/climatechange/index.htm

Tribal Climate Resilience Resources are available online. https://toolkit.climate.gov/tribal

Estate Planning   The American Indian Probate Reform Act of 2004 (AIPRA) made many changes to the way trust or restricted land and property is inherited. It also made changes that affected land management and purchases. The BIA Web site provides information describing how AIPRA affects wills and inheritance. https://www.bia.gov/yourland/estateplanning/index.htm

Events   A calendar of events is available online. https://www.bia.gov/Calevents/index.htm

Freedom of Information Act (FOIA)   Before submitting a written FOIA request, verify that the desired information is not already publicly available. "FOIA REQUEST" must be clearly written on the envelope, and the requester should be as specific as possible in identifying the record or records being sought. He or she should also include a brief description of the reason for the request because the Department of the Interior may use it as a basis for fee reduction or discretionary release of otherwise exempt materials. Requests made under the FOIA become part of the public record and may be placed in BIA public files. A FOIA request should be addressed to the Indian Affairs FOIA Officer, Assistant Secretary–Indian Affairs, 1849 C Street NW., MS 3070–MIB, Washington, DC 20240. Phone, 202-208-3135 or 202-208-5097. Fax, 202-208-6597. https://www.bia.gov/FOIA/index.htm | Email: foia@bia.gov

Frequently Asked Questions (FAQs)   The BIA posts answers to FAQs on its Web site. https://www.bia.gov/FAQs/index.htm

The BIA Web site also features a "How Do I" informational Web page. https://www.bia.gov/WhereIsMy/index.htm

Library   An online document library features frequently requested documents and links. https://www.bia.gov/DocumentLibrary/index.htm

News   The BIA posts joint statements, statements, and other news items on its Web site. https://www.bia.gov/News/index.htm

The BIA maintains a social media presence on Facebook. https://www.facebook.com/USIndianAffairs211979362167761

Regional Offices   Contact information for the 12 BIA regional offices is available online. https://www.bia.gov/WhoWeAre/RegionalOffices

Site Map   The Web site map allows visitors to look for specific topics or to browse content that aligns with their interests. https://www.bia.gov/SiteMap/index. https://www.bia.gov/ContactUs/index

For further information, contact the Office of the Assistant Secretary for Indian Affairs, Office of Public Affairs, Department of the Interior, MS–3658–MIB, 1849 C Street NW., Washington, DC 20240. Phone, 202-208-3710.

Bureau of Indian Education

Department of the Interior, 1849 C Street NW., Washington, DC 20240
Phone, 202-208-3710. Internet, http://www.bie.edu.

Director	ANN MARIE BLEDSOE DOWNES, ACTING

The Bureau of Indian Education (BIE) provides quality educational opportunities for eligible American Indian and Alaska Native elementary, secondary, and postsecondary students from federally recognized tribes. The Bureau directs and manages education functions, including forming policies and procedures, supervises program activities, and approves the expenditure of funds appropriated for education functions.

The BIE educates approximately 48,000 American Indian and Alaska Native children at 183 elementary and secondary schools on 64 reservations in 23 States. The Bureau operates 57 of these schools. The other 126 schools are tribally operated under the Indian Self-Determination and Education Assistance Act of 1975 (25 U.S.C. 450 et seq.) or the Tribally Controlled Schools Act of 1988 (25 U.S.C. 2501 et seq.). The BIE oversees two postsecondary schools—Haskell Indian Nations University in Lawrence, KS, and Southwestern Indian Polytechnic Institute in Albuquerque, NM—and it funds the Navajo and United Tribes Technical Colleges.

Sources of Information

Career Opportunities American Indian children deserve a quality education—and that starts with highly qualified, dedicated staff and educators. The BIE employees nearly 4,500 professionals in careers that offer unique and diverse cultural and lifestyle experiences. Phone, 505-563-5304. https://www.bie.edu/Jobs/index.htm | Email: staffing@bie.edu

Directory The BIE "National Directory" (SEP 2016) is available in Portable Document Format (PDF) online. https://www.bie.edu/cs/groups/xbie/documents/document/idc2045002.pdf

Divisions and Programs The BIE Web site features a web page with a list of the agency's divisions and programs and links to their web sites. https://www.bie.edu/Programs/index

Freedom of Information Act (FOIA) FOIA requests for BIE records should be sent to the Indian Affairs FOIA Officer. Phone, 202-208-3135 or 202-208-5097. https://www.bia.gov/FOIA/index.htm | Email: foia@bia.gov

News The BIE posts news items on its Web site. https://www.bie.edu/NewsEvents/index.htm

The BIE has a Facebook page. https://www.facebook.com/Bureauofindianeducation

The BIE tweets on Twitter. https://twitter.com/BureauIndianEdu

Reports Performance and special education reports and school report cards are accessible online. https://www.bie.edu/HowAreWeDoing/index.htm

Resources BIE education line officers, school superintendents, principals, teachers, and staff can access program guidance, handbooks, templates, and training provided in various formats—WebEx or PowerPoint—to refresh professional skills. These online documents and presentations are provided to supplement staff training throughout the school year. https://www.bie.edu/Resources/index.htm

Scholarships The BIE Web site provides information on scholarship opportunities for American Indian students. https://www.bie.edu/ParentsStudents/Grants/index.htm

Site Map The Web site map allows visitors to look for specific topics or to browse content that aligns with their interests. https://www.bie.edu/SiteMap/index.htm. https://www.bie.edu/ContactUs/index.htm

For further information, contact the Office of the Assistant Secretary for Indian Affairs, Office of Public Affairs, Department of the Interior, 1849 C Street NW., MS–3658–MIB, Washington, DC 20240. Phone, 202-208-3710.

Bureau of Land Management

Department of the Interior, 1849 C Street NW., Washington, DC 20240
Phone, 202-208-3801. Internet, http://www.blm.gov.

Director	VACANTA

The Bureau of Land Management (BLM) was established July 16, 1946, by the consolidation of the General Land Office (created, 1812) and the Grazing Service (formed, 1934). https://www.blm.gov/about

The Bureau sustains the diversity, health, and productivity of America's public lands for the benefit of present and future generations through a mandate of multiple-use and sustained-yield. It manages 1 of every 10 acres of land across the United States, about 245 million acres of land, most of which is located in Alaska and 11 other Western States. The Bureau also manages about 30 percent or 700 million acres of the Nation's subsurface mineral estate. The Bureau oversees conventional and renewable energy development, livestock grazing, recreation, and timber harvesting, and it protects cultural, historical, and natural resources. Many of these resources are found on National Conservation Lands, a subset of BLM lands that are federally designated, that cover 32 million acres, and that include 223 wilderness areas and 25 national monuments. https://www.blm.gov/programs/national-conservation-lands

BLM management responsibilities and activities are broad in scope and diverse. It manages Federal onshore coal, gas, and oil operations—and also vast stretches of public lands that will play a significant role in the Nation's emerging renewable energy portfolio. The BLM is already 75 percent of the way to reaching President Obama's Climate Action Plan goal of approving projects that will generate 20,000 megawatts of renewable energy by 2020. The Bureau also contributes to wildland fire management to protect the public and the Nation's natural resource landscape, recreational areas, and wildlife habitat. https://www.blm.gov/programs/energy-and-minerals

The Bureau manages livestock on 155 million acres of land, administering nearly 18,000 permits and leases held by ranchers who graze mostly cattle and sheep. Under the Wild Free-Roaming Horses and Burros Act of 1971, it also manages herds of wild horses and burros on public rangelands. https://www.blm.gov/programs/natural-resources/rangelands-and-grazing. https://www.blm.gov/programs/wild-horse-and-burro

Recreation is also part of the BLM's portfolio. Birdwatchers, campers, hang gliders, horseback riders, hunters, mountain bikers, photographers, whitewater rafters, and visitors to cultural and natural heritage sites recreate on hundreds of millions of acres of public lands. The Bureau estimates that it receives approximately 62 million recreational visits per year. https://www.blm.gov/programs/recreation

The Bureau's broad management responsibilities require balancing public land uses and protection of public land resources. Working with State and local and tribal governments, stakeholder groups, and the public, the BLM creates land use plans, referred to as Resource Management Plans, to guide decisions for approved uses of and actions affecting public lands. https://www.blm.gov/programs/planning-and-nepa

Sources of Information

Adoption Schedule The BLM offers wild horses and burros for adoption or purchase at events nationwide throughout the year. The most current adoption event schedule is accessible online. https://www.blm.gov/programs/wild-horse-and-burro/adoption-and-sales/adoption-events

Business Opportunities The National Operations Center in Denver, Colorado, and the Oregon/Washington State Office handle most procurements over $150,000 and also award and administer all Indefinite Delivery / Indefinite Quantity (IDIQ) contracts that are national in scope.

Government contracting and financial assistance information and resources for small businesses are available online. https://www.blm.gov/services/acquisition/contractingl

Career Opportunities The BLM relies on people with diverse skills and professional backgrounds—administration and management, biological sciences, business services, cadastral survey and geological sciences, fire and aviation, law and realty, petroleum engineering, and more—to carry out its mission. https://www.blm./careersl

Information on BLM Pathways programs for students and recent graduates is available online. https://www.blm.gov/careers/students-and-grads/pathways-program-coordinators

Freedom of Information Act (FOIA) Instructions to submit a FOIA request for agency records are available on the BLM Web site. https://www.blabout/foia

General Land Office Records The General Land Office Records Automation Web site provides access to Federal land conveyance records for the Public Land States, including image access to more than five million Federal land title records issued between 1820 and the present. The Web site also has survey plat- and field note-related images that date back to 1810. Please note: The Web site does not currently contain every Federal title record issued for the Public Land States. https://www.glorecords.blm.gov/default.aspx

Reading Rooms State offices provide facilities where visitors may examine status records, tract books, and other records of public lands and their resources.

Recreation The National Conservation Lands program offers online recreational guides for a convenient connection to public lands. https://www.blm.gov/visit

The BLM Web site provides resources for mountain bikers. These resources include the BLM Top 20 Mountain Biking Opportunities list and interactive mountain biking maps for trails on BLM lands. https://www.blm.gov/mountainbike/

Renewable Energy   The BLM Web site features a table that contains the locations and other details of the renewable energy projects approved since 2009 on public lands.

Site Maps   An index of BLM site maps is available online. A site map allows Internet visitors to look for specific topics or to browse content that aligns with their interests.

Speakers   Upon request from organizations within their areas of jurisdiction, local offices will arrange for speakers to explain BLM programs.

Statistics   Public Land Statistics documents according to year and starting with 1996 are accessible online. http://www.blm.gov/public_land_statistics/index.htm

Tables and spreadsheets with data that include the numbers of BLM-administered oil and gas leases, of applications for permit to drill, and of oil and gas wells are accessible on the BLM Web site. Most of the statistics presented cover Fiscal Years 1988–2015. https://www.blm.gov/about/data/public-land-statistics. https://www.blm.gov

For further information, contact the Office of Public Affairs, Bureau of Land Management, Department of the Interior, 1849 C Street NW., Washington, DC 20240. Phone, 202-208-3801.

Bureau of Ocean Energy Management

Department of the Interior, 1849 C Street NW., Washington, DC 20240-0001
Phone, 202-208-6474. Internet, http://www.boem.gov.

Director   ABIGAIL ROSS HOPPER

The Bureau of Ocean Energy Management (BOEM) was created on October 1, 2011, as directed by Secretarial Order No. 3299, as amended.

The Bureau assesses marine-related activities on the Outer Continental Shelf (OCS) and the nature, extent, recoverability, and value of energy resources and minerals located there. It promotes responsible marine-related activities, including exploring, inventorying, and developing energy and mineral resources; analyzes the potential environmental effects of proposed resource management operations; conducts and oversees environmental studies to inform policy decisions on OCS energy and marine mineral resources management; develops and implements leasing and resource evaluation and management regulations; and oversees the financial accountability of lessees, operators, and operating-rights holders to ensure that they meet financial and contractual commitments.

The Bureau promotes cooperation among the Federal Government, State and tribal governments, and native communities on national, regional, and local issues relevant to the scope of its responsibilities. BOEM activities also support national policy priorities: energy security, environmental protection, and social and economic development. http://www.boem.gov/About-BOEM

Sources of Information

Business Opportunities   Information on doing business with the Bureau is available online. http://www.boem.gov/Doing-Business-with-BOEM

Calendar   The BOEM Web site features a calendar of upcoming events. http://www.boem.gov/Upcoming-Events

Career Opportunities   The BOEM relies on professionals with engineering and science backgrounds for ensuring the safe and environmentally responsible development of the Nation's offshore energy and marine mineral resources. http://www.boem.gov/employment

The BOEM posts vacancy announcements on its Web site. http://www.boem.gov/vacancies

Educational Resources   BOEM teacher resources are available online. http://www.boem.gov/Environmental-Studies-Program-Teacher-Resources

Freedom of Information Act (FOIA)   Instructions for submitting a request for BOEM records under the FOIA are available online. The BOEM operates a FOIA requester service center. Phone, 703-787-1818. http://www.boem.gov/Requesting-Access-to-BOEM-Records

Glossary   The BOEM maintains an online resource evaluation glossary. http://www.boem.gov/Resource-Evaluation-Glossary

Historic Preservation   Archaeologists in Office of Renewable Energy Programs coordinate studies and conduct National Historic Preservation Act reviews to identify and protect archaeological sites and other historic properties. OCS historic properties include aircraft, lighthouses, precontact (European contact with Native Americans) archaeological sites, and shipwrecks. Historic properties onshore come under review when a proposed renewable energy project may affect them. To learn more about investigating the steamship "City of Houston" and German submarine "U–576" and other preservation activities, visit the "Historic Preservation Activities" Web page. https://www.boem.gov/Renewable-Energy/Historic-Preservation-Activities

Library   The BOEM Web site has an electronic library. http://www.boem.gov/Library

Marine Minerals   Mineral resources from the OCS are used in coastal restoration projects to address erosion. The BOEM has conveyed rights to millions of cubic yards of OCS sand for coastal restoration projects in multiple States. These projects have restored hundreds of miles of the Nation's coastline, protecting both infrastructure and ecological habitat. The BOEM posts key marine mineral statistics on its Web site. http://www.boem.gov/MMP-Current-Statistics | Email: MarineMinerals@boem.gov

Newsroom   The BOEM newsroom features congressional testimony, factsheets, Frequently Asked Questions (FAQs), leadership presentations, media advisories, notes to stakeholders, science notes, statistics and facts, technical announcements, and videos. http://www.boem.gov/BOEM-Newsroom

Oil and Gas Energy   The BOEM has posted the 2012–2017 lease sale schedule and information on specific lease sales on its Web site. http://www.boem.gov/Oil-and-Gas-Energy-Program/Leasing/Five-Year-Program/Lease-Sale-Schedule/2012---2017-Lease-Sale-Schedule.aspx

Posters   Colorful BOEM posters that promote maritime history, ocean science and stewardship, and awareness of marine animals and their habitats are available from the Gulf of Mexico Public Information Office. Phone, 800-200-4853. http://www.boem.gov/BOEM-Posters

Renewable Energy   The offshore renewable energy guide provides background information on ocean renewable energy resources, the Outer Continental Shelf, and alternate uses for oil and gas platforms. http://www.boem.gov/Offshore-Renewable-Energy-Guide

A list of leases that the BOEM has executed since the inception of its renewable energy program is available online. http://www.boem.gov/Lease-and-Grant-Information

The BOEM collaborates with States on offshore energy development and is in the process of coordinating Federal-State task forces in certain coastal States. A summary of the status of activity in the various States is available online. https://www.boem.gov/Renewable-Energy-Program/State-Activities/Index.aspx

Regional Offices   The BOEM operates three regional offices, one for the Alaska Outer Continental Shelf (OCS) region, one for the Pacific OCS region, and one for the Gulf of Mexico and Atlantic OCS regions. Phone, 907-334-5200 (Alaska). Phone, 805-384-6305 (Pacific). Phone, 800-200-4853 (Gulf of Mexico and Atlantic).

Shipwrecks   The BOEM Alaskan shipwreck table is the most comprehensive compilation of Alaskan shipwrecks to date. The table offers a list of wrecks that occurred in Alaskan waters from 1741 to 2011. The "Shipwrecks Off Alaska's Coast" Web page also features maritime history, ship, and shipwreck links to external Web sites. http://www.boem.gov/Alaska-Coast-Shipwrecks **Site Map** The Web site map allows visitors to look for specific topics or to browse content that aligns with their interests. http://www.boem.gov/Sitemap. http://www.boem.gov/Contact-Us | Email: BOEMPublicAffairs@boem.gov

For further information, contact the Office of Public Affairs, Bureau of Ocean Energy Management, Department of the Interior, 1849 C Street NW., Washington, DC 20240-0001. Phone, 202-208-6474.

Bureau of Reclamation

Department of the Interior, 1849 C Street NW., Washington, DC 20240
Phone, 202-513-0575. Internet, http://www.usbr.gov.

Commissioner	ESTEVAN LÓPEZ

The Bureau of Reclamation was established pursuant to the Reclamation Act of 1902 (43 U.S.C. 371 et seq.). The Bureau is the largest wholesale water supplier and the second largest producer of hydroelectric power in the United States, with operations and facilities in the 17 Western States. Its operations and facilities also support recreation and flood control and benefit fish and wildlife. http://www.usbr.gov/main/about/mission.html

Sources of Information

Business Opportunities The Bureau of Reclamation purchases a wide range of products and services and supports various Federal socioeconomic development programs by reaching out to and assisting businesses. The Bureau also provides financial assistance for programs related to conservation, Endangered Species Act mitigation, rural water, and water management and reclamation and reuse. http://www.usbr.gov/mso/aamd/doing-business.html

The Acquisition and Assistance Management Division is responsible for the Bureau's acquisition and financial assistance policy, acquisition and financial assistance operations, and property programs. Phone, 303-445-2431. http://www.usbr.gov/mso/aamd/org-contact.html

Career Opportunities The Bureau relies on professionals with expertise in administration, engineering and design, environmental protection, research, wildlife management, and other disciplines to carry out its mission. Career-related information is available from the nearest regional office or the Diversity and Human Resources Office, Denver, CO. Phone, 303-445-2684. http://www.usbr.gov/hr

Environment The Bureau maintains a list of links to online resources that provide environmental information. http://www.usbr.gov/environmental

Freedom of Information Act (FOIA) Contact information for the Bureau's regional FOIA coordinators is available online. http://www.usbr.gov/foia/contacts.html

The Bureau maintains an electronic reading room that contains frequently requested records and documents that are currently of special interest. http://www.usbr.gov/foia/readroom.html

Glossary Definitions for terms commonly used by the Bureau are accessible in its online glossary. http://www.usbr.gov/library/glossary

The Bureau maintains a separate online glossary of recreation-related terms. http://www.usbr.gov/recreation/glossary.html

News The Bureau posts news releases and stories on its Web site, which also features congressional testimony, factsheets, photos, and speeches. http://www.usbr.gov/newsroom/newsrelease

Publications Publications for sale are available through the National Technical Information Service. Phone, 800-553-6847. http://www.ntis.gov

Reclamation Manual   The Bureau's Web site has an online tool that allows users to search for keywords and terms in the "Reclamation Manual." The manual comprises a series of policy and directives and standards, which collectively assign program responsibility and establish and document agencywide methods of doing business. http://www.usbr.gov/recman

Recreation   Recreation.gov provides information on all recreation facilities on Federal lands, including those owned and managed by the Bureau of Reclamation or one of its partners. Internet visitors can use Recreation.gov to make reservations at facilities that require them. http://www.recreation.gov/unifSearch.do

The Bureau's Web site features a list of publications on recreation-related topics. http://www.usbr.gov/recreation/publications.html

Regional Offices   Contact information for the Washington, DC, and Denver, CO, based offices and Upper Colorado, Great Plains, Lower Colorado, Mid-Pacific, and Pacific Northwest regional offices is available on the "Addresses and Contacts" Web page. http://www.usbr.gov/main/offices.html

Water Conservation   The WaterSMART program allows all Department of the Interior bureaus to work with States, tribes, local governments, and nongovernmental organizations to pursue a sustainable water supply for the Nation by establishing a framework that provides Federal leadership and assistance on the efficient use of water, that integrates water and energy policies to support the sustainable use of all natural resources, and that coordinates the water conservation activities of the various Department offices. http://www.usbr.gov/watersmart/water.html. https://www.doi.gov/watersmart. http://www.usbr.gov/main/offices.html

For further information, contact the Office of Public Affairs, Bureau of Reclamation, Department of the Interior, 1849 C Street NW., Washington, DC 20240-0001. Phone, 202-513-0575.

Bureau of Safety and Environmental Enforcement

Department of the Interior, 1849 C Street NW., Washington, DC 20240
Phone, 202-208-3985. Internet, http://www.bsee.gov.

Director   Brian M. Salerno

The Bureau of Safety and Environmental Enforcement (BSEE) was created on May 19, 2010, by Secretarial Order No. 3299, as amended. https://www.bsee.gov/who-we-are/history

The BSEE promotes safety, protects the environment, and conserves resources on the Outer Continental Shelf (OCS) through regulatory oversight and enforcement. The Offshore Regulatory Program develops standards and regulations to improve operational safety and to strengthen environmental protection. The Oil Spill Preparedness Division develops standards and guidelines for offshore operators. It also collaborates with sister agencies on spill response technologies and capabilities.

Three regional offices support the Bureau. Their personnel inspect gas and oil drilling rigs and production platforms to ensure compliance with safety requirements. Inspection teams are multiperson, and the expertise of their members spans a range of disciplines. https://www.bsee.gov/what-we-do

Sources of Information

Business Opportunities   Information on doing business with the BSEE is available online. http://www.bsee.gov/About-BSEE/Doing-Business-with-BSEE/index

Career Opportunities   The BSEE relies on professionals with backgrounds in biology, geology, geophysics, engineering, and other fields to carry out its mission. http://www.bsee.gov/careers

Freedom of Information Act (FOIA)   The FOIA gives the public the right to request

Federal agency records and requires Federal agencies to make certain records available. The BSEE Web site serves as the portal to the agency's FOIA program. The FOIA is based on the principle of openness in Government: Any person has a right of access to Federal agency records, except to the extent that such records or portions of them are protected from disclosure by exemption or by special law-enforcement record exclusion. https://www.bsee.gov/newsroom/library/foia

The BSEE maintains an electronic FOIA reading room. https://www.bsee.gov/newsroom/library/FOIA-Reading-Rooom

Frequently Asked Questions (FAQs) The BSEE promotes safety, protects the environment, and conserves resources offshore through regulatory oversight and enforcement. To accomplish this mission, the Bureau relies on a wide range of world-class professionals. The Frequently Asked Questions (FAQs) Web page offers a sample of the questions that BSEE experts address and answers that they have provided. https://www.bsee.gov/newsroom/library/frequently-asked-questions | Email: webmaster@bsee.gov

Glossary This glossary contains common oil and gas exploration and leasing terms, many of which are unique to the drilling industry. https://www.bsee.gov/newsroom/library/glossary

News The BSEE newsroom contains feature stories, media advisories, news briefs, photos and videos, press releases, and posts from the Director. The briefing room contains annual reports, congressional testimony, factsheets, speeches, statements, and technical presentations. https://www.bsee.gov/newsroom

The BSEE tweets announcements and other newsworthy items on Twitter. https://twitter.com/BSEEgov

Offshore Statistics The BSEE Web sites features a section dedicated to offshore statistics and facts. https://www.bsee.gov/stats-facts

Reading Room The Bureau's Deepwater Horizon electronic reading room contains documents that deal with the BP/Deepwater Horizon explosion and ensuing oil spill and that have been cleared for public release. https://www.bsee.gov/newsroom/library/archive/deepwater-horizon-reading-room

Regional Offices Information on the BSEE's three geographic regions—Alaska OCS, Gulf of Mexico OCS, and Pacific OCS—and their respective regional offices is available on the "BSEE Regions" Web page. http://www.bsee.gov/About-BSEE/BSEE-Regions/BSEE-Regions

Site Map The Web site map allows visitors to look for specific topics or to browse content that aligns with their interests. https://www.bsee.gov/sitemap. http://www.bsee.gov/About-BSEE/Contact-Us/Contact-Us

For further information, contact the Office of Public Affairs, Bureau of Safety and Environmental Enforcement, Department of the Interior, 1849 C Street NW., Washington, DC 20240-7000. Phone, 202-208-3985.

National Park Service

Department of the Interior, 1849 C Street NW., Washington, DC 20240
Phone, 202-208-6843. Internet, http://www.nps.gov.

Director	JONATHAN B. JARVIS

The National Park Service (NPS) was established in the Department of the Interior on August 25, 1916 (16 U.S.C. 1). http://www.nps.gov/aboutus/index.htm

The National Park Service protects the natural and cultural resources and values of the National Park System for the benefit of present and future generations. The National Park System comprises 401 units. These units include national parks, monuments and memorials, battlefield sites and national military parks, scenic parkways, preserves and reserves, trails and riverways, rivers and lakeshores and seashores, recreation areas, and historic sites of American or international importance. The Service also manages a variety of national and international programs to promote natural and cultural resource conservation and to expand the benefits of outdoor recreation.

The NPS develops and implements park management plans and staffs the areas under its administration. Through exhibits, films, publications talks, tours, and other interpretive media, it promotes the natural values of these areas and communicates their historical significance to the public. The NPS operates a range of visitor facilities, including campgrounds, and provides a variety of food, lodging, and transportation services.

The National Park Service also administers the State portion of the Land and Water Conservation Fund, State comprehensive outdoor recreation planning, nationwide outdoor recreation coordination and information, the National Register of Historic Places and the National Trails System, natural area programs, national historic landmarks and historic preservation, technical preservation services, the historic American engineering record and buildings survey, interagency archeological services, and planning and technical assistance for the national wild and scenic rivers system.

Sources of Information

America the Beautiful Passes   A pass may be used at more than 2,000 Federal recreation sites. A pass covers entrance fees at national parks and national wildlife refuges, as well as standard amenity fees and day use fees at national forests and grasslands and at lands managed by the Bureaus of Land Management and Reclamation and the U.S. Army Corps of Engineers. Five types of America the Beautiful passes are available: access, annual, annual fourth grade, senior, and volunteer. https://www.nps.gov/planyourvisit/passes.htm

Business Opportunities   Visit the "Doing Business With Us" Web page to find information on commercial tours, contracts and procurement, National Park concessions, and special park uses, including commercial filming. http://www.nps.gov/aboutus/doingbusinesswithus.htm

Career Opportunities   To find permanent and seasonal NPS career opportunities online, visit USAJobs, the Federal

Government's official source for Federal job listings. https://my.usajobs.gov

Additional information on internships, permanent careers, seasonal opportunities, and volunteering is available on the "Work With Us" Web page. http://www.nps.gov/aboutus/workwithus.htm

Directories   An online text box allows Internet visitors to search for NPS employees by last name. https://www.nps.gov/directory

A park directory (SEP 2016) that includes park addresses, codes, phone numbers, and superintendents is available online in Portable Document Format (PDF). https://www.nps.gov/aboutus/upload/NPS-Park-Listing-09-01-16.pdf

Find a Park   Visitors to the NPS Web site may search for a park by name or by State. https://www.nps.gov/findapark/index.htm

Freedom of Information Act (FOIA)   Instructions for submitting a FOIA request to obtain NPS records are available online. https://www.nps.gov/aboutus/foia/index.htm

The NPS Web site features an electronic FOIA library. https://www.nps.gov/aboutus/foia/foia-reading-room.htm

Frequently Asked Questions (FAQs)   The NPS Web site has answers to these questions. https://www.nps.gov/aboutus/faqs.htm

Glossaries   The NPS's National Center for Preservation Technology and Training maintains an extensive glossary of building stone terms. https://ncptt.nps.gov/buildingstone/glossary

The online series "Defining the Southwest" includes a glossary of terms that are often encountered in discussions of the cultures and environments of the American Southwest. https://www.nps.gov/articles/southwest-glossary.htm

A glossary of geologic terms that the NPS and U.S. Geological Survey western Earth surface processes team compiled is available on the NPS Web site. http://www.nature.nps.gov/geology/usgsnps/misc/glossaryAtoC.html | Email: parkgeology@den.nps.gov

Grants   Information is available online for grants authorized under the Land and Water Conservation Fund. Phone, 202-354-6900. http://www.nps.gov/lwcf/index.htm

Information is also available online for grants authorized under the Historic

Preservation Fund. Phone, 202-354-2067. http://www.nps.gov/preservation-grants

News   The NPS posts new releases online. https://www.nps.gov/aboutus/news/news-releases.htm

The NPS Web site features a multimedia section that includes audio, photographs, videos, and webcam. https://www.nps.gov/media/multimedia-search.htm

The NPS tweets announcements and other newsworthy items on Twitter. https://twitter.com/natlparkservice

The NPS maintains a Facebook page. https://www.facebook.com/nationalparkservice

Publications   To explain decisions, document information, and disseminate knowledge, the NPS uses a variety of publications, many of which are accessible online. For example, "The National Parks: Index 2012–2016" can be downloaded as a PDF. The "Publications" Web page offers online access to contemporary and historic reports, periodicals, virtual stacks, and public databases. http://www.nps.gov/aboutus/publications.htm

Some publications are available for purchase in hardcopy from the U.S. Government Bookstore. Phone, 202-512-1800. Phone, 866-512-1800. https://bookstore.gpo.gov/agency/222 | Email: contactcenter@gpo.gov

Regional Offices   Contact information is available online for NPS regional offices and parks and the Washington office. http://www.nps.gov/aboutus/contactinformation.htm. https://www.nps.gov/aboutus/contactus.htm

For further information, contact the Office of Communications, National Park Service, Department of the Interior, 1849 C Street NW., Washington, DC 20240. Phone, 202-208-6843.

Office of Surface Mining Reclamation and Enforcement

Department of the Interior, 1951 Constitution Avenue NW., Washington, DC 20240
Phone, 202-208-2565. TDD, 202-208-2694. Internet, http://www.osmre.gov.

Director	JOSEPH PIZARCHIK

The Office of Surface Mining Reclamation and Enforcement (OSMRE) was established in the Department of the Interior by the Surface Mining Control and Reclamation Act of 1977 (30 U.S.C. 1211). http://www.osmre.gov/about.shtm

The OSMRE carries out the requirements of the Surface Mining Control and Reclamation Act in cooperation with States and tribes. The Office protects people and the environment from the adverse effects of coal mining. The OSMRE assures that land is restored to beneficial use after mining operations cease, and it mitigates the effects of past operations by reclamation of abandoned coal mines. The Office mainly oversees State mining regulatory and abandoned-mine reclamation programs, assists States in meeting the objectives of surface mining law, and regulates mining and reclamation activities on Federal and Indian lands and in those States opting not to assume primary responsibility for regulating coal mining and reclamation activities within their borders.

The Office establishes national policy for the surface mining control and reclamation program, reviews and approves amendments to previously approved State programs, and reviews and recommends approval of new State program submissions. It also manages the collection, disbursement, and accounting of abandoned-mine land reclamation fees; administers civil penalties programs; establishes technical standards and regulatory policy for reclamation and enforcement; offers guidance for environmental considerations, research, training, and technology transfers; and monitors and evaluates State and tribal regulatory programs, cooperative agreements, and abandoned-mine land reclamation programs.

Sources of Information

Abandoned Mine Land Inventory System To provide information for implementing the Surface Mining Control and Reclamation Act of 1977, the OSMRE maintains an inventory of land and water affected by past mining. The inventory contains information on the location, type, and extent of abandoned mine land impacts, as well as information on the reclamation costs. The inventory is based on field surveys by State, tribal, and OSMRE program officials. https://amlis.osmre.gov/About.aspx

Business Opportunities Information to assist small business operators and owners is available online. For additional information, contact the Acquisition Management Branch. Phone, 202-208-2902. http://www.osmre.gov/contacts/business.shtm

Career Opportunities To find employment opportunities at the OSMRE, visit the "Jobs at OSMRE" Web page and click on the USAJobs quick link. http://www.osmre.gov/contacts/jobs.shtm

Freedom of Information Act (FOIA) A FOIA request for OSMRE records may be submitted via electronic or postal mail or by using the Department of the Interior's electronic request form and selecting "Office of Surface Mining" in the drop-down menu. http://www.osmre.gov/lrg/foia.shtm | Email: foia@osmre.gov

Frequently Asked Questions (FAQs) The OSMRE posts answers to FAQs on its Web site. http://www.osmre.gov/resources/FAQs.shtm

The OSMRE Web site also features a "How Do I?" section. http://www.osmre.gov/howdoi.shtm

Grants Information on regulatory program grants and abandoned mine land grants is available on the OSMRE Web site. http://www.osmre.gov/resources/grants.shtm

Library The general public may use the OSMRE online library catalog to locate legal and technical information. http://o10007.eos-intl.net/O10007/OPAC/Index.aspx

Mine Maps The National Mine Map Repository collects and maintains mine map information and images for the entire country. http://mmr.osmre.gov

An index that includes over 180,000 maps of closed and abandoned mines is available online. The index serves as an inventory for determining which maps are available. To obtain actual copies of maps, contact the National Mine Map Repository. Fax, 412-937-2888. http://mmr.osmre.gov/MultiPub.aspx

Most Requested Content The OSMRE Web site features a collection of links to its most frequently requested Web pages. http://www.osmre.gov/resources/mostRequested.shtm

Newsroom The newsroom features OSMRE stories and news releases. http://www.osmre.gov/resources/newsroom.shtm

The OSMRE tweets announcements and other newsworthy items on Twitter. https://twitter.com/OSMRE

The OSMRE has a Facebook page. https://www.facebook.com/Office.of.Surface.Mining.Reclamation.Enforcement

Regional Offices Appalachian Region Office. http://www.arcc.osmre.gov/contacts.shtm

Mid-Continent Region Office. http://www.mcrcc.osmre.gov/contacts.shtm

Western Region Office. http://www.wrcc.osmre.gov/contacts.shtm

Resources The OSMRE Web site features a section dedicated to electronic, informational resources. http://www.osmre.gov/resources.shtm

Site Map The Web site map allows visitors to look for specific topics or to browse content that aligns with their interests. http://www.osmre.gov/resources/sitemap.shtm

An A–Z index is also available to help visitors find the information that they seek on the OSMRE Web site. http://www.osmre.gov/resources/AtoZ.shtm

Top Priorities The OSMRE Web site features a section on the agency's top priorities. http://www.osmre.gov/topPriorities.shtm. http://www.osmre.gov/contacts.shtm | Email: getinfo@osmre.gov

For further information, contact the Office of Communications, Office of Surface Mining Reclamation and Enforcement, Department of the Interior, 1951 Constitution Avenue NW., Washington, DC 20240. Phone, 202-208-2565. TDD, 202-208-2694.

United States Fish and Wildlife Service

Department of the Interior, 1849 C Street NW., Washington, DC 20240
Phone, 703-358-4545. Internet, http://www.fws.gov.

Director   DANIEL M. ASHE

[For the United States Fish and Wildlife Service statement of organization, see the Code of Federal Regulations, Title 50, Subchapter A, Part 2]

The U.S. Fish and Wildlife Service (USFWS) is the principal Federal agency dedicated to fish and wildlife conservation. The Service's history spans 145 years, dating from the establishment of its predecessor agency, the Bureau of Fisheries, in 1871. First created as an independent agency, the Bureau of Fisheries was later placed in the Department of Commerce. A second predecessor agency, the Bureau of Biological Survey, was established in 1885 in the Department of Agriculture. In 1939, the two Bureaus and their functions were transferred to the Department of the Interior. In 1940, they were consolidated into one agency and redesignated the Fish and Wildlife Service by Reorganization Plan No. 3 (5 U.S.C. app.). http://training.fws.gov/history/USFWS-history.html

The USFWS works with others to conserve, protect, and enhance fish, wildlife and plants and their habitats for the continuing benefit of the American people. The Service manages the 150-million-acre National Wildlife Refuge System, which comprises 563 refuges and 38 wetland management districts. It operates 72 national fish hatcheries, a historic national fish hatchery, 65 fishery resource offices, and 81 ecological service field stations. The USFWS enforces Federal wildlife laws, administers the Endangered Species Act, manages migratory bird populations, restores nationally significant fisheries, conserves and restores wildlife habitats, and assists foreign governments with conservation. It also collects excise taxes on fishing and hunting equipment and distributes the revenues to State fish and wildlife agencies.

The Service improves and maintains fish and wildlife resources by proper management of wildlife and habitat. It also helps meet public demand for wildlife dependent recreational activities

by maintaining public lands and restoring native fish and wildlife populations.

Wildlife and fishery resource programs support the management of wildlife refuges on public lands. Wildlife-related activities include population control, migration and harvest surveys, and law and gaming enforcement for migratory and nonmigratory birds and mammals. Fishery-related activities include hatchery production monitoring, stocking, and fishery management. Fishery resource programs also provide technical assistance for coastal anadromous, Great Lakes, and other inland fisheries.

The USFWS identifies, protects, and restores endangered fish, wildlife, and plant species. It maintains Federal lists of endangered and threatened wildlife and plants that are published in the Code of Federal Regulations (50 CFR 17.11 et seq.), conducts status surveys, prepares recovery plans, and coordinates national and international wildlife refuge operations.

The Service protects and improves land and water environments to benefit living natural resources and to enhance the quality of human life. It administers grant programs that help imperiled species, assists private landowners restore habitat, asses environmental impact and reviews potential environmental threats, manages Coastal Barrier Resource System mapping, monitors potential wildlife contaminants, and studies fish and wildlife population trends.

Public use and information activities include preparing informational brochures and maintaining public Web sites; coordinating environmental studies on USFWS lands; operating visitor centers, self-guided nature trails, observation towers, and display ponds; and promoting birdwatching, fishing, hunting, wildlife photography, and other forms of wildlife-dependent outdoor recreation.

The Wildlife and Sport Fish Restoration Program supports the conservation and enhancement of the Nation's fish and wildlife resources. Excise taxes on sporting arms and fishing equipment fund these efforts.

Sources of Information

Blog   The USFWS Web site features "Open Spaces—A Talk on the Wild Side." https://www.fws.gov/news/blog

Business Opportunities   An online guide explains how to find business opportunities and to compete for them. Information is also available from regional offices and from the Division of Contracting and General Services in Falls Church, VA. Phone, 703-358-2500. http://www.fws.gov/cfm/Small%20Business/BusinessWith.html | Email: small_business_opts@fws.gov

Career Opportunities   Information on careers in conservation is available on the USFWS Web site. Additional information is available from USFWS regional offices and the Human Capital Office in Falls Church, VA. Phone, 703-358-1743. https://www.fws.gov/humancapital

Climate Change   The USFWS Web site provides a collection of links and informational sources for learning about climate science and conservation in a changing climate. https://www.fws.gov/home/climatechange/resources.html

Contaminants   The USFWS Web site features a section dedicated to contaminants—for example, metals and pesticides—and their effects on wildlife. https://www.fws.gov/ecological-services/habitat-conservation/contaminants.html

Endangered Species   The USFWS Web site features a search tool for learning about and identifying endangered species. The text boxes can search for an endangered species based on the State, U.S. Territory, or county where it lives, or according to its common or scientific name. https://www.fws.gov/endangered/?ref=topbar

An online subscription form is available to receive breaking news affecting endangered species, endangered species news stories, and the "Endangered Species Bulletin" via email. https://visitor.r20.constantcontact.com/manage/optin?v=001ip3iEJ-xkvrgM_ZzpwhxaKQXTq4Cp14J

Energy Development   The USFWS Web site features a section dedicated to the development of domestic energy sources and its effect on wildlife. https://www.fws.gov/ecological-services/energy-development/energy.html

Freedom of Information Act (FOIA)   The USFWS makes records available to the public to the greatest extent possible. The records that are being sought already may be posted online. If the information cannot be found online or if the location of the desired records is uncertain, consider contacting the USFWS FOIA public liaison before submitting a FOIA request. https://www.fws.gov/irm/bpim/foia.html | Email: fwhq_foia@fws.gov

The USFWS does not have a centralized records system. Most data and records are kept in field offices. Instructions on where to send a FOIA request for USFWS records are available online. https://www.fws.gov/irm/bpim/foiawhere.html

Glossaries   Ecological Services maintains an online glossary of terms found in environmental legislation. https://www.fws.gov/ecological-services/about/glossary.html

The Midwest Region maintains an online glossary of terms associated with endangered species. https://www.fws.gov/midwest/endangered/glossary/index.html

The Midwest Region also maintains a glossary of terms associated with freshwater mussels of the Upper Mississippi River System. https://www.fws.gov/midwest/mussel/glossary.html

The USFWS Web site features a short glossary of National Environmental Policy Act (NEPA) terms in Portable Document Format (PDF). https://www.fws.gov/r9esnepa/Intro/Glossary.PDF

National Wildlife Refuges   For information on the National Wildlife Refuge System, including information on specific wildlife refuges and wetland management districts, visit the "National Wildlife Refuge System" Web site. Phone, 800-344-9453. http://www.fws.gov/refuges/index.html

News Media Inquiries   Journalists, reporters, and other media professionals seeking information or to arrange an interview should contact a regional public

Activities

Coverage   The Corporation insures most private sector defined-benefit pension plans that provide a pension benefit based on factors such as age, years of service, and salary.

It administers two insurance programs, separately covering single-employer and multiemployer plans. More than 40 million workers and retirees participate in nearly 24,000 covered plans.

Single-Employer Insurance   Under the single-employer program, the Corporation guarantees payment of basic pension benefits if an insured plan terminates without sufficient assets to pay those benefits. The law limits, however, the total monthly benefit that the PBGC may guarantee for one individual to $5,011.36 per month for a 65-year-old individual in a pension plan that terminates in 2015. The law also sets other restrictions on PBGC's guarantee, including limits on the insured amount of recent benefit increases. In certain cases, the Corporation may pay some benefits above the guaranteed amount depending on the funding level of the plan and amounts recovered from employers.

A plan sponsor may terminate a single-employer plan in a standard termination if the plan has sufficient assets to purchase private annuities to cover all benefit liabilities. If a plan does not have sufficient assets, the sponsor may seek to transfer the pension liabilities to the PBGC by demonstrating that it meets the legal criteria for a distress termination. In either termination, the plan administrator must inform participants in writing at least 60 days prior to the date the administrator proposes to terminate the plan. Only a plan that has sufficient assets to pay all benefit liabilities may terminate in a standard termination. The Corporation also may institute termination of underfunded plans in certain specified circumstances. http://www.pbgc.gov/wr/benefits/guaranteed-benefits.html

Multiemployer Insurance   Under title IV, as revised in 1980 by the Multiemployer Pension Plan Amendments Act (29 U.S.C. 1001 note), which changed the insurable event from plan termination to plan insolvency, the Corporation provides financial assistance to multiemployer plans that are unable to pay nonforfeitable benefits. The plans are obligated to repay such assistance. The act also made employers withdrawing from a plan liable to the plan for a portion of its unfunded vested benefits. http://www.pbgc.gov/prac/multiemployer.html

Premium Collections   All defined-benefit pension plans insured by the PBGC are required to pay premiums to the Corporation according to rates set by Congress. The per-participant flat-rate premium for plans starting in 2015 is $57.00 for single-employer plans and $26.00 for multiemployer plans. Underfunded single-employer plans must also pay an additional premium equal to $24 per $1,000 of unfunded vested benefits. A termination premium of $1,250 per participant per year applies to certain distress and involuntary plan terminations, payable for 3 years after the termination. http://www.pbgc.gov/prac/prem/premium-rates.html

Sources of Information

Blog   The PBGC Web site features the "Retirement Matters" blog. http://www.pbgc.gov/about/who-we-are/retirement-matters

Business Opportunities   The PBGC tries to give a fair share of its procurement awards and subcontracting opportunities to small businesses. The PBGC regularly procures accounting, actuarial, auditing, benefits administration, legal, and information technology services.

The agency utilizes various types of contract vehicles that are outlined in the "Federal Acquisition Regulation". These types of contract vehicles include agreements, commercial contracts, major contracts, orders against other Government contracts, and purchase orders. http://www.pbgc.gov/about/procurement.html

Career Opportunities   The PBGC relies on accountants, actuaries, administrative personnel, analysts, attorneys, auditors, employee benefits law specialists, information technology experts, public affairs specialists, and other professionals to carry out its mission. http://www.pbgc.gov/about/jobs.html

Fraud Alerts   The PBGC, with support from its Office of the Inspector General, posts fraud alerts to spread awareness of scams. http://www.pbgc.gov/wr/other/pg/fraud-alerts.html

Freedom of Information Act (FOIA)   The PBGC participates in FOIAonline, which allows information seekers to submit electronic FOIA requests, to track the status of requests, to search for requests submitted by others, to access released records, and to generate agency-specific processing reports. https://foiaonline.regulations.gov/foia/action/public/home

FOIA requests must be in writing and may be submitted also by email, fax, or by regular mail to the Disclosure Officer, Pension Benefit Guaranty Corporation, 1200 K Street NW., Suite 11101, Washington, DC 20005. Fax, 202-326-4042. http://www.pbgc.gov/about/pg/footer/foia.html | Email: disclosure@pbgc.gov

Glossary   The PBGC maintains a glossary of terms with simplified definitions. Some terms and their definitions are PBGC-specific in usage. http://www.pbgc.gov/about/pg/header/glossary.html

Insured Pension Plans   A list of pension plans that recently paid premiums to the PBGC is available online. http://www.pbgc.

gov/wr/find-an-insured-pension-plan/pbgc-protects-pensions.html

Open Government   The PBGC posts datasets that are useful for increasing agency accountability, public knowledge of the agency and its operations, and economic opportunity. http://www.pbgc.gov/open/index.html | Email: opengov@pbgc.gov

Plain Language   PBGC writers and editors are committed to using plain language in new communications and revising confusing or unclear language in existing material. Send them a note via email if a sentence or paragraph's clarity could be improved. http://www.pbgc.gov/about/pbgc-in-plain-english.html | Email: webmaster@pbgc.gov

Press Room   The PBGC posts press releases on its Web site. http://www.pbgc.gov/news/press.html

An online subscription form is available to sign up for the latest news, delivered via email, from the PBGC. http://www.pbgc.gov/about/stay-informed.html

Site Map   PBGC Web site visitors may use the site map to look for specific topics or to browse for content that aligns with their interests. http://www.pbgc.gov/pbgc-sitemap.html. http://www.pbgc.gov/about/pg/contact/contact.html

For further information, contact the Pension Benefit Guaranty Corporation, 1200 K Street NW., Washington, DC 20005-4026. Phone, 202-326-4000 or 800-400-7242 .

Postal Regulatory Commission

901 New York Avenue NW., Suite 200, Washington, DC 20268-0001
Phone, 202-789-6800. Fax, 202-789-6861. Internet, http://www.prc.gov.

Chair	ROBERT G. TAUB
Vice Chair	MARK ACTON
Commissioner	NANCI E. LANGLEY
Commissioner	TONY HAMMOND
Commissioner	(VACANCY)
Director, Office of Accountability and Compliance	MARGARET CIGNO
Director, Office of Public Affairs and Government Relations	ANN FISHER
Director, Office of Secretary and Administration	STACY L. RUBLE
General Counsel	DAVID A. TRISSELL
Inspector General	JOHN F. CALLENDER

[For the Postal Regulatory Commission statement of organization, see the Code of Federal Regulations, Title 39, Part 3002]

The above list of key personnel was updated 06–2017.

The Postal Regulatory Commission develops and implements a modern system of postal rate regulation.

The Postal Regulatory Commission is the successor agency to the Postal Rate Commission, which was created by the Postal Reorganization Act, as amended (39 U.S.C. 101 et seq.). The Commission was established as an independent agency in the executive branch of Government by the Postal Accountability and Enhancement Act (39 U.S.C. 501). It comprises five Commissioners, appointed by the President with the advice and consent of the Senate, one of whom is designated as Chair.

The Commission promulgates rules and regulations, establishes procedures, and takes other actions necessary to carry out its obligations. It considers complaints received from interested persons relating to United States Postal Service rates, regulations, and services. The Commission also has certain reporting obligations, including a report on universal postal service and the postal monopoly. http://www.prc.gov/about

Sources of Information

Case Information   Active cases and daily listings are accessible online. A docket search tool is also available. http://www.prc.gov/dockets/active. http://www.prc.gov/dockets/daily. http://www.prc.gov/dockets/search | Email: prc-dockets@prc.gov

Employment   The Commission relies on the professional services of accountants, attorneys, economists, industrial engineers, marketing specialists, statisticians, and administrative and clerical personnel to fulfill its mission. http://www.prc.gov/employment-opportunities

Freedom of Information Act (FOIA)   A FOIA request form is available online. http://www.prc.gov/foia/onlinerequest

Newsroom   The Commission posts congressional submissions, papers, press releases, speeches, and upcoming events online. http://www.prc.gov/press-releases

Reading Room   Facilities for inspection and copying of records, viewing automated daily lists of docketed materials, and accessing the Commission's Web site are located at 901 New York Avenue NW., Suite 200, Washington, DC. The room is open on weekdays, excluding legal holidays, 8 a.m.–4:30 p.m.

Practice / Procedure   Practice and procedure rules governing the conduct of proceedings before the Commission may be found in parts 3001, 3010, 3015, 3020, 3025, 3030, 3031, 3050, and 3060 of title 39 of the "Code of Federal Regulations." http://www.ecfr.gov/cgi-bin/text-idx?SID=a34266c229a4a7b3c470845f8da08605&node=39:1.0.2.15.2&rgn=div5. http://www.prc.gov/offices/osa

For further information, contact the Secretary, Postal Regulatory Commission, 901 New York Avenue NW., Suite 200, Washington, DC 20268-0001. Phone, 202-789-6840.

Railroad Retirement Board

844 North Rush Street, Chicago, IL 60611-1275
Phone, 312-751-4777. Fax, 312-751-7154. Internet,http://www.rrb.gov | Email: opa@rrb.gov.

Chair	VACANT
Labor Member	WALTER A. BARROWS
Management Member	STEVEN J. ANTHONY
Inspector General	MARTIN J. DICKMAN
Director, Administration	KEITH B. EARLEY
Director, Equal Opportunity	LYNN E. COUSINS
Director, Human Resources	MARGUERITE V. DANIELS
Director, Public Affairs	MICHAEL P. FREEMAN
Chief, Acquisition Management	PAUL T. AHERN
Facility Manager	SCOTT L. RUSH
General Counsel	ANA M. KOCUR
Director, Legislative Affairs / Legislative Counsel	BEVERLY BRITTON FRASER
Director, Hearings and Appeals	RACHEL L. SIMMONS
Secretary to the Board	MARTHA P. RICO

Chief Actuary	FRANK J. BUZZI
Chief Information Officer	RAM MURTHY
Chief Financial Officer	VACANT
Director of Field Service and Senior Executive Officer	DANIEL J. FADDEN
Director, Programs	MICHAEL A. TYLLAS
Director, Policy and Systems	KIMBERLY PRICE-BUTLER
Director, Program Evaluation and Management Services	JANET M. HALLMAN
Director, Retirement and Survivor Benefits	VALERIE F. ALLEN
Director, Disability Benefits	SHERITA P. BOOTS
Director, Unemployment and Programs Support	MICHEAL T. PAWLAK

[For the Railroad Retirement Board statement of organization, see the Code of Federal Regulations, Title 20, Part 200]

The Railroad Retirement Board administers comprehensive retirement-survivor and unemployment-sickness benefit programs for the Nation's railroad workers and their families.

The Railroad Retirement Board (RRB) was originally established by the Railroad Retirement Act of 1934, as amended (45 U.S.C. 201-228z-1).

The RRB derives statutory authority from the Railroad Retirement Act of 1974 (45 U.S.C. 231-231u) and the Railroad Unemployment Insurance Act (45 U.S.C. 351-369). It administers these acts and participates in the administration of the Social Security Act and the Health Insurance for the Aged Act insofar as they affect railroad retirement beneficiaries.

The RRB comprises three members whom the President appoints with the advice and consent of the Senate: one upon the recommendations of representatives of railroad employees; one upon the recommendations of railroad employers; and one, the Chair, as a public member.

Activities   The Railroad Retirement Act provides for the payment of annuities to individuals who have completed at least 10 years of creditable railroad service, or 5 years if performed after 1995, and have ceased compensated service upon their attainment of specified ages or at any age if permanently disabled for all employment. In some circumstances occupational disability annuities or supplemental annuities are provided for career employees.

A spouse's annuity is provided, under certain conditions, for the wife or husband of an employee annuitant. Divorced spouses may also qualify.

Survivor annuities are awarded to the qualified spouses, children, and parents of deceased career employees, and various lump-sum benefits are also available under certain conditions.

Benefits based upon qualifying railroad earnings in a preceding 1-year period are provided under the Railroad Unemployment Insurance Act to individuals who are unemployed in a benefit year, but who are ready and willing to work, and to individuals who are unable to work because of sickness or injury.

The RRB maintains, through its field offices, a placement service for unemployed railroad personnel.

Sources of Information

Benefit Inquiries   The RRB provides personal assistance to railroad employees and railroad retirement beneficiaries through its field offices. Staff can explain benefit rights and responsibilities on an individual basis, assist employees in applying for benefits, and answer questions about benefit programs. (Railroad labor groups and employers also help railroad personnel stay informed about benefit programs.) Most field offices are open to the public during the week, 9 a.m.–3:30 p.m. They close at noon on Wednesdays, however, and do not open on Federal holidays. To locate an office, see "Field Offices" below and use the online Zip Code locator or call the automated phone system. Phone, 877-772-5772. http://www.rrb.gov/mep/ben_info.asp

Congressional Inquiries   Members of Congress or their staff may inquire about constituents, benefit claims, and filed applications by contacting the

Congressional Inquiry section of the Office of Administration. Phone, 312-751-4970. Fax, 312-751-7154. https://www.rrb.gov/opa/rrbcongress_contacts.asp | Email: opa@rrb.gov

Data The RRB posts actuarial, financial, and statistical data on its Web site. It also publishes datasets on the Web site Data.gov. https://www.rrb.gov/act/historical.asp. https://www.rrb.gov/data

Employment Contact the RRB's Bureau of Human Resources. Phone, 312-751-4580. Email: recruit@rrb.gov

The RRB posts online railroad job vacancies that have been reported to its field offices. https://www.rrb.gov/PandS/Jobs/rrjobs.asp

Field Offices Field offices are located throughout the country. Staff members answer questions about Medicare and Social Security benefits for railroad workers and their families, retirement benefits, sickness and unemployment benefits, survivor benefits, and tax withholding and statements. A Zip Code locator is available online for finding the nearest field office. https://www.rrb.gov/field/field.asp

Freedom of Information Act (FOIA) A FOIA request may be made by fax, letter, or online request form. A record description must contain sufficient detail—author, date, subject matter, type of record—to allow RRB staff to locate the record with reasonable effort. https://www.rrb.gov/blaw/foia/foia_guide.asp. https://secure.rrb.gov/efoia

Glossary A glossary of RRB terms is available online. https://www.rrb.gov/general/glossary.asp

Hotline To report the illegal receiving of RRB benefits or to file a complaint about misconduct relating to the RRB, its programs or employees, contact the Office of Inspector General. Phone, 800-772-4258. Fax, 312-751-4342. https://www.rrb.gov/OIG/hotline.asp | Email: hotline@oig.rrb.gov

Legislative Affairs For information on legislative matters, contact the Office of Legislative Affairs. Phone, 202-272-7742. Fax, 202-272-7728. The office is open Tuesday–Thursday, 9 a.m.–3:30 p.m., eastern standard time, except on Federal holidays. http://www.rrb.gov/org/ogc/ola.asp | Email: ola@rrb.gov

Publications Booklets, pamphlets (English and Spanish), and forms of interest to beneficiaries and railroad workers are available online. Pamphlets also are available from the RRB's field offices and Chicago headquarters. https://www.rrb.gov/mep/ben_forms.asp | Email: opa@rrb.gov

Telecommunications Devices for the Deaf (TDD) The RRB provides TDD services: beneficiary inquiries (Phone, 312-751-4701); equal opportunity inquiries (Phone, 312-751-4334). https://www.rrb.gov/general/contact_us.asp | Email: opa@rrb.gov

For further information, contact Public Affairs, Railroad Retirement Board, 844 North Rush Street, Chicago, IL 60611-1275. Phone, 312-751-4777. Fax, 312-751-7154.

Securities and Exchange Commission

100 F Street NE., Washington, DC 20549
Phone, 202-551-7500. Internet, http://www.sec.gov.

Chair	W. Jay Clayton
Commissioner	Michael S. Piwowar
Commissioner	Kara M. Stein
Commissioner	(vacancy)
Commissioner	(vacancy)
Division Heads	
Codirector, Enforcement	Stephanie Avakian
Codirector, Enforcement	Steven Peikin
Director, Corporation Finance	William Hinman
Director, Economic and Risk Analysis / Chief Economist	Jeffrey Harris

Director, Investment Management	DALIA BLASS
Director, Trading and Markets	HEATHER SIEDEL, ACTING

Office Heads

Associate Executive Director, Human Resources	LACEY DINGMAN
Chief Accountant	WESLEY BRICKER
Chief Administrative Law Judge	BRENDA P. MURRAY
Chief Financial Officer	CARYN KAUFFMAN, ACTING
Chief FOIA Officer	BARRY D. WALTERS
Chief Operating Officer	KENNETH JOHNSON, ACTING
Chief Technology Officer	PAMELA DYSON
Director, Acquisitions	VANCE CATHELL
Director, Compliance Inspections and Examinations	PETER DRISCOLL, ACTING
Director, Credit Ratings	THOMAS BUTLER
Director, Equal Employment Opportunity	PETER HENRY, ACTING
Director, International Affairs	PAUL LEDER
Director, Investor Education and Advocacy	LORI J. SCHOCK
Director, Legislative and Intergovernmental Affairs	KEITH CASSIDY
Director, Minority and Women Inclusion	PAMELA GIBBS
Director, Municipal Securities	JESSICA KANE
Director, Public Affairs	JOHN NESTER
Director, Strategic Initiatives	MARK AMBROSE
Director, Support Operations	BARRY D. WALTERS
Ethics Counsel	SHIRA P. MINTON
General Counsel	ROBERT STEBBINS
Inspector General	CARL W. HOECKER
Investor Advocate	RICK A. FLEMING
Secretary	BRENT J. FIELDS

[For the Securities and Exchange Commission statement of organization, see the Code of Federal Regulations, Title 17, Part 200]

The Securities and Exchange Commission protects investors, facilitates capital formation, and maintains efficient, fair, and orderly markets.

The Securities and Exchange Commission (SEC) was created under authority of the Securities Exchange Act of 1934 (15 U.S.C. 78a–78jj) and was organized on July 2, 1934. The Commission serves as adviser to United States district courts in reorganization proceedings for debtor corporations in which a substantial public interest is involved. The Commission also has certain responsibilities under section 15 of the Bretton Woods Agreements Act of 1945 (22 U.S.C. 286k–1) and section 851(e) of the Internal Revenue Code of 1954 (26 U.S.C. 851(e)). https://www.sec.gov/about/laws.shtml

The Commission is vested with quasi-judicial functions. Persons aggrieved by its decisions in the exercise of those functions have a right of review by the United States courts of appeals. https://www.sec.gov/about/whatwedo.shtml

Activities

Full and Fair Disclosure   The Securities Act of 1933 (15 U.S.C. 77a) requires issuers of securities and their controlling persons making public offerings of securities in interstate commerce or via mail to file registration statements containing financial and other pertinent data about the issuer and the securities being offered with the SEC. There are limited exemptions, such as government securities, nonpublic offerings, and intrastate offerings, as well as certain offerings not exceeding $1.5 million. The effectiveness of a registration statement may be refused or suspended after a public hearing if the statement contains material misstatements or omissions, thus barring sale of the securities until it is appropriately amended.

Regulation of Investment Advisers   Persons who, for compensation, engage in the business of advising others with respect to securities must register with the Commission. The Commission is authorized to define what practices are considered fraudulent or deceptive and to prescribe means to prevent those practices.

Regulation of Mutual Funds and Other Investment Companies

The Commission registers investment companies and regulates their activities to protect investors. The regulation covers sales load, management contracts, composition of boards of directors, and capital structure. The Commission must also determine the fairness of various transactions of investment companies before they actually occur.

The Commission may institute court action to enjoin the consummation of mergers and other plans of reorganization of investment companies if such plans are unfair to securities holders. It may impose sanctions by administrative proceedings against investment company management for violations of the act and other Federal securities laws. It also may file court actions to enjoin acts and practices of management officials involving breaches of fiduciary duty and personal misconduct and to disqualify such officials from office.

Regulation of Securities Markets

The Securities Exchange Act of 1934 assigns to the Commission broad regulatory responsibilities over the securities markets, the self-regulatory organizations within the securities industry, and persons conducting a business in securities. Persons who execute transactions in securities generally are required to register with the Commission as broker-dealers. Securities exchanges and certain clearing agencies are required to register with the Commission, and associations of brokers or dealers are permitted to register with the Commission. The act also provides for the establishment of the Municipal Securities Rulemaking Board to formulate rules for the municipal securities industry.

The Commission oversees the self-regulatory activities of the national securities exchanges and associations, registered clearing agencies, and the Municipal Securities Rulemaking Board. In addition, the Commission regulates industry professionals, such as securities brokers and dealers, certain municipal securities professionals, Government securities brokers and dealers, and transfer agents.

Rehabilitation of Failing Corporations

In cases of corporate reorganization proceedings administered in Federal courts, the Commission may participate as a statutory party. The principal functions of the Commission are to protect the interests of public investors involved in such cases through efforts to ensure their adequate representation and to participate in legal and policy issues that are of concern to public investors generally.

Representation of Debt Securities Holders

The Commission safeguards the interests of purchasers of publicly offered debt securities issued pursuant to trust indentures.

Enforcement Activities

The Commission's enforcement activities are designed to secure compliance with the Federal securities laws administered by the Commission and the rules and regulations adopted thereunder. These activities include measures to do the following: compel compliance with the disclosure requirements of the registration and other provisions of the relevant acts; prevent fraud and deception in the purchase and sale of securities; obtain court orders enjoining acts and practices that operate as a fraud upon investors or otherwise violate the laws; suspend or revoke the registrations of brokers, dealers, investment companies, and investment advisers who willfully engage in such acts and practices; suspend or bar from association persons associated with brokers, dealers, investment companies, and investment advisers who have violated any provision of the Federal securities laws; and prosecute persons who have engaged in fraudulent activities or other willful violations of those laws.

In addition, attorneys, accountants, and other professionals who violate the securities laws face possible loss of their privilege to practice before the Commission.

To this end, private investigations are conducted into complaints or other indications of securities violations. Established evidence of law violations is used in appropriate administrative proceedings to revoke registration or in actions instituted in Federal courts to restrain or enjoin such activities. Where the evidence tends to establish criminal fraud or other willful violation of the securities laws, the facts are referred to the Attorney General for criminal prosecution of the offenders. The Commission may assist in such prosecutions. https://www.sec.gov/litigation.shtml

Sources of Information

Business Opportunities The Office of Acquisitions' Web page features links to help those who seek business opportunities with the SEC. Phone, 202-551-7300. https://www.sec.gov/oacq

Career Opportunities The SEC relies on accountants, attorneys, economists, examiners, industry specialists, information technology specialists, and other professionals to carry out its mission. Applicants must apply for a specific vacancy and complete a process of competitive selection. This process does not apply, however, to attorney vacancies. The Commission runs a college and law school recruitment program that relies on campus visits and student interviews. http://www.sec.gov/careers

For more information, contact the Office of Human Resources. Phone, 202-551-7500. Fax, 202-777-1028. https://www.sec.gov/ohr

Electronic Data Gathering, Analysis, and Retrieval (EDGAR) The EDGAR database provides free public access to corporate information such as prospectuses, registration statements, and quarterly and annual reports. https://www.sec.gov/edgar.shtml

Events A schedule of upcoming SEC meetings, public appearances by SEC officials, and public hearings is available online. http://www.sec.gov/about/upcoming-events.htm

Fast Answers The SEC maintains a list of the terms for which SEC Web site visitors search most frequently. https://www.sec.gov/fast-answers

Freedom of Information Act (FOIA) The Office of Freedom of Information Act Services makes SEC records available to the public to the greatest extent possible under the FOIA. The Office receives nearly 17,000 requests per year for Commission documents and records. For more information, contact the FOIA public service center. Phone, 202-551-7900. Fax, 202-772-9337. https://www.sec.gov/page/foia

Many records—no-action and interpretive letters, public comments on proposed rules, registration statements and reports filed by regulated companies and individuals, SEC decisions and releases, and staff manuals—can be read and printed for free by using the SEC online search feature. An electronic request form is available for obtaining nonpublic records: consumer complaints, records compiled in investigations, and staff comment letters. The SEC will release nonpublic records, except when they are protected by a FOIA exemption. The electronic request form may be used also for obtaining older records that the SEC has not posted on its Web site—records usually dated before 1996. https://tts.sec.gov/cgi-bin/request_public_docs

Glossary The Office of Investor Education and Advocacy maintains an online glossary. https://investor.gov/glossary

Investment Adviser Public Disclosure The SEC provides an online tool to search for an investment adviser firm and to view the registration or reporting form (Form ADV) that the adviser filed. The tool also allows an investor to search for an individual investment adviser representative and to view his or her professional background and conduct. http://www.adviserinfo.sec.gov/IAPD/default.aspx#

Investor Education The Office of Investor Education and Advocacy offers services to and provides tools for investors. The Office cannot tell an investor how or where to invest money, but it can help him or her invest knowledgeably and avoid fraud. Phone, 800-732-0330. Fax, 202-772-9295. https://www.investor.gov | Email: help@sec.gov

The Office of Investor Education and Advocacy tweets on Twitter. https://twitter.com/SEC_Investor_Ed

The SEC maintains a list of external educational web sites. https://www.sec.gov/investor/links.shtml

The SEC maintains a list of investor calculators and tools that are available on external web sites. https://www.sec.gov/investor/tools.shtml

Links The SEC Web page "Other Links" contains links to other Web sites—government and nongovernment—that may be of interest to Internet visitors. https://www.sec.gov/links

Newsroom The SEC posts press releases, public statements, speeches, testimonies, and web casts on its Web site. A subscription form is available online to receive news alerts via email. https://www.sec.gov/news | Email: news@sec.gov

Open Government The SEC supports the Open Government initiative by promoting the principles of collaboration, participation, and transparency. https://www.sec.gov/open | Email: opengov@sec.gov

Organizational Chart The SEC's organizational chart is available in Portable Document Format (PDF) for viewing and downloading. https://www.sec.gov/images/secorg.pdf

A text version of the SEC's organizational chart also is available. https://www.sec.gov/about/orgtext.htm

Plain Language Like other Federal agencies, the SEC must compose documents in plain writing. According to the Plain Writing Act of 2010, writing should be "clear, concise, well-organized" and follow "other best practices appropriate to the subject or field or audience." SEC writers and editors want to know if agency documents and Web pages are difficult to understand. Contact them by email to leave a comment or make a suggestion. https://www.sec.gov/plainwriting.shtml | Email: PlainWriting@sec.gov

Publications SEC publications are available in Chinese, English, and Spanish in Portable Document Format (PDF). https://www.investor.gov/publications-research-studies/publications

Regional Offices Regional offices can provide investors with information and assist them with complaints. Contact information for the SEC's 11 regional offices is available online. https://www.sec.gov/page/sec-regional-offices

RSS Feeds RSS feeds are an online resource for keeping abreast of the most recent materials posted to the SEC Web site. https://www.sec.gov/about/secrss.shtml

Site Map The Web site map allows visitors to look for specific topics or to browse content that aligns with their interests. https://www.sec.gov/sitemap.shtml

Small Business Activities Information for small businesses—information on legal obligations when they sell securities and on financial and other reporting obligations when their securities are traded publicly—is available online. Contact the Office of Small Business Policy for more information. Phone, 202-551-3460. http://www.sec.gov/info/smallbus.shtml

Social Media The SEC maintains a presence on Flickr, LinkedIn, Pinterest, Twitter, and YouTube. https://www.sec.gov/opa/social_media.html

Tips / Complaints Members of the public can inform the SEC of possible violations of U.S. securities laws by completing the online questionnaire. https://www.sec.gov/complaint.shtml

Votes The final votes of SEC Commissioners on decisions, orders, rules and similar actions are posted online. https://www.sec.gov/about/commission-votes.shtml. https://www.sec.gov/contact.shtml

For further information, contact the Office of Public Affairs, Securities and Exchange Commission, 100 F Street NE., Washington, DC 20549. Phone, 202-551-4120. Fax, 202-777-1026.

Selective Service System

National Headquarters, Arlington, VA 22209-2425
Phone, 703-605-4100. Internet, http://www.sss.gov.

Director	DONALD M. BENTON
Deputy Director	ADAM J. COPP, ACTING
Chief Information Officer	SCOTT W. JONES
Chief of Staff	RODERICK R. HUBBARD, ACTING
General Counsel	RUDY G. SANCHEZ, JR.
Associate Directors	
Financial Management / Chief Financial Officer	RODERICK R. HUBBARD
Operations	ADAM J. COPP
Public and Intergovernmental Affairs	(VACANCY)

[For the Selective Service System statement of organization, see the Code of Federal Regulations, Title 32, Part 1605]

The Selective Service System supplies the Armed Forces with manpower in an emergency and operates an Alternative Service Program for men classified as conscientious objectors.

The Selective Service System was established by the Military Selective Service Act (50 U.S.C. app. 451-471a). The act requires the registration of male citizens of the United States and all other male persons who are in the United States and who are ages 18 to 25. The act exempts members of the active Armed Forces and nonimmigrant aliens. Proclamation 4771 of July 20, 1980, requires male persons born on or after January 1, 1960, and who have attained age 18, but have not attained age 26 to register. Registration is conducted at post offices within the United States, at U.S. Embassies and consulates outside the United States, and online at the Selective Service System's Web site.

The act imposes liability for training and service in the Armed Forces upon registrants who are ages 18 to 26, except those who are exempt or deferred. Persons who have been deferred remain liable for training and service until age 35. Aliens are not liable for training and service until they have remained in the United States for more than 1 year. Conscientious objectors who are opposed to all service in the Armed Forces are required to perform civilian work in lieu of induction into the Armed Forces.

The authority to induct registrants, including doctors and allied medical specialists, expired on July 1, 1973. https://www.sss.gov/About

Sources of Information

Business Opportunities   For information on opportunities for small businesses, call 703-605-4038.

Employment   The Selective Service System offers competitive wages, the Thrift Savings Plan with matching funds, health care benefits, paid vacation time, and work-life benefit options that include telework, as well as alternate and flexible work schedules for most positions. For more information, visit the "Careers" Web page or contact the Office of Human Resources. Phone, 703-605-4040. https://www.sss.gov/Careers

The Selective Service System posts the results of past Federal employee viewpoint surveys on its Web site. https://www.sss.gov/Reports-and-Notices/Human-Capital-Survey

Forms   Frequently requested forms are available on the Selective Service System's Web site. https://www.sss.gov/Forms

Freedom of Information Act (FOIA)   An information seeker should submit his or her request in writing; include his or her name, address, and telephone number; indicate that the request is being made under the Freedom of Information Act; provide specific information for identifying the records sought; and send the request to the FOIA Officer, Selective Service System, National Headquarters, Arlington, VA 22209-2425. https://www.sss.gov/Reports/FOIA

The Selective Service System maintains a FOIA electronic reading room. https://www.sss.gov/Reports/FOIA/FOIA-Electronic-Reading-Room

Newsletter   The Selective Service System's quarterly newsletter "The Register" is available online. https://www.sss.gov/Public-Affairs/The-Register-Newsletter

Plain Language   The Selective Service System adheres to Federal plain language guidelines. If a document or Web page is poorly written and difficult to understand, contact the agency by email. https://www.sss.gov/Reports-and-Notices/Plain-Language | Email: Information@sss.gov

Publications   The Selective Service System posts reports, including its "Annual Report to the Congress of the United States," online. https://www.sss.gov/Reports

Registration   Men, age 18–25, with a valid social security number, may use the online registration form. A fillable registration form that can be returned by mail is also available for immigrant males (documented or undocumented), for men who cannot use the online registration form because of a faulty social security number, and for men without a social security number. https://www.sss.gov/Home/Registration. https://www.sss.gov/contact.htm | Email: information@sss.gov

For further information, contact the Office of Public and Intergovernmental Affairs, Selective Service System, Arlington, VA 22209-2425. Phone, 703-605-4100.

EDITORIAL NOTE

The Small Business Administration did not meet the publication deadline for submitting updated information of its activities, functions, and sources of information as required by the automatic disclosure provisions of the Freedom of Information Act (5 U.S.C. 552(a)(1)(A)).

Small Business Administration

409 Third Street SW., Washington, DC 20416
Phone, 202-205-6600. Fax, 202-205-7064. Internet, http://www.sba.gov.

Administrator	LINDA MCMAHON
Deputy Administrator	(VACANCY)
Assistant Administrators	
Office of Faith-Based Community Initiatives	(VACANCY)
Office of Hearings and Appeals	DELORICE PRICE FORD
Office of the National Ombudsman and Regulatory Enforcement Fairness	EARL L. GAY
Associate Administrators	
Office of Capital Access	ANN MARIE MEHLUM
Office of Communications and Public Liaison	BRIAN WEISS
Office of Congressional and Legal Affairs	DANIELLE L. JIMENEZ
Officer of Disaster Assistance	JAMES RIVERA
Office of Entrepreneurial Development	TAMEKA MONTGOMERY
Office of Field Operations	CHRISTOPHER L. JAMES
Office of Government Contracting and Business Development	JOHN SHORAKA
Office of International Trade	EILEEN SÁNCHEZ
Office of Investment and Innovation	MARK L. WALSH
Office of Native American Affairs	NATHAN SEGAL
Office of Veterans Business Development	BARBARA CARSON
Chief Counsel for Advocacy	DARRYL L. DEPRIEST
Chief Financial Officer	TAMI PERRIELLO
Chief Operating Officer	MATTHEW VARILEK
General Counsel	MELVIN F. WILLIAMS, JR.
Inspector General	PEGGY E. GUSTAFSON

[For the Small Business Administration statement of organization, see the Code of Federal Regulations, Title 13, Part 101]

The Small Business Administration aids, assists, and counsels entrepreneurs and protects their business interests; preserves free and competitive enterprise; and maintains and strengthens the overall economy of the Nation.

The Small Business Administration (SBA) was created by the Small Business Act of 1953 and derives its present existence and authority from the Small Business Act (15 U.S.C. 631 et seq.) and the Small Business Investment Act of 1958 (15 U.S.C. 661). https://www.sba.gov/about-sba/what-we-do/history

Activities

Advocacy   The Office of Advocacy carries a congressional mandate to serve as an independent voice within the Federal Government for the approximately 28 million small businesses nationwide. The Chief Counsel for Advocacy, whom the President appoints with the advice and consent of the Senate, from the private sector, presents the concerns, interests, and views of the small business community to White House administrators, Members of the Congress, and Federal and State regulators.

The Office reports annually on Federal compliance with the Regulatory Flexibility Act (RFA), which requires agencies to analyze the effect of their regulations on small businesses and to consider less burdensome alternatives. Executive Order 13272 requires Federal agencies to take the Office's comments into consideration before finalizing proposed regulations. It also requires the Office to train Federal staff on RFA compliance.

The Office serves as one of the best sources of information on the state of small businesses nationwide and on the issues that affect success and growth. It conducts economic and statistical research on jobs that small businesses create; on the effect of

Federal laws, regulations, and programs; and on factors that influence their competitive strength. The Office then recommends measures that address the special needs of small businesses to policymakers.

Regional advocates facilitate communication between the Chief Counsel for Advocacy and the small business community. As the Chief Counsel's direct link to local business owners, State and local government agencies, State legislatures, and small business organizations, these advocates identify emerging problems and issues by monitoring the effect of Federal and State regulations and policies on business activity in their respective regions. https://www.sba.gov/advocacy | Email: advocacy@sba.gov

For further information, contact the Office of Advocacy. Phone, 202-205-6533.

Business and Community Initiatives The Office of Business and Community Initiatives develops and cosponsors counseling, education, training, and information resources for small businesses. It partners with the private sector to promote entrepreneurial development. The Office supports the Service Corps of Retired Executives (SCORE) nationwide, nonprofit association (www.score.org). SCORE volunteers, who number over 11,000, help small businesses start and grow by providing free or low cost educational services: mentoring and business counseling, tools, and workshops. The Office also provides online information for young entrepreneurs (www.sba.gov/teens).

For further information, contact the Small Business Administration. Phone, 202-205-6600.

Business Development The Office of Business Development oversees the 8(a) Business Development program. The Office assists with contracts and loans, counsels, expands access to capital and credit, gives technical guidance, and offers training workshops. One of its principal business development tools is the Mentor-Protégé program, which allows participants to benefit from business development assistance provided by successful companies. https://www.sba.gov/offices/headquarters/obd/resources

For further information, contact the Office of Business Development. Phone, 202-205-5852.

Capital Access The Office of the Associate Administrator for Capital Access increases the availability of capital through banks and other lending partners. It oversees SBA programs that help small businesses gain access to capital. These programs include the 7(a) general business guarantee, 504 Certified Development Company, SBA surety bond guarantee, and microlending. https://www.sba.gov/offices/headquarters/oca

For further information, contact the Office of Capital Access. Phone, 202-205-6657.

Disaster Assistance The SBA serves as the Federal disaster bank for nonfarm, private sector losses. It lends money to disaster survivors for repairing or replacing their most damaged property. The agency makes direct loans with subsidized interest rates to individuals, homeowners, businesses of all sizes, and nonprofit organizations. https://www.sba.gov/content/disaster-assistance

For further information, contact the Office of Disaster Assistance. Phone, 202-205-6734.

Field Operations The Office of Field Operations is responsible for the provision of SBA services and availability of its products: It serves as the critical link between SBA policymakers and small businessmen and women. The Office provides policy guidance and oversight to regional administrators and district directors for achieving agency goals and objectives and for solving problems in specific operational areas. It plays a liaison role and expedites issues for the regional and district offices when dealing with the central office, coordinating the presentation of views from the field. It also establishes and monitors district performance goals and organizes reviews of the field offices. A complete listing of the regional, district, and disaster field offices—including addresses, telephone numbers, and key officials—is available online. https://www.sba.gov/about-sba/sba-locations

For further information, contact the Office of Field Operations. Phone, 202-205-6808.

Financial Assistance The SBA gives its guarantee to lending institutions and certified development companies that make loans to small businesses. These businesses can then use the money for working capital and financing the acquisition of land and buildings, constructing new and improving existing facilities, and purchasing equipment and machinery.

Under the SBA's microloan program, the Administration provides indirect, small-scale financial and technical assistance to very small businesses through loans and grants to intermediary nonprofit organizations (www. sba.gov/content/microloan-program). https:// www.sba.gov/tools/local-assistance

For further information, contact the nearest Small Business Administration district office.

Government Contracting Through various programs and services, the SBA assists small businesses—including HUBZone certified firms and disadvantaged, women-owned, and service-disabled veteran-owned small businesses—with receiving Government procurement. The contracting liaison helps small-scale entrepreneurs secure an equitable share of the natural resources that the Federal Government sells. The Administration also works with the Office of Management and Budget and other Federal agencies to establish policy and regulations affecting small business access to Government contracts. https://www. sba.gov/category/navigation-structure/ contracting

For further information, contact the nearest Office of Government Contracting. Phone, 202-205-6460.

Historically Underutilized Business Zones The Historically Underutilized Business Zone (HUBZone) program was enacted into law as part of the Small Business Reauthorization Act of 1997. The program fosters economic development and employment in HUBZones, which include Indian reservations, through the establishment of preferences. The program provides greater access to Federal contracting opportunities for qualified businesses. The SBA regulates and implements the program: It determines which businesses are eligible to receive HUBZone contracts, maintains a list of qualified businesses that Federal agencies can use to locate venders, adjudicates protests of contract eligibility, and reports to the Congress on the program's effect on employment and investment in the zones. https://www.sba.gov/content/understanding-hubzone-program | Email: HUBZone@sba. gov

For further information, contact the HUBZone Help Desk. Phone, 202-205-8885.

International Trade The Office of International Trade makes American small businesses more competitive in the global marketplace by developing international trade opportunities for small enterprises. It collaborates with other Federal agencies and public and private sector groups to promote small business exports and to help entrepreneurs who seek opportunities to export. The Office—through 19 U.S. Export Assistance Centers, SBA district offices, and service-provider partners—coordinates and directs the Administration's export initiatives. https://www.sba.gov/offices/headquarters/oit

For further information, contact the Office of International Trade. Phone, 202-205-6720.

Native American Affairs The Office of Native American Affairs assists and encourages the creation, development, and expansion of small businesses owned by Native Americans. It develops and implements initiatives designed to address specific business challenges encountered by Native American entrepreneurs. The Office's Web page features information on programs and tools to promote reservation-based small business activity. https://www.sba.gov/offices/headquarters/naa

For further information, contact the Office of Native American Affairs. Phone, 202-205-7364.

Regulatory Fairness Program Congress established the National Ombudsman and 10 Regulatory Fairness (RegFair) Boards in 1996 as part of the Small Business Regulatory Enforcement Fairness Act. The National Ombudsman assists small businessmen and women when they experience excessive or unfair Federal regulatory enforcement action. The National Ombudsman receives comments from small businesses and acts as a liaison between them and Federal agencies. These comments are forwarded to the appropriate Federal agencies for review and consideration of the fairness of their enforcement actions. The National Ombudsman sends a copy of an agency's response to the small business owner. In some cases, fines are reduced or eliminated and decisions changed in favor of the business owner.

Each of the RegFair Boards comprises five volunteer members who are owners, operators, or officers of small enterprises. The SBA Administrator appoints board members for 3-year terms. Each RegFair Board meets at least annually with the Ombudsman, reports to the Ombudsman on substantiated instances of excessive or unfair enforcement, and comments on the annual report to Congress prior to its publication. https://www.sba.gov/ombudsman

For further information, contact the Office of the National Ombudsman. Phone, 888-734-3247.

Research Investment and Technology Transfer   The Office of Investment and Innovation manages the Small Business Investment Research (SBIR) and Small Business Technology Transfer (STTR) programs. These two programs together provide billions of dollars per year for small enterprises to participate in federally funded research and development and to cooperate with 11 Government agencies and hundreds of research institutions and universities. The SBIR and STTR programs stimulate the creation of intellectual property with potential for commercialization and with applications in a broad range of sectors in the Nation's economy. https://www.sba.gov/offices/headquarters/ooi/about-us

For further information, contact the Office of Investment and Innovation. Phone, 202-205-6510.

Small Business Development Centers   The Office of Small Business Development Centers funds, oversees, and supports the nationwide Small Business Development Center (SBDC) network. The SBDC program provides one-stop management assistance to current and prospective small business owners in central and easily accessible branch locations. The program relies on the cooperation of the private sector, the educational community, and Federal, State, and local governments.

The SBDC program delivers up-to-date counseling, technical help, and training in all aspects of small business management. Its services include assistance with feasibility studies and with engineering, financial, marketing, organization, production, and technical challenges. Special SBDC activities include international trade assistance, procurement assistance, rural development, venture capital information, and technical assistance. https://www.sba.gov/offices/headquarters/osbdc

For further information, contact the Office of Small Business Development Centers. Phone, 202-205-6766.

Surety Bonds   The Surety Bond Guarantee program helps small and emerging contractors obtain the bonding necessary for bidding on and receiving contracts up to $5 million. The SBA guarantees bonds that participating surety companies issue and reimburses between 70–90 percent of losses and expenses incurred should a business default on the contract. Construction, service, and supply contractors are eligible for the program if they meet certain standards. https://www.sba.gov/surety-bonds

For further information, contact the Office of Surety Guarantees. Phone, 202-205-6540.

Venture Capital   The Small Business Investment Company (SBIC) program was created in 1958 to bridge the gap between venture capital availability and the needs of startups and expanding small businesses. SBICs are privately owned and managed venture capital funds, which the SBA licenses and regulates. They use their own capital combined with SBA guaranteed funds to make equity and debt investments in qualifying small businesses. Fund managers may invest only in small businesses having net worth of less than $18 million and average aftertax income for the previous 2 years of less than $6 million. The New Markets Venture Capital (NMVC) program is a sister program centering on low-income areas. It augments the contribution made by SBICs to small businesses in the United States.

The Federal Government neither invests directly in nor targets industries for inclusion in the SBIC program. Qualified private fund managers are responsible for fund portfolio management and investment decisions. To obtain an SBIC license, an experienced team of private equity managers must secure minimum commitments from private investors. https://www.sba.gov/category/lender-navigation/sba-loan-programs/sbic-program-0 | Email: askSBIC@sba.gov

For further information, contact the Investment Division. Phone, 202-205-6510.

Veterans Business Development   The Office of Veterans Business Development (OVBD) formulates, executes, and promotes policies and programs that provide assistance to small businesses owned and controlled by veterans and service-disabled veterans, including reserve component members of the U.S. military. The Office also serves as an ombudsman, advocating for veterans. OVBD personnel are involved in every SBA program to ensure that veterans receive special consideration in the operation of that program. The Office provides resources, services, and tools: the Vet Gazette newsletter, Reserve and Guard business assistance kits, program design assistance, training, and counseling. The Office manages five Veterans Business Outreach Centers to provide outreach, directed referrals, and tailored entrepreneurial development services to veterans, including service-disabled veterans, and reservists. The OVBD also coordinates SBA collaborative efforts with veterans service organizations; the Departments of Defense, Labor, and Veterans Affairs; the National Veterans Business Development Corporation; State veterans affairs departments; the National Committee for Employer Support of the Guard and Reserve; the Department of Defense Yellow Ribbon Reintegration Program; and other civic, private, and public organizations. https://www.sba.gov/content/veteran-service-disabled-veteran-owned

For further information, contact the Office of Veterans Business Development. Phone, 202-205-6773.

Women's Business Ownership   The Office of Women's Business Ownership (OWBO) enables and empowers women entrepreneurs through advocacy, outreach, education, and support. OWBO programs offer business training and counseling, access to credit and capital, and marketing opportunities, including Federal contracts.

In 1988, the SBA established the Women's Business Center (WBC) program to help women overcome barriers to success. Today, WBCs offer SBA services in almost every State. WBCs tailor their services to the needs of their communities. They provide financial, Internet, management, and marketing training, as well as offering access to SBA financial and procurement assistance programs. https://www.sba.gov/offices/headquarters/wbo | Email: owbo@sba.gov

For further information, contact the Women's Business Ownership representative in your SBA district office. Phone, 202-205-6673.

Sources of Information

Business Opportunities   Information on selling to the Government and qualifying for Government contracts is available online. The SBA also provides online resources for small businesses and posts information on Government contracting programs on its Web site. https://www.sba.gov/contracting

The Office of Government Contracting maintains a glossary that defines program-related terms that may be unfamiliar. https://www.sba.gov/offices/headquarters/ogc/resources

Electronic Updates   An online subscription form is available to sign up for electronic updates on upcoming events and business tips. https://www.sba.gov/updates

Career Opportunities   The SBA offers Federal Government health benefits, flexible work schedules, and paid leave. It also promotes a work-life balance. https://www.sba.gov/about-sba/sba-team/jobs-sba

In 2016, the SBA ranked 26th among midsize agencies in the Partnership for Public Service's Best Places To Work Agency Rankings. http://bestplacestowork.org/BPTW/rankings/detail/SB00

Resource Guide   English (2015) and Spanish (2012) versions of the "Resource Guide for Small Business" are available online in Portable Document Format (PDF). https://www.sba.gov/about-sba/what-we-do/resource-guides

Freedom of Information Act (FOIA)   Instructions for submitting a FOIA request are available online. https://www.sba.gov/about-sba/sba-performance/open-government/foia

Newsroom   The SBA newsroom features congressional testimonies, media advisories, press releases, speeches, and weekly lending reports. https://www.sba.gov/about-sba/sba-newsroom

Open Government   The SBA supports the Open Government initiative by promoting the principles of collaboration, participation, and transparency. https://www.sba.gov/about-sba/sba-performance/open-government

Plain Language   SBA writers and editors are committed to producing documents in plain language. If documents or Web pages are unclear or difficult to understand, contact the SBA by email. https://www.sba.gov/about-sba/sba-performance/open-government/other-plans-reports/plain-language-page | Email: plain.language@sba.gov

Public Affairs   The SBA public affairs team responds to questions from the media and general public, arranges interviews with appropriate program staff, and provides referrals and other information. To find an SBA local or regional spokesperson, visit the "Regional and Local Media" Web page. For public inquiries and small business advocacy affairs, contact the Office of Public Communications and Public Liaison. Phone,

202-205-6740. https://www.sba.gov/about-sba/sba-newsroom/regional-local-media
Site Map   The Web site map allows visitors to look for specific topics or to browse content that aligns with their interests. https://www.sba.gov/sitemap. https://www.sba.gov/about-sba/what-we-do/contact-sba | Email: answerdesk@sba.gov

For further information, contact the Office of Public Communications and Public Liaison, Small Business Administration, 409 Third Street SW., Washington, DC 20416. Phone, 202-205-6740.

Social Security Administration

6401 Security Boulevard, Baltimore, MD 21235
Phone, 410-965-1234 / 800-772-1213. 800-325-0778 (TTY). Internet, http://www.socialsecurity.gov.

Commissioner	NANCY A. BERRYHILL, ACTING
Deputy Commissioner	(VACANCY)
Chief of Staff	BEATRICE M. DISMAN, ACTING
Deputy Commissioners	
Budget, Finance, Quality, and Management	MICHELLE A. KING
Communications	JAMES C. BORLAND, ACTING
Disability Adjudication and Review	THERESA L. GRUBER
Human Resources	MARIANNA LACANFORA
Legislation and Congressional Affairs	ROYCE B. MIN, ACTING
Operations	MARY L. HORNE, ACTING
Retirement and Disability Policy	MARK J. WARSHAWSKY
Systems / Chief Information Officer	RAJIVE K. MATHUR
Chief Actuary	STEPHEN C. GOSS
Counselor to the Commissioner	FRANK A. CRISTAUDO
Director, Equality Employment Opportunity	KOJUAN L. ALMOND
Executive Secretary	DARLYNDA K. BOGLE
General Counsel	ASHEESH AGARWAL
Inspector General	GALE S. STONE, ACTING

[For the Social Security Administration statement of organization, see the Code of Federal Regulations, Title 20, Part 422]

The above list of key personnel was updated 09–2017

The Social Security Administration manages the retirement, survivors, and disability insurance programs that are known as Social Security; it administers the Supplemental Security Income program for the aged, blind, and disabled; and it assigns Social Security numbers to U.S. citizens and maintains earnings records based on those numbers.

The Social Security Administration (SSA) was established by Reorganization Plan No. 2 of 1946 (5 U.S.C. app.), effective July 16, 1946. It became an independent agency in the executive branch by the Social Security Independence and Program Improvements Act of 1994 (42 U.S.C. 901), effective March 31, 1995. https://www.ssa.gov/history

The SSA is headed by a Commissioner whom the President appoints with the advice and consent of the Senate.

The Deputy Commissioner assists in administering the programs necessary to accomplish the Administration's mission. The Deputy Commissioner performs duties that the Commissioner, Chief Financial Officer, Chief Information Officer, General Counsel,

Chief Actuary, and Inspector General assign or delegate to him or her. https://www.ssa.gov/OP_Home/ssact/title07/0702.htm

The Administration's operations are decentralized to provide local services. Each of the 10 SSA regions has a network of field offices and call centers. These offices and centers provide liaison between the SSA and public. The Administration operates 10 regional offices, approximately 1,230 field offices, 33 teleservice centers, 15 Social Security card centers, 6 processing centers, and 2 additional processing centers in its central office. https://www.ssa.gov/org/index.htm

Activities

Black Lung By agreement with the Department of Labor, the SSA assists in the administration of the black lung benefits provisions of the Federal Coal Mine Health and Safety Act of 1969, as amended (30 U.S.C. 901). https://www.ssa.gov/OP_Home/rulings/di/09/SSR73-24-di-09.html

Hearings and Appeals The SSA administers a nationwide hearings and appeals program that offers a way for those who are dissatisfied with determinations affecting their rights to and amounts of benefits or their participation in programs to seek remedy through the Social Security Act. The act allows for administrative appeals of these determinations in accordance with the requirements of the Administrative Procedure and Social Security Acts. The SSA operates approximately 166 hearing offices, including 2 satellite offices; 5 national hearing centers; and 4 national case assistance centers within in its 10 administrative regions. http://www.ssa.gov/appeals/about_odar.html

Medicare While the administration of Medicare is the responsibility of the Centers for Medicare and Medicaid Services, the SSA provides Medicare assistance to the public through SSA field offices and call centers. It adjudicates requests for hearings and appeals of Medicare claims. http://www.ssa.gov/medicare

Old-Age, Survivors, and Disability Insurance The SSA administers social insurance programs that provide monthly benefits to retired and disabled workers, to their spouses and children, and to survivors of insured workers. Financing is under a system of contributory social insurance, whereby employees, employers, and the self-employed pay contributions that are pooled in special trust funds. When earnings stop or decrease because the worker retires, dies, or becomes disabled, monthly cash benefits are paid to supplement the family's reduced income. https://faq.ssa.gov/ics/support/splash.asp

Supplemental Security Income The SSA administers this needs-based program for the aged, blind, and disabled. A basic Federal monthly payment is financed by general revenue, rather than from a special trust fund. Some States, choosing to provide payments to supplement the benefits, have agreements with the Administration under which it administers the supplemental payments for those States. http://www.ssa.gov/disabilityssi/ssi.html

Sources of Information

Business Opportunities The Office of Acquisition and Grants serves as the SSA's principal procurement office. http://www.ssa.gov/oag

Career Opportunities The SSA offers opportunities for various career paths: acquisitions, contracts, and grants; administrative support; facilities and physical security; finance and accounting; human resources; information technology; law enforcement; legal; and public contact. http://www.ssa.gov/careers

In 2016, the SSA ranked 9th among 18 large agencies in the Partnership for Public Service's Best Places To Work Agency Rankings. http://bestplacestowork.org/BPTW/rankings/detail/SZ00

Fraud Hotline The Office of the Inspector General (OIG) operates a toll-free hotline, 10 a.m.–4 p.m., eastern standard time, for reporting allegations of abuse, fraud, and waste affecting SSA programs and operations. Phone, 800-269-0271. TTY, 866-501-2101. Fax, 410-597-0118. https://oig.ssa.gov/report-fraud-waste-or-abuse

An online form also is available to file a report. https://www.ssa.gov/fraudreport/oig/public_fraud_reporting/form.htm

Freedom of Information Act (FOIA) An online guide discusses important FOIA-related topics: how to request information and records, information that the SSA cannot disclose, and the fees associated with making a request. https://www.ssa.gov/foia

Frequently Asked Questions (FAQs)   The SSA posts answers to FAQs and offers information on popular help-topics. https://faq.ssa.gov/ics/support/default.asp?deptID=34019&_referrer=https://www.ssa.gov/ask

Glossary   A glossary of Social Security terms is available online. https://www.ssa.gov/agency/glossary

Multilanguage Gateway   The SSA tries to eliminate or reduce, as much as possible, barriers of language that impede the delivery of its services. Social Security information is available on the SSA Web site in the following languages: American Sign Language, Arabic, Armenian, Chinese, Farsi, French, Greek, Haitian Creole, Hmong, Italian, Korean, Polish, Portuguese, Russian, Somali, Spanish, Tagalog, and Vietnamese. The SSA provides free interpreter services for conducting Social Security-related business. https://www.ssa.gov/multilanguage

News   The SSA posts press releases on its Web site. https://www.ssa.gov/news/press/releases

An online newsletter also is available. https://www.ssa.gov/news/newsletter

Online Services   The SSA offers a growing number of services electronically through its Web site. https://www.ssa.gov/onlineservices

Open Government   The SSA supports the Open Government initiative to create a more open and transparent Government by promoting the principles of collaboration, participation, and transparency. https://www.ssa.gov/open | Email: open.government@ssa.gov

Organizational Chart   The SSA's organizational chart is available in Portable Document Format (PDF) for viewing and downloading. https://www.ssa.gov/org/ssachart.pdf

Plain Language   The Plain Writing Act of 2010 requires Federal agencies to communicate in a manner that the public can understand and use. SSA writers and editors welcome suggestions for improving agency forms, notices, pamphlets, or pages from its Web site. https://www.ssa.gov/agency/plain-language | Email: PlainWriting@ssa.gov

Publications   Many SSA publications in English, Spanish, and other languages are accessible online. http://www.socialsecurity.gov/pubs

Site Map   The Web site map allows visitors to look for specific topics or to browse content that aligns with their interests. https://www.ssa.gov/sitemap.htm

Speakers   Under certain circumstances, the SSA can provide a speaker free of charge, generally available during business hours, to explain benefits, programs, and services. An online form is available to initiate a request. http://www.ssa.gov/agency/ask-for-a-speaker.html. https://www.ssa.gov/agency/contact | Email: OPI.Policy.Coordination@ssa.gov

For further information, contact the Office of Public Inquiries, Social Security Administration, 6401 Security Boulevard, 1106 West High Rise Building, Baltimore, MD 21235. Phone, 410-965-0709. Fax, 410-965-0695.

Surface Transportation Board

395 E Street SW., Washington, DC 20423
Phone, 202-245-0245. Internet, http://www.stb.gov/stb/index.html

Board

Chair	ANN D. BEGEMAN, ACTING
Vice Chair	(VACANCY)
Member	DEBRA L. MILLER
Member	(VACANCY)
Member	(VACANCY)

Directors

Office of Economics	WILLIAM J. BRENNAN, ACTING
Office of Environmental Analysis	VICTORIA J. RUTSON
Office of Proceedings	SCOTT ZIMMERMAN, ACTING
Office of Public Assistance, Governmental Affairs and Compliance	LUCILLE L. MARVIN
Office of the General Counsel	CRAIG KEATS
Office of the Managing Director	RACHEL D. CAMPBELL, ACTING

The above list of key personnel was updated 10–2017.

The Surface Transportation Board adjudicates and resolves railroad rate and service disputes and reviews proposals for railroad mergers.

The Surface Transportation Board (STB) is the successor agency to the Interstate Commerce Commission (ICC), which was created in 1887. The ICC Termination Act of 1995 established the STB as an independent adjudicatory body within the Department of Transportation. It remained administratively aligned with the Department for nearly two decades. On December 18, 2015, the Surface Transportation Board Reauthorization Act of 2015 established the STB as a wholly independent Federal agency (49 USC 1301 et seq.). https://www.stb.gov/stb/about/overview.html

The STB comprises five members whom the President appoints and the Senate confirms for 5-year terms. The President also designates one of the members to serve as the Board's chair. https://www.stb.gov/stb/about/board.html

Activities

The STB adjudicates disputes and regulates interstate surface transportation through various laws governing the different modes of surface transportation. Its general responsibilities include the oversight of firms engaged in interstate and foreign commercial transportation—to the extent that it takes place within the United States, or between or among points in the contiguous United States and points in Alaska, Hawaii, or U.S. Territories or possessions. The STB's jurisdiction generally extends over railroad rate and service issues, rail restructuring transactions, including mergers and line abandonments, construction, and sales, and labor matters related thereto; some moving van, trucking, and noncontiguous ocean shipping company rate matters; some intercity passenger bus company financial, operational, and structural matters; and pipeline matters that the Federal Energy Regulatory Commission does not regulate.

The STB promotes substantive and procedural regulatory reform, provides a forum for the resolution of disputes, and facilitates appropriate market-based business transactions. Through rulemakings and case disposition, it develops improved and efficient ways of analyzing problems, reducing costs associated with regulatory oversight, and encouraging private sector negotiations and resolutions.

Sources of Information

Annual Reports The STB posts activity reports that it prepares for Congress every few years and annual reports on its Web site. https://www.stb.gov/stb/about/annual.html

Career Opportunities Current job openings are posted online. https://www.stb.gov/stb/about/jobs.html

In 2016, the STB was ranked number 16 among 29 small Government agencies in the Partnership for Public Service's Best Places To Work Agency Rankings. http://bestplacestowork.org/BPTW/rankings/detail/TX00

Electronic Filing As an alternative to submitting paper filings, consider filing electronically. E-filing may not be used for initial filings in a proceeding, filings requiring a fee (with the exception of recordations), and large evidentiary filings. https://www.stb.gov/stb/efilings.nsf

Environment The Office of Environmental Analysis's Web page features links to cases, correspondence, rules, and other resources related to environmental matters. https://www.stb.gov/stb/environment/sea.html

Freedom of Information Act (FOIA) The STB Web site features an online form for submitting FOIA requests. Phone, 202-245-0271. Fax, 202-245-0464. https://www.stb.gov/stb/efilings.nsf/FOIARequest?OpenForm | Email: FOIA.privacy@stb.gov

Frequently Asked Questions (FAQs) The STB posts answers to FAQs on its Web site. https://www.stb.gov/stb/faqs.html

Glossary The STB Web site features a glossary of terms associated with environmental issues. https://www.stb.gov/glossary.nsf/emletterweb?OpenView&RestrictToCategory=a

Historic Preservation The National Environmental Policy and National Historic

Preservation Acts and other Federal environmental laws require the STB to consider the impact of its licensing decisions on historic properties. The Office of Environmental Analysis develops guidance that clarifies the STB's historic preservation review requirements and posts it on the STB's Web site. https://www.stb.gov/stb/environment/preservation.html

Industry Data   The STB posts financial and statistical reports containing economic data on its Web site. https://www.stb.gov/stb/industry/econ_reports.html

Rail carriers must file a summary of each contract entered into for the transportation of agricultural products. Beginning with the first quarter of 2008, filed contract summaries are available on the STB's Web site in Portable Document Format (PDF) and grouped by railroad. https://www.stb.gov/econdata.nsf/8B5F6EFB897D7C218525743 4003D44A2 | Email: rcpa@stb.gov

Library   The library is open to the public on weekdays, excluding Federal Holidays, 10 a.m.–3 p.m. Phone, 202-245-0406. http://www.stb.dot.gov/stb/public/inquiries_library.html | Email: rcpa@stb.gov

The STB's Web site features an electronic library whose resources can be accessed by opening the "E–Library" drop-down menu on the home page. https://www.stb.gov/stb/index.html

Maps   The Railroad Map Depot features links to railroad maps. The railroad map information is based on publicly available maps and data that government agencies, railroads, and other stakeholders produce. https://stb.maps.arcgis.com/home/index.html

News   The STB posts announcements and other noteworthy items on its "What's New" Web page. https://www.stb.gov/stb/news/whatsnew.html

Organizational Chart   An organizational chart is available in the "About STB" section of its Web site. https://www.stb.gov/stb/about/orgchart.html#

Publications   Consumer pamphlets are available in Portable Document Format (PDF) from the electronic library. http://www.stb.dot.gov/stb/elibrary/epubs.html

Railroad Rates   Experts in the Office of Economics monitor patterns of average rail rates that the Nation's railroads charge. Multiyear studies address the key factors behind rate increases and decreases and assess the effects on consumers, shippers, and the Nation as a whole. A small collection of rail rate studies in Portable Document Format (PDF) is available on the STB Web site. https://www.stb.gov/stb/industry/econ_rateindex.html

Testimony / Speeches   The Office of Public Assistance, Governmental Affairs, and Compliance posts the testimony and speeches of STB officials online. https://www.stb.gov/stb/news/speeches_testimony.html. https://www.stb.gov/stb/contact.html | Email: rcpa@stb.gov

For further information, contact the Surface Transportation Board, Office of Public Assistance, Governmental Affairs, and Compliance, 395 E Street SW., Washington, DC, 20423. Phone, 202-245-0238.

Tennessee Valley Authority

400 West Summit Hill Drive, Knoxville, TN 37902
Phone, 865-632-2101. Internet, http://www.tva.com.

Board of Directors

Chair	RICHARD C. HOWORTH
Director	MARILYN A. BROWN
Director	V. LYNN EVANS
Director	VIRGINIA T. LODGE
Director	ERIC M. SATZ
Director	RONALD A. WALTER
Director	(VACANCY)
Director	(VACANCY)
Director	(VACANCY)

Executive Leadership

President / Chief Executive Officer	WILLIAM D. JOHNSON
Executive Vice President / Chief Financial Officer	JOHN M. THOMAS III
Executive Vice President / General Counsel	SHERRY A. QUICK
Executive Vice President, External Relations	VAN M. WARDLAW
Executive Vice President, Generation	JOSEPH P. GRIMES
Executive Vice President, Operations	MICHAEL D. SKAGGS
Senior Vice President / Chief Communications and Marketing Officer	JANET J. BREWER
Senior Vice President / Chief Human Resources Officer	SUSAN E. COLLINS
Inspector General	RICHARD W. MOORE

The Tennessee Valley Authority conducts a unified program of resource development to advance economic growth in the Tennessee Valley region.

The Tennessee Valley Authority (TVA) is a wholly owned Government corporation created by the act of May 18, 1933 (16 U.S.C. 831-831dd). All functions of the Authority are vested in its nine-member Board of Directors, whose members the President appoints with the advice and consent of the Senate. The Board designates one of its members to serve as the Chair. https://www.tva.com/About-TVA

Activities

The TVA's activities are diverse: They range from economic development and environmental stewardship to electric power production and transmission, flood control, navigation, recreation improvement, and to water supply and water quality management.

The TVA's electric power program is financially self-supporting and operates as part of an independent system with the Authority's system of dams on the Tennessee River and its larger tributaries. These dams provide flood regulation on the Tennessee River and contribute to regulation of the lower Ohio and Mississippi Rivers. The system maintains a continuous 9-foot-draft navigation channel for the length of the 650-mile Tennessee River main stream, from Paducah, KY, to Knoxville, TN. The dams harness the power of the rivers to produce electricity. They also provide other benefits, notably outdoor recreation and water supply.

The Authority operates the river management system and provides assistance to State and local governments in reducing local flood problems. It also works with other agencies to encourage full and effective use of the navigable waterway by industry and commerce.

The TVA is the wholesale power supplier for 154 local municipal and cooperative electric systems serving customers in parts of 7 States. It supplies power to 58 industries and Federal installations whose power requirements are large or unusual. Power to meet these demands is supplied from dams, coal-fired powerplants, nuclear powerplants, natural gas combined-cycle powerplants, combustion turbine and diesel installations, solar energy sites, wind turbines, a methane gas facility, and a pumped-storage hydroelectric plant; U.S. Corps of Engineers dams in the Cumberland Valley; and Brookfield Renewable Energy Partners dams, whose operations are coordinated with the TVA's system.

Economic development is at the heart of the TVA's mission of making the Tennessee Valley a better place to live. A healthy economy means quality jobs, more investment in the region, sustainable growth, and opportunities for residents in the southeastern region to build more prosperous lives. TVA economic development takes a regional approach to economic growth by partnering with power distributors and both public and private organizations to attract new investments and quality jobs, supporting retention and growth of existing businesses and industries, preparing communities for leadership and economic growth, and providing financial and technical services.

Sources of Information

Business Opportunities The TVA partners with power distributors, suppliers, and other individuals and organizations. It seeks business relationships with firms offering reliable products and services at competitive prices. The TVA encourages businessmen and women of diverse backgrounds—minorities, service-disabled-veterans, veterans, as well as small business owners and entrepreneurs in historically underutilized business zones—to learn about available opportunities. For more information, contact Supply Chain, BR 4A–C, 1101 Market Street, Chattanooga, TN 37402. Phone , 423-751-7903. https://www.tva.com/Information/Doing-Business-with-TVA

Career Opportunities The TVA is a service-oriented agency that relies on diverse and talented professionals to carry out its mission. https://www.tva.com/Careers

In 2016, the Office of Inspector General ranked first among 305 agency subcomponents in the Partnership for Public Service's Best Places To Work Agency Rankings!. http://bestplacestowork.org/BPTW/rankings/detail/TV01

Economic Development TVA Economic Development serves the seven States of the TVA service area—AL, GA, KY, MS, NC, TN, and VA. Through partnerships with other economic development organizations, the TVA fosters capital investment and job growth in its service area. Information is available online, or contact TVA Economic Development, 26 Century Boulevard, Suite 100, Nashville, TN 37214. Phone, 615-232-6051. https://www.tva.com/Economic-Development

Environmental Reviews The TVA conducts environmental reviews to consider the effects of its proposed projects on the human and natural environment before making final decisions. The TVA's environmental projects are open for public review. https://www.tva.com/Environment/Environmental-Stewardship/Environmental-Reviews

Freedom of Information Act (FOIA) The TVA operates a FOIA requester service center. Phone, 865-632-6945. https://www.tva.com/Information/Freedom-of-Information | Email: foia@tva.gov

Historic Photographs From the earliest days of the TVA, photographers captured images of the agency's work and the cultural changes that followed. The TVA collection contains over 20,000 black-and-white negatives and over 5,000 original file prints. Its images span half a century, from 1933 to 1983. https://www.tva.com/Environment/Environmental-Stewardship/Land-Management/Cultural-%2B-Historic-Preservation/TVA-Historic-Photograph-Collection

Library Services Visitors may use the TVA Research Library by appointment. Contact the TVA Research Library, 400 W. Summit Hill Drive, Knoxville, TN 37902-1499. Phone, 865-632-3464. https://tva.com/Our-TVA-Story/Nancy-Proctor | Email: corplibknox@tva.gov

Native American Tribes Native Americans have a cultural and historical interest in the Tennessee Valley. The TVA consults with 18 federally recognized tribes when it undertakes projects that could affect their cultural sites. https://www.tva.com/Environment/Environmental-Stewardship/Land-Management/Cultural-%2B-Historic-Preservation/Native-Americans

Newsroom The TVA posts news stories and press releases online. https://www.tva.com/Newsroom

Oversight The Office of the Inspector General from the TVA posts reports and data on Oversight.gov, a text-searchable repository of reports that Federal Inspectors General publish. The Council of the Inspectors General on Integrity and Efficiency operates and maintains the website to increase public access to independent and authoritative information on the Federal Government. https://oversight.gov

Public Engagement The TVA benefits from engaged citizens. It encourages comments, feedback, and input. Contact TVA Communications, 400 W. Summit Hill Drive, Knoxville, TN 37902-1499. Phone, 865-632-2101. https://www.tva.gov/About-TVA/Contact-Us | Email: tvainfo@tva.gov

Site Map The website map allows visitors to look for specific topics or to browse content that aligns with their interests. https://www.tva.com/Index

Social Media The TVA has a Facebook account. https://www.facebook.com/TVA

The TVA tweets announcements and other newsworthy items on Twitter. https://twitter.com/tvanews

The TVA posts videos on its YouTube channel. https://www.youtube.com/user/TVANewsVideo

TVA Kids   The TVA maintains the website tvakids.com, which is a colorful online resource for students and teachers. The site covers topics like green power, making electricity, and saving energy. It also has a section of "Cool Stuff" that includes games, videos, and warnings about energy vampires. https://www.tvakids.com. https://www.tva.gov

For further information, contact the Tennessee Valley Authority at 400 W. Summit Hill Drive, Knoxville, TN 37902-1499. Phone, 865-632-2101. Or, contact the Tennessee Valley Authority at 500 North Capitol Street NW., Suite 200, Washington, DC 20044. Phone, 202-898-2999.

Trade and Development Agency

1000 Wilson Boulevard, Suite 1600, Arlington, VA 22209-3901
Phone, 703-875-4357. Fax, 703-875-4009. Internet, http://www.ustda.gov.

Director	ENOH T. EBONG, ACTING
Deputy Director	ENOH T. EBONG
Administrative Officer	CAROLYN HUM
Chief of Staff	VACANT
Chief, Office of Acquisition Management	GARTH HIBBERT
Director, Congressional Affairs and Public Relations	THOMAS R. HARDY
Director, Finance	KATHLEEN NEUMANN
General Counsel	KENDRA LINK, ACTING
Chief Information Officer	BENJAMIN BERGERSEN
Special Advisor to the Director	CLARK JENNINGS

Regional Directors

East Asia	Carl B. Kress
Latin America and Caribbean	Nathan Younge
Middle East, North Africa, Europe and Eurasia	Carl B. Kress
South and Southeast Asia	Henry D. Steingass
Sub-Saharan Africa	Lida Fitts
Director, Global Programs	Andrea Lupo
Director, Office of Program Monitoring and Evaluation	Diana Harbison

The Trade and Development Agency advances economic development and U.S. commercial interest in developing and middle-income countries.

The Trade and Development Program was established on July 1, 1980, as a component organization of the International Development Cooperation Agency. Section 2204 of the Omnibus Trade and Competitiveness Act of 1988 (22 U.S.C. 2421) made it a separate component agency. The organization was renamed the Trade and Development Agency (USTDA) and made an independent agency within the executive branch of the Federal Government on October 28, 1992, by the Jobs Through Exports Act of 1992 (22 U.S.C. 2421).

The USTDA is a foreign assistance agency that delivers its program commitments through overseas grants and contracts with U.S. firms. The Agency helps companies create U.S. jobs through the export of U.S. goods and services for priority development projects in emerging economies. The Agency links U.S. businesses to export opportunities by funding project planning activities, pilot projects, and reverse trade missions while creating sustainable infrastructure and economic growth in partner countries.

The USTDA provides grant funding to overseas project sponsors for the planning

TRADE AND DEVELOPMENT AGENCY

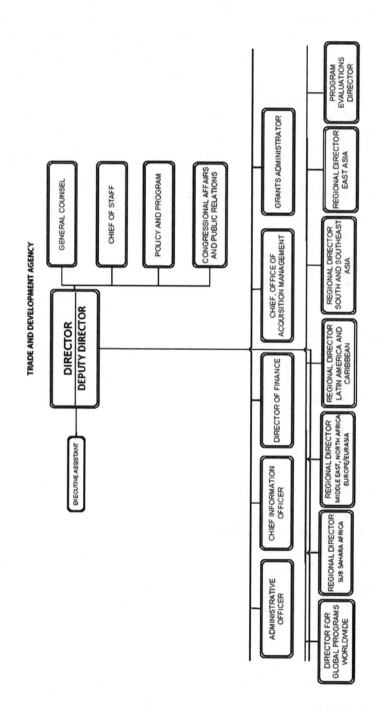

of projects that support the development of modern infrastructure and an open trading system. The hallmark of USTDA development assistance is building partnerships between U.S. companies and overseas project sponsors. These partnerships facilitate the application of proven private sector solutions to developmental challenges.

The Agency works with other U.S. Government agencies to bring their particular expertise and resources to a development objective. These agencies include the Departments of Commerce, Energy, State, Transportation, and the Treasury; Office of the U.S. Trade Representative; Export-Import Bank of the United States; and Overseas Private Investment Corporation. https://www.ustda.gov/about/mission

Activities   The USTDA funds various forms of technical assistance, training, early investment analysis, reverse trade missions, and business workshops that support the development of a modern infrastructure and a fair and open trading environment. The Agency works closely with foreign project sponsors and makes its funds available to them for contracting with U.S. businesses. This arrangement gives American firms market entry, exposure, and access to information. It helps them establish positions in markets that are otherwise difficult to penetrate. The USTDA is involved in many sectors, including energy, transportation, and information and communications technologies.

USTDA-funded studies evaluate the technical, economic, and financial aspects of a development project. They provide the host nation with information on the availability of U.S. goods and services. Financial institutions also use these studies for assessing the creditworthiness of an undertaking. Grants are based on an official request for assistance: Either the sponsoring government or a private sector organization in a developing or middle-income nation can make the request. https://www.ustda.gov/program

Sources of Information

Business Opportunities   Overseas project sponsors can select U.S. firms to carry out USTDA-funded work through a competitive proposal process that relies on the Federal Business Opportunities Web site (FedBizOpps.gov) or through "sole-source" grants, which allow an overseas project sponsor to identify a U.S. firm as a partner or preferred supplier. More information is available on the "Project Proposals" Web page. https://www.ustda.gov/program/project-proposals

Employment   Job openings and information on internships are posted online. https://www.ustda.gov/about/career-opportunities. https://www.ustda.gov/about/career-opportunities/internships

Freedom of Information Act (FOIA)   A FOIA request must be submitted in writing by email, fax, or mail, and clearly identified as a "FOIA REQUEST." Staff is available to answer questions and help formulate a request over the phone; however, the USTDA does not accept phone requests. Mail a request to the FOIA Requester Service Center, U.S. Trade and Development Agency, 1000 Wilson Boulevard, Suite 1600, Arlington, VA 22209-3901. Phone, 703-875-4357. Fax, 703-875-4009. https://www.ustda.gov/about/resources/foia | Email: foia@ustda.gov

Library   The USTDA maintains a collection of reports on infrastructure development projects from emerging economies worldwide. Contact the library by email to obtain a report: Most reports can be sent electronically. These reports are accessible also online. Phone, 703-875-4357. https://www.ustda.gov/ustda-library | Email: library@ustda.gov

Newsletter   To provide timely information on Agency supported activities, the USTDA distributes an electronic newsletter containing business opportunities, events, and updates. A subscription form is available online. https://www.ustda.gov/connect/subscribe-ustda-news-and-alerts

Regional Programs   The USTDA is organized into five international regions. Information on each region is available on the Agency's Web site. Questions should be addressed to the appropriate regional director or country manager. Phone, 703-875-4357. http://www.ustda.gov/program/regions/index.asp. https://www.ustda.gov/about/contact | Email: info@ustda.gov

For further information, contact the U.S. Trade and Development Agency, 1000 Wilson Boulevard, Suite 1600, Arlington, VA 22209-3901. Phone, 703-875-4357. Fax, 703-875-4009.

United States African Development Foundation

1400 I Street NW., Suite 1000, Washington, DC 20005
Phone, 202-233-8800. Fax, 202-673-3810. Internet, http://www.usadf.gov.

Board of Directors

Chair	John W. Leslie, Jr.
Vice Chair	John O. Agwunobi
Board Member	Ward Brehm
Board Member	Morgan M. Davis
Board Member	Iqbal Paroo
Board Member	(vacancy)
Board Member	(vacancy)

Staff

President / Chief Executive Officer	C.D. Glin
General Counsel	June B. Brown
Managing Director, Finance and Administration	Mathieu Zahui, Acting

[For the United States African Development Foundation statement of organization, see the Code of Federal Regulations, Title 22, Part 1501]

The United States African Development Foundation promotes development in Africa to empower marginalized and underserved communities.

The United States African Development Foundation was established by the African Development Foundation Act (22 U.S.C. 290h) as a Government corporation to support African-led development. The Foundation is led by the Board of Directors, which comprises the Chair, the Vice Chair, and five Board Members whom the President nominates with the advice and consent of the Senate. http://www.usadf.gov/adfact

The Foundation invests in private and nongovernmental organizations in Africa to promote and support innovative enterprise development, generate jobs, and increase incomes of the poor. It seeks to expand local institutional and financial capacities to foster entrepreneurship, ownership, and community-based economic development among marginalized and underserved populations in sub-Saharan Africa.

Sources of Information

Blog   The United States African Development Foundation has a blog. http://www.usadf.gov/blog

Career Opportunities   Vacancy announcements are posted online. http://www.usadf.gov/open-positions

Country Portfolios   The Foundation has 20 country programs and special initiatives that extend its reach to a total of 30

African countries. http://www.usadf.gov/wherewework

Events   Information on Foundation-related events is available online. http://www.usadf.gov/events

Frequently Asked Questions (FAQs)   Answers to FAQs are posted on the Foundation's Web site. http://www.usadf.gov/faq

Grants   Information on grants is available online. An applicant may download an application in English or French. Once completed, the application may be submitted by email or postal mail. http://www.usadf.gov/apply

News   Press releases are available online. http://www.usadf.gov/pressreleases

Resources / Results   Information on the Foundation's effectiveness, efficiency, investment return, and successful enterprises is included in its 2016 impact sheet. http://www.usadf.gov/results

Sectors   The Foundation supports African-led agricultural development that benefits community enterprises. http://www.usadf.gov/agriculture

The Foundation supports the development of affordable and renewable energy to benefit rural African communities. http://www.usadf.gov/off-grid

The Foundation invests in the next generation of youth-led African enterprises. http://www.usadf.gov/youth

Social Media   The United States African Development Foundation has a Facebook account. https://www.facebook.com/USADF

The Foundation tweets announcements and other newsworthy items on Twitter. https://twitter.com/USADF

The Foundation posts videos on its YouTube channel. https://www.youtube.com/channel/UCvhwYYAN6WGK4rlmiWAfEAA. http://www.usadf.gov/contact-us | Email: info@usadf.gov

For further information, contact the Office of the President, U.S. African Development Foundation, 1400 I Street NW., Suite 1000, Washington, DC 20005-2248. Phone, 202-673-3916. Fax, 202-673-3810.

United States Agency for International Development

1300 Pennsylvania Avenue NW., Washington, DC 20523
Phone, 202-712-0000. Internet, http://www.usaid.gov

Administrator	WADE WARREN, ACTING
Deputy Administrator	(VACANCY)
Counselor	THOMAS H. STAAL
Chief of Staff	WILLIAM R. STEIGER
Executive Secretary / National Security Advisor	NEILESH SHELAT
Assistant Administrator, Bureau for Global Health	JENNIFER ADAMS
Assistant Administrator, Bureau for Africa	CHERYL ANDERSON, ACTING
Executive Director, U.S. Global Development Lab	HARRY BADER, ACTING
Assistant Administrator, Bureau for Management	ANGELIQUE M. CRUMBLY
Assistant to the Administrator, Bureau for Food Security / Deputy Coordinator for Development, Feed the Future	BETH DUNFORD
Assistant Administrator, Bureau for Europe and Eurasia	MARGOT ELLIS, ACTING
Assistant to the Administrator, Bureau for Policy, Planning and Learning	SUSAN FINE, ACTING
Assistant Administrator, Bureau for Legislative and Public Affairs	DON GRESSETT, ACTING
Assistant Administrator, Bureau for Democracy, Conflict and Humanitarian Assistance	ROBERT JENKINS, ACTING
Chief Human Capitol Officer	KIMBERLY A. LEWIS
Assistant Administrator, Bureau for the Middle East	MARIA LONGI, ACTING
Assistant Administrator, Bureau for Latin America and the Caribbean	SARAH-ANN LYNCH, ACTING
General Counsel	DAVID H. MOORE
Assistant Administrator, Bureau for Economic Growth, Education and Environment	CHARLES NORTH, ACTING
Assistant Administrator, Bureau for Asia	GLORIA STEELE, ACTING
Associate Administrator	ERIC G. POSTEL

[For the Agency for International Development statement of organization, see the Federal Register of Aug. 26, 1987, 52 FR 32174]

The United States Agency for International Development works to eradicate extreme global poverty and to enable resilient and democratic societies to realize their potential.

The United States Agency for International Development (USAID) is an independent Federal agency established by 22 U.S.C. 6563. Its principal statutory authority is the Foreign Assistance Act of 1961, as amended (22 U.S.C. 2151 et seq.). The Agency serves as the focal point within the Government for economic matters affecting U.S. relations

UNITED STATES AGENCY FOR INTERNATIONAL DEVELOPMENT

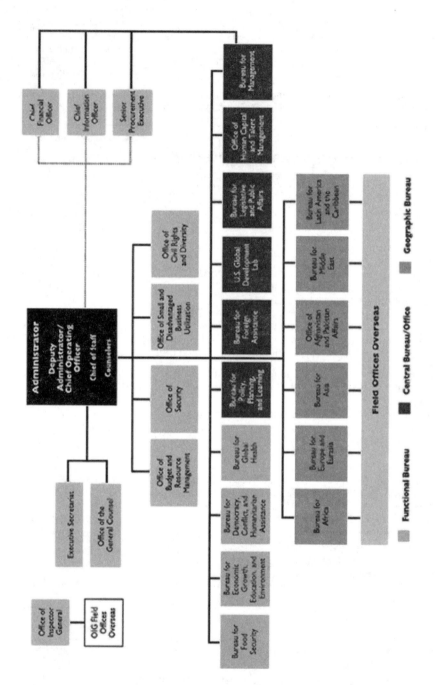

with developing countries. It administers international economic and humanitarian assistance programs. The Administrator is under the direct authority and foreign policy guidance of the Secretary of State. https://www.usaid.gov/who-we-are/usaid-history

Programs

The Agency works in over 100 countries to promote broadly shared economic prosperity, strengthen democracy and good governance, protect human rights, improve global health, advance food security and agriculture, increase environmental sustainability, further education, help societies prevent and recover from conflicts, and provide humanitarian assistance in the wake of natural and manmade disasters. https://www.usaid.gov/what-we-do

Democracy   The Agency promotes the transition to and consolidation of democratic regimes throughout the world. Programs focus on such problems as human rights abuses; misperceptions of democracy and free-market capitalism; lack of experience with democratic institutions; the absence or weakness of intermediary organizations; nonexistent, ineffectual, or undemocratic political parties; disenfranchisement of women, indigenous peoples, and minorities; failure to implement national charter documents; powerless or poorly defined democratic institutions; tainted elections; and inability to resolve conflicts peacefully. http://www.usaid.gov/what-we-do/democracy-human-rights-and-governance

Economic Growth   The Agency promotes broad-based economic growth by addressing factors that enhance the capacity for growth and by working to remove obstacles that obstruct individual opportunity. Programs concentrate on strengthening market economies, expanding economic opportunities for the disadvantaged in developing countries, and building human skills and capacities to facilitate broad-based participation. http://www.usaid.gov/what-we-do/economic-growth-and-trade

Environment   Environmental programs support two strategic goals: 1) reducing long-term threats to the biosphere, particularly loss of biodiversity and change in climate; 2) promoting sustainable economic growth locally, nationally, and regionally by addressing shortsighted environmental, economic, and developmental practices. Globally, USAID programs focus on reducing sources and enhancing sinks of greenhouse gas emissions and on promoting innovative approaches to the conservation and sustainable use of the planet's biological diversity. The approach adopted to address national environmental problems differs from county to country, depending on its environmental priorities. Strategies may include improving agricultural, industrial, and natural resource management practices; strengthening public policies and institutions; dialoguing with governments and international agencies; and environmental research and education. http://www.usaid.gov/what-we-do/environment-and-global-climate-change

Global Health and Population   The Agency improves access and quality of services for maternal and child health, nutrition, voluntary family planning, and reproductive health. It prevents and treats HIV/AIDS, malaria, and tuberculosis. It assists countries in the design and implementation of state-of-the-art public health approaches to end preventable child-maternal deaths and achieve an AIDS-free generation. The Agency takes advantage of economies of scale in procurement, technical services, and commodities. To promote sustainability, the Agency helps expand health systems and the health workforce by adopting and scaling-up proven health interventions across programs and countries. It also contributes to a cooperative global effort to stabilize world population growth and support women's reproductive rights. The types of population and health programs supported vary with the particular needs of individual countries and the kinds of approaches that local communities initiate and support. http://www.usaid.gov/what-we-do/global-health

Humanitarian Assistance and Post-Crisis Transitions   The Agency gives humanitarian assistance to save lives, reduce suffering, help victims return to self-sufficiency, and reinforce democracy. Programs focus on disaster prevention, preparedness, and mitigation; timely delivery of disaster relief and short-term rehabilitation supplies and services; preservation of basic institutions of civil governance during a disaster crisis; support for democratic institutions during periods of national transition; and building and reinforcement of local capacity to anticipate disasters and better cope with their aftermath. http://www.usaid.gov/what-we-do/working-crises-and-conflict

Overseas Organizations   USAID country organizations are located in countries where a bilateral program is being implemented. The in-country organizations are subject to the direction and guidance of the chief U.S. diplomatic representative in the country, usually the Ambassador. The organizations report to the appropriate assistant administrators according to geographic bureaus: Africa, Asia and the Near East, Europe and Eurasia, and Latin America and the Caribbean.

The overseas program activities that involve more than one country are administered by regional offices. These offices may also have country organizational responsibilities for assigned countries. Generally, the offices are headed by a regional development officer.

Coordination and representative offices for development assistance provide liaison with various international organizations and represent U.S. interests in development assistance matters. These offices may be only partially staffed by USAID personnel and may be headed by employees of other U.S. Government agencies. http://www.usaid.gov/where-we-work

Sources of Information

Business Opportunities   For information on contracting opportunities, contact the Office of Small and Disadvantaged Business Utilization, USAID, Washington, DC 20523-0001. Phone, 202-567-4730. Fax, 202-567-4740. https://www.usaid.gov/work-usaid/how-to-work-with-usaid

Comments   Comments, complaints, feedback, ideas, questions, and

recommendations may be submitted by using an online form. http://www.usaid.gov/comment

Congressional Affairs   Congressional inquiries should be directed to the Bureau for Legislative and Public Affairs. Phone, 202-712-4340. http://www.usaid.gov/who-we-are/organization/bureaus/bureau-legislative-and-public-affairs

Employment   USAID employs professionals with a variety of managerial, operational, and technical skills to achieve its international development goals. Its workforce includes direct-hire and contract employees based in the United States and at field missions worldwide. http://www.usaid.gov/careers

Forms   An electronic forms page features a selection of up-to-date USAID forms that are arranged according to form number. https://www.usaid.gov/forms

Freedom of Information Act (FOIA)   FOIA requests must be submitted in writing: email, fax, mail, or via the Public Access Link web portal. USAID Government information specialists are available to answer questions; however, the Agency does not accept verbal FOIA requests. Phone, 202-712-0960. Fax, 202-216-3070. https://www.usaid.gov/foia-requests | Email: foia@usaid.gov

News   USAID posts news and information—congressional testimonies, events, factsheets, photographs, podcasts, speeches, and videos, as well as its "Frontlines" magazine, "Impact Newsletter", and "Impact" blog—online. https://www.usaid.gov/news-information

Open Government   USAID supports the Open Government initiative by posting data, records, and reports online. https://www.usaid.gov/open. https://www.usaid.gov/work-usaid/take-action

For further information, contact the U.S. Agency for International Development, 1300 Pennsylvania Avenue NW., Washington, DC 20523-0001. Phone, 202-712-0000.

United States Commission on Civil Rights

1331 Pennsylvania Avenue NW., Suite 1150, Washington, DC 20425
Phone, 202-376-8128. Fax, 800-977-8339 (FedRelay). Internet, http://www.usccr.gov.

Chair	Catherine E. Lhamon
Vice Chair	Patricia Timmons-Goodson
Commissioner	Debo P. Adegbile
Commissioner	Gail Heriot
Commissioner	Peter N. Kirsanow
Commissioner	David Kladney
Commissioner	Karen K. Narasaki
Commissioner	Michael Yaki
Staff Director	Mauro A. Morales

[For the Commission on Civil Rights statement of organization, see the Code of Federal Regulations, Title 45, Part 701]

The Commission on Civil Rights informs the development of national civil rights policy and enhances enforcement of Federal civil rights laws.

The Commission on Civil Rights was first created by the Civil Rights Act of 1957, as amended, and reestablished by the United States Commission on Civil Rights Act of 1994, as amended (42 U.S.C. 1975). http://www.usccr.gov/about/index.php

Activities

The Commission conducts hearings on important civil rights issues, including issuing subpoenas for the production of documents and the attendance of witnesses; publishes studies and reports on a wide range of civil rights issues to inform and advise policymakers; holds public briefings, issues press releases, makes information publicly available online, and provides a complaint referral service to promote greater public awareness of civil rights issues, protections, and enforcement; and sustains advisory committee involvement in the national program planning to strengthen factfinding. http://www.usccr.gov/about/powers.php

Regional Programs   The Commission maintains 51 State Advisory Committees (SACs), one for each State and the District of Columbia. Each SAC is composed of citizen volunteers who are familiar with local and State civil rights issues. SAC members assist the Commission with factfinding, investigating, and disseminating information. The Commission ensures that advisory committees are diverse and represent a variety of backgrounds, skills, experiences, and perspectives. This diversity promotes debate and broadens exploration of the issues. All appointments are made in

a nondiscriminatory manner. http://www.usccr.gov/about/sac.php

Sources of Information

Complaints   The complaint referral service helps place individuals in contact with the appropriate office for obtaining information on the complaint process. Phone, 202-376-8513 or 800-552-6843. http://www.usccr.gov/filing/complaint.php | Email: referrals@usccr.gov

Employment   Career opportunities—vacancy announcements and available internships—are posted online. Contact the Human Resources Division for more information. Phone, 202-376-8364. http://www.usccr.gov/about/careers.php | Email: careers@usccr.gov

Freedom of Information Act (FOIA)   Information on how to file a FOIA request is available online. A request may be sent by email or fax, or by mail to the FOIA Officer, U.S. Commission on Civil Rights, 1331 Pennsylvania Avenue NW., Suite 1150, Washington, DC 20425. Phone, 202-376-8351. Fax, 202-376-1163. http://www.usccr.gov/foia/index.php | Email: foia@usccr.gov

Library   The Robert S. Rankin Memorial Library welcomes visitors. It is open on weekdays, 10 a.m.–4 p.m. (except on Federal holidays). For more information, contact the Robert S. Rankin Memorial Library, 1331 Pennsylvania Avenue NW., Washington, DC 20425. Phone, 202-376-8110. Fax, 202-376-7597. http://www.usccr.gov/about/library.php | Email: publications@usccr.gov

Publications   For a complete list of Commission publications, consult the online catalog. It includes briefings; clearinghouse publications; hearings, consultations, and conferences; periodicals; publications in Spanish; staff reports; State advisory committee reports; and statutory and interim reports. To order a publication, contact the U.S. Commission on Civil Rights, 1331 Pennsylvania Avenue, NW., Suite 1150, Washington, DC 20425. Phone: 202-376-8128. http://www.usccr.gov/pubs/index.php | Email: publications@usccr.gov

Regional Offices   A list of the six regional offices—including addresses, telephone numbers, and areas served—is available online. http://www.usccr.gov/contact/regional.php. http://www.usccr.gov/contact/index.php

For further information, contact the Office of the Staff Director, U.S. Commission on Civil Rights, 1331 Pennsylvania Avenue NW., Suite 1150, Washington, DC 20425. Phone, 202-376-7700. Phone, 800-977-8339 (FedRelay).

United States International Trade Commission

500 E Street SW., Washington, DC 20436
Phone, 202-205-2000. Internet, http://www.usitc.gov.

Chair	RHONDA K. SCHMIDTLEIN
Vice Chair	DAVID S. JOHANSON
Commissioner	IRVING A. WILLIAMSON
Commissioner	MEREDITH M. BROADBENT
Commissioner	(VACANCY)
Commissioner	(VACANCY)
Chief Administrative Law Judge	CHARLES E. BULLOCK
Director of Operations	CATHERINE B. DEFILIPPO
Director, Office of Economics	WILLIAM M. POWERS
Director, Office of Industries	JONATHAN R. COLEMAN
Director, Office of Investigations	MICHAEL G. ANDERSON
Director, Office of Tariff Affairs and Trade Agreements	JAMES R. HOLBEIN
Director, Office of Unfair Import Investigations	MARGARET D. MACDONALD
Director, Office of Analysis and Research Services	JAMES KENNEDY
General Counsel	DOMINIC L. BIANCHI
Director, Office of External Relations	LYN M. SCHLITT
Chief Information Officer	KIRIT AMIN
Chief Administrative Officer	STEPHEN MCLAUGHLIN
Director, Office of Human Resources	ERIC MOZIE
Director, Office of Security and Support Services	ROBERT N. RIESS
Chief Financial Officer	JOHN M. ASCIENZO
Director, Office of Procurement	DEBRA BRIDGE
Director, Office of Finance	DEREK HENDERSON
Director, Office of Budget	CHRIS SWETZ
Secretary	LISA R. BARTON
Inspector General	PHILIP M. HENEGHAN
Director, Office of Equal Employment Opportunity	ALTIVIA JACKSON

The United States International Trade Commission provides the President, the U.S. Trade Representative, and the Congress with independent analysis of and information on tariffs, international trade, and the Nation's competitiveness; makes determinations in proceedings involving imports that may harm a domestic industry or violate U.S. intellectual property rights; and maintains the Harmonized Tariff Schedule of the United States.

The United States International Trade Commission (USITC) is an independent agency created by the Revenue Act (39 Stat. 795) and originally named the United States Tariff Commission. The name was changed to the United States International Trade Commission by section 171 of the Trade Act of 1974 (19 U.S.C. 2231).

With the advice and consent of the Senate, the President appoints six commissioners for 9-year terms, unless the appointment is made to fill an unexpired term. The Chair and Vice Chair are designated by the President for 2-year terms, and succeeding Chairs may not be of the same political party. The Chair generally is responsible for the administration of the Commission. Not more than three Commissioners may be members of the same political party (19 U.S.C. 1330). https://www.usitc.gov/press_room/about_usitc.htm

Activities

The Commission performs a number of functions pursuant to the statutes referred to above. Under the Tariff Act of 1930, the Commission has broad powers of investigation relating to the customs laws of the United States and foreign countries; the volume of importation in comparison with domestic production and consumption; the conditions, causes, and effects of foreign industrial competition with United States industries; and all other factors affecting competition between articles of the United States and imported articles. The Commission is required, whenever requested, to convey its available information to the President, the House Committee on Ways and Means, and the Senate Committee on Finance. The President, Congress, or the two committees mentioned can direct the Commission to undertake investigations and studies.

To carry out these responsibilities, the Commission engages in extensive research, conducts specialized studies, and maintains a high degree of expertise in all matters relating to the commercial and international trade policies of the United States.

Imported Articles Subsidized or Sold at Less Than Fair Value The Commission conducts preliminary-phase investigations to determine whether imports of foreign merchandise allegedly being subsidized or sold at less than fair value injure or threaten to injure an industry in the United States. If the Commission's determination is affirmative and the Secretary of Commerce determines there is reason to believe or suspect such unfair practices are occurring, then the Commission conducts final-phase investigations to determine the injury or threat of injury to an industry.

Under the Uruguay Round Agreements Act, the Commission also conducts sunset reviews. In these reviews, the Commission evaluates whether material injury to a U.S. industry would continue or recur if the antidumping duty or countervailing duty order under review were revoked. Such injury reviews must be conducted on all antidumping duty and countervailing duty orders every 5 years for as long as the orders remain in effect.

Unfair Practices in Import Trade The Commission applies U.S. statutory and common law of unfair competition to the importation of products into the United States and their sale. If the Commission determines that there is a violation of law, it will direct that the articles involved be excluded from entry into the United States, or it may issue cease-and-desist orders directing the person engaged in such violation to stop.

Trade Negotiations The Commission advises the President as to the probable economic effect on the domestic industry and on consumers of modification of duties and other barriers to trade that may be considered for inclusion in any proposed trade agreement with foreign countries.

Generalized System of Preferences With respect to articles that may be considered for preferential removal of the duty on imports from designated developing countries, the Commission advises the President as to the probable economic effect such removal will have on the domestic industry and on consumers.

Industry Adjustment to Import Competition (Global Safeguard Actions) The Commission conducts investigations upon petition on behalf of an industry, a firm, a group of workers, or other entity representative of an industry to determine whether an article is being imported in such increased quantities as to injure or threaten to injure the domestic industry producing an article like or directly competitive with the imported article. If the Commission's finding is affirmative, it recommends to the President the action that would address such a threat and be most effective in facilitating positive adjustment by the industry to import competition. The President determines if import relief is appropriate.

The Commission reports on developments within an industry that has been granted import relief and advises the President of the probable economic effect of the reduction or elimination of the tariff increase that has been granted. The President may continue, modify, or terminate the import relief previously granted.

Imports From NAFTA Countries (Bilateral Safeguard Actions)   The Commission investigates whether, as a result of the reduction or elimination of a duty provided for under the North American Free Trade Agreement (NAFTA), a Canadian article or a Mexican article, is being imported in such increased quantities and under such conditions that imports of the article cause serious injury or (except in the case of a Canadian article) a threat of serious injury to the domestic industry producing an article that is like or directly competitive with the imported article. If the Commission's determination is in the affirmative, the Commission recommends to the President the relief that is necessary to prevent or remedy serious injury. Commission investigations under these provisions are similar procedurally to those conducted under the global safeguard action provisions.

Market Disruption From Communist Countries   The Commission conducts investigations to determine whether increased imports of an article produced in a Communist country are causing market disruption in the United States. If the Commission's determination is in the affirmative, the President may take the same action as in the case of serious injury to an industry, except that the action would apply only to imports of the article from the Communist country. Commission investigations conducted under this provision are similar procedurally to those conducted under the global safeguard action provisions.

Import Interference With Agricultural Programs   The Commission conducts investigations, at the direction of the President, to determine whether imports or potential imports may interfere with the Department of Agriculture's agricultural programs or reduce the amount of any product processed in the United States. After investigating, the Commission discloses findings and makes recommendations. The President may then restrict the imports in question by imposing import fees or quotas. Such fees or quotas may be applied only against countries that are not members of the World Trade Organization.

Uniform Statistical Data   The Commission, in cooperation with the Secretary of the Treasury and the Secretary of Commerce, for statistical purposes, enumerates articles imported into and exported from the United States and seeks to compare such data with domestic production statistical programs.

Harmonized Tariff Schedule of the United States, Annotated   The Commission issues a publication containing the U.S. tariff schedules and related matters and considers questions concerning the arrangement of such schedules and the classification of articles. https://www.usitc.gov/tata/hts/index.htm

International Trade Studies   The Commission conducts studies, investigations, and research projects on a broad range of topics relating to international trade, pursuant to requests of the President, the House Ways and Means Committee, the Senate Finance Committee, either branch of the Congress, or on its own motion. Public reports of these studies, investigations, and research projects are issued in most cases.

The Commission also keeps informed of the operation and effect of provisions relating to duties or other import restrictions of the United States contained in various trade agreements. Occasionally, the Commission is required by statute to perform specific trade-related studies.

Sources of Information

Business Opportunities   Most USITC contract opportunities are reserved for small businesses. They are typically for experienced contractors in the areas of administrative services, facilities management, information technology, and management consulting. The Office of Procurement oversees all procurements. Phone, 202-205-2252. https://usitc.gov/procurement/doing_business_with_usitc.htm

Career Opportunities   The USITC relies on accountants, analysts and specialists, attorneys, economists, and other professionals to carry out its mission. For more information, contact the Director, Office of Human Resources. Phone, 202-205-2651. https://www.usitc.gov/employment/positions.htm | Email: hr@usitc.gov

Freedom of Information Act (FOIA)   A FOIA request form is available online. https://pubapps.usitc.gov/applications/foia/request.asp

Glossary   The USITC maintains an online glossary. https://usitc.gov/glossary.htm

Investigations   A list of active antidumping and countervailing duty investigations is available online. https://www.usitc.gov/trade_remedy/731_ad_701_cvd/investigations.htm

337Info is an information retrieval system containing data on USITC Section 337 investigations. https://pubapps2.usitc.gov/337external | Email: 337InfoHelp@usitc.gov

The Electronic Document Information System (EDIS) contains all documents that have been filed in relation to USITC investigations. EDIS provides the capabilities to file documents for an investigation and to search for documents that have been submitted to the USITC. https://edis.usitc.gov | Email: EDIS3Help@usitc.gov

News   The USITC posts news releases on its Web site. https://www.usitc.gov/press_room/news_release/news_release_index.htm

Open Data   The USITC helps increase the Federal Government's efficiency and transparency by making its operational information more accessible and useful. https://www.usitc.gov/data/index.htm

Reading Rooms   Reading rooms are open to the public in the Office of the Secretary and the USITC Main Library. The USITC Law Library is publicly accessible by prior arrangement. Call 202-205-3287 to schedule a visit.

Popular Topics   The "Popular Topics" Web page features links to frequently visited USITC Web pages. Popular topics include calendar events, commissioner biographies, "Federal Register" notices, hearing protocols, jobs, and news releases. https://usitc.gov/popular_topics.htm

Publications   The Commission publishes results of investigations on various commodities and subjects. Other publications include an annual report to the Congress on the operation of the trade agreements program and an annual review of Commission activities. Specific information on these publications can be obtained from the Office of the Secretary. https://usitc.gov/research_and_analysis/commission_publications.htm. http://www.usitc.gov/secretary.htm

For further information, contact the Secretary, United States International Trade Commission, 500 E Street SW., Washington, DC 20436. Phone, 202-205-2000.

United States Office of Special Counsel

1730 M Street NW., Suite 218, Washington, DC 20036-4505
Phone, 202-804-7000, 800-872-9855, 202-653-5151. Internet, http://www.osc.gov

Leadership Tables

Special Counsel	TRISTAN LEAVITT, ACTING
Principal Deputy Special Counsel	TRISTAN LEAVITT
Deputy Special Counsel of Litigation and Legal Affairs	(VACANCY)
Deputy Special Counsel of Policy and Congressional Affairs	(VACANCY)
General Counsel	SUSAN ULLMAN

Administrative Services Division

Chief Operating Officer	BRUCE GIPE
Chief Financial Officer	KARL P. KAMMANN
Chief Human Capital Officer	JAMES J. WILSON
Chief Information Officer / Information Branch Chief	JENNIFER LI
Clerk	KENNETH HENDRICKS

General Law Division

Associate Special Counsel	ANNE WAGNER
Chief of Alternative Dispute Resolution Unit	JANE JULIANO
Chief of Complaints Examining Unit	BARBARA J. WHEELER
Chief of Disclosure Unit	CATHERINE A. MCMULLEN
Chief of Diversity, Outreach and Training Unit	SHIRINE MOAZED

Investigation and Prosecution Division—Field

Associate Special Counsel	BRUCE D. FONG
Chief of Field Office–Dallas	ANNE GULLICK
Chief of Field Office–Detroit	CHRISTOPHER T. TALL
Chief of Field Office–San Francisco Bay Area	JOSEPH SIEGELMAN

Investigation and Prosecution Division—Headquarters

Associate Special Counsel	LOUIS LOPEZ
Chief of Hatch Act Unit	ANA GALINDO-MARRONE
Chief of Investigation and Prosecution Division–Team A	MARIAMA LIVERPOOL
Chief of Investigation and Prosecution Division–Team B	RACHEL VENIER
Chief of Investigation and Prosecution Division–Team C	DARSHAN SHETH
Chief of Retaliation and Disclosure Unit	KAREN GORMAN
Chief of Retaliation and Disclosure Unit	ELIZABETH MCMURRAY
Director of Uniformed Services Employment and Reemployment Rights Act Enforcement / Senior Counsel	PATRICK H. BOULAY

The United States Office of Special Counsel investigates allegations of certain activities prohibited by civil service laws, rules, or regulations and litigates before the Merit Systems Protection Board.

The U.S. Office of Special Counsel (OSC) was established on January 1, 1979, by Reorganization Plan No. 2 of 1978 (5 U.S.C. app.). The Civil Service Reform Act of 1978 (5 U.S.C. 1101 note), which became effective on January 11, 1979, enlarged its functions and powers. Pursuant to provisions of the Whistleblower Protection Act of 1989 (5 U.S.C. 1211 et seq.), the OSC functions as an independent investigative and prosecutorial executive branch agency that litigates before the Merit Systems Protection Board. https://osc.gov/Pages/about.aspx

Activities

The OSC safeguards the merit system in Federal employment by protecting employees and applicants from prohibited personnel practices, especially from reprisal for whistleblowing. The Office operates a secure channel for Federal whistleblower disclosures of gross waste of funds or mismanagement, substantial and specific danger to public health and safety, and violations of laws, regulations, or rules. The OSC also issues advice on the Hatch Act and enforces its restrictions on political activity by Government employees. It protects the civilian employment and reemployment rights of military servicemembers under the Uniformed Services Employment and Reemployment Act. The OSC enhances Government accountability and performance by the realization of a diverse, inclusive Federal workplace where employees embrace excellence in service, uphold merit system principles, are encouraged to disclose wrongdoing, and are protected against reprisals and other unlawful employment practices. https://osc.gov/Pages/WhatWeDo.aspx

Sources of Information

Business Opportunities The OSC relies on the Department of Interior for performing assisted procurements. The OSC posts contract opportunities online by using Government acquisition vehicles like GSA Ebuy. It posts open market opportunities on the Federal Business Opportunities Web site. https://osc.gov/Pages/Contact-Contract.aspx

Career Opportunities The agency employs approximately 110 employees who work in Washington, DC, or in the Dallas, Detroit, and Oakland field offices. To carry out its mission, the OSC relies heavily on attorneys, investigators, and personnel management specialists.

The OSC seeks law students year-round for internships in Dallas, TX; Detroit, MI; Oakland, CA; and Washington, DC. https://osc.gov/Pages/Contact-Employment.aspx

In 2016, the OSC ranked 15th among 29 small agencies in the Partnership for Public Service's Best Places To Work Agency Rankings. http://bestplacestowork.org/BPTW/rankings/detail/FW00

Electronic Filing The E–Filing System makes filing a complaint with the OSC easier and faster. https://osc.gov/pages/file-complaint.aspx

En Español The OSC posts information in Spanish on its "Para Información En Español" Web page. https://osc.gov/Pages/ParaInformacionEnEspanol.aspx

Freedom of Information Act (FOIA) FOIA requests must be submitted in writing by email, fax, or U.S. postal mail or other delivery service. The OSC provides a Public Access Link portal that allows information seekers to submit a request online and to receive confirmation of and updates on a pending request. https://osc.gov/Pages/FOIA-Resources.aspx

Frequently Asked Questions (FAQs) The OSC posts answers to FAQs on its Web site. https://osc.gov/Pages/Resources-FAQ.aspx

Hatch Act Advisory Opinions Advice that the OSC has given to individuals on the Hatch Act is publicly accessible online. https://osc.gov/Pages/Advisory-Opinions.aspx

News The OSC posts news releases online. https://osc.gov/Pages/News.aspx

Open Government The OSC supports the Open Government initiative by promoting the principles of collaboration, participation, and transparency. https://osc.gov/OpenGov/OpenGov.aspx

Prohibited Personnel Practices The OSC provides information on personnel practices that are prohibited within the Federal workplace. https://osc.gov/Pages/PPP.aspx

Site Map The Web site map allows visitors to look for specific topics or to browse content that aligns with their interests. https://osc.gov/Pages/SiteMap.aspx

Social Media The OSC tweets announcements and other newsworthy items on Twitter. https://twitter.com/US_OSC

Speakers To request a speaker, contact the OSC by phone or fax. Phone, 202-804-7000. Fax, 202-254-3711.

Whistleblower Files The OSC posts documents from closed investigations on its Web site. These documents are based on whistleblower disclosures. https://osc.gov/Pages/Resources-PublicFiles.aspx

2302(c) Program Certification The White House has required all Federal agencies to certify that they are educating their employees about the rights of whistleblowers. Phone, 703-466-0259. https://osc.gov/Pages/Outreach-2302Cert.aspx | Email: 2302c@osc.gov. https://osc.gov/Pages/contact.aspx

For further information, contact the U.S. Office of Special Counsel, 1730 M Street NW., Suite 218, Washington, DC 20036-4505. Phone, 202-804-7000 or 800-872-9855. Fax, 202-653-5151.

United States Postal Service

475 L'Enfant Plaza SW., Washington, DC 20260
Phone, 202-268-2000. Internet, http://www.usps.gov

Board of Governors

Chair	(VACANCY)
Vice Chair	(VACANCY)
Governor	(VACANCY)
Governor	(VACANCY)
Governor	(VACANCY)
Governor	(VACANCY)
Governor	(VACANCY)
Governor	(VACANCY)
Governor	(VACANCY)
Postmaster General / Chief Executive Officer	MEGAN J. BRENNAN
Deputy Postmaster General / Chief Government Relations Officer	RONALD A. STROMAN
Secretary	JULIE S. MOORE

Officers

Postmaster General / Chief Executive Officer	MEGAN J. BRENNAN
Deputy Postmaster General / Chief Government Relations Officer	RONALD A. STROMAN
Executive Vice Presidents	
Chief Customer and Marketing Officer	JAMES COCHRANE
Chief Financial Officer	JOSEPH CORBETT
Chief Human Resources Officer	JEFFREY WILLIAMSON
Chief Information Officer	KRISTIN SEAVER
Chief Operating Officer	DAVID E. WILLIAMS
General Counsel	THOMAS J. MARSHALL
Chief Postal Inspector	GUY COTTRELL
Judicial Officer	GARY E. SHAPIRO
Vice Presidents	
Controller	MAURA A. MCNERNEY
Corporate Communications	JANICE D. WALKER
Delivery Operations	KEVIN L. MCADAMS
Digital Solutions / Chief Information Security Officer	GREGORY S. CRABB
Employee Resource Management	SIMON STOREY
Engineering Systems	MICHAEL J. AMATO
Enterprise Analytics	ISAAC S. CRONKHITE
Facilities	THOMAS SAMRA
Finance and Planning	LUKE GROSSMANN
Information Technology	JEFFREY C. JOHNSON
Labor Relations	DOUGLAS TULINO
Mail Entry and Payment Technology	PRITHA MEHRA
Marketing	STEVEN W. MONTEITH
Network Operations	ROBERT CINTRON
Pricing and Costing	SHARON OWENS
Product Innovation	GARY C. REBLIN
Retail and Customer Service Operations	KELLY M. SIGMON
Sales and Customer Relations	CLIFF RUCKER
Supply Management	SUSAN M. BROWNELL

Vice Presidents—Area Operations

Capital Metro Area	LINDA M. MALONE
Eastern Area	JOSHUA D. COLIN
Great Lakes Area	JACQUELINE M. KRAGE STRAKO
Northeast Area	EDWARD PHELAN, JR.
Pacific Area	LARRY MUÑOZ, ACTING
Southern Area	SHAUN E. MOSSMAN
Western Area	GREGORY GRAVES, ACTING
Inspector General	TAMMY L., WHITCOMB, ACTING

[For the United States Postal Service statement of organization, see the Code of Federal Regulations, Title 39, Part 221]

The United States Postal Service provides the American public with affordable, reliable, and universal mail service.

The Postal Service was created as an independent establishment of the executive branch by the Postal Reorganization Act (39 U.S.C. 101 et seq.), approved August 12, 1970. The present United States Postal Service commenced operations on July 1, 1971.

In Fiscal Year 2016, the Postal Service had approximately 508,908 career employees and handled over 153 billion pieces of mail. The chief executive officer of the Postal Service, the Postmaster General, is appointed by the nine Governors of the Postal Service. The President appoints the nine Governors with the advice and consent of the Senate. The Governors and the Postmaster General appoint the Deputy Postmaster General, and these 11 appointees constitute the Board of Governors.

In addition to the national headquarters, area and district offices oversee more than 35,000 post offices, branches, stations, contract postal units, village post offices, and community post offices throughout the United States. http://about.usps.com/welcome.htm

Activities

To expand and improve service to the public, the Postal Service engages in customer cooperation activities, including the development of programs for both the general public and major customers. The consumer advocate, a postal ombudsman, represents the interests of the individual mail customer in matters involving the Postal Service. The advocate brings complaints and suggestions to the attention of top postal management and solves the problems of individual customers. To provide services responsive to public needs, the Postal Service operates its own planning, research, engineering, real estate, and procurement programs, and it maintains close ties with international postal organizations.

The Postal Service is the only Federal agency whose employment policies are governed by a process of collective bargaining under the National Labor Relations Act. Its Office of Human Resources, including the Labor Relations Division, administers labor contract negotiations that affect bargaining unit personnel, as well as personnel matters involving employees not covered by collective bargaining agreements.

The U.S. Postal Inspection Service, a Federal law enforcement agency, has jurisdiction in criminal matters affecting the integrity and security of the mail. Postal inspectors protect all postal employees and enforce more than 200 Federal statutes involving mail fraud, mail bombs, child pornography, illegal drugs, mail theft, and other postal crimes. http://about.usps.com/what-we-are-doing/welcome.htm

Sources of Information

Business Opportunities   Suppliers can learn about doing business with the Postal Service online. Information on rights and permissions (the use of trademarked material) and licensing products is also available online. http://about.usps.com/doing-business/welcome.htm

Career Opportunities   Information on careers—including information for veterans and reservists, for students and recent graduates—is available on the Postal Service's Web site or at the nearest post office. http://about.usps.com/careers/welcome.htm

The U.S. Postal Inspection Service posts career opportunities on its Web site. https://postalinspectors.uspis.gov/employment/positions.aspx

Consumer Information   For general information, call the "ASK USPS" line. Phone, 800-275-8777. To buy stamps, calculate postage prices, change addresses, find answers to frequently asked questions, locate ZIP Codes, print postage, shop at the Postal Store, and track packages, visit the Postal Service's Web site. http://about.usps.com/news/welcome.htm

Fraud / Theft   Postal inspectors can be located by Zip Code on the U.S. Postal Inspection Service's locator Web page. http://locator.uspis.gov/locator

Complaint forms to report identity and mail theft, mail fraud, and unsolicited sexually oriented advertising are accessible online. Phone, 800-275-8777. https://postalinspectors.uspis.gov/contactUs/filecomplaint.aspx

Freedom of Information Act (FOIA)   Information and guidance on the Freedom of Information and the Privacy Acts and on Postal Service records management, as well as access to an electronic FOIA reading room are available online. http://about.usps.com/who-we-are/foia/welcome.htm

The Postal Service maintains an online FOIA reading room. Before submitting a FOIA request to access records, check the electronic reading room to see if the desired information is immediately available. https://about.usps.com/who-we-are/foia/readroom/welcome.htm

History   Benjamin Franklin and the Postal Service, what was the nature of their association? Visit the "Postal History" Web page to learn just how close it was. http://about.usps.com/who-we-are/postal-history/welcome.htm

The National Postal Museum houses one of the largest and most significant philatelic and postal history collections in the world and one of the most comprehensive library resources on philately and postal history. The museum's exhibition galleries present America's postal history from Colonial times to the present. Its collections contain prestigious international and U.S. postal issues and specialized collections, archival postal documents, and three-dimensional objects. https://postalmuseum.si.edu

Inspector General   The Office of Inspector General has a toll-free hotline and online complaint form for reporting fraud, mismanagement, and waste. Phone, 888-877-7644 or 866-644-8398 (hearing impaired). Complaints also may be sent to the U.S. Postal Service, Office of Inspector General Hotline, 10th Floor, 1735 N. Lynn Street, Arlington, VA 22209-2020. https://www.uspsoig.gov/hotline | Email: hotline@uspsoig.gov

Newsroom   The Postal Service maintains an online newsroom that features broadcast and audio downloads, leadership biographies, national and local news, service alerts, testimonies and speeches, and a photo gallery. http://about.usps.com/news/welcome.htm

Organizational Chart   The "Postal Leadership" page has links leading to two Portable Document Format (PDF) files containing organizational charts, one with leadership photographs and the other without them. http://about.usps.com/who-we-are/leadership/officers.htm

Passports   Thousands of post offices accept passport applications on behalf of the Department of State. These post offices offer the products and services needed to acquire a first-time passport or renewal. At some locations, a passport photograph can be taken for an additional fee. https://www.usps.com/international/passports.htm

Philatelic Sales   For information on available stamps, philatelic items, and collectibles, visit the "Stamps" Web page. https://www.usps.com/stamps

Publications   Information on mailability, on postage rates and fees, and on other topics is available at the nearest post office. Most postal regulations affecting domestic and international mail, employee and labor relations, and purchasing can be found in Postal Service manuals and in the "Code of Federal Regulations." A wide range of publications—including annual reports to Congress, handbooks, manuals, notices, periodicals, and posters—is available online. http://about.usps.com/periodicals-publications/welcome.htm

Reading Areas   Reading areas are maintained in the library at USPS Headquarters on the 11th Floor. The library's holdings include historic, legal, regulatory, and other documents. Visitors must schedule an appointment—weekdays, 9 a.m.–4 p.m. (except Federal holidays)—before accessing the library .Phone, 202-268-2906.

Site Map   The Web site map allows visitors to look for specific topics or to browse content that aligns with their interests. http://about.usps.com/sitemap.htm

Social Media   The Postal Service has a Facebook account. https://www.facebook.com/USPS

The Postal Service tweets announcements and other newsworthy items on Twitter. https://twitter.com/usps

The Postal Service posts videos on its YouTube channel. https://www.youtube.com/user/uspstv/custom. https://www.usps.com/help/contact-us.htm

For further information, contact the U.S. Postal Service, 475 L'Enfant Plaza SW., Washington, DC 20260. Phone, 202-268-2000.

QUASI-OFFICIAL AGENCIES

Legal Services Corporation

3333 K Street NW., Washington, DC 20007
Phone, 202-295-1500. Fax, 202-337-6797. Internet, http://www.lsc.gov.

President	JAMES J. SANDMAN
Chief of Staff	REBECCA FERTIG COHEN
Vice Presidents	
Government Relations and Public Affairs	CAROL A. BERGMAN
Grants Management	LYNN A. JENNINGS
Legal Affairs / General Counsel / Corporate Secretary	RONALD S. FLAGG
Chief Information Officer	REBECCA FERTIG COHEN, ACTING
Directors	
Office of Compliance and Enforcement	LORA RATH
Office of Data Governance and Analysis	CARLOS A. MANJARREZ
Office of Human Resources	TRACI HIGGINS
Office of Institutional Advancement	NADIA ELGUINDY
Office of Program Performance	EDWARD CASPAR
Treasurer / Comptroller	DAVID L. RICHARDSON
Inspector General	JEFFREY E. SCHANZ

The above list of key personnel was updated 09–2017.

The Legal Services Corporation promotes equal access to justice and provides civil legal assistance to low-income persons.

The Legal Services Corporation (LSC) is a private, nonprofit corporation established by the Legal Services Act of 1974, as amended (42 U.S.C. 2996), to promote equal access to justice under the law for all Americans. http://www.lsc.gov/about-lsc/who-we-are

Appointed by the President and confirmed by the Senate, the 11-member Board of Directors heads the LSC. By law, it is bipartisan and no more than six members may be of the same political party. http://www.lsc.gov/about-lsc/board-members

Congressional appropriations fund the LSC to provide legal services through grants to independent, local legal services provider programs. These programs are selected through a system of competition. In 2017, the LSC funded 133 programs. Together,

they serve every county and congressional district in the Nation, as well as the U.S. Territories. Some of these programs address the particular needs of Native Americans and migrant farmworkers. http://www.lsc.gov/what-legal-aid/how-we-work

The legal services delivery system is based on several principles: local priorities, national accountability, competition for grants, and a strong public-private partnership. Local programs are governed by their own boards of directors, which set priorities and determine the types of cases that will be handled subject to restrictions set by Congress. A majority of each local board is appointed by local bar associations, and one-third of each local board is composed of client representatives appointed by client groups. Each board hires its own executive director. Programs may supplement their LSC grants with additional funds from State and local governments and other sources. They further leverage Federal funds by involving private attorneys in the delivery of legal services for the poor, mostly through volunteer pro bono work.

LSC-funded programs neither handle criminal cases nor accept fee-generating cases that private attorneys are willing to accept on a contingency basis. In addition, in 1996, a series of new limitations were placed upon activities in which LSC-funded programs may engage on behalf of their clients, even with non-LSC funds. All programs must comply with laws enacted by Congress and the implementing regulations promulgated by the LSC. http://www.lsc.gov/about-lsc/what-we-do

Sources of Information

Blog The LSC maintains a blog. http://www.lsc.gov/media-center/blog
Board Meetings Board meeting documents and information are available online. http://www.lsc.gov/about-lsc/board/board-meetings
Business Opportunities The LSC regularly seeks the assistance of vendors to purchase products and contractors to carry out special projects. The LSC is eligible for General Services Administration schedule pricing and posts requests for proposals on eBuy and FedBizOpps.gov. http://www.lsc.gov/about-lsc/doing-business-lsc-rfps
Campaign for Justice The campaign for justice funds initiatives that strengthen the work of civil legal aid providers nationwide. https://lsc40.lsc.gov
Career Opportunities The LSC is an organization of socially aware professionals who serve the unrepresented and promote equal justice. Information on career opportunities and working at the LSC is available online. http://www.lsc.gov/about-lsc/careers
Civil Legal Outcomes The LSC developed its civil legal outcomes toolkit to help legal aid programs with defining, collecting, and reporting on metrics that describe their effectiveness. The toolkit includes detailed instructions, electronic learning modules, examples, and additional resources for implementing an outcomes management system. http://clo.lsc.gov
Client Success Stories An interactive map allows website visitors to browse client success stories by State. http://www.lsc.gov/what-legal-aid/client-success-stories
Data Detailed national and local level information on client characteristics, expenditures, funding, private attorney involvement, service area demographics, services provided, staffing, and the use of technology is available on the "Grantee Data" web pages. http://www.lsc.gov/grants-grantee-resources/grantee-data
Donations Tax-deductible donations to the LSC support the use of technology innovations in legal services, provide law fellows for civil legal aid programs in need, raise public awareness of the legal aid system crisis, and support research into the effectiveness and need of civil legal aid. http://www.lsc.gov/support-lsc/donate-now
Events A list of upcoming events is available online. http://www.lsc.gov/meetings-and-events/calendar
Facts What percentage of the population is eligible for LSC-funded assistance? What is the average annual salary of LSC grantee staff attorneys? To learn the answers to these questions and others, visit the "Quick Facts" web page. http://www.lsc.gov/quick-facts
Find Legal Aid An online search tool is available to find the nearest LSC-funded legal aid organization by address, city, or ZIP Code. http://www.lsc.gov/what-legal-aid/find-legal-aid
Freedom of Information Act (FOIA) The FOIA grants any person the right to request access to Federal agency records or information. U.S. Government agencies are required to disclose records after they receive a written request for them; however, the statute shields certain records from disclosure. The LSC complies with the FOIA and releases records to information seekers, as long as the desired records are shielded. A FOIA request must be made in writing and may be submitted by electronic submission form, email, fax, or postal service. The request should be clearly marked: "Freedom of Information Act Request." Fax, 202-337-6519. http://www.lsc.gov/about-lsc/foia | Email: FOIA@lsc.gov

The LSC maintains a FOIA reading room online. Before submitting a FOIA request, information seekers should search the reading room for records that are immediately accessible. http://www.lsc.gov/

about-lsc/foia/foia-electronic-public-reading-room

Grant Programs   Descriptions of the LSC's seven grant programs—basic field, disaster relief emergency, technology initiative, and veterans appeals pro bono grants; leadership development and loan repayment assistance programs; and pro bono innovation fund—are available online. http://www.lsc.gov/grants-grantee-resources/our-grant-programs

Justice Gap   The justice gap represents the difference between the level of civil legal assistance that is available and the level that is necessary to meet the legal needs of low-income individuals and families. To learn more about the justice gap, visit the "The Unmet Need for Legal Aid" web page. http://www.lsc.gov/what-legal-aid/unmet-need-legal-aid

News   The LSC posts press releases on its website. http://www.lsc.gov/media-center/press-releases

Organizational Chart   An organizational chart is available on the "LSC Leadership" web page. http://www.lsc.gov/about-lsc/lsc-leadership

Oversight   The Office of the Inspector General from the LSC posts reports and data on Oversight.gov, a text-searchable repository of reports that Federal Inspectors General publish. The Council of the Inspectors General on Integrity and Efficiency operates and maintains the website to increase public access to independent and authoritative information on the Federal Government. https://oversight.gov

Publications   Annual reports, budget requests, factbooks, and reports are accessible online. http://www.lsc.gov/media-center/publications

Social Media   The LSC has a Facebook account. https://www.facebook.com/LegalServicesCorporation

The LSC tweets announcements and other newsworthy items on Twitter. https://twitter.com/lsctweets. http://www.lsc.gov/about-lsc/contact-us

For further information, contact the Office of Government Relations and Public Affairs, Legal Services Corporation, 3333 K Street NW., Washington, DC 20007-3522. Phone, 202-295-1500. Fax, 202-337-6797.

Smithsonian Institution

1000 Jefferson Drive SW., Washington, DC 20560
Phone, 202-633-1000. Internet, http://www.si.edu.

Board of Regents

Citizen Regents	
Chair	David M. Rubenstein
Vice Chair	Steve M. Case
	Barbara M. Barrett
	John Fahey
	Roger W. Ferguson
	Michael Govan
	Risa J. Lavizzo-Mourey
	Michael M. Lynton
	John W. McCarter, Jr.
Congressional Regents	
Representatives	Thomas J. Cole
	Samuel Johnson
	Doris Matsui
Senators	John Boozman
	Patrick J. Leahy
	David Perdue
Ex Officio Regents	
Chief Justice of the United States	John G. Roberts, Jr.
Vice President of the United States	Michael R. Pence

Chief of Staff to the Regents	PORTER WILKINSON

Senior Executives

Secretary	DAVID J. SKORTON
Chief Financial Officer	ALBERT G. HORVATH
Provost	JOHN H. DAVIS, ACTING
Assistant Secretary, Advancement	ZULLY DORR, ACTING
Assistant Secretary, Communications and External Affairs	CAROLYN MARTIN, ACTING
Assistant Secretary, Education and Access	PATTY BARTLETT, ACTING
Director, Equal Employment and Minority Affairs	ERA L. MARSHALL
General Counsel	JUDITH E. LEONARD

Administration / Program Directors

Under Secretary For Finance And Administration	ALBERT G. HORVATH
Chief Information Officer	DERON BURBA
Chief Investment Officer	AMY CHEN
Director, Contracting and Personal Property Management	THOMAS DEMPSEY
Director, Finance and Accounting	JEAN GARVIN
Director, Human Resources	WALTRUNETTE GARDNER, ACTING
Director, Planning, Management and Budget	DAVID VOYLES
Director, Policy and Analysis	H. WHITNEY WATRISS, ACTING
Director, Smithsonian Exhibits	SUSAN ADES
Director, Smithsonian Facilities	NANCY BECHTOL
Director, Sponsored Projects	TRACEY FRASER
President, Smithsonian Enterprises	CHRIS LIEDEL

Museums / Research Centers

Under Secretary For Museums And Research	JOHN H. DAVIS, ACTING
Directors	
Anacostia Community Museum	LORI D. YARRISH, ACTING
Archives of American Art	KATE HAW
Center for Astrophysics	CHARLES R. ALCOCK
Center for Folklife and Cultural Heritage	MICHAEL A. MASON
Cooper Hewitt, Smithsonian Design Museum	CAROLINE BAUMANN
Freer Gallery of Art and Arthur M. Sackler Gallery	JULIAN RABY
Hirshhorn Museum and Sculpture Garden	MELISSA CHIU
National Air and Space Museum	JOHN R. DAILEY
National Museum of African American History and Culture	LONNIE G. BUNCH III
National Museum of African Art	CHRISTINE KREAMER, ACTING
National Museum of American History	JOHN GRAY
National Museum of Natural History	KIRK JOHNSON
National Museum of the American Indian	KEVIN GOVER
National Portrait Gallery	KIM SAJET
National Postal Museum	ELLIOT GRUBER
National Zoological Park	DENNIS KELLY
Smithsonian American Art Museum and Renwick Gallery	STEPHANIE STEBICH
Smithsonian Asian Pacific American Center	LISA SASAKI
Smithsonian Environmental Research Center	ANSON H. HINES
Smithsonian Institution Archives	ANNE VAN CAMP
Smithsonian Institution Traveling Exhibition Service	MYRIAM SPRINGUEL
Smithsonian Latino Center	EDUARDO DÍAZ
Smithsonian Libraries	NANCY E. GWINN
Smithsonian Marine Station	VALERIE J. PAUL
Smithsonian Museum Conservation Institute	ROBERT J. KOESTLER

Smithsonian Tropical Research Institute	MATTHEW LARSEN
Inspector General	CATHY L. HELM

The above list of key personnel was updated 09–2017.

The Smithsonian Institution increases the fund of human knowledge and diffuses that knowledge among people.

The Smithsonian Institution was created by an act of Congress on August 10, 1846 (20 U.S.C. 41 et seq.), to carry out the terms of the will of British scientist James Smithson (1765–1829), who in 1826 had bequeathed his entire estate to the United States "to found at Washington, under the name of the Smithsonian Institution, an establishment for the increase and diffusion of knowledge among men." On July 1, 1836, Congress accepted the legacy and pledged the faith of the United States to the charitable trust.

In September 1838, Smithson's legacy, which amounted to more than 100,000 gold sovereigns, was delivered to the mint at Philadelphia. Congress vested responsibility for administering the trust in the Secretary of the Smithsonian and the Smithsonian Board of Regents, composed of the Chief Justice, the Vice President, three Members of the Senate, three Members of the House of Representatives, and nine citizen members appointed by joint resolution of Congress. To carry out Smithson's mandate, the Institution executes the following functions: conducts scientific and scholarly research; publishes the results of studies, explorations, and investigations; preserves for study and reference more than 137 million artifacts, works of art, and scientific specimens; organizes exhibits representative of the arts, the sciences, American history, and world culture; shares Smithsonian resources and collections with communities throughout the Nation; and engages in educational programming and national and international cooperative research.

The Smithsonian Institution is an independent trust instrumentality of the United States that comprises the world's largest museum and research complex. It includes 19 museums and galleries, the National Zoo, and nine research facilities in several States and the Republic of Panama. The Institution is dedicated to public education, national service, and scholarship in the arts, sciences, history, and culture. Smithsonian activities are supported by its trust endowments and revenues; gifts, grants, and contracts; and funds appropriated to it by Congress. Admission to the museums in Washington, DC, is free. http://www.si.edu/About/History

Activities

Anacostia Community Museum   The Museum, located in the historic Fort Stanton neighborhood of Southeast Washington, serves as a national resource for exhibitions, historical documentation, and interpretive and educational programs relating to the impact of history and contemporary social issues on urban communities. http://anacostia.si.edu | Email: ACMinfo@si.edu

For further information, contact the Anacostia Community Museum, 1901 Fort Place SE., Washington, DC 20020. Phone, 202-633-4820.

Archives of American Art   The Archives contains the Nation's largest collection of documentary materials reflecting the history of visual arts in the United States. On the subject of art in America, it is the largest archives in the world, holding more than 16 million documents. The Archives gathers, preserves, and microfilms the papers of artists, craftsmen, collectors, dealers, critics, and art societies. These papers include manuscripts, letters, diaries, notebooks, sketchbooks, business records, clippings, exhibition catalogs, transcripts of tape-recorded interviews, and photographs of artists and their work. http://www.aaa.si.edu

For further information, contact the Archives of American Art, Suite 2200, 750 Ninth Street NW., Washington, DC 20001. Phone, 202-633-7940.

Arthur M. Sackler Gallery   This Asian art museum opened in 1987 on the National Mall. Changing exhibitions drawn from major collections in the United States and abroad, as well as from the permanent

SMITHSONIAN INSTITUTION

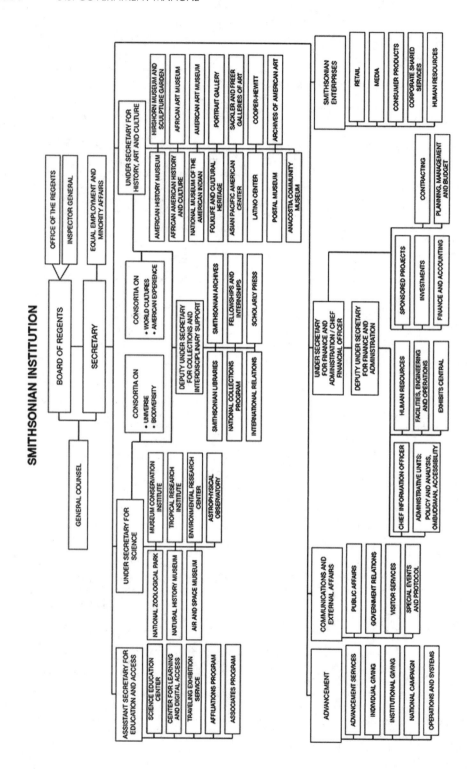

holdings of the Sackler Gallery, are displayed in the distinctive below-ground museum. The Gallery's growing permanent collection is founded on a group of art objects from China, South and Southeast Asia, and the ancient Near East that were given to the Smithsonian by Arthur M. Sackler (1913–1987). The Museum's current collection features Persian manuscripts; Japanese paintings; ceramics, prints, and textiles; sculptures from India; and paintings and metalware from China, Korea, Japan, and Southeast Asia. The Sackler Gallery is connected by an underground exhibition space to the neighboring Freer Gallery. http://www.asia.si.edu | Email: publicaffairsAsia@si.edu

For further information, contact the Arthur M. Sackler Gallery, 1050 Independence Avenue SW., Washington, DC 20560. Phone, 202-633-4880.

Center for Astrophysics

The Smithsonian Astrophysical Observatory and the Harvard College Observatory have coordinated research activities under a single director in a cooperative venture, Harvard-Smithsonian Center for Astrophysics. The Center's research activities are organized in the following areas of study: atomic and molecular physics, radio and geoastronomy, high-energy astrophysics, optical and infrared astronomy, planetary sciences, solar and stellar physics, and theoretical astrophysics. Research results are published in the Center Preprint Series and other technical and nontechnical bulletins and distributed to scientific and educational institutions around the world. http://www.cfa.harvard.edu/sao

For more information, contact the Smithsonian Astrophysical Observatory, 60 Garden Street, Cambridge, MA 02138. Phone, 617-495-7463.

Center for Folklife and Cultural Heritage

The Center is responsible for research, documentation, and presentation of grassroots cultural traditions. It maintains a documentary collection and produces Smithsonian Folkways Recordings, educational materials, documentary films, publications, and traveling exhibits, as well as the annual Smithsonian Folklife Festival on the National Mall. Recent Folklife festivals have featured a range of American music styles, a number of State tributes, and performers from around the world. Admission to the festival is free. The 2-week program includes Fourth of July activities on the National Mall. http://www.folklife.si.edu

For further information, contact the Center for Folklife and Cultural Heritage, Capital Gallery, Suite 2001, 600 Maryland Avenue SW., Washington, DC 20024. Phone, 202-633-1000.

Cooper Hewitt, Smithsonian Design Museum

The Museum is the only museum in the country devoted exclusively to historical and contemporary design. Collections include objects in such areas as applied arts and industrial design, drawings and prints, glass, metalwork, wallcoverings, and textiles. Changing exhibits and public programs seek to educate by exploring the role of design in daily life. http://cooperhewitt.org

For further information, contact the Cooper Hewitt, Smithsonian Design Museum, 2 East Ninety-First Street, New York, NY 10128. Phone, 212-849-8400.

Freer Gallery of Art

The building, the original collection, and an endowment were the gift of Charles Lang Freer (1854–1919). The Gallery houses one of the world's most renowned collections of Asian art, an important group of ancient Egyptian glass, early Christian manuscripts, and works by 19th- and early 20th-century American artists. The objects in the Asian collection represent the arts of East Asia, the Near East, and South and Southeast Asia, including paintings, manuscripts, scrolls, screens, ceramics, metalwork, glass, jade, lacquer, and sculpture. Members of the staff conduct research on objects in the collection and publish results in scholarly journals and books for general and scholarly audiences. http://www.asia.si.edu | Email: publicaffairsAsia@si.edu

For further information, contact the Freer Gallery of Art, Jefferson Drive at Twelfth Street SW., Washington, DC 20560. Phone, 202-633-4880.

Hirshhorn Museum and Sculpture Garden

From cubism to minimalism, the Museum houses major collections of modern and contemporary art. The nucleus of the collection is the gift and bequest of Joseph H. Hirshhorn (1899–1981). Supplementing the permanent collection are loan exhibitions. The Museum houses a collection research facility, a specialized art library, and a photographic archive, available for consultation by prior appointment. The outdoor sculpture garden is located nearby on the National Mall. There is an active program of public service and education, including docent tours, lectures on contemporary art and artists, and films of historic and artistic interest. http://www. hirshhorn.si.edu | Email: hmsginquiries@ si.edu

For further information, contact the Hirshhorn Museum and Sculpture Garden, Seventh Street and Independence Avenue SW., Washington, DC 20560. Phone, 202-633-4674.

Museum Conservation Institute   The Institute researches preservation, conservation, and technical study and analysis of collection materials. Its researchers investigate the chemical and physical processes that are involved in the care of art, artifacts, and specimens and attempt to formulate conditions and procedures for storage, exhibit, and stabilization that optimize the preservation of these objects. In interdisciplinary collaborations with archeologists, anthropologists, and art historians, natural and physical scientists study and analyze objects from the collections and related materials to expand knowledge and understanding of their historical and scientific context. http://www.si.edu/mci

For further information, contact the Museum Conservation Institute, Museum Support Center, Suitland, MD 20746. Phone, 301-238-1240.

National Air and Space Museum   Created to memorialize the development and achievements of aviation and spaceflight, the Museum collects, displays, and preserves aeronautical and space flight artifacts of historical significance, as well as documentary and artistic materials related to air and space. Among its artifacts are full-size planes, models, and instruments. Highlights of the collection include the Wright brothers' "Flyer," Charles Lindbergh's "Spirit of St. Louis," a Moon rock, and Apollo spacecraft. The exhibitions and study collections record the human leap into the air, the sky, and space beyond. They offer a concentrated presentation of flight

craft of all types, spaceflight vehicles, and propulsion systems. The Museum's IMAX Theater and domed Einstein Planetarium are popular attractions. The Museum's Steven F. Udvar-Hazy Center, at Washington Dulles International Airport, features artifacts that include a space shuttle and the "Enola Gay" World War II bomber. http://airandspace. si.edu | Email: NASMVisitorServices@si.edu

For further information, contact the National Air and Space Museum, Sixth Street and Independence Avenue SW., Washington, DC 20560. Phone, 202-633-2214.

National Museum of African American History and Culture   Established in 2003, the Museum is the first national museum that documents exclusively African American art, culture, history, and life. http://www. nmaahc.si.edu | Email: NMAAHCinfo@ si.edu

For further information, contact the National Museum of African American History and Culture, Capital Gallery, Suite 7001, 600 Maryland Avenue SW., Washington, DC 20024. Phone, 202-633-1000.

National Museum of African Art   This is the only art museum in the United States that portrays exclusively Africa's creative, visual traditions. Its research components, collection, exhibitions, and public programs make the Museum a primary source for the examination and discovery of African arts and culture. The collection includes works in wood, metal, fired clay, ivory, and fiber. The Eliot Elisofon Photographic Archives includes slides, photos, and film segments on Africa. There is also a specialized library. http:// africa.si.edu

For further information, contact the National Museum of African Art, 950 Independence Avenue SW., Washington, DC 20560. Phone, 202-633-4600.

National Museum of American History   In pursuit of its fundamental mission to inspire a broader understanding of the United States and its people, the Museum provides learning opportunities, stimulates the imagination of visitors, and presents challenging ideas about the Nation's past. The Museum's exhibits provide a unique view of the American experience. Emphasis is placed upon innovative individuals representing a wide range of cultures, who have shaped our heritage, and upon science and the remaking of our world through technology. Exhibits draw upon strong collections in the sciences and engineering, agriculture, manufacturing, transportation, political memorabilia, costumes, musical instruments, coins, Armed Forces history, photography, computers, ceramics, and glass. Classic cars, icons of the American Presidency, First Ladies' gowns, the Star-Spangled Banner flag, Whitney's cotton gin, Morse's telegraph, the John Bull locomotive, Dorothy's ruby slippers from "The Wizard of Oz," and other American icons are highlights of the collection. http://www.americanhistory.si.edu | Email: info@si.edu

For further information, contact the National Museum of American History, Fourteenth Street and Constitution Avenue NW., Washington, DC 20560. Phone, 202-633-1000.

National Museum of Natural History
Dedicated to understanding the natural world and the place of humans in it, the Museum's permanent exhibitions focus on human cultures, Earth sciences, biology, and anthropology, with the most popular displays featuring gem stones such as the Hope Diamond, dinosaurs, insects, marine ecosystems, birds, and mammals. In 2010, the Museum celebrated its 100th anniversary with the opening of a new permanent exhibition, the David H. Koch Hall of Human Origins. An IMAX theater offers large-format films. The Museum's encyclopedic collections comprise more than 126 million specimens, making the Museum one of the world's foremost facilities for natural history research. The Museum's seven departments are anthropology, botany, entomology, invertebrate zoology, mineral sciences, paleobiology, and vertebrate zoology. Doctorate-level staff researchers ensure the continued growth and value of the collection by conducting studies in the field and laboratory. http://www.mnh.si.edu | Email: naturalexperience@si.edu

For further information, contact the National Museum of Natural History, Tenth Street and Constitution Avenue NW., Washington, DC 20560. Phone, 202-633-1000.

National Museum of the American Indian
The Museum was established in 1989, and the building on the National Mall opened September 2004. Much of the collection of the Museum is comprised of the collection of the former Heye Foundation in New York City. It is an institution of living cultures dedicated to the collection, preservation, study, and exhibition of the life, languages, literature, history, and arts of the Native peoples of the Americas. Highlights include Northwest Coast carvings; dance masks; pottery and weaving from the Southwest; painted hides and garments from the North American Plains; goldwork of the Aztecs, Incas, and Maya; and Amazonian featherwork. The National Museum of the American Indian also operates the George Gustav Heye Center at the Alexander Hamilton U.S. Custom House in New York City. http://americanindian.si.edu | Email: NMAI-info@si.edu

For further information, contact the National Museum of the American Indian, Fourth Street and Independence Avenue SW., Washington, DC 20560. Phone, 202-633-1000.

National Portrait Gallery
The Gallery was established in 1962 for the exhibition and study of portraiture depicting men and women who have made significant contributions to the history, development, and culture of the United States. The Gallery contains more than 19,000 works, including photographs and glass negatives. The first floor of the Gallery is devoted to changing exhibitions from the Gallery's collection of paintings, sculpture, prints, photographs, and drawings as well as to special portrait collections. Featured on the second floor are the permanent collection of portraits of eminent Americans and the Hall of Presidents, including the famous Gilbert Stuart portrait-from-life of George Washington. The two-story American Victorian Renaissance Great Hall on the third floor of the Gallery houses an exhibit of 20th-century Americans and is used for special events and public programs. The Gallery shares a large library with the Smithsonian American Art Museum and the Archives of American Art. The education department offers public programs; outreach programs for adult groups; and walk-in and group tours. http://www.npg.si.edu | Email: npgnews@si.edu

For further information, contact the National Portrait Gallery, Eighth and F Streets NW., Washington, DC 20001. Phone, 202-633-8300.

National Postal Museum   The Museum houses the Nation's postal history and philatelic collection, the largest of its kind in the world, with more than 13 million objects. The Museum is devoted to the history of America's mail service, and major galleries include exhibits on mail service in colonial times and during the Civil War, the Pony Express, modern mail service, automation, mail transportation, and the art of letters, as well as displays of the Museum's priceless stamp collection. Highlights include three mail planes, a replica of a railway mail car, displays of historic letters, handcrafted mail boxes, and rare U.S. and foreign-issue stamps and covers. http://postalmuseum.si.edu

For further information, contact the National Postal Museum, 2 Massachusetts Avenue NE., Washington, DC 20001. Phone, 202-633-1000.

National Zoological Park   The National Zoo is an international leader in wildlife conservation, education, and research. Home to more than 2,000 animals, the Zoo encompasses 163 acres along Rock Creek Park in Northwest Washington. Exhibits include the David M. Rubenstein Family Giant Panda Habitat, where the giant pandas Mei Xiang and Tian Tian reside with their cub Bao Bao. Built to mimic the animals' natural habitat in China, it is part of the Zoo's Asia Trail, which also takes visitors through the habitats of red pandas, Asian small-clawed otters, fishing cats, sloth bears, and clouded leopards. Other highlights include the Elephant Trails, home to the Asian elephant Kandula, who was born at the Zoo in 2001; Amazonia, a 15,000-square-foot rain forest habitat; the Reptile Discovery Center, featuring African pancake tortoises and the world's largest lizards, Komodo dragons; and the Great Ape House, home to gorillas, orangutans, and other primates. http://nationalzoo.si.edu

For further information, contact the National Zoo, 3001 Connecticut Avenue NW., Washington, DC 20008. Phone, 202-633-4888.

Renwick Gallery   The Gallery, a branch of the Smithsonian American Art Museum, is dedicated to exhibiting crafts of all periods and to collecting 20th-century American crafts. It offers changing exhibitions of American crafts and decorative arts, both historical and contemporary, and a rotating selection from its permanent collection. The Gallery's grand salon is elegantly furnished in the Victorian style of the 1860s and 1870s. http://www.americanart.si.edu/renwick | Email: AmericanArtRenwick@si.edu

For further information, contact the Renwick Gallery, Seventeenth Street and Pennsylvania Avenue NW., Washington, DC 20006. Phone, 202-633-7970.

Smithsonian American Art Museum   The Museum's art collection spans centuries of American painting, sculpture, folk art, photography, and graphic art. A major center for research in American art, the Museum has contributed to such resources as the Inventory of American Paintings Executed Before 1914, the Smithsonian Art Index, and the Inventory of American Sculpture. The library, shared with the National Portrait Gallery, contains volumes on art, history, and biography, with special emphasis on the United States. The Donald W. Reynolds Center for American Art and Portraiture is home to the Smithsonian American Art Museum, the National Portrait Gallery, and the Archives of American Art. Hundreds of images from the collection and extensive information on its collections, publications, and activities are available on the Museum's Web site. http://www.americanart.si.edu | Email: AmericanArtInfo@si.edu

For further information, contact the Smithsonian American Art Museum, Eighth and F Streets NW., Washington, DC 20006. Phone, 202-633-7970.

Smithsonian Asian Pacific American Center   The Center seeks to enrich the appreciation of America's Asian Pacific heritage and empower Asian Pacific American communities in their sense of inclusion within the national culture. http://smithsonianapa.org | Email: apac@si.edu

For further information, contact the Asian Pacific American Center's administrative office, Capital Gallery, Suite 7065, MRC 516, P.O. Box 37012, Washington, DC 20013-7012. Phone, 202-633-2691.

Smithsonian Environmental Research Center (SERC)   The Center is the leading national research center for understanding environmental issues in the coastal zone. SERC is dedicated to increasing knowledge of the biological and physical processes that sustain life on Earth. The Center, located near the Chesapeake Bay, trains future generations of scientists to address ecological questions of the Nation and the globe. http://www.serc.si.edu

For further information, contact the Smithsonian Environmental Research Center, 647 Contees Wharf Road, Edgewater, MD 21037. Phone, 443-482-2200.

Smithsonian Institution Archives   The Smithsonian Institution Archives acquires, preserves, and makes available for research the official records of the Smithsonian Institution and the papers of individuals and organizations associated with the Institution or with its work. These holdings document the growth of the Smithsonian and the development of American science, history, and art. http://siarchives.si.edu

For further information, contact the Smithsonian Institution Archives, Capital Gallery, Suite 3000, 600 Maryland Avenue SW., Washington, DC 20024. Phone, 202-633-5870.

Smithsonian Institution Traveling Exhibition Service (SITES)   Since 1952, SITES has been committed to making Smithsonian exhibitions available to millions of people who cannot view them firsthand at the Smithsonian museums. Exhibitions on art, history, and science travel to more than 250 locations each year. http://www.sites.si.edu

For further information, contact the Smithsonian Institution Traveling Exhibition Service, Suite 7103, 470 L'Enfant Plaza SW., Washington, DC 20024. Phone, 202-633-3120.

Smithsonian Latino Center   The Center promotes Latino presence within the Smithsonian Institution. It is not represented in one physical location; rather, it works collaboratively with the Institution's museums and research centers to ensure that the contributions of the Latino community in the arts, history, national culture, and scientific achievement are celebrated, explored, presented, and preserved. The Center supports collections and archives, exhibitions, public and educational programs, research, and Web-based content and virtual platforms. It also manages leadership and professional development programs for emerging scholars, museum professionals, and Latino youth. http://latino.si.edu/Home

For further information, contact the Smithsonian Latino Center at Capital Gallery, 600 Maryland Avenue SW., MRC 512, Washington, DC 20013-7012. Phone, 202-633-1240.

Smithsonian Libraries   The Smithsonian Institution Libraries include more than 1 million volumes (among them, 40,000 rare books) with strengths in natural history, art, science, humanities, and museology. Many volumes are available through interlibrary loan. http://library.si.edu

For further information, contact the Smithsonian Institution Libraries, Tenth Street and Constitution Avenue NW., Washington, DC 20560. Phone, 202-633-2240.

Smithsonian Marine Station at Fort Pierce   The research institute features a state-of-the-art laboratory where Station scientists catalog species and study marine plants and animals. Among the most important projects being pursued at the site is the search for possible causes of fishkills, including Pfiesteria and other organisms. http://www.sms.si.edu

For further information, contact the Smithsonian Marine Station–Fort Pierce, 701 Seaway Drive, Fort Pierce, FL 34949. Phone, 772-462-6220.

Smithsonian Tropical Research Institute (STRI)   The Institute is a research organization for advanced studies of tropical ecosystems. Headquartered in the Republic of Panama, STRI maintains extensive facilities in the Western Hemisphere tropics. It is the base of a corps of tropical researchers who study the evolution, behavior, ecology, and history of tropical species of systems ranging from coral reefs to rain forests. http://www.stri.org

For further information, contact the Smithsonian Tropical Research Institute, 1100 Jefferson Drive SW., Suite 3123, Washington, DC 20560. Phone, 202-633-4700. Phone, 011-507-212-8000 (Panama).

Sources of Information

Business Opportunities   Information on procurement of supplies, property management and utilization services for Smithsonian Institution organizations, and construction contracts may be obtained from the Director, Office of Contracting, Smithsonian Institution, 2011 Crystal Drive,

Suite 350, Arlington, VA 22202. Phone, 202-633-7290. http://www.si.edu/se/seproductsubmissions.aspx

Career Opportunities   Employment information is available from the Office of Human Resources, Smithsonian Institution, Capital Gallery, Suite 5060, 600 Maryland Avenue SW., Washington, DC 20560. Phone, 202-633-6370. http://www.sihr.si.edu

In 2016, the Smithsonian Institution ranked 7th among 27 midsize Government agencies in the Best Places To Work Agency Rankings. http://bestplacestowork.org/BPTW/rankings/detail/SM00

Education / Research   Write to the Directors of the following offices at the Smithsonian Institution, Washington, DC 20560: Office of Fellowships and Internships, Smithsonian Center for Folklife and Cultural Heritage, Smithsonian Science Education Center, and Smithsonian Center for Learning and Digital Access. http://www.smithsonianofi.com. http://www.folklife.si.edu. https://ssec.si.edu. http://smithsonianeducation.org

Frequently Asked Questions (FAQs)   The Smithsonian Institution posts answers to FAQs on its website. https://www.si.edu/faqs

Media Affairs   Members of the press may contact the Smithsonian Office of Public Affairs, 1000 Jefferson Drive SW., Washington, DC 20560. Phone, 202-633-2400. http://newsdesk.si.edu/contacts

Memberships   For information on the Friends of the Smithsonian, write to PO Box 37012, MRC 712 Washington, DC 20013-7012. Phone, 202-633-6300. http://smithsonianmembership.com | Email: membership@si.edu

For information on the Resident Associate Program, write to Smithsonian Associates, PO Box 23293, Washington, DC 20026-3293. Phone, 202-633-3030. http://residentassociates.org

For information on the Smithsonian National Associate Program, call 800-766-2149. http://www.si.edu/Membership

For information on the National Air and Space Society, call 202-633-2603. http://www.nasm.si.edu/getinvolved/membership | Email: MembershipNASM@si.edu

For information on the Friends of the National Zoo, call 202-633-3038. http://nationalzoo.si.edu/Audiences/Members

For information on National Museum of the American Indian membership, call 800-242-6624. http://americanindian.si.edu | Email: NMAImember@si.edu

Organizational Chart   The Smithsonian Institution's organizational chart is accessible online in Portable Document Format (PDF) for viewing and downloading. https://www.si.edu/Content/Pdf/About/Smithsonian-organizational-chart.pdf

Photographs   Photographs and slides from the Smithsonian photographic archives are available to researchers, publishers, Government agencies, and the general public. A searchable database of images is available online. Purchase or use of images may require permission from the Smithsonian curatorial unit that holds copyright. For assistance, contact Smithsonian Photographic Services. Phone, 202-633-1933. http://www.si.edu/Collections | Email: photos@si.edu

Publications   The Smithsonian Institution's annual reports, starting with the year 2004, are available online as Portable Document Format (PDF) files. For information on acquiring hardcopies of reports, call 202-633-1000. http://www.si.edu/About/Annual-Report | Email: info@si.edu

Smithsonian Books, in collaboration with the Smithsonian Institution, publishes narrative nonfiction books on culture, history, science and technology, and the arts, as well as signature illustrated books based on Smithsonian museums and their collections. Random House Publisher Services distribute these titles. http://www.smithsonianbooks.com

Smithsonian Institution Scholarly Press, in conjunction with Rowman and Littlefield Publishing Group, Inc., publishes the research and other scholarly contributions of Smithsonian authors. http://www.scholarlypress.si.edu

Subscribe to the "Smithsonian Magazine" online. Phone, 800-766-2149. http://www.smithsonianmag.com | Email: smithsonian@customersvc.com

Subscribe to "Air and Space Magazine" online. Phone, 800-513-3081. http://www.airspacemag.com/?no-ist | Email: airandspace@customersvc.com

Social Media   The Smithsonian Institution has a Facebook account. https://www.facebook.com/Smithsonian

The Smithsonian Institution tweets announcements and other newsworthy items on Twitter. https://twitter.com/smithsonian

The Smithsonian Institution posts videos on its YouTube channel. https://www. youtube.com/user/SmithsonianVideos

Tours For information on museum and gallery tours, contact the Smithsonian Information Center, 1000 Jefferson Drive SW., Washington, DC 20560. Phone, 202-633-1000. School groups are welcome. The benefits of various memberships and their levels include special guided tours. http:// www.si.edu/Visit/GroupTours

Visitor Information The Smithsonian Information Center, located in the original Smithsonian building, commonly known as The Castle, provides general orientation through films, computer interactive programs, and visitor information specialists to help members and the public learn about the national collections, museum events, exhibitions, and special programs. Write to the Smithsonian Information Center, 1000 Jefferson Drive SW., Washington, DC 20560. Phone, 202-633-1000. http://www.si.edu/ Visit/Hours

An accessibility map of Smithsonian museums on and near the National Mall is available online. https://www.si.edu/content/ ovs/accessmapsindd.pdf

Volunteer Opportunities The Smithsonian Institution welcomes volunteers and offers a variety of service opportunities. For information, write to the Office of Visitor Services, 1000 Jefferson Drive SW., Washington, DC 20560. Phone, 202-633-1000. http://www.si.edu/Volunteer. http:// www.nga.gov/content/ngaweb/contact-us/ department-list

For further information, contact the Smithsonian Information Center, 1000 Jefferson Drive SW., Washington, DC 20560. Phone, 202-633-1000. TDD, 202-357-1729.

John F. Kennedy Center for the Performing Arts

John F. Kennedy Center for the Performing Arts, Washington, DC 20566
Phone, 202-467-4600. Internet, http://www.kennedy-center.org.

Chair	DAVID M. RUBENSTEIN
President	DEBORAH F. RUTTER
National Symphony Orchestra	
Music Director	GIANANDREA NOSEDA
The Suzanne Farrell Ballet	
Artistic Director	SUZANNE FARRELL
Washington National Opera	
Artistic Director	FRANCESCA ZAMBELLO

The above list of key personnel was updated 09–2017.

The Kennedy Center is the only official memorial to President John F. Kennedy in Washington, DC. The Center presents a year-round program of dance, drama, music, and opera from the United States and abroad.

Sources of Information

Business Opportunities Opportunities are posted on the Federal Business Opportunities Web site. For more information, contact The John F. Kennedy Center for the Performing Arts, Washington, DC 20566. https://www. fbo.gov

Career Opportunities Job descriptions of open positions are available online. http:// www.kennedy-center.org/jobs

The John F. Kennedy Center for the Performing Arts offers internships for undergraduate and graduate students and for recent college graduates. http://education. kennedy-center.org/education/internships/ overview.html

In partnership with American University, the Center offers a merit-based, 9-month fellowship in art management. http:// education.kennedy-center.org/education/ internships/fellowships.html

Education / Research   For information on education programs, contact The John F. Kennedy Center for the Performing Arts, Washington, DC 20566. Phone, 202-416-8000. http://www.kennedy-center.org/education

Free Performances   Free performances are given every day at 6 p.m. on the Millennium Stage in the Grand Foyer. https://www.kennedy-center.org/video/upcoming

History   In January of 1964, not long after the death of President John F. Kennedy, Congress designated the National Cultural Center as a "living memorial" to the slain President and authorized 23 million dollars to help build what is known today as the John F. Kennedy Center for the Performing Arts. Before the end of that year, enough artwork, building materials, and additional funds had been donated to start construction. With a gold-plated spade that had been used to break ground at both the Lincoln and Jefferson Memorials, President Lyndon B. Johnson symbolically removed the first soil from the new site. The Center opened to the public in 1971, more than a decade after President Dwight D. Eisenhower and legislators, from both parties, had taken initial steps toward realizing this vision. To learn more about the people who imagined a cultural center for the Nation, those who supported its realization, and the emergence of the John F. Kennedy Center for the Performing Arts as an iconic institution of the arts, visit the "History" Web page. http://www.kennedy-center.org/pages/about/history

Live Streaming   The Center live streams artists while they perform. http://www.kennedy-center.org/video/live

Memberships   For information on national and local activities, including the bimonthly "Kennedy Center News" for members, visit an information desk inside The John F. Kennedy Center for the Performing Arts. Or, contact Member Services, The John F. Kennedy Center for the Performing Arts, Washington, DC 20566. Phone, 202-416-8310. http://www.kennedy-center.org/membership | Email: membership@kennedy-center.org

Social Media   John F. Kennedy Center for the Performing Arts has a Facebook account. https://www.facebook.com/KennedyCenter

The Center tweets announcements and other newsworthy items on Twitter. https://twitter.com/KenCen

The Center posts videos on its YouTube channel. https://www.youtube.com/user/TheKennedyCenter

Special Functions   For information on using the facilities for special functions, contact the Office of Special Events, The John F. Kennedy Center for the Performing Arts, Washington, DC 20566. Phone, 202-416-8000. https://www.kennedy-center.org/rental

Theater Operations   For information on using the theaters, contact the booking manager at The John F. Kennedy Center for the Performing Arts, Washington, DC 20566. Phone, 202-416-8032. http://www.kennedy-center.org/pages/theaterrental

Tickets   Tickets for admission to performances may be purchased at the box office, by mail, by phone using instant-charge, or online. Phone, 202-467-4600. TTY, 202-416-8524. https://www.kennedy-center.org/tickets

The Center posts answers to frequently asked ticket-related questions. http://www.kennedy-center.org/contact/topic/1

Tours   The Friends of the Kennedy Center volunteers provide visitor services. Tours are available free of charge on weekdays, 10 a.m.–5 p.m., and on weekends, 10 a.m.–1 p.m. https://www.kennedy-center.org/pages/visitor/tours

Videos   The Center regularly posts short videos of artists performing. Its Web site has an expanding collection of over 2,000 selections. http://www.kennedy-center.org/Video/recentVideos

Volunteer Opportunities   For information on volunteer opportunities, contact Friends of the Kennedy Center, 2700 F Street NW, Washington, DC 20566. Phone, 202-416-8000. http://www.kennedy-center.org/support/volunteers. http://www.kennedy-center.org/contact

For further information, contact The John F. Kennedy Center for the Performing Arts. Phone, 202-467-4600.

National Gallery of Art

4th and Constitution Avenue NW., Washington, DC 20565
Phone, 202-737-4215. Internet, http://www.nga.gov.

President	FREDERICK W. BEINECKE
Director	EARL A. POWELL III

Activities

The National Gallery of Art administers a world-class collection of painting, sculpture, and the graphic arts. The West Building includes European (13th–early 20th century) and American (18th–early 20th century) works. An extensive survey of Italian painting and sculpture, including the only painting by Leonardo da Vinci in the Americas, is on display in the Gallery. Rich in Dutch masters and French impressionists, the collection offers superb surveys of American, British, Flemish, Spanish, and 15th- and 16th-century German art, as well as Renaissance medals and bronzes, Chinese porcelains, and about 117,000 works of graphic art from the 12th century to the present day. The East Building collections and Sculpture Garden contain important works by major 20th-century artists. The Gallery relies on public and private resources. Federal appropriations support its operations and maintenance. Private donations and funds allow it to acquire artwork, as well as to offer a variety of special programs. For example, a fellowship program promotes graduate and postgraduate research, an extension service provides free education resources to millions of people each year, and other programs educate schoolchildren and the public.

Sources of Information

Business Opportunities For more information, contact the National Gallery of Art, Office of Procurement and Contracts, 2000B South Club Drive, Landover, MD 20785. Phone, 202-842-6745. Fax, 202-312-2792. https://www.fbo.gov/index?s=main&mode=list&tab=list

Calendar The full calendar of events is available online. To subscribe to the quarterly brochure of seasonal exhibition and programming highlights, visit the Gallery's Web site or call 202-842-6662.

http://www.nga.gov/content/ngaweb/calendar.html | Email: calendar@nga.gov

Career Opportunities The National Gallery of Art relies on approximately 1,000 employees to carry out its mission. Some positions require a background in art history or design; however, other positions—like salesperson, security guard, and visitor services aide—support the museum's daily operations and are less specialized. The National Gallery of Art also employs accountants, administrators, facilities managers, fundraisers, information systems specialists, librarians, and other professionals with technical expertise. Phone, 202-842-6282. http://www.nga.gov/content/ngaweb/opportunities/employment-opportunities.html | Email: staffing@nga.gov

The National Gallery of Art offers internships and opportunities for fellows. Conservation and curatorial fellowships are available, as well as Center for Advanced Study in the Visual Arts (CASVA) fellowships. http://www.nga.gov/content/ngaweb/opportunities/interns-and-fellows.html

The National Gallery of Art offers a range of volunteer opportunities. Volunteers serve as docents, manage the information desks at the entrances to the East and West Buildings, work in the library, and help in the horticulture division. Local high school students can participate in the teen volunteer program. http://www.nga.gov/content/ngaweb/opportunities/volunteer-opportunities.html

Center for Advanced Study in the Visual Arts (CASVA) The CASVA is a research institute that supports study of the production, use, and cultural meaning of architecture, art, artifacts, film, photography, and urbanism. It offers fellowships, organizes scholarly meetings, produces publications, and supports research. These activities are privately funded through endowments and grants to the National Gallery of Art. Phone, 202-842-6480. http://www.nga.gov/content/

ngaweb/research/casva.html | Email: casva@
nga.gov

Concerts   Concerts by accomplished
musicians are open to the public without
charge. Seating starts 30 minutes before the
performance on a first-come, first-seated
basis. Phone, 202-842-6941. http://www.
nga.gov/content/ngaweb/calendar/concerts.
html

Educational Resources   The Gallery's free
loan program allows community groups,
educational institutions, individuals, and
nonprofit television stations nationwide
to borrow teaching packets and DVDs.
Dozens of lessons and activities are also
accessible on the Gallery's Web site.
For more information, including the free
catalog of education resources, contact
the Department of Education Resources,
National Gallery of Art, 2000B South Club
Drive, Landover, MD 20785. Phone, 202-
842-6273. http://www.nga.gov/content/
ngaweb/education/learningresources.html |
Email: edresources@nga.gov

Family Programs   The Gallery offers free
family programs—children's films, music
performances, storytelling, and workshops—
that are suitable for children ages 4 and up.
Phone, 202-789-3030. http://www.nga.gov/
content/ngaweb/education/families.html |
Email: family@nga.gov

Films   An ongoing program of classic
cinema, documentary, avant-garde, and
area premieres takes place each weekend.
Seating is on a first-come, first-seated
basis, and admission is free. Doors open
approximately 30 minutes before each show.
Visiting filmmakers and scholars discuss
films with the audiences following some
screenings. Phone, 202-842-6799. http://
www.nga.gov/content/ngaweb/calendar/film-
programs.html | Email: film-department@
nga.gov

Frequently Asked Questions (FAQs)   The
National Gallery of Art posts answers to
FAQs on its Web site. http://www.nga.gov/
content/ngaweb/contact-us.html

Ice-Skating Rink   Each winter, the National
Gallery of Art opens its ice rink in the
Sculpture Garden. The seasonal skating
schedule is posted online in November.
http://www.nga.gov/content/ngaweb/visit/
ice-rink.html

Image Collections   The Department of
Image Collections serves as the National
Gallery of Art's research center for images of
Western art and architecture. The collections
now contain over 14 million digital images,
microforms, negatives, photographs, and
slides, making this resource one of the
largest of its kind. Gallery staff, Center for
Advanced Study in the Visual Arts (CASVA)
members, visiting scholars, and serious adult
researchers regularly use the collections. The
library is accessible by appointment every
Monday, noon–4:30 p.m., and Tuesday–
Friday, 10 a.m.–4:30 p.m., except on Federal
holidays. Phone, 202-842-6026. http://www.
nga.gov/content/ngaweb/research/library/
imagecollections.html

Lectures   Lecture events are open to the
public, and admission is free. Seating is
available on a first-come, first-seated basis.
http://www.nga.gov/content/ngaweb/
calendar/lectures.html

Library   The National Gallery of Art Library
maintains a collection of more than 400,000
books and periodicals on the history, theory,
and criticism of art and architecture. The
collection's holdings emphasize Western
art from the Middle Ages to the present
and American art from the colonial era to
the present. The library is accessible by
appointment every Monday, noon–4:30
p.m., and Tuesday–Friday, 10 a.m.–4:30
p.m., except on Federal holidays. Phone,
202-842-6511. http://www.nga.gov/content/
ngaweb/research/library/About.html

Memberships   The Gallery offers three
membership levels of annual giving: The
Circle, The Tower Project, and The Exhibition
Circle. Circle members contribute to
conservation programs, special exhibitions,
and research. Tower Project members
promote contemporary artists by supporting
modern and contemporary exhibitions
in the Tower Gallery of the East Building.
Exhibition Circle members provide funding
for exhibitions. For more information on
membership levels and their benefits,
contact The Circle, National Gallery of Art,
2000B South Club Drive, Landover, MD
20785. Phone, 202-842-6450. Fax, 202 789-
4577. http://www.nga.gov/content/ngaweb/
support/membership.html | Email: circle@
nga.gov

News   The National Gallery of Art posts recent news releases on its Web site. http://www.nga.gov/content/ngaweb/press.html | Email: pressinfo@nga.gov

An online subscription form is available to sign up for announcements, newsletters, notifications, and updates on acquisitions and exhibitions; activities, projects, and programs; and other topics. http://subscribe.nga.gov/subscription_form_ngart.cfm

NGAkids   NGAkids offers interactive activities and adventures with artwork from the Gallery's collection and an animated tale set in the Gallery's Sculpture Garden. http://www.nga.gov/content/ngaweb/education/kids.html

Photographs   Photographs that are not on display may be viewed by appointment. Phone, 202-842-6144. Email: photographs@nga.gov

Publications   The Gallery Shops sell publications on the Gallery's collections and quality reproductions of artwork. Purchases may be made online or by calling 800-697-9350. https://shop.nga.gov

Public Wi-Fi   Wireless internet service is available throughout the Gallery to visitors who are 18 years old and older or at least 13 years old with permission from a parent or guardian. The network name is "NGA_Public_WiFi," and a password is not needed. A user must, however, supply his or her own Internet device and agree to the "Terms and Conditions of Use." http://www.nga.gov/content/ngaweb/visit/public-wifi.html

Tours   The education division offers daily guided talks and tours in the galleries. Phone, 202-842-6247. http://www.nga.gov/content/ngaweb/visit/tours-and-guides.html

Visitor Services   The Visitor Services Office assists those with special needs, responds to written and telephone requests, and helps visitors plan their stay in the Washington, DC, area. For more information, contact the National Gallery of Art, Office of Visitor Services, 2000B South Club Drive, Landover, MD 20785. Phone, 202-842-6691. http://www.nga.gov/content/ngaweb/visit.html

Works on Paper   Works of art on paper that are not on display may be viewed by appointment. Phone, 202-842-6380 (European works). Phone, 202-842-6605 (American works). http://www.nga.gov/content/ngaweb/research/make-an-appointment.html | Email: printstudyrooms@nga.gov. http://www.nga.gov/content/ngaweb/contact-us.html

For further information, contact the National Gallery of Art. Phone, 202-737-4215.

Woodrow Wilson International Center for Scholars

Scholar Administration Office, Woodrow Wilson Center, One Woodrow Wilson Plaza, 1300 Pennsylvania Avenue NW., Washington, DC 20004-3027
Phone, 202-691-4000. Fax, 202-691-4001. Internet, http://www.wilsoncenter.org.

Director / President / Chief Executive Officer	JANE HARMAN

Activities

Created by an Act of Congress in 1968, the Woodrow Wilson International Center for Scholars is a national, living memorial honoring the legacy of President Woodrow Wilson. The Wilson Center, headquartered in Washington, DC, and supported by both public and private funds, provides a strictly nonpartisan space for scholars and policymakers to interact. By conducting relevant, timely research and promoting dialogue from diverse perspectives, the Center works to address critical current and emerging challenges confronting the United States and the world. https://www.wilsoncenter.org/about-the-wilson-center

Sources of Information

Career Opportunities   Career opportunities at the Center are posted online. For more information, contact the Office of Human Resources, One Woodrow Wilson Plaza,

1300 Pennsylvania Avenue NW., 3d Floor, Washington, DC 20004-3027. http://www.wilsoncenter.org/opportunities/Job | Email: jobs@wilsoncenter.org

Donations   An online form is available for making tax-deductible contributions to support dialogue and scholarship in public policy. Gifts may be directed to a specific program by using the "Designation" drop-down menu. "Unrestricted" gifts allow the Center to build its overall capacity and meet areas of greatest need. Phone, 202-691-4171. https://support.wilsoncenter.org/donation_form | Email: development@wilsoncenter.org

Fellowships   The Center offers residential fellowships that allow academics, public officials, journalists, business professionals, and others to pursue their research and writing at the Center while interacting with policymakers in Washington. The Center also invites public policy scholars and senior scholars from a variety of disciplines to conduct research for varying lengths of time in residence. Phone, 202-691-4000. http://www.wilsoncenter.org/fellowships-grants

Internships   The Center has a year-round need for interns to assist the program and projects staff and to act as research assistants for scholars and fellows. Phone, 202-691-4053. http://www.wilsoncenter.org/opportunities/Internship

Media Affairs   Members of the press may contact the Center at 202-691-4217. http://www.wilsoncenter.org/media-access-to-the-wilson-center

Multimedia   Wide ranging in scope, "Wilson Center On Demand" serves as a hub for insightful analysis of and commentary on ideas and issues. https://www.wilsoncenter.org/wilson-center-demand

Presidential Memorial Exhibit   The Center houses the Woodrow Wilson Presidential Memorial Exhibit, which features memorabilia, historical information, photographs, several short films, and a memorial hall with quotations. The exhibit is open weekdays, 8:30 a.m.–5 p.m. Admission is free. Phone, 202-691-4000. http://www.wilsoncenter.org/woodrow-wilson-presidential-memorial-exhibit-and-learning-center | Email: wwics@wilsoncenter.org

Publications   The Center publishes policy briefs and research reports, as well as books written by staff and visiting scholars and fellows, through the Wilson Center Press. Phone, 202-691-4000. http://www.wilsoncenter.org/publications

Every 3 months, "The Wilson Quarterly" magazine releases a cluster of content exploring a single topic from diverse perspectives. This free, online magazine examines culture, current events, ideas, and the people affected by them. http://wilsonquarterly.com/quarterly | Email: wq@wilsoncenter.org

Research   The Center's "Research" Web page allows visitors to explore the pressing global challenges confronting the U.S. policy community and general public today. https://www.wilsoncenter.org/research

Social Media   The Center maintains an account on Facebook. https://www.facebook.com/woodrowwilsoncenter

The Center posts openings for jobs and internships on its LinkedIn page. https://www.linkedin.com/company/woodrow-wilson-international-center-for-scholars

The Center tweets announcements, news, and other noteworthy items on Twitter. https://twitter.com/thewilsoncenter

The Center posts videos on its YouTube channel. https://www.youtube.com/user/woodrowwilsoncenter

Visitor Services   Events, unless otherwise noted, are free and open to the public. Photo identification is required for entry. A listing of events at the Center is available online. http://www.wilsoncenter.org/events. http://www.wilsoncenter.org

For further information, contact the Woodrow Wilson International Center for Scholars, One Woodrow Wilson Plaza, 1300 Pennsylvania Avenue NW., Washington, DC 20004-3027. Phone, 202-691-4000. Fax, 202-691-4001.

State Justice Institute

11951 Freedom Drive, Suite 1020, Reston, VA 20190
Phone, 571-313-8843. Internet, http://.www.sji.gov.

Board of Directors

Chair	CHASE T. ROGERS
Vice Chair	DANIEL J. BECKER
Member	DAVID V. BREWER
Member	ISABEL FRAMER
Member	JONATHAN LIPPMAN
Member	WILFREDO MARTINEZ
Member	MARSHA J. RABITEAU
Member	CHASE T. ROGERS
Member	HERNÁN D. VERA
Secretary	GAYLE A. NACHTIGAL
Treasurer	JOHN B. NALBANDIAN

Officers

Executive Director	JONATHAN D. MATTIELLO

The above list of key personnel was updated 07–2017.

The State Justice Institute supports the Nation's judicial system and the public that it serves.

The State Justice Institue (SJI) was established by the State Justice Institute Authorization Act of 1984 (42 U.S.C. 10701 et seq.) as a private, nonprofit corporation to further the development and improvement of judicial administration in the State courts.

An 11-member Board of Directors supervises the SJI. The President appoints the members with the advice and consent of the Senate. By law, the Board is composed of six judges, a State court administrator, and four members of the public—no more than two of the four public members can be affiliated with the same political party. http://www.sji.gov/about-sji

The SJI develops solutions to common issues faced by State courts; provides practical products to judges and court staff; ensures that effective approaches in one State are quickly and economically shared with other courts nationwide; and supports national, regional, and instate educational programs to speed the transfer of solutions.

To accomplish these broad objectives, the SJI is authorized to provide funds through grants, cooperative agreements, and contracts to the State courts and to court support organizations. http://www.sji.gov/priority-investment-areas

Sources of Information

Forms Documents to view and print are posted online in Portable Document Format (PDF). These documents include a number of forms: assurances, consultant rate, disclosure of lobbying activities, grant application, project budget, reimbursement request, and State approval certificate. http://www.sji.gov/forms

Grants Information on various award and grant types—curriculum adaptation and training grants, the education support program, project grants, and technical assistance grants—is available online. http://www.sji.gov/grants

Newsletter Readers may subscribe to the monthly "SJI Newsletter" online. http://www.sji.gov/newsletter-archives. http://www.sji.gov | Email: contact@sji.gov

For further information, contact the State Justice Institute, 11951 Freedom Drive, Suite 1020, Reston, VA 20190. Phone, 571-313-8843.

United States Holocaust Memorial Museum

100 Raoul Wallenberg Place, SW., Washington, DC 20024-2126
Phone, 202-488-0400. TTY, 202-488-0406. Internet, http://www.ushmm.org.

U.S. Holocaust Memorial Council

Chair	HOWARD M. LORBER
Vice Chair	ALLAN M. HOLT
Members	WALTER R. ALLEN, JR.
	LAURENCE M. BAER
	DANIEL BENJAMIN
	TOM A. BERNSTEIN
	ELISA SPUNGEN BILDNER
	JOSHUA B. BOLTEN
	MICHAEL S. BOSWORTH
	ETHEL C. BROOKS
	LEE T. BYCEL
	SARA DAREHSHORI
	SHEFALI RAZDAN DUGGAL
	NORMAN L. EISEN
	LEE A. FEINSTEIN
	RAFFI FREEDMAN-GURSPAN
	JORDAN T. GOODMAN
	SAMUEL N. GORDON
	GRANT T. HARRIS
	SARAH K. HURWITZ
	PRISCILLA L. KERSTEN
	HOWARD KONAR
	JONATHAN S. LAVINE
	EDWARD P. LAZARUS
	ALAN B. LAZOWSKI
	STUART A. LEVEY
	ERICA A. LEVINE
	SUSAN G. LEVINE
	SUSAN E. LOWENBERG
	DAVID M. MARCHICK
	LESLIE MEYERS
	TAMAR NEWBERGER
	DEBORAH A. OPPENHEIMER
	ERIC P. ORTNER
	CHERYL PEISACH
	DANA M. PERLMAN
	MICHAEL P. POLSKY
	MICHAEL H. POSNER
	RICHARD S. PRICE
	RONALD RATNER
	BENJAMIN J. RHODES
	MELISSA ROGERS
	DANIEL J. ROSEN
	MENACHEM Z. ROSENSAFT
	MICHAEL P. ROSS
	ELLIOT J. SCHRAGE
	MAUREEN SCHULMAN
	IRVIN N. SHAPELL
	CINDY SIMON SKJODT

SCOTT STRAUS
MICHÈLE TAYLOR
HOWARD D. UNGER
CLEMANTINE WAMARIYA
ANDREW J. WEINSTEIN
JEREMY M. WEINSTEIN
DANIEL G. WEISS
(VACANCY)

Congressional Members

REP. THEODORE E. DEUTCH
REP. DAVID F. KUSTOFF
REP. ILEANA ROS-LEHTINEN
REP. BRADLEY S. SCHNEIDER
REP. LEE M. ZELDIN
SEN. ALAN S. FRANKEN
SEN. ORRIN G. HATCH
SEN. BERNARD SANDERS
(VACANCY)
(VACANCY)

Ex Officio Members—Nonvoting
Department of Education	PHILIP H. ROSENFELT
Department of State	THOMAS K. YAZDGERDI
Department of the Interior	(VACANCY)
General Counsel to the Council	GERARD LEVAL

Council Staff
Museum Director	SARA J. BLOOMFIELD
Internal Auditor	MEL SCHWARTZ

Museum Administration
Museum Director	SARA J. BLOOMFIELD
Chief Development Officer	JORDAN TANNENBAUM
Chief Financial Officer	POLLY POVEJSIL HEATH
Chief Information Officer	JOSEPH KRAUS
Chief Marketing Officer	MICHELLE STEIN, ACTING
Chief Museum Operations Officer	TANELL COLEMAN
Chief Program Officer	SARAH OGILVIE
Director, Collections	MICHAEL GRUNBERGER
Director, International Affairs	PAUL SHAPIRO
Director, Levine Institute for Holocaust Education	KRISTINE DONLY, ACTING
Director, Mandel Center for Advanced Holocaust Studies	WENDY LOWER, ACTING
Director, National Institute for Holocaust Documentation	MICHAEL GRUNBERGER
Director, Planning	DARA GOLDBERG
Director, Simon-Skjodt Center for the Prevention of Genocide	CAMERON HUDSON
General Counsel	RONALD F. CUFFE

The United States Holocaust Memorial Museum promotes documentation, study, and interpretation of the Holocaust and maintains a permanent living memorial to its victims.

The United States Holocaust Memorial Museum (USHMM) was established by the act of October 7, 1980 (36 U.S.C. 1401-1408). It received permanent authorization as an independent establishment by the act of October 12, 2000 (36 U.S.C. 2301 et seq.).

UNITED STATES HOLOCAUST MEMORIAL MUSEUM

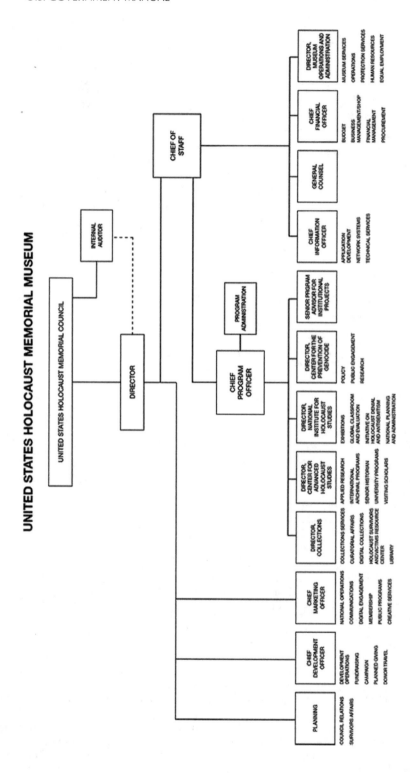

The United States Holocaust Memorial Council, which serves as a board of trustees, governs the USHMM. The Council's 55 members are appointed by the President to staggered 5-year terms. Additionally, five members are appointed from each Chamber of the Congress. There are also three nonvoting ex-officio members from the Departments of Education, State, and the Interior.

The USHMM operates as a public-private partnership. Its activities and programs are supported by planned giving, endowments, and revenues; gifts, grants, and contracts; and Federal funding. https://www.ushmm. org/information/about-the-museum

Activities

Jack, Joseph and Morton Mandel Center for Advanced Holocaust Studies   The Center works with the United States Holocaust Memorial Council's Academic Committee to support research projects and publications on the Holocaust, provide access to Holocaust-related archival materials for study and new research, sponsor fellowship opportunities for pre- and postdoctoral researchers, and offer seminars, summer research workshops, conferences, lectures, and symposia. http://www.ushmm.org/ research/the-center-for-advanced-holocaust-studies/about-the-center-for-advanced-holocaust-studies

For further information, contact the Jack, Joseph, and Morton Mandel Center for Advanced Holocaust Studies. Phone, 202-488-0400. TTY, 202-488-0406.

Simon-Skjodt Center for the Prevention of Genocide   The Center raises awareness of genocide, influences policymaking on genocide prevention, and stimulates worldwide action to prevent genocide and related mass atrocities. It seeks to make genocide prevention a national and international priority by increasing public awareness and mobilizing worldwide support to avert these crimes against humanity. http://www. ushmm.org/confront-genocide/about | Email: genocideprevention@ushmm.org

For further information, contact the Simon-Skjodt Center for the Prevention of Genocide. Phone, 202-488-0400. TTY, 202-488-0406.

William Levine Family National Institute for Holocaust Education   The Institute promotes a variety of resources and programs to help educators, professionals, and students increase their knowledge of Holocaust history and understand its relevance today. Educational outreach programs provide teachers with classroom strategies and resources for teaching students about the Holocaust. http://www.ushmm. org/educators/teaching-about-the-holocaust

For further information, contact the National Institute for Holocaust Education.

Programs

Law, Justice, and the Holocaust Program   This program examines the decisions German jurists made and the pressures they faced under the Nazi regime. This is a one-day program for judges, prosecutors, and court administrators. http:// www.ushmm.org/professionals-and-student-leaders/judiciary

For further information, contact the Law, Justice, and the Holocaust Program.

Civic and Defense Initiatives Program   This program explores the ways in which the military can work to prevent genocide today. http://www.ushmm.org/professionals-and-student-leaders/military-professionals

Law Enforcement and Society: Lessons of the Holocaust Program   This program examines the role that law enforcement professionals played in the Holocaust. It also challenges them to reflect on their professional and personal responsibilities in a democracy today. http://www.ushmm. org/professionals-and-student-leaders/law-enforcement

For further information, contact the Lessons of the Holocaust Program.

Programs on Ethics, Religion, and the Holocaust   These programs focus on the response of churches to the Holocaust and the ways in which religious institutions, leaders, and theologians have addressed this history and its legacy. http://www.ushmm. org/research/the-center-for-advanced-holocaust-studies/programs-ethics-religion-the-holocaust

For further information, contact the Programs on Ethics, Religion, and the Holocaust.

Youth and Community Initiatives

Program   This program introduces students to Holocaust history and helps them develop leadership skills for confronting hatred and promoting human dignity. http://www. ushmm.org/professionals-and-student-leaders/student-leaders

For further information, contact the Student Leaders Program.

Sources of Information

Café   The Museum Café is open daily, 8:30 a.m.–4:30 p.m., except on Yom Kippur and Christmas Day. Visitors may not bring food into it or the Museum. The café serves breakfast, salads, sandwiches, and soups, including vegetarian and kosher options. Kosher food is prepared and sealed offsite under rabbinical supervision. https://www. ushmm.org/information/visit-the-museum/museum-cafe

Calendar of Events   For information on upcoming events, see the Museum's online calendar. http://www.ushmm.org/online/calendar

Career Opportunities   The museum employs people with diverse professional experience: collections, education, exhibits, fundraising, marketing, programing, and other areas. A list of current job openings is available on the "Careers" Web page. https://www.ushmm.org/information/career-volunteer-opportunities/careers

Unpaid internship opportunities are available. https://www.ushmm.org/information/career-volunteer-opportunities/careers/internships

Collections / Exhibitions   The Museum's holdings include art, books, pamphlets, advertisements, maps, film and video historical footage, audio and video oral testimonies, music and sound recordings, furnishings, architectural fragments, models, machinery, tools, microfilm and microfiche of government documents and other official records, personal effects, personal papers, photographs, photo albums, and textiles. The self-guided permanent exhibition spans three floors and presents a narrative history

of the Holocaust with historical artifacts, photographs, and film footage. Special exhibitions include Remember the Children: Daniel's Story (for children 8 and up) and Some Were Neighbors: Collaboration and Complicity in the Holocaust. The Museum's traveling exhibitions have gone to numerous cities, States, and countries. These exhibitions extend the history of the Holocaust beyond the Museum's walls. More information on the Museum's collections and exhibitions is available on its Web site. http://www.ushmm.org/information/exhibitions

Encyclopedia   An encyclopedia of the Holocaust is available on the Museum's Web site. https://www.ushmm.org/learn/holocaust-encyclopedia

Frequently Asked Questions (FAQs)   The Museum posts answers to FAQs on its Web site. https://www.ushmm.org/research/ask-a-research-question/frequently-asked-questions

Multilingual Resources   At the top of the Museum's home page is a "Language" drop-down menu that allows non-English readers to access resources in a number of languages: Arabic, Bahasa, Chinese, French, Greek, Hungarian, Italian, Japanese, Korean, Portuguese, Russian, Spanish, and Turkish. https://www.ushmm.org

News   The Museum posts press releases on its Web site. https://www.ushmm.org/information/press/press-releases

To receive electronic Museum news, invitations to special programs and exhibitions, and updates on genocide prevention and other initiatives, subscribe using the online form. https://engage. ushmm.org/subscribe.html

Organizational Chart   The USHMM's organizational chart is accessible online in Portable Document Format (PDF) for viewing and downloading. https://www.ushmm. org/m/pdfs/ushmm-org-chart.pdf

Plan a Visit   The Museum is open every day, except on Yom Kippur and Christmas. Admission is free; however, timed passes are required to enter the permanent exhibition from March through August. No passes are required for other Museum exhibitions. The "Plan Your Visit" Web pages contain a trove of useful information on accessibility, admission and tickets, group reservations, hours, location, transportation, and more. https://www.ushmm.org/information/visit-the-museum/plan-your-visit

Social Media The Museum relies on social media to share information on its programs and resources; to memorialize the victims of Nazism; to launch discussion on the Holocaust and its relevance today; and to raise awareness that antisemitism, genocide, and hatred are persistent threats and that everybody has a role in combating them. https://www.ushmm.org/information/connect-with-the-museum#guidelines

Support the Mission Annual membership gifts help the Museum confront antisemitism and answer Holocaust denial, expand educational outreach, and preserve historical artifacts. https://www.ushmm.org/support

The Museum uses its resources to confront hatred and genocide, to educate students and provide classroom resources for teachers, and to rescue Holocaust evidence and make additional historic documents available in digital format. An online contribution, one-time or monthly, supports these activities immediately and directly. https://engage.ushmm.org/support.html

Volunteer Opportunities The Museum welcomes volunteers and offers a variety of service opportunities. http://www.ushmm.org/information/career-volunteer-opportunities/volunteering. https://www.ushmm.org/online/form/contact-the-museum/input

For further information, contact the U.S. Holocaust Memorial Museum, 100 Raoul Wallenberg Place, SW., Washington, DC 20024-2126. Phone, 202-488-0400. TTY, 202-488-0406.

United States Institute of Peace

2301 Constitution Avenue NW., Washington, DC 20037
Phone, 202-457-1700. Fax, 202-429-6063. Internet, http://www.usip.org.

Board of Directors

Chair	Stephen J. Hadley
Vice Chair	George E. Moose
Member	Judy Ansley
Member	Eric S. Edelman
Member	Joseph Eldridge
Member	Kerry Kennedy
Member	Ikram U. Khan
Member	Stephen D. Krasner
Member	John A. Lancaster
Member	Jeremy A. Rabkin
Member	J. Robinson West
Member	Nancy Zirkin
Secretary of State (ex officio)	Rex W. Tillerson
Secretary of Defense (ex officio)	Gen. James Mattis, USMC
President, National Defense University (ex officio)	Maj. Gen. Frederick M. Padilla, USMC
President, U.S. Institute of Peace (ex officio)	Nancy Lindborg

Officials

President	Nancy Lindborg
Executive Vice President	William B. Taylor
Director, Congressional Relations	Anne Hingeley, Acting
Director, Public Affairs and Communications	Liz Callihan Acting
Vice President, External Relations	Diane Zeleny

The United States Institute of Peace prevents, mitigates, and resolves violent conflicts around the world.

The United States Institute of Peace (USIP) is an independent nonprofit corporation established by Congress pursuant to title XVII of the Defense Authorization Act of 1985, as amended (22 U.S.C. 4601-4611), to develop, apply, and foster cost-effective strategies and tools to prevent, mitigate, and resolve violent international conflicts, particularly those that threaten or harm America's strategic and security interests. The United States Institute of Peace Act defines the organization's mission: "to serve the people and the government through the widest possible range of education and training, basic and applied research opportunities, and peace information services on the means to promote international peace and the resolution of conflicts among nations and peoples of the world without recourse to violence." http://www.usip.org/vision-mission-core-principles

With the confirmation of the Senate, the President appoints the Institute's bipartisan Board of Directors. It comprises 12 members from outside the Federal service—plus four ex officio members, three from the State Department, Department of Defense, and National Defense University, and the fourth is the President of the Institute. The Board governs the Institute and appoints its President. No more than eight voting members may be from the same political party. http://www.usip.org/aboutus/board.html

Activities

The Institute supports U.S. national security and foreign affairs through conflict management and peacebuilding operations, training in conflict management and peacebuilding tradecraft and best practices, and conflict research and analysis. The USIP operates on the ground in conflict zones. It facilitates dialogue among parties in conflict, builds conflict management skills and capacity, identifies and disseminates best practices in conflict management,

promotes the rule of law, reforms and strengthens education systems, strengthens civil society, and educates the public through media and other outreach activities. The USIP works in partnership with the State and Defense Departments, the U.S. Agency for International Development, nongovernmental organizations, higher and secondary educational institutions, foreign governments, and international organizations to promote collaborative problemsolving through conflict management operations, training and analysis, facilitated dialogue, Track 1.5 diplomacy, and special events. The Institute conducts practitioner training in conflict management, including mediation and negotiating skills for government and military personnel, civil society leaders, and staff of nongovernmental and international organizations. The Institute extends its reach through grants, fellowships, and scholarships to nonprofit organizations in the United States and overseas. http://www.usip.org/issue-areas

Sources of Information

Employment The USIP relies on knowledgeable, talented professionals to carry out its mission. A recent graduate typically starts as a program assistant. The ideal candidate is a high academic achiever; has a background in international relations or a related field; and possesses administrative, computer, research, and writing skills. Regional specialization and language skills may be required for some positions. http://www.usip.org/jobs

Grants / Fellowships Information on USIP grants and fellowship programs is available online. http://www.usip.org/grants-fellowships

Publications USIP articles, publications, and tools are accessible online. http://www.usip.org/publications. http://www.usip.org/newsroom

For further information, contact the U.S. Institute of Peace, Office of Public Affairs and Communications, 2301 Constitution Avenue NW., Washington, DC 20037. Phone, 202-457-1700.

INTERNATIONAL ORGANIZATIONS

African Development Bank

Avenue Jean-Paul II, 01 BP 1387, Abidjan 01, Côte d'Ivoire
Phone, +225 20 26 10 20. Internet, http://www.afdb.org | Email: afdb@afdb.org.

President   AKINWUMI ADESINA

The above list of key personnel was updated 09–2017

The African Development Bank stimulates sustainable economic development and social progress in regional member countries to mitigate poverty and its effects.

The African Development Bank (AFDB) was established in 1964. By charter amendment, the AFDB expanded its membership to include nonregional countries in 1982. The admission of nonregional countries boosted AFDB capital resources by more than twofold.

The Bank's mandate centers on the economic development and social progress of its regional members. AFDB membership totals 80 countries: 54 African and 26 nonregional countries.

The African Development Fund, established in 1972 and operational in 1974, complements AFDB operations by providing concessional financing for high-priority development projects. Contributing countries provide the Fund with resources to improve economic and social conditions in beneficiary countries. These beneficiaries include countries that are increasing in economic capacity and en route to becoming the new emerging markets or that are regarded as fragile states and require special assistance for basics levels of service delivery. http://www.afdb.org/en/about-us/mission-strategy

Sources of Information

Career Opportunities Grade and salary data and information on current job vacancies are available online. http://www.afdb.org/en/about-us/careers

Documents The AFDB posts documents on its website. http://www.afdb.org/en/documents

Environmental and Social Assessments The AFDB website features relevant documents in a database that may be filtered and sorted by country, topic and sector, or both. https://www.afdb.org/en/documents/environmental-social-assessments/cop

Field Offices Contact information for AFDB field offices is available online. http://www.afdb.org/en/about-us/organisational-structure/complexes/country-regional-programs-policy/field-offices/field-office-contacts

Français The AFDB website offers information and resources for visitors who read French. https://www.afdb.org/fr

Frequently Asked Questions (FAQs) The AFDB posts answers to FAQs on its website. http://www.afdb.org/en/about-us/frequently-asked-questions

Glossary The AFDB website features a glossary of acronyms. http://www.afdb.org/en/glossary

News / Events The AFDB website features events, interviews, loan and grant announcements, multimedia, news, press releases, project stories, and speeches. http://www.afdb.org/en/news-and-events

Organizational Chart   The AFDB's organizational chart is available in Portable Document Format (PDF) for viewing and downloading. https://www.afdb.org/fileadmin/uploads/afdb/Documents/Generic-Documents/AFDB_ORGANIZATION_CHART_2_MAY_2017.pdf

Site Map   The website map allows visitors to look for specific topics or to browse content that aligns with their interests. http://www.afdb.org/en/sitemap

Social Media   The AFDB has a Facebook account. https://www.facebook.com/AfDBGroup/?ref=ts

The AFDB tweets announcements and newsworthy items in English and French on Twitter. https://twitter.com/AfDB_Group

Statistics   Defining achievable goals and setting realistic targets, as well as evaluating the effects of projects, depend heavily on reliable data. The AFDB promotes improvement in the quality and quantity of statistical data on all aspects of development. https://www.afdb.org/en/knowledge/statistics

Web TV   The AFDB's Web TV features programs in English and French. http://www.afdb.tv

Where the AFDB Works   The AFDB's website features a list of African countries where the Bank is active. http://www.afdb.org/en/countries

---

Asian Development Bank

Headquarters: 6 ADB Avenue, Mandaluyong City, 1550 Metro Manila, Philippines
Phone, +632 632-4444. Fax, +632 636-2444. Internet, http://www.adb.org | Email: information@adb.org.

ADB North American Representative Office: 900 17th Street NW., Suite 900, Washington DC 20006
Phone, 202-728-1500. Fax, 202-728-1505.

President   TAKEHIKO NAKAO

The above list of key personnel was updated 09–2017.

The Asian Development Bank stimulates sustainable economic development and social progress in member countries to mitigate poverty and its effects.

The Asian Development Bank (ADB) commenced operations on December 19, 1966. It comprises 67 members: 48 regional and 19 nonregional countries.

The ADB works to eradicate poverty in Asia and the Pacific. As a multilateral development finance institution, it provides grants, loans, and technical assistance. The Bank serves its member countries, which are also its shareholders. Through equity investments and loans, the ADB also provides direct assistance to private enterprises of developing member countries.

To maximize the effects of its assistance on development, the ADB facilitates policy dialogues, offers advisory services, and mobilizes financial resources through cofinancing operations involving official, commercial, and export sources of credit. ABD operations promote three complementary agendas: environmentally sustainable growth, inclusive economic growth, and regional integration. The Bank's core areas of development activity are education, environment, finance, infrastructure, and regional cooperation and integration. http://www.adb.org/print/node/179940

Sources of Information

Business Opportunities   ADB projects rely on the goods and services of consultants, contractors, manufacturers, and suppliers. http://www.adb.org/site/business-opportunities/main

Career Opportunities   The "Careers" Web page features access to the ABD career and employment system, information on its young professional program and internships, descriptions of current job vacancies, and a summary of what the ADB looks for in a potential employee. http://www.adb.org/site/careers/main

Chinese   The ADB website offers information and resources for visitors who read Chinese. https://www.adb.org/zh

Climate Change   Production and use of energy from nonrenewable sources and the unsustainable development and consumption of other natural resources destabilize the climate and undermine long-term prosperity in Asia and the Pacific. Devastating storms, droughts, floods, and rising sea levels disproportionately affect poor communities. While climatologists forecast that extreme climate events will become more frequent and intense, the ADB continues its support of sustainable growth in the region through financing and innovative technologies. https://www.adb.org/themes/climate-change-disaster-risk-management/main

History   Conceived in the early 1960s as a financial institution that would be Asian in character and foster economic growth and cooperation in one of the poorest regions in the world, the ADB opened in the Philippine capital of Manila in 1966. To learn about the Bank's initial achievements and those of more recent decades, visit the "ADB History" web page. https://www.adb.org/about/history

Members   The ADB posts a list of its regional and nonregional members and descriptions of them on its website. https://www.adb.org/about/members

Organizational Chart   The ADB's organizational chart is available in Portable Document Format (PDF) for viewing and downloading. https://www.adb.org/sites/default/files/page/203876/adb-org-chart-20170720.pdf

Publications   The ADB website offers information on books, brochures and flyers, conference proceedings, guides, papers and briefs, policies and plans, reports, and statutory reports and official records. http://www.adb.org/publications

Social Media   The ADB has a Facebook account. https://www.facebook.com/AsianDevBank

The ADB tweets announcements and other newsworthy items on Twitter. https://twitter.com/ADB_HQ

The ADB posts videos on its YouTube channel. https://www.youtube.com/user/AsianDevelopmentBank

Statistical Database System   The ADB maintains a central statistical database to store macroeconomic and social data of its developing member countries. https://sdbs.adb.org/sdbs | Email: sdbs@adb.org

European Bank for Reconstruction and Development

One Exchange Square, London EC2A 2JN, United Kingdom
Phone, +44 20 7338 6000. Internet, http://www.ebrd.com.

President   Sir Suma Chakrabarti

The above list of key personnel was updated 09–2017

The European Bank for Reconstruction and Development develops open and sustainable market economies in democratic countries.

The European Bank for Reconstruction and Development (EBRD) is a multilateral development bank that supports projects in over 30 countries, from central Europe to central Asia and to the southern and eastern Mediterranean. Investing primarily in private sector clients whose needs cannot be met fully by commercial credit and equity markets, the EBRD promotes entrepreneurship and fosters transition toward open and sustainable market economies.

The London-based EBRD has a political mandate: It assists countries that are committed to and apply the principles of multiparty democracy and pluralism. The Bank also conducts its affairs with a commitment to environmental protection and sustainable energy development. In addition to benefiting the countries that receive its investments, the Bank also serves its shareholders' interests: 66 countries from five continents, the European Union, and the European Investment Bank. http://www.ebrd.com/who-we-are/history-of-the-ebrd.html

Sources of Information

Business Opportunities   Information on opportunities for consultants, contractors, and suppliers is available on the EBRD website. http://www.ebrd.com/work-with-us/procurement.html

Career Opportunities   Information on job locations and types, benefits and rewards, and internships is available on the EBRD website. http://www.ebrd.com/careers-at-the-ebrd.html

Contact Information   Department and country contacts are listed on the "EBRD Contacts" Web page. http://www.ebrd.com/contacts.html

Economic Data   Economic teams publish macroeconomic and structural data series, and they survey data affecting the Bank's countries of operation. http://www.ebrd.com/what-we-do/economic-research-and-data/data.html

Environmental and Social Sustainability   EBRD financing supports sustainable development projects that are designed and operated in compliance with good international practices. To help clients meet sustainability goals, the EBRD posts downloads and resources on its website. http://www.ebrd.com/key-sustainability-downloads.html

Green Economy Transition (GET)   By 2020, the GET approach seeks to increase the volume of green financing to 40 per cent of EBRD annual business investment. Safeguarding the environment and strengthening ecosystems help market economies function better and, therefore, are central to the transition process that the EBRD has promoted since its inception. http://www.ebrd.com/what-we-do/get.html

History   In October of 1989, a month before German citizens dismantled parts of the Berlin Wall, President François Mitterrand of France proposed the establishment of a European bank to meet the challenges of emergent economic and political realities. In less than 2 years, the EBRD opened for business with its headquarters in London. To learn more about the role played by the EBRD in the transition from the end of the Cold War to a new European era, visit the "History of the EBRD" web page. http://www.ebrd.com/who-we-are/history-of-the-ebrd.html

Organizational Chart   The EBRD's organizational chart is available on the "Structure and Management" web page in Portable Document Format (PDF) for viewing and downloading. http://www.ebrd.com/who-we-are/our-structure.html

Products / Services   Information on the EBRD's advisory services, policy reform dialogue services, and financial products is available online. http://www.ebrd.com/what-we-do/products-and-services.html

Reports   The EBRD posts annual, donor, financial, sustainability, and transition reports on its website. http://www.ebrd.com/news/publications.html

Sectors / Topics   The EBRD website features a section that brings together the topics that most concern the Bank and the sectors in which it is most active. http://www.ebrd.com/what-we-do/sectors-and-topics.html

Social Media   The EBRD tweets announcements and other newsworthy items on Twitter. https://twitter.com/ebrd

The EBRD maintains a Facebook account. https://www.facebook.com/ebrdhq

Where EBRD Works   The EBRD website features the list of countries where the Bank is active. http://www.ebrd.com/where-we-are.html

---

Inter-American Defense Board

2600 Sixteenth Street NW., Washington, DC 20441
Phone, 202-939-6041, 202-319-2791. Internet, http://iadb.jid.org | Email: protocol@jid.org.

Chair   VICE ADM. GONZALO NICOLÁS RÍOS POLASTRI

The Inter-American Defense Board is the oldest permanently constituted, international military organization in the world. It was founded by Resolution XXXIX of the Meeting of Foreign Ministers at Rio de Janeiro in January 1942. The Board is governed according to Statutes that the General Assembly of the Organization of American States approved in March 2006. Senior armed forces officers from the member nations staff the various agencies of the Board. Its three major components are the Council of Delegates, the Secretariat, and the Inter-American Defense College. http://iadb.jid.org/quienes-somos/resena-historica-de-la-sede-de-la-jid

The Board studies and recommends to member governments measures it deems necessary for the safety and security of the hemisphere. It also acts as a technical military adviser for the Organization of American States and is involved in projects such as disaster preparedness and humanitarian demining programs in Central and South America.

Established in 1962, the Inter-American Defense College is located on Fort Lesley J. McNair, whose buildings and furnishings the United States Government donated. The United States hosts the College, which prepares senior military officers and civilian functionaries for positions in their respective governments. The College offers an 11-month, professionally-oriented, and fully accredited Masters of Science degree. Multidisciplinary in content, the curriculum centers on the Western Hemisphere's most pressing defense and security issues. http://www.colegio-id.org/index.php

Sources of Information

Documents Documents are posted online to increase the transparency of Inter-American Defense Board activities. http://iadb.jid.org/documents-and-publications
Events Symposia and seminars are posted on the Board's Web site. A calendar of meetings also is available on the Web site's home page. https://sites.google.com/a/jid.org/iadb/eventos/simposios-y-seminarios
News News items are available on the home page of the Board's Web site. http://iadb.jid.org
Regional Organizations Links to regional organizations are accessible on the "Strategic Links" Web page. http://iadb.jid.org/strategic-links. http://iadb.jid.org/quienes-somos/contactos | Email: jid@jid.org

For further information, contact the Inter-American Defense Board, 2600 Sixteenth Street NW., Washington, DC 20441. Phone, 202-939-6041. Fax, 202-319-2791.

Inter-American Development Bank

Headquarters: 1300 New York Avenue NW., Washington, DC 20577
Phone, 202-623-1000. Fax, 202-623-3096. Internet, http://www.iadb.org.

President	LUIS A. MORENO

The above list of key personnel was updated 09–2017

The Inter-American Development Bank (IDB) was established in 1959 to help accelerate economic and social development in Latin America and the Caribbean.

The Bank has 48 member countries, 26 of which are borrowing members in Latin America and the Caribbean. http://www.iadb.org/en/about-us/about-the-inter-american-development-bank,5995.html

Sources of Information

Business Opportunities IDB projects in Latin America and the Caribbean create contract opportunities for businesses and consultants. http://www.iadb.org/en/projects/project-procurement,8148.html
Career Opportunities The IDB relies on professionals with expertise in economics, education, energy, environmental sustainability, financial markets, institutional capacity, investment funds, rural development and disaster risk, science and technology, social protection and health, transport, water and sanitation, and other fields to carry out its mission. http://www.iadb.org/en/careers/careers-at-the-idb,1165.html

Data The IDB posts datasets on its Web site. https://data.iadb.org

Glossary The IDB maintains a glossary on its Web site. http://www.iadb.org/en/projects/glossary,18952.html

Key Facts To learn at glance who leads the IDB, how many people it employs, how many countries are members, who are its clients, and recent annual levels of its approved lending, visit the "Key Facts" section. http://www.iadb.org/en/about-us/key-facts,18246.html

Learning Resources Online courses are accessible on the IDB Web site. http://www.iadb.org/en/courses/home,20468.html

Looking for Something? Try finding it by using the "What Are You Looking For" Web page. http://www.iadb.org/en/projects/what-are-you-looking-for,18944.html?

Publications A variety of publications—annual reports, books, catalogs and brochures, databases and datasets, discussion and working papers, journals, magazines, monographs, newsletters—is available online. https://publications.iadb.org/facet-view?field=type_view

Social Media The IDB tweets announcements and other newsworthy items on Twitter. https://twitter.com/the_IDB

The IDB has a Facebook account. https://www.facebook.com/IADB.org

Inter-American Investment Corporation

Headquarters: 1350 New York Avenue NW., Washington, DC 20577
Phone, 202-623-3901. Internet, http://www.iic.org/en.

Chair, Board of Executive Directors	LUIS A. MORENO
Chief Executive Officer	JAMES P. SCRIVEN

The above list of key personnel was updated 09–2017

The Inter-American Development Bank promotes development in Latin America and the Caribbean through the private sector.

The Inter-American Investment Corporation (IIC), an affiliate of the Inter-American Development Bank based in Washington, DC, was established in 1985 to promote the economic development of its Latin American and Caribbean members by financing small- and medium-size private enterprises. The IIC provides project financing in the form of direct loans and equity investments, lines of credit to local financial intermediaries, and investments in local and regional investment funds.http://www.iic.org/en/who-we-are/about-us#.WGLh5H0rLIU

The IIC has 45 member countries, of which 28 are in the Western Hemisphere, including Canada and the United States, and 17 are outside the region. http://www.iic.org/en/what-we-offer#.VumT0H0rLIU

Sources of Information

Career Opportunities The ICC relies on talent and experience to carry out its mission. It recruits, hires, and maintains a staff of diverse, motivated, and qualified professionals with expertise, leadership potential, and strong interpersonal and teamwork skills. Current job opportunities are posted online. http://www.iic.org/en/about-us/careers

History A three-part history, from 1985 to 1999, from 2000 to 2012, and from 2013 to the present, is available on the IIC's Web site. http://www.iic.org/en/who-we-are/our-history-timeline#.WD9-D30rLIV

Key Initiatives The IIC's Web site features a section on its most important initiatives. http://www.iic.org/en/initiatives

Library The IIC's Web site features a photo library. http://www.iic.org/en/media/photo-library#.WD94730rLIU

Member Countries The IIC Web site features two lists of member countries: regional members and other members. An interactive map complements the two lists. http://www.iic.org/en/countries

News The IIC posts news items on its Web site.

Projects IIC projects may be searched by country or year. http://www.iic.org/en/projects

Publications   Brochures, factsheets, and reports—some in English and Spanish, some also in French and Portuguese—are available online. http://www.iic.org/en/media/publications#.VumPI30rLIU

Transaction Cycle   A description of the five stages of a successful IIC transaction—business origination, eligibility review, due diligence and approval, closing

and disbursement, and supervision and evaluation—is available online. http://www.iic.org/en/what-we-offer/transaction-cycle#.WD9_p30rLIU

Social Media   The IIC tweets announcements and other newsworthy items in Spanish on Twitter. https://twitter.com/GrupoBID_CII

The IIC has a Facebook account. https://www.facebook.com/CIIGrupoBID

Editorial Note

The International Monetary Fund did not meet the publication deadline for submitting updated information of its activities, functions, and sources of information as required by the automatic disclosure provisions of the Freedom of Information Act (5 U.S.C. 552(a)(1)(A))

International Monetary Fund

700 Nineteenth Street NW., Washington, DC 20431
Phone, 202-623-7000. Fax, 202-623-4661. Internet, http://www.imf.org.

Managing Director / Chair of the Executive Board	CHRISTINE LAGARDE
First Deputy Managing Director	DAVID LIPTON
Deputy Managing Director / Chief Administrative Officer	CARLA GRASSO
Deputy Managing Director	MITSUHIRO FURUSAWA
Deputy Managing Director	MIN ZHU

The International Monetary Fund fosters global monetary cooperation, secures financial stability, facilitates international trade, promotes employment and sustainable economic growth, and reduces poverty worldwide.

The Final Act of the United Nations Monetary and Financial Conference, signed at Bretton Woods, NH, on July 22, 1944, set forth the original Articles of Agreement of the International Monetary Fund (IMF). The Agreement became effective on December 27, 1945, when the President, authorized by the Bretton Woods Agreements Act (22 U.S.C. 286), accepted membership for the United States in the IMF. The inaugural meeting of the Board of Governors was held in March 1946, and the first meeting of the Executive Directors was held May 6, 1946.

On May 31, 1968, the Board of Governors approved an amendment to the Articles of Agreement for the establishment of a facility based on Special Drawing Rights (SDR) and for modification of certain rules and practices. The amendment became effective on July 28, 1969, and the Special Drawing Account opened on August 6, 1969. The Special Drawing Rights Act (22 U.S.C. 286

et seq.) authorized the United States to accept the amendment and participate in the Special Drawing Account.

On April 30, 1976, the Board of Governors approved a second amendment to the Articles of Agreement, which became effective on April 1, 1978. This amendment gave members the right to adopt exchange arrangements of their choice while placing certain obligations on them regarding their exchange rate policies, which the IMF was to monitor closely. The official price of gold was abolished, and the Special Drawing Account was promoted as the principal reserve asset of the international monetary system. The Bretton Woods Agreements Act Amendments (22 U.S.C. 286e-5) authorized the United States to accept this amendment.

On June 28, 1990, the Board of Governors approved a third amendment to the Articles of Agreement, which became effective on November 11, 1992. Under this amendment, a member's voting rights and certain related rights may be suspended by a 70-percent majority of the executive board if the member country has been declared ineligible to use the Fund's general resources and persists in its failure to fulfill any of its obligations under the Articles.

The IMF has 189 member countries. It promotes international monetary cooperation through a permanent forum for consultation and collaboration on international monetary problems; facilitates the expansion and balanced growth of international trade; promotes exchange rate stability; assists in the establishment of an open multilateral system of payments for current transactions among members; and gives confidence to members by making IMF resources temporarily available to them under adequate safeguards.

The IMF helps member countries correct imbalances in their international balances of payments. It periodically examines the economic developments and policies of its members, offers policy advice, and at a member's request and upon executive board approval, provides financial assistance through a variety of financial facilities designed to address specific problems. These financing mechanisms provide access to the Fund's general resources and offer short-term assistance during crises of market confidence, compensatory financing to countries suffering declines in export earnings, emergency assistance for countries recovering from natural disasters or armed conflict, and low-interest rate resources to support structural adjustment and promote growth in the poorest countries. The IMF also provides technical assistance and training to member countries. http://www.imf.org/external/about.htm

Sources of Information

Career Opportunities In addition to economists and research assistants, the IMF relies on professionals with skills and expertise in a range of other fields— communications, facilities management, finance and accounting, human resources, information technology, language services, legal, library and archives, office assistance, procurement, security, and transportation and hospitality. Information on careers, current job vacancies, and recruitment programs is available online. http://www.imf.org/external/np/adm/rec/recruit.htm

Country Information The IMF is an organization comprising 189 countries that, together, work to promote monetary cooperation, financial stability, international trade, employment and sustainable economic growth, and to reduce poverty. An alphabetical index of the participating countries and information on those countries are available on the IMF's Web site. http://www.imf.org/external/country/index.htm

Glossary The IMF maintains an online glossary of financial terms and acronyms. http://www.imf.org/external/np/exr/glossary/index.asp

Publications The IMF's "Finance and Development" magazine and "Fiscal Monitor" biannual report are available online in Portable Document Format (PDF). Its "New and Noteworthy" newsletter and other publications are also accessible online. http://www.imf.org/external/publications/index.htm

Videos The IMF posts videos in Arabic, Chinese, English, French, Russian, and Spanish on its Web site. http://www.imf.org/external/mmedia/index.aspx. http://www.imf.org | Email: publicaffairs@imf.org

For further information, contact the Chief of Public Affairs, International Monetary Fund–Communications Department, 700 Nineteenth Street NW., Washington, DC 20431. Phone, 202-623-7300. Fax, 202-623-6278.

International Organization for Migration

Headquarters: 17 Route des Morillons, C.P. 17, CH-1211 Geneva 19, Switzerland. Mailing address, P.O. Box 71, CH-1211, Geneva 19, Switzerland
Phone, 011-41-22-717-9111. Internet, http://www.iom.int | Email: hq@iom.int.

Washington Office: Suite 700, 1752 N Street NW., Washington, DC 20036
Phone, 202-862-1826. Email: IOMWashington@iom.int.

New York Office: 122 E. 42d Street, 48th Floor, New York, NY 10168
Phone, 212-681-7000. Email: newyork@iom.int.

Director General	WILLIAM LACY SWING
Deputy Director General	LAURA THOMPSON
Chief of Mission–Washington, DC	LUCA DALL'OGLIO
Permanent Observer to the United Nations	ASHRAF EL NOUR

The above list of key personnel was updated 09–2017

The International Organization for Migration addresses the underlying issues of migration, answers the operational challenges of migration management, promotes economic and social development through migration, champions the dignity and well-being of migrants, and challenges the xenophobic narrative directed at them.

Established in 1951, the International Organization for Migration (IOM) is the leading intergovernmental organization in the field of migration. With 166 member states, an additional 8 states holding observer status, and offices in over 100 countries, the IOM promotes humane and orderly migration for the benefit of all. It does so by providing services and advice to migrants and governments, while working in close cooperation with governmental, intergovernmental, and nongovernmental partners. The IOM has observer status to the United Nations.

The Organization works with its partners in the following areas: meeting the operational challenges of migration management, increasing understanding of migration issues, encouraging social and economic development through migration, and upholding the human dignity and well-being of migrants.

The Organization has been at the forefront of emergency response to ensure assistance and protection to stranded migrants and displaced persons. It has a lead role under the UN Cluster Approach in camp coordination and management in natural disasters and is a key partner in emergency shelter, logistics, health, protection, and early recovery.

IOM expertise and services support the following activities: secure, reliable, and cost-effective assistance for migrating persons; humane and orderly management of migration and the effective respect for migrants' human rights; technical cooperation and operational assistance for building national capacities and facilitating cooperation on issues relevant to migration; helping states to integrate migrants into their new environment and to engage diasporas as development partners; advising states in the development and delivery of programs and technical expertise to combat migrant smuggling and human trafficking; working with national health systems to reduce mortality, morbidity, and disabilities and to enhance access to rights-based health and well-being services throughout the migration cycle; and partnering with states to address labor migration. http://www.iom.int/about-iom

Sources of Information

Blog The IOM maintains a blog on its Web site. http://weblog.iom.int

Business Opportunities Information on procurement opportunities is available online. https://www.iom.int/procurement-opportunities

Career Opportunities Current job vacancies in various countries are posted online. https://recruit.iom.int/sap/bc/webdynpro/sap/hrrcf_a_unreg_job_search?sap-client=100&sap-language=EN&sap-wd-configid=ZHRRCF_A_UNREG_JOB_SEARCH#

Countries IOM maintains more than 480 country offices and sub-offices worldwide. http://www.iom.int/countries

Español / Français Spanish and French versions of the Web site can be accessed by using language links at the top of the home page. http://www.iom.int

Glossary A list of key migration terms that is based on the IOM's "Glossary on Migration" is available online. http://www.iom.int/key-migration-terms

History Originally known as the Provisional Intergovernmental Committee for the Movement of Migrants from Europe, the IOM got its start amidst the chaos and displacement caused by WWII. Today, the

IOM is the leading international agency working to advance the understanding of migration issues, encourage social and economic development through migration, and uphold the human dignity and well-being of migrants. To learn more of the IOM story, which began in 1951, visit the "IOM History" page. http://www.iom.int/iom-history

Organizational Chart The IOM's organizational chart is available in Portable Document Format (PDF) for viewing and downloading. http://www.iom.int/sites/default/files/Organigram.pdf

Press Room The IOM posts featured stories, news, radio and television interviews, and more on its Web site. http://www.iom.int/press-room

Publications Visit the online bookstore to see IOM publications in English, French, and Spanish. http://publications.iom.int

Regional Geographic Coverage A map of IOM regional geographic coverage is available online. http://www.iom.int/sites/default/files/about-iom/IOM_Regional_Geographical_Coverage.jpg

A list of IOM regional geographic coverage also is available online. http://www.iom.int/sites/default/files/about-iom/Coverage-of-ROs-Feb2016.pdf

Regional Offices Regional office staff reviews and endorses projects and provides technical support to Country Offices. Descriptions of and contact information for the IOM's nine regional offices are available online. http://www.iom.int/regional-offices

Social Media The IOM has a Facebook account. https://www.facebook.com/IOM

The IOM tweets announcements and other newsworthy items on Twitter. https://twitter.com/UNmigration

The IOM posts videos on its YouTube channel. https://www.youtube.com/user/IOMMigration

United Nations Information on the IOM's Office to the United Nations is available online. http://unofficeny.iom.int | Email: unofficeny@iom.int. http://www.iom.int/contact-us | Email: hq@iom.int

For further information, contact the International Organization for Migration–Headquarters, P.O. Box 71, CH–1211, Geneva 19, Switzerland.

EDITORIAL NOTE

Organization of American States did not meet the publication deadline for submitting updated information of its activities, functions, and sources of information as required by the automatic disclosure provisions of the Freedom of Information Act (5 U.S.C. 552(a)(1)(A))

Organization of American States

Seventeenth Street and Constitution Avenue NW., Washington, DC 20006
Phone, 202-370-5000. Fax, 202-458-3967. Internet, http://www.oas.org/en.

Secretary General	Luis Almagro Lemes
Assistant Secretary General	Nestor Mendez
Secretary for Strengthening Democracy	Francisco Guerrero Aguirre
Executive Secretary for Integral Development	Kim Hurtault-Osborne
Secretary for Multidimensional Security	Claudia Paz y Paz
Secretary for Administration and Finance	Jay Anania
Secretary for Legal Affairs	Jean Michel Arrighi
Secretariat for Access to Rights and Equity	(vacancy)
Secretariat for Hemispheric Affairs	(vacancy)

The Organization of American States seeks an order of peace and justice among its member states, promotes their solidarity and strengthens their collaboration, and defends their sovereignty, territorial integrity, and independence.

The Organization of American States (OAS) brings together the countries of the Western Hemisphere to strengthen cooperation and advance common interests. At the core of the OAS mission is a commitment to democracy. Building on this foundation,

OAS works to promote good governance, strengthen human rights, foster peace and security, expand trade, and address the complex problems caused by poverty, drugs, and corruption. Through decisions made by its political bodies and programs carried out by its General Secretariat, OAS promotes greater inter-American cooperation and understanding.

OAS member states have intensified their cooperation since the end of the cold war, taking on new and important challenges. In 1994, the region's 34 democratically elected presidents and prime ministers met in Miami for the First Summit of the Americas, where they established broad political, economic, and social development goals. They have continued to meet periodically since then to examine common interests and priorities. Through the ongoing Summits of the Americas process, the region's leaders have entrusted the OAS with a growing number of responsibilities to help advance the countries' shared vision.

With four official languages—English, Spanish, Portuguese, and French—the OAS reflects the rich diversity of peoples and cultures across the Americas. The OAS has 35 member states: the independent nations of North, Central, and South America, and of the Caribbean. Since 1962, Cuba has been barred from participation by resolution of the Eighth Meeting of Consultation of Ministers of Foreign Affairs. Countries from all around the world are permanent observers, closely following the issues that are critical to the Americas and often providing key financial support for OAS programs.

Member states set major policies and goals through the General Assembly, which gathers the hemisphere's foreign ministers once a year in regular session. The Permanent Council, made up of ambassadors appointed by member states, meets regularly at OAS headquarters in Washington, DC, to guide ongoing policies and actions. The chairmanship of the Permanent Council rotates every 3 months, in alphabetical order of countries. Each member state has an equal voice, and most decisions are made through consensus.

Also under the OAS umbrella are several specialized agencies that have considerable autonomy: the Pan American Health Organization in Washington, DC; the Inter-American Children's Institute in Montevideo, Uruguay; the Inter-American Institute for Cooperation on Agriculture in San Jose, Costa Rica; and the Pan American Institute of Geography and History and the Inter-American Indian Institute, both in Mexico City.

In 1948, at the Ninth International Conference of American States, 21 nations of the hemisphere signed the OAS Charter: Argentina, Bolivia, Brazil, Chile, Colombia, Costa Rica, Cuba (barred from participation), Dominican Republic, Ecuador, El Salvador, Guatemala, Haiti, Honduras, Mexico, Nicaragua, Panama, Paraguay, Peru, United States of America, Uruguay, and Venezuela.

Subsequently, 14 other countries joined the OAS by signing and ratifying the Charter. They were Barbados, Trinidad and Tobago, Jamaica, Grenada, Suriname, Dominica, Saint Lucia, Antigua and Barbuda, Saint Vincent and the Grenadines, the Bahamas, Saint Kitts and Nevis, Canada, Belize, and Guyana. This brings the number of member states to 35. http://www.oas.org/en/about/who_we_are.asp

Sources of Information

Conferences A calendar of conferences is available online. http://www.apps.oas.org/oasmeetings/default.aspx?Lang=EN

Documents The most important OAS documents, including its founding Charter and the Inter-American Democratic Charter, are available on its Web site. Along with these essential documents, links to other key reference material—such as annual reports of the Secretary General, OAS resolutions, agreements, and treaties—are also available. http://www.oas.org/en/information_center/default.asp

Employment Information on career opportunities, consultancies, and internships is available online. http://www.oas.org/dhrs/dhr/employment_opportunities.asp

History A short history of the OAS is available on its Web site. http://www.oas.org/en/about/our_history.asp

Language Assistance The OAS maintains English and Spanish versions of its Web site. Some Web pages are also available in French and Portuguese. Language tags appear above the search box in the top right corner of most of the site's Web pages. http://www.oas.org/en

Members States   Information on the 35 independent states of the Americas—all of which have ratified the OAS Charter and are member states—is available on the OAS Web site. http://www.oas.org/en/member_states/default.asp

News   The OAS posts press releases on its Web site. http://www.oas.org/en/media_center/press_releases.asp

The OAS posts newsletters on its Web site. http://www.oas.org/en/media_center/newsletters.asp

The OAS posts video news on its Vimeo channel. https://vimeo.com/channels/oasvideonews

The OAS posts speeches by OAS leadership on its Web site. http://www.oas.org/en/media_center/speeches.asp

Permanent Representatives   A list of permanent representatives to the OAS is available on its Web site. http://www.oas.org/en/about/authorities.asp

Publications   OAS publications in English and Spanish are available on its Web site. http://www.oas.org/en/information_center/publications.asp

Scholarships   Information on OAS scholarships is available online. http://www.oas.org/en/scholarships

Social Media   The OAS tweets announcements, news, and other noteworthy items on Twitter. https://twitter.com/oas_official

The OAS has a Facebook account. https://www.facebook.com/OASofficial

Staff Directory   The OAS Web site features an online staff directory. To see the complete directory, leave all fields blank and click on the search button. http://www.oas.org/teldir

Topics   The OAS Web site features a "Topics" Web page to help visitors find information that they seek or material that aligns with their interests. http://www.oas.org/en/topics/default.asp. http://www.oas.org/en/contactus.asp

For further information, contact the Organization of American States, Seventeenth Street and Constitution Avenue NW., Washington, DC 20006. Phone, 202-370-5000. Fax, 202-458-3967.

United Nations

United Nations, New York, NY 10017
Phone, 212-963-1234. Internet, http://www.un.org.

United Nations Office at Geneva: Palais des Nations, 1211 Geneva 10, Switzerland

United Nations Office at Vienna: Vienna International Centre, P.O. Box 500, A–1400, Vienna, Austria

Washington, DC: United Nations Information Centre, Suite 400, 1775 K Street NW., Washington, DC 20006
Phone, 202-331-8670. Fax, 202-331-9191. http://www.unicwash.org | Email: unicdc@unic.org.

Secretary–General	ANTÓNIO GUTERRES
Deputy Secretary-General	AMINA J. MOHAMMED
Director-General, United Nations Office at Geneva	MICHAEL MØLLER
Director-General, United Nations Office at Vienna	YURY FEDOTOV
Director, Washington DC Information Centre	ROBERT SKINNER

The above list of key personnel was updated 09–2017.

The United Nations supports tolerance and peaceful coexistence among the nations; seeks to maintain peace and security among them; opposes the use of armed force, except in the common interest; and promotes the economic and social advancement of all peoples.

The United Nations is an international organization that was set up in accordance with the Charter drafted by governments represented at the Conference on International Organization meeting at San Francisco. The Charter was signed on June 26, 1945, and came into force on October 24, 1945, when the required number of ratifications and accessions had been made by the signatories. Amendments increasing membership of the Security Council and the Economic and Social Council came into effect on August 31, 1965.

The United Nations now consists of 193 member states, of which 51 are founding members.

The purposes of the United Nations set out in the Charter are to maintain international peace and security; to develop friendly relations among nations; to achieve international cooperation in solving international problems of an economic, social, cultural, or humanitarian character and in promoting respect for human rights; and to be a center for harmonizing the actions of nations in the attainment of these common ends.

The principal organs of the United Nations are the Economic and Social Council, General Assembly, International Court of Justice, Secretariat, Security Council, and Trusteeship Council. http://www.un.org/en/sections/about-un/overview/index.html

Economic and Social Council   This organ is responsible, under the authority of the General Assembly, for the economic and social programs of the United Nations. Its functions include making or initiating studies, reports, and recommendations on international economic, social, cultural, educational, health, and related matters; promoting respect for and observance of human rights and fundamental freedoms for all; calling international conferences and preparing draft conventions for submission to the General Assembly on matters within its competence; negotiating agreements with the specialized agencies and defining their relationship with the United Nations; coordinating the activities of the specialized agencies; and consulting with nongovernmental organizations concerned with matters within its competence. The Council consists of 54 members of the United Nations elected by the General Assembly for 3-year terms; 18 are elected each year.

The Council usually holds two regular sessions a year. It has also held a number of special sessions. https://www.un.org/ecosoc/en

General Assembly   All states that are members of the United Nations are members of the General Assembly. Its functions are to consider and discuss any matter within the scope of the Charter of the United Nations and to make recommendations to the members of the United Nations and

other organs. It approves the budget of the organization, the expenses of which are borne by the members as apportioned by the General Assembly.

The General Assembly may call the attention of the Security Council to situations likely to endanger international peace and security, may initiate studies, and may receive and consider reports from other organs of the United Nations. Under the "Uniting for Peace" resolution adopted by the General Assembly in November 1950, if the Security Council fails to act on an apparent threat to or breach of the peace or act of aggression because of lack of unanimity of its five permanent members, the Assembly itself may take up the matter within 24 hours—in emergency special session—and recommend collective measures, including, in case of a breach of the peace or act of aggression, use of armed force when necessary to maintain or restore international peace and security.

The General Assembly normally meets in regular annual session from September through December. It also has met in special sessions and emergency special sessions. http://www.un.org/en/ga

International Court of Justice   The International Court of Justice is the principal judicial organ of the United Nations. It has its seat at The Hague, the Netherlands. All members of the United Nations are ipso facto parties to the Statute of the Court. Nonmembers of the United Nations may become parties to the Statute of the Court on conditions prescribed by the General Assembly on the recommendation of the Security Council.

The jurisdiction of the Court comprises all cases that the parties refer to it and all matters specially provided for in the Charter of the United Nations or in treaties and conventions in force.

The Court consists of 15 judges known as members of the Court. They are elected for 9-year terms by the General Assembly and the Security Council, voting independently, and may be reelected. http://www.icj-cij.org/homepage/index.php?lang=en

Secretariat   The Secretariat consists of a Secretary-General and "such staff as the Organization may require." The Secretary-General, who is appointed by the General Assembly on the recommendation of the

Security Council, is the chief administrative officer of the United Nations. He acts in that capacity for the General Assembly, the Security Council, the Economic and Social Council, and the Trusteeship Council. Under the Charter, the Secretary-General "may bring to the attention of the Security Council any matter that in his opinion may threaten the maintenance of international peace and security." http://www.un.org/en/sections/about-un/secretariat/index.html

Security Council   The Security Council consists of 15 members, of which 5—the People's Republic of China, France, Russia, the United Kingdom, and the United States of America—are permanent members. The 10 nonpermanent members are elected for 2-year terms by the General Assembly. The primary responsibility of the Security Council is to act on behalf of the members of the United Nations in maintenance of international peace and security. Measures that may be employed by the Security Council are outlined in the Charter.

The Security Council, together with the General Assembly, also elects the judges of the International Court of Justice and makes a recommendation to the General Assembly on the appointment of the Secretary-General of the organization.

The Security Council first met in London on January 17, 1946, and is so organized as to be able to function continuously. http://www.un.org/en/sc

Trusteeship Council   The Trusteeship Council was initially established to consist of any member states that administered trust territories, permanent members of the Security Council that did not administer trust territories, and enough other nonadministering countries elected by the General Assembly for 3-year terms to ensure that membership would be equally divided between administering and nonadministering members. Under authority of the General Assembly, the Council considered reports from members administering trust territories, examined petitions from trust territory inhabitants, and provided for periodic inspection visits to trust territories.

With the independence of Palau, the last remaining United Nations trust territory, the Trusteeship Council formally suspended operations after nearly half a century. The

Council will henceforth meet only on an extraordinary basis, as the need may arise. http://www.un.org/en/decolonization/trusteeship.shtml

Sources of Information

A–Z Index   An alphabetical index is available on the United Nations' Web site to help visitors search for specific topics or browse content that aligns with their interests. http://www.un.org/en/sections/about-website/site-index/index.html

Career Opportunities   United Nations Secretariat staff members work in a dynamic, multicultural environment that fosters a broader understanding of countries and cultures worldwide. The United Nations welcomes applications from nationals of all of its Member States and encourages women to apply. http://www.un.org/en/sections/resources/job-seekers/index.html

Documents   Launched in 1993 and updated in 2016, the Official Document System (ODS) is an online database of United Nations documents that has full-text, born-digital documents published from 1993 onward. The ODS also includes scanned documents that were published between 1946 and 1993. Documents are available in the official languages of the United Nations. Some documents are also available in German. https://documents.un.org/prod/ods.nsf/home.xsp

Frequently Asked Questions (FAQs)   The United Nations posts answers to FAQs on its Web site. http://www.un.org/en/sections/about-un/frequently-asked-questions/index.html

Global Issues   The "Global Issues Overview" Web page offers convenient access to a trove of information on ageing, atomic energy, children, climate change, decolonization, democracy, food, population, refugees, water, women, and more. http://www.un.org/en/sections/issues-depth/global-issues-overview/index.html

Human Rights   The Universal Declaration of Human Rights and a short history of this document are posted on the United Nation's Web site. http://www.un.org/en/universal-declaration-human-rights

Library   The Dag Hammarskjöld Library is accessible online. https://library.un.org

Multimedia United Nations Radio is accessible online. In addition to English, listeners may opt to hear programs in Arabic, Chinese, French, Russian, Spanish, and other languages. http://www.unmultimedia.org/radio/english

United Nations Video is accessible online and features documentaries, as well as coverage of events, news developments, and issues at the United Nations. http://www.un.org/en/sections/news-and-media/un-video/index.html

News The News Centre provides breaking news coverage of developments around the United Nations system, offering quick access to news-related products and resources. http://www.un.org/News

Non-English Readers The United Nations provides versions of its Web site in Arabic, Chinese, French, Russian, and Spanish. Language options are available on the Web site's welcome page. http://www.un.org

Publications Books, reports, and data are available from the online bookshop. https://shop.un.org

Resources by Audience The United Nations groups information and resources on its Web site according to categories of people who may be interested in them. Audiences include academics, businessmen and women, delegates, job seekers, journalists, representatives of civil society, students, and visitors. http://www.un.org/en/sections/resources-different-audiences/index.html

Social Media Official United Nations social media include Facebook, Flickr, Tumblr, Twitter, YouTube, and other accounts. http://www.un.org/en/sections/about-website/un-social-media/index.html

Sustainable Development The United Nations promotes 17 sustainable development goals to end poverty, to ensure prosperity for all people, and to protect Earth's biosphere as part of a development agenda. http://www.un.org/sustainabledevelopment/sustainable-development-goals

Where We Work The United Nations is a global organization that affects billions of people. It and the components comprising the United Nations system have a worldwide presence to ensure that timely assistance can reach people who most need it. The activities of the United Nations are divided into five geographical regions: Africa, Americas, Asia and the Pacific, Europe and Central Asia, and the Middle East. An overview of each area and links to relevant offices, agencies, and programs are available on the "Where We Work" Web page. http://www.un.org/en/sections/where-we-work/index.html

World Bank Group

Headquarters: 1818 H Street NW., Washington, DC 20433
Phone, 202-473-1000. Fax, 202-477-6391. Internet, http://www.worldbank.org.

President   JIM YONG KIM

The World Bank Group's personnel tables were updated 09–2017.

The World Bank Group promotes shared global prosperity and seeks to end extreme poverty.

The World Bank Group consists of five institutions: the International Bank for Reconstruction and Development (IBRD), the International Development Association (IDA), the International Finance Corporation (IFC), the Multilateral Investment Guarantee Agency (MIGA), and the International Centre for the Settlement of Investment Disputes (ICSID). The two primary economic and social development institutions are the IBRD and the IDA. Donor countries and countries with borrowing rights, a total of 189 countries, support and benefit from these two development banks. The other three institutions complement the activities of the IBRD and the IDA. These World Bank Group institutions are working collectively to end extreme poverty within a generation and boost shared prosperity and equality in the developing world.

Sources of Information

A–Z Topics The World Bank's Web site features an alphabetical list of topics that helps visitors learn about the Banks many and diverse activities. http://www.worldbank.org/en/topic

Blog The World Bank posts items by featured bloggers on its Web site. http://blogs.worldbank.org

Career Opportunities The World Bank typically hires people with strong academic backgrounds, a broad understanding of development issues, and international work experience. In more than 170 countries, it employees professionals who specialize in economics, education, engineering, finance, public health, and many other fields. About 40 percent of World Bank staff members work in more than 110 developing countries. http://web.worldbank.org/WBSITE/EXTERNAL/EXTJOBSNEW/0,,pagePK:8454306~theSitePK:8453353,00.html

Countries / Regions The Web site features a browse-by-country tool and roll-over-to-navigate world map to help visitors explore World Bank activities around the globe. http://www.worldbank.org/en/country

Data The World Bank's Web site gives visitors free and open access to global development data. http://data.worldbank.org

The microdata library facilitates access to data collected through sample surveys of households, business establishments, and other facilities. These sets of microdata may also be derived from agricultural, housing, or population censuses or through an administrative data collection processes. The Library also contains supporting documentation from censuses and surveys that the World Bank and other international organizations, statistical agencies, and other agencies in low and middle-income countries conducted or supported. http://microdata.worldbank.org/index.php/home

History The "World Bank Group Archives" Web site supports the institutional memory of the World Bank Group and provides access to records of the International Bank for Reconstruction and Development and the International Development Association. The Web site also features online historical resources and information products: exhibits on the Archives' collection and World Bank history, General International Standard Archival Description (ISAD(G)) finding aids, and transcripts of oral history interviews. http://www.worldbank.org/en/about/archives

Libraries The World Bank Group and International Monetary Fund libraries collaborate to provide information services and make available resources to World Bank Group and International Monetary Fund staff. These libraries provide limited services to external researchers and visitors. http://jolis.worldbankimflib.org/external.htm

News The World Bank posts press releases and other newsworthy items on its Web site. http://www.worldbank.org/en/news

Open Learning Campus The Open Learning Campus offers educational opportunities that allow diverse audiences to learn at their own pace. It helps prepare people seeking to address the tough development challenges of the 21st century. https://olc.worldbank.org

Podcasts The World Bank's features a trove of podcasts on a variety of topics: climate change, energy development, indigenous communities, immigration and forced displacement, sustainability, and more. http://www.worldbank.org/en/news/multimedia?multimedia_class_exact=Audio&qterm=&lang_exact=English

Projects The World Bank's Web site allows visitors to browse or search for projects by country or area, sector, or theme. http://projects.worldbank.org

Publications The World Bank's Web site features an "Open Knowledge Repository" that allows users to browse and search for thousands of publications. http://www.worldbank.org/en/publication/reference

Research The World Bank Web site features research program datasets and analytical tools on its Web site. http://econ.worldbank.org/WBSITE/EXTERNAL/EXTDEC/EXTRESEARCH/0,,contentMDK:20388241~menuPK:665266~pagePK:64165401~piPK:64165026~theSitePK:469382,00.html

Social Media The World Bank tweets announcements and other newsworthy items on Twitter. https://twitter.com/worldbank

The World Bank has a Facebook account. https://www.facebook.com/worldbank

The World Bank posts videos on its YouTube channel. https://www.youtube.com/WorldBank

Speaker's Bureau The Speaker's Bureau serves as the official liaison between the

World Bank Group and its visitors, who include business leaders, governmental representatives, students and teachers, youth organizations, and other professionals. http://

www.worldbank.org/en/about/speakers-bureau | Email: speakersbureau@worldbank.org

---

International Bank for Reconstruction and Development

Internet, http://www.worldbank.org/en/about/what-we-do/brief/ibrd.

The International Bank for Reconstruction and Development (IBRD) officially came into existence in 1944.

The Bank promotes economic, social, and environmental progress in developing nations by reducing poverty so that their people may live better and fuller lives. The Bank lends funds at market-determined interest rates, provides advice, and serves as a catalyst to stimulate outside investments. Its resources come primarily from funds raised in the world capital markets, its retained earnings, and repayments on its loans.

Sources of Information

Countries   The Governments of the 189 member countries own the IBRD.http://www.worldbank.org/en/about/leadership/members

Bonds   The IBRD issues World Bank bonds in the international capital markets to fund development projects in member countries. http://treasury.worldbank.org/cmd/htm/index.html

---

International Centre for Settlement of Investment Disputes

Headquarters: 1818 H Street NW., MSN J2-200, Washington, DC 20433
Phone, 202-458-1534. Fax, 202-522-2615. Intermet, http://icsid.worldbank.org/ICSID |
Email: ICSIDsecretariat@worldbank.org.

President	JIM YONG KIM
Secretary-General	MEG KINNEAR

The International Centre for Settlement of Investment Disputes (ICSID), an autonomous international institution affiliated with the World Bank Group, was established under the Convention on the Settlement of Investment Disputes Between States and Nationals of Other States. The Convention sets forth ICSID's mandate, organization, and core functions. The primary purpose of ICSID is to provide facilities for conciliation and arbitration of international investment disputes.

The ICSID Convention is a multilateral treaty formulated by the Executive Directors of the International Bank for Reconstruction and Development (the World Bank). The treaty entered into force in 1966. There are currently 159 signatory states to the ICSID Convention of which 150 countries also deposited their instruments of ratification, acceptance, or approval of the Convention.

International Development Association

Internet, http://ida.worldbank.org.

The International Development Association (IDA) came into existence in 1960 as an institution of the World Bank Group.

The Association's resources consist of subscriptions and supplementary resources in the form of general replenishments on a

3-year revolving cycle, mostly from its more industrialized and developed members; special contributions by its richer members; repayments on earlier credits; and transfers from IBRD's net earnings.

The Association promotes economic development, reduces poverty, and raises the standard of living in the least developed areas of the world. It does this by financing their developmental requirements on concessionary terms, which are more flexible and bear less heavily on the balance of payments than those of conventional loans, thereby furthering the objectives of IBRD and supplementing its activities.

Sources of Information

Articles of Agreement The IDA's Articles of Agreement became effective in 1960. They are available online in Portable Document Format. http://ida.worldbank.org/sites/default/files/IDA-articles-of-agreement.pdf
Climate Climate change threatens poorer people globally, with the potential to force more than 100 million people back into poverty by 2030. The IDA is making plans to help manage this threat of enormous scope and scale. http://ida.worldbank.org/theme/climate
Countries Seventy-seven countries are eligible to receive IDA resources. In addition, India is receiving transitional support. http://ida.worldbank.org/about/borrowing-countries

A list of the approximately 50 contributor countries is available on the IDA's Web site. http://ida.worldbank.org/about/contributor-countries
History A short history of the IDA is available on its Web site. http://ida.worldbank.org/about/history
News / Publications The IDA posts press releases and other newsworthy items on its Web site. http://ida.worldbank.org/news
Results The IDA's Web site features an overview of the results of the IDA's efforts in the world's poorest countries by country, theme, or topic. http://ida.worldbank.org/results

---

International Finance Corporation

Headquarters: 2121 Pennsylvania Avenue NW., Washington, DC 20433
Phone, 202-473-7711. Fax, 202-974-4384. Internet, http://www.ifc.org.

President	JIM YONG KIM
Executive Vice President / Chief Executive Officer	PHILIPPE LE HOUÉROU

The International Finance Corporation (IFC), a World Bank Group institution, was established in 1956 to promote productive private enterprise in developing member countries.

The Corporation pursues its objective principally through direct debt and equity investments in projects that establish new businesses or expand, modify, or diversify existing businesses. It also encourages cofinancing by other investors and lenders.

Additionally, advisory services and technical assistance are provided by IFC to developing member countries in areas such as capital market development, privatization, corporate restructuring, and foreign investment.

Sources of Information

Career Opportunities The IFC posts career opportunities on its Web site. http://www.ifc.org/wps/wcm/connect/Careers_Ext_Content/IFC_External_Corporate_Site/IFC+Careers
Climate The IFC is increasing its climate-related investments to address climate change—a fundamental threat to development, with the potential to impact millions, threatening agricultural livelihoods, increasing the incidence of natural disasters and affecting water, energy, and food supplies. http://www.ifc.org/wps/wcm/connect/Topics_Ext_Content/IFC_External_Corporate_Site/Climate+Business
Contact Information General information is available on the IFC's Web site. http://

www.ifc.org/wps/wcm/connect/corp_
ext_content/ifc_external_corporate_site/
about+ifc_new/contacts
Countries   The IFC operates in more than
100 countries. An online interactive map
presents the scope of its activities. http://
www.ifc.org/wps/wcm/connect/corp_
ext_content/ifc_external_corporate_site/
about+ifc_new/Where+We+Work
History   Opened in 1956 with $100 million
in capital, the IFC has been creating jobs
and raising living standards for six decades.

http://www.ifc.org/wps/wcm/connect/corp_
ext_content/ifc_external_corporate_site/
about+ifc_new/ifc+history
Transparency / Accountability   The IFC
provides information on its investment
and advisory services activities to clients,
partners, and stakeholders. http://www.
ifc.org/wps/wcm/connect/Topics_Ext_
Content/IFC_External_Corporate_site/
Sustainability+and+Disclosure/
Disclosure+Portal

Multilateral Investment Guarantee Agency

Headquarters: 1818 H Street NW., Washington, DC 20433
Phone, 202-458-2538. Fax, 202-522-0316. Internet, http://www.miga.org.

President	JIM YONG KIM
Executive Vice President / Chief Executive Officer	KEIKO HONDA

The Multilateral Investment Guarantee
Agency (MIGA), a World Bank Group
institution, was formally constituted in 1988.
   Working with public and private insurers,
MIGA promotes foreign direct investment in
developing countries to support economic
growth, reduce poverty, and improve the
quality of people's lives. Due to its status
as a World Bank Group institution, MIGA's
guarantees protect investments against
noncommercial risks and help investors gain
access to funding sources with improved
financial terms and conditions.

Sources of Information

Career Opportunities   The MIGA advertises
available positions on the World Bank's job
vacancies page. https://www.miga.org/who-
we-are/careers
Contact Information   General information
is available on the MIGA's Web site. https://
www.miga.org/contact

Convention   The "Convention Establishing
the Multilateral Investment Guarantee
Agency" went into effect on April 12,
1988. The Council of Governors amended
it in 2010. The Convention is available
online in Portable Document Format (PDF).
https://www.miga.org/who-we-are/miga-
convention
Frequently Asked Questions (FAQs)   The
MIGA posts answers to FAQs on its Web
site. https://www.miga.org/who-we-are/
frequently-asked-questions
History   A timeline and short history of the
MIGA are available on its Web site. https://
www.miga.org/who-we-are/history
Member Countries   The names of the 181
member countries—156 developing, 25
industrialized—are available on the MIGA's
Web site. https://www.miga.org/who-we-are/
member-countries
News   The MIGA posts press releases on its
Web site. https://www.miga.org/news/press-
releases